D1261148

Flotilla

Johns Hopkins Books on the War of 1812
Donald R. Hickey, *Series Editor*

Flotilla

THE PATUXENT NAVAL CAMPAIGN
IN THE WAR OF 1812

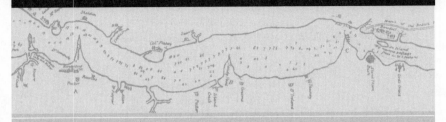

Donald G. Shomette

Foreword by

Fred W. Hopkins, Jr.

The Johns Hopkins
University Press
Baltimore

© 2009 The Johns Hopkins University Press
All rights reserved. Published 2009
Printed in the United States of America on acid-free paper
2 4 6 8 9 7 5 3 1

The Johns Hopkins University Press
2715 North Charles Street
Baltimore, Maryland 21218-4363
www.press.jhu.edu

Originally published 1981
by Calvert Marine Museum Press
as *Flotilla: Battle for the Patuxent*

Library of Congress Cataloging-in-Publication Data
Shomette, Donald.
   Flotilla : the Patuxent naval campaign in the War of 1812 / Donald G. Shomette ;
foreword by Fred W. Hopkins, Jr.
       p. cm.
   Includes bibliographical references and index.
   ISBN-13: 978-0-8018-9122-9 (hardcover : alk. paper)
   ISBN-10: 0-8018-9122-1 (hardcover : alk. paper)
   1. Patuxent River Valley (Md.)—History—War of 1812. 2. Barney, Joshua,
1759–1818. 3. United States—History—War of 1812—Naval operations. 4. United
States—History—War of 1812—Riverine operations. I. Title.
   E355.6.S53 2009
   973.5'2—dc22   2008022415

A catalog record for this book is available from the British Library.

Special discounts are available for bulk purchases of this book.
For more information, please contact Special Sales
at 410-516-6936 or specialsales@press.jhu.edu.

The Johns Hopkins University Press uses environmentally friendly book
materials, including recycled text paper that is composed of at least 30 percent
post-consumer waste, whenever possible. All of our book papers are
acid-free, and our jackets and covers are printed on paper
with recycled content.

*To all those who have placed themselves in harm's way
for our nation, liberty, and justice*

If men could learn from history,
what lessons it might teach us!
But passion and party blind our eyes,
And the light which experience gives
is a lantern on the stern,
which shines only on the waves behind us!

Samuel Taylor Coleridge
December 18, 1831

CONTENTS

Within eight months of the outbreak of hostilities in the War of 1812, the British Royal Navy had successfully instituted a blockade of the Chesapeake Bay and with startling regularity was soon sending raiding parties over the length and breadth of this most strategic waterway. No available American naval force seemed capable of contesting for control of the Maryland–Virginia Tidewater against the invader's 74-gun ships-of-the-line, frigates, and sloops-of-war threatening the major ports of Norfolk, Annapolis, and Baltimore and the capital of the United States itself, the still infant city of Washington, D.C. One man of vision, however, Baltimore's own Joshua Barney, a veteran seaman of renown and a naval hero of the Revolution, detected a possible weak link in British plans for bringing the bay region to its knees.

Much of the Chesapeake, with its myriad complex of islands, rivers, and shoals—indeed, its full eight thousand miles of intricate tidal shoreline—was accessible only to shallow-draft vessels. British raiding parties had to be ferried from point to point in armed ship's barges to carry on their nefarious depredations ashore. While conducting their operations in such shoally areas, these small, lightly armed craft were of necessity often well beyond the protective umbrellas of the 74s and frigates and vulnerable. Barney's plan was simple: build a flotilla of heavily armed, shallow-draft row galleys or barges that would not be held prisoner to wind and tide and could attack the enemy's vulnerable barge force whenever it left the cover of the Royal Navy warships. In this manner, the debilitating British attacks, which were bringing the Tidewater's economy to a veritable standstill, might be blunted and, with some luck, even defeated.

A reluctant but grateful secretary of the navy immediately accepted Barney's plan for the defense of the Chesapeake Bay, and Barney was given independent command of the Chesapeake Flotilla in the newly created U.S. Flotilla Service. Though the flotilla had to be constructed from scratch, manned, tested, and fielded in a matter of months, under adverse conditions, and with little in the way of funding or manpower available, there appears to have been little alternative. In *The Naval War of 1812*, Theodore Roosevelt points out that this little force was, in truth, conceived in total desperation and as a

ix

result failed to achieve its military objectives. The British, though hindered, were not deterred in their expeditions against the Tidewater. Scores of towns, plantations, and farms readily fell victim to the enemy's swift assaults while the flotilla, bottled up in Maryland's Patuxent River, struggled valiantly to free itself. Roosevelt acknowledged that it was not for lack of courage that the flotilla failed in its mission. The bravery of the five hundred flotillamen and marines who manned it throughout its short life was proven time and again as they turned back wave after wave of the numerically superior and better-armed foe seeking to destroy it, and they even elicited a singularly impossible victory against a considerable frigate force at St. Leonard's Creek. The stand Barney and his men made at Bladensburg in August 1814, a gallant effort that sparked one of the few memorable incidents in that otherwise dark day in the history of American arms, and their heroic roles in the defense of Baltimore at Fort McHenry and its outer defenses are barely remembered. The ambitious plan to defend the Chesapeake at a minimum of expense, doomed to failure from the start, has also been all but forgotten. The reasons for that failure cannot be found in the able and courageous man who commanded the flotilla or in the steadfast seamen who manned it. The answer lies elsewhere.

In 1890 Captain Alfred Thayer Mahan published his monumental work, *The Influence of Sea Power upon History, 1660–1783,* in which he set forth the conditions affecting a nation's relative success as a power on the high seas. Perhaps one way to evaluate the apparent lack of success Barney had in achieving his military objectives is to apply Captain Mahan's conditions to the microcosm of America's greatest estuary system, the Chesapeake Bay, and one of its chief tributaries, the Patuxent River, upon which the main focal point of naval confrontation in the theater was to be centered during the summer of 1814.

It has been stated that the flotilla was doomed even before its construction began as a result of Mahan's principle of "physical conformation." The entrance to the Chesapeake Bay at the Virginia Capes is relatively narrow, and several excellent anchorages are afforded just inside the mouth itself. These peculiar features of the coast made it extremely easy for the Royal Navy to blockade the bay during both the American Revolution and the War of 1812. With the entrance to the Tidewater under blockade, the numerically inferior U.S. Navy stood little chance of forcing its way in to provide even limited support for the flotilla. Indeed, no material move to assist or reinforce Barney's naval force with ships or boats—or to even resupply it—from within the bay or from without was even considered. The vast system of navigable rivers and the embayment itself, a watery highway over which the great wealth and commerce of the region was channeled, Mahan points out, which in times of peace permits the growth of a nation's internal trade, also provides an enemy, in times of war, with easy access to the interior. Given the numbers of available British vessels, and later on troops, and the minuscule size of the flotilla sent to oppose them, it appears that there was little of significance that Barney might have done to stem the tide. Nevertheless, he did manage to succeed in maintaining a potent force, which tied up a significant portion of the Royal Navy squadron employed in the Tidewater during the three months he was engaged on the Patuxent River. Despite the flotilla's fierce determination and discipline, however, it was helpless to prevent the continued British depredation against the vulnerable shores of Maryland and Virginia and, for a period, up the navigable length of the lower Patuxent itself.

In examining the characteristics of a nation's population as it affects maritime power, Mahan points out the need for a sufficient number of individuals familiar with the seafaring trade. It initially appeared that procuring skilled seamen to man his flotilla, once built, would be the least of Barney's problems. Was not the bay area famous for its privateersmen and mariners? Such was not the case, however. As the following pages will show, Barney encountered severe problems in recruitment that were directly attributable to competition from the regular navy and privateering syndicates and to the incredibly hard duty and well-known dangers inherent in small craft warfare, which many unemployed seamen were unwilling to endure. When he finally put to sea, many barges were left behind in Baltimore for lack of crewmen. Indeed, manpower proved critical to the effective use of the flotilla throughout its existence.

A second aspect of a nation's population impact on its military and overall strategy is its trained reserve force. With respect to Barney's flotilla and its defense of the Patuxent, it becomes necessary to extend Mahan's principle to the militia system and the local citizen-soldiers required to support the squadron's shoreward forces. The vivid descriptions of the David and Goliath battles in St. Leonard's Creek in June 1814 and the accounts of Barney's later predicaments and ultimate retreat up the Patuxent thoroughly demonstrate the necessity of unified action between land and sea forces in a riverine situation and a clear chain of command to coordinate it. Yet the militia, and even the regular army, repeatedly failed to act with the flotilla in a militarily compatible manner. Only once, during the Second Battle of St. Leonard's, was such an effort undertaken, albeit with astonishingly positive results despite poor performances by both the army and militia. However, militia and civilian support by the planters and townspeople of the Patuxent region failed to materialize, largely owing to the political and social schism wrought by the unpopular war and by the enormously effective British campaign of terror. The cost to Maryland was an almost total exhaustion of resolve in the countryside and millions of dollars in property losses. The failure to act measurably hastened the ruination, if not total destruction, of nearly every town and plantation of the Patuxent Valley and ultimately of the flotilla itself, the scars of which would remain for a century or more.

Finally, Mahan points out that the "character of the government" is significantly instrumental in the development and support of a country's sea power. One might well question the prospects for successfully instituting a blockade of the Chesapeake or even the need for a flotilla had the government of Thomas Jefferson not adopted its famous but unsuccessful "gunboat" policy. Had the nation moved ahead with the development of a conventional bluewater naval force suitable to contend with another oceanic force such as that fielded by the Royal Navy, the story might have been different. But the few traditional fighting ships, frigates, sloops-of-war, and the like—which, when deployed, acquitted themselves with incredible success—were not to be had on the Chesapeake, with the exception of those entirely blockaded and useless in its rivers, and the American government was obliged to experiment in the mosquito warfare proposed by Barney under extreme wartime conditions. There were no other options.

Though in retrospect the Barney flotilla failed to provide the means for the blunting of British depredations in the Tidewater, its effectiveness as a viable tactical fighting force in the environment for which it was designed was astonishing. The flotilla itself, though extremely vulnerable to both weather and enemy broadsides, even when locked in St. Leonard's Creek, an unknown backwater tributary of the Patuxent, proved capable of bearding the British lion time and again and, when finally freed, continued to present a dangerous threat to his rear and flanks that could not be ignored. It was soon conceded that, as long as Barney's force continued to exist, British offensive operations in the Tidewater, and particularly in the Patuxent, would be seriously jeopardized. The planned expedition against the capital of the United States of America could not be made with a prospect of success as long as the flotilla could fight. But in the end, its destruction was not to be at the hands of the enemy but under the direct orders of a panic-stricken government.

The following pages are not simply a day-to-day history of the inception, fielding, fighting, and ultimate destruction of the Chesapeake Flotilla but a comprehensive bird's-eye view of the complex nature and incredible impact of the naval war of 1812 as it was played out in the turbid waters of the Patuxent River.

The battle for the Patuxent was the first and only series of fleet engagements between national navies to be fought in Maryland waters. It was a desperate, even gallant, experiment in naval development, which, though ably managed and heroically conducted, was ultimately condemned to failure, a forgotten yet ultimately instructive chapter in the development of our nation's great naval and maritime evolution.

Fred W. Hopkins, Jr.

The original keel of this modest volume, first laid down in 1979 and launched two years later, was not fielded, like the U.S. Chesapeake Flotilla that it sought to document, under duress. But as with all good ships whose sails and masts, after long service, are deemed in need of a refit, it has become necessary to haul it into drydock for a few adjustments and improvements. It was born, in its first incarnation as *Flotilla: Battle for the Patuxent*, as the conscious outgrowth of a larger effort that attempted to archaeologically investigate and record the tangible remnants of the maritime heritage of one of Maryland's most historic waterways, the Patuxent River. The fruits of that grand endeavor, known as the Patuxent River Submerged Cultural Resources Survey, have over the last quarter century directly influenced the way we have explored, studied, recorded, and managed our incredibly rich historical and archaeological resources. But more important, it has also provided a better understanding of how we, as Americans, came to be who we are today. One of those fruits was the publication of the first comprehensive account of a forgotten but important component of American naval history, the U.S. Chesapeake Flotilla.

As we approach the bicentennial of the War of 1812, it is fitting that this new and revised edition of *Flotilla* not only incorporates important historical data that has come to light over the years since the original publication first appeared but also has benefited immensely from a veritable surge of fresh views and scholarly works on that important conflict in our nation's formative years. Moreover, in the course of revising and expanding the original text for this edition, I have had the joy of revisiting the many thousands of pages of original documents, manuscripts, and published works first examined at least three decades ago. In so doing I frequently encountered data that was either overlooked or ignored, or for some reason or other set aside and never picked up again, much of which has been mined for this edition. With these assets in hand, it has been possible to provide a substantially enhanced and, I hope, sharper perspective on the Patuxent naval campaign and the experiment in riverine gunboat warfare that it embraced, fought nearly two centuries ago by an infant America almost torn asunder by conflict and its first major crisis of direction.

The Chesapeake Flotilla was a small squadron belonging to a short-lived and independent arm of the navy called the U.S. Flotilla Service, a naval defense force conceived in desperation, but led and fought with incredible valor and ability against overwhelming odds. The men who built it, manned it, and ultimately destroyed it were among the first responders in a national military emergency on American soil every bit as harrowing and divisive by degrees as the War for Independence and the Civil War. In this work I have sought to present the astonishing story of the birth, life, and death of that diminutive fleet, and its incredible influence on the course of a conflict some have called America's Second War for Independence. It is, indeed, the tale of an eighteen-boat squadron of gunboats, row galleys, and barges, the five hundred men who manned it, and a commander, Commodore Joshua Barney, whose resolution, bravery, and fighting leadership prevailed time and again against all likelihood of failure. Sadly it was also an American experiment in naval warfare tragically doomed from the beginning, but one whose very failure was instructive in redirecting the course of future naval development.

This work was never intended to present the entire history of the naval war of 1812 as it was fought on the Chesapeake, of the overall Chesapeake theater on land and water, or of the U.S. Flotilla Service. Nor was it written as a biographical homage. Rather it was calculated to present a holistic picture, from both American and British perspectives, warts and all, of the Patuxent Campaign and its consequences, including the only fleet engagements between national navies ever fought in Maryland waters, ultimately leading to the British march on Washington. The effects of the flotilla's very existence were substantial. Indeed, the three-month-long David and Goliath contest between the flotilla and the British Royal Navy on the waters of the Chesapeake Bay and Patuxent River would directly influence the course of the War of 1812 and ultimately American history itself.

Though it is the usual form for historians to present quoted material as in the original, replete with random capitalization, incorrect punctuation, misspellings, arcane abbreviations, and the like, I have often found such to be cumbersome and difficult for the lay reader to digest. Hence, I have corrected the more egregious of these errors by placing most quoted material in its modern form and sentence structure, without altering the wording, intent of the message, or data. The names of towns, villages, and other geographic locations are addressed in their modern forms to also avoid confusion. For those

readers who wish to try to navigate through the original documents or manuscript text, or for further reference by student and scholar, I have provided
comprehensive endnotes and bibliography. In producing the endnotes I have,
as in the original edition, made reference to several substantial collections of
manuscript transcripts when I did not have access to the originals. The most
notable of these were the Cockburn Papers in the Manuscript Division of the
Library of Congress and a large number of Royal Navy ship logs, journals,
and letters published in various editions of the *Chronicles of St. Mary's,* the
originals of which are in the Admiralty Collection, Public Record Office,
in London. A considerable number of official U.S. government and military
communications and reports, war damage claims, congressional hearings,
and the like, the originals of which are housed in various collections in the
Washington, D.C., and Suitland, Maryland, branches of the National Ar-
chive and Record Service, were published in several elephant-size volumes of
the *American State Papers.* Though I have examined most of the originals and
microfilm copies of original manuscripts, I have found the published versions
to be, with a few exceptions, quite as good, and have generally cited them as
they are more readily available to the reader. The exception is in the navy letters to and from the secretary of the navy, many of which I transcribed from
microfilm in 1980, but which have since been published in the U.S. Naval
History Division's marvelous multivolume bible of the war at sea, *The Naval
War of 1812: A Documentary History.*

In documenting the history of the U.S. Chesapeake Flotilla and its role
in the Patuxent Campaign, and the archaeological discovery of its physical
remains in June 1980 and July 1997, I have been directed and assisted from the
beginning by several individuals and institutions without whose input and encouragement this work would never have come to fruition. First and foremost
among these is my close friend and associate Dr. Ralph E. Eshelman who,
while director of the Calvert Marine Museum many years ago, provided not
only his, but the museum's robust support in first publishing my history of the
flotilla. His strong encouragement, honest criticism, and judicious prodding
were then as now welcomed stimulants for me to keep on going. Dr. Fred W.
Hopkins, Jr., graduate dean emeritus, of the University of Baltimore, my dear
friend and mentor for countless years, generously contributed for inclusion in
the first edition of this book the fruits of his own considerable research on the
War of 1812 and the men who fought it as well as the insightful introduction.
He has never ceased providing me with the benefits of his opinions, knowledge, and gifted perception, for which I am truly indebted to him. This new

edition has also benefited greatly by the wonderful work of the U.S. Naval Historical Center and its superb historians, William S. Dudley and Michael J. Crawford, and their dedicated staff, notably Christine F. Hughes, Tamara Moser Melia, Charles E. Brodine, and Carolyn M. Stalling. Their monumental three-volume work, *The Naval War of 1812: A Documentary History,* will stand as the centerpiece for all future works on the naval war of 1812. I have also greatly enjoyed over the years a rewarding association with my longtime friend and colleague Scott S. Sheads, historian and ranger, Fort McHenry National Monument and Historic Shrine, whose perspective and freely given knowledge on the history of the War of 1812, which has greatly influenced and enhanced my own, is second to none. I would also like to acknowledge Mary C. Lethbridge, former director of the Library of Congress Information (now Public Affairs) Office. In helping me, many years ago, hone the original manuscript, from which this new volume has ultimately emerged, I was fortunate to have been ably assisted by Jennifer Rutland, for whose services I am still eternally grateful. I would be remiss if I did not extend a word of gratitude to the late Hulbert Footner, whose wonderful biography of Commodore Joshua Barney, *Sailor of Fortune,* first inspired me to dip my toes into the muddy waters of the Patuxent in search of his noble flotilla, and to the late Walter Lord, whose history of America's earliest and darkest hour, *The Dawn's Early Light,* is a model still without equal.

I would also like to extend my sincere appreciation to the notable national, state, and regional institutions in which the great bulk of archival material, which it has been both a chore and a pleasure to examine, rests. These include the National Archives and the Library of Congress in Washington, D.C.; the Maryland Historical Society, in Baltimore, Maryland; the Pennsylvania Historical Society in Philadelphia, Pennsylvania; the Public Record Office in London, England; and the Calvert County, Prince George's County, and St. Mary's County, Maryland Historical Societies. And finally, I would like to express thanks to my wife Carol for putting up with the chaos imposed by the "mad historian."

The voyage has been wonderful for me, and I hope will prove of interest to the reader.

Flotilla

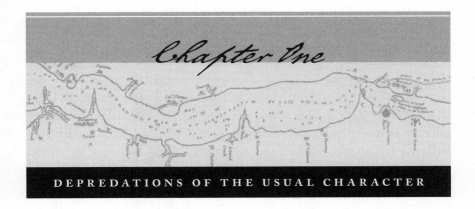

Chapter One

DEPREDATIONS OF THE USUAL CHARACTER

When the vanguard of a powerful British fleet entered the Virginia Capes on the morning of February 4, 1813, the last thing on the minds of the farmers of the fertile Patuxent River Valley of the Maryland Tidewater a hundred miles to the north was war.[1] The contest into which the United States had cast itself, recklessly some said, was now more than seven months old. Everyone was confident that the battle lines that had been drawn across the Canadian frontier would continue to serve as the focal point of conflict, and its progress was no longer the main topic of conversation in rural Southern Maryland, where the war had been quietly opposed from the beginning. No one suspected that the slowly silting backwater region of the Tidewater called the Patuxent would ever assume a prominent role in anything but the harvesting of the fine tobacco for which it was justly famous, for it had been assumed that, even if the British did decide to carry the war to the Chesapeake, there were certainly more appropriate targets elsewhere to attract their attention.

Yet, ever since President James Madison's war message to the Congress of the United States on June 1, 1812, in which he detailed for the nation a strong indictment of British policies and actions inimical to the well-being of America, the current had been inexorably gathering a momentum that would inundate the Tidewater in one of the most bitter episodes of a conflict history would remember only as the War of 1812.[2] The immediate response to the president's address was exhibited on June 4, when the House of Representatives passed a bill by a margin of seventy-nine to forty-nine, declaring a state of war between the United States and Great Britain. On June 17 the Senate passed the bill by a vote of nineteen to thirteen, and the following day Madison placed his signature on the momentous declaration.[3]

Few nations that have willingly thrown their resources, livelihood, and future into the swirling cauldron of war have been as unprepared for the contest as the United States was at the outset of this conflict. The active naval forces available for service boasted only seven frigates, a handful of smaller warships, and several diminutive mosquito fleets of gunboats, most of which were old, unseaworthy, and totally unsuitable for duty. Federalist opponents of the war (and there were many in Maryland and Virginia) were quick to point out the state of unpreparedness in which the young nation now found itself. They hastened to accentuate in many quarters of the country the unpopular nature of the commitment Madison had grudgingly set into action. "Without funds, without taxes, without an army, navy, or adequate fortifications," noted the editors of one staunch anti-war advocate, the *Federal Republican*, "with one hundred and fifty million of our property in the hands of the declared enemy, without any of his property in our power, and with a vast commerce afloat, our rulers have promulgated a war against the clear and decided sentiments of a vast majority of the nation."[4]

Despite the stated reasons justifying the war, such as the illegal impressment of American seamen by British warships, violations of American sovereignty, and the interference with American trade, large portions of the population were undeniably opposed to military action. The first rumblings of a national belief in what would later be called "manifest destiny," that the entirety of the North American continent, including Canada, was fated to become part of the American Union, only compounded the dissension. The loose-knit fabric of nationhood, so recently stitched together, seemed about to unravel.

Militarily, the United States appeared to stand little chance of victory, especially at sea, for the Royal Navy, though momentarily embroiled in a deadly struggle with France, numbered more than a thousand ships. The British army, it was said, was resolutely capable of engaging and defeating the best that France or any nation could throw at it. What chance did American arms have against such a foe?

In Maryland the war had polarized the population into opposing political camps, with advocates and opponents vociferously airing their cases in both public and private forums. The powerful and wealthy pro-war elements were centered in and about the Port of Baltimore and were quite vocal in their sentiments, as were their opponents. Declarations of support and dissent were daily espoused in the press and at citizens' meetings. Occasionally, riotous actions, beatings, even tarring-and-featherings and murders erupted in ugly confrontations that accentuated the passionate and partisan differences of opinion. On one occasion, the publication of a Federalist anti-war newspaper was halted when the publisher's offices were stormed and several men defending it were killed, maimed, or cruelly tortured by the mob. The issue of freedom of the press was brought to the fore, and the Maryland state elections that followed soon afterward resulted in the swearing in of a strong anti-war element that came to dominate the Executive Office as well as much of the Statehouse.[5]

Yet in Southern Maryland, along the rural lower Patuxent and Potomac drainages, far removed from the storm of controversy and public confrontation, the inhabitants, largely Federalists in political persuasion, seemed altogether uninterested in the crisis of dissent and even less in the progress of the war.

There were, however, certain advantages to be had in America's otherwise untimely entrance into open conflict. Most of Great Britain's sizeable military establishment was tied up in a costly war with France and for the moment seemed unable to cope with the surprising, although small, surge of American naval aggressiveness. The borders of Britain's Canadian dominions, upon which American eyes had been covetously cast since the days of the American Revolution, lay seductively open and apparently ripe for plucking. And long-untended British violations of American rights begged to be swiftly avenged before the enemy was capable of preparing an appropriate military response.

While the United States could never have hoped to rival Britain in terms of conventional sea power, there was a singularly important alternative that might, in the long run, help to balance the incredibly lopsided odds. That option, which was to prove of considerable import in attracting enemy attentions to the Tidewater, was nothing less than the institution of the time-honored practice of issuing letters of marque and reprisal to privately owned and armed warships. It was hoped that this practice, commonly referred to as privateering, which had been employed with often stunning success during the Revolution, might injure Britain's commerce to such an extent that she would be obliged to sue for peace on American terms. It was not unusual that the United States should adopt such a method to wage war on the high seas. The concept and practicality of employing privately owned vessels to wage war against an enemy, of course, was not new. Indeed, its antecedents extended back to the days of King Edward I, and it had been employed by the great and minor powers of Europe ever since. From the very onset of the colonial period in America, English and colonial letters of marque vessels and privateers had canvassed the oceans in quest of Spanish, French, Dutch, and Portuguese prizes during the numerous wars that had blighted the Western

Hemisphere. The British, in fact, had employed privateering right up to the wars with Napoleon, and it was certainly not considered out of the ordinary that their Yankee cousins should do the same.

The issuance by a national government of a letter of marque and reprisal, an official warrant or commission, authorized a designated agent to search, seize, or destroy the assets and property belonging to a national government or party that had committed some offense under the accepted laws of nations against the citizens of the issuing nation. The commission usually granted the right for private parties operating under the commission to raid and capture merchant shipping of an enemy nation at war. Quite literally, the formal statement of the warrant authorized the agent to pass beyond the borders of the nation ("marque" meaning frontier or boundary), where he might engage in searching for, capturing, or destroying the assets, resources, or personnel of the adversarial party. Technically, the measure might not always be against a nation but a foreign party, and might, on certain occasions, be considered a retaliatory procedure short of a full declaration of war, intended to vindicate the action to other sovereign nations in the context of undeclared hostilities ("reprisal"). It was, however, often legally and politically a delicate undertaking, and it was always one fraught with unexpected consequences. Without the formal assurance of such warrants or commissions or proof thereof being present, the agents could indeed be, and sometimes were, considered as pirates under the commonly accepted laws of nations (though the line was often thin and occasionally overstepped). As with the issuance of a warrant for domestic search, seizure, arrest, or death, the commission necessarily had to contain a certain degree of specificity to guarantee that the designated agent would not exceed his authority and the intent of the issuing agency or government. It thus surprised no one that in the very declaration of war itself, the president was empowered "to issue to private armed vessels of the United States commissions or letters of marque and general reprisal in such form as he shall think proper, and under the seal of the United States, against the vessels, goods, and effects of the government of the said United Kingdom of Great Britain and Ireland, and the subjects thereof."[6]

Within a month of the declaration of war, there were no less than sixty-five such privately armed and owned American ships at sea actively capturing British commerce vessels and decimating enemy trade with astonishing skill and seamanship. Among the most successful of the privateers were those belonging to Maryland. Vessels commissioned in this state were wreaking havoc upon the enemy with such incredible efficiency that the state itself, and in particular the Port of Baltimore that spawned them, grew in notoriety with every new success. Though accurate counts vary, in the course of the war at least 117 privateers were commissioned from Maryland, more than half of which were fitted out at Baltimore—the largest number from any single port in the United States. Maryland vessels captured more than 455 prizes, and according to one reliable source perhaps more than 500 of the 1,338 enemy vessels, or more than a third of the total known taken as prizes by American privateers.[7]

Maryland captains such as Joshua Barney, George Coggeshall, James Dooly, and Thomas Boyle were rocketed to fame almost overnight for their deeds of daring and often for the incredible fortunes gained while privateering. Barney alone, in the course of a single voyage aboard an old 206-ton, 12-gun Baltimore-built schooner named *Rossie*, accounted for the capture of 4 ships, 8 brigs, 3 schooners, and 3 sloops, valued with their cargoes at nearly $1.5 million. Seven of the prizes were burnt at sea for want of sufficient prize crews to man them, and 217 prisoners were sent to Newfoundland aboard one of the prizes for lack of space or security aboard the captor's ship to carry them away. Captain Boyle, an ex-patriot New Englander, having adopted Maryland as his home state, while commanding the 14-gun schooner *Chasseur*, captured or destroyed more than 30 vessels valued at millions of dollars, and on several occasions even engaged in pitched battles with regular British warships.[8]

The successes of the American privateers, in particular those belonging to Maryland, could not be denied. Even the federal government was astonished at the devastating achievements of these vessels so early in the war. Buoyed by hopes of forcing the British mercantile community to bring further pressure on its government, many important Americans, such as Thomas Jefferson, encouraged not just the capture of enemy commerce vessels but also their total destruction "to make the merchants of England feel and squeal and cry out for peace."[9]

In early 1813 the federal government enlarged upon the public's right to participate in actions against the British navy and marine when on March 3, Congress passed an act making it lawful for anyone "to burn, sink, or destroy any British armed vessel of war" except cartels or flag-of-truce ships. Moreover, all citizens were authorized to use "torpedoes, submarine instruments, or any other destructive machine whatsoever" to accomplish such ends. To sweeten the deal, a bounty of one half the value of the vessels destroyed, as well as their guns, cargo, tackle, and apparel, would be paid by the U.S. Treasury to whomever accomplished such ends.[10]

The one singularly negative aspect of the Maryland privateering effort was the venomous hatred their successes were earning from the British, and even from several New England states violently opposed to the war. It was obvious that English merchants could not long withstand such economically disruptive activities; they soon were obliged to beseech their government for protection and help. It was not until October 13, 1812, however, that the British administration could bring itself to reciprocate the American hostilities and formally declare war on the United States.

That the declaration of war by a young upstart nation such as the United States against a major world power such as Great Britain had at first been taken somewhat less than seriously was perhaps best evidenced by the delay of nearly seven months before the British government issued a formal declaration of its own. Indeed, not until January 9, 1813, did the British officially state their own justification for war with America. While denying any intention of conquest or involvement in promoting native uprisings on the American frontier, the government had given as the principal reason for seizing seamen from American ships that, in its own fight for survival against Napoleonic France, it had been forced to search neutral ships and remove English sailors. The American military campaign against Canada, it was believed in London, could not be long sustained. Moreover, and quite fortunately for Great Britain, Napoleon's army was on the retreat from Russia and in such a devastated condition that the great dictator's days were likely to be few. If there was ever a time to mount a concerted offensive against America, it was now.[11]

The pressure to act specifically against the privateers increased, and many merchants suggested that moves be taken to close the principal outlets from which the bulk of American privateering vessels sailed, namely the Chesapeake and Delaware. More important, the vulnerability of the Chesapeake and its proximity to the center of American government, as well as its incredibly rich commerce and shipping, had considerable appeal to British military planners. Thus, on December 26, 1812, Vice Admiral Sir John Borlase Warren, the elderly commander-in-chief of the North American Station, was directed to undertake a singularly monumental task, namely "to establish the most complete and vigorous blockade of the ports and harbours of the Bay of Chesapeake and of the River Delaware, and to maintain and enforce the same according to the usages of war."[12]

Though the mission required diverting ships from critical wartime service in the Mediterranean and the English Channel, and blockade duty on the

Bay of Biscay, barely five weeks later the vanguard of a fleet of warships under the command of Admiral George Cockburn entered the Virginia Capes and cast anchor in Hampton Roads. Cockburn himself arrived off Lynnhaven Bay on March 3. A working commander who shared with his men the privations and dangers of war at sea and ashore, the admiral had only recently been conducting operations on the coast of Spain when given command of the Chesapeake theater and instructed to first report to Bermuda. His orders were formidable. He was not only to institute a total blockade of the Chesapeake and Delaware bays, but also to capture or destroy the American shipping in the James, York, Rappahannock, and Potomac rivers, and, off Baltimore, to secure intelligence regarding American land and sea forces, acquire pilots knowledgeable about the Chesapeake, find a safe and defensible anchorage for his squadron, figure out some means of capturing the USS *Constellation* then outfitting in the Elizabeth River, cut off trade with Long Island Sound, maintain regular communications with other British naval forces, and send all prizes taken to Bermuda.[13] The squadron was indeed imposing to see. They consisted of the admiral's flagship HBMS *Marlborough*, 74, Captain Charles B. H. Ross commanding; *Dragon*, 74, Captain Robert Barrie commanding; *Poictiers*, 74, Commodore John P. Beresford commanding; *Victorious*, 74, Captain John Talbot commanding; *Statira*, 38, Captain Hassard Stackpole commanding; *Maidstone*, 36, Captain George Burdett commanding; *Belvidera*, 36, Captain Richard Byron commanding; *Narcissus*, 32, Captain John R. Lumly commanding; *Lauristinus*, 21, Captain Thomas Graham commanding; and *Tartarus*, 16, Captain John Pasco commanding.[14] Yet, if the forces initially at Cockburn's disposal were considerable, owing to their size and draft, quite suitable for oceanic warfare, they were ill suited for the shallow-water environment of the Chesapeake Tidewater.

George Cockburn, though born of privilege to a family of influence, and only forty-one years of age, was a daring, resourceful, and altogether aggressive commander. He was eager to carry out the war against the Tidewater and its nests of privateers in the most appropriate and propitious manner possible. An acolyte of Hardy, Hood, and Lord Nelson, he was a handsome officer and a strict disciplinarian who was commanding in presence, ruthless, politically astute, and intelligently persuasive in debate or battle. Nelson himself had paid the ultimate compliment by calling him a skilled seaman and man of action. A veteran of combat in the Mediterranean, India, the West Indies, and northern Europe, his life had indeed been one of constant and intrepid motion, and it was not long before his traits came to epitomize to his foes in

America the ultimate enemy. Napoleon Bonaparte, whom the admiral was later to escort on his voyage to St. Helena, though perhaps not the most objective of observers, described him as "rough, overbearing, vain, choleric and capricious." Yet it was because of all of these qualities that he was perhaps the most adequately suited man available for the dirty little war that was to ensue in the Tidewater. Cockburn easily contrasted those about him, superiors and inferiors alike. The once able, though now aged Vice Admiral John Borlase Warren, his superior, seemed relatively placid and unimaginative, indeed even timid, when placed in the same ocean with him.[15]

Cockburn was well aware that although the British squadron was substantially superior to any American naval defense available for the Chesapeake, it was, in truth, serving as but a diversion to frighten the U.S. government into withdrawing troops from the Canadian frontier. Locked in mortal combat with Napoleonic France, Great Britain could spare few troops for North America, but having more or less disposed of the French navy was more readily capable of waging war against the United States at sea. Yet, Cockburn was confident that it was but a portent of the future and a virtual guarantee of trouble ahead for the rich and vulnerable planters and plantations, hamlets and cities alike of the Tidewater that might influence the very outcome of the war.

Working in the admiral's favor was a complete lack of American unity of command in the Chesapeake Tidewater. The governors of Virginia, Maryland, and Delaware seemed totally incapable of coordinating action. Only the U.S. secretary of the navy seemed intent on organizing a formal defensive posture, but without regulars, with only militia to rely upon for coastal protection, and with total domination of the waters by the Royal Navy's effective blockade, every effort was met with frustration.

In March, when Cockburn's forces, which had quickly put a crimp on the flow of Baltimore privateers into the open ocean, were substantially reinforced with the arrival of Warren, aboard HBMS *San Domingo*, 74, Captain Charles Gill commanding, with a number of lesser vessels in company, the invaders' objectives began to take form. While the British blockaders as yet possessed land troops, they could boast of a body of perhaps the best marines in the world. And with these Cockburn was itching to undertake more than a few projects with which to substantially occupy and injure his foes. Thus, with the onset of spring his squadron moved up the Chesapeake from its anchorage at Lynnhaven Bay. Early in April he began sending tenders and small boats into nearly every navigable inlet on the Chesapeake, looting and burning, as well as sounding and charting the area for later use, as he proceeded. Often the local militia was called out to defend this or that township, plantation, or landing, hastily traded a few shots with the Royal Marines, and just as quickly ran off into the woods, disbanding after the immediate threat had subsided.[16]

In April, Cockburn launched his first large-scale expedition into Maryland waters. The British seemed to have been born to plunder, and they enjoyed free rein from the Susquehanna and Elk to the Chesapeake Capes. In a matter of days Sharp's Island was assailed and looted. On April 16 the Port of Baltimore was menaced when the British hove to off the Patapsco to establish a blockade and take soundings, and the citizens of the city flocked to raise half a million dollars for the city defenses, which were rushed ahead. Fortunately, the approach to Fort McHenry, guarding the city harbor, proved too much for the deep draft line-of-battle ships. On April 23 Spesuite Island, near the head of the Chesapeake at the mouth of the Susquehanna River, was occupied, and three days later an attack on Annapolis was rumored to be in the making. On April 27 Royal Marines landed on Poplar Island, and the following day occupied Tilghman Island, to the immediate south.[17]

On April 29 Frenchtown, opposite Elkton, was assaulted, plundered, and burned to the ground. A packet ship and four smaller vessels, along with a great quantity of flour, army clothing, saddles, bridles, and other military equipment, were also destroyed. On May 3, again bypassing Baltimore, the admiral bombarded, captured, and sacked the thriving little port of Havre de Grace with but slight resistance offered by a brave lone gunner named John O'Neill. Unfortunately, the fact that any resistance at all had been made was excuse enough for the enemy to burn between forty and sixty dwellings in the town. Soon afterward the marauders rowed up the Susquehanna River to assail the Principio Iron Works, one of the principal cannon foundries in the country. On the morning of May 6, the twin ports of Georgetown and Fredericktown, facing each other on opposite sides of the Sassafras River, were assaulted and totally destroyed. Such hit-and-run raids brought terror to the shores of the northern regions of the Chesapeake as the enemy moved about, capturing farms and towns seemingly at will, destroying or stealing tobacco, livestock, and grain, and burning or taking as a prize every vessel encountered. Although there had been a few sharp engagements with American privateers and revenue cutters on the waters, overall opposition in the Tidewater had been nil. With little more for defense than the Virginia and Maryland militias, which were usually unreliable at best, a few antiquated and poorly manned federal gunboats at Baltimore, Washington, and Norfolk, the blockaded U.S. Navy frigate *Constellation* at Norfolk, the frigate *Adams* at the Washington Navy Yard, and four privateer schooners at Baltimore hired by the government, there seemed little that could be done against the new masters of riverine warfare in North America.[18]

On June 1 Admiral Warren, who had quit the Chesapeake for Bermuda with forty prizes in hand on May 17, returned to the Tidewater with a large naval reinforcement, together with a substantial body of marines and soldiers under the command of Sir Thomas Sidney Beckwith. Beckwith's force, which the British government fervently hoped would serve to divert American attentions from the Canadian theater, consisted of a detachment of 1,800 marines, 300 Royal Marine artillerymen (50 with special training in Congreve rocketry), 300 infantrymen belonging to the 102nd Regiment, and 250 Independent Foreigners, or Canadian "chasseurs." The chasseurs were, in fact comprised largely of French prisoners of war who had chosen service with their captors rather than rotting away in a British prison.[19]

Earl Bathurst himself had prepared Beckwith's instructions. He ordered Sir Thomas to use his army as directed by Admiral Warren, but once ashore he was to be in complete command. He was also directed to remember that his mission was to be one of harassment and he was to avoid any general action or occupation of any place. He might exact money from any individuals he felt appropriate but was not to attempt to do so from governments. Moreover, he could receive runaway slaves as free persons but was under no circumstances to encourage slave insurrection.[20]

With this force available, it was decided that an offensive operation be carried out against Norfolk to capture the Portsmouth Navy Yard and the USS *Constellation*, at anchor and blockaded in the Elizabeth River. The project was temporarily delayed by a surprise but failed American gunboat attack against HBMS *Junon* on June 20. The expedition, when it finally got under way two days later, proved to be something of a disaster for the invaders. Proceeding up the Elizabeth, the British had encountered a strongpoint at Craney Island, guarding the waterway's mouth. Here, the Virginians had established a fortification upon the small, shoally sandspit close to the west side of the river but controlling the channel that checked the Royal Navy's advance. Failing in his endeavors against Norfolk, the enemy turned his attentions and frustrations against the tiny port of Hampton, ten miles up the James River. After a brief American resistance, the town was captured on June 25 by amphibious assault, looted, and pillaged, innocent civilians were murdered outright, and

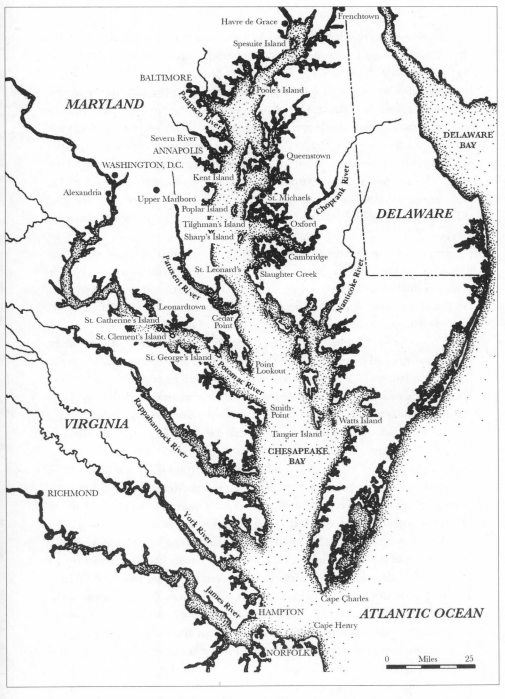

The upper Chesapeake theater of operations, 1813–14. *Map by Donald G. Shomette.*

several women were allegedly raped by two companies of French chasseurs. The chasseurs were returned to the fleet in utter disgrace, never to fight again in the Tidewater.[21]

Inexorably, the focus of war began to creep toward the Patuxent-Potomac axis of Southern Maryland. During the spring and summer of 1813 the British began to consider the hitherto untouched St. Mary's County fulcrum of Maryland's western shore as fertile grounds for foraging and watering expeditions. The county was skirted on all but one side by water and lay dangerously exposed to attack by enemy naval forces at almost any given point. The danger was all but ignored by the federal government, although as early as March 20, 1813, feeble local efforts had been under way to establish a defensive posture.[22]

Responding to the threat of enemy incursions into the upper reaches of the Chesapeake, officers of the St. Mary's County Militia, in late March, were notified of a meeting to be convened at Leonardtown, the county seat, on April 3 to consider defensive measures and to prepare for mobilization. On March 25 U.S. Postmaster General Gideon Granger directed that a forward observation post be established at Point Lookout, the strategic, sandy, mosquito-infested peninsular tip of the county formed by the conflux of the Potomac River and Chesapeake Bay. From this vantage point, an agent could monitor the movements of any enemy vessels arriving or departing the Maryland Tidewater, observe their activities, note their armaments, and otherwise provide a continuous stream of critical intelligence to Washington, Annapolis, and Baltimore. An agent named Henry Weitz was appointed but was replaced in June by an eager volunteer by the name of Thomas Swann. To facilitate the smooth transfer of intelligence, postmasters at all of the post offices on the route between the point and Washington were sternly ordered to "help forward the express with the greatest possible speed."[23]

Alarms were to become frequent from the beginning of April onward. On the evening of April 8 Lieutenant Colonel Athanasius Fenwick, commander of the 12th Regiment, Fifth Brigade, Maryland Militia, from his "Alarm Post at Leonardtown," dispatched an express to Captain James Forrest, commander of the Leonardtown Troop of Horse, informing him "that a part of the enemy's squadron was at [the] Point." When the order to turn out was disseminated, however, few if any of the militia that mustered were equipped with swords, pistols, or the least munitions of war. The citizen-soldiers of St. Mary's County, it would appear, were completely unprepared to repel even the smallest incursion against their territory.[24]

Fortunately for the county, the British were for the moment intent on targets farther up the Chesapeake. Nevertheless, much of Southern Maryland had developed a serious case of war jitters. Many succumbed to the well-founded fear that the foe would certainly turn his attention on the region before all was said and done. On the banks of St. Inigoes Creek, just up from the mouth of the St. Mary's River, the priests of the old Jesuit Mission of St. Inigoes were panic-stricken. Flocks of young novitiates were herded aboard a small boat belonging to one Captain Coad and shipped off to the safety of Georgetown, D.C. Their departure, it appeared, was perhaps not a bit too soon.[25]

"Hardly had the Novices been removed," wrote one of the priests afterward, "when the British cruisers made up the Chesapeake." Then Brother Mobberly, "who had charge of St. Ingo's [*sic*], could be seen in a terrible bustle, shouting his commands to this and that, loading his ox carts, and hustling his patient steers at a double quick step to the cellars of his neighbors."[26] The frightened priest deposited a sizeable store of the mission's yearly food supply in the cellars of at least three of his parishioners, Cornelius Fish, John Leach, and Peter Thompson. Barrels of whiskey, port wine, herring, hams, beef, flour, sugar, codfish, and even candles were hidden away for safekeeping.[27]

Despite calls for government protection, St. Mary's County remained exposed and unprotected. Yet, when the British seemingly ignored the region, the initial panic soon turned to a contagious malaise. The only visible federal action came on July 19, when Postmaster General Granger finally arranged for a regular express to be carried to and from the government agent at Point Lookout. Thomas Swann was directed to dispatch a daily status report to the capital from the Ridge Post Office, just north of his post on the point, and would in return receive a daily communication or instructions from the War Department. With the express rider no longer obliged to make regular stops, dispatches could be carried one way in only twenty-three hours.[28]

It was well that the lines of communication had been improved, for on the same day that Granger upgraded the express system, Admiral Cockburn finally decided to pay a visit to the shores of Southern Maryland. The British efficiently proceeded to throw up a blockade of the Patuxent, while entering the Potomac in force on July 14 to take soundings and proceed upriver as far as possible. After a brief but fierce encounter with the U.S. Navy schooner *Asp*, which was taken and burned (but later retaken by the Americans), several small islands were immediately seized without opposition. On Blackistone and St. Catherine's islands wells were sunk to secure fresh drinking water for the fleet. St. George's Island, at the conflux of the St. Mary's River and the Potomac, fared a bit worse when considerable looting was carried out. Penetration upriver as far as Cedar and Maryland points were conducted, and several successful disembarkations carried out under Beckwith's direction on both the Virginia and Maryland shorelines.[29]

Yet the British were not invincible. When they attempted a raid across the Potomac against the Virginia shore settlements along Mattox Creek, a light infantry company commanded by Captain John Hungerford drove them back with some losses. Another probe was made into Rozier Creek, but also successfully met by Hungerford. Despite the skirmishes, Cockburn was not shaken. He proceeded to launch another invasion, this time against the geographic apex of Southern Maryland, the Point Lookout Peninsula. Captain James Forrest of the Leonardtown Troop of Horse, St. Mary's County Militia, reported that the enemy landed between two and three thousand men upon the point, from which it was expected raids would be carried out with impunity against the surrounding countryside.[30]

Though early estimates of the enemy's strength were often exaggerated, reports of the lootings, burnings, and kidnappings, which they perpetrated, were usually not. Plundering raids by small, mobile parties were soon under way against many of the private estates along both the shores of the Potomac and the lower Patuxent. During foraging expeditions without opposition, the invaders robbed homes, small farms, and great plantations alike. Stocks of cattle, hogs, and sheep were driven before the raiders and carried aboard their ships. *Niles' Weekly Register,* a barometer gauging the levels of British destruction since their arrival in the Chesapeake, noted of the Point Lookout–based forays: "Their depredations were of the usual character—they plundered anything and everything, robbing even the women and children of their clothes, and destroying such articles as it did not suit them to carry away." Local residents, such as Benjamin Williams, Robert Armstrong, Mordecai Jones, and James Biscoe, were kidnapped, labeled as prisoners of war, and trundled off and incarcerated in the foul holds of Royal Navy warships or sent to Halifax.[31]

When the British decided to loot a dwelling, they ignored nothing. The home of William and Elizabeth Smoot, for example, was among the many to suffer visitation by the invaders. Not only did the enemy carry off the Smoots' only livestock, a cow and a yearling, but he also took anything and everything else that struck his fancy. Even the most mundane items were not overlooked. A small looking glass, two knives and three forks, two metal spoons, an earthen pitcher of cream and a glass salt sellar, two new piggins, a bucket, two tea cups, a cream cup, a towel and tea cloth, two pairs of yarn gloves, a pocket comb, a fine-toothed comb, a large stone jug, a small pair of scissors, a saw, a new neck handkerchief, and a bridle were among the personal objects stolen. Inventories of this sort, though they seemed insignificant to the better-established citizens of the region, were of concern to poor dirt farmers such as the Smoots. Such thefts seemed disgraceful in their pettiness and without military justification. They did, however, serve to thoroughly terrorize and demoralize the population as Cockburn had anticipated.[32]

With every new day of occupation the list of estates, plantations, and private dwellings pillaged by the enemy grew. The Widow Locker, James Kirk, Robert Duncanson, Josiah Biscoe, McKay Biscoe, Tyler Thomas, Benjamin Williams, Robert Armstrong, Ann Bennett, and the Richardson family all suffered under the heel of British plundering forays.[33]

If the loss of property by the citizenry of the Maryland Tidewater wasn't bad enough for many farmers, the loss of their slaves was practically unbearable. By mid-summer, so many runaways had fled to British shipping in the bay, it had become more than a nuisance for Cockburn, who had to feed and shelter them from the finite larders of his squadron. His orders in this regard had been specific: he could not return any Negro against his will to slavery. They were to either be enlisted in the British military service or be shipped out as colonists to British possessions, although specifically which British colonies would receive them and at whose expense had been left open. The only real concession the admiral had was to allow slave owners to come aboard the shipping to try to persuade their ex-slaves to return.[34]

Enemy raids were one thing, but rumors of their other objectives while visiting the countryside were something else. Tall tales and hearsay were running rampant throughout the region. One such story claimed that it was the enemy's intention to locate all the Irishmen they could, claim them as His Majesty's subjects, and impress them into military service. It was said that one particular individual, a certain Mr. Clarke, had been fixed upon as a likely Irishman suitable for induction, a proposal that was vigorously protested by the subject in question. A British officer stepped up and insisted that the man was indeed of Irish origin. "Well, Sir," the man replied, "if I thought that I had a drop of Irish blood in me, I would bleed myself to death in order to draw it out." The reply so thoroughly amused the British officer that Clarke was released.[35]

Contrary to the popular consensus fostered by the war hawks in Washington and Baltimore, the British were often very selective in their depredations, and at Cockburn's order quite frequently paid hard cash for provisions or livestock sold to them by local inhabitants (which also ensured the survival of their homes and estates). One Royal Navy officer recorded the method in which such transfers of goods, especially cattle, smaller livestock, and fowls, were carried out, even with the rank-and-file of militia units. "The plan agreed on was this," he wrote. "They were to drive them down to a certain point, when we were to land and take possession—for the inhabitants being all militiamen, and having too much patriotism to sell food to 'King George's men'—they used to say 'put the money under such a stone or tree, pointing to it and then we can pick it up and say we found it.'" Even Colonel Michael Taney of the Calvert County Militia, brother of future Supreme Court Justice Roger Brooke Taney and brother-in-law to Francis Scott Key, was later accused of participating in the nefarious commerce, thereby saving the Taney family estate on the Patuxent at Battle Creek.[36] There were indeed, as the British officer noted, "more ways than one to cheat the old gentleman."[37] Despite such dealings, both collaborators and foes of the British suffered much the same. On July 27, after more than a week of raiding around the mouths of the Potomac and the Patuxent, the enemy re-embarked aboard his fleet. Three days later the squadron mercifully stood up the Chesapeake.[38]

The desperate need for organized defense in St. Mary's and in heretofore-untouched neighboring Calvert and Charles counties was blatantly obvious, as it was soon to be for all of the counties of Maryland. Yet the Maryland Militia system had, in fact, been organized under the Act of 1793 to accommodate just such an emergency. In 1811 two additional acts "for regulating and governing the militia of the State" strengthened the established act and made provision for an appropriate and viable division of forces for each county. The entire establishment was divided into 12 brigades, each composed of 4 regiments. Each regiment was made up of 2 battalions, and each battalion was comprised of 5 companies. Every company was to consist of 64 privates, 4 sergeants, 4 corporals, a drummer, and a fifer or bugler. Thus, a full-strength brigade could muster, on paper at least, nearly 3,000 men. Into this organization all white males between the ages of 18 and 45 were obliged to enroll. There were certain exceptions, however. Civil officers, pilots, sailors in the coasting trade, professors in schools and colleges, and conscientious religious objectors were exempt. Unfortunately, the command structure of the Maryland Militia system was divided between the Eastern and Western Shores, and its forces were neither experienced nor well armed.[39]

The counties situated along the vulnerable reaches of the Patuxent and Potomac drainages were to ultimately rely on three units: the Fourth Brigade, comprised of the 14th, 17th, 18th, and 19th Regiments (Prince George's and lower Montgomery counties); the Fifth Brigade, comprised of the 1st, 12th, 43rd, and 45th Regiments (St. Mary's and Charles counties); and the Eighth Brigade, comprised of the 2nd, 22nd, 31st, and 32nd Regiments (Calvert and Anne Arundel counties).[40]

A detached cavalry organization, however, provided for eleven districts, with a separate squadron of horse for far-off Alleghany County. Montgomery and Prince George's counties formed the Second Cavalry District, Calvert and Anne Arundel the Third, and Charles and St. Mary's the Fourth. Each of these districts was allocated a single regiment commanded by a lieutenant colonel and composed of two squadrons of horse under the charge of a major. Each squadron was made up of two troops apiece. A troop was to be composed of two lieutenants, a coronet, a quartermaster sergeant, four regular sergeants, four corporals, a farrier, a saddler, a trumpeter, and thirty-two privates commanded by a captain.[41]

On paper the militia defense of the Patuxent-Potomac axis consisted of nearly 9,000 infantry and 1,150 cavalry. Unfortunately, few if any of these units were to operate at anywhere near full strength at any given period of the war. And it was painfully apparent from the very outset that those enrolled in the militia in Southern Maryland were only half-heartedly in support of the war effort at best. The system was found entirely deficient in its ability to field sufficient forces, but equally significant was its notable lack of esprit de corps.

A single regular U.S. Army unit, the 36th Infantry Regiment, which had been sent into St. Mary's County during the first days of the war, was soon removed to assist in the defense of Baltimore, where it was thought the enemy's main attempts would be made. Even General Philip Stuart's command, the Fifth Brigade, Maryland Militia, which would normally have been charged with the defense of the St. Mary's County peninsula, the strategic fulcrum of Southern Maryland, was ordered to watch, instead, over a reach extending from Baltimore County, through Anne Arundel County, and into Calvert County—all on the exposed bay side of the Patuxent drainage.[42]

The virtual abandonment of the underbelly of Maryland was based on strategic reality, and for purely military reasons the U.S. War Department was not enthusiastic about maintaining a strong force on the St. Mary's peninsula. Superior mobility on the water and naval supremacy along the many peninsular "necks" and islands of the Tidewater provided the British with the means to easily envelop or flank a force on any side they wished. The St. Mary's peninsula contained no major cities of significance and provided little in the way of industrial support, and was therefore deemed of little importance to the general war effort. The same was true with the narrow Calvert County peninsula, the western side of which was bordered by the Patuxent River and the eastern side by the Chesapeake.

With the bulk of the nation's regular fighting force being employed or earmarked for duty along the Canadian frontier, Washington, Baltimore, and Annapolis were the centerpieces of defense considerations in the region, and even they would have to depend on all the local help they could muster. Yet Washington, at least at the outset of the war with its population of only 5,904 whites, 867 free blacks, and 1,437 slaves, had been confident of its own security and certain that no sizeable navel force could make it beyond the intricate and deadly matrix of shoals on the lower Potomac; if it did, it would have to contend with a major fortification, Fort Washington (formerly Fort Warburton), several miles below the city itself. Baltimore was defended by Fort McHenry, which guarded the entrance to Baltimore harbor. Annapolis, the third point in the strategic triangle, though defended by several small but poorly situated forts and perhaps the most vulnerable of all, was centrally located and could be rapidly reached and reinforced by land forces from the other two points. It was thus obvious to the citizens of Southern Maryland, who were already tepid in their zeal for the war, that they would have to largely fend for themselves. As a consequence, whatever support there had been for the government's military policy in the beginning was quickly eroded by the virtual abandonment of the region to the untender mercies of the Royal Navy.

Many in St. Mary's County sought redress, and, through the efforts of a committee selected to represent them, presented a ten-point petition of grievance to the Maryland state legislature in which they cited the danger to the county from its exposed situation and its military abandonment by both state and federal governments. It was the committee's opinion that there was justification for the federal government to furnish a regiment of regular infantry for the defense of the region, not only to shield against attack, but also to provide an annoyance to the enemy. "In the name of justice," the petitioners wrote, "we solicit it to rescue and save us. In the name of God we crave it for the sake of suffering humanity."[43]

...

When the British evacuated their Point Lookout base and stood up the Chesapeake Bay, both Annapolis and Baltimore were immediately threatened but left untouched. After a brief incursion against Sandy Point, near the state capital, however, the enemy came to rest, reportedly with three thousand men, on Kent Island on the Eastern Shore. The island had been taken without major incident and most of its civilian population had fled. From their perch in the upper Chesapeake the enemy proceeded to probe along the Eastern Shore while launching a campaign of bellicose political propagandizing and electioneering. It had become Cockburn's stated intention that should there not be a change of administration by the election of a Federalist to the presidency of the United States, he would personally destroy Baltimore and lay both shores of the Chesapeake so desolate that they would never again prosper.[44]

On August 10 Cockburn began to test the mettle of the Eastern Shore defenses by organizing a thrust against the diminutive seaport of St. Michaels on the Miles River. For only the second time were the British checked in a large-scale assault, where the Maryland militia made a credible stand. During the brief artillery engagement Cockburn's favorite nephew was killed, and the admiral began to have second thoughts about campaigning on the Eastern Shore. Three days later, when Royal Marines attempted to cut off and destroy a detachment of several hundred militiamen near Queenstown, they returned frustrated. Owing to the massing of American militia troops in Baltimore and Annapolis, and having met with opposition on the Eastern Shore, the admiral decided to abandon Kent Island and finally bring to a close major operations of the 1813 campaign in Maryland waters, though a return to the Potomac for forage and watering purposes was in order. In September respite for most of the Tidewater was granted when Cockburn and the greatest part of the British fleet sailed for Bermuda to refit and reprovision. A small squadron under Captain Robert Barrie, consisting of one ship-of-the-line, two frigates, two brigs, and three schooners, was left behind to maintain the winter blockade at the Virginia Capes and conduct nuisance raids whenever possible.[45]

It appeared to his American opponents that Cockburn's principal objectives had been primarily to gratify himself and his men with plunder and prizes (and as a consequence secure their support and loyalty) and to harass the citizens of Maryland into a union with anti-war proponents to sue for peace on any terms. Yet the 1813 campaign season, though successful in terms of destruction of largely rural property, had failed to achieve any solid objectives. Baltimore, Annapolis, and Washington were still intact. Virginia, though repeatedly tarnished by enemy incursions, was resisting vigorously. Privateers were still managing to slip through the blockade whenever northerly gales provided cover and the war on the Canadian frontier continued to drag on. In truth, however, the admiral had simply been marking time in the most profitable fashion possible, defining the weaknesses of his opponents, charting the bay and its many tributaries, and learning lessons that would be put to good use in the following and final campaign season.

In early November, before the onset of winter, the attentions of the small British force remaining in the bay again centered on the Potomac, where fresh water was to be found and where a number of sloops and schooners heavily laden with flour were captured. Hitherto, the British had failed to employ their talents as master incendiaries against the rural setting of the Southern Maryland underbelly, but now, in a last fling of the year, they set about to initiate the region as they had so many other areas of the Tidewater. On November 2 they paid a visit to St. George's Island to take on water and left it in smoldering ruin.[46]

Father Francis X. Neale of the St. Inigoes Jesuit mission wrote sadly of his own inspection of the island immediately after the enemy's departure:

> Last Wednesday I visited St. George's Island, & viewed with affliction the great devastation made by the English in their last visit to that place. From the face of things they could have had no other view than to have completely destroyed the whole of the property. They have burnt every house. I found that a fire reached on the south and west sides of the island from end to end. The island is about 3 miles in length. They had cut down 25 to 26 large oak, all white oaks excepting two or three. The stocks of nearly all of them were carried off; 5 or 6 large stocks of hickories, the stocks taken away; a great variety of pines cut down, the stocks of some of them were not to be found. The fire was still alive in four or five different places. They burnt as much of the fencing as they could, as also the marshes. In a word they have left sufficient proof that they would have destroyed the whole had it laid in their power.[47]

Unknown to Father Neale, some of the timber had been cut to serve in the construction of war barges and masts and for the use of British shipping constructors in Europe. But to the priest, the denuding of the island and the burning of its farms and houses were nothing less than ruthless, wanton destruction, and, indeed, a sad forecast of what might still lie ahead.

On November 7, as a parting gesture, Barrie embarked 120 freed slaves onboard his ship, HBMS *Dragon,* and sailed down to Lynnhaven Bay for the winter. For the British, the Chesapeake campaign had been a success. Admiral Warren was confident in his assurances to General Prevost that the operations on the bay had prevented at least 25,000 Americans from marching on Canada and had substantially weakened the United States. More than six hundred slaves had flocked to the British standard, most of which had been sent off to Bermuda. American trade, both oceanic and coastal, had been brought to a virtual standstill. And finally the overall blockade of key American ports had bottled up most of the small U.S. Navy at Bristol, Portsmouth, New York, Norfolk, Baltimore, and Washington.[48]

Though constantly obliged to find new sites for replenishing their water reserves, British control of the Chesapeake was to last well into the following spring, when strong reinforcements would be returning to the bay. This time, however, they would return to face a novelty: organized American naval resistance.[49]

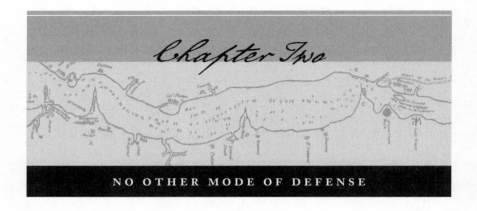

Chapter Two

NO OTHER MODE OF DEFENSE

During the spring of 1813 U.S. Secretary of the Navy William Jones had grown increasingly anxious—indeed, exasperated—over America's inability to challenge British control of the Chesapeake. Modest, hardworking Jones was well aware of the dangerous implications inherent in permitting the bay to remain a British lake for much longer. Should the enemy be able to throw a large body of troops into the region, their tactical and strategic advantages, already considerable, would be enormous and would have predictably disagreeable consequences for the Tidewater and the nation. At the very least, Norfolk, Baltimore, and even Washington itself would be at risk.

The U.S. Navy needed money, men, and ships, all of which were in critically short supply. But most of all, Jones needed a plan of action for the Chesapeake that stood a modest chance of success in fending off the enemy and a man capable and determined enough to institute it. The individual selected would have to be resourceful enough to muster a force practically from scratch, popular enough to recruit experienced seamen to sail it, and skillful enough to whip the more powerful enemy at his own game. The man Jones finally selected was to fit the job description superbly.

Joshua Barney was almost fifty-three years old at the outbreak of the war, and one of the few native Maryland sea captains who could justifiably be termed a national hero. Born in Baltimore when the town was little more than a rude hamlet on the Patapsco River, the man later to be called "the prince of privateers and adventurers" had gone to sea as a boy of twelve and took command of his first vessel at the age of sixteen. He gained his military experience early on. While still in his first command he and his ship were detained at Alicante and temporarily impressed into service by the Spanish in the celebrated expedition of Count Alexander O'Reilly against Algiers. Upon his return to America, he learned of the outbreak of the revolt against

England and, still in his teens, enlisted as master's mate aboard the sloop-of-war *Hornet*. Initially assigned to recruit seamen for what would turn out to be the only true fleet operation of the infant Continental Navy, he was the first to hoist the new American flag in Maryland. During the ensuing years of the Revolution he had served aboard and successfully commanded both privateers and Continental vessels, and at seventeen became the youngest man to ever take command of a Continental Navy frigate. Thrice a prisoner of the British and once exchanged, he had twice cleverly contrived escape to return to the service of his country. In April 1782, while in command of the 16-gun Pennsylvania privateer *Hyder Ally*, he engaged in what was to be one of the last major naval encounters of the war. The battle was termed "one of the best fought actions on record" and resulted in the defeat of the British warship *General Monk* off Cape May, New Jersey. Soon afterward he was entrusted to carry important dispatches to Benjamin Franklin in Paris, where he was introduced at the court of Louis XVI. In 1795, as a result of his fame, reputation, and prominence as a daring naval commander, he accepted a post in the French navy as commodore of the West Indies squadron. Five years later, having bore witness to and participated in many momentous events, he retired from French naval service and returned to his native Maryland and the life of a prosperous trader.[1]

Though handsome in his youth, in his later years Barney's appearance evoked an impression more befitting a country squire than a grizzled, hard-fighting seadog. Nonetheless, he was still, by any measure, a formidable man of action. He possessed all of the virtues of a born leader: a crisp mind, resourcefulness, an unerring capability to rise to any occasion despite the odds, and a willingness to fight with every ounce of strength available to him. He could be as strong (his enemies would say tyrannical) as necessary, but he was always a source of stability to those who followed him. His men adored him and were not dismayed by the discipline he required in surmounting every obstacle. Even his military adversaries were impressed by his resolve and cunning. Yet, like other great commanders, especially those with decided points of view, he had jealous rivals, often in places of authority and power. Though normally tolerant, Barney had suffered continued sniping and often outright opposition throughout his life from lesser men and political adversaries, and occasionally revealed his one flaw in reply. Generally able to overlook the pettiness of others, the commodore was on occasion given to base narrow-mindedness that sometimes distorted his normally balanced, straightforward approach to personalities and events.

The one thing Joshua Barney could not overlook was what he construed to be weakness in an individual's, or even in a nation's, character or morals. There were no grays in the course of human events as he viewed them, only black and white, right and wrong, good and bad. His greatest ally was the common seaman, and his enemy throughout his entire adult life was England. Sentiment played little part in his schemes, and he could easily abandon military territory or personal gain for which he had bitterly contested in the field, on the seas, in the counting room, or in the courts if it was expedient or necessary to do so. Patriotism, honor, courage, tenacity, and force of will were second nature to him, and he naturally expected those who followed him to exhibit the same characteristics.

In May 1812, as the promise of open hostilities with Great Britain ripened, Barney sold his home in the city of Baltimore and retired with his wife to a farm at Elkridge, on the upper Patuxent River, in Anne Arundel County. Here he wished for nothing more than to assume the domestic tranquility of a simple gentleman farmer. Yet the old commodore was among those of democratic-republican leanings who had been vociferously in favor of a face-off with England, but had long since despaired of such an eventuality during the remaining years of his life. Yet he had scarcely ensconced himself in his new home and acquired the trappings of a domestic lifestyle when the exciting news of Congress's declaration of war against his old nemesis, Great Britain, reached him.[2]

Barney's reaction was instantaneous. "To content himself with following the plough, watching the growth of corn, or shearing the merinos, while the blast of war was blowing in his ears," his adoring niece Mary Barney would write nearly two decades later, "would have been an effort beyond his philosophy [and] altogether contrary to his nature. He did not even allow time for such an idea to suggest itself, but instantly packing up a few changes of linen and other little comforts he hurried off to the city of Baltimore, and in less than three weeks from the publication of the important manifesto by Congress, he was once more on the broad theatre of his glory, in command of an armed cruiser."[3]

Barney had despaired of obtaining a command in the American navy due to his loss of tenure and seniority on the navy lists and because of his controversial service under the flag of France, a nation now under the dominion of the tyrant Napoleon, who many in high places despised as much as England. Thus, he sought and accepted command of the next best thing—a privateer. The old warrior's adventurous cruise aboard the intrepid little 12-gun *Rossie*,

Commodore Joshua Barney. *Oil painting by Rembrandt Peale, 1819 (copy from original owned by the Mayor and City Council of Baltimore), Maryland Historical Society, Baltimore, Maryland. Photograph by Donald G. Shomette.*

the first letter of marque vessel to depart Baltimore in the war, need not be recounted here in full. Suffice it to say that the voyage proved to be one of the more injurious privateering ventures of the conflict and a model many sought to emulate. Eighteen British vessels, the total tonnage of which was computed at 3,698, and valued at well over $1.5 million, were captured, burned, sunk, or ransomed. During the course of the expedition Barney fought two spirited engagements, one against the British letter-of-marque *Jeannie,* and another against His Britannic Majesty's packet-ship *Princess Amelia.* Both vessels (one after a somewhat bloody contest) were defeated and taken.[4]

Barney's success was such that immediately upon his return to Baltimore on November 23, 1812, numerous privateering syndicates solicited him to engage in another cruise. Unfortunately, though the cruise of *Rossie* had proved an astonishing success in terms of the number of enemy vessels captured or destroyed, when the final accounts were drawn up, and after the inordinate expenses incurred in condemning and disposing of the prizes and the heavy duties at that time imposed on the prize goods by the Congress were included, the profits realized were pitifully small. Barney was not happy with the outcome. As his niece later noted, "there was really no adequate motive to encounter the privateers and discomforts of the small vessels then employed as privateers." The old commodore respectfully declined the offers and returned to his home and sheep at Elkridge.[5]

...

Throughout the turbulent spring of 1813 Barney had flinched with every British foray against the soil of his native Maryland. By early May, following the enemy attacks on Frenchtown, Havre de Grace, Georgetown, and Fredericktown, the crisis in the Maryland Tidewater was coming to a head. The State of Maryland was politically divided between the anti-war Federalist Party, which controlled the Executive Office and the House of Delegates, and the pro-war Democratic-Republican Party, centered in Baltimore, which controlled the Senate. The City of Baltimore, the seat of the "war hawks" and privateering and in the eye of the storm, lacked both major federal and state support for its protection and had determined early on to defend itself on land and sea if necessary. Its champion had been U.S. Senator Samuel Smith of Maryland, chairman of the powerful Senate Naval Committee, major general in the Third Division of the Maryland Volunteer Militia, head of the Baltimore Committee of Safety, designated by Governor of Maryland Levin Winder as commander for the defense of Baltimore, and an unrepentant hawk. Smith, like Barney, was a Revolutionary War hero from Baltimore (who also served as the principal spokesman for his city's merchant and shipping interest), and was a mighty force to be reckoned with. Acting at the behest of the Baltimore Committee of Public Safety he had organized a Corps of Seamen, and moved to have built a naval force of six to eight armed war barges and one row galley. The Baltimore City fleet was rapidly assembled at city expense, even as the divided Maryland legislature was being called into a thirteen-day special session on May 17 by Governor Winder to address the crisis. On May 18 Smith informed the Baltimore Committee of Public Supply that each vessel of the city fleet was to be "from 65 to 70 feet long, prepared for oars, to mount a 32-pounder in the bow and stern and constructed to sail equally well with either end for a bow." All were to be built under contract, with the first being in the water in three weeks' time. Each vessel was to be assigned a number and an American flag. A numbered flag, to be painted by a professional painter named Thomas Galloway and assigned to each vessel, was to fly beneath the American colors.[6]

As the special session of the legislature moved forward and contracts were let in Baltimore for the city defense fleet, the Democratic-Republicans, unhappy with the national government's inability to protect state waters, aggressively moved on numerous fronts to address Maryland's overall weak military position. Twenty-three measures were enacted, including the calling up of the Maryland Militia and borrowing money from private banks to pay for it. Resolutions were passed condemning the British for acts against humanity and national honor. A thousand dollars was voted for the relief of Havre de Grace and seven hundred more for Fredericktown. But the core problem of coastal protection on Maryland waterways was something else.[7]

The shadow, if not the actual imprint, of both Sam Smith and Joshua Barney was manifest in every action regarding the state's naval defense. On May 26, 1813, Senator Levi Hollingsworth of Baltimore introduced a bill in the state legislature entitled "An Act for the building of Barges for the defense of the Chesapeake Bay." The act, as proposed, authorized and required the governor and council to purchase or build, as soon as possible, twenty war barges for the protection of state waters. Each vessel was to be not less than fifty feet or more than seventy feet keel length. Each was to be armed with either a single long 18- or 24-pounder cannon, and outfitted with "such other armament as they may deem proper, and masts, sails, oars, and other suitable equipment." A special barge commission comprised of some of the state's leading mariners, shipbuilders, and most experienced naval and military officers, including Joshua Barney, John Eager Howard, Solomon Frazier, Perry Spencer, Samuel Sterett, George Stiles, and Thomas Tennant, would be appointed to direct the building and equipping of the fleet. The commissioners were also to be authorized to make any alterations deemed beneficial for the service in the dimensions, form, construction, and armament of this unique state squadron. The governor and council were authorized and required to appoint one captain, one first lieutenant, one second lieutenant, and the requisite warrant officers for each barge. A suitable crew of seamen, ordinary seamen, and landsmen were also to be enlisted for a period of one year. One or more surgeons or surgeon's mates would be appointed for each barge, provided that the whole number of officers and crew did not exceed one hundred men per vessel.[8]

In order to compete with the recruitment efforts of the U.S. Navy, the act required that all officers and enlisted men be entitled to receive the same pay, clothing, and rations as if they were in the regular navy, provided that the pay and rations of the captains and other officers in the barge force did not exceed that of the commanders and other officers in gunboats in the national service. Furthermore, all prize money was to be distributed among the officers and men according to the rules and proportions prescribed by the United States in relation to the navy. As an inducement to enlist in state service, a bounty of $10 would be offered for each enlistee. Officers and crews could be discharged whenever the governor and council deemed their services no longer necessary. If disabled while in service, both officers and men were to be entitled to half pay for the rest of their lives.[9]

And finally, once the legislation was passed, the governor and council were to be requested to immediately transmit a copy of the act to the president of the United States with an entreaty that the aid of the general government—that is, its financial support—be sought to carry the act into effect. If, in the event the general government procured and appointed, without delay, a force similar to that contemplated by the Maryland legislature, the act would not go into operation. Moreover, if the United States appointed officers and men, and provided for the same to man the barge fleet, the governor and council would be authorized and requested to deliver the barges to the U.S. government.[10]

That Maryland would move to create its own navy, in itself, was not unique. During the American Revolution, eleven of the thirteen states, including Maryland and Virginia, had formally established and fielded their own naval forces when the Continental Navy proved inadequate for the purpose of defending state waters, and the current action was undoubtedly guided by the experience gained by the deployment of such vessels during the last war. It was also in keeping with the Jeffersonian policy of using small, inexpensive, shallow-draft naval vessels suitable for protection of coastal waters rather than large and costly blue-water offensive sloops-of-war, frigates, and ships-of-the-

line. Jefferson's minimalist and controversial naval program had been intended to keep America from becoming involved in European affairs, militarily
and politically, to allow the nation time to grow. It had, in effect, relegated the
United States to maintaining only a very small blue-water fleet and relying
heavily on coastal gunboat defense. As a reflection of earlier national policy,
the Maryland Barge Act was a measure that was more likely than any other to
garner support from the Federalists in the House of Delegates. Moreover, the
proposed legislation was designed to act as a spur to stimulate federal action
even if it failed to pass. Indeed, it may have even been introduced with the
legislature's full knowledge that it would never get to the governor's desk, and
if it did, being a Federalist and opponent to the war, he would probably not
sign it.

On the day that it was introduced, the Barge Act passed the Maryland
Senate, but on May 28, 1813, it failed to pass the House of Delegates, much
to the consternation of many influential Marylanders. Among the numerous
critics of the delegates' rejection of the bill was Joshua Barney, who bitterly
declared that the failure to act "means our bay harbours and cities lay exposed
to the fury of the enemy."[11]

Despite the Federalists' defeat of the Barge Act, powerful forces continued
to press for a fleet of such craft to defend the Chesapeake. Soon after the failure of the barge bill in the Maryland state legislature, Sam Smith took the issue directly to the U.S. Navy. With an eye toward seeing to the security of his
own constituency while also assessing the national situation as chairman of
the Senate Naval Committee, Smith had already requested the new secretary
of the navy, William Jones, to provide his committee with a complete return
of all gunboats already in naval service and a list of their stations. He did so
with a view of proposing the development of a "special defence" naval force "of
Barges or Galleys" for the protection of coastal areas, including, of course, his
own city of Baltimore.[12] Jones, who had been appointed by President James
Madison in November 1812 to replace Secretary Paul Hamilton, had himself
once been a sea captain, as well as a merchant, banker, and U.S. congressman,
but had inherited only a skeletal staff and no professional naval officers to
serve as advisors. He nevertheless had set out upon a determined course that
would overall serve the nation well, and was politically astute enough to pay
special attention to Smith's requests.

Among some of his many goals, Smith wished to explore the possibility
of having the national government take over the expenses of maintaining
the war barges built by Baltimore "during the late excitement" or still un-

der construction. It was a strategy that the navy secretary was quite familiar with. Indeed, he had been besieged by numerous similar requests from other politicians, and had been in frequent correspondence with "corporations and committees from Maine to Georgia," all hoping to secure the services of the U.S. Navy for local defense, or at least for the navy to pick up the bill for local naval defense initiatives similar to Baltimore's. Not surprisingly, with only limited funds and fewer physical resources at his command, the secretary had, until Smith's solicitation, sought to ward off such pressures. "I consider it indispensable," he wrote President Madison on June 6 regarding the query, "to resist the pretensions of local bodies who undertake to prescribe not only the extent but the natures and manner of employing the public force." But the chairman of the Senate Naval Committee was another matter.[13]

Personally charged by Governor Levin Winder on May 19 with the defense of Baltimore, Smith diligently pursued his objective of securing the navy's commitment for a stronger defense of the state's most important seaport. On June 10, undoubtedly with his beloved city in mind, he dispatched another note to Jones regarding the possibility of employing sunken hulks, booms, or other impediments to facilitate the water defenses of American harbors. But it was in the possible deployment of large number of armed barges for local naval forces, "capable of carrying 18 and 32 pounders, and of such a construction as that they may row as fast as the barges of the enemy," that the Naval Committee and its chairman appeared to be most interested in. Coming more to the point, the committee wanted to know how many barges would be necessary to defend the ports of the United States and how much it would cost to build both a fifty-foot and a seventy-foot class of the vessel.[14]

Secretary Jones took a week to assemble his data before responding, though his personal support of the barge concept was minimal at best. Although he noted that the "barges (or rather galleys) contemplated by the committee are certainly a very useful class of vessels as an auxiliary force," it was necessary that they be attached to support craft capable of providing accommodations necessary for the health and comfort of the men needed to man them. Without comfortable accommodations, he predicted, it would be impossible to secure crews for them or to retain them even if procured. Indeed, such vessels could not hope to be fielded without a substantial support element, and he was not remiss in informing the committee as to why:

> The form necessary to produce the greatest celerity of movement by the impulse of the oar must be long, narrow, and shallow; consequently such vessels being open and of small capacity, cannot afford to a numerous crew, the accommodations

necessary to lodge and protect them from the weather, or to prepare their provisions and carry the necessary supplies. Hence it results that if these vessels are to be employed distinctly, a given number will require a store ship, hospital ship and receiving ship, in which to prepare the provisions, and shelter the crew from the inclemency of the weather, otherwise disease will be the inevitable consequence.

If such a force as envisioned by the committee were to be attached to gunboats and other vessels already being employed in harbor defense, and manned from those same vessels as necessary, the utility of both the fifty- and seventy-foot classes of barges would be retained, the difficulty of procuring additional crews obviated, the expenditure only moderately increased since the same crews would perform alternate duty on both classes of vessels, "and the accommodation and comfort of both . . . improved." Yet, it was the secretary's opinion that the only field advantage to be derived from barges would be when they were employed in calm or very moderate weather, for when the wind blew strongly, they might be easily outsailed by any fast sailing vessel. "It is," he warned, "impracticable to combine in the same vessels the qualities of very fast rowing and sailing."

Jones's litany of objections to barges as a replacement for traditional men-of-war was lengthy. Not only were there disadvantages to the vessel type, he believed, but there were innumerable obstacles to adequately manning them. Principal among these were not only the lack of accommodations, but the hard labor at the oars. The major objection, however, was the absence of any pecuniary advantages for seamen who were already being tempted into service in the navy or aboard privateers "by the stimulus of prize money, the éclat of our navy victories, and the preference which seamen naturally give to vessels better adapted to their habits and comfort." Indeed, recruiting efforts to man gunboats already in service in Philadelphia, Baltimore, and Norfolk, even with the aid of bounties, had proceeded with miserable success. Much of the difficulty stemmed from extant prejudices against gunboats, which were justifiably reputed among mariners to be poor sailers. Yet even gunboats possessed better accommodations for the comfort of seamen than did barges. It was thus likely that the difficulties to be experienced in manning barges would be at least equal to if not worse than manning gunboats. The secretary admonished:

> This small and scattered species of force is the most expensive and least susceptible of the economical controul [sic] of this department of any that can be devised. The rank and character of the persons commanding on detached and remote stations ensure no responsibility. Small agencies and offices must be multiplied, and

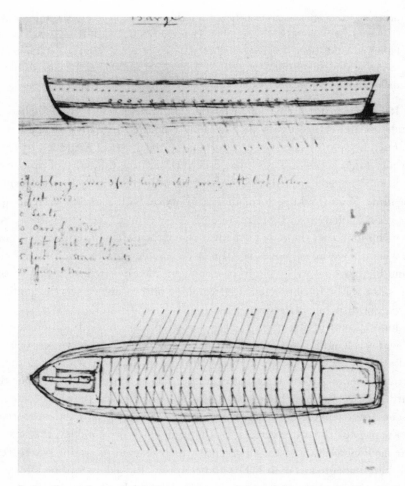

Joshua Barney's sketch for a barge accompanied his July 4, 1813, plan for the defense of the Chesapeake. *National Archives and Records Administration, Washington, D.C.*

in every view the nature of the service is incompatible with the rank, duties and indispensable acquirements of the officers of the navy, and of the existing regulations of the naval establishment.

If this system of harbour defence is to be extended, the public interest will be promoted by rendering the system distinct from that of the naval establishment.

If Congress under existing circumstances shall determine to employ a certain number of barges, I would recommend their being attached to and manned from the force already employed for harbour defence, as occasion may require.

The secretary, however, was well aware that the Naval Committee did not agree with his views regarding reliance upon gunboats rather than a barge force for coastal defense, but the Senate remained unmoved. Jones thus dutifully provided facts and figures on what it would take to field an adequate barge fleet. He informed the committee that in the event Congress deemed it necessary to field barges for the defense of American harbors, a total of fifty-five such craft dispersed throughout the nation would be satisfactory. Eight of the vessels should be employed on the upper Chesapeake and another eight on the lower bay. Basing his estimates on comparisons of costs incurred by a committee of the citizens of Philadelphia, which had, like Baltimore, ordered a number of barges built for the defense of their own city, the secretary reported that a 36-ton first-class barge, 70 feet in length, 14 feet abeam, and 4 feet deep in hold, with sails, rigging, oars, "and every thing complete except armament," would cost about $2,500. It would be capable of carrying a long 24-pounder on one end and a 36-pounder carronade on the other. Such a vessel would be propelled by 36 oars, double-banked, and would carry a crew of 54 officers and men. The second-class barge, of 19 tons, 50-foot length, 12-foot beam, and 3.5-foot depth in hold, complete except for armament, would cost $1,250. This class of vessel would mount but a single long, light 18-pounder, and would be propelled by 12 oars, double-banked. It would be manned by a crew of 42. A small 9-ton third-class barge of 36-foot length, 8-foot beam, and 3-foot depth of hold could be produced for $625, and would be armed with a single 12-pounder carronade. The third-class barge would be propelled by 20 oars, double-banked, and require a crew of only 30 officers and men. All 3 classes would be double ended, that is "constructed both ends alike to row with equal facility and velocity either way." All vessels employed in warm southern waters such as the Chesapeake would have to be copper fastened and copper sheathed to prevent damage from shipworms that could destroy an unprotected hull in a single season. The sheathing work would increase the cost of a first-class barge by $750, a second-class by $500, and a third-class by $300.

. . .

By July it had become obvious to all that the government was still floundering about helplessly in its modest efforts to defend the Tidewater. British depredations and actions in the lower bay were continuing without letup and threatened to spill over into Maryland waters, even as the Senate Naval Committee moved steadily forward in crafting legislation to field a barge force—despite Secretary Jones's lack of enthusiasm. News from the south had been disturbing. On June 20, the same day as the arrival of 3 line-of-battle ships, 4 frigates, a naval transport, 5 sloops, army transports, and tenders, American gunboats had unsuccessfully assaulted the 38-gun frigate *Junon* in Hampton Roads. Two days later 50 British barges with 1,500 British soldiers and marines had attacked and been repelled by American forces on Craney Island, in the Elizabeth River, in a costly effort to capture Norfolk. On June 25 the invaders exacted revenge, this time landing at Hampton, which was captured and brutally sacked. Now they were moving up toward the Potomac. The Naval Committee's barge initiative now hung in the balance. But there was one vocal and highly visible champion of the effort who would help put it over the top.

Joshua Barney could restrain himself no longer. On Independence Day public citizen Barney penned, for the perusal of the secretary of the navy, a detailed plan that largely mirrored in many respects but enlarged upon the Naval Committee's views on the development, deployment, and service of a fleet of barges. The plan, laid out by a man of the sea who had fought as many if not more naval battles against the British than any American alive, was entitled simply "Defence of Chesapeake Bay."[15]

The plan, he noted, was merely his outline of a comprehensive scheme for both offensive and defensive operations in the Chesapeake Tidewater, the details of which he felt could be better explained and all of its advantages pointed out in person. Nevertheless, the plan was offered replete with a sketch of the vessel type he suggested be employed in its institution. It was a marvel of strategic and tactical comprehension that seemingly addressed all of the dangers of the present military emergency with the limited resources available, incorporated the views of the Naval Committee, and appeared flexible enough to meet any future situation that might arise. It effectively countered many of the lukewarm arguments the secretary of the navy had mounted against a barge defense of the Chesapeake.

Barney began by noting that the enemy had 11 ships-of-the-line, 33 frigates, 38 sloops-of-war, and a number of schooners and other vessels on the American Station (presumably available for service in the bay). With each line vessel carrying a complement of 110 marines, each frigate 50, and each sloop-of-war 20, together with 2,000 additional marines, 2 battalions of Royal Artillery, and 2 battalions of seamen momentarily expected from England, the enemy would soon have available a landing force estimated at 8,200 men. "The object of the enemy (well-known)," he noted, "is the destruction of the city and navy yard at Washington, the city and navy yard at Norfolk, and the

Secretary of the Navy William Jones. *Naval Historical Center, Washington, D.C.*

city of Baltimore." It was to be expected, he reasoned, that the enemy would be obliged to employ frigates, sloops-of-war, and schooners, with barges and small craft, against all of these places. The attempt against any one of them, he felt certain, awaited only the arrival of Admiral Sir John Borlase Warren from Bermuda with the reinforcements (which had, in fact, just arrived). "He has already tried our waters, knows our channels, received information, and will no doubt speedily return prepared for mischief."

The question was how to meet such an overwhelming force with any probability of success. There were only two frigates available, *Adams* at Washington and *Constellation* at Norfolk, both of which were incapable of acting owing to the strong blockade. The older gunboats already in service were too heavy to row and too clumsy to sail. They were fit only to lay moored, protect a narrows, or assist in the defense of a fort, but little more. "I am therefore of [the] opinion the only defence we have in our power, is a kind of barge or row-galley, so constructed, as to draw a small draft of water, to carry oars, light sails, and one heavy gun. These vessels may be built in a short time (say 3 weeks), men may be had, the city of Baltimore alone, could furnish officers and men for twenty barges, without difficulty. We have in Baltimore 150 mas- ters and mates of vessels, all of whom have seen and some of them been out [in] such kind of vessels in Sweden and Denmark, and among the Spaniards. Such men can be relied upon, and when no further service would be required from them, would again return into merchant service, by which means the officers of the U.S. Navy would not be called into service."

But how could such a tiny mosquito fleet contend with such an enormously powerful foe, indeed the mightiest navy on the planet?

"Let as many of these barges be built as can be manned, form them into a flying squadron, let them be continually watching and annoying the enemy in our waters, where we have the advantage of shoal water and flats in abundance throughout the Chesapeake Bay." The enemy could be followed wherever he went, but dare not dispatch his own smaller vessels while such an American menace lay in the vicinity. Each of the barges or galleys, armed with a single 24-pounder and small arms, he suggested, could carry 50 officers and men and 25 or more soldiers at one time. Thus, a squadron of 20 barges might provide a highly mobile force of 1,000 seamen and marines, and an additional 500 to 1,000 land troops. "With such a force, there would be no necessity for camps being formed at any given point, as this force would always be hovering around the enemy, and prevent any partial attacks on our bay shore or within our waters."

It was quite conceivable that such a force of vessels might even succeed in driving the British from the Chesapeake altogether. During the summer months they could harass the enemy at night. Attacking in the dark, they could fire at the big warships with impunity. The barges, being small and fast, would make poor targets themselves and would consequently suffer little damage. If properly outfitted, the barges would not even have to fear en- emy boarding attempts. Three or four light, fast fireships added to the flotilla might with ease, under cover of the barges, "be run on board any of the en- emies ships, if they should attempt to anchor, or remain in our narrow rivers or harbours." During the winter months, Barney felt, the enemy would not act, and the barge flotilla might be quartered in the York River, at Hampton, or at any other place strategically convenient to the mouth of the bay.

As for defending the major ports of the Tidewater, the flotilla would more than prove its worth. "Should the enemy land all their forces with a design on any of our large cities, they must be met in the field, but unless their heavy ships can cover the landing, and receive them on board again, the barge squadron might, and would cut off a retreat, by acting in concert with our troops on shore."

Barney considered it of great importance that scuttling vessels or other obstructions, as suggested by Smith, be carried out immediately to block the channel of the Potomac River below Washington. The frigate *Adams* and all of the old gunboats still in service might be stationed above the obstructions with a floating battery to defend the passage through. Another line of vessels or obstructions, he suggested, could also be sunk at Hawkins Point a few miles below Fort McHenry, near Baltimore. Armed schooners already in service and several floating batteries prepared with furnaces for hot shot could defend the passage there with facility. As for Norfolk, he had been informed that appropriate measures had already been taken into consideration for the protection of that place. Defense works, such as Fort Norfolk, were finished or already nearing completion, and no comment was necessary.

Countering Jones's insinuation that such a fleet would prove too expensive, Barney noted that the price tag for constructing a barge force would be minuscule in comparison to the cost of preparing a large, elaborate, and time-consuming conventional naval force. A single barge might not cost more than $3,000, and after its military service was completed, it could be refitted and sold as a commercial coaster. Fifty barges would cost less than half the price of a conventional frigate, and the officers and men, recruited specifically for the flotilla service, would be on the government payroll but a short time and would have no further claim on the government after the war.

The marine forces necessary, Barney envisioned, would be entirely separate from and totally unconnected with the flotilla navy, and would be so organized as to have a single regiment of troops annexed to them. The marines would be under the command of a capable marine officer and a colonel "with powers to correspond, not only with the general government, but with the Governors of Virginia and Maryland, and act in concert whenever circumstances required."

Barney reminded the secretary that a plan for the outfitting and manning of twenty barges had been laid before the Maryland General Assembly only a few weeks earlier. Although the Senate had passed the bill, the House of Delegates had rejected it. The consequences of this action, he noted, left the harbors and cities of the Tidewater exposed to the full wrath of the enemy.

Yet, should the national government adopt his scheme, it would prove to be a cut-rate plan for defense that just might work. "In fact," he wrote forebodingly, "we have no other mode of defense left us."

Stung by the repeated assaults of the enemy in the Chesapeake and elsewhere, and with the navy seemingly powerless to reply, the barge flotilla concept, personally championed by such illustrious figures as Barney and Smith and with the Senate Naval Committee's blessing, was finally embraced. The construction of a force of such vessels, under a new (albeit temporary) branch of the U.S. Navy to be called the U.S. Flotilla Service, was officially authorized on July 5, only one day after Barney's plan had been submitted. Congress promptly appropriated $250,000 for the construction of a national barge fleet, with each vessel to be no less than forty-five feet in length and capable of carrying heavy guns. Both Barney and Smith, though often adversaries in political life, were undoubtedly united in their elation.[16]

...

In August Barney traveled north to Newport, Rhode Island, on business. One of the prizes taken by *Rossie* had been sent into port there, and being a man ever mindful of his own financial interests, the old privateersman was obliged to attend to matters concerning its disposition. While at Newport, he was pleased to receive a formal response to his plan from Secretary Jones dated August 20. Given the fact that Barney had been one of the principal champions of the barge flotilla concept, he could not have been too surprised by its contents.

"The President of the United States," it read, "reposing special trust and confidence in your patriotism, valor, fidelity and abilities, has directed this special letter appointing you an Acting Master Commandant in the Navy of the United States for the special purpose of the distinct and separate command (subject only to the direct orders of the Secretary of the Navy) of the United States flotilla in the upper part of the Chesapeake to consist of such vessels as shall be designated by the Department of the Navy, which command you will hold during the pleasure of the President."[17]

Barney undoubtedly read the justification for the appointment with delight.

> The nature of the force, necessary for the defence of the extensive bays and rivers of the United States, and the means of manning and employing that force, require an organization, in some degree, different from the general naval establishment.

The President of the U. States, in order more effectually to accomplish the objects of the legislature, as contemplated in the late law, providing for the building or procuring, and employing, such number of barges, as he may deem necessary, has determined to select for the special command of the flotilla, on the upper part of the Chesapeake, a citizen, in whose fidelity, skill, local knowledge, and commanding influence with the marines [mariners] of the district, reliance may be placed, in case of great emergency.[18]

By Barney's appointment to the nonpermanent rank of acting master commandant the elderly veteran was to have a position, if accepted, separate from the regular naval establishment, but would be entitled to the pay, rations, and emoluments of a master commandant in the regular navy. His command was to consist of the barges, "now building by contract at Baltimore for this department, such of the city barges, as may be purchased, or taken into the service of the U[nited] States, and such other barges, gun boats, or vessels, as may, from time to time, be attached thereto, by orders of this department."[19]

The officers immediately subordinate to the commandant were to be sailing masters in the regular naval establishment, and such subordinate and petty officers as the Navy Department directed. The petty officers and crews were to be "regularly shipped" as in the regular naval establishment, and would be entitled to the rights, privileges, and advantages of the Navy Pension Fund, Navy Hospital, distribution of prize money, pay, rations, and so forth, as in any other branch of the service. But all were to be shipped "for the special service of the flotilla" for a period of only twelve months. Moreover, they would not be liable to draft by any other service during that period.[20]

Barney's reaction to the letter can be imagined. Thus assured of a command, answerable only to the secretary of the navy, and not liable to interference from younger officers who might possess greater tenure on the navy list, he hurried home to Elkridge as quickly as possible, and then to Washington, where he was to "learn more at large the nature of the service expected of him." Upon meeting with Jones, he was reassured that his was indeed to be a separate command, unconnected with the regular navy establishment and subject only to direct orders from the government. His basic concept for the creation and fielding of a flotilla squadron had been accepted.[21]

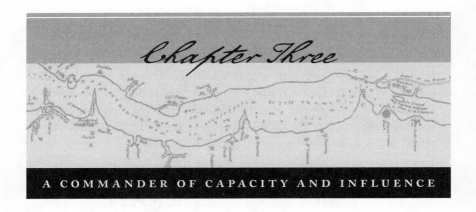

A COMMANDER OF CAPACITY AND INFLUENCE

Though having acquiesced to the fielding of a national barge force, Secretary Jones was deliberate in his directions as to how it should be built, especially the Chesapeake squadron, and quickly communicated his wishes to Barney. The secretary wanted the barges to be constructed and equipped along the lines of the new galley *Black Snake*, recently built at and now lying at the Washington Navy Yard. He urged the new commandant to examine the vessel in person, for actually seeing it, he informed Barney, "will have conveyed to you a more perfect idea of the manner in which I wish them to be armed and equipped, than any written description." The secretary fully intended, if the movements of the enemy permitted, on sending the galley around to Baltimore. There, he reasoned, "completely fitted, to the most minute article, ready for action," the new vessel would serve as a model "from which all the rest can be fitted in exact conformity." In the event that *Black Snake* could not be sent, either the navy's master boat builder or Chief Naval Constructor James Doughty would attend Barney in Baltimore to give directions. The commandant was also to be provided with the dimensions, description, and drawings of the masts, spars, sails, and so forth.[1]

Jones provided some description of the few vessels already building on the Patapsco, which were, from that point on, interchangeably referred to as either barges or galleys.

> The galleys building at Baltimore are upon the same plan and construction as those here, except that the former are a little fuller at each end, the better to enable them to bear the heavy metal [of guns] without hogging. The *Black Snake*, now with everything on board, ready for service, draws 21 inches water. Much pains have been taken to perfect those built here, in order to serve as an exact guide for those built elsewhere; and I am perfectly satisfied with them, in all respects, that every possible effort will be made, to get them round to Baltimore in due time. I

40

not only rely upon your exertions, to equip them in the shortest possible time; but upon your judgment, care, and economy, in doing it to the best advantage. The three galleys, building here, will be added to your squadron, together with the *Scorpion* cutter, schooner *Asp,* and two or three gunboats. Also such of the barges belonging to the city of Baltimore, as come within the description of the Act of Congress, provided the [naval] agent and [Baltimore] committee can agree upon terms.[2]

Barney was quick to follow the secretary's lead. Upon his arrival in the capital, one of his first acts was to inspect the recently completed *Black Snake,* built at the Washington Navy Yard. On August 27 Jones gave him more details on the vessels authorized for construction at Baltimore, where Navy Agent James Beatty had just contracted for eight barges. He then instructed him to find out exactly "what the builders have engaged to perform" and then to personally superintend the construction and equipping of the fleet. As for arming it, Beatty had already been ordered to transport a number of 24-pounders to Baltimore, four of which were to be employed onboard the four largest galleys. Each first-class craft was also to be equipped with a single 42-pounder carronade, a short, stubby gun, lighter in weight than a long gun of equal caliber, limited in range but devastating in close in fighting. These were to be shipped if possible (barring difficulties from British blockaders) from the Washington Navy Yard. If the 42-pounders could not be sent, however, Barney was instructed to substitute four 32-pounder carronades from Baltimore. The smaller second-class vessels were to be armed with long 18-pounders, which were also to be dispatched from Washington.[3]

Jones urged Barney to take measures to secure his ammunition, small stores, and the like. Casting of grape shot for his guns should be done immediately. Small arms for each of the largest barges were to include 36 muskets and 36 boarding axes, and 26 muskets and an equal number of boarding pikes for the second-class vessels. Ammunition for each long gun was to consist of 80 rounds of shot and 30 stands of grape shot. Ammunition for each carronade was to consist of 60 rounds of shot, 30 stands of grape shot, and 30 cannister shot. Ten rounds of powder and shot were to be reserved for target practice.[4]

Not all of Barney's time in the capital pertained to navy business. While attending to his mission, he learned of efforts by a number of his longstanding enemies in Baltimore to discredit him in the eyes of the Navy Department and have his appointment rescinded. One of those so engaged was Colonel Lemuel Taylor, a prominent Baltimore merchant and one-time friend of the commandant, who had taken care of him in France and nursed him through an illness "with the sedulity and affection of a brother." But that was in the past. Now, it seems, Taylor had written to Jones casting an abundance of aspersions on the commandant's character and abilities. Among other things, he categorized the commandant as "a most abandoned rascal both as to politics and morals and that he is despised by 9/10 of all that have taken an active part in the defence of Baltimore."[5]

For reasons unknown, Jones himself informed Barney of the letter and its author. Deeply incensed, Barney did what many men of honor in that period did: he immediately challenged the merchant to a duel. The challenge was accepted and the two adversaries agreed upon the already famed dueling grounds near Bladensburg, Maryland, just beyond the Washington city limits, as the field of honor. As word quickly circulated about the impending contest, however, and dueling was illegal in Maryland, "the marshal having been apprised of their intent, met them at Bladensburg, and pursued them on till they passed without his jurisdiction." The new location selected was a half-mile outside of Alexandria, Virginia, and just beyond the borders of the District of Columbia. On the afternoon of September 3 the two men met. As the challenged party was given the choice of weapons, Colonel Taylor selected pistols at five paces. Despite the short distance between them, the first fire was without effect, with both duelists missing their mark. Neither man flinched and witnesses later reported that "both gentlemen exhibited uncommon firmness" as they prepared for a second round. This time, Barney's bullet struck Taylor in the chest, albeit not fatally. The colonel was carried to Alexandria, where his wound was dressed, and then proceeded on to Washington. Though the wound was severe, Barney later noted, his opponent "survived it long enough to repent," indeed long enough to participate in the defense of Baltimore a year later. As for Barney, his honor having been satisfied, and without breaking stride, he hurried off to see to the business of building a fleet.[6]

Upon his arrival on the Patapsco, Barney fell to work with tireless vigor. On August 30 he received more of Jones's written instructions and immediately conferred with Beatty. The two men then went to examine the first few barges already under construction. *Black Snake* had yet to arrive and the shipbuilding project had suffered from the lack of a model. The commandant was not pleased with the progress, as the vessels "are very backward" and only one was nearly ready to launch. Some were merely floored. Others had only frames up and were neither floored nor planked. The commandant glumly predicted that they probably wouldn't be completed in less than a month. "The contractors," he sarcastically reported, "appear to me, either not to understand what they are about, or will not understand, which will make it absolutely necessary to have either Mr. Doughty or the [navy's] master boat builder here to give directions, and the sooner the better." If *Black Snake* could be brought around, "many difficulties, and much time & trouble would be avoided, and the work done in a more masterly stile." If she were not, he declared, "I must come again to Washington, to see her, and make these thick skulls here do their duty."[7]

Barney, who had, for unknown reasons, yet to receive Jones's instructions regarding armaments, informed the secretary that he was still unaware of what guns he would actually be obliged to mount upon the barges. None having been brought around as yet, he could not order ammunition for them, although he had ordered grapeshot and cannister stools to be cast immediately for every size, all of which could be assembled at Washington. As for small arms, he requested that pistols and sabers be added to the requisition of muskets and pikes. He also suggested that a gunner be sent from the Washington Navy Yard to be put to work fitting "every article of gunnery" while the barges were under construction.[8]

On September 29, since Baltimore had earlier contracted for barges and row galleys for its own defense, the U.S. Navy moved to purchase for the Chesapeake Flotilla the city row galley *Vigilant,* Captain John Rutter commanding, for $1,800. The commandant also managed to acquire, also through outright purchase from the city, two armed barges. These were Baltimore Flotilla barges *No. 5,* costing $1,725, and *No. 6,* Captain William Flanagan commanding, costing $1,875. Though not much to go on, it was a start.[9]

From early September on, Jones and Barney exchanged many views on the technical details of vessel construction. Doughty, who had gone to Washington to secure additional supplies, returned to Baltimore with the much-needed ordnance, albeit armed with barge design and size alterations from the original order. The first-class barges were lengthened to 75 feet. Instead of 24-pounders, 4 18-pounders, such as carried aboard *Black Snake,* were to be sent for the 4 first-class barges, along with 4 shorter, lighter 18-pounders and 4 24-pounder carronades for the second-class barges. The 42-pounder carronades for the first-class barges, apparently now being deemed too heavy, were to be replaced by 32-pounder carronades, although not for all. The 32-pound-

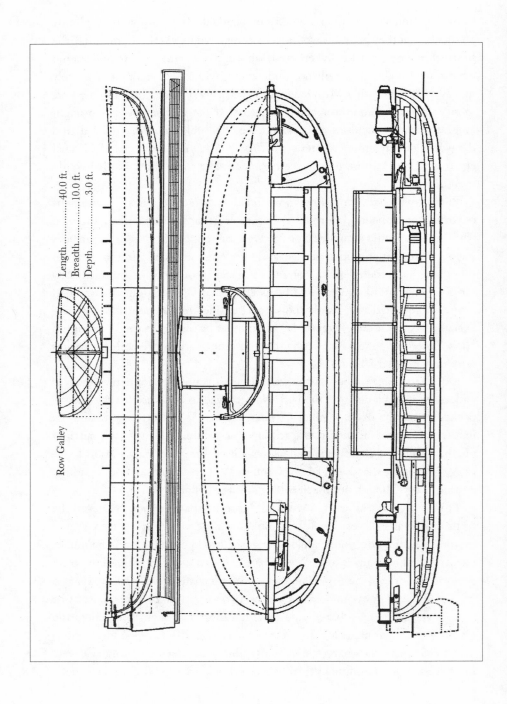

Row Galley

Length..........40.0 ft.
Breadth..........10.0 ft.
Depth..........3.0 ft.

ers, however, produced by the foundry of John Dorsey, would be specially delivered in person by Naval Agent James Beatty. The ordnance from the capital was to be shipped onboard the U.S. Navy cutter *Scorpion* and schooner *Asp*, which, together with *Black Snake*, were to sail immediately from the Washington Navy Yard. Although all three vessels were to be officially attached to the Chesapeake Flotilla, both *Scorpion* and *Asp*, having been manned in part by the crew of the warship *Adams* at Washington, were under orders, after making delivery, to proceed on detached duty to guard the mouth of the Potomac. Though delighted with *Scorpion*, the commandant was not the least bit happy with the acquisition of *Asp*, a 3-gun, 57-ton schooner purchased in February in Alexandria, Virginia. In mid-July, while on the Potomac, both vessels had been chased by two British brig-sloops, *Contest* and *Mohawk*. *Scorpion* had escaped up the bay, but *Asp*, a poor sailer, had retreated into the Yeocomico River, where she was captured, set afire, and abandoned. As soon as the enemy had departed, the Americans had retaken her and put out the flames. Though she had been repaired, Barney claimed that she was now "a miserable tool, and will never be anything but an expense." Not surprisingly, the vessel was seldom employed in any of his subsequent operations and generally proved more of a liability than an asset to the navy.[10]

. . .

Not all of the outfitting went smoothly. Barney was to be almost immediately frustrated in his request for pistols and cutlasses, for Secretary Jones disagreed with him on the necessity of providing the barges with them at all. "With muskets and pikes, I do not see much necessity for pistols and cutlasses," he wrote, "indeed pistols are not to be had." However, he promised to send grape and canister from the Washington Navy Yard.

On September 2, now that the building program was under way, Jones instructed the commandant to "open a rendezvous," or recruitment center, to enlist "as many men as will man the whole of the new and old barges." He

Facing page
Naval constructor William Doughty's plan for a typical row galley. Note the carronade on the bow and the long gun on the stern, both of which were mounted on wooden slides rather than carriages. This vessel, propelled only by oars, could be covered by a removable awning to protect the oarsmen from the elements as needed. *Drawing by Donald G. Shomette after Howard I. Chapelle.*

also formalized for the first time the complements, ranks, and pay scales for men serving on both the first- and second-class barges. The following was the authorized complement of officers and men for the barge fleet and their monthly pay:

75-foot barges (first-class)
1 Sailing Master (commanding)
1 Master's Mate ($20)
1 Gunner ($20)
1 Boatswain ($20)
1 Steward ($18)
1 Cook ($18)
10 Seamen ($12)
34 Ordinary Seamen ($6 to $10)

50-foot barges (second-class)
1 Sailing Master (commanding)
1 Master's Mate ($20)
1 Gunner ($20)
1 Boatswain ($20)
1 Steward ($18)
1 Cook ($18)
8 Seamen ($12)
26 Ordinary Seamen ($6 to $10)[11]

As all of the Baltimore City Flotilla's experienced officers and men were about to be paid off by the city and might even be disbanded, Barney saw an opportunity that could not be ignored and quickly sought Jones's approval to secure their continued service for his own force. His request had merit, for although he had entertained frequent applications from masters of many vessels in port for positions with the as-yet-to-be completed U.S. Flotilla, he now preferred the veterans of the city fleet, many of whom he undoubtedly knew, who had experience in both the city and tiny federal defense force of barges, hired schooners, and old gunboats. He adroitly made it known that he wished to enlist as many as possible, even though he had no vessels of his own ready for any of them, and was eager to "prepare a place for them until called into service." If the navy was willing to appoint the commanders of the barges right away, they could be put to work superintending the building of their own vessels, as was customary, and in recruiting their crews at the same time.

The Navy Department responded both immediately and positively to Barney's request. Of the seven commanders of the city vessels (the row galley *Vigilant* and barges *Nos. 1, 2, 3, 4, 5,* and *6*), one former and six active captains (some of them Revolutionary War veterans) enlisted with the Chesapeake Flotilla. These included Captains Claudius (or Claude) Besse, James Sellers, William Martin, Henry Worthington, John Warner, Jesse Huffington, and John Kiddall. A number of junior officers, such as Lieutenants John Besse and Girard Gorsuch, followed suit. Some, such as Huffington and Gorsuch, already had experience as privateersmen under their belts. On September 10 Claudius Besse, a veteran privateersman of the last war and until recently a barge commander in the Baltimore City Flotilla, became the first sailing master enrolled to command one of Barney's barges. Six days later one John Geoghegan, who would prove to be one of the ablest officers in the fleet, came aboard and was soon given command of gunboat *No. 138.*[12] Ironically, Barney's own commission beyond "acting" status would not be fixed for almost eight months!

In the meantime, contracts continued to be let to a variety of firms to provide the necessary equipage, supplies, and labor. One of the commandant's former agents and part-owner in *Rossie,* Christopher Deshon, was awarded the contract to provide any additional cannons and muskets. Ironwork was to be provided by Philip Cronmiller and Richard Laurence. The Mount Aetna Furnace Company would provide grape and 18-pound shot, while the Bellona Gunpowder Mill was contracted to provide the necessary gunpowder. Ammunition would be produced and delivered by William Conway. Sails were to be produced by Miles Ray, and masts and yards by Donald Best. James Belt, who had already provided ship chandlery for *Vigilant* while in city service, would provide rope and caulking. Leather cartouche boxes were ordered from William Graham. And so it went. Every necessity, no matter how small or large, was considered and contracts awarded accordingly. General work and miscellaneous requirements of a dozen varieties were to be supplied by at least five separate contractors: James Ganteume, George Waggoner, Thomas Cockwell, Levi Jones, and Joseph Lotz.[13]

Barney by now had eight vessels well under way, all barges or galleys. It was now determined in yet another revision of plans that each first-class vessel would be armed with a 24-pounder long gun at one end and a 42-pounder carronade at the other. The smaller barges were to be armed with a single 18-pounder and one 24- or 32-pounder apiece. Yet, as the construction progressed armament characteristics, it was proved, would be subject as much to availability (determined by the competing needs of regular naval vessels) as to suitability. Carronades were transferred in lieu of the long guns ordered earlier for several of the vessels and firepower, especially for close-in fighting, was substantially improved. Soon the long guns of the vessels also varied widely in caliber, being 42-, 32-, 24-, 18-, or 12-pounders. The carronades were also of various calibers, 42-, 32-, or 24-pounders. Caliber determination of guns for each vessel, it would appear, would be largely based upon both class and mobility of the specific vessel.[14]

Most of the vessels in the flotilla were extremely light and trim, averaging only 5 tons net weight per ship, not the 36 that Jones had predicted, but were heavily burdened with cannon, each weighing somewhat over 1½ tons or more. The carronades averaged ¾ of a ton per gun. Each vessel carried more than 1½ tons of shot and 2 tons of rigging. Thus, an average vessel's net weight approached 12 tons overall.[15]

One of the prime contractors for the basic construction of at least three barges, and possibly many more, was the firm of Thomas Kemp, a highly reputed Baltimore shipbuilder. Kemp was famed for his construction of the privateers *Rossie, Chasseur, Comet, Patapsco, Midas,* and *Rolla,* as well as the U.S. Navy sloops *Erie* and *Ontario.* In his yard at Washington and Aliceanna streets, on Fells Point, he built at least one of the early fifty-foot craft and two of the seventy-five-foot vessels, the latter at a cost of $2,350 apiece, and provided masting for a number of others. His brother Joseph, living in Wades Point, near St. Michaels, would also gain at least one if not more naval contracts.[16]

At the end of the summer the initial barge off the ways was subjected to its first sea trial. Secretary Jones was less than impressed. "It is vain to expect to combine excellence in every quality in a vessel of this kind," he wrote on September 15. The cause of the poor performance, he said, was "her long shallow body, and trimming on an even keel." The resistance of the water on the lee bow pressed her to windward, "having so little hold of the water abaft, [as] to resist her flying to." The way to remedy this, he suggested, was by "adding a lee board on her quarter, or adding a scag to her keel abaft, which would greatly injure her other qualities." Whether or not any of the suggested corrections were made is unknown. A description of the boats as they appeared in October indicated that they possessed a wide gangway but were open amidships, and rowed double-banked. They were by then covered by cedar awnings, with curtains at the sides, which afforded complete shelter to the men during the night and from the sun during the day while sailing under oars only. The awnings could be quickly dismantled whenever the vessel was preparing to proceed under sail or stripping for action. "They row either end foremost, indifferently, and draw, with all on board, but 22 inches water."[17]

After the trial, in which ordnance testing was undoubtedly conducted, Barney himself suggested heavier construction to better withstand the shock of heavy artillery discharges. Constantly adding his own experience and insight to the building program, he suggested, perhaps as a result of observing certain failings of the Baltimore City barges, that the new vessels be built a little fuller at both ends to better bear the weight of cannon without hogging amidships. Doughty went back to the drawing boards and prepared yet another design, this time for a sturdier vessel 75 feet in length, 15 feet abeam, and 4 feet deep. Later in the year he prepared yet a third design for a third-class vessel 40 feet in length, 10 feet abeam, 3 feet deep, and fitted for oars only.[18]

That Jones was more satisfied with Barney's barges than before, especially after alterations had been started, may be illustrated by instructions to Thomas Macdonough, commander of the U.S. Navy forces on Lake Champlain, written on December 7, to build fifteen galleys "similar to those now constructing here, at Baltimore, for the flotilla of the Chesapeake." He had already directed Master Commandant Daniel T. Patterson, commanding the U.S. Navy gunboats at New Orleans, that if the antiquated fleet under his command from the old Jeffersonian-era navy was in too great a state of decay to be serviceable, that it should not be repaired but be replaced by a squadron of barges similar to those on the Chesapeake. Indeed, it appears that whatever personal concerns the secretary may have initially held for the barge fleet had been dispelled, and he soon began to press for the construction of an additional six or eight second-class craft to supplement the Chesapeake Flotilla. On December 8 he instructed Barney to confer with Beatty respecting the building of additional barges on the Eastern Shore at St. Michaels, in Talbot County, as he was of the opinion "that every possible exertion must be made during the winter to meet the enemy with vigor in the spring." A week later, Barney wrote to Perry Spencer, owner of the Spencer Hall Shipyard, "the only builder of note on the Eastern Shore." The letter was carried by Spencer's son, a delegate in the Maryland General Assembly, who assured the commandant that his father would undertake the work. Spencer's yard at or near St. Michaels, in Talbot County, would eventually be awarded a contract to construct a large number of second-class barges, the crews of which were also to be raised on the Eastern Shore.[19]

...

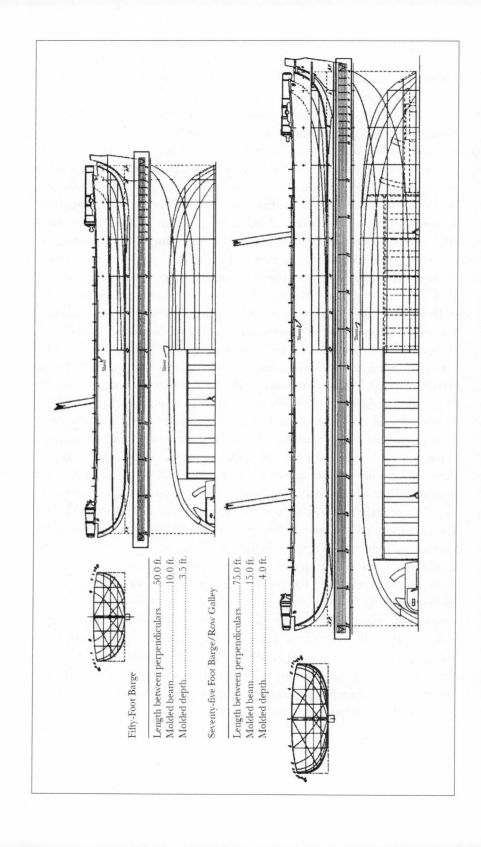

Fifty-Foot Barge

Length between perpendiculars.......50.0 ft.
Molded beam...............................10.0 ft.
Molded depth..............................3.5 ft.

Seventy-five Foot Barge/Row Galley

Length between perpendiculars.......75.0 ft.
Molded beam...............................15.0 ft.
Molded depth..............................4.0 ft.

Although enormous emphasis had been placed upon the construction of the barge fleet, the Chesapeake Flotilla squadron, charged with the defense of the upper bay, was not to be composed entirely of that class of warcraft. A number of vessels specifically designated as gunboats were also employed.

Many historians have used the terms *gunboat* and *barge* interchangeably. This is definitely incorrect. At least two gunboats that would see service with the flotilla, *Nos. 137* and *138,* had been constructed at Baltimore many years earlier by one William Price. Both had been built along the lines of plans prepared by Commodore James Barron in 1806. These sloop-rigged gunboats, unlike the typical schooner-rigged vessels of an even earlier design, were capable of being propelled by more than twenty sweep of twenty-foot-long oars. They were unquestionably also of the class that Barney claimed from the very beginning to be slow and cranky under sail.[20]

Both *Nos. 137* and *138* belonged to a series of 177 gunboats contracted for by the U.S. government before the beginning of 1809, and the second and third of ten such constructed in a series (*Nos. 136* to *145*) in the William Price yard at the east end of Thames Street, on Fells Point, between 1806 and 1808. When originally awarded the contract, Price was considered well equipped to handle the job, having already produced several gunboats to navy specifications as early as 1804. Barron had called for each boat to be 60 feet between perpendiculars, 56 feet on keel, 48 feet straight rabbet, 16.5 feet abeam, and 6.5 feet in depth of hold. Unlike the double-ended, lateen-rigged barges, they were to be square-sterned and sloop-rigged, and would have been similar in appearance to small pilot boats, although shoaler and flatter on the bottom. Each was to

Facing page

Top: William Doughty's plan for a second-class, fifty-foot-long, single-masted lateen rigged barge, mounting a carronade and a long gun and propelled by both sail and oars. Both first- and second-class barges were later equipped with washboard collars to protect the oarsmen from heavy seas, obliging them to row from a standing position. *Bottom:* William Doughty's first-class, seventy-five-foot-long, double-masted barge became the workhorse of the Chesapeake Flotilla. Like the second-class vessel, its fixed rudder assembly, aft the long-gun mount, was probably managed from a yoke system forward of the gun deck. It is possible that leeboards may have been employed in the barge design as suggested by a sketch of the vessels later employed during the defense of Fort McHenry. See the pencil sketch of the bombardment of Fort McHenry in this book. *Drawings by Donald G. Shomette after Howard I. Chapelle.*

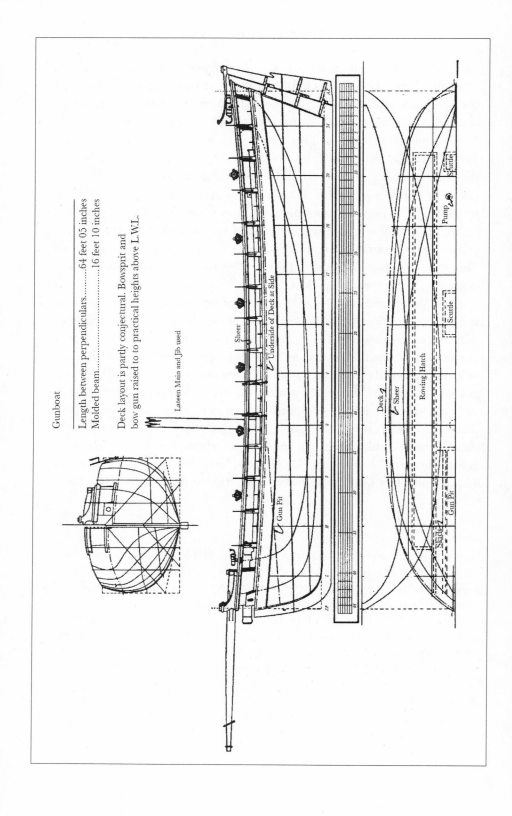

Gunboat

Length between perpendiculars........64 feet 05 inches
Molded beam.........................16 feet 10 inches

Deck layout is partly conjectural. Bowsprit and
bow gun raised to to practical heights above L.W.L.

Lateen Main and Jib used

Sheer

Underside of Deck at Side

Gun Pit

Deck

Sheer

Rowing Hatch

Scuttle

Pump

Scuttle

Side

Gun Pit

be armed with a single 32-pounder long gun. Captain Samuel Evans of the U.S. Navy supervised the construction of both vessels.[21]

In February 1813 *No. 137,* under the command of Sailing Master Moses Middleton, and *No. 138,* had been assigned to the Potomac Flotilla and based at the Washington Navy Yard, under the overall command of Master Commandant Arthur Sinclair, and later Lieutenant Edmund P. Kennedy. The mission of this small force, ultimately composed of three gunboats and a schooner, was to repel any enemy incursions into the river. Yet, the squadron had occasionally ventured into the Chesapeake, once as low as the Piankatank River, Virginia. In the early spring 1813 it had experienced its first two brief enemy encounters. Soon afterward, *No. 138* was transferred back to Baltimore to assist in the city's naval defense, and later participated in yet another reconnaissance, this time as far south as New Point Comfort, Virginia. In September *No. 138* was assigned to Barney's still infant flotilla, whether he wanted her or not. Six months later, in March 1814, *No. 137* followed suite. Although never stated, it seems probable that Jones hoped the two vessels would serve as the central corps of the flotilla rather than auxiliaries or tenders. If so, he was to be greatly disappointed.

None of the Price vessels had met the approval of their previous commanders. One had complained: "The gunboats sail & work very heavily & it will be necessary to observe some caution lest in the event of pursuit by a superior force, they should be cut off or separated. It will require some circumspection lest you should come in contact with some of our private armed vessels in the bay, which by the imprudence of the commander of one of them, was the case during the late [April 1813] cruise of the [Potomac] Flotilla, it is known that some of the gunboats under your command, are lateen rigged, which is conspicuous & sufficient distinction of itself."[22]

Facing page

Captain James Barron's 1806 design for a gunboat in the series in which *Nos. 137* and *138* were constructed. These vessels were notoriously bad sailers and were considered a handicap to the flotilla squadron by both Commodore Barney and Navy Secretary Jones. Barney's flagship *Scorpion,* formerly gunboat *No. 59,* once converted to a topsail sloop or cutter rig, proved quite suitable for service on the open water but inadequate for use in the confines of the Patuxent River. *Drawing by Donald G. Shomette after Howard I. Chapelle.*

Barney's flagship was to be the USS *Scorpion*, variously described as a gun-boat, large topsail sloop, block-sloop, and cutter. This vessel, which was fi-nally dispatched to permanently join the fleet on February 18, 1814, was the oldest in the squadron. Originally constructed for the navy as gunboat *No. 59*, she was one of the series contracted for by the U.S. government well before the beginning of 1809 and along the lines of one of the several aforementioned prototype plans produced by Captain James Barron. In late July 1806 Barron let contracts for the construction of four gunboats, to be numbered 58 through 61, all to be produced to the design of his own aforementioned plan and speci-fications. Builder George Hope, of Hampton, Virginia, was awarded con-tracts for the construction of at least two vessels in the series, *Nos. 58* and *59*. Hope apparently considered adjustments to Barron's plans the following year with suggestions that the gunboats in the series be altered to a fifty-foot deck, a fifteen-foot beam, and a five-foot hold. Whether these adjustments were carried out is unknown. When first contracted for, their hulls, masts, and the like, were each projected to cost approximately $5,000. Fully equipped and outfitted, however, the total cost of *No. 59* approached $11,000. On April 21, 1806, Congress appropriated money for the construction program, but the plans, and Hope's probable alterations to them, may have been irrevocably tied to reductions of funding. Nevertheless, the two gunboats were launched at Hampton in late December of the same year. By mid-January 1807 they had been taken to Norfolk for outfitting. Unlike some, James Barron was quite pleased with the Hope gunboats. "I think," he wrote approvingly, "it will not be presuming too far to say, that, the two, so far finished, as to form a correct opinion of them, will bear a comparison with any vessels of the de-scription, ever built, in this country." Just five years later, in March 1812, "the old gunboat *No. 59*" was hauled up to the wharf at the Washington Navy Yard "and thence rebuilt with much improvement." Her hull, which may have been lengthened at this time, was caulked, coppered, and launched. Then, "rigged completely new" as a cutter, she was fitted out with boats, water casks, and all necessary armaments and stores and renamed *Scorpion*.

It has been suggested that the vessel may have then been refitted again as a block-sloop, a vessel type basically employed in stationary harbor defense, more along the lines of a floating battery than a sailing man-of-war; if that was the case, she was but one of two known block-sloops to be in naval ser-vice at the outbreak of the War of 1812. If so, however, she was destined not to remain in that category for long and soon underwent further alterations. Although few records have been found pertaining to her actual construction, the plan of one block-sloop, which was undoubtedly only a proposal, has survived from this period. This particular plan suggests a vessel measuring 48 feet, 8 inches on deck, 17 feet, 8 inches molded beam, 18 feet, 8 inches extreme beam, and about 4 feet, 6 inches in the hold. Speed under oars or sails for such vessel types was generally sacrificed in order that they might carry heavy cannon. Intended and equipped for static defense, they were given high bulwarks specifically to resist boarders and to protect the crews from small arms fire. Navy lists indicate that *Scorpion* was initially assigned four guns and a crew of twenty-five seamen, but observations by the British in 1814 suggest that she was a fairly large vessel and may have been pierced to carry additional artillery, though she apparently never received all of them.[23]

When *Scorpion* was finally transferred from Washington to the Baltimore Station, about March 1814, Acting Master Commandant Barney immediately ordered her hauled out and again refitted to his own specifications at the Lazaretto, on the north side of the city harbor entrance, approximately six hundred yards opposite Fort McHenry. Already unhappy with the naval contractors, he informed Secretary Jones that the cutter was to be fitted out "with our own hands, and will cost but a trifle." Already armed with a single 24-pounder long gun, one 18-pounder gunnade, and two 12-pounder carronades, he felt that she was unsuitable for mounting a great 42-pounder bronze howitzer that the Navy Department had wanted. The gun was promptly transferred to the USS *Adams,* which was almost destitute of armament, then outfitting at Washington. Apparently pleased with *Scorpion's* sailing qualities and size, Barney selected the ex-gunboat-turned-cutter as his flagship. From mid-April 1814 onward, it would be intimately tied to every event in the life and death struggles of the U.S. Chesapeake Flotilla.[24]

. . .

Building and manning an entire flotilla, practically from scratch, was obviously an incredibly demanding undertaking. There were a thousand and one details to attend to, and Barney was finding himself inundated by jobs normally delegated to others, but, lacking a sufficient staff to carry out such tasks, was obliged to do them himself. The difficulties of the job, moreover, were often compounded by Secretary Jones, who had a nettlesome penchant for second guessing the commandant, alternately questioning and then imposing his strong "opinions" as to what he should do next, while attempting to micromanage the assemblage of the fleet from afar.

Barney persisted. He requested the Navy Department provide him with a purser to deal with the squadron's accounts and supplies as Purser Robert Ormsby, who had been assigned to the flotilla since its inception, had long before been transferred to the USS *Erie,* although he would be technically carried on the flotilla muster until April 6, 1815. In September 1813, when a small enemy squadron ravaged sections of the bay and caused a flurry of excitement in Baltimore, Barney never broke his stride. Work on the flotilla at Fells Point and St. Michaels continued unabated. Unfortunately, even with many seamen out of work owing to a standing embargo by the government, recruiting was going badly.[25]

As the construction program accelerated, Barney's success in meeting the manpower needs of his fleet for the coming spring had borne little fruit. The problem was caused by the far better prospects for prize money offered to seamen by privateering syndicates. Moreover, few men in their right minds, claimed some, wanted to take up service in open gunboats and barges that mounted only one or two guns and were exposed not only to the weather but also the shot and shell of an enemy frigate or 74-gun man-of-war, the largest killing machines ever invented. By December 15, 1813, Barney had decided upon a new recruitment tactic. "I have turned my views to the best means of procuring men," he informed Secretary Jones, "and beg leave to ask permission to employ Captain Solomon Frazier a [Maryland State] Senator, now here, from the Eastern Shore, he is well known as a character, perhaps the most popular among the seafaring men of the Eastern Shore, of any man in Maryland; he was in the service of the [Maryland] State [Navy] the latter end of the [Revolutionary] War, and commanded at that time a galley, in which service he behaved on several occasions with great gallantry and honour to himself—he is rich and at his ease, but declares if you will give him an appointment, he will quit the senate and serve under me."[26]

Frazier was, indeed, a popular veteran sailor and fighter. During the Revolution he had commanded the Eastern Shore barge *Fearnaught,* which had been turned over to the Maryland State Navy for the defense of state waters. He later commanded the state galley *Defence,* and fought fearlessly at the famous Battle of Kedges Straits in the Chesapeake. Barney was quite aware of the political value of having the well-known state senator serving under him, and consented to give him command of a whole division of the barge fleet if the Navy Department approved of his appointment. But it was Frazier's popularity that Barney felt was his most important attribute. The recruitment value on the Eastern Shore in having as a division commander in the fleet such a respected, experienced, and well-regarded old hand, willing to resign his position in the Maryland Senate to serve his state and nation, was inestimable. That he might procure enough seamen to fully man his division while superintending the building project at the Spencer Shipyard at or near St. Michaels would be an added bonus. Frazier would be put on an equal footing with the commandant's second in command, Solomon Rutter, who had been appointed on September 15 as acting lieutenant in the U.S. Flotilla Service after transferring from the Baltimore City Flotilla. Rutter had earlier commanded a company of seventy-five seamen in a unit organized by General Smith called the Corps of Seamen, had been responsible for laying a boom from the Lazaretto to Whetstone Point to impede the main channel approach to Baltimore, and had commanded a unit of Marine Artillery.

Jones quickly approved of Frazier's nomination, and on December 17 authorized Naval Agent Beatty, with Barney's "advice and assistance," to contract for ten more second-class barges at the Spencer Shipyard at St. Michaels, "to be built as fast as possible, under the superintendence of Mr. Frazier." He also recommended that the constructor's drawings be sent from Baltimore to St. Michaels, but if these were not on hand, and if one of the completed and fitted second-class barges at Baltimore was available, "it will be well to send her as a model."[27]

By Christmas, advertisements had begun to regularly appear in the newspapers, drumming up volunteers by pointing out the benefits of enlistment. One typical ad in the Baltimore *American & Commercial Daily Advertiser* read:

CHESAPEAKE FLOTILLA

Where an honorable and comfortable situation offers to men out of employ during the Embargo; where Seamen and Landsmen, will receive two months pay advanced, and their wives to receive half-pay monthly, and single men can provide for aged parents, and widows for helpless children, in the same manner; with the advantage of being near their families, and not to be drafted into the militia, or turned over into any other service. Apply to the recruiting officer, or JOSHUA BARNEY

Com'dt of U.S. Flotilla[28]

Despite such promotional efforts and the exertions of Frazier, recruitment of regular flotillamen failed to progress as smoothly as Barney had anticipated the previous July. Not surprisingly, nepotism was rife among the senior officers in filling out positions of rank. Barney himself brought on his own brother Louis as a clerk, and his son William B. Barney, a major in the 5th

Regimental Cavalry District, who would eventually serve as a sailing master of the flagship *Scorpion*. No fewer than six Fraziers (five of whom were officers) and six Rutters (all of whom were officers) were eventually to appear on the flotilla muster. As the weeks passed and recruitment continued to lag, anyone, experienced or not, was taken on. Even a small number of blacks, both freemen and slaves, were recruited, the former of their own free will and the latter apparently placed aboard by their masters in return for their pay.[29]

Though Secretary Jones had considerable confidence in the abilities of Joshua Barney, he too worried constantly over the progress of the Flotilla Service recruitment program. In February he had written to John Galliard, the new chairman of the Senate Naval Committee who had replaced outgoing Sam Smith, concerning the obstacles being encountered. "We have a right, sir, to anticipate, during the ensuing summer the most urgent occasion for the vigorous employment of the flotilla for the defense of the waters of the United States; and it has become a very interesting question how that force is to be commanded with the best effect. That service is, at best, unpopular with the regular officers of the navy . . . There are other intrinsic difficulties in this service, which are unknown on board our ships of war. The temptations to insubordination and vice are much greater in this scattered and amphibious kind of force; and the rigors of naval discipline, unless tempered with judgment and great moderation discourage the recruiting for this service." There was, however, one advantage in hand. "Bay and river craftsmen, seamen, ordinary seamen, who have families, riggers, and naval mechanics out of employ, will engage in this service, under a local commander of capacity and influence, when they will not engage for the regular naval service."[30] Joshua Barney was, fortunately, a commander of just such merits. And progress *was* being made even as the days and hours diminished before the enemy, who had, with the exception of a small naval force, wintered in Bermuda, returned to the bay in force.

In the meantime, Barney continued his recruitment campaign. He soon began working with sympathetic Maryland legislators in Annapolis to secure $30,000 in state funding for bounties to induce men to join up, even though the force fell under the direction of the U.S. Navy Department. Competition continued to be keen for the average able-bodied seaman's services, not only from the privateering interests, but also from the regular navy itself. In March 1814 at least two U.S. Navy 44-gun warships, *Java* and *Columbia,* were under construction and nearing completion in Baltimore but were without adequate manpower to field them. Another named *Erie,* of 21 guns, being readied for sea, was in a similar situation. A fourth, the USS *Ontario,* 18 guns, lay at her berth ready to sail but was only partially manned. Eyeing such a manpower pool, small as it was, lying useless on the Baltimore waterfront, was too much for Barney. He complained bitterly to Jones that the officers of these vessels, especially those under construction, refused to temporarily release what sailors they had for flotilla duty, even though their own ships stood little chance of putting to sea in the near future. Barney's repeated complaints soon bore fruit. Jones was obliged to intercede on the old seadog's behalf, though the commandant had conveniently ignored the fact that the flotilla and the regular navy were to operate as two discrete services. The navy secretary ordered the release of eighty-five petty officers, regular and ordinary seamen, and boys from *Ontario* to help fill out the flotilla's complement, and Barney breathed a bit easier, albeit only briefly. He was not amused when forty of the transfers arrived completely drunk at the Lazaretto to report for duty on the night of April 13, throwing the remainder of the flotillamen into the utmost confusion. The following day another twenty-eight arrived in the same shape. Enraged, Barney slapped most of them in irons to sober up. Seventeen more that had arrived were in such poor physical condition that he had to send them to the hospital.[31]

Among his many recruitment schemes, Barney had actively pursued the idea of having the U.S. Sea Fencibles, an independent Baltimore unit, attached to his marine unit. At first, Captain Matthew Simmones Bunbury and his second, Lieutenant Caleb R. Robinson, in command of the Baltimore-based unit, and Captain William H. Addison, seemed outwardly anxious to join, but the commandant soon found them intractable. By spring Bunbury, whose services had also been wooed by General Samuel Smith, had become decidedly intent on maintaining his own separate command. Indeed, he had come to oppose the idea of serving under Barney so much that he was advertising in his own recruitment notices that those who enlisted in the Fencibles were not liable to transfer to the flotilla, or to any other corps for that matter. Barney was soon calling Bunbury's unit the most scurrilous epithet he could think of—landsmen.[32]

There was also stiff competition from the army and the militia, not just for manpower but also for equipment. General Smith, now charged by Governor Winder with the defense of Baltimore, demanded that three former city-owned vessels that Barney had taken over be returned and placed under his direct command. Local politics were equally injurious. On the Eastern Shore, where Lieutenant Frazier was busily engaged in recruiting and superintending barge construction, politicians representing the state's two political parties, which were roughly equal in strength there, sparred over the morality of the war in general and, needing votes, actively discouraged local recruitment altogether until after the election season was over. Discouraged by the poor enrollment, Frazier requested instructions from his superior. Assuming that half a loaf was better than none at all, Barney wryly told him to promise that all Democrats would be home in time to vote on October 1.[33]

By March 4, 1814, it was reported that the Chesapeake Flotilla had ready for service thirteen barges and a pilot boat schooner called *Shark* lying at Baltimore. By March 25 it was publicly acknowledged that the U.S. Flotilla construction effort was progressing well, not only at Baltimore and on the Eastern Shore, but throughout the Chesapeake and Delaware tidewaters. Six barges had been purchased at Philadelphia for defense of the Delaware, 4 more at Baltimore, and one at Norfolk for the Flotilla Service. Four had been purchased at Baltimore from the city flotilla, and 8 vessels abuilding there were nearing completion. Ten barges were under construction at St. Michaels and 4 more at Washington. By April 4, Barney was pleased to report, 2 of the barges built at the Washington Navy Yard had joined him at Baltimore, 4 of the vessels constructed at St. Michaels had also come up, and 4 more were expected within the week. In all, the Chesapeake Flotilla at Baltimore would ultimately include a total of at least 26 barges, with another 18 assigned to the Norfolk squadron. The fleet, however, had not taken the 3 weeks to build as Barney had so optimistically predicted, but nearly 9 months!

Moreover, the difficulty in recruiting and arming his squadron continued. The commandant was "cruelly disappointed" with the retarded delivery of the 18-pounders, which were brought in on March 31 by John Dorsey from his foundry on Curtis Creek, five miles from the city, and complained that the gunfounder "has trifled with us from the first, with promises from day to day . . . no dependence can be put upon his word." Nevertheless, he now boasted that "nothing will be wanting but men" and a purser to handle accounts. Yet, even as late as March 24, 1814, he was obliged to inform Jones that for want of funds his men were without clothes, and payment of wages and procurement of provisions were still being personally handled by himself. Moreover, the ongoing recruitment effort was further retarded when President Madison requested Congress to repeal the trade embargo that had forced many able seamen into unemployment, thereby creating the manpower pool from which Barney had been enlisting men. "We were doing very well in procuring men," he soon lamented, "untill the news of raising the embargo arrived." Nevertheless, on April 14 Congress complied with the president's request, effectively drying up the source of many seamen who otherwise might have enrolled. The news was, unfortunately, published for all to see, including the British.[34]

Uppermost in everyone's mind was what the enemy's plans in the Chesapeake Tidewater would be for the coming season of war. Secretary Jones, sitting in his diminutive office in Washington, had no illusions. He had been bombarded with pleas from every shore in the region, crying out for a barge here and another there to protect local interests. Nevertheless, he maintained that it would be necessary to concentrate the available naval forces at hand. Convinced that the enemy possessed a strong desire "to destroy this place," Washington, he had already informed Barney in mid-February, that they would assuredly make an effort to that end. It was thus imperative that the flotilla keep the enemy south of the Potomac to prohibit any advance on the capital. "Your force is our principal shield, and all eyes will be upon you." [35]

. . .

In early April news arrived of the enemy's return to the Chesapeake in some force. He was, it was reported, erecting fortifications on islands in the bay and preparing for offensive action. When informed Acting Master Commandant Joshua Barney's reply was terse: "I am anxious to be at them."[36]

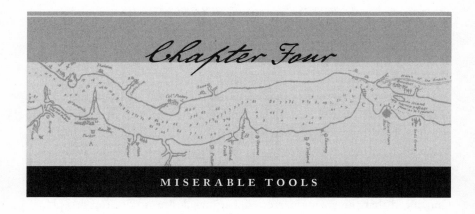

Chapter Four

MISERABLE TOOLS

On April 12, 1814, the Chesapeake Flotilla's new purser, John Stuart Skinner, of Calvert County, whose services had been requested long before, finally arrived in Baltimore to assist Barney. His appearance on the scene prompted little celebration, however, for that same day distressing news from the south appeared in the city newspapers. A certain Captain Allen, commander of the schooner *Eliza Ann,* while en route from Baltimore to Norfolk, had dispatched a letter dated April 6 that noted that while attempting to pass Tangier Straits he had encountered a British frigate, a brig, and a tender lying in the channel off Watts Island. The enemy had three prizes in their possession, and had obviously considered that *Eliza Ann* would soon become the fourth. The fact that such a force lay about Tangier was not surprising in itself, as the British had frequented the area during the previous winter and into the spring. What was of concern was that Allen's schooner had been pursued not only by a tender but by a small force of barges. Moreover, the enemy's line was said to extend clear across the Chesapeake from Watts Island to the mouth of the Potomac. The last heard from the captain was that he had been obliged to take shelter in the Patuxent River from the pursuing enemy.[1]

Immediately on the heels of Allen's information came more bad news in a communiqué also dated April 6, this time from Norfolk. It was reported that an enemy reinforcement squadron composed of two large ships, probably frigates or ships-of-the-line, two brigs, three schooners, and possibly other vessels, had entered the bay and were heading north. The following day word arrived in the city that the squadron had come to anchor off the mouth of the Potomac.[2]

That British reconnaissance units were swarming about and probing the Western Shore from an anchorage on the Potomac was soon confirmed when intelligence regarding their activities on the bay shore of St. Mary's County arrived at Baltimore. A city schooner owned by one Charles Barker, it was reported in the papers, had been stopped by an enemy barge poking about inside St. Jerome's Creek on the bay shores of St. Mary's County. When the enemy attempted boarding, a fight ensued during which a British officer and one seaman were killed. Barker and his schooner escaped northward.[3]

From Accomac County, it was belatedly reported that on April 4 an enemy frigate, a brig, and two schooners had arrived in Pocomoke Sound and were taking soundings near the entrances of Onancock and Pungoteague creeks, had raided Watts and Tangier islands for their livestock, and were already throwing up breastworks upon one of the islands on which they had planted cannon. Construction of a hospital, barracks, and even a large fort were under way, and an invasion of the county mainland was feared.[4]

Secretary Jones, who had just dispatched the schooner *Asp* down the Potomac from Washington laden with cannon for the defense of Frenchtown on the Eastern Shore (which had already been savaged once) and masting for the frigate *Java,* then abuilding at Baltimore, was obliged to send off a fast sloop to call her back lest she fall into enemy hands. From the new British anchorage off the Eastern Shore, he knew a move across the bay to the entrance of the Potomac was but a few hours' sail. Fearing a shift into the river and the potential threat to the capital itself, he directed Barney to be ready to sail at a moment's notice. Almost as an afterthought, he informed him that he was to receive for the use of the squadron surgeon, Dr. Thomas Hamilton, a medicine chest and surgical tools from *Ontario*, "which you will preserve in perfect order to be returned to the ship when prepared for service," as well as such slops and stores to be transferred from the USS *Erie* as needed. "I am all anxiety to see you under way in order to keep those fellows in check below—Your present force I trust is sufficient to repel all the boats the enemy can muster and I hope to hold his ships uneasy under certain circumstance." If the British entered the Potomac, Barney was ordered to "hang upon his rear."[5]

A spate of even worse news arrived on April 14, when Lieutenant Rutter came in from St. Michaels in an open barge with thirty Eastern Shore recruits for the flotilla. While en route he had passed a British 74-gun man-of-war and two schooners a few miles below Sandy Point, near Annapolis, narrowly escaping observation. Only two days before the enemy had been waiting off St. Michaels in hopes of learning of the American barges, and possibly to snag a few in the process. The British, he reported, had already captured and burned a number of bay craft before moving on, and were now believed to be in Herring Bay.[6] It was clear to all that the enemy had returned with the same arrogant panache he had exhibited the previous year.

Whether his squadron was ready or not, Barney was determined to have a look for himself. On April 17, even before receiving the secretary's orders, a completed and manned segment of the Chesapeake Flotilla set out on its maiden voyage, a shakedown cruise with ten barges, gunboat *No. 138,* and the flagship *Scorpion.* Owing to the manpower shortage, *Vigilant* was unable to accompany the fleet. *No. 137,* undergoing refitting as a much-needed storeship, also remained behind. Arriving at Annapolis soon afterward, the commandant discovered that the enemy, after having burned and captured a number of small craft off Kent Island, had apparently retired south to the Piankatank River in Virginia. Nevertheless, the flotilla pressed on toward the Patuxent, arriving there soon afterward without event. Two days later it returned to Baltimore. Nevertheless, the short cruise had proved of value since defects in several of the vessels were discovered before they were exposed to battle conditions.[7]

Barney was particularly unhappy with the performance of the second-class barges, the fifty-footers. They were simply not as seaworthy as he had wished, and had shipped far too much water during choppy weather. Even before the squadron had departed the Patapsco on the first outing, several of the vessels had already twisted their rudder heads off and had to be left behind in Baltimore.[8]

The flotilla was still under-manned, with each barge at least ten men shy of a full complement. Indeed, there were not more than 550 men in the entire force fit for duty, and the enemy was already making his lethal presence once more felt on the bay. Though discouraged, Barney had still not given up in his efforts to secure the services of the Sea Fencibles to flesh out his manpower needs, but with each failed attempt he grew more and more frustrated. "If I had the Sea Fencibles which are doing worse than nothing at the fort [Fort McHenry], I could man five more barges." But every effort was in vain. With the secretary of war and General Smith both actively maneuvering in every possible way to secure their services as well, and with little support forthcoming from Jones, Barney quietly admitted defeat in the matter on April 22.[9]

There were, unfortunately, other problems, not as clear-cut as his vessels' performance or recruitment, which bothered the commandant. Throughout the long months that he had labored to field the flotilla, he had worried over the nebulous status of his rank in relation to the regular navy. His two able lieutenants, Solomon Frazier and Solomon Rutter, were in much the same situation, although neither had made serious inquiry concerning their status as acting lieutenants. On April 16, however, the day before Barney sailed on the first shakedown cruise, the U.S. Congress, after considerable lobbying by the Navy Department, clarified the situation, much to the approbation if not total satisfaction of all parties concerned. On that date an act of Congress was passed authorizing the formal appointment of officers in the Flotilla Service. By virtue of the act the president was empowered to appoint four captains and twelve lieutenants to be employed in the Flotilla Service of the United States, not only on the Chesapeake but on the Delaware and in New England waters as well, "without rank in the navy, but with the same rank and authority in the flotilla service as officers of the same grade are entitled to in the navy of the United States."[10]

Ten days later, on April 26, Jones informed Barney of his official status and rate as of the previous day. "Herewith you will receive a commission from the President as Captain in the Flotilla Service of the United States. You will be entitled to seventy five dollars per month and six rations per day, being the pay and subsistence of a Captain in the Navy commanding a ship of 20 and under 32 guns, and governed by the rules and regulations provided for the government of the Navy." Both Frazier and Rutter were also officially appointed on the same day to posts of lieutenants in the Flotilla Service. As commander of the Baltimore squadron, Captain Joshua Barney, USFS, would henceforth be formally addressed as commodore.[11]

...

While Barney and his men raced to prepare the flotilla, the enemy continued his nefarious depredations. On April 20 a large fleet of bay craft that were as yet unaware of the British presence on Tangier Sound attempted to enter Pocomoke River on the Eastern Shore. The enemy had quickly sighted them, and the order to give chace was issued. Between forty and fifty vessels, mostly fishing craft, taken by complete surprise, fled helter-skelter in a desperate effort to escape into the Great and Little Annamessex rivers. The following day a squadron of British barges entered the Little Annamessex and easily captured or burned seven vessels, five of which belonged to the little port of Onancock. One of those destroyed, it was later reported, had a number of cannon aboard, which were thrown overboard to prevent capture.[12] That the enemy could threaten at will the Potomac, gateway to the U.S. capital itself, and only twenty miles west of the Little Annamessex, was now painfully obvious to the public as well as the government.

Barney resolved to take his entire force on another sortie down the bay to the Potomac, but logistics, always a concern on naval forays, provided yet another obstacle. As Jones had predicted, without the capability of carrying provisions for an extended period at sea, the flotilla was extremely limited in its striking range. The fleet, Barney knew, could not sail until *Asp*, decrepit as she was, had arrived from Washington to serve as a supply ship until a replacement could be found. He had already discovered that *No. 137*, though refitted to carry provisions, was only partially adequate for the task, though still preferable to the schooner. Thus, on April 25, soon after word of the depredations on the Little Annamessex reached Baltimore, he dispatched his lookout boat and the row galley *Vigilant* down the bay to reconnoiter. Four days later *Vigilant* returned with the disturbing news, confirming everyone's fears, that an enemy force comprised of two ships and several smaller vessels was already in the Potomac. The lookout boat had remained behind to keep a watch on them.[13]

The commodore immediately decided to make a sprint southward with the stated objective of convoying the schooner *Asp* safely to Baltimore. The run down the bay, of course, would not be without risk. Without the fast lookout boat to serve as his forward eyes or *Asp* as a storeship, the time he could keep the squadron at sea, hence his range of operations, was limited. "I cannot remain long as we are unable to carry more than twelve days of provisions . . . it is impossible to put provisions, other than salt, onboard the gunboats, they have no hold or place to put bread, which is very bulky, nor dare I trust liquors or small stores among the crews of any." Nevertheless, leaving Lieutenant Rutter to superintend affairs at Baltimore and—for want of men to sail them—several first-class barges mounting 42-pounder carronades and 24-pounder long guns, Barney departed the Patapsco with *Scorpion*, both gunboats, and a dozen barges on April 29. With a gale-force wind nipping at his heels, he arrived in the Patuxent two days later. Although his primary mission was to escort *Asp*, he blithely informed Secretary Jones that he was prepared to let himself "be guided by circumstances."[14]

The run down the bay was not without cost. The gale had ripped a mast from one of the barges, which had to be replaced. Upon his arrival in the Patuxent on the afternoon of May 1, Barney received onboard the latest local intelligence from the Potomac, albeit somewhat skimpy and already two days old: a British ship and several schooners had been there, and the lookout boat was still somewhere to the south. The following morning he dispatched his own observer overland through St. Mary's County to Point Lookout, at the confluence of the Potomac and Chesapeake, for more specific information on the enemy, but no new particulars regarding either *Asp* or the British were forthcoming. In the meantime, he waited anxiously for the return of his lookout boat.[15]

...

While the commodore was occupied in gauging the threat to the Potomac, the most direct water route to Washington, the enemy had continued his raids along the Eastern Shore unabated and virtually unopposed. Stealth, experience, and sheer bravado were often second nature to seasoned Royal Navy tars and marines used to fighting and prevailing over the mightiest power on the European Continent, namely the French. The pitiful resistance usually offered, with but a few exceptions, on the backwaters of the Chesapeake must have seemed to many like swatting flies at a picnic. When one of Cockburn's commanders, Captain George Edward Watts, of HBM brig-sloop *Jaseur,* received intelligence that an American privateer was in the East River, he immediately took action that proved a considerable embarrassment to his foe. Shortly before dawn on April 30, *Jaseur* moved quietly into the little waterway and within sight of the letter-of-marque ship without being discovered. Under muffled oars, a launch commanded by First Lieutenant Henry West, RN, with twenty-four men, was dispatched on a surprise cutting-out expedition. Although the privateer was under the protection of a shore battery of several field pieces, the experience and panache of the British raiders was telling. The privateer, whose skipper, one Captain Knapp, had been keeping watch with seven men while twenty more were asleep below, was taken by complete surprise. Lieutenant West and six men had managed to board the vessel undetected, and in a lightning assault drove the watch below, fastened down the hatches, and "brought [the ship] safely out, before they even knew on shore that she was boarded." The prize, which was preparing to run the blockade the next day, proved to be the 228-ton *Grecian,* a veteran sea raider owned by Baltimore shipping magnet Isaac McKim, a friend and supporter of Joshua Barney's during his epic foray in *Rossie.* Captain Watts was delighted with his prize, which he described as "one of the fleetest and most beautiful schooners in America, coppered and copper fastened [and] pierced for 20 guns" although only four guns and five swivels had been mounted. A bonus prize, a vessel transporting a supply of guns and munitions for the U.S. Army, had also been taken.[16]

...

Unaware of the action just a few miles across the bay, and anticipating an extended stay in the middle bay region, Joshua Barney took the opportunity of dispatching *No. 137* back to Baltimore for provisions with orders to return as soon as possible to the Patuxent. Finally, after several days' wait, the squadron was rejoined by the lookout boat, and Barney pressed on for the Potomac, where he intended on sending her up to join *Asp*. Unhappily, the spring weather continued to make things difficult. The run between the Patuxent and Potomac proved even more taxing than the voyage down the bay, with cold, heavy seas continually washing over the gunnels of the barges. Simply to move on, he was obliged to transfer everything out of the barges except fifteen rounds of shot each to the larger *Scorpion* and *No. 138*. By the time the fleet had arrived on the Potomac, about May 7, unfortunately in concert with another spate of foul weather, it was running low on provisions, with more than half already consumed.[17]

The enemy, Barney discovered, who had entered the river on April 27 to take on water and establish a temporary blockade, had already departed. In truth, Cockburn, hoping to blunt any opposition to his presence in the bay, had assigned the commander of the foray, Captain Robert Barrie of *Dragon*, "to ascertain whether the enemy has any force there within our reach, and to do him any mischief, which you may find to be within your power either in St. Marys or in any other part of the river below the Kettle Bottoms [Shoals]." On May 8 reports from Westmoreland County, Virginia, dated six days earlier, reached Baltimore with news of the enemy's arrival in the river. "The ship came too [*sic*] off Ragged Point and very near the Virginia shore. The tenders ran farther up, and have been cruizing about from Blackstone's Island down every day since they came in. The ship dropped down after one day's stay, about St. George's Island, where she now lives. A large topsail schooner has also been up as far as Blackstone's Island, and is now with the ship."[18]

The news had reached Baltimore soon after Barney's departure, so Colonel Henry Carberry, commander of the 36th U.S. Infantry Regiment, immediately dispatched a detachment under the command of Major Alexander Stuart to Leonardtown. Intelligence sources suggested that it was the enemy's intention to establish a fortification on Blackistone Island "with the view of landing their sick." Exciting rumors flew about the city that Carberry's men had been sent not simply to watch the invaders, but to dislodge them. Barney's flotilla was somewhere near the mouth of the Potomac, and many anticipated a showdown.[19]

It was not to be. At least, not yet.

The British, it was soon learned in more detail, had left the river just before Barney's arrival, taking with them upwards of one hundred runaway slaves aboard *Dragon*. They had run as far up the river as Montebello, the estate of Major William C. Somerville, of the 12th Regiment, St. Mary's County Militia. They had also sent in a cutting-out expedition into Breton Bay but were reportedly repulsed by the local militia. Afterward, as earlier reported, the invaders had taken possession of both Blackistone (also known as St. Clement's) and St. George's islands to take on water. While reconnoitering in the area, several barges had engaged two American privateers off Peckatone plantation, in Westmoreland County, Virginia.[20] By the narrowest of margins, the Chesapeake Flotilla had missed sighting the British squadron, and undoubtedly did not learn of the consequences of its visit to the Potomac until returning to Baltimore.

With the flotilla's provisions nearly expended, Barney had little choice but to head back up the bay, fighting adverse winds all the way, in hopes of meeting *No. 137* in the Patuxent so that the cruise might be extended. Upon his arrival there, he found the river empty. Once again he gave the order to press north. On May 10, a little below Annapolis, the flotilla finally encountered the gunboat, laden with a cargo of saltwater-soaked and now useless bread. With his provisions expended and his men hungry, Barney had little choice but to return to Baltimore, where he arrived on the evening of May 11, "which was very lucky as we have had a terrible night."[21]

The second shakedown cruise had been a sobering if learning experience regarding the capabilities of the little cockleshell war boats. Barney had quickly discovered en route down, much to his chagrin, that the second-class barges still swam far too deep, were nearly swamped during the first gale, and were simply unsafe. While lying at anchor off Point Lookout, he reported, "I was very near losing them, as they took in great quantities of water." All of the vessels had often been awash in turbulence, which generated considerable discontent among their crews, who were now "very unwilling to remain in them in their present state." The exposure to the cold and wet had sickened many of the men, and out of the now six hundred in service, at least twenty to thirty would likely be laid up sick at any given time because of it. To remedy the problem, eight-inch washboards had to be constructed around each of the craft to increase their freeboard. Experience would eventually show that the washboards would have to be raised another eleven inches to keep the rolling waters of the Chesapeake out. Moreover, some could not safely mount 18-pounders, and upon his return to Baltimore Barney determined to have them replaced with smaller and lighter 12-pounders, which was speedily accomplished on four vessels.²²

The flotilla had other limitations that were not as easily corrected. Only a very small amount of supplies and munitions could be carried aboard each barge, and no provision had been made to carry medical personnel, the sick, or the wounded. Barney made a point of requesting a special vessel to accommodate the latter. When he examined the waterlogged stores aboard *No. 137*, he discovered that a great quantity of the bread supplies had been completely spoiled by leaks in the deck, which obliged him to unload the whole ship and have it recaulked. It was, indeed, the gunboats that caused him the most consternation. Both vessels were deemed "such miserable tools I do not know what to do with them, [as] they cannot carry any thing more than their own armament, as 3500 lbs bread bags filled her [*No. 137*], the salt moved on deck where the men were obliged to sleep, and they sail so bad, that I am afraid to trust them out of my sight ahead or astern."²³

The enemy were reported to be lying below Smith Point, Virginia, and off Watts Island, on the Eastern Shore, which was now said to be defended by a fort with seventeen guns. The island, some intelligence stated (incorrectly as it was later proved), was being used as a hospital for the sick and as a sanctuary for at least three hundred Negroes, men, women, and children. Cockburn was avowed to be "much onshore fishing and amusing himself." Moreover, the enemy had just taken a merchant schooner that had earlier accompanied the flotilla down to the Patuxent. The admiral, who had apparently learned of Barney's motion, possibly through the Russian ambassador to Washington, who had paid him a visit, seemed well aware of American military impotence in the area.²⁴

. . .

Rear Admiral George Cockburn, recently promoted to Admiral of the White, had returned to the Chesapeake, after wintering at Bermuda, with all the promise of another season of unopposed plundering and general mayhem at the expense of the citizens of the Maryland–Virginia Tidewater. His promotion had not gone unnoticed by his enemies. "The ruffian," suggested *Niles' Weekly Register*, "will be anxious to deserve this distinction by some act of great atrocity and meanness."[25] Yet, from aboard his 74-gun flagship, HBMS *Albion,* he rested secure in the knowledge that it would only be a matter of time before a very large reinforcement of ships and marines would be at his disposal. With these a concerted effort against a major city might be made before the war came to its inevitable conclusion. The erection of the new island base in mid-Chesapeake, not on Watts but on Tangier, had heralded a new day for Cockburn and the British war effort in the Tidewater, albeit not without some planning difficulties.

In November 1813 the Admiralty had ordered the uninspired Admiral Warren, commander-in-chief of the American Station, to step down. He had been criticized, among other things, for being too lenient with the American citizenry and for failure to regularly report on the disposition of his ships and to equitably allocate his resources. His replacement, Vice Admiral Sir Alexander Forrester Inglis Cochrane, was to be sent to Bermuda to succeed him. The aged Warren, however, refused to relinquish command to his successor, who arrived on March 6, 1814, until he was himself on the way to England. Thus, it was not until April 1 that the new commander officially took the reins of the Royal Navy in American waters, having enjoyed but three weeks with which to make preparations for the coming campaign. Not until April 28 did Cockburn officially receive orders to place himself under the new commander-in-chief. One of Cochrane's first orders was for Cockburn to find a suitable place in the Chesapeake to serve as a fixed base of operations.[26]

Cochrane was not merely a new commander, but a representative of the British government's newly honed war plans for the contest in North America. Moreover, he was burning to avenge the recent disasters the Royal Navy had suffered on the high seas at the hands of the infant U.S. Navy. The string of defeats in major ship-to-ship combats, the successful depredations of American privateers (even in British home waters), and the invasions of Canada all demanded retribution. After a year of largely defensive actions on the Canadian frontier, it was time to take the war to the Americans—not just the hit-and-run tactics practiced along coastal areas such as the Chesapeake, but major offensive operations with whole armies. "I have it much at heart," Cochrane had said, "to give them a complete drubbing before peace is made."[27] To do so, and in concert with his government's strategy, he would seek to divert American military attention from the Canadian theater, in which His Majesty's forces had been sorely pressed, and to wear down the U.S. government and public at large, physically and economically. By creating a significant and sizeable diversion in the Chesapeake Bay, seizing and fortifying one of its major islands, he would certainly draw the attention of the Madison government. But if he could facilitate the desertion of the main labor pool and source of economic stability of the Tidewater to his base and shipping, namely the slave population of the region, the results could be devastating for America. He had successfully recruited and employed blacks a few years earlier from the islands of Marie Galante and Guadeloupe in the West Indies, and as early as 1812 had suggested to the First Lord of the Admiralty that the slaves in Virginia were "British in their hearts." The freed slaves could be given the opportunity of enlisting in His Majesty's service—thereby enlarging the already stressed military forces available in the United States—or settling in one of the British colonies, such as Trinidad or Canada. The prospects of facing their own slaves under arms would likely make the Americans abandon their Canadian campaign and cry out for peace at any price for fear of a general revolt.[28]

To facilitate the scheme, Cochrane issued a proclamation on April 2, the day after assuming command, while in Bermuda, with a thousand copies sent to Cockburn via HBMS *Asia* for distribution throughout the Chesapeake. The announcement was directly aimed at the disaffected anti-war citizenry and the slave population of the United States. Incredibly, the document was published almost verbatim in many of the American newspapers, both pro- and anti-war publications, and gave notice that all persons wishing to emigrate from the country with their families would be received aboard any of His Majesty's ships or vessels of war or at any military posts upon or near the coast of America. It further declared that all would be welcomed to serve in either His Majesty's land or sea forces, but that those not so inclined would be sent as free settlers to British possessions in North America or the West Indies.[29] The inducement to fly to the British standard and freedom and to take up arms against their former masters was not wasted on many slaves in Maryland and Virginia who might be able to escape to British vessels in the bay or to their new island base in Tangier Sound.

Cockburn was already well aware of the intended change in policy regarding slaves since his own departure from Bermuda. Hitherto, when slaves had fled to British vessels, they had sometimes been returned to their masters upon request, as a matter of form. Now, even before the proclamation had arrived, he had instituted a new policy. When a party of twenty-three slaves from Mathews County, Virginia, had boarded the British squadron in early 1814, a flag of truce was sent out by the local militia commander to negotiate their return as had been usual protocol. This time, however, the protocol was altered. On March 24 Cockburn replied to the officer, Lieutenant Colonel Leaven Gayle: "I have the honor to inform you that circumstances have determined me no longer to subject H.B.M. ships in the Chesapeake to similar visitations [of flags of truce] on the subject of slaves supposed to have escaped to them." From then on the trickle of slaves to the British banner would quickly grow into a veritable flood.[30]

Cockburn had arrived off Tangier Island on April 4 and commenced sounding out the surrounding waters and laying buoys to mark the channel, "and found it to be safe and practicable." The following day, a New York schooner called *Hiram*, taken earlier as a prize, was anchored at Tangier Spit to serve as a floating navigational aid. To her masts were nailed large boards with a chart of Tangier Harbor drawn on them, along with the course and distance to the principal rivers and harbors in the bay. To this vessel all ships coming up the bay would send their boats for information. Unfortunately for the British, the simple scheme had not counted on the violent spring storms that occasionally swept the Tidewater, and within the month *Hiram* had been driven onto the beach between Nandua and Pungoteague creeks.[31]

Two days after Cockburn had begun taking soundings, he brought his flagship *Albion* to anchor "in a perfectly secure berth in 15 fathoms of water about a mile to the eastward of the south end of Tangier Island." It was soon apparent that the island would prove far superior to Watts as a base of operations. Though Watts Island, which was but four miles distant, had plenty of wood, the water supply there was bad. And unlike Watts, drinking water on Tangier was "readily found in every part we have dug for it." It was also the only island in mid-bay that provided a decent deepwater anchorage nearby for the larger warships and at which small craft and boats could land "with perfect facility at all times and in all weather." With a single ship placed in the main bay channel on the west side, between the island and Smith Point, Virginia, he informed his superior, "it becomes almost impracticable for any thing whatever to slip by us." With another ship situated at a similarly advantageous position just within the Virginia Capes, it would even be possible to stop up all enemy communications by water. Moreover, it was perfectly situated as a location from which any and all operations against both the Eastern and Western Shores, in either Maryland or Virginia, could be launched that both Cockburn and Cochrane might contemplate.[32]

There were, however, drawbacks. The island, he wrote, "is chiefly swampy low land intersected with numerous creeks and marshes, but these being all salt water and kept in constant motion by the tides it seems [to] prevent their producing pernicious effects." Less than a month later he began to consider the effects of the bane of most bay islands, namely the mosquitoes that swarmed in veritable clouds, but dismissed them as little more than a nuisance that would disappear as they cleared the brush and bracken while building their new base of operations.[33]

After deciding to establish his base on Tangier rather than Watts, Cockburn had immediately set Lieutenant Thomas Fenwick of the Royal Engineers to constructing a fort, a guardhouse, barracks, and other buildings on the southernmost end of the island. The project was facilitated by the capture in the Potomac of a schooner, laden with lumber and shingles. Other timber-laden prizes would soon add to the inventory of building materials. Watering parties were set to work digging wells at numerous locations along the beach. It was soon clear to the Americans that the invaders had come to stay for some time. Within days, the Eastern Shore was in a state of near panic. Soon afterward, the admiral moved to sow even more discontent by "bribing" a number of escaped slaves to return to the mainland and spread the news amidst their brethren that the British were establishing a major base on Tangier and were ready to offer protection and put arms in their hands. He was, no doubt, well aware that their white masters would also learn of the move and thereafter unintentionally sow further seeds of panic among the general population.[34]

Within a short time, the methodology of enticing slaves to escape from their masters was refined to a fine art. By mid-May it would become standard procedure to send freed blacks ashore with money to tempt their own to go over to the British. The actual escape plan itself was simple. After dark, barges were sent near an appointed shore. Those slaves who wished to go on board would make signals by raising a light. Sometimes a gun or lighted candle would serve as the sign. The barges would then pick them up and carry them to their ship or to the island, where they would be fed and housed, and then, if they enlisted, issued uniforms, weapons, and training as Royal Marines. Those who refused enlistment were employed in working parties.[35]

American reports reaching Barney claimed that no less than three hundred blacks were already on the island. Certainly, many Marylanders must have felt that fighting white Englishmen was one thing, but fighting one's escaped slaves was an entirely different matter. As a result, a very real fear of slave insurrection began to wrap its fingers around the throat of the Tidewater, though the actual number of Negroes who had fled to the British was far less than reported. In truth, by the end of April only a hundred men, women, and children had managed to reach sanctuary on Tangier Island and were proving as much an inconvenience as an asset to the enemy. All had to be fed and clothed from the already limited larders of HBMS *Albion*. Moreover, the women and children, who far outnumbered the men, were little more than a drain on provisions and patience, as they served no practical purpose to their liberators. Though the success of the emancipation had the Americans in a dither, the practicality of the action for the British was telling. By April 27 Cockburn reported that because of the extra burden his men had already been placed on reduced rations as provisions were running short. At one point he had been obliged to requisition a cargo of flour from a recent capture to help feed the new arrivals, an action that was not popular among the men who had taken the prize. Frequent foraging raids ashore for provisions had now become a necessity.[36]

Barney's principal concern, however, was not on the flight of the slave population to the enemy, but enemy barges reportedly abuilding on the island. A strike against Tangier, for the moment defended only by *Albion*, which would be obliged to keep to the main channels, and a tender or two, was an inviting prospect. If the fleet kept to the shoally waters where the big enemy warships couldn't swim, it might possibly be enough to bombard his island base on Tangier Sound or, under the right conditions, even take on the lone British man-of-war. Such an attack would have the effect of injuring or destroying the base before it matured, and at the very least discouraging or deflecting the flight of escaped slaves to the island. To put a crimp in the growth of the newly forming black Colonial Corps of Marines, or His Majesty's Ethiopian Regiment as it was occasionally called, might retard the enemy's ability to conduct raids ashore throughout the Tidewater. Afterward the commodore's force could link up with a small flotilla squadron already on the Norfolk Station and, when combined, pose a major obstacle to further British depredations in the bay.[37]

The earlier narrow miss with the British on the Potomac had perhaps been fortuitous, for the American squadron had obviously not been ready for a fight. Even now there were still barely enough men to adequately fit out half of the completed or nearly completed flotilla vessels. Yet again, as he had done so many times in his life, Commodore Joshua Barney resolved to throw himself in harm's way with the forces in hand whatever the consequences. Duty demanded it.

Numbering thirteen war barges, two gunboats, a row galley, a lookout boat, and the flagship *Scorpion*, accompanied by a covey of merchantmen intent on slipping through the blockade, the U.S. Chesapeake Flotilla again set sail from Baltimore on May 24. For lack of men to sail them, at least eleven barges and the schooner *Asp*, which had finally come up, were left behind. There were less than a month's provisions aboard the crowded fleet and stuffed aboard one of the older gunboats, and many of the vessels were still unseaworthy. But delay was no longer possible. The following morning the squadron departed the Patapsco and proceeded south for several days without encountering hostile forces. On or about May 31 it entered the familiar waters of the Patuxent River to secure shelter and an overnight anchorage under Drum Point. In so doing Barney was unaware that he had set the stage for the first round of the Patuxent Campaign, a struggle that would ultimately define the course of the war on the Chesapeake and, indeed, American history itself.

Chapter Five

SAILS AND OARS

On the evening of May 31 Captain Robert Barrie, commander of HBMS *Dragon*, directed the armed schooner *St. Lawrence*, 13, under Lieutenant David Boyd, and the schooner *Catch-up a Little*, a tender to *Dragon*, to rendezvous with him off the sandy maw of the Potomac River near Point Lookout. His avowed intention was to conduct a reconnaissance in force along the coast between the mouths of the Potomac and Patuxent rivers, concentrating in particular on the St. Jerome's Creek area.[1] The investigation was not to be undertaken lightly, for his orders from Admiral Cockburn, sent the previous day along with an auxiliary force of men and vessels as reinforcement, included troublesome news. An informer had alerted the admiral that he had sighted Commodore Barney's flotilla a few miles north of Point Lookout, Maryland, above the entrance to the Potomac River, and Barrie was being sent to investigate. In the event Barney was not encountered, the captain was to look into the St. Mary's and Yeocomico rivers and to "do any mischief on either side of the Potomac which you may find within your power." Indeed, the captain was to be given freedom to extend his operations as far north of Point Lookout or as far west of it as he wished, and was to consider himself "at full liberty to act as circumstance may point out to you as being most advisable for the service."[2]

The captain embarked aboard his gig at 8:00 p.m. off Smith Point, Virginia, and proceeded north across the mouth of the Potomac and up toward the creek in company with three barges commanded by Lieutenant George C. Urmston, which had been loaned to him from *Albion* by Admiral Cockburn, and four of his own barges under the command of Lieutenant George Pedlar. At about daybreak on June 1, after a hard pull across the wide mouth of the Potomac River and up the Chesapeake shore of St. Mary's County, Barrie arrived at the rendezvous point well in advance of the reconnaissance squadron.

By 5:00 a.m., however, enough of his force had assembled to permit the exploration of St. Jerome's to begin. *St. Lawrence*, formerly an American privateer named *Atlas* captured the previous year at Ocracoke, North Carolina, and which had recently been engaged in transporting runaway slaves to Tangier Island, came to anchor off the creek, and small boat parties were dispatched to begin their investigations.[3]

The wind was from the north, light and inclined to calm. Several hours passed as Barrie's men perused the shoreline at a leisurely pace. Then, at about nine o'clock in the morning the lookout suddenly sighted several strange sails standing down the Chesapeake apparently intent on reaching Hooper's Straits. Activity aboard the English vessels was instantly charged with electricity generated by the promise of fresh prizes.[4]

Unknown to the British, Commodore Joshua Barney, having got under way at 3:00 a.m., had come out of the Patuxent River five hours later ready to fight. The row galley *Vigilant* and the lookout boat, racing ahead, apparently sighted Barrie before the main flotilla did and signaled the commodore that a brig and a schooner were in the offing, but as they closed, they identified the vessels as two schooners, one full-rigged and showing nine ports to a side. The commodore smelled blood and immediately ordered "sails and oars," and brought his force about to close. Simultaneously, Barrie issued the same order, wishing to sound out the Americans and obviously not expecting the flotilla to be the well-armed naval force it was. He immediately discovered, almost too late, that, with the force in hand, to close would be biting off more than he could reasonably consume.[5]

Barrie's first sighting of the flotilla counted twenty-five sails. Of these he noted "sixteen appeared to be large lateen rigged vessels, rowing from 30 to 40 oars, the rest were sloops and schooners. One of the sloops carried a broad pendant, and shewed six ports of a side. One of the lateen vessels carried a French flag at the fore."[6] The British commander found his scattered force dangerously vulnerable, with his small boat parties away reconnoitering up St. Jerome's Creek; they were in serious danger of being cut off from the schooners. Signals were immediately hoisted and guns fired aboard the ships to alert *Dragon*, off Smith Point, and to summon back the recon parties. The winds now became variable as Barrie commenced picking up his men, but they favored the Americans, who were closing fast. At 1:00 p.m. Barney came up off St. Jerome's Creek, but Barrie had wisely fallen back toward the Potomac. The Americans now discovered the presence of *Dragon*, which had got under way, and the approach of seven barges responding to Barrie's alarm.

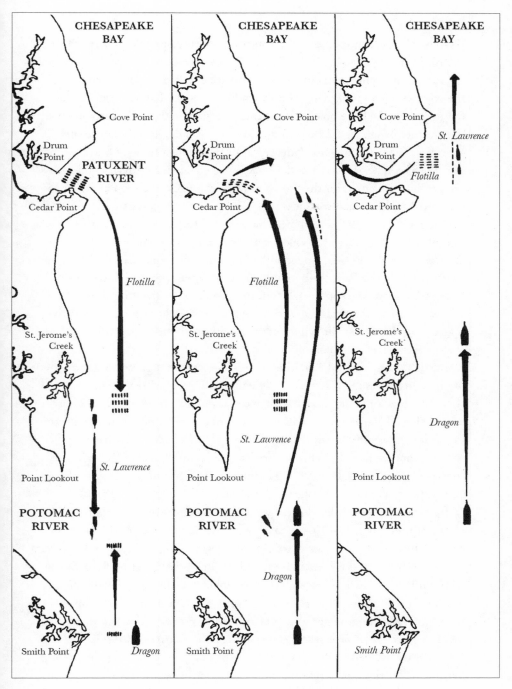

The Battle of Cedar Point, June 1, 1814. *Map by Donald G. Shomette.*

Desperately, the commodore raced southward for the open Potomac as the big British 74 struggled to cut him off from the river's closest access.[7]

At that moment the wind shifted dramatically and began to blow out of the southwest, bringing with it a threatening squall that made its presence felt in full on the little boats of the American flotilla. Barrie's ships now had the weather gauge, and *Dragon,* under a press of sail, was taking the speediest course she could toward Point Lookout in an effort to deny Barney entry into the Potomac. The commodore had little choice but to retire and reluctantly made the signal for the flotilla to withdraw back into the Patuxent. The rainsquall had brought with it a stiff wind and rough waters dangerous for vessels such as Barney's diminutive barges, and the enemy, with a third-rate line-of-battle ship, three schooners, and seven barges, was now in full pursuit. At 4:00 p.m. the flotilla, under full sail, doubled around Cedar Point, the southern lip of the Patuxent's mouth. Again the wind shifted, blowing fresh out of the west as if to oppose American entry into the river. Barney resorted to oars only and the flotilla rowed up under the weather shore. *Scorpion* had managed well against the wind and was worked in with little difficulty, but the enemy's forces were coming up fast.[8]

Barrie's trump card, the floating fortress *Dragon,* though under a full press of sail, had also found the shift in the wind, combined with adverse tides and shoally waters, difficult to cope with and was obliged to come to anchor eight miles below Cedar Point. Unwilling to hazard a general engagement with the forces at hand against a numerically superior squadron, the British commander tried another tactic. "I endeavoured to tempt him," Barrie later reported, "to separate his forces, by directing Lieutenant Pedlar with the *Dragon's* barge and cutter, to cut off a schooner under Cove Point."[9]

Barney's gunboats, the slowest vessels of the squadron, were among the rearmost units coming in, and one of these, *No. 137,* was of considerable concern to the commodore, as she was in the rear carrying the great bulk of the fleet's provisions and the enemy was only a little astern of her. Like Barrie, whose mission had been to merely reconnoiter the flotilla, the commodore too was unwilling to risk a general engagement in a squall. Yet, fearing that he might lose the gunboat and the squadron's precious provisions, he immediately brought *Scorpion* and *No. 138* to anchor. A party of flotillamen was hurriedly dispatched to the straggler to assist her crew in rowing and towing her in against the tide and wind. Simultaneously a signal was raised for the remainder of the squadron, which had already moved ahead, to return and reinforce *Scorpion.* Within minutes of the call for assistance, the flagship and

No. 138 had opened a brisk fire on *St. Lawrence* and the enemy barges. Immediately the schooner bore up and got her boats ahead to tow her off. The American barges now rowed down on the enemy schooner force and commenced a peppery fire from long range, albeit too far to cause the enemy damage, while the storeship was extracted from harm's way. "We then gave up the chase, got under way with the *Scorpion* & gunboats, and returned into port with all the flotilla."[10]

Although the original objective of his mission had been thwarted, Barney could take some consolation in the fact that his squadron had come away from the skirmish intact. Yet the engagement had produced a few surprises that neither the commodore nor anyone else in the flotilla had anticipated. During one phase of the combat the British had advanced a barge fitted to throw rockets which, though erratic and inaccurate, possessed superior range to any of the guns aboard the American vessels. They had fortunately thus far caused little or no damage to the squadron. Nevertheless, Barney was concerned and confided later to the secretary of the navy that he was fearful that "this will be their mode of warfare against the flotilla."[11]

The new enemy weapon in question was the invention of a British artillery officer by the name of Sir William Congreve. And it was actually quite a simple affair—a metal tube filled with powder and capped with a warhead of desired size. A long stick, employed for stabilizing the missile's flight, was attached. The weapons were portable and a single seaman or soldier could carry three 12-pounders. Firing was equally simple, for all that was necessary was a single tube and tripod arrangement. Some modification was required for utility at sea, but barges such as those employed by the British on the Chesapeake were apparently ideal. The commodore was eventually able to secure an expended missile and send it to Washington for study. The stick attached to his prize was fifteen feet in length.[12]

The deployment, for the first time, of a unit of ex-slaves trained on Tangier and placed under the command of Acting Ensign and Adjutant William Hammond, RM, who "evinced the greatest eagerness, to come to action with their former masters," had drawn the highest praise from Barrie and even notice by the admiral.[13] For the Americans, however, the new enemy auxiliaries would prove a source of unending concern, almost as worrisome as the enemy's new weapon of terror, the Congreve rocket.

For his own part, Barney regretted that he had no furnaces for heating his shot. He suggested that any troops that might be in the vicinity should be sent to the Patuxent immediately to cooperate with his flotilla should he

A Congreve rocket barge. *Reprint from William Congreve,* The Details of the Rocket System *(London: J. Whiting, 1814).*

be obliged to remain in the river. He was still unhappy with the unsuitability of the gunboats for the service required of them, as the dangerous rescue of *No. 137* had so vividly illustrated. "To save *No. 137* I was near being exposed in bad weather, to a general engagement with a heavy force . . . may I now be permitted," he requested of the Navy Department, "to ask you for a vessel to carry provisions, such as will not be the means of disaster or disgrace. If you will allow me one she can be had of Mr. William O'Neal in Washington. She is now here having been under my convoy, and her captain has gone on to Washington—she is a fine vessel, sails well & will carry about 450 barrels. The captain who is half owner will go in her, and says you may have her very cheap (hired) as he has nothing to employ her with." The commodore added that he was already employing the vessel at only $12 a day.[14]

Particulars of the engagement off Cedar Point varied slightly with the source. Barney claimed that he was opposed by three schooners, seven barges, and *Dragon*, which, providentially for him, had not entered the fray. Barrie noted that the forces under his command included *St. Lawrence*, seven barges, his own gig, and *Dragon*'s cutter. Other points of difference, however, were of significance. Barney claimed his flotilla escaped entirely unscathed, but

Barrie reported of the vessel he had sought to cut off: "Commodore Barney allowed the schooner to be burnt in the face of the flotilla, without attempting a rescue." In fact, Barney had saved *No. 137,* but never mentioned the loss of another vessel. It is possible that the schooner in question was one of the merchantmen convoyed under the flotilla's wing, the loss of which may have seemed inconsequential to the commodore. Barrie had, after all, noted a total of twenty-five sails in the American force when first sighted, seven more than the actual military force in the commodore's entire squadron. This suggests that a convoy of at least seven merchantmen had come out of the Patuxent with the flotilla, one of which may have been destined for destruction.[15]

Barney retired to an anchorage three miles up the river, and Barrie boarded *Dragon* and anchored south of the river mouth with *St. Lawrence* and the barge force which, the American commodore observed, "play about all day." The remaining enemy vessels were sent down the bay to obtain reinforcements "in which case some attempt may probably be made to attack us . . . In a day or two I expect the enemy will make their arrangements."[16]

Captain Barrie was indeed fixing upon a movement against the flotilla, but not in the manner Barney supposed and with a certain degree of trepidation. "It is my intention," he informed Admiral Cockburn, "to take advantage of the first opportunity to move the *Dragon* into the mouth of the Patuxent . . . I fear it will be impossible to follow the Flotilla up the river in the *Dragon,* and as the schooners and boats are by no means equal to it, may I request you . . . to reinforce me with the *Jaseur* & one of the frigates, than I think we may venture up the river, as our boats would be able to tow the frigate should it be necessary."[17]

In the meantime, Barrie decided to allow his men a bit of shore leave—of a sort. On the evening of June 3 a landing party was fitted out and a raid carried out against the plantation of Nicholas Sewall, at Cedar Point, and several blacks and a considerable quantity of livestock were carted off as plunder. A second landing was at Rousby Hall Creek (modern Mill Creek) on the Patuxent, where the invaders cut out and destroyed a vessel. In response to Barney's request and the immediate danger to the public welfare a force of three hundred men of the 36th Infantry Regiment under Major Alexander Stuart was immediately mobilized at Leonardtown, in St. Mary's County, and marched to the rescue. Following a course that was to become all too familiar in the days and weeks ahead, however, they arrived a day too late.[18]

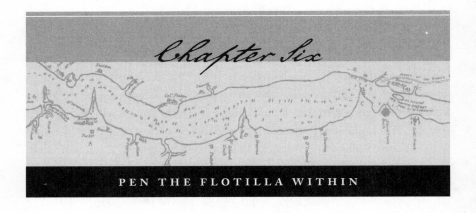

Several days of bad weather, thick and blowing, which had followed the action off Cedar Point had conspired to prevent Commodore Barney from adequately monitoring the enemy's motions. Nevertheless, he remained anchored under Drum Point defiantly awaiting the enemy's next move, the need to preserve his flotilla as a strong force being paramount in his mind.[1] Captain Barrie, however, was not about to afford his counterpart the luxury of such considerations, much less an opportunity to escape. He had, after all, by sheer luck, managed to corner within the confines of the Patuxent River the only potentially serious menace to Royal Navy operations on the upper Chesapeake Bay, and was not about to begin playing the game recklessly. Conservative tactics, based on the premise of never attacking without the benefit of overwhelming odds, or, when the odds were not favorable, attempting a move only against a foe of proven timidity, had generally stood the British in good stead thus far in the Tidewater. And there was now certainly no need to deviate from such battle-tested methods.

Though perhaps less than pleased that Barrie had been unable to bring *Dragon* up against the Americans at the skirmish off Cedar Point, Cockburn took some satisfaction that they had been forced into the Patuxent. It was, he informed the captain, "of all the rivers in the Chesapeake the best to have them in and I only hope you will be able to keep them there, till we are strong enough to follow them up it, with small craft." It was, in fact, at 110 miles in length, the longest river within the state of Maryland, and was navigable for approximately fifty miles into the very heart of the region. Along its banks were ensconced at least six ports and scores of major tobacco plantations and warehousing complexes. Thus, the admiral moved quickly to provide Barrie with whatever he needed to blockade the Patuxent by ordering up every available ship that could be spared in the Chesapeake. Some measure of the importance he placed on locking the flotilla within the river may be gauged from the fact that he gambled on bringing every vessel up from Lynnhaven Bay, except HBMS *Acasta*, Captain Alexander Kerr commanding, and the tender *Warrington*, which had been left to prevent the escape of the USS *Constellation* from the Elizabeth River.[2]

By June 6 Barrie's expected reinforcements were beginning to converge. *Dragon* had finally hove to, joining *St. Lawrence* and her tender off the mouth of the Patuxent. HBM sloop-of-war brig *Jaseur*, 18, Captain George Edward Watts commanding, had arrived only hours afterward from station off Smith Island (where her men had been cutting fascines for fortifications being built on Tangier Island). Late in the afternoon, HBMS *Loire*, Captain Thomas Brown commanding, joined the growing squadron, having come up from Lynnhaven Bay. American observers noted that *Loire* was a razee, a modified frigate whose spar-deck had been removed and a larger spar-plan provided, making her an exceptionally swift vessel for her size. Though rated to carry thirty-eight guns, she was reported by a deserter to be armed with fifty cannon. Barrie now had his odds, better than four-to-one in artillery alone, and more ships had been promised as they came in from Bermuda and elsewhere. Upon receiving a letter from Cockburn dated June 3, he must have felt his confidence justified. "You may depend on my sending every thing to you as it arrived," the admiral had written, "as the destruction of these fellows would be a point of great importance." By evening Barney, painfully aware of the growing strength of his foe and judging the enemy to be intent on an immediate assault, deemed it prudent to retire upriver.[3] He had, in fact, little choice, for on the wide, deep waters off Drum Point, where the enemy could easily maneuver and bring to bear overwhelming firepower, his own tiny force stood little chance of survival.

By daylight on June 7 Barrie's force, finally assembled, slowly but methodically prepared for its move against the American flotilla. The sky was overcast, and a morning rain began to pepper the waters of the bay as guard boats, sent out the night before to prevent untoward surprises such as floating torpedoes, fireships, or sudden American assault, were summoned in. By noon the weather had moderated, but the British took their time, carefully preparing for every eventuality and developing their plan of attack. By 7:00 p.m. *Loire*, in company with *Jaseur*, *St. Lawrence*, and *Dragon*'s tender and seven boats belonging to both *Albion* and *Dragon*, had weighed anchor and entered the Patuxent, proceeding as far as Somervell's (now Solomon's) Island. As a precautionary measure, one that would be employed throughout the Patuxent

Campaign, guard boats were again sent out and kept in continual motion, rowing about the warships throughout the night.[4]

At 4:00 a.m. on June 8 Barrie transferred his flag to the lighter-draft *Loire*, leaving *Dragon* to patrol the mouth of the river. The rain had finally stopped, although a cloudy, gunmetal-gray sky lingered. Barney's flotilla still lay in the main waterway, though now anchored farther upriver near Point Patience, a boney finger of sand projecting into the 130-foot-deep channel a mile north of Somervell's Island. An hour later, the British were on the move with their ships and fifteen barges, four of which had been loaned from Cockburn's own flagship. At 7:00 a.m. the Americans, much to Barrie's chagrin, were discovered to also be in motion, working up toward a small tributary called St. Leonard's Creek on the eastern side of the river. Within a short time Barney had entered the creek and pressed up it approximately two miles before bringing his boats to anchor in a line abreast across the channel and prepared for action. The British commander immediately ordered signals raised for *Jaseur* and *St. Lawrence* to take up pursuit. *Loire* and seven armed barges belonging to *Dragon* and *Albion* followed in short order.[5]

Large sailing ships without a pilot could not easily navigate the way up the Patuxent, and Barrie possessed no charts of the river to assist him in his task. In her crew's eagerness to overtake the American flotilla, *St. Lawrence* was accidentally run aground on a shoal. Without hesitation, Barrie ordered the barges sent ahead to take soundings and left the big war schooner to get off as best she could. The opportunity of isolating the entire American naval force in a backwater creek and destroying it at leisure was simply too inviting to pass up, and the British commander was not about to let an accident of this nature inflict further delay. Thus, at the mouth of St. Leonard's "every exertion was made to anchor the *Loire* and *Jaseur* . . . so as to pen the flotilla within."[6]

Though Barney's selection of St. Leonard's as a refuge may, in light of subsequent events, be questioned from a strategic point of view, its tactical utility as a defensive position for his shallow-draft vessels was superb. The direct approach to the creek's main channel was shielded by a long, tongue-like bar swooping southward from the northern lip of land and caused no end to British navigational difficulties. Barrie, on his first encounter with the bar, hastily concluded that the water was "too shoal to admit of even the *Jaseur* being carried into the creek," although, in actuality, there was a perfectly safe approach for light-draft watercraft close to the southern lip of the entrance. Tall bluffs overlooked the mouth of the creek on both its northern and southern shores, and the waterway was noted to be "in few places more than a musquet shot wide, and in many not above two cable lengths."[7] The banks on either side, almost as far as its headwaters, were generally high, in some places reaching an elevation of sixty feet or more. A heavy forested ridge lined both shores, providing excellent cover for riflemen wishing to clear the decks of passing warships or barges below, although cultivated plains suitable for massing troops lay behind the trees. Moreover, the protected waterway was usually mirror-calm, the perfect environment for Barney's shallow-draft warcraft under oars. It was indeed a defensive position that would make any sensible commander charged with conducting an attack against it shudder.

Yet to the British, the placid, mirror-calm waters of St. Leonard's Creek appeared at the outset to be nothing more than another obscure, provincial backwater in which, by chance, they had managed to block up a potent American naval force. The waterway had, in fact, a history of greater import than they could have known. The land had been settled along the adjacent river in many places for centuries, first by aboriginal natives and later by the white man. Barely more than 150 years before, peaceful Indian tribes such as the Patuxent, Mattapanient, and Acquintanackuak had raised corn, fished for oysters and bass, and later helped the pathetically ill-equipped white newcomers to build their modest hovels. When Captain John Smith first explored the Patuxent in 1608, he had found on or near the opposing entrance elevations of the creek two major Patuxent Indian towns, Opanient and Quomocac. These were lands to which the turmoil and religious quarrels of faraway Europe had been transferred and played out in violent miniature. They were lands that had been fruitful to the newcomers and profitable to their descendants. And they were lands that British forces had once before, during the American Revolution, sought to lay in ruin. Situated near the mouth of this quiet, fish-hook-shaped estuary, and perched upon a slight hillside overlooking a wide belly in its bend, was a modest plantation estate known as Johnson's Fresh, or to some as the Brewhouse, on which had been born Thomas Johnson, one of Maryland's great patriot leaders. Johnson was chiefly remembered as the man who made the speech nominating George Washington to the post of commander-in-chief of the Continental Army. Yet he himself had served not only as a member of the Continental Congress, but also as the state's first elected governor, a member of the Constitutional Convention, one of three commissioners who laid out the City of Washington, and ultimately as a justice of the U.S. Supreme Court.[8] Directly opposite Johnson's birthplace, on a steep bluff overlooking a secluded, well-protected anchorage in the southern curve of the fishhook's bend, lay the rambling estate of Spout Farm, owned by an arm of the prolific Parran family. Since the seventeenth century, sailing ships had come to the cove beneath the great manor house to take on fresh water from the natural springs, for which the manor was named, before departing on long Atlantic voyages. And here, too, slave ships had come to deposit their sad human cargoes in the early days of the Maryland slave trade.[9]

At the head of the waterway, situated on a sloping peninsula formed by two small streams, Mill Creek and Upper St. Leonard's Creek, lay the old port of St. Leonard's Town. Its antecedent had originally been established at the entrance of the waterway in 1683, but was reestablished at the headwaters in 1706, where it continued as an official Maryland port of entry, a title that had been repeatedly renewed with reassuring regularity by the old colonial government. Indeed, the little port had risen to some prominence as an important export center for Calvert County by the beginning of the eighteenth century, and in 1735 it was officially enlarged by act of Assembly to include additional lands east of Mill Creek. The town's harbor facilities were also apparently substantial, and in 1747 the site was selected to host one of twelve tobacco inspection stations on the Patuxent.[10]

It was now to play host to an American naval force upon whose success or failure the town's very survival depended.

. . .

Upon his arrival off the mouth of St. Leonard's at 8:00 a.m., Barrie sent in a screening force of barges while the great warships in the squadron were occupied in locating an adequate anchorage in the unfamiliar waters. Although he would be unable to move in force against the Americans before noon, he seemed confident that Barney would try to make a fight of it, but doubted the commodore's men, like most Americans he had encountered over the last nine months, would have the heart.[11]

Barney had taken the brief opportunity offered by Barrie's delay at the mouth of the creek to position his squadron, which had already been divided into three divisions, each with its own distinctive flag color, in a line formation across the creek. The commodore's own unit was red; Lieutenant Solomon Rutter commanded the white; and Lieutenant Solomon Frazier directed the blue.[12] Major William B. Barney, the commodore's son, was placed in acting command of the *Scorpion* cutter when the commodore, perhaps hoping to set an example, chose to fight from aboard an open-decked barge.[13]

When Barrie moved, he too chose to personally direct operations from aboard an armed barge, even while his ships were going about the business of securing their anchorage. His immediate intentions were first to establish Barney's position and strength, and then, if fortune smiled, to draw the Americans into a decisive fight. Once under way, the British barges wasted little time in moving up the creek, with the rocket barge in the lead, and about noon made contact with their foe. They opened the fray with a long-range rocket attack from a considerable distance, and then general cannon fire from their barges, but neither with any effect. Barrie may have been somewhat dismayed to find the Americans apparently eager for battle, and showed little disposition to engage them at close quarters when the flotilla barges sprinted down to dispute the field. Barney fired several shots to establish range and then moved with only his thirteen barges to "approach the enemy within the power of his guns." The tactic met with frustration as the British, using both sails and oars, adroitly slipped back every time he advanced. Momentarily, having taken some measure of their respective opponents, both sides disengaged and retired to their anchorages to determine the next maneuver.[14]

The British renewed the engagement with a somewhat larger force later in the afternoon. It was soon obvious that Barrie would be continually enlarging his barge fleet as time progressed, and was placing a strong reliance on his rockets to terrorize the Americans. Not surprisingly, Barney was quite uneasy at the prospect of opposing an enemy armed with such novel long-range weaponry. "This kind of fighting," he wrote with some discouragement, "is much against us as they can reach us when we cannot reach them, and when we pursue them their light boats fly before us."[15]

It was, in fact, more than a little disconcerting when enemy rockets, inaccurate as they were, began to fall amidst the American line, and downright disastrous when they scored an occasional hit. When one of the fiendish devices landed onboard barge *No. 4,* one of the former Baltimore City boats in Rutter's division, passing through the body of a hapless seaman named Thomas P. Gilbert, the vessel was immediately set ablaze. The flames spread rapidly, igniting a barrel of powder and another loaded with musket cartridges. The resultant explosion hurled seamen into the water in every direction. Three men were wounded, one of whom was burned "perfectly crisp" on his hands, face, and other exposed portions of his body. The two magazines onboard were set afire, and the barge's commander, accompanied by officers and crew, hastily abandoned ship.[16]

The commodore immediately ordered another officer to board the stricken vessel in an attempt to halt the blaze before the craft was entirely consumed.

At that moment Major Barney hailed his father and requested permission to take charge of the burning vessel. Although the duty was considered a "forlorn hope," the commodore rescinded the order to the other officer and granted permission to his son to board—as a volunteer. The young man, undoubtedly accompanied by a few others, immediately clambered over the burning boat's gunnels and, by sheer dint of active labor bailing and rocking the vessel from side to side, succeeded in dousing the fire. The old commodore was both astonished and pleased, for his son had taken on a project challenging death itself and had emerged triumphant. It was, indeed, reminiscent of the personal daring the commodore himself had exhibited on numerous occasions throughout his life.[17]

Barrie contented himself now, having determined what he believed to be the full measure of his opponent, with retiring to the mouth of the creek, most certainly taking with him a revised impression of the flotilla.

Barney's force of armed warcraft, not counting the merchantmen and hired craft locked up in the creek with him, totaled eighteen vessels. These were as follows:

- 3 75-foot barges each mounting a single long 24-pounder and one 42-pounder carronade
- 4 75-foot barges each mounting a single long 18-pounder and one 32-pounder carronade
- 2 50-foot barges each mounting a single long light 18-pounder and one 24-pounder carronade
- 4 50-foot barges each mounting a single long 12-pounder and one 24-pounder carronade
- 1 row galley, *Vigilant,* mounting a single 18-pounder gunnade
- 2 gunboats, *Nos. 137* and *138,* each mounting a single 24-pounder
- 1 sloop, *Scorpion,* mounting a single 24-pounder long gun, one 18-pounder gunnade, and two 12-pounder carronades
- 1 lookout boat mounting a single 18-pounder gunnade[18]

It was obvious that the British barge force, now enlarged to fifteen vessels and growing every hour, would find it difficult to contend with the well-armed flotilla despite the advantage of rockets. And, Barrie unhappily discerned, the creek was definitely too shallow and narrow to admit penetration by any of his principal ships of war, with the possible exception of the schooners. He was not hesitant in expressing his newfound fears to the admiral that it might not be in his power to do anything, unless perchance he might deploy a bomb-ship, in which case the destruction of the flotilla would be certain. But there were no bomb-ships in the Chesapeake (although one might be on the way from Europe). He was undoubtedly heartened by the news that *St. Lawrence* had been refloated and that *Loire* had taken an American lumber schooner prize while he had been fighting in the creek; yet he now flinched at the thought of having to contend with Barney's well-chosen position.[19] "Finding it impossible to attack the enemy in our boats with the most distant prospect of success," he wrote afterward, "I had nothing left but to endeavour by every means in my power to annoy him from our boats and provoke him to chace them within gun shot of the frigate. With this view every scheme I could think of was practised both night and day."[20]

Barrie methodically prepared his approach by working the warships closer in toward the mouth of the creek, tightening the noose more securely than ever. The vessels were anchored on spring lines to facilitate rapid shifts in firing positions from a stationary anchorage simply by loosing or tightening the cables. The lumber schooner was stripped of her cargo and armed with a 32-pounder carronade and added to the barge fleet, while several barges were sent out to take soundings in the lower creek. If Barrie couldn't get in, Barney certainly wasn't going to be let out—except to fight.[21]

. . .

It was nearing 4:00 p.m. on June 9 when Joshua Barney brought to a close his report to Secretary Jones concerning the events of the last few days. The last enemy attack, that morning, the third thus far, had been much like the ones the day before, and the commodore, attempting to take stock of the situation, was unable to find any particularly shining prospects. He had provisions enough for less than a few days, and as his time was taken up both day and night in commanding the flotilla, he had been unable to attend to the difficult, time-consuming duty of securing necessities. He requested that his purser, John Skinner, who had not sailed with the fleet, be sent down to attend to such matters. The commodore also noted that a strong force of regular infantry, perhaps Major Alexander Stuart's unit belonging to the 36th Infantry Regiment, should be dispatched from St. Mary's County to secure the flotilla's flanks on either shore of the creek. Such a force might cross in safety higher up the Patuxent and would be invaluable if positioned along the key points of the creek's shores. The local Calvert County guard, the 31st Maryland, under Colonel Michael Taney, were on the alert, but would they be enough and could they be counted upon? The commodore was dead certain about one thing: the enemy was absolutely determined to destroy the flotilla and was waiting only for a reinforcement to assist the forces at hand to finish the job.[22]

No sooner had Barney completed the letter than the British were again sighted moving up the waterway in force. On they came, now twenty barges strong, this time with *St. Lawrence* coming up behind. The commodore had repositioned his fleet even farther up St. Leonard's after the last skirmish, obliging the enemy to pass through a narrower front than before. Again the engagement opened with a rocket attack. The British were obviously delighted with their new weapon, and Barrie was again placing some hope on the chance that it would prove to be the prod needed to draw the Americans into a confrontation with his big ship, at the creek's entrance. The commodore had made the mistake of looking upon Barrie's game of baiting the Americans down-creek as a feeling-out process preliminary to an all-out attack, but refused to take the hook. Nevertheless, he aggressively assailed the invaders until he had driven them back to the safety of the frigates. The last skirmish of June 9 was concluded at about 6:30 p.m. much as those before had ended.[23]

It would not be the same the next time.

...

June 10 was born with clear skies, fine weather, and, for the Americans, favorable winds out of the north. For the British, the morning's advent was initiated with a concern wrought by a flurry of American activity on the western shores of the Patuxent opposite St. Leonard's Creek. In the vicinity of a rather grand plantation belonging to Colonel John Rousby Plater, one of the more venerable landmarks of St. Mary's County, American forces had been gathering for some time. Barrie saw it as a hotbed of military activity that, if left untended, promised to grow even hotter. At 8:00 a.m. the British commander grew more alarmed when he observed a concentration of soldiers and covered wagons down by the water's edge and, worse, a number of boats convoying troops across the river. Barrie was well aware that should Barney be permitted to reinforce his flanks, his position at the head of St. Leonard's Creek would become impervious to attack.[24]

Unknown to the British, the commodore had already begun to prepare two positions, a modest marine bivouac on his left flank and a battery on his right. The first, protected by seventy-five flotilla marines, was being established on a high bluff overlooking the eastern shore of the creek at a narrows barely half a mile below the town. The flotilla itself now lay anchored in a single line across the waterway and abreast of the camp.[25]

If Barrie was disturbed by the American attempt to cross the Patuxent from the Plater plantation, he did not allow it to hinder his judgment. A boat force was immediately dispatched to bring a stop to such imprudent motions. He then turned his full attention to the American flotilla. Having received yet another reinforcement of barges the previous evening, the captain again set out to chastise Barney or to lure him down the creek. Although the British commander did not know it, the old commodore was this time fully prepared and more than happy to oblige.[26]

Barney had quietly girded his squadron to greet the next enemy offensive operation with a surprise counterattack. If the enemy refused to close, then he would redouble his own efforts. He had streamlined his midget armada by removing the sails from the barges so that they could move faster under oars.[27] The British, he hoped, would not be expecting the additional speed and might be caught unaware. The active frontline force selected for the job consisted of thirteen barges manned by less than five hundred men. The two gunboats and *Scorpion* were to be left behind in the upper creek owing to the difficulty of management of these vessels in the shoally water and to the crankiness of the gunboats when speed was a necessity. The initial disposition of *Vigilant* is not recorded, although there is some indication that she may have been among several vessels employed in transporting troops across the creek at about this time, possibly some of those that made it safely across the Patuxent before the enemy had closed off the traffic.[28]

The flotilla maintained its divisional designations of red, white, and blue. Barney's division consisted of six vessels and occupied the center of the American line of battle, while the two units under Frazier and Rutter, occupying the left and right flanks respectively, were comprised of three or four vessels each.[29]

At 8:00 a.m., unaware that the Americans had prepared to respond to their next tickle with a sledgehammer, the British got ready to throw every available barge into the assault force and sent them "up the creek to annoy the enemy." At 2:00 p.m., a cursory reconnaissance having preceded it, the main force moved up. Barrie's flotilla consisted of twenty-one barges and boats, a rocket barge, and two schooners under tow, the whole manned and fought by six to seven hundred marines and seamen of the Royal Navy.[30] The attack was launched in grand style as His Majesty's flotilla, with a "band of music" playing, flags flying, and spirits high, ascended the creek. The two schooners, armed with 32-pounder carronades, were towed by the barges in orderly procession and came to anchor well out of American range to permit the usual

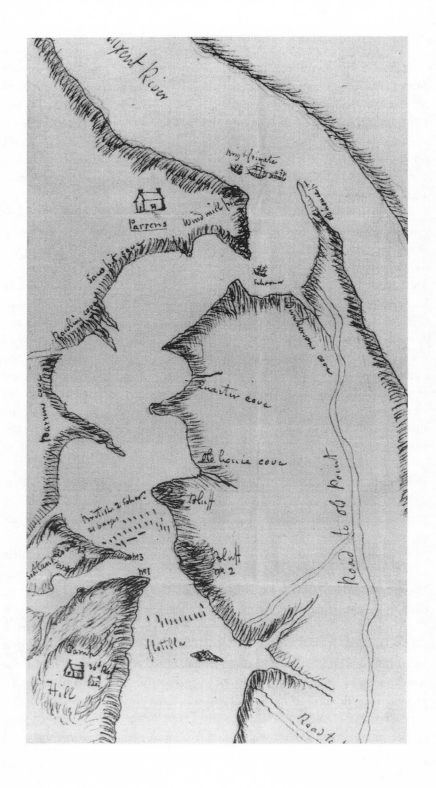

Pen-and-ink sketch map by Joshua Barney showing lower St. Leonard's Creek, June 10, 1814, just before battle and the disposition of American and Royal Navy forces. Note the position of the British squadron at the entrance of the waterway (*top*), the British schooner and barge force arrayed above the Chesapeake Flotilla, and the campsite of the 36th U.S. Infantry (*bottom left*). *National Archives and Records Administration, Washington, D.C.*

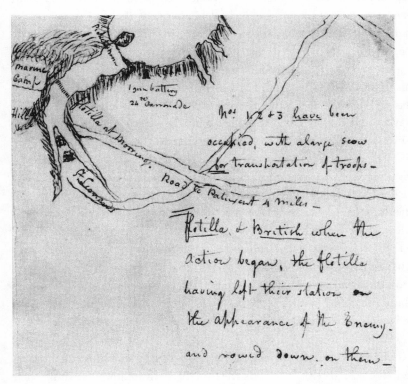

Pen-and-ink sketch map by Joshua Barney showing upper St. Leonard's Creek, June 10, 1814, depicting the location of a picket boat line at a narrows in the waterway, shore batteries, the campsite of Barney's marines, the flotilla's mooring position when not deployed, and St. Leonard's Town. *National Archives and Records Administration, Washington, D.C.*

opening rocket barrage. This time, however, Barney had given the signal to meet the enemy as soon as he had entered the creek, and now suddenly upped anchor, quitted his position, and rowed down on the unsuspecting foe.[31]

The British flotilla formed three lines strung out laterally across the creek just below a tributary flowing into it two miles south of the town. Barney's forces formed as well, but in a single line of battle just above the lip of the tributary and less than a thousand feet from the enemy. Within minutes, every boat in his force was engaged. Never one to conduct a fight from the rear, the commodore stood upon the deck of his barge at the very center of the conflict, amidst rocket and cannon fire, directing the course of action. His son lingered nearby in a small dispatch boat and was seen from time to time rowing about, exposing himself to fire, delivering his father's messages to the various vessels of the squadron. For a seemingly interminable period the two flotillas lay opposite each other trading shots. This time the British did not draw away, and Barney noted that the enemy "kept up a smart fire for some-time and seemed determined to something decisive."[32]

The engagement was fierce as the sky was shredded by rockets, cannonballs, and canister shot. Although Sailing Master Besse's barge was sunk and one of the flotilla's big guns burst, the commodore's gunners soon began to gall the enemy so badly that he was obliged to retire down the creek—or so later American reports concluded. To the 450 flotillamen directly engaged it appeared that the enemy, overestimated at eight hundred strong, "struck with sudden confusion, began to give way, and turning their prows, exerted all their force to regain the covering ships." In point of fact, however, Barney's line may have been mistaking bait for blood, and with all the eagerness nurtured by an assured victory, followed as if on cue the very scenario laid out by Barrie.[33]

Unfortunately for the British, the blockaders at the entrance to St. Leonard's Creek were not quite prepared. At 3:30 p.m. the warships caught sight of the moving engagement even as the Americans were hotly pursuing their retiring foe downstream.[34] A heavy fire was observed being maintained by both sides, and it was apparent that the battle would soon spill over the creek's entrance. *St. Lawrence* had been anchored so as to directly fire into the throat of the waterway, yet fall beneath the protective shield of the frigate guns farther out, and was expected to offer a strong measure of security to the fleeing barges. Nevertheless, *Loire*'s springs were hauled taut and her broadsides were brought to bear directly on the creek's entrance.[35]

It took little more than twenty minutes for a Royal Navy frigate crew to convert a dormant sailing vessel into a mechanical engine of destruction.

At the commander's order, the boatswain would bellow "all hands!" A roll tapped out by a drummer, usually no older than a schoolchild, galvanized all aboard into instant activity. Hundreds of feet slapped the decks as gun crews rushed to their stations. Marines clambered into the fighting tops, cracking open cartons of hand grenades to toss down on the decks of the enemy's vessels should he attempt to close or board. Deep within the heart of the ship, aproned gunner's mates passed along flannel-covered powder cartridges to young powder monkeys, who in turn slipped the cartridges into leather containers called "salt boxes." Countless sprints up and down ladders to waiting gun crews were required to fuel the voracious appetites of the enormous iron cannons poking their muzzles toward the enemy. Aft, in the cockpit, a midshipmen's mess table was converted into a surgeon's operating table and buckets were brought, into which severed limbs and other amputated sections could be dumped for disposal. On the gun decks, sand was spread to prevent seamen and gunners who were to be engaged in battle from slipping upon their own blood and gore. In the moments before battle, innumerable hands, all orchestrated by the twin experiences of harsh discipline and Royal Navy tradition, were engaged in a thousand and one activities, any one of which could mean life or death for the participants, and even victory or defeat.[36]

At 4:00 p.m. Barney's advancing line hove within range of the mighty broadsides of *Loire* and *Jaseur*, but the commodore was intent on more accessible prey. *St. Lawrence* now lay in his direct path, and a heavy American fire quickly began to concentrate on her. In danger of being overwhelmed, the schooner attempted to beat out of the creek, but everything seemed to go wrong for her at once. Her commander, undoubtedly stunned by the ferocity of the American attack that had obliged him to fall back, momentarily lost control of his vessel. Suddenly, *St. Lawrence* "grounded with a falling line and lay completely exposed to the fire of the flotilla without being able to bring more than one gun to act against."[37]

The orderly retirement of the British line instantly turned into a panic-stricken rout. One of the small schooners carrying several 32-pounders was raked by a shot from her aft as she fled. Onward Barrie's barges ran, passing the grounded *St. Lawrence*, totally unimpeded by thoughts of attempting to tow her off or defend her. Even as they fled, Barrie's gig was practically cut in two and the rocket barge shattered by a direct hit. Frantically the invaders sought the sanctuary offered by the iron umbrellas of *Loire* and *Jaseur*—which had yet to open.[38]

For a few devastating moments American attention focused entirely on the crippled and helplessly stranded schooner. Several shots seriously injured her main boom and her foremast, practically cutting it off halfway up. Her guns were dismounted, her decks torn apart, and her hull perforated under the larboard quarter at the water's edge. A number of seamen, trying to escape the practically point-blank fire of the Americans, were killed or wounded. The order to abandon ship was given.[39]

At that moment a deafening roar resounded up and down the Patuxent. His Majesty's men-of-war had opened their broadsides on Barney's flotilla, finally bringing the nearly abandoned schooner under the protection of a wall of British fire. The frigate's cannonading soon became general, and the pounding could not long be ignored. It was now the Americans' turn to run for cover. Retreating to the eastern shore and sheltered by the creek's tree-lined highland on its southern shore, the boats assumed a temporary mantle of invisibility. The British, on the other side of the highland, were suddenly at a loss for targets.[40]

Barrie coolly countered the American maneuver by ordering officers stationed in his fighting tops to direct *Loire*'s fire over the point of land from aloft, taking aim on the American mastheads. Barney immediately ordered the masts unstepped and taken down, but the galling fire continued. By this time Barrie had already dispatched a party of Royal Marines under the overall command of Captain Thomas Carter, from his own ship and *Jaseur*, to the mouth of the creek to seize command of the bluff overlooking the American position. The intolerably heavy fire from the warships, however, had already begun to have a telling effect on the commodore's staying power. The fight, having lasted nearly six hours and traversing the entire length of the creek, had undoubtedly wearied Barney's flotillamen. No less than seven hundred shots had been thrown at them by the two big warships alone, and now the danger of being enfiladed by Carter's shore party was simply too much. At 7:00 p.m. the commodore gave the order to retire up creek. A gaggle of British barges pursued, nipping ineffectually at his heels the entire way.[41]

British and American accounts of Barney's disengagement differ. According to the British, the commodore retired in "great disorder" and confusion. American accounts suggest an orderly retreat, as the flotilla barges were lighter and rowed faster with their masts down. Whatever the mode of the moment may have been, the Chesapeake Flotilla finally came to rest at its protected anchorage below St. Leonard's Town. Here it was to lie "secure & defended by strong parties of regulars & militia, stationed on each side of the creek behind trees."[42]

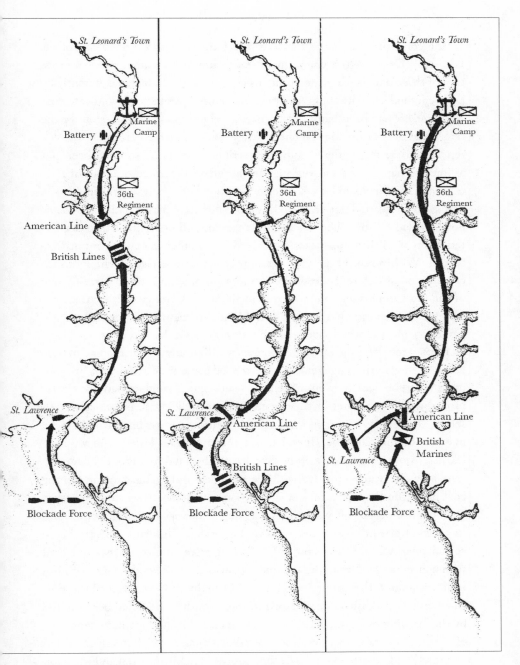

The First Battle of St. Leonard's Creek, a three-day series of engagements, was concluded on June 10, 1814, with the near destruction of HBMS schooner *St. Lawrence* by the Chesapeake Flotilla and the beginning of a two-week standoff. *Map by Donald G. Shomette.*

The consequences of the Battle of the Barges, or the First Battle of St. Leonard's Creek as the engagement later came to be called, the culmination of three days of almost continuous combat, were evaluated differently by both contenders. Although American accounts optimistically indicate that *St. Lawrence* had been badly cut to pieces and put out of commission for the remainder of the campaign, if not the war, the schooner, according to Barrie's report, had in fact suffered only four serious hits. True, she had been put ashore, perhaps to prevent sinking, and if left to the tender mercies of Barney's flotillamen would have been either captured or totally destroyed. Yet she was neither captured nor destroyed. A half hour after Barney's retreat, *Jaseur's* boats hauled off the schooner, and the morning following the battle carpenters from the brig-sloop were put aboard to commence making immediate repairs. Within several days the vessel was again in service on the Patuxent carrying on as before. Indeed, she would soon be employed in carrying one of the most important communiqués of the war. As for casualties, the British officially reported but half a dozen killed and less than a dozen seriously wounded, most of which had been aboard *Jaseur* and the schooner.[43]

Barney reported the outcome somewhat differently. "That the enemy suffered severely in this engagement," he recalled some time afterward, "was too manifest to be denied, even if their own subsequent conduct had not clearly proved the fact. Several of their boats were entirely cut to pieces, and both schooners were so damaged as to render them unserviceable during the remainder of the blockade. They had a number of men killed, and we have learned from an eye witness of the fact that the hospital rooms of the flag-ship were long afterwards crowded with the wounded in this engagement. On the part of the flotilla, not a man was lost—one of the fleet was sunk by a shot from the enemy, but she was taken up again on the very day of the action, and two days afterwards was as ready as ever for service." Unfortunately, the barge commander, Claude Besse, possibly suffering from combat stress, "appeared so much deranged" that the commodore was later obliged to remove him from command, though he would not be formally discharged until the Flotilla Service was disbanded on April 15, 1815. Another barge had been injured by the bursting of a gun, which was soon replaced by a 24-pounder from one of the gunboats not in service. The row galley *Vigilant*, which finally managed to enter the fight, was injured by a shot but was quickly repaired and was soon "more formidable than ever."[44]

Whatever the final score actually was, Barrie had developed a healthy respect for his foe, for as Barney noted, "the enemy made no further efforts to disturb the tranquility of the flotilla, but contented themselves with converting the siege into a blockade, by mooring in the mouth of the creek." By June 13, in fact, Barney's flanks had finally been strengthened with the arrival of Major Stuart and elements of the 36th Regiment, which had taken up positions along the little waterway to annoy the enemy if he ventured up. He had also erected a small battery near the mouth of Johns Creek, from which he now anchored his fleet in a line across St. Leonard's. Piles had been driven into the bottom and a log boom laid across the narrowest part of the waterway to stifle any surprise approach by the British. Even should the enemy's force increase, the commodore informed Jones, "we have little to fear from an attack by boats, no matter how numerous."[45]

Perhaps angered by the draw contest, Captain Barrie meant to do more than that. There seemed little recourse but to find another way to compel Barney to come out of the creek and fight. However, finding that the Americans in St. Leonard's had secured themselves at the head of the creek, with military protection on the shores, and "showed no disposition to again venture from its fastness," the British commander decided that "by destroying some of the tobacco stores, the inhabitants would be induced to urge Commodore Barney to put out and defend their property."[46] Having thus determined on this new stratagem, Captain Robert Barrie commenced a program, later taken up and modified by his fellow commanders, of systematic destruction of property on both shores of the Patuxent so intensive and thorough that its foul scars would not be eradicated—or forgotten—for more than a century.

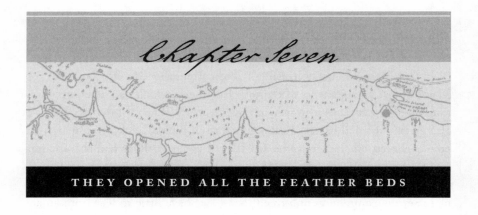

Chapter Seven

THEY OPENED ALL THE FEATHER BEDS

From the highlands around the entrance to St. Leonard's Creek, the view of the wide Patuxent on a cloudless summer day can be exhilarating. And with a good glass and a steady hand one can readily explore the intriguing sequence of nooks and crannies that indent the far shoreline. In the summer of 1814, on either side of the river, fields of Indian corn and meadows of the most luxuriant pasture abounded. A few neat wooden whitewashed houses, surrounded by orchards and gardens, provided an impressive counterpoint to the seemingly boundless forests that formed a backdrop to the scene. One overawed British observer noted that the countryside produced "the most delightful mixture of art and nature that can possibly be conceived."[1]

Although the land appeared newly cleared in many areas, the spring growth of heath and bushy tanglewood had not yet been removed, nor had the roots of recently felled trees. The local citizenry was simply too occupied with its own survival this year to undertake such work. Though lands close to the water's edge had long before given way to man's cultivation, the lines between the tamed earth and the forests were still quite distinct. Fields and farms, however, were neatly divided by "the most beautiful hedge-rows and boundaries" but produced a uniform appearance on both sides of the river for only a half-mile or so inland, where the forests reigned supreme.[2]

The sojourner arriving at the edge of these forests, it would appear, might find penetration by eye extremely difficult, and by foot or horseback simply out of the question—unless over the few crude dirt roads that linked the towns of the Patuxent drainage. "Here," remarked a British officer with great admiration, "nature is seen in her grandest attire; civilized man in his most pitiful state. The rivers and forests are sublime beyond description, whilst the tiny spots, brought under the dominion of culture and civilization, appear only like petty thefts, from the wild beasts and wilder human inhabitants of these savannas, which they care not to resent, because they are unworthy of their notice."[3]

Now they were lands on the verge of total desecration by fire and sword.

. . .

On the morning after the battle Captain Robert Barrie wasted little time in setting out upon his scheme to draw Commodore Barney into another round of open combat—on Royal Navy terms. Before the sun was high he had already ordered out a squadron of barges that promptly and systematically commenced laying waste to both sides of the creek entrance in the immediate vicinity, only to be foiled by an alarm.

At 1:30 p.m. British reconnaissance vessels, dispatched up St. Leonard's Creek to raid and keep an eye on Barney, were hastily called back to the main fleet anchorage. The Americans, restlessly shifting about in the upper reaches, were reportedly "making a show of coming down." It had rained again during the early morning hours and the frigates' sails had been loosed to dry, but upon the sounding of the alarm they were hastily furled and the decks cleared for action. Springs were once more hauled taut and broadsides brought to bear on the creek entrance.[4]

The alarm proved false.

At 4:00 p.m. Barrie again sent out armed boats on a raid, this time to the far north shore of the creek. Several storehouses were burned and a number of hogsheads of tobacco were carried off. The expedition returned three hours later, having encountered not the least resistance.[5] Among the private properties destroyed by the British was a plantation belonging to a certain Mr. James John Pattison and another belonging to Barney's own purser, John Stuart Skinner.[6] And Barrie was just getting warmed up.

. . .

It was a fine home that stood at Hallowing Point, in Calvert County, barely a dozen miles north of the entrance of St. Leonard's Creek, at an ancient landing opposite the old riverport town of Benedict, which had been established in 1683. In addition to the main house, a sizeable frame dwelling estimated by the owner to be worth $6,000, there was a separate kitchen valued at $1,000, the usual outbuildings valued at between $500 and $660, and $200 worth of grain in storage. The house had been erected on a substantial tract of land first granted to one John Ashcomb in 1653, and had once been the site of one of the earliest ferry operations on the river. A small island stood near the opposite shore, beyond which lay the port of Benedict. Legend had it that one could summon the ferry from the opposite side of the river (more likely from the island) by simply calling across, hence the name Hallowing Point. It was also said the house had been built by one Benjamin Mackall, who had acquired the land and settled there some years later. Benjamin was a planter of considerable importance who had served in the Maryland Assembly and as chief justice of Calvert County. His son was Colonel Benjamin Mackall, who had also served in the Assembly, as a justice of the county, and during the American Revolution as a member of the local Committee of Safety. Now it belonged to Captain John G. Mackall, a dashing cavalry officer in the county militia.[7]

Owing to the recent arrival of the enemy on the shores of Calvert County, Captain Mackall had not been home much. Yet, owing to its position at the narrows and opposite Benedict, his house had more than once been visited by militia units from both Charles and Calvert counties. Ever since Barney's flotilla had arrived on the river, a line of communications with the militia operations in St. Mary's and Charles counties had been maintained via the vital Benedict–Hallowing Point narrows. Messengers bearing the latest intelligence or news would embark aboard a ferryboat at the former, disembark at Mackall's, where they could procure fresh horses, and press on for the head of St. Leonard's Creek.

On June 11 a small party from the 45th Maryland Militia Regiment, consisting of Major John Walker, Captain George McWilliams, a handful of men from Captain William T. Lee's company, and Lieutenant William G. Neale of the U.S. Army, crossed over to Mackall's, where they obtained fresh mounts and rode on with messages for the commodore from St. Mary's and Charles. Upon completion of their mission they turned for home, but not before a chance encounter with Captain Mackall, from whom they solicited and received permission to refresh themselves at his home.[8]

During the return trip to Hallowing Point, Walker's party apparently became strung out, and upon reaching the Mackall house, found some of its members had yet to come up. It was thus decided to lodge there for the night and cross the Patuxent the next morning, when the whole party had finally been reassembled. Most of the militiamen were wearing their civilian garb, and only one among them, Lieutenant Neale, was wearing a full uniform or carrying a sword. Yet, it was enough to identify the group to the enemy as a military unit and the Hallowing Point estate as a bona fide target.[9]

When the troopers began crossing the river on the morning of June 12, they did so at some hazard, for while they were on the boat they sighted several of Barrie's barges making for the shoreline they had just left. After Walker's men had fired a few shots, the two antagonists separated. The Americans there had been entirely unaware of the mission of the enemy, who had, in fact, been dispatched under a flag of truce to the St. Mary's shore a few miles lower down to demand of the local inhabitants a quantity of cattle "with a threat that they would destroy the houses if they were not furnished." The envoy had been summarily refused. It was an act that would produce dire consequences. The presence of American soldiers at Hallowing Point, even temporarily, had also been duly noted by the enemy and was not to be forgotten![10]

. . .

Barrie was not going to accept the kind of refusal his men had received in St. Mary's without providing a suitable reply. Thus, he immediately formed another expedition comprised of 140 Royal Marines and 30 black Colonial Marine corpsmen in 17 barges to chastise the Americans for their rudeness. This time both Captains Barrie and Watts went along to personally superintend the entire operation. The party quietly proceeded toward a tobacco storage depot approximately 4 miles above the mouth of St. Leonard's Creek, in the neighborhood of Broome's Island, where an estimated 500 American militiamen had assembled. The landing was uncontested although a few shots were fired. The estate of Captain John Broome VII, of the 31st Maryland Militia, was destroyed. "The enemy," Barrie later reported, "did not think it prudent to face this force but allowed the tobacco store and their houses which were most excellent military posts to be burnt without opposition."[11]

Barrie had presumed correctly the alarm his forays would have throughout the region. Often hopelessly intermingled, rumors and reports reached Washington and painted the worst possible picture, often exaggerating the extent of the enemy's depredations entirely beyond reasonable proportions. One such account claimed that the British had ascended the river in their barges and had put the ports of Benedict and Lower Marlboro to the torch, and were even then hovering in sight of their next target, the Port of Nottingham.[12]

Barrie did not intend on letting up. Two days later, five boatloads of marines under the command of the able Captain Carter were again sent ashore, this time on the St. Mary's side of the river near Colonel Plater's plantation, to take the livestock denied them on June 12. Again, American militiamen, three hundred strong, were reported collecting near Colonel Plater's plantation, "but the enemy being aware of our intentions fled into the woods." Captain Carter returned later in the day, unimpeded, with livestock in hand.[13]

A British landing party in the Chesapeake Tidewater. *Library of Congress, Washington, D.C.*

Spurred by successes of this sort, British plundering expeditions on the Patuxent were to increase drastically. "Tobacco, slaves, farm stock of all kinds, and household furniture, became the objects of their daily enterprises, and possession of them in large quantities was the reward of their honorable achievements. What they could not conveniently carry away, they destroyed by burning. Unarmed, unoffending citizens were taken from their very beds—sometimes with bed and all—and carried on board their ships, from which many of them were not released until the close of the war."[14]

Barrie soon received a substantial reinforcement to assist him in his romps along the Patuxent. At 11:00 a.m. on June 13 an unidentified warship was observed at anchor near the mouth of the river. Upon investigation, the ship was discovered to be HBMS *Narcissus,* 32, Captain John Richard Lumly commanding. The new arrival had just come in from the Delaware without fuel and supplies, seeking provisions before returning to her former station, but Cockburn, seeing an opportunity to box in or destroy the only significant opposition he had encountered on the upper bay, ordered her to remain on the Chesapeake. Anxious to prevent the new arrival's meeting the same difficulties he himself had experienced in ascending the river, Captain Barrie courteously dispatched *Dragon*'s tender with a master and pilot to assist her. Even then, two full days were required to warp the frigate safely around Point

Patience and upriver to St. Leonard's Bar. *Jaseur* was then obliged to move farther out to provide the newcomer elbowroom and a clear shot at the creek entrance. Not until sunset on June 15 was *Narcissus* comfortably anchored.[15] For Barrie the reinforcement, bringing along 5 more boats and 260 more men, including 31 newly minted black marines from Tangier, was a welcome addition indeed.[16]

Even before Lumly's ship had come to anchor, Barrie sought to put the reinforcements (at least the marines) to work. Another raiding force, comprised of 160 Royal Marines from *Loire* and *Narcissus* and the newly arrived contingent of Colonial Marines, was fitted out. This force proceeded up the Patuxent in three divisions of boats, each consisting of five vessels. The first division was under the command of Captain Watts, the second, Lieutenant Alexander of *Dragon,* and the third, Lieutenant Urmston of *Albion.* For support, *Dragon*'s tender was also sent along, undoubtedly to facilitate the removal of plunder should the expedition meet with success.[17]

The British embarked aboard their boats at 1:00 p.m. on June 15, and after several hours of hard rowing, arrived at Benedict, a dozen miles above St. Leonard's Creek, but on a narrow strip of land on the western shore belonging to Charles County and directly opposite Hallowing Point. The quiet little town had been of considerable importance to the tobacco commerce of the middle Patuxent region, but like many sites along the river whose trade was rapidly being gobbled up by the City of Baltimore, had seen finer days. Yet much of the leafy wealth of Southern Maryland still managed to find its way to the town's warehouses for transshipment elsewhere. It was indeed an alluring subject for the untender attentions of the Royal Navy.[18]

"Here," Barrie later reported, "a party of regulars were stationed who fled on our approach, leaving several musquets, knapsacks and part of their camp equipage behind them. They also left a six pounder which was spiked." The local inhabitants had largely deserted the town, along with the militia, which Barrie had mistaken for regulars. The townsfolk had trundled off whatever they could, but Barrie was delighted to discover more than 360 hogsheads of tobacco, a veritable treasure trove of enormous value on the European markets, still intact in the town warehouse.[19]

Hallowing Point was not to be ignored either. Not long after Major Walker had passed through, a small detachment of sixty soldiers belonging to the 43rd Regiment of the St. Mary's and Charles County Militia, under the command of Captain John F. Gray, had been sent across to establish some protection for the site. The manor house itself had been left by Mackall in the care of a "schoolmaster" named Crane, a private tutor no doubt for the captain's children, who was permitted to live there. The teacher had protested the presence of the soldiers, stating that Mackall had requested he stay at the house and endeavor to protect it. Crane persisted and a compromise was reached: the soldiers established a camp within 150 yards of the Mackall home but not at the house itself. Not surprisingly, when the British barges again appeared on the opposite side of the river, he demanded the militiamen leave, least they attract the enemy's brutal attentions. Though Gray and a colleague named Denton tried to persuade the teacher they should stay, he remained adamant. The Americans, he claimed, were far too weak in numbers to repel an attack. Finally the persistent tutor prevailed and Gray ordered the company's retreat, but it was already too late. As the militiamen began to pull back, they were spotted by the enemy and fired upon, suffering one wounded. Within a short time, the invaders had landed at Hallowing Point, and the ancestral home of Benjamin Mackall had been put to the torch.[20]

...

The raiders were just beginning to hit their stride. Leaving behind a heavy boat party and *Dragon*'s tender under the supervision of a certain Lieutenant Fitzmaurice (or Fitzmorris), "an active zealous officer," to protect the prize tobacco taken at Benedict lest the Americans attempt a recapture, Barrie pushed farther north up the river toward the port of Lower Marlboro. Here, he had learned, were several large warehouses literally bulging with tobacco, and other valuable property as well, "and as Marlborough is near the Seat of Government I thought an attack on this town would be a sad annoyance to the enemy and oblige the regulars and militia to try their strength with us."[21]

Lower Marlboro was another of the numerous Patuxent River ports that had reached its peak of prosperity in days gone by and was now in decline. Like St. Leonard's Town, its antecedent, known as Coxtown, had been designated an official Maryland port of entry by the Act of 1683 and for a century or more had functioned as one of the principal ports of the Patuxent watershed, primarily serving Lyons Creek Hundred, one of the wealthiest and most productive tobacco regions in the state. The town was well situated for river commerce in earlier times but, with the rise in importance and influence of the city on the Patapsco, its life blood, like Benedict and many other river towns throughout the Tidewater, had begun to flow more slowly. Still, the enormous storehouses of tobacco made the site an inviting target for the plunder-hungry British.[22]

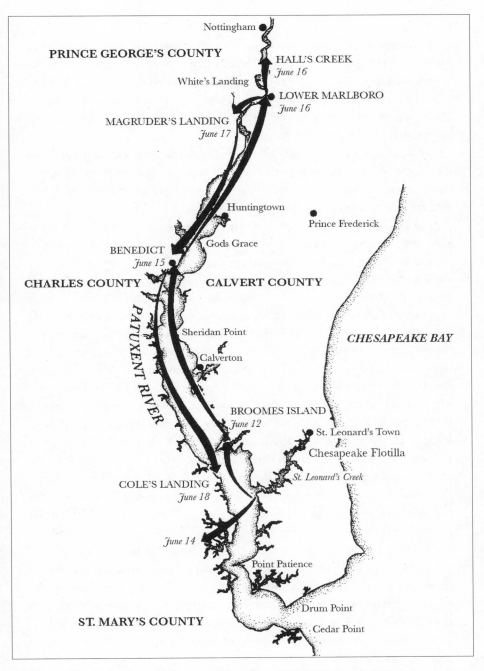

PRINCE GEORGE'S COUNTY

Nottingham

HALL'S CREEK
June 16

White's Landing

LOWER MARLBORO
June 16

MAGRUDER'S LANDING
June 17

Huntingtown

Prince Frederick

BENEDICT
June 15

Gods Grace

CHARLES COUNTY

CALVERT COUNTY

PATUXENT RIVER

CHESAPEAKE BAY

Sheridan Point

Calverton

BROOMES ISLAND
June 12

St. Leonard's Town

Chesapeake Flotilla

St. Leonard's Creek

COLE'S LANDING
June 18

June 14

Point Patience

ST. MARY'S COUNTY

Drum Point

Cedar Point

Captain Barrie's raids on the Patuxent River, June 1814. *Map by Donald G. Shomette.*

Positioned on a rising ground on the river's eastern shore and overlooking the water barely five miles north of Benedict, the site afforded an easy defense for those inclined to offer the enemy opposition. Although an elevated shoreline just south of the village at a pinched bend in the river provided a superior command of the narrow funnel through which enemy barges must navigate to strike, no defense was made.

About 6:00 p.m. on Thursday evening, June 16, Barrie, having been joined by *Jaseur*, was permitted to "take quiet possession" of Lower Marlboro, "a town admirably situated for defence," even as the militia and local population fled terror-stricken into the nearby woods.[23]

The British were not delicate in their activities in and about the town despite the uncontested landing, and caroused throughout the entire night in an orgy of wanton destruction. One unhappy resident documented some of their ruthless meanderings in detail. "They opened all the feather beds they could find, broke the doors and windows out and so tore the houses to pieces inside as to render them of very little value; 4 barges that night came as high as Hall's Creek, and more landed above [Lower] Marlborough. We moved our beds and principal furniture to Caicard's [*sic*, William Molleson Carcaud] and put the rest in the house." A small detachment consisting of a single British officer and five men probed three miles into the countryside "and stole with impunity from a widow lady, thirteen slaves, and done considerable damage by the destruction of furniture, &c. at other places." In the town itself, the British spent the night unmolested. While in the vicinity of the town pillaging was also conducted at Kent's and Ballards Landings, the latter entirely stripped of black slaves, and at Graham's Patuxent Manor, where all of Mr. Graham's hogs and sheep were taken off. It was later estimated that at least a thousand hogsheads of tobacco, valued at $50 each, had also been destroyed during the latter part of the raid.[24]

The following morning Barrie's marines commenced loading tobacco and cattle aboard a small schooner. The vessel had been captured along with the town and belonged to Captain John David, a veteran commander in the Maryland State Navy in the Revolution and now an innkeeper on the waterfront. They then proceeded to burn the tobacco-swollen warehouses. At 8:00 a.m. on June 17 more than 2,500 hogsheads of the leaf, the value of which was estimated at more than $125,000, went up in smoke.[25]

Having thus single-handedly obliterated a sizeable chunk of Southern Maryland's economic future in one modest exercise of bravado, Barrie ordered the expeditionary force to re-embark for Benedict, taking with them a civilian hostage named J. W. Reynolds, possibly for later exchange purposes. At this juncture, however, intelligence was received via several runaway slaves informing the captain that a body of American regulars, 360 strong, believed to belong to the 36th Regiment, and a party of militiamen, were assembling downriver to effect an ambush of his forces from the heights of Holland's Cliffs, overlooking the narrows.[26]

Captain Carter and a small party of Royal Marines were promptly dispatched to flush out the reported ambushers and "to take the enemy in flank should he shew himself." The marines, however, were able to traverse the cliffs and embark downstream without the least molestation. Whether or not there was a force of American regulars in the neighborhood is open to question. As Carter's boats pulled away from the shore below the cliffs, they were saluted with the only opposition thus far—a few ineffective parting shots from the tree-lined heights they had just descended.[27] It seemed the least their American hosts could do—the very least.

The return trip was uncontested. Barrie left no stone unturned and, adding insult to injury, stopped long enough at Magruder's Landing, a mile below Lower Marlboro but on the western shore, to burn Moil's and Magruder's warehouses containing three hundred hogsheads of tobacco. Upon his arrival at Benedict, he found that Lieutenant Fitzmaurice had held the port without difficulty. After leaving a few boats for the lieutenant to patrol the town and ferry landing with, Barrie pressed on. Other stops later were also in order such as Cole's Landing, in St. Mary's County, where further depredations were conducted in the usual manner.[28]

The incursions of the enemy, allegedly as far north as Hall's Creek, had alarmed most of the American military forces in the region as well as the civilian population. At the port of Nottingham, on the western shores of the river, it was reported, furniture of all kinds was removed from private homes, and it was said not a bed remained in the village. While the British were devastating Lower Marlboro, Colonel Decius Wadsworth of the U.S. Army, en route to join Barney with two pieces of artillery, arrived at Nottingham. "Finding the barges of the enemy" wrote one correspondent in the town to a merchant in New York, "about halfway between Lower Marlborough and Nottingham he scaled his pieces—the enemy, on hearing the canon, advanced no farther. This no doubt saved the warehouse and other property there . . . The militia are collecting in considerable numbers, at Nottingham, but I trust the enemy will not again return."[29] In nearby Upper Marlboro, Prince George's County officials were equally panicked. The county public records and official papers were removed for safe keeping by Colonel William Bradley Beanes in horse-drawn carts, at a charge of $7 per cart, eight miles to the countryside estate of Dennis Magruder called Mount Lubentia. Some, hidden in the rafters, would remain there for nearly two centuries.[30]

...

While Barrie amused himself by laying waste to the venerable towns and plantations of the lower and middle Patuxent, Commodore Barney, helpless to assist in upriver defense, attempted to glean all of the intelligence he could regarding British intentions. He was as much concerned with his foe's long-range strategy as with his own tactical limitations, and sought to gather every scrap of information possible.

From six deserters who had taken the opportunity offered by weakened ship's security aboard *Narcissus* to defect, the commodore learned that the British were still not prepared to undertake a major strike against any of the principal cities in the Maryland Tidewater until a reinforcement of regulars arrived from Bermuda.[31] This he had undoubtedly already surmised, since the enemy was able to field fewer than two hundred marines in his own immediate vicinity (not counting the black recruits), and was probably as hard put to do likewise elsewhere.

The commodore deployed his flotilla as often as possible, and occasionally traded shots with guard boats protecting the anchored frigates or attacked vessels venturing into the creek at night to spy, hunt for fresh water, or conduct nuisance raids with their rockets and guns. On the evening of June 13, for instance, five British barges rowed up the creek on a reconnaissance foray, fired eight 18-pounders and three rockets without causing the least damage, and were then chased out of the waterway helter-skelter.[32] On another occasion Barney had moved his own barges quietly downcreek to the shelter of a cove beneath the bluffs of Spout Farm. At about 10:00 a.m. an enemy barge, either on a reconnaissance mission or in search of fresh water, was observed entering the creek. The commodore waited until the vessel was well within gunshot before exposing his little armada. One can well imagine the surprise exhibited by the unwary foe. "She then discovered us," Barney later reported, "but our round shot was very near destroying her. I saw two oars cut off and was told two men fell over board, or jumped over. Several bodies of dead men," he added, "have floated ashore in the creek and river since the 10th inst."[33] The evening forays gave the commodore reason to believe that if the enemy were to conduct another full-fledged assault, it would likely have to be undertaken at night.[34]

The Americans' logistical problems were almost as frustrating as was their strategic neutralization by the enemy. There were neither horses nor oxen remaining within several miles of St. Leonard's Creek, nor were there persons able or willing to lend the flotilla support. Everyone, it seemed, was on the run from the enemy or cowering in their homes. And worse, many of the people had reportedly removed their effects to avoid ill-treatment and plundering, not only by the enemy, but as often as not, it was said, by the U.S. Infantry, notably the 36th Regiment.[35]

An air of semi-permanent occupation had been established at the head of the creek by the flotillamen. A small tent city had been thrown up at the foot of the peninsula upon which the town stood and around a local tobacco warehouse owned by a farmer named John Ireland. The rafters of the warehouse itself were being used to dry the sails from the squadron. Dr. Thomas Hamilton, the fleet surgeon, had established a hospital of sorts in a house owned by one Mary Frazier and in a small, unoccupied building nearby. From procurement records later provided by the good doctor, it would appear that the only medication available for the sick and wounded consisted of sugar, chocolate, and whiskey procured locally.[36]

With the iron fist of British control now extending upriver as far as Lower Marlboro, and direct passage across the river below that place entirely cut off, supplies were all but impossible to acquire, and those that were had to be carted in with great difficulty. Barney had been obliged to take whatever wagons were available, most of which belonged to the U.S. Marine Corps, and send for provisions from the south, which his purser, John Skinner, had sent from Baltimore. Normally, the Marine Corps would have secured its own supplies owing to the independent nature of Barney's command. But they too had been nearly severed from normal support. The commodore thus found it necessary to issue the few marines in his company rations from his own rapidly dwindling larders.[37] "We are much at a loss," he lamented, "for some person to purchase articles & procure supplies. The waggoners want money advanced them, and horses to ride express. I am not provided with money for that purpose, nor is Mr. Skinner here to make the supplies."[38]

The commodore had been obliged to make do with the little resources he had at hand. Even before the Battle of Cedar Point and the near capture of his cranky storeship, *No. 137*, he had been casting about for a replacement. One merchant vessel that seemed to fit the bill had fled into the fastness of St. Leonard's Creek with him. The vessel in question had been a Georgetown, D.C., schooner called *Islet*, owned by William O'Neale and commanded by a skipper and co-owner named Robert Taylor. Barney undoubtedly had been negotiating with the owners before the fleet left Baltimore with *Islet* in company, and after the fray off Cedar Point had sought approval from the secretary of the navy to hire her. Finally, on June 6, even as the American fleet was being hotly pursued into St. Leonard's, Jones was writing to inform the commodore of his concurrence, accompanied by an order to send the lethargic, slow-moving gunboats to Baltimore "when you have a convenient opportunity."[39]

"Since nine of yesterday," he wrote Barney the following day, "I have seen Mr. O'Neale and the captain of the schooner you wish to hire for a store-ship. The captain will hand you this letter, and you will hire the best vessel of him, by the month, for such time as you may require her service, and on the best terms you can agree for." The vessel was hired out to the navy at the rate of $12 a day, "free of all other charge and responsibility on the part of the United States," and was to be navigated by a sufficient number of hands and at the sole expense and charge of the owners. Negotiation of the actual contract was left to Barney. O'Neale and Taylor proposed to assume all risks and fully man the ship. Barney counter-offered. His conditions for hiring the vessel required the owners "to find a sufficient number of seamen to navigate the vessel, the captain of the vessel to be under the orders of the commander of the flotilla, to carry such quantity of naval stores as was agreed on, and her safety, in every respect, to be at the risk of the owners; for which services and risk the United States agreed to give to the [owners] the sum of ten dollars per day."[40]

The owners and the commodore finally agreed upon a deal, but "the confusion existing at that time prevented it [the agreement] being committed to writing" and the contract was concluded verbally after some additional bargaining. The owners were to receive the reduced sum proposed by Barney rather than their original asking price. Unfortunately, the actual contract for the services of *Islet* would not be finalized until July 7, for combat would repeatedly get in the way of palaver.[41]

...

Barney's land support left much to be desired. The Calvert County Militia, the 31st Maryland, under Lieutenant Colonel Michael Taney, of course, had been called up immediately after the flotilla had become boxed in St. Leonard's Creek, but seemed, to the commodore at least, to continually cover itself with dishonor. Several companies of the regiment had been raised, including one under the command of Captain John Broome (whose plantation on Island Creek had also succumbed to British raiders) and another from up-county under the command of Major Stephen Johns, but they seemed to be entirely unsuitable for the duty required of them. Barney hosted a strong repugnance for the militia, and particularly the Calvert County Militia, which, with the exception of a single company, had left the scene by June 13. They were, he noted, "to be seen everywhere but just where they were wanted—whenever the enemy appeared they disappeared: but their commander was never able to bring them into action." Barney recognized Major Johns as an active, zealous individual who labored hard to inspire his men, but noted that the unit had rendered little assistance to the flotilla, "nor did they even attempt to defend their own houses or plantations from pillage and conflagration."

The 36th U.S. Infantry Regiment, under the overall command of Colonel Henry Carberry, had arrived on June 14 in response to the commodore's plea for regulars. The regiment had occupied a superb position "commanding three points of the creek, the ground very high, and within 400 yards of the flotilla," with the men quartered in a barn. Barney saw its conduct, however, as little more worthy of praise than that of the militia, although several of the unit's officers, such as Major Alexander Stuart, seemed well disposed to meet the enemy on any terms. The soldiers of the 36th possessed neither discipline nor subordination, and received no check for their irregularities from their commanding officers, most of which were themselves without any military experience. Indeed, the undisciplined troops, who left camp at will, were almost as bad as the British, ranging themselves through the countryside, committing depredations upon the local inhabitants and their property. They "gave themselves up to disgraceful inaction, so that the presence of this regiment added nothing to the effective force of the commodore."[42]

From the outset, an intense and mutual disdain existed between Barney and Carberry. The commodore accused the colonel of publicly finding fault with the flotilla for coming into the creek in the first place, and, once, for withdrawing his own troops from their superb position overlooking the creek without informing him. Terse notes were exchanged between the two commanders as hostilities grew. "For eight days every officer and man with the exception of one or two have been on guard," Carberry informed the commodore when accused of inaction. Barney replied that he had personally been in the colonel's camp "every day, watching the movements of the enemy . . . but I had not the pleasure of seeing you during the day." Fatigue may have been partly responsible for the tension. The commodore, for one, had not so much as touched a bed during the entire time he had been in St. Leonard's.[43]

From the flotilla commander's point of view, the 36th Infantry, and Carberry in particular, had thus far been counterproductive to the efforts of the navy. The colonel's conduct, Barney believed, did not stem from patriotic motives, and "his conversation respecting the flotilla to every individual in these parts leads me to believe he would willingly see it sacrificed."[44] Although the security of the naval force depended upon the maintenance of troops on one or both sides of St. Leonard's Creek, Carberry cared little for the entire business, and even less for the commodore and his boats. He undoubtedly felt that there was more important work to be done elsewhere. On June 15, citing fatigue among his men, Carberry abandoned his position on the creek and retired a mile inland.[45]

For Barney, the one shining light had been the arrival of the detachment of about 110 U.S. Marines and three light 12-pounders under Captain Samuel Miller on the evening of Thursday, June 16. Miller's march had been difficult in the extreme. Having left Washington the previous Sunday morning, he and his men had marched northeast to the little river town of Queen Anne's "as there are no means of passing the artillery over the river lower down" at the usual ferry crossing at Nottingham, presumably because of British control of the waterway. Upon their arrival at St. Leonard's Town, they had promptly encamped therein, tired but eager to test their mettle against the enemy.[46]

. . .

On June 18, as the British ransacked the upriver towns, Carberry informed Barney that he was abandoning his position on the shores of the creek and was marching off to the northern reaches of the county where the enemy seemed to be. This would, of course, in the navy's view, leave the flotilla in serious jeopardy should the British discover Barney's predicament and choose to land their own marines to take full advantage of it. The commodore immediately dashed off a note to Secretary Jones, together with Carberry's letter, and held his breath. Fortunately, the enemy were simply too preoccupied in tending their prize tobacco and pillaging the Patuxent shoreline to pay much attention to their chief rival. Carberry, however, was as good as his word, and proceeded to march away the same evening he informed the commodore of his intentions. And to add insult to injury, he impressed one of the few wagons the navy had been able to hire to haul provisions.[47]

The commodore's problems were not entirely with the Royal Navy and the U.S. Army. He also had to contend with the cold and unwelcoming Federalist population of Southern Maryland as well, into whose midst he had been cast. To many supporters of the war, being a Federalist was now tantamount to being a traitor or, in its mildest term, pro-British. It was, in fact, bandied about in some circles that the Madison administration had intentionally directed the navy to lay the conflict in the laps of those less-than-lukewarm patriots of Southern Maryland, "to make the federalists feel the pressure of the war they abhor." The enemy's ability to move about and destroy at will on the Patuxent had, in fact, begun early on to draw vehement criticism in Federalist circles and even in the anti-war press as nearby as Georgetown. Such criticism was quickly transmitted to Europe and echoed with relish in the British press, most notably in the London *Times*. The fact that a large American army could be spared to invade Canada, but not to protect the seacoasts and river ports of the United States, or even the Chesapeake Bay, from depredations of the foe, caused considerable ire, and some critics of the war claimed it was "the intention of Government to invite the enemy to lay them in ashes."[48]

In truth, governmental intentions *had* focused on the campaign in Canada, and the Chesapeake was largely left to its own devices, or, more appropriately, to the protection of a feckless militia and a less than aggressive army regiment or two, whose commanders appeared both incompetent and little devoted to their duty. And Barney and the citizens of Southern Maryland were left to face the consequences. Directly, the more serious of these difficulties was the inability to conduct operations in security in the semi-hostile Federalist environment of St. Leonard's Creek. Secrecy was impossible, and spies and traitors abounded.

The commodore was infuriated, in particular, by the machinations of a certain John Parran, a local resident living at the entrance to the creek whom he claimed was "a Violent Fed." Paying an unsolicited visit to the American camp near St. Leonard's Town, Parran claimed that he and his brother had recently been taken prisoners aboard the enemy flagship and had secured their release only upon the stipulation that they urge the local inhabitants to stay in their homes. He informed Barney that the enemy had vowed not to molest the citizenry if they remained in their residences, but should they flee, their homes and all of their property would be utterly destroyed, as had been done to the homes of several uncooperative local citizens. And to reinforce his statement, he reminded the commodore that the property of the flotilla's own purser, John Skinner, had been destroyed specifically for those reasons the day after the big battle on June 10.[49]

Parran, however, appeared just a little too inquisitive for Barney's mind, and asked a few too many questions. But when he let slip that he was returning to the enemy's flagship, the commodore smelled a rat and placed him under immediate arrest. An express was dispatched to Washington to ask what should be done with the probable traitor. Jones consulted with Attorney General Richard Rush on the matter and, much to the commodore's dismay, sent a reply back ordering the prisoner's release. Barney's superiors reasoned that Parran's incarceration would pose a greater danger by antagonizing the local population than the spy himself posed to the flotilla's security! Barney adroitly circumvented the order. "I have released Mr. Par[r]an," he informed Washington, "but he chooses to remain as if under restraint for his own purposes."[50]

. . .

The commodore continued to monitor British naval activity on the river even though he was powerless to act against it. On June 20 he reported that "the brig has moved up above Benedict, that several small schooners (prizes) returned onboard the frigates, laden with goods, tobacco, stocks, etc., and immediately returned upriver again."[51] It was apparent that the enemy was systematically stripping the countryside of every removable article, or destroying it if it couldn't be carted off.

Among the vessels the commodore had observed heading up the Patuxent were *Jaseur*, *St. Lawrence*'s boats, and practically all of *Loire*'s boats and barges.[52] Soon the river traffic formed by Barrie's flotilla began to ebb and flow with distressing regularity, pumping tobacco, livestock, slaves, and goods downstream and leaving behind a wasted, burned-out countryside.

. . .

After having thoroughly ransacked the warehouses and town of Lower Marlboro and dispatched probes almost as far north as the port of Nottingham, Captain Barrie's force had retired downriver toward Benedict, pillaging every landing and plantation along the way. On June 17, while stopping briefly at Benedict, to permit his men to carry on the business of plundering the town, a planter of considerable means and influence on the banks of the Patuxent, one Clement Dorsey by name, arrived on the hills overlooking the town.[53]

Whether Dorsey was there on his own accord, or at the behest of Brigadier General Philip Stuart, commander of the Maryland 5th Brigade, is open to conjecture. His stated purpose now was merely to attend to the property of the Widow Forbes, a Benedict resident, while she was away on personal business in Philadelphia. Whatever his reasons may have been, his visits to the enemy lines may have provided the catalyst that ultimately saved the town from destruction.

Dorsey had left Bryantown, Maryland, on horseback at noon on June 17 unarmed except for a single pistol, taking the most direct route to Benedict. As he galloped along, he discovered the entire countryside in a frenzied state of alarm. Upon reaching the gentle slopes above the Patuxent, he found a few of his neighbors "collected there from curiosity," with but a single musket among them, intently watching the British in the town below. They could plainly see the enemy's vessels in the river, perhaps a dozen or more barges and other craft, including Captain David's schooner, decks crowded with plunder and practically awash from the weight of their burdens, coming down from Lower Marlboro and Magruder's Landing. Other vessels lay at the Benedict wharf. The enemy, Dorsey learned, had been burning and plundering wherever they touched shore. Even the barns of the helpless Widow Mackall, over in Calvert County, had been put to the torch. Dorsey undoubtedly conjectured that the enemy's intentions toward the town below would be much the same, especially since the site had served as a military post for the county militia.[54]

Immediately struck by the impending danger to the public property, "the immense amount of tobacco and the value of the private buildings" that faced destruction, as well as by the blatant absence of any military force to offer opposition, Dorsey resolved to personally attempt to dissuade the enemy from following his usual incendiary practices in the town. Despite later aspersions to the contrary, Dorsey claimed no financial interest in either Benedict or its warehouse and apparently acted out of humanity toward his fellow Marylanders. After unsuccessfully soliciting a number of persons to accompany him into the British-held village under a flag of truce, he finally encountered a willing compatriot, a certain Thomas Lancaster. The two men promptly mounted their horses and rode down the hill toward the town. He was met by Captain Barrie himself at the entrance to the village.

"Sir, my name is Dorsey," announced the farmer as he dismounted.

"What," Barrie demanded haughtily, "do you want?"

"I wish to see the commander of this detachment."

"I am he."

"I," the farmer stated proudly, "am a citizen of Maryland."

"What do you want?" the captain again demanded.

"I want, if practicable, to suggest you reason sufficient to induce you not to burn this property."

"Who told you we were to burn it?"

"Nobody, but if you intend to do so, I tell you that property," he said, pointing to the Widow Forbes's house, "belongs to a widow lady, now attending a dying child in Philadelphia. To save it I have hastened here."

It was apparently all the farmer could think of to call upon the captain's sense of decency. Perhaps if he spared one home he might spare them all.

"I doubt," sneered Barrie, "your ability and disposition to make a good speech . . ."

"It will not again be repeated to you," interrupted Dorsey as he started to remount, his humanitarian request obviously rebuffed.

Barrie restrained him. "If there is any design to burn, there could be no distinction. People leaving their habitation, and the military bring their field pieces, and then cowardly abandoning them . . ."

Dorsey angrily broke in. "If the government order military establishments and then abandon them, the citizens cannot help it. You must pursue your own course."

With that, Dorsey and Lancaster remounted and inquired whether or not it was necessary to retain their flag as they left.

"I have sentries everywhere," Barrie replied icily.

. . .

Frustrated, Clement Dorsey rejoined his neighbors congregating on the hills west of the town. Soon after coming up with his friends, he learned, to his astonishment and indignation, that others had apparently sought to exact their own form of revenge upon the enemy for his malevolent machinations. Several barrels of liquor, thoroughly laced with arsenic, had been left behind in the village for the enemy to consume. Dorsey was aghast at this most uncivilized action, especially since the discovery by the British of such a crude trick would undoubtedly engender retribution and guarantee the total destruction of the town and everything about it for miles.

"But a few minutes passed," he recalled later, "before I determined on my course. I considered the American character as deeply implicated in this horrible deed, so inconsistent with humanity and the established usages of nations, that its immediate disclosure was called for, lest its effects might produce the intended design, and thus give to our . . . situation a more desolating complexion."

Thus determined to disclose the deadly deception, Dorsey returned to the town accompanied by two volunteers, Dr. William Hatch Dent and James Brawner, under another flag of truce. Once again he was met by Captain Barrie, himself on horseback and attended by a marine private. Dorsey got right to the point of his return.

"I come to ask no favors. I come to discharge what I deem a duty," the farmer announced. "Since I left you I have heard, with astonishment, that some person has most wickedly poisoned four barrels of whiskey . . ."

"But one," interjected Dr. Dent sheepishly.

". . . and left them here. The fact, if true, may be ascertained by your physician."

"Be it so, sir," Barrie replied knowingly. "The whiskey is stoved. It was a most beastly act."

There it was. The British commander already knew, and the destruction of Benedict, as retribution, was probably already contemplated.

Unexpectedly, the officer continued. "I thank you, sir, for making your communication. No more than every honorable man ought to make."

"I have but few friends collected," said Dorsey. "I have done this upon my own responsibility." He paused for a moment. It was just possible that his modest act in the name of common humanity might yet sway the enemy commander from issuing the fatal order if the blame for the poisoning could be placed other than at the feet of the local population, or if the local citizenry, as personified by himself, might disassociate itself from the actions of the government. Fortunately, Barrie was unaware that Dorsey had, as early as January 1812, been appointed to collect all firearms in Charles County that might be usable in case of war, and had been an ardent supporter of the government's war policy since the start.

"I shall," he continued, "communicate it to my government, if that approves of it, it will be to me a consolation; if not I have the approbation of my own breast."

Barrie had warmed readily to his informant and now assumed a considerably friendlier posture than he had earlier. If the farmer had been willing to save British marines from an act of treachery, he might be keen to report valuable military information, as had many of his fellow Marylanders.

"I have heard," the captain began, "that there was military and artillery here . . ."

"The only fact I can communicate with honor, sir," the farmer interjected, "is that the fact was not perpetrated by a citizen."

Although Dorsey did not know it at the time, the poisoning had, in fact, been carried out by a local resident who feared that if the liquor fell into the hands of Barrie's Colonial Marines, former slaves, they "might commit greater excesses from the too free use of it."[55] Thus, without giving away military information, Dorsey had, perhaps, partially convinced the British commander that vengeance against the town of Benedict was not justified. Again, the interview was concluded, and the three Americans galloped off, not knowing whether their efforts had been useful or in vain.

Dorsey was to provide yet one more service to the citizenry of Benedict.

Some distance from the town the trio stopped by the roadside to reclaim Dorsey's pistol, which had been hidden in the bush before they had ridden into the town lest it be confiscated by the enemy. While halted, Dent and Brawner simultaneously spotted a party of four British seamen marching toward the residence of a certain Mr. Sothron. The seamen were loudly making it known that they had the fullest intention of destroying the house. Dorsey raced after a party of fleeing, terrorized citizens, "calling upon them to return, and asking them if it was possible for them to permit a neighbor's house to be destroyed by four men."[56]

The inhabitants continued on in their mad flight, paying no heed to Dorsey. With his own party possessing but a single firearm, and that with but a single shot and nothing to reload it with, Dorsey immediately devised a ruse to save the house.

"We heard them breaking open the doors," the farmer later reported. "We were entirely ignorant, whether they had any force concealed. I begged them [Dent and Brawner] to fire the gun, and called out loudly as I could, for the cavalry and artillery to advance and gave orders evidencing the presence of a great force. They ran with great precipitation, and when I saw them they were near the town. They [the British] appeared to be sailors; but the distance was too great for me to speak with certainty on the subject. Shortly afterwards their marines in full uniform were discovered in the marsh, at the place where these men must have crossed; and as they have not advanced higher up, I suppose them to have stationed them to prevent any straggling parties from advancing into the country."

Dorsey retired to a position three miles beyond the town and waited, half expecting to see the glow of a burning village silhouetted against the evening sky. By 7:00 p.m., however, he was buoyed by the absence of any conflagration as he prepared a long dispatch to General Stuart. Perhaps his efforts had not been in vain after all. But his warning of events to come seemed ominous in the extreme.

"I cannot but believe but this system of plunder is permitted in order to attach the men to their officers preparatory to a combined attack by land and water upon Barney's flotilla."[57]

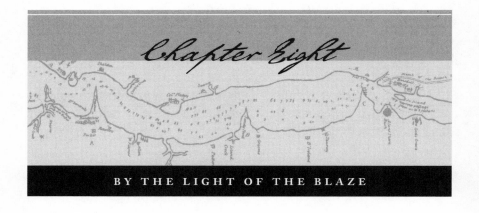

Washington was again alarmed at the proximity of the enemy to the capital city. At 3:00 a.m. on June 18 an express, the first of several to arrive from the Patuxent during the day, reached the city from Nottingham informing Secretary of War John Armstrong of the enemy's latest ascent up the river in considerable force and requesting immediate assistance. A number of false reports arrived as well claiming that the towns of Benedict, Lower Marlboro, and Nottingham had been burned. Still others noted that there were no arms to be had within a five-mile circumference of Benedict, where it was thought the enemy still lay with between twelve and fifteen barges.[1] Rumors and facts entwined so rapidly that only verification by troops on the scene could separate the two.

The secretary of war issued instructions to Major General John P. Van Ness, commander of the District of Columbia Militia, and within an hour necessary orders were distributed to all available unit commanders. With amazing alacrity, a force of 280 men, consisting of Major George Peter's Georgetown Artillery with six field pieces, Captain John J. Stull's Georgetown Riflemen, Captain John C. William's Georgetown Hussars, Captain William Thornton's Columbian Dragoons, and Captain Elias B. Caldwell's Washington Light Horse, were ready to march by 10:00 a.m., the whole under the command of Major Peter. This force, together with the local militia units hovering somewhere about the Benedict region, when supplied with four or five hundred stand of arms, was deemed "adequate to stop the progress of the incendiaries & drive them back." Just to be certain, however, detachments from the 36th and 38th U.S. Infantry stationed on the South River were ordered to also proceed to Nottingham.[2]

. . .

Even as Major Peter's forces were mustering in Washington, Captain Robert Barrie, in *Dragon*'s tender, attended by a covey of barges and the two prize schooners, all heavily laden with tobacco, retired downriver to the St. Leonard's Bar anchorage.[3] Barrie, however, had no intention of abandoning Benedict quite yet. After stripping the two schooners of their cargoes, he dispatched the prizes back upriver to fetch more plunder from the town. Yet his continued and most profitable management of affairs on the river were about to come to an end. Upon his return to the mouth of St. Leonard's, he was handed orders from Cockburn directing him to bring *Dragon* and "such other force as may not be absolutely required" for the blockade of the flotilla "and rejoin the admiral at Tangier Island." Command of the blockade was to be turned over to Captain Brown.[4]

Barrie remained for the night onboard *Loire*, anchored off St. Leonard's Bar, where he read the new orders penned on the 17th. The admiral, after having stripped most of his forces from the mouth of the bay (which had kept the American frigate *Constellation* tightly locked up in the Elizabeth River) to strengthen the blockade of Barney on the Patuxent, was beginning to feel the pressure increase on his small squadron. Logistical, personnel, and health problems abounded. "The fatigues we have undergone here & the sudden changes of the weather from excessive heat to coolness has tried our constitutions a little." The wells on Tangier Island had turned brackish and bad, and many men were down with the flux. The admiral himself had been unwell for some time, and his trusted skipper of *Albion*, Captain B. H. Ross, had become so ill that Cockburn was obliged to send him off to Bermuda to recuperate.[5] With only *Albion* to protect the island base until the arrival of reinforcements, it was absolutely necessary to do some shifting about. Yet he was not unaware of the stress that some of his forces, most notably *Dragon*, had been under since the very beginning of the war. Barrie and his crew had been on constant duty in the Chesapeake without letup for more than nine months, and the admiral had resolved to send both the ship and her men to Bermuda for much needed relief and refit.[6]

Yet work on the Tangier Island base had progressed despite the handicaps, as well as labor and supply shortages. Construction on the fort and support facilities, all of which had reportedly been planned in England, had moved forward. Three sides of the fascine, timber, and earthen fort, each 250 yards long, had been completed. Eight 24-pounder and 6-pounder field pieces (the latter captured in a raid on Pungoteague on May 29) had been mounted. An additional number of 18- and 24-pounders had been brought in and recently

Rear Admiral George Cockburn. *Mezzotint by C. Turner, 1819. Library of Congress, Washington, D.C.*

landed from HBMS *Endymion,* and more were expected with the next reinforcement. A hospital capable of housing a hundred sick had just been constructed, as well as a church and twenty dwellings, "all laid out in streets." In the salt meadows, at least eighteen bullocks grazed. And finally, a number of large gardens had been planted with "vegetables of all sorts growing in great perfection."[7]

It was not the slow progress of work on Tangier that bothered the admiral most but the American flotilla. That the arrival of the American flotilla squadron had caused him to reorganize is not extraordinary. That he was now obliged to temporarily waylay for service any of His Majesty's warships that touched in the bay, and even countermand orders from Admiral Cochrane himself, is also not surprising. When HBMS *Armide,* Captain Thomas E. Trowbridge commanding, appeared briefly under orders from the commander-in-chief for duty elsewhere, Cockburn immediately countered them on the grounds that "a very formidable flotilla . . . fitted out by the monied men of Baltimore, has made its appearance in the bay since my last communication to the commander in chief." Thus *Armide*'s orders, much to Captain Trowbridge's displeasure, had to be temporarily postponed because "of this late great addition to the enemy's force in this neighbourhood."[8]

With but five major warships and a handful of schooners and brigs to maintain control of the nearly 200-mile reach of Chesapeake Bay, Rear Admiral George Cockburn was stretched to the limit. The arrival of the hard-fighting Chesapeake Flotilla on the scene had, for the first time, truly challenged the free rein on the bay he had enjoyed the previous year. He now openly complained to Cochrane "how sharply and unexpectedly Jonathan has exerted himself in putting forth his marine armaments in this bay" and just how much he had "been puzzled to cut & contrive to meet them at all points and cause all his efforts to recoil on himself." Had he more ships, he suggested, the situation would not be so dire. He had already given up the idea of outright destroying the flotilla in its lair or drawing it out into the open, at least for the time being. Indeed, "the great force and active power of the Baltimore Flotilla" was such "as to render it decidedly an over match for any of our smaller ships," and thus required a blockade by the frigates *Loire* and *Narcissus* and the schooner *St. Lawrence*. Nevertheless, he was well aware of the divisiveness his raiding had caused. He estimated that British depredations had early on destroyed vast stores of property worth $700,000 to $800,000 on the river, as well as guard stations and military posts. All of the towns on the river's shores had been virtually abandoned, and over the last month alone the raids had cost the Americans more than $1 million. *Dragon* was "loaded literally with prize goods" and there was more stored on Tangier Island than the admiral knew what to do with. He begged Cochrane to send some transports to haul it away. Fortunately for the British, the "great armament" of the Americans, the Chesapeake Flotilla, was locked up tight "where it can do no harm but to its friends." Baltimore and the rest of the upper bay region were now fully exposed to incursions. When Cochrane finally arrived with a strong fleet and more men, he assured his superior, Baltimore would most certainly be destroyed.[9]

If there was one bright spot for Cockburn in the whole situation—aside from the incredibly rich plunder that he had acquired—it was the performance of the slaves-turned-soldiers. He had been authorized not only to train and deploy them, but to outfit them in the red jackets of Royal Marines, "as their gay appearance may act as an inducement to others to come off." Barrie had reported that the black troopers had been acquitting themselves on the Patuxent with the "utmost order, forbearance and regularity," and uniformly volunteered for any operation wherein they might meet their former masters. The admiral himself had been delighted by "how uncommonly and unexpectedly well the Blacks have behaved in the several engagements in which they have now joined with us." They had not even flinched when some of their own fell in recent skirmishes on the Eastern Shore. Though he had once dismissed their usefulness, he now hoped to form them into a regular Corps of Colonial Marines because they were reliable in battle and dare not desert as long as they were in the Chesapeake. Indeed, "as they are stronger men and more trust worthy," he much preferred them to Royal Marines, many of whom had deserted to the enemy. Moreover, when properly trained, "they make excellent skirmishers for the woods in the neighbourhood."[10]

...

On June 20 Barrie sailed for Tangier in *Jaseur* accompanied by "all the boats of the different ships of the squadron," each laden with as much spoils and runaway slaves as could be carried. Overwhelmed by the extent and value of the prize tobacco and black manpower he had taken in only a few days' time, the captain had been happily obliged to make room aboard the crowded Patuxent armada by transporting the prize goods down the bay to the main British base on Tangier. *Dragon* would follow. He had left behind him in St. Leonard's Creek, he informed Cockburn, a flotilla of no less than twenty-four enemy vessels (undoubtedly including in his count merchantmen locked in with it), averaging about sixty men each, with a regiment of soldiers attached to it. As far as he could determine there were "four large sloops of light d[ra]ft of water with 4 or 5 guns of a side, the others carry a long 24 pr. each and are tolerably well handled & managed." It was thus deemed necessary to leave at least two frigates and a brig or schooner behind to hold the keys to St. Leonard's.[11]

Barrie's departure left Captain Thomas Brown, the skipper of *Loire*, in overall command of the Patuxent squadron, and he too was more than a little interested in continuing the campaign of depredations and in accumulating the rich plunder of the river valley. Thus on June 21, *St. Lawrence* and several small boats, with marines from *Loire* and *Narcissus,* were ordered upriver to further deplete the warehouse stocks lying at Benedict. The pillage of the Patuxent was, for the British, beginning to take on the aspects of a long Sunday outing, with vessels shuttling merrily up and down the river as if on the Thames itself.[12]

As *St. Lawrence* ascended the Patuxent she passed the two prize schooners taken earlier by Barrie coming down fully laden, of course, with sixty-eight hogsheads of tobacco.[13] Shortly after noon on the 21st she came to anchor off Benedict, and landing parties were dispatched to bring off the remaining tobacco stores left in the town. While busily engaged in this prosperous, if now tedious, enterprise, the shore parties were met with a totally unexpected surprise—American resistance.

...

Major George Peter's forces had had a time of it. After they formed on the morning of the 18th, word reached the city of Washington that Barrie had already retired down the Patuxent from Benedict. The District militiamen were then permitted to go home. Almost immediately afterward, however, another express arrived informing the government that the enemy had again returned to the town. On the morning of the 19th Peter's force once more formed and this time took up the march to Nottingham. By late that evening a vanguard of the Georgetown Dragoons, approximately seventy-five strong, reached the port after a forced march and joined some 250 local militiamen already assembled there. Miraculously, fully expecting to find the village in ashes, the dragoons discovered it still intact.[14]

Perhaps it had come close to being just that, yet had been preserved "by unexpected interposition from destruction" by a tiny detachment of regular infantry, armed with several 18-pounders, under the command of Lieutenant Thomas L. Harrison of the 36th U.S. Infantry. Harrison's unit had crossed the river at Nottingham only a short time before en route to reinforce Carberry, at the time thought to be on St. Leonard's Creek. Soon after crossing, however, the unit's commander, for some unknown reason, had been persuaded to linger briefly in the vicinity. While his tiny force was still near the town, which at that time was totally unprotected, a number of British barges hove in sight of nearby Hall's Creek. The lieutenant quickly turned his guns on the enemy and after a few shots had the pleasure of seeing the foe retire with alacrity down the river.[15]

Harrison's presence apparently served as a nucleus around which a growing body of Prince George's County Militia had gathered. The lieutenant and his guns, however, moved on; but the fact that the enemy had penetrated nearly as high up as Nottingham had a shattering effect on the local population. A near flood of humanity seemed to pour onto the roads as upriver towns such as Upper Marlboro and Pig Point were deserted almost overnight. Soon after the little skirmish it was reported that "every one [is] moving or preparing to move their effects of every kind."[16]

At 8:00 a.m. on June 20 the Georgetown Dragoons were ordered to move out and proceed with alacrity downriver to Benedict, where it was reported that the enemy was again in full possession of the town and several miles of the surrounding countryside. Barely four hours after the dragoons' departure, Major Peter's main force of artillery and infantry marched into the streets of Nottingham from Washington. Within two hours of his arrival, the major was also alerted to the enemy's return to Benedict. A portion of his unit, mostly Alexandria riflemen, was instantly put in motion toward the beleaguered town. His main force remained at Nottingham to counter any designs the enemy might have on that place, one of the few on the Patuxent yet to suffer injury.[17]

Late in the afternoon, advance elements of the District Volunteers, as they liked to refer to themselves, primarily the dragoons, reached the hills overlooking Benedict and discovered General Stuart there with a company of riflemen and a few cavalry and infantrymen from the local militia keeping watch on the enemy below.[18]

Down by the river Lieutenants James Scott of *Narcissus* and Sampson Marshall of *Loire*, in joint command of the British shore parties, were blissfully unaware of the gathering American forces. Since 2:00 p.m. the work of loading the vessels had been progressing smoothly. Then, at precisely 4:00 p.m., just as the seventeenth hogshead of tobacco had been sent aboard one of the barges, the thunder of hooves was heard. Sailors and marines alike formed a line as the Georgetown Dragoons, followed by a rag-tag mélange of infantry, swept down upon the plain without apparent form or plan. The British line evaporated almost instantly, even before the dragoons closed in, partly owing to the nature of the ground but primarily because of the massive odds against it. The plain provided a superb platform for cavalry attack, and the simplest navy tar knew he stood little chance on foot against the oncoming American horsemen. For a change, the British fled panic-stricken, clambering over a fence line that posed the only barrier between themselves and certain death or capture. A sergeant and four marines and sailors, however, found themselves surrounded and were taken prisoner before escape could be effected. The dragoons advanced swiftly, pulling down the fence in minutes, and continued the pursuit.[19]

Not all of the British fled. Sergeant Mahiou of the Royal Marines bravely stood his ground, firing his musket at the charging Americans until entirely surrounded by a sea of horsemen and infantrymen. One of the Alexandria troopers, Francis Wise, crumpled in a bloody heap, felled by Mahiou's shot. General Stuart and another Alexandria trooper rushed the marine in an instant. Mahiou, with no time to reload, defended himself with his bayonet, holding his attackers at bay with cold steel. But there were simply too many. In a last-ditch effort, the sergeant hurled his weapon at another American trooper, who collapsed to the ground wounded. Now the target of many American guns, the brave unarmed marine turned his attention to Stuart and nearly overpowered the general before finally being struck and killed by a shot.[20]

Pursuit of the British marauders continued for only a few more minutes, until the bulk of the enemy, including Lieutenant Marshall, was driven into a nearby marsh into which the cavalry could not follow. Seven British barges loaded with reinforcements were now seen approaching the shore, but the field, swarming with dragoons, riflemen, and artillery, obliged them to have second thoughts. The barges beat a hasty retreat to their mother ship. The field was now cleared of enemy forces, although no one seemed to know how many, if any, were still in the town. The riflemen present, and a small, ill-organized company of artillery with two of the three field pieces, quickly began to regroup on the plain four hundred yards from the town to await orders for their next move.[21]

Within minutes, *St. Lawrence* and her gaggle of barges opened up on Stuart's forces, concentrating a very brisk fire of round and grape on the field for more than a quarter of an hour. The bombardment was the first that many in the American line had ever experienced, "very few of whom probably ever heard the whistling shot about their ears, but who stood their ground with much steadiness." The fire from the enemy shipping was answered by two American field pieces, but only briefly. The Royal Navy gunners were obviously the more capable and numerous of the two forces, and soon obliged Stuart to issue an order to retire from the field. The retreat was carried out in good order, and the general had the final satisfaction of observing the enemy barges scurrying downriver in company with the big war schooner.[22]

Concerned that some of the enemy might yet linger about the town or that the warships might return long enough to blow it apart from the river, the general dispatched an urgent express to Major Peter at Nottingham requesting his full and immediate assistance. Upon receipt of the order, the major set off for Benedict with his entire force, reaching his destination before daybreak of June 21 after an all-night forced march. Soon after his arrival, a reconnaissance party was dispatched to investigate the town and happily discovered its abandonment by the enemy.[23]

The British had not suffered severely from the skirmish at Benedict. Losses were put at one seaman and five marines captured or killed. General Stuart, however, reported five prisoners and one deserter taken, all of which were transported to Washington and committed to the custody of the marshal. British reports of the incident seemed totally unimpressed by the American effort, though an unsuccessful attempt was made to trade J. W. Reynolds, the civilian taken prisoner at Lower Marlboro, for Mahiou, whom the British believed to be still alive. The affair, in fact, left little remark in the enemy's records other than the usual list of accolades for the officers involved.[24]

The fact that American arms had successfully assisted in repelling an enemy, despite the insignificant size of that force, was heartily welcomed in Washington. The effects of the Benedict skirmish were perhaps more injurious in the long run, however, than the actual damage done to the British. A belief in the invincibility of the American militiamen had long been an accepted premise in the young nation's defense-making policy, despite the unalterable fact that militia had proved of only limited value in practically every campaign since the Revolution. Their record thus far in the defense of Maryland had been atrocious. But in a single moment all of that was forgotten and the militiaman was again considered by most to be the state's military backbone. Dinners were held in behalf of the District Volunteers and innumerable toasts were raised in their honor. In Alexandria, that venerable riverport on the Potomac whose sons had actively and energetically fought at Benedict, the skirmish created quite a sensation, and "many of our young men are at this moment preparing for the scene of action."[25]

The citizenry of the town itself treated the saviors of Benedict somewhat less than royally. "This is a beautiful country at this season," wrote one District man stationed there, "but I cannot say much of the liberality of the people of the neighborhood, from whom we received no thanks for defending them though we pay most liberally for every thing we consume. In return for our services they (with honorable exceptions) charge us the most extortionate prices for every article of subsistence."[26]

. . .

The effective neutralization of Barney's flotilla, the terrible depredations being incurred on both shores of the Patuxent, and the generally disgraceful manner in which the militia forces in the vicinity (with the exception of the District Volunteers at Benedict) were conducting themselves were points of considerable consternation in more than a few upper-echelon circles in Washington. The enemy's plundering had begun to inflict terribly high economic losses on Maryland. One estimate calculated that the "royal firm, Cockburn and Barrie," had carried off nearly four thousand hogsheads of tobacco valued at approximately a quarter of a million dollars and were certain to find a ready market in Europe owing to the vacuum created by the Chesapeake blockade.[27] Yet, the Tidewater theater of operations continued to take a back seat to the northern campaigns. The consensus still seemed to be that whatever measures were to be taken in Maryland, they would have to be carried out by the forces already there, primarily the militia.

Secretary Jones, lacking the equivalent of militia for the navy, was obliged to grasp at straws for the Chesapeake's naval defense. Unfortunately, his main forces were tied up either at Baltimore, Norfolk, and Washington or in the Patuxent, and he seemed unable to maintain focus on occasion, often second guessing his field officers from afar. Soon after learning that Barney had been forced on June 7 to retire into St. Leonard's with the British hot on his heels, the secretary had sent a rather chiding letter. While promising to send reinforcements, some light artillery, and the detachment of U.S. Marines under Samuel Miller, "as good troops as can be found," he obliquely reproached the commodore on his strategic judgment. "I have no doubt that the motives which induced you to enter that creek in preference to ascending the Patuxent," he wrote, "will be found justified by the occasion though the former in my present view would have had the effect of leading them farther into the country, and of multiplying the chances of annoying & obstructing them in their descent."[28] On June 14, however, he suggested a rather creative concept that might permit the release of at least one of those forces, Barney's flotilla, into the bay.

Why couldn't the flotilla, he queried the commodore, be transported from St. Leonard's Creek on wheels across the narrow peninsular neck of Calvert

County and be refloated in the bay? The vessels were certainly small enough that they might be carried on wagons, and the Calvert County peninsula was at its narrowest, less than half a mile in a straight line, albeit several miles by road, between the headwaters of the creek and the Chesapeake. After all, the British had carried out a similar feat during the American Revolution when they transported part of an entire gunboat flotilla overland between the St. Lawrence River and Lake Champlain to defeat an American naval force at the Battle of Valcour Island. Indeed, many of the U.S. Navy gunboats currently in service had been built in Maine, where they had been hauled overland four or five miles to the sea by oxen. From St. Leonard's Town, he wrote, "I am told the road is good and free from any serious impediment." He estimated that one of the first-class barges, when stripped of every removable article, would weigh less than six tons. Fitted with a stout pair of dray wheels ordered from Baltimore and a proper bolster and chock assembly, such a vessel could easily be moved by oxen with the assistance of manual labor. Having grown increasingly enamored with the idea, the secretary even envisioned enhancing the mobility of the flotilla over wider ranges of both land and sea. "If it is practicable," he waxed hopefully to the commodore, "it will be highly gratifying, and produce an excellent effect, for if you can transport them four miles you may twenty, and thus the enemy will see the futility of any attempt to blockade you in any of the numerous inlets into which circumstances may force you."[29]

Behind his growing defenses and promised reinforcements, the conservative Barney was skeptical of the idea, considering an overland portage of the fleet impractical. He had already begun to take measures to secure his position by obstructing passage into the creek at its entrance. One defender noted, "our guns all bear upon it at short cannister distance or long musket shot, so that an assault by night, of no matter what force, would meet with defeat; in the day time they dare not look at us." Sam Miller's marines, who had arrived on the evening of June 16, had constructed a considerable breastwork on the flotilla's left flank, in which the navy placed "great confidence." A boom across the narrowest section of the creek and a row of piles driven into the bottom would further retard any advance of the enemy. The defensive posture seemed impervious.[30]

Dutifully, however, the commodore addressed the navy secretary's directive about moving the fleet overland. Immediately upon receipt of Jones's orders, he sent his son William, now sailing master of *Scorpion*, to reconnoiter the terrain and roads leading from St. Leonard's Creek to the bayside of Calvert County. The major returned to report that there was, indeed, an excellent road, two and a half miles in length, running from the head of the creek to the bay.[31]

The commodore informed Jones that if the portage idea were in fact put into execution it would undoubtedly result in the loss of *Scorpion,* the two gunboats, and the lookout boat, a pilot boat schooner, all of which were simply too large to move overland. Moreover, it would be difficult, if not impossible, to transport the artillery, which, if left behind, would probably be spiked by the disaffected inhabitants "as at Benedict." And by the time the vessels were ready to be launched in the bay, the Royal Navy, with its big guns and superior-ranged rockets, would have gotten wind of the plan from some local spy within four hours after preparations to move began, and be there to meet the flotilla on the bay side before it could be launched and rearmed to escape. Unprotected by shoals, and with many miles to travel northward in the bay before they would encounter the first inlet on the western shore large enough to offer protection, the flotilla would again be at the untender mercy of the enemy on open water. However, Barney concluded, leaving the onus of decision for probable failure on the secretary's shoulders, "if you think proper we can make the attempt, and send to Baltimore for wheels, blocks, falls, etc."[32]

Jones was not deterred and turned the decision back upon Barney. "It is for you to determine," he wrote on June 18, but strongly suggested that the commodore order dray wheels from Baltimore anyway. When he had the wheels in hand, then he would be better able to determine the expediency of their use. In the event they were not used for transporting the fleet across the land, he might employ them as gun carriages! In any event, should the enemy increase his force in the bay, it would probably be necessary to secure the flotilla in St. Leonard's if possible, but transfer the men to the barges that had been left behind or built at Baltimore and Washington since the end of May.[33]

Two days later Barney informed the secretary that he would do whatever was ordered but that if the fleet was to be moved overland to the bay, "we shall sacrifice the *Scorpion,* 2 gunboats & look out boat" unless troops were provided to protect them. And that, he knew, was not likely.[34]

· · ·

Jones reluctantly surrendered to the commodore's reasoning, but with the new round of destructive raids he was again under pressure to do something, anything. Perhaps, he reasoned, if there was no longer a flotilla to attract British attention, the enemy would simply go away! It was a head-in-the-sand line of thought many Southern Maryland Federalists had cherished since Barney first dipped his oars in the Patuxent, and one which, to the harried secretary of the navy, seemed to grow more attractive (repugnant as it was at base) every day.

Finally, on June 20 Barney received an express from Washington with another incredible order from the Navy Department more drastic than the last. In a lengthy letter Jones systematically laid out his reasoning for his decision, undoubtedly aware that the commodore would be less than receptive, before giving the order itself. With the enemy concentrating his forces in the vicinity "for the real or ostensible purpose of destroying or blockading the flotilla," and more expected at any moment from Bermuda, the secretary wrote, it was time to reassess the situation. The strategy of providing for the defense of the flotilla as an end in itself was no longer a viable one. The enemy, he noted, "certainly appears to attach much more importance to the blockade of a few barges, than the distinct and intrinsic object can justify—hence I believe he has other and greater designs." Moreover, the Calvert County peninsula, on either side of which he could land at will, was simply indefensible. The enemy could ascend as far as Nottingham, as already proven, and from there even threaten Washington itself. The flotilla, tied up under blockade by a few frigates, was helpless to respond. Without enough flotillamen to protect the approach to the city by water with the new barges available there, Baltimore was vulnerable on all sides. Even Fort McHenry was open to long-range rocket attack, against which it would be powerless to respond. The danger of any of the flotilla vessels falling into British hands was also foremost in his mind. "Their loss would be nothing compared with the consequences of such formidable weapons of annoyance in the hands of the enemy." Thus, he determined that the flotilla must be stripped of every moveable article and effectually destroyed. The flotillamen were to be sent to Baltimore to man three new barges and a new hundred-ton 7-gun schooner called *Lynx* being readied there. The monetary value of the squadron in the Patuxent was, with all its armament removed, reasoned the secretary, paltry. The gunboats, their hulls "being old and so sluggish as to endanger any force they may act with, are better burnt than preserved." Six first-class and seven second-class barges and *Scorpion* could be replaced for an estimated $25,500, the cost of a single Baltimore schooner, "which nobody would think of defending even at the expense already incurred." Almost as an afterthought, the secretary accorded the commodore an escape clause. Should the enemy change his position and permit the overland escape to be executed as earlier contemplated, the flotilla might yet be saved, "otherwise you will carry it [the destruction] into execution forthwith."[35]

The depression that this singular command imposed on the commodore was unbearable. "I acknowledge the justness of the reasoning, and the precaution in your orders," he replied upon receiving the formal directive, "but I feel a depression of spirits on the occasion, indescribable." Unable to bring himself to superintend the demise of a force that he had worked so hard and long to build, man, and field, which had tied up a great portion of the Royal Navy forces on the bay for weeks, seemed madness promulgated by sheer panic. Not surprisingly, the commodore briefly delayed execution of the command, keeping it a secret for the moment. He feared the effects such an order would have on his men, for as he looked about him he observed them even then to be "in the highest spirits and anxious to meet again the enemy they looked on as defeated and beaten."[36]

The destruction of the flotilla, salvage of its armaments, provisions, and other items, and retirement from the peninsula would not be without difficulty. As there were no wagons to be had to transport materials, they would have to be sent down from the northward. Everything saved would have to be sent up to Herring Bay, West or South rivers, for transshipment to Baltimore. The cannon would be the most difficult to remove, but if left behind would most certainly "be rendered useless by the disaffected inhabitants." The flotillamen, except for a detachment to be diverted to Washington to man three barges there, would proceed with the wagons.[37]

A day passed before Barney reluctantly did his duty and gave the order to dismantle the squadron. *Scorpion,* the two gunboats, the lookout boat, and six second-class barges were quickly broken down and those parts that were movable were carried ashore for temporary storage under canvas until wagons arrived from the northward.[38]

Distasteful as this mission was, Barney had disposed of more than half the flotilla with typical efficiency when a countermanding order arrived at 11:00 a.m. the following morning, offering the chance for a reprieve. American spirits in St. Leonard's Creek soared as flotillamen, undoubtedly grumbling about the capriciousness of high command in Washington, went about the work of reassembling the vessels.[39]

Even better news was forthcoming. Reinforcements were on the way from Baltimore with heavy artillery to "annoy" the enemy and hopefully end the standoff. Jones ordered the commodore to meet with the commander of the unit coming down, Colonel Decius Wadsworth, to determine "if any decisive course could be adopted, to terminate the blockade, and spare the destruction of the flotilla." Barney must have grimaced at the rejoinder. If such an end could not be speedily achieved, however, the secretary's previous order was to be instituted.[40]

The commodore's facile mind, perhaps racing ahead lest the seemingly fickle warlords in the capital might in turn countermand the last order, began considering his next move, an offensive one that might set the enemy on his ears. It was not likely that he would now permit either the British or Washington to put an end to his flotilla, at least not without a fight. Upon reading the secretary's latest directive, he immediately ordered all of the guns reshipped, ammunition distributed, and the fleet prepared for action. Sails, rigging, water casks, and other articles that could, if necessary, be carried overland to a depot a dozen miles upstream, at Huntingtown Court House, were left ashore. The fleet would fight light and under oars, relying upon speed and surprise to compensate for inferior firepower. By 2:30 p.m. the flagship and every barge was again ready for battle.[41]

On June 22 Commodore Joshua Barney wrote to his brother Louis that Captain Barrie "has gone down to the Admiral to consult what means they are to take for my destruction," and then added almost as an afterthought, "but sooner than they shall do it, I will put the fire to the flotilla and walk off by the light of the blaze."[42]

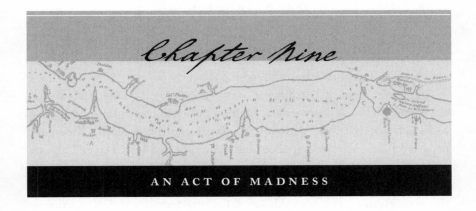

Colonel Decius Wadsworth, commissary general of Ordnance, U.S. Army, was sympathetic to the plight of Barney's Chesapeake Flotilla and appeared to be one of the few military men unwilling to let inter-service rivalry and bitterness get in the way of his duty. The colonel had a reputation as a good officer, and was a military engineer of some note as well who had designed and built some of the defense works at Baltimore. He seemed quick to grasp the utility of applying one of the principal maxims of tactics to the St. Leonard's impasse, one that everyone but Secretary Jones had thus far ignored. That maxim was simply to seize the high ground.

Wadsworth's proposal was elementary. If batteries could be established on the opposite highland bluffs at the mouth of the creek, from which points American artillery fire could be directed onto the very decks of the enemy warships, the British might be driven from their anchorage and permit Barney's flotilla to escape. It was, in fact, an approach that had been brought up several weeks earlier by Jones. "Is there any prominent point," he had asked Barney on June 10, "upon which a breastwork could be thrown up below the enemy, and the guns from the gun boats be mounted thereon? We could soon send you two or three truck carriages, if traveling carriages are not to be had. What means does the country afford of transporting the guns without carriages to the desired point?"[1]

Both Wadsworth's proposal and the secretary's observation were founded in good, common, military sense. Yet it was a tactical move already anticipated by the British. "Should the enemy possess a decent proportion of spirit and enterprise," Captain Brown had only days before noted, "I imagine from the thick woods near the entrance of the creek, and on the opposite bank of the river, they might get guns that would oblige us to drop further out, and perhaps eventually out of the river."[2] Though the British recognized the danger, they were virtually powerless to prohibit its inception, as they lacked a land force sufficient to seize and hold the terrain.

The government in Washington was concerned, especially after word of the enemy's latest depredations as high up as Benedict and Lower Marlboro had reached the city, and Wadsworth's plan was readily accepted. The colonel departed from the capital at about the same time as Major Peter's force, but with only two 18-pounders, several small field pieces, and a traveling furnace suitable for quick erection and capable of providing hot shot to toss at enemy shipping. Adding muscle to this force, the secretary of war directed the 2nd Battalion, 38th Infantry Regiment, under Colonel Peter Little, be sent down to the creek from Baltimore and placed under Wadsworth's command. Carberry's 36th Infantry was also ordered to return to the creek from up-county. Secretary of the Navy Jones had already dispatched a hundred marines under the command of Captain Samuel Miller, an aggressive, toe-to-toe fighter badly needed by Barney, with an additional three cannon. Miller, however, was directed to act only "under the immediate and exclusive orders" of the Navy Department that were to be issued from time to time, and to confer with Barney only "on the best manner of protecting the flotilla and annoying the enemy." Not a word was mentioned concerning the Marine Corps' acting relationship with the U.S. Army or even with Colonel Wadsworth.[3]

Even as this sizeable reinforcement was marching, Barney entertained his own notions of how to effectively turn the tables on the enemy. "If three or four truck carriages could be sent on from Washington for 24 pounders, we might make good use of them," he wrote. "There is a fine point below this called Point Patience where the river is very narrow not more than 200 yards wide. This point will be shown to Col. Wadsworth when he arrives." A battery at Point Patience, the commodore believed, might hinder British naval movements in the vicinity, and perhaps even cut Brown off from the rear should he be obliged to retreat.[4]

Barney may have done more than simply theorize about establishing a battery on Point Patience. On June 20 he sent an urgent order for equipment suitable for moving heavy artillery. The articles were to be sent down the bay from Baltimore as quickly as possible to South River, West River, Herring Bay, or Plumb Point "according to circumstances" and then carried by wagons overland to St. Leonard's. Whether the equipment was destined for a battery at Point Patience or for the portage of the flotilla was left open. The request was not a secret for long.[5]

British intelligence sources in predominantly Federalist Southern Maryland were, of course, quite good, and around St. Leonard's Creek they were excellent. Barney's hint of establishing a battery at Point Patience was immediately picked up and transmitted to Captain Brown, possibly by two black refugees who boarded *St. Lawrence* on June 22. They reported that American troops seemed to be mustering on both sides of the river. Brown had been keeping an eye on the point for some days and from the ship had been unable to detect any activity there, especially military construction work. To his undoubted dismay, he now learned that "they are beginning to erect batteries and also on the opposite side of the river." He quickly dispatched Lieutenant Boyd to personally investigate with *St. Lawrence* (while en route to Tangier Island laden with plunder), just to be certain. "You may depend upon my using every exertion," Brown assured Admiral Cockburn, "to check their operations."[6]

Barney's Point Patience plan was never mentioned again.

The two black runaways apparently brought with them a useful bulk of information, but an American turncoat, possibly Parran, brought even more. Coming aboard *Loire* on the night of June 22, he informed Captain Brown that American military might in the region was increasing daily, and that strong forces were mustering at a variety of positions up and down the river securing tobacco stocks and making any thrust against Barney's flotilla, without adequate land support, out of the question. And without vessels armed with long guns but drawing less than eight feet of water, any naval thrust up the creek would be sheer suicide.[7] Brown, however, was confident and failed to suspect that the Americans had anything more than defensive measures in mind.

Yet the British were beginning to recognize the dangerous implications posed by the ostensibly neutralized flotilla. Should any major amphibious operations on the river be considered, the flotilla would ultimately have to be dealt with. And should Barney be permitted to escape, it would not only be downright embarrassing for the Royal Navy, it would place future operations in the region in considerable jeopardy.

"Should you have any hopes of an army arriving that could attack their Capital," Brown had written to Cockburn, "it would be very necessary that Barney's flotilla should be pent up the creek as so strong a force up the river where boats only could approach might be a considerable annoyance to any force going there."[8]

Barney, however, had no intention of remaining penned up in St. Leonard's Creek.

...

Though local Federalists seemed to be feeding the British practically every scrap of intelligence available, all that was really necessary would have been a subscription to a Baltimore or Washington newspaper. Here they would have found the latest news concerning the comings and goings of militia units and regular troops, shipping notices, and sundry other items of considerable military import. Some newspapers had distinct Federalist leanings and blatantly printed news inimical to the best interests of the country, although just within the bounds of actual sedition. Others, such as Washington's *Daily National Intelligencer*, assiduously condemned the Federalist papers but proceeded to print the latest military dispatches, troop movements, and the like, without the slightest concern for security. If Wadsworth had counted on moving down to St. Leonard's unnoticed, he was sadly mistaken, for on June 22 the following article appeared in the *Intelligencer* and was soon picked up and reprinted in the Baltimore *American* word for word.

> We understand that the artillery and rifle companies from this district reached Nottingham on Monday, about twelve o'clock, and were the same day ordered to Benedict, from which point the enemy contrived to plunder the country. Colonel Wadsworth, of the Ordnance Department, who left this city several days ago with a traveling furnace, two 18-pounders, and some small field pieces, will command the troops from this district and such others as may be detached thither. The dragoons under Major Peter arrived at Nottingham late on the evening of their departure from this city and early the next morning proceeded in quest of the enemy. In addition to the troops already in that neighbourhood, we understand that eight 18-pounders with a suitable number of artillerymen have been ordered to the Patuxent from Baltimore, the whole to set under the orders of Colonel Wadsworth.[9]

His movements thus publicly announced, Colonel Wadsworth and his artillery, Captain Miller with the marines and field guns, and the battalion of infantry due from Baltimore reinforced the morale of the flotillamen at St. Leonard's with unvarnished zeal. "The patriotism and spirit of the men of Baltimore," wrote one sailor, "of which we have just received advice, have infused into the minds of all ranks of flotillamen, a congenial warmth. We now hope, by their aid, to collect such a force on the headlands commanding the entrance of the Creek, as shall drive these robbers who live only on plunder and devastation, from its shores, and leave the gallant Barney and his brave associates once more a free expanse on their favorite element, to meet the enemy on something like equal terms, and again drive them before him as they [the British] have valiantly done the sheep and oxen of the inoffensive inhabitants on the shores of the Patuxent."[10]

Barney was not about to waste the positive sentiments of the moment on mere camaraderie. Upon their arrival on June 24, he immediately convened a conference with Wadsworth and Miller to discuss appropriate measures to drive the enemy from the mouth of the creek. For once, the commodore and an officer of another service managed to agree on basic strategy.[11] It was decided "that a battery and furnace should be erected on the commanding height near the mouth of the creek, upon which the colonel's two 18-pounders should be placed, and that, on the 26th before daylight, a simultaneous attack should be made by the flotilla and battery upon the blockading ships." It was Barney's full intention for the flotilla to force its way into the Patuxent "providing the enemy were not closer than round shot distance."[12] Any closer and the men on the unprotected decks of the barges would be sitting ducks for British grape and canister shot. The commodore did not fear the loss of a vessel, but he agonized over the danger to his brave men.

Wadsworth was at a loss for gunners to man his artillery and pitched upon Barney for the loan of several gun crews. The commodore agreed and placed one of his best officers, Sailing Master John Geoghegan, skipper of *No. 138*, and twenty handpicked flotillamen to be placed under the direct command of the colonel for the specific purpose of manning the two big 18s.[13]

· · ·

Everything was a-bustle aboard the American flotilla as preparations for the coming battle were made. The men were in high spirits and everyone seemed impatient for the hour of decision to arrive. On the evening of June 25 Barney commenced preparations for moving the squadron silently down the creek "that he might be near the enemy at the appointed hour next morning." Once again he divided his force into three squadrons, under the same officers as before.[14] All went well aboard the flotilla in the waning hours before the coming fight.

Ashore, however, all was not proceeding quite as smoothly, for though the strategy appeared sound, the devil was in the details.

At 5:00 p.m. on the evening of the 25th, Sailing Master Geoghegan disembarked with his special duty detachment of flotillamen and a District of Columbia volunteer, accompanied by a youth by the name of J. T. Blake (later to become Congressman Blake of Indiana), to join Colonel Wadsworth.

Shortly after 6:00 p.m. the party fell in with the colonel's personal servant, who informed them that his master was already on the way to the mouth of the creek. The detachment hurried on, hoping to overtake the colonel on the way. Blake, who had been detached to Wadsworth as an aide, was sent ahead on horseback to deliver Barney's last-minute messages and final disposition before the battle. At about sunset, as the flotilla glided slowly down the creek under oars only to its jump-off position, the little detachment ashore arrived at Miller's encampment of marines and was cordially greeted. Wadsworth came up soon afterward and the entire force, sans a marine officer, a sergeant, and ten men left to guard the camp, continued on toward the point together. In the gathering darkness, 117 men stumbled along the dirt road leading to the highland from which they were to fight. Wadsworth galloped ahead, mulling over plans for the erection of the furnace, but halted long enough for the marines and flotillamen to overtake him. Orders were given to begin collecting combustible materials to burn in the furnace as they proceeded, and the nearest fence posts became the first victims. About half a mile from the north shore point of the creek the party came to a halt at the intended site for the furnace. Wadsworth and Geoghegan moved on alone to reconnoiter forward positions appropriate for the battery. At 11:00 p.m., having located a site he considered suitable for the battery, the sailing master retired slightly to the rear, where the colonel was busy laying out the furnace, to secure instructions as to the exact place the guns should be situated.[15]

"As you are to command and fight them," Wadsworth curtly informed the flotillaman, "place them where you please."[16]

Wadsworth was at that moment surrounded by a unit of Colonel Carberry's regiment, the 36th, under a certain young captain, Thomas Carberry, and had already at his disposal a supply of planks, spades, and other necessaries required for the erection of both battery and furnace. All of the guns had finally been brought up, including the marines' 12-pounders, and Geoghegan quickly retired to his selected site to begin work on a gun platform. Miller followed in short order and began constructing a similar work to the right of the main battery.[17]

"I got 7 spades and the same number of pick axes, and commenced heaving up a breast work," Geoghegan later reported. "The regulars & part of my men [were] employed bringing plank for the platform, bricks and wood for the furnace and &c. My men continued digging without any assistance from the soldiers altho frequent application was made for help and for more shovels, but without effect. At about ½ past 3 a.m. the place was not so deep as intended it should be for want of assistance. The guns came down soon after and the necessary preparations were made."[18]

Wadsworth took measures to prevent the enemy from being alarmed by any undue activity ashore, and all movements were carried out with the utmost secrecy and silence. The colonel ordered the ammunition wagons and carts held up a quarter of a mile from the main battery site, and all supplies, even the bricks for the furnace, were passed along by hand over the entire distance. Although undoubtedly fatiguing to the men, silence and concealment were the keys to surprise—surprise upon which the attack's success or failure might hinge. "I felt certain," the colonel wrote afterward, "if the enemy should open upon us even a random fire, it would be impossible to get anything done for the confusion it would create."[19]

As Geoghegan's emplacement was nearing completion, Wadsworth appeared on the scene to inspect, and, much to the weary flotillamen's disgust, entirely disapproved of the position "as being too much exposed to the enemy's fire." He then ordered the guns placed several feet to the rear of the completed works, behind the summit of the hill overlooking the enemy ships. Geoghegan immediately complained that the guns would be mounted in soft sand in that position and would be difficult, if not impossible, to fire with accuracy. Wadsworth was obdurate. Geoghegan unhappily but dutifully proceeded to carry out the new order.[20]

The flotillamen began work on another battery site, although without much help from the nearby infantrymen. It mattered little to the tired marines or sailors that many of the troopers in their immediate rear were new recruits and bone-sore from a forced march. Those to Miller's immediate right and rear belonged to the 38th Infantry and perhaps had good reason to be recalcitrant in their eagerness to pitch in. The men of the 38th had been in motion, almost without respite, for the better part of three days. On the morning of June 23 the major portion of the unit present, the 2nd Battalion, under the command of Major George Keyser, which had been comfortably quartered in Howard Parks, near Baltimore, had boarded the transport ship *Stephen Decatur* bound for Annapolis. From there the unit, 260 strong, marched to the town of Friendship, where they were bivouacked. On the morning of the 25th they again took up the march toward St. Leonard's, but while on the road learned of the impending attack upon the enemy and resolved to reach the creek by nightfall to help. The thirty-mile march from Friendship was arduous in the extreme, and no stops were made for either rest or refreshment. Keyser's men arrived at 10:00 p.m. that evening "completely exhausted and the whole excessively fatigued and famished."[21]

Immediately upon reaching St. Leonard's Town, Keyser was ordered by Wadsworth to place himself under the direct command of Colonel Carberry, whose regiment had just returned from up-county. Within two hours of their arrival, the 38th was again on the march, in company with the 36th, toward a flat plain behind the main battery site on the point. Keyser soon discovered the plain to be completely exposed to the river, from which the enemy, if he chose to, could move up and bombard at will. The infantry took small consolation in the presence of three 12-pounder field pieces brought up under the command of Lieutenant Thomas L. Harrison.[22] Nevertheless, Keyser's troops manfully took up their assigned positions, precarious as they were.

Wadsworth may have had some justification for his concern over the exposed location of the battery; he was definitely not enthusiastic over the tactical extreme its situation called for. "The ground I was obliged to occupy for a battery," he complained, "consisted of a high bluff point having the Patuxent on the right and St. Leonard's Creek on the left, with which the communication was over a flat piece of ground subject to be enfiladed from the Patuxent to the hill on which the guns were placed, and liable to a severe fire from the same quarter; therefore, in case of an attack, the enemy might render our situation very uncomfortable by stationing a small vessel so as to command the low ground I speak of."[23] But the colonel, despite the misgivings of the flotillamen, stoutly defended the repositioning of the battery. "We commenced in the height an epaulement to cover our guns; but the work progressed so slowly from the shortness of time, I did not think it best to occupy it. We stationed our guns so as to barely allow the muzzles to peep over the hill. This brought us on descending ground in a ploughed cornfield."[24]

From the very outset, Wadsworth was not overly optimistic about the chances of completing the battery in the allotted time. Early in the evening he dispatched young Blake with a message for Barney. He informed the flotilla commander that the "Commodore need not be in a hurry, as he, (Col. W.) was not positively certain that the fort would be ready to co-operate with the flotilla the next morning." As a consequence of this notice, Barney did not drop down to the extreme mouth of the creek as planned, but crept to within a mile of the entrance at nearly sunset and anchored in a line.[25] Wadsworth's miscalculation would have important repercussions in the coming engagement.

Near daybreak, as Geoghegan's new position neared completion, the sailing master divided his men equally among the big guns. The gun crews, however, were still short of the necessary number of men to handle each unit, and several soldiers were recruited to fill out each complement, "but not enough to work the guns as they should have been." Yet even before the first swash of morning gray began to streak the sky, the flotillamen and the marines to their right had readied their positions as well as could be expected, loaded their cannons, and anxiously awaited the signal to open fire.[26]

...

At 4:00 a.m. the American masked batteries opened with rude suddenness on the dark, hulking warships lying below in the Patuxent, less than six hundred yards distant. The sleeping enemy was taken by complete surprise, momentarily stunned by the Americans' "point blank shot" and immediately frustrated at their own inability to readily reply. The opening shots had been fired by Geoghegan's 18-pounders, followed immediately after by Miller's 12-pounders. The British guns were aimed up the throat of the creek in anticipation of an assault by water, not from the shore. Barney was nowhere to be seen, and Captain Brown immediately placed his position in tactical perspective. He realized that if he were to hold his position at the mouth of the creek, it was imperative that he knock out the batteries on the heights. But the grogginess of sleep, combined with the stunning success of the surprise, had taken its toll. The British were a full quarter of an hour preparing their guns, swinging on their cables, and arranging spring lines to bring them to bear on the heights. In that same time each of the American guns had fired no less than three uncontested rounds apiece. With the masked battery hidden from the British line of sight, Brown's guns were obliged to simply "fire at where the smoke issued from."[27]

Unfortunately for the Americans, the British immediately deemed Wadsworth's fire considerably less than effective. Although Captain Miller's guns, commanded by Captain Grayson and Lieutenants Richardson and Nichols, were admirably served and judiciously fought (firing four rounds to every one of Geoghegan's, Miller later boasted), their effect was trifling. And the main battery guns, Barney observed bitterly after the contest, "being placed on a declevity, must either fire directly into the hill, or be elevated so high in the air . . . they were rendered useless. At the very first fire, the guns recoiled halfway down the hill and in this situation they continued to fire in the air at random."[28]

Even Wadsworth was forced to admit that the recoil of the guns down-
ward every time they were fired gave his men excessive labor in bringing them
back to their position. "In every respect," he added in his own defense, "it
answered admirably. The enemy found it impossible to hit us; every shot either
fell short and struck the bank or flew clear over us." Indeed, the situation of
the newly raised regiment in the field behind Geoghegan and Miller, which
had also been selected by Wadsworth to protect the rear of the battery, and
onto which much of the enemy shot was falling, was precarious.[29] What he
failed to mention was that his own shots, with perhaps the exception of one
or two hot shots—and even these were later contested—were also failing to
hit the British.

Captain Brown, finding that he could not immediately dislodge the battery, but cognizant of the danger should the Americans begin to find their
mark, dispatched a rocket barge and several of *Loire*'s launches full of marines
to flank the battery on its exposed Patuxent side, just as feared. He also adopted the method of employing smaller charges of powder to simply lob the
shot over the crest of the hill. British fire on the battery was intense, and one
observer estimated that more than six hundred shot were fired against it during the course of the engagement.[30]

But where was Barney?

The American flotilla was delayed in its arrival at the scene of battle by a
full forty-five minutes as a result of Wadsworth's message, and, one suspects,
Barney's own innate distrust of the army's ability to carry out an operation of
the sort being undertaken. Even as the commodore had begun moving down
before the opening of the engagement, his pessimism on this point was clearly
displayed when he was overheard to declare "that he expected to receive no
assistance from the land battery but that he was determined to do his duty by
forcing his way into the Patuxent if not at the imminent hazard of having his
flotilla destroyed."

Barney's delay, whether intentional or not, had aborted the stunning impact
a combined assault would have delivered to the enemy, but when he finally
arrived, there was no stopping him. Encouraged by the continuing thunder
of guns from the direction of the point, his flotillamen were eager to join in
the "Chorus." Concealed from the enemy's view until the last moment when
it rounded the southern lip of the creek entrance, the flotilla "now seemed to
fly under the rapid strokes of the oar," and in a few minutes reached the mouth
of the creek, where the barges assumed a head-on line of battle formation and
opened fire upon the moored ships. Totally dismayed by the second surprise

of the morning, Brown hastily dropped farther back into the river and turned his broadsides on Barney. The initial onslaught of the flotilla, however, had been costly to the British. *Loire* was quickly hulled in at least seven places before she could bring her own guns to bear on the American barges and the smaller craft about her suffered heavily.[31]

Barney's position in the creek fully exposed him to the brunt of enemy firepower, and in particular to the horribly destructive, man-killing grape shot. The flotilla had rowed to within four hundred yards of the enemy before Brown dropped farther out; and the mouth of the creek was here so narrow that only eight of the commodore's largest barges could be admitted abreast at one time and still be capable of using their guns. The moment the flotilla appeared, the big British guns ceased their fire upon the batteries, Barney later informed his brother Louis, "and poured it into us, seeming to have just waked." The seamen were entirely unprotected by any form of bulwarks, and the "warm reception they met with," in the form of grape and cannister

A conjectural view of the Second Battle of St. Leonard's Creek, June 26, 1814, by watercolorist Irwin Bevan. The illustration is somewhat inaccurate in that it shows no less than eight rocket barges deployed against the American naval force, when there were but two such vessels known to have been deployed at the time. *Photocopy, Naval Historical Center, Washington, D.C.*

shot, rained down upon them in seemingly endless showers. The waters literally churned from the downpour of the British bombardment. Yet the flotilla
gunners matched the enemy's fire in intensity, returning each shot with interest. Even Captain Brown grudgingly acknowledged the American fire to be
well directed. The battle soon became, as Barney noted, "a scene to appall the
inexperienced and the faint hearted."[32]

. . .

From the point, Miller's and Geoghegan's guns had begun serving up hot shot
in hopes of setting the enemy ships afire. After the engagement, considerable
discussion was raised over the effectiveness of their work, with proponents
claiming that the frigates were ablaze on several different occasions. Others
charged that none of the shot had even come close to hitting the foe. British
records are silent on the point. Yet the two batteries continued to fire despite
their obvious handicaps.[33]

A short time after Geoghegan's battery was opened, two officers, one of
whom was Lieutenant William Carter, the sailing master's second in command, had his arm blown off when a gun fired prematurely while being loaded
with hot shot. With the exception of one man assigned to guard the seamen's
muskets, the main battery's effective manpower was cut to sixteen men. But
still they continued to fire, although with negligible effect. Most of the damage was now being inflicted by the flotilla.[34]

At about this time Captain Miller, on Geoghegan's right, received intelligence that enemy barges were landing to his right and in the rear of the main
battery. Similar reports had been coming up for some time, but little attention
had been paid them since Colonel Carberry's and Keyser's forces, the 36th
and 38th Regiments, and Harrison's three 12-pounders had been stationed in
the plain to counteract such attentions in that quarter. In truth, two enemy
barges and the rocket boats had been spotted moving up the Patuxent on the
battery's right, firing grape and round shot at the battery as they moved, apparently attempting to intimidate and distract the forward American position
into thinking a landing was about to be undertaken. Miller, whose attention
had been absorbed by the frigates lying below, paid little heed until his supply of round shot gave out. He now sought to put his own three guns to use
elsewhere on the field of battle; but before he could move, another near tragic
accident occurred.[35]

Geoghegan had continued to blast away for some time, even though
Miller's guns had ceased. As one of the 18-pounders was firing a hot shot,

a 32-pounder ball from the enemy met it in mid-flight, split it in pieces, and forced one of the fragments through a small ammunition box, later claimed by Wadsworth to have been poorly placed, at the rear of the guns. The box had been covered by a tarpaulin and contained cannister, a few grape shot, and a quantity of wadding, but fortunately no explosive cartridges of any kind. The box was instantly covered by flames, and splinters from it and the shattered projectiles sprayed the area. Geoghegan was wounded in the knee and another gunner, a midshipman named Aynan Dunan, was also hit. A number of observers had at first mistaken the freak accident to be the result of a well-guided enemy rocket that had struck the "injudiciously placed" ammunition box. But the sailing master's guns kept firing.[36]

Devoid of round shot and seeking to be of use on the field in some active capacity or other, Miller observed that the three 12-pounders under Lieutenant Harrison on the plain "had been injudiciously permitted to remain in a distant part of the field, without orders for firing a single shot, or instructions to be placed in a battery to resist any attack from the barges." The marine thus deemed it advisable to occupy a position from which resistance might be given to the threatened enemy landing in the rear. Wadsworth had momentarily left the main battery, presumably to investigate the impact of the bombardment in the field, and Miller was unable to inform the colonel of his intentions. Secure in the belief that he and his men were operating independently and in concert with but not under Wadsworth, he first consulted Geoghegan on the nature of the movement while "observing, at the same time, that if I could render him any possible service, I would postpone it." The flotillaman concurred that the marines, without a further supply of shot, could no longer be of any use in their present position, whereupon Miller ordered his guns limbered and moved down to the open ground on his right and in the main battery rear.[37]

The new position was dangerously exposed to the fire from both the frigates and the barges, which lobbed shot over the hill out of sight of the new position and completely out of range of any grape or cannister that could be thrown by the Americans. Miller reported,

> Thus situated, I was compelled once more to seek a position sanctioned by military propriety, and commensurate with the nature and extent of my forces such as one presented itself directly in my rear, near the defile which entered upon the road [to the point]; I therefore pointed out to Capt. Grayson the ground I wished to take, and my reasons for so doing; but before I had reached half way to the spot, I discovered the infantry retiring in good order along the low ground. It instantly

occurred to me that Col. Wadsworth was possessed of some important movement of the enemy's frigates (for in the low ground they were completely out of sight) which I justified him in directing the whole of the troops under his command to retire. I, therefore, from the unfortunate movement of the battalion of infantry, became one of the moving number from the field.[38]

What had started out as a movement to counter the insignificant danger posed by the enemy barges had become a general retreat facilitated by a breakdown in the chain of command. When Miller had moved toward his first new position, he passed through Keyser's 38th Infantry, informing them that his ammunition had been expended and that he was leaving the main battery. At the same time he informed them that enemy barges were maneuvering to land in the rear. The 38th promptly attempted to shift alignment to present a front to the place where the enemy was to land. The movement, however, proved simply too much for the green, untested troops who had been subjected to hours of enemy bombardment after an arduous forced march. By the time Miller was moving toward his next position, "every description of troops were leaving the field and the battery was abandoned." With no directions from Wadsworth forthcoming, the 38th acted under orders received the preceding evening, which were simply that they should be guided by the movements of the 36th—and the 36th had already commenced marching off the field. Many officers in the 38th noted that their battalion was the last to leave, and then only while under the impression that they were taking up a new position.[39]

But a retreat was still a retreat.

In the meantime, Wadsworth had returned to the main battery, and suddenly found himself with barely enough men left to work a single gun, which he quickly ordered turned to the rear to hold the enemy barges in check.[40]

At this juncture Geoghegan discovered that the infantry was in full flight and immediately informed the colonel of the obvious. Wadsworth grimly replied that he had ordered a detachment of the 36th to march down to repel the approaching barges should they attempt a landing; his orders, however, had been ignored, and the troops, apparently spurred by the seeming evacuation of the main battery, had kept on going. The battery itself was now in serious danger of being cut off from behind, and an immediate retreat was agreed upon. Then on finding that the teamsters and horses, which had hauled the guns up, had also departed, and that the danger of abandoning artillery to an enemy who might turn it upon the retiring Americans being a distinct possibility, Wadsworth ordered the guns spiked.[41]

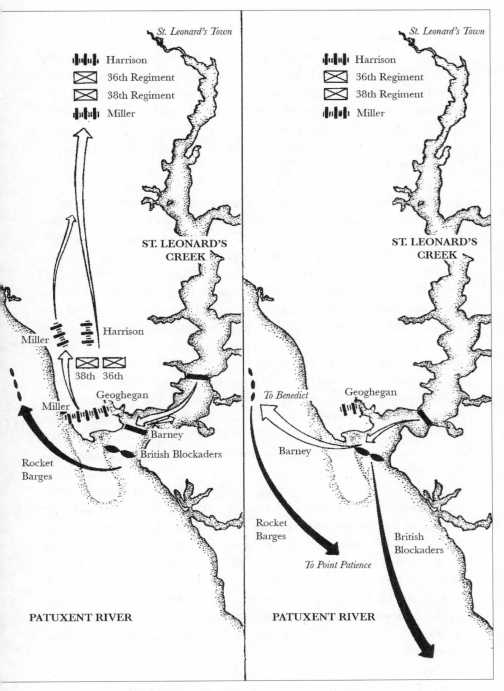

St. Leonard's Town

	Harrison
	36th Regiment
	38th Regiment
	Miller

ST. LEONARD'S
CREEK

Miller   Harrison

38th   36th

Miller   Geoghegan

Barney

British Blockaders

Rocket
Barges

PATUXENT RIVER

St. Leonard's Town

	Harrison
	36th Regiment
	38th Regiment
	Miller

ST. LEONARD'S
CREEK

To Benedict   Geoghegan

Barney

Rocket
Barges   British
                          Blockaders

To Point Patience

PATUXENT RIVER

The Second Battle of St. Leonard's Creek, June 26, 1814. *Map by Donald G. Shomette.*

Several batterymen now joined in the general exodus from the field; but others, entirely fatigued by the labors of the last twenty-four hours, reportedly collapsed by their guns and slept. Those who retreated immediately encountered the infantry on the road, and soon afterward came up with the horses and limbers belonging to the big guns.[42] From all appearances the battle was not faring at all well for the Americans.

But events were soon to take an unexpected twist that no one, least of all Commodore Joshua Barney, fully expected.

During the last minutes in which the guns of Wadsworth's battery had been firing, Barney had also been heavily engaged. The commodore, during this period, was "surprised and mortified to observe that not a single shot from the battery fell with assisting effect." Now, with a menacing silence falling from the point, the flotilla experienced the undivided attention of British firepower. Three of the barges, under Sailing Masters Worthington, Kiddall, and Sellers, suffered heavily. Barney was certain that his casualties numbered over a hundred men, but later reported that only seven men, including a young midshipman by the name of George Asquith, had been killed and four wounded. Three more of the flotillamen had been wounded in the battery.[43] Shortly after the battery was quieted, Barney was obliged to disengage, for, as he later wrote, "it would have been an act of madness in such a force, unassisted, to contend against two frigates, a brig, two schooners, and a number of barges, in themselves equal to the force that could be brought into action from the flotilla."[44] Within minutes the flotilla had retired less than three-quarters of a mile up creek and had drawn up in a line, bravely awaiting the inevitable denouement.[45]

Immediately after Barney's withdrawal, T. P. Andrews, a young volunteer and compatriot of Mr. Blake, Wadsworth's aide, left the flotilla and went ashore with the intention of volunteering to assist in withstanding the expected enemy assault on the fort. En route, he encountered the retreating army but was unable to discover the cause of the movement. He soon fell in with Lieutenant Carter, Geoghegan's second in command, who was weak from his wounds and fearful of fainting. The officer requested the youth to conduct him to the flotilla and, along the way, he related the account of the confusion at the battery. Upon boarding the fleet, Andrews "surprised the Commodore, not a little, by informing him of the retreat."[46]

Miraculously, at that very moment and unknown to Barney, the critically mauled British too had decided to retire. The Americans were unaware of the extent of enormous damage they had inflicted upon the enemy. *Loire,* in particular, had been badly battered during the engagement. She had been hulled at least fifteen times, severely crippling her, and her mizzen topmast had been shot away. One shot had ripped into her copper sheathing just above the waterline and another just below. A third shot had struck her near the bridle port and had torn off her planking in that area. Her yawl, gig, and whaleboat had been seriously mangled. An observer who had the opportunity of boarding her later in the day noted that "he found them hard at work pumping, in plugging the shot holes to keep her from sinking, and painting them over as fast as plugged of the color of the vessel." *Narcissus* did not escape unscathed either and was reported as "very much cut up below the bends," and her crew kept employed in pumping desperately to keep her afloat.⁴⁷

Within a few minutes of Barney's retirement up St. Leonard's, about six o'clock, the British were also perceived to be in motion—but, astonishing as it may have seemed, they were standing downriver. One of the frigates was observed to be severely damaged and had four of her pumps working at once. Beyond that, nothing was certain except that, for the Americans, a miracle had delivered them the field of battle and victory at the very moment they had expected defeat.⁴⁸

If the amazing turn of events came as a blessing to Commodore Barney and his indefatigables, to Captain Brown it was a defeat difficult to explain away. Indeed, he hardly tried. In his official report, composed on June 27, he explained his motions rather tersely. "Judging we might be harassed by the battery again opening on us, and the ships having been frequently hulled, and part of the rigging shot away I thought it prudent to weigh and drop down the river to a place called Point Patience, where I again anchored about three miles below in hopes the flotilla might be induced to follow."⁴⁹ Though Brown was obviously attempting to downplay his failure to maintain the blockade of St. Leonard's Creek, his retirement from that position could not be considered as anything less than a singular American feat of arms, simply because Barney still commanded the mouth of the creek. If Brown was, as he said, counting on the Americans to come out against him at this point, he was either a fool or a man of very poor judgment. And he was certainly neither of these.

By 8:00 a.m. the British had warped around and come to anchor off the south side of Point Patience, where *Loire* got her spring lines ashore and began operations to prevent her foundering. Now even the weather conspired against them. While the enemy desperately attempted to repair *Loire* enough to perhaps reinstate the blockade, a sudden calm fell over the river. The only manner of movement afloat was now by oars.⁵⁰

Barney made an immediate decision. Captain Brown later reported the results of the commodore's actions thus: "I had the mortification to observe them rowing down the creek, and up the river, the whole consisting of one sloop and eighteen row boats." However, one of the boats was observed to return to the creek and it was believed that the vessel had sustained damages that had prohibited escape after the engagement. In fact, two vessels, *Nos. 137* and *138*, deemed to be too slow to safely escape, were ordered to remain behind at the town waterfront.[51]

Embarrassed and frustrated by the Americans' evacuation, the enraged British took out their anger on the nearest target. A landing party was sent ashore to destroy the first American house it came to. The unfortunate estate proved to be that belonging to Dr. William D. Somervell at Point Patience, who also lost at least nine of his slaves.[52]

. . .

Brown's official report of the battle was embarrassingly short. He had permitted a vastly inferior American force, heavily outgunned, outnumbered, and outmanned, to escape a perfect entrapment, and at the very moment that victory had been assured retired downriver. For the sake of his own preservation, the entire affair was underplayed with skillful understatement. There was only one positive aspect to the outcome, and even that in itself accentuated the defeat that had been inflicted. "I am happy to say," he wrote, "the only person wounded is the boatswain of the *Narcissus* who has lost a leg."[53] Only one casualty, and Brown had permitted practically the entire American flotilla to escape to cause unending worry to the Royal Navy.

. . .

Aboard the flotilla jubilation reigned. Young Blake was given the mission of taking the first word of victory to Washington. The commodore's letters told it all. "Thus we have again beat them and their rockets, which they did not spare. You see we improve: first we beat off a few boats, which they thought would make an easy prey of us. Then they increased the number. Then they added schooners. And now behold the two frigates, all, all, have shared the same fate. We next expect ships of the line. No matter we will do our duty . . . Thanks to hot & cold shot the blockade has been raised."[54]

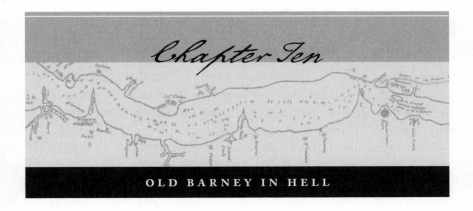

The thunderous clamor of battle had resounded with stunning clarity for miles up the Patuxent Valley. At Benedict, the District of Columbia Volunteers kept an anxious vigil at the water's edge, and from the nearby hills lookouts strained for a glimpse of an occasional masthead piercing the heavy smoke blanketing the St. Leonard's Creek region. By mid-morning a stillness had fallen over the river and the 260 militiamen in the town contested with a stranglehold of anxiety over the outcome of the battle.[1]

At 3:00 p.m. a fleet of barges with a topsail sloop in the lead was spotted making its way up the river directly toward the town as fast as oars could carry it. The militia, perceiving the approaching force to be the enemy bent on revenging himself upon the town for the "little scratch" inflicted earlier, momentarily froze in place. However, Major Peter, "that vigilant and scientific officer," immediately snapped the men from their malaise and began arranging the several companies present to meet the expected enemy assault. Peter had determined to contest the British landing even though the enemy was thought to be seven or eight hundred strong.[2]

"The moment of expectation was serious," wrote one of the town's defenders to a friend in the District, "but it was not wasted in idleness. Every man prepared himself for a re-encounter which was deemed unavoidable; and it was not until the barges had approached within two miles of the shore and our videttes expected every moment to be fired upon, that an express from General Stuart reached us, informing that Barney had got out with his flotilla. You may well conceive this information was most acceptable. The fleet or flotilla anchored opposite Benedict at 8 o'clock in the evening, and for the first time since we left you, we slept without apprehension of a visit from the enemy."[3]

Barney had little inclination or time to rest. As the barges moved up toward their new anchorage, Captain Miller came on board the commodore's boat to relate a firsthand account of the proceedings at the Wadsworth battery. The commodore was painfully aware that there had been mismanagement somewhere, but satisfied himself, upon the arrival of Geoghegan's official report sometime later, that the mistakes on the point were not committed by his officers or men.[4] But then, there were none of the colonel's men there to provide their points of view of the affair.[5]

Wadsworth himself later frankly admitted to much of the mismanagement.

> We committed a great many blunders during the action, or our success would probably have been more complete. I forbear to enter into minute particulars lest I should cast an indiscreet censure of some of the officers, perhaps undeserved. But the fact is, the infantry and light artillery decided upon a retreat without my orders before they had lost a single man killed or wounded, and at the time, too, when the enemy was manoeuvering to the rear of our position with their barges. The consequence of this movement was very disadvantageous; the men at the guns perceiving the infantry retreating and the enemy getting into the rear, their numbers sensibly to diminish, and I was pretty soon left with only men enough to work one gun, which I was necessitated to turn to the rear for the sake of keeping the barges in check. Finally the few men that remained were so exhausted with fatigue, we found it impracticable to fire any more and the limbers and horses, which had been ordered down the hill, having disappeared and gone, I know not where, I found myself under the painful necessity of spiking the guns to prevent their being used by the enemy, should he get possession of them. I might in justice to the infantry, acknowledge that they did not take to flight, but quitted the ground in perfect order; after a while I was able to halt them and bring them back. In the meantime the enemy were getting underway and retiring down the river—from the precipitancy of his retreat, I infer he must have suffered considerably. From some untoward circumstances I had it not in my power to observe the effect of each shot fired, otherwise I think [sic] destruction would be complete . . . I hope on the whole, taking into consideration our not being fully prepared, the excessive fatigue of the men, and that we have attained the object in view, which was the release of Commodore Barney's flotilla, the affair will not reflect dishonor on our troops.[6]

Although Commodore Barney had nothing good to say about the activities of the infantry, he was not worried that his own officers and flotillamen or Miller's marines might bear any dishonor, and was generous in his praise of their performance, noting that "it was my men alone that fought there" and he "had but little reason to complain of any officer whatever; never did men behave better, or with more subordination, bravery, or coolness."[7] Nevertheless, on July 7 Jones ordered a court of inquiry into Miller's conduct after receiving a disparaging letter from Wadsworth regarding his behavior during the battle. Both Barney and Geoghegan, neither of whom could be spared from the field, were ordered to Washington to testify. Barney reluctantly allowed the invaluable Geoghegan to go. But as Lieutenant Frazier was in ill health and the enemy was in force below but one good tide away, the situation, Barney pointed out, "will not admit of my absence at this time." He would provide whatever evidence he could in writing, but simply could not be away from the fleet for an extended court case. When the inquiry was finally conducted it went on for nearly three weeks, at the conclusion of which Captain Miller was honorably acquitted when the full account was made known.[8]

The Second Battle of St. Leonard's Creek, despite the facts that Barney's flotilla had escaped intact and that fewer than a score of men had been injured or killed, wrought considerable criticism in the press for the manner in which it was conducted. The lateness of the flotilla in arriving at the mouth of the creek, the purported bungling at the Wadsworth battery, and the retreat by the infantry without orders became bones of heated contention among various factions involved in the battle. Public bickering continued for weeks, much of which was published in the pages of the *Intelligencer* and the Baltimore *American,* adding little in the way of public confidence in the federal government's defense capabilities despite the victory.[9]

...

On St. Leonard's Creek the reality of the British retreat had not been immediately understood or even recognized by Colonel Wadsworth's forces. Even as Captain Brown was taking stock of his damaged shipping and preparing to get under way toward Point Patience, a small detachment from Colonel Carberry's regiment was finally halted a mile and a half from the field by Wadsworth, and the retreat ground to a stop. The detachment volunteered to return to the battery with horses and limbers to retrieve the spiked cannon though the enemy's intentions against that place were still of considerable concern. Young Captain Thomas Carberry and ten or twelve men (including two Georgetown volunteers, John Lee and a certain Lockerman) accomplished this mission with alacrity and not only brought off the artillery, but also the furnace, sponges, and other accoutrements. Several wounded infantrymen left behind in the bushes during the army's flight were also carried out and given medical attention. It was said, though never verified, that when Wadsworth heard of their action, undertaken despite the expectation that the enemy had landed in the interval, he cried out to the captain: "I make you a colonel on the spot." It was even claimed by some that the captain's movements to reclaim the artillery had been the very thing that had frightened the British away, fearful as they were that Carberry was there to serve up more hot shot instead of remove cannons.[10] Soon after the captain's return, Wadsworth was finally able to rally his men and then march back to the field to repel the enemy should he make another attempt.[11]

Sailing Master Geoghegan characteristically subordinated his weakness and injuries to duty and proceeded toward Captain Miller's encampment, where he left his wounded. He then returned with the remainder of his fatigued officers and men to the gunboats. Barney was not about to make the enemy a present of any useful item, much less a gunboat or two, and had dispatched Rutter to bring off whatever he could as quickly as possible. That which couldn't be saved was to be destroyed. The masting from the barges and the boom from *Vigilant*, which had been left behind as those vessels had gone into battle under oars only, were still in the upper waterway. These were "launch'd into the creek" and "push'd up so as to conceal them from the enemy." The gun slides from the gunboats were then dumped. Then, the two vessels that had been little more than a hindrance ever since the campaign had begun were ordered scuttled to prevent enemy capture. At 5:00 p.m. on June 26 Geoghegan hauled up *No. 138* alongside *137* at the foot of the town and, "agreeable to orders received from Lieutenant Rutter," both vessels were sunk.[12]

The two gunboats scuttled in upper St. Leonard's Creek were among several vessels that had returned to or simply remained near the town after the battle, and everyone knew that it was only a matter of time before the enemy came back to complete a job that he had weeks before set out to do. Nevertheless, Rutter, Geoghegan, and the handful of men left behind were soon employed in loading spars and iron kentledge—all of which had been taken off the barges sometime earlier to facilitate speed in battle—aboard a schooner lying at the head of the waterway. This work was completed by June 30, after which Rutter intended to proceed down the creek and up the Patuxent to rejoin the flotilla.[13]

In the meantime, Geoghegan, left in charge of St. Leonard's Town, had taken the precaution of ordering a reconnaissance down the creek to keep a watch for the enemy. He was soon informed by the scouts that two British warships, accompanied by several small schooners, "had drop'd a little above the mouth of the creek about 4 o'clock that evening." This circumstance destroyed any possibility of Rutter's schooner gaining the Patuxent with a reasonable chance of success. Thus, on the morning of July 1 the spars and iron were all offloaded again and stored ashore in their former position. Geoghegan joined the lieutenant in his encampment at the Calvert County Court House in Prince Frederick to discuss their next move. On the morning of July 2, it was decided, Geoghegan would march back to St. Leonard's Town with a work party and several wagons and remove whatever masting and kentledge still remained there.[14]

The sailing master returned to the town with a guard of eight men, but had barely completed the loading of a single wagon when a report was received that the enemy was approaching in force. He immediately broke off the loading work and sent the wagons away with orders for those coming up to turn back. "Thirteen masts of our barges and the yards belonging to the galley," he later reported, "were then launch'd into the creek & push'd up so as to conceal them from the enemy. Care had also been taken to send off the [gun] slide belonging to Gun Boat *No. 138*" to prevent it being taken and used in arming one of the enemy's vessels. Geoghegan's small party then proceeded to assume a post on the peninsular point of land upon which the St. Leonard's warehouse was situated, from which he intended to harass the British approach.[15]

The enemy, already twice stung, had cautiously awaited the arrival of further reinforcements before again venturing into the fastness of St. Leonard's Creek. On June 27 HBMS *Severn* was sighted by *Loire* coming in from the Chesapeake. Overall command of His Majesty's forces on the Patuxent now evolved to Captain Joseph Nourse, commander of *Severn*, a new 56-gun ship built of fir. Three days later *St. Lawrence* returned from Tangier Island and rejoined the squadron.[16]

British intentions now focused on mopping up whatever remained of American resistance still in the creek and ignoring, for the moment, Barney's main force. After reviewing the circumstances and results of the last engagement on the creek, Captain Nourse rightly had "reason to suppose the enemy had not removed all his vessels from thence," and prepared to send a force in to dispose of whatever remained.[17] The move was necessary, for should a thrust be undertaken upriver, it would certainly not do to have an enemy force, even a few small gunboats, in one's rear. Indeed, judging from the damage already inflicted by the little American vessels when united, it was certainly advisable to destroy them in detail whenever the opportunity presented itself.

The following afternoon *Loire, Severn, St. Lawrence,* and several small schooners weighed and sailed up the Patuxent, finally coming to anchor abreast and slightly north of the mouth of the creek. Unfortunately for the British, their operations were again retarded by the grounding of *St. Lawrence* on a mudbank. Nevertheless, the work of arming two of the smaller schooners with carronades and a large 12-pounder in preparation for another penetration into St. Leonard's was undertaken without delay. At 11:00 p.m., after six hours of labor, *St. Lawrence* was freed.[18]

Saturday morning, July 2, was ruffled only by fresh breezes and cloudy skies. Captain Nourse had already dispatched several guard boats up the creek to reconnoiter American motions and strength. These were undoubtedly the same vessels reported on by the advance American scouts. By 11:00 a.m. all of *Loire*'s and *Severn*'s barges, as well as the two schooners, were loaded with 150 marines and made ready to move up. "Captain Brown with the marines of both ships," Nourse recorded, "landed about two miles up the creek & proceeded for the town while the boats under the orders of my first lieutenant Wm. Gammon pushed up. *St. Lawrence* was again anchored in the main throat of the creek just in case a retreat might be necessary."[19]

As soon as the leading British vessels were within musket shot, the Americans saluted them with a well-directed volley. The greeting was promptly answered by a thunderstorm of round and grape. Geoghegan prudently ordered his men to retire, leaving a forward observer, an officer, to watch the motions of the enemy from a safe distance. On July 3, the officer employed on this mission joined the sailing master and presented a full report. Upon the enemy's arrival at the head of the creek, he said, "they commenced by burning the small vessels lying there, they then landed and a party remained upon the point who employ'd themselves in removing the few Hhds. [hogsheads] of tobacco which were left in the warehouses, some of which they placed in a launch, & the remainder, they either roled [*sic*] into the water, or left to be consumed in the house to which they set fire."[20]

In the meantime, the landing party proceeded directly to the town, which they promptly set afire, burning all of the buildings "except that where the doctor had his quarters with the store adjoining, and another immediately opposite." Absolutely nothing else was spared in this venerable old village—not even the slave quarters, the hen houses, or the pigsties. The British officers eagerly inquired of the few terrified remaining inhabitants who it was that had fired the volleys from the shore on their approach, and when told it had been the flotillamen, sneered: "It was like them, that they regrettably had not stayed a little longer."[21]

The invaders immediately boarded one of the gunboats that had been dismantled and sunk with her gunnels level with the water, and attempted to blow up part of her deck. They worked diligently at their plan of destruction, and ultimately both gunboats as well as several small merchantmen were reported "destroy'd." At 6:00 p.m. the raiders re-embarked on their vessels, having loaded one of the schooners with forty hogsheads of captured tobacco, and proceeded back down the creek. By 8:30 p.m. they had safely returned with their booty and reached the security of the frigate anchorage off the creek's entrance.[22]

The morning following the British withdrawal, Rutter and Geoghegan commenced reloading their wagons with the spars and rigging sequestered from the enemy for carriage up-county to the little river port of Huntingtown on Hunting Creek, from which they could be sent by water to the flotilla.[23] On going down to inspect the condition of the scuttled boats, which they hoped could be raised and placed back into service after the immediate emergency had subsided, Geoghegan "met a number of the inhabitants who had been onto the gunboats, & tore up & plunder'd every piece of iron and copper &c they could get at." The flotillaman was furious and immediately seized the filched goods. He observed in his report of the incident to Barney that "they were more anxious to plunder the property of the U.S. than to defend their own, which is certainly the case as there were more men collected for that purpose than has been seen together since we lay in the creek."[24]

. . .

Notwithstanding the reverberations of vengeance bestowed upon the local population by the British for their own defeat in the recent battle, the Americans had achieved several important advantages by escaping from St. Leonard's Creek. First, the flotilla was still intact, a force in being and obviously a force to be reckoned with. Second, now that this force was no longer penned up, but lay in the main river, it blocked British access into the heartland of the state via the Patuxent and controlled the approach to strategic overland junctions leading to Washington, Annapolis, and Baltimore. Third, logistical support was now more readily available via direct overland passage to Washington and Baltimore. In fact, almost as soon as the flotilla dropped anchor off Benedict, Barney fired off a letter to the secretary of the navy requesting provisions. On June 28 five barrels of pork, five of beef, and thirty of bread were loaded on two wagons at the Washington Navy Yard by Navy Store Keeper Buller Cocke to be sent to the flotilla—the first fresh supplies delivered in weeks.[25]

Soon after his arrival at Benedict, Barney received an express from Jones with a single line of congratulations on raising the blockade, followed by orders to come to Washington to plan the next move, "as this can be decided with a more full and satisfactory discussion by an hours conversation than by partial correspondence." Before departing, the commodore directed the flotilla to be brought upriver to Lower Marlboro, where it would be more centrally located and could control the strategic narrows below the town with greater facility than any position lower down. Immediately after his arrival in the capital, on the evening of June 30, the commodore found himself immersed in strategy conferences. His views concerning the disposition of the flotilla, the probable intentions of the enemy, and what measures would be necessary to protect the capital and Baltimore were discussed at length.[26]

The precise proceedings of the Washington conference are unknown but the results were soon manifest. What is clear, however, is that both the secretary of the navy and Commodore Barney were at a crossroads of commitment. That the flotilla had escaped upriver from St. Leonard's Creek had solved nothing. The river was still under a blockade. St. Leonard's Town had been destroyed. And all that the flotilla, which would have to remain on the defensive, could hope for was to keep an eye on the enemy. If the British received substantial reinforcements from Europe, Bermuda, or elsewhere, as expected, both Washington and Baltimore were still likely to be targets, and the flotilla would be helpless to intervene.

As a result of the Washington conference, it was decided that the thirteen barges, *Scorpion*, and five hundred flotillamen would remain on the river. Barney's able second, Lieutenant Rutter, was to be dispatched to take charge of fourteen recently or nearly completed new barges and five hundred men newly recruited at Baltimore for the defense of that city. The commodore was undoubtedly happy for his lieutenant but would sorely miss that capable officer's services. Yet in the event of an assault on either Washington or Baltimore, it had been quickly agreed upon that the flotillamen at either place could march to the aid of the others.[27]

Barney returned to the Patuxent after a two-day absence and immediately ordered Rutter to his new post. He then directed his own flotilla to up anchor and retire even farther upriver to a point just off the Nottingham waterfront, where another narrows below the town could easily be monitored by American guns and where he might be in closer communication with Washington. At Nottingham, however, he found the inhabitants in a frantic state of alarm and confusion. The District Volunteers had been ordered back to the capital (into which they marched with considerable pomp and ceremony), causing the local citizenry to take their departure as a sign of abandonment. As in Calvert County, Barney quickly discovered the local Prince George's County militia to be less than useless and, as he bitterly noted, "were here and there, but never where the enemy was."[28]

There was, perhaps, good reason for the commodore to be perturbed by the inaction of the local home guard. On one occasion a call had gone out to muster forty of the Nottingham Militia that were to be stationed at the Tanyard, near the town. Out of this number, fewer than six men turned out. One local farmer, Clement Hollyday, a supporter of the government, was embarrassed by the poor showing and beseeched a relative to whom he had written not to mention it to anyone. "It would give them a bad opinion of our part of the county," he wrote. Then, perhaps by way of excuse, he noted, "Nottingham has been & is now very sickly. The inhabitants has the flux & measles."[29]

The poor showing of the Nottingham Militia, however, was only symptomatic of the deep-seated anti-government attitude smoldering amidst the grassroots of Southern Maryland. If Barney was angered by the militia and the local citizenry, the feeling was mutual. Many, whose homes had been destroyed or looted by the British or who stood to lose should the enemy again ascend the river, believed that their plight had been triggered by the presence of one man—Joshua Barney.

One citizen of Calvert County named Thomas E. King summed up the violent hatred that many inhabitants of Southern Maryland had developed for the commodore and his flotilla in a letter to his brother Benjamin, a new resident of the District of Columbia:

> I am sorry to see you are so much influenced by Dr. [James H.] Blake [mayor of Washington] as to change your political sentiments and have such a mean opinion of the citizens of Calvert [County], the place that gave you birth, to think that the militia could not fight for looking at the mean marines that came down for the defense of old Barney, who has been the means of ruining Calvert, for if he had never of come in the Patuxent the British would never have thought nor had any idea that they could come as high as Lower Marlboro in the world, but his going down the Bay and giving them a challenge as it were, he could not think they would let him return without following him up, and he pitched on the Patuxent as a place of safety, and as he knew Calvert, St. Mary's, Charles and Prince George' Counties were all Federalist, he thought it would be the means of making them all advocates of old Jim Madison, but it has enraged them so that a great many that were in favor of him now are abusing him every day, but I think when I tell the mischief the British have done it will be enough to make you and every man abuse Jim Madison and old Barney in Hell if you could.[30]

Chapter Eleven

LEVIATHAN AWAKENED

At the beginning of July, Admiral George Cockburn's flagship, HBMS *Albion,* lay anchored off the main British land base in the Chesapeake at Tangier Island in company with her tender, *Warrington,* engaged in a number of last-minute tasks before moving to join the Patuxent squadron. Tangier Shoals, ever since the loss of the schooner *Hiram* in the spring, had proved to the British to be a dangerous hazard to the support shipping unfamiliar with the bay, and Cockburn had found it necessary to erect a temporary beacon south of the island as a warning. On July 2 the tender was dispatched to sound out the shallows, after which a prize sloop loaded with three tons of iron ballast was scuttled in the most appropriate position on the shoals to serve as a visual warning to approaching vessels. Lanterns were undoubtedly hung from her exposed mast at night and a pennant by day to ward off endangered shipping.[1]

Cockburn had been eager to resume his format of depredations of the previous year in the Tidewater—a program being carried out with great facility by his lieutenants on the Patuxent—at least until promised reinforcements arrived from Bermuda with which he could undertake even greater projects of destruction. Yet, for the time being, his forces were stretched to the limits. On June 24 the arrival of HBMS *Severn,* Captain Joseph Nourse commanding, bearing letters from Cochrane helped some, but owing to American stirrings in Norfolk, even *Dragon* had been forced at the last minute to remain in Lynnhaven Bay. The American threat, perceived or real, seemed to be increasing in several quarters, causing the admiral considerable anxiety. The day before the battle on St. Leonard's Creek, he had been obliged to dispatch an expedition to destroy an American post and battery being established at Chesonesex, on the Eastern Shore, immediately abreast of the forward British post on Watts Island. "I found it impossible," he informed Cochrane, in justifying his requisition of *Severn*, indeed every vessel that came into the bay, "to guard *at Norfolk* the *Constellation* thirty gun vessel two privateer brigs and other craft said to have been lately armed there, in *the Potowmack* the Washington gun boats, *in the Patuxent* the new Baltimore Flotilla and to take care of and forward the works on *this island* . . . with only this ship [*Albion*] two frigates [*Acasta* and *Loire*] a brig [*Jaseur*] and schooner [*St. Lawrence*]." Moreover, he had been obliged to employ his precious picket boats as store ships owing to the retarded progress in construction on Tangier Island because of a paucity of manpower. And there were other problems.[2]

One necessity the Royal Navy was continually obliged to consider was that of drinking water. The water supply requirements of a vessel the size of *Albion*, especially during the sizzling hot summers encountered on the Chesapeake, were enormous. Daily consumption by the crew and livestock aboard, as well as an abundance of other needs, accounted for nearly two to three tons of water per day. *Albion*'s supply, though not critically low, was dwindling as the water from the Tangier wells was proving to be both inadequate and increasingly bad. A visit to the western shore of the bay, where supplies around Drum Point had already been found, would answer the ship's needs. Moreover, the recent defeat on the Patuxent required a firsthand look by the admiral himself.

Thus, temporarily taking leave of the business at and about Tangier Island, Cockburn ordered *Albion* to weigh anchor on July 3 and stand up the bay under full sail. An hour after the big warship made sail, three bay craft were sighted in the mouth of the Potomac River northwest of Smith Point. A barge, *Albion*'s launch, and the ship's gig were sent off in pursuit. That evening the sky was pregnant with lightning and thunder. Heavy rainsqualls followed in the traditional sequence familiar to mariners since time immemorial, and there was undoubtedly some concern aboard the flagship for the safety of the three tiny craft. Finally, the barge and launch returned in company, though the gig did not arrive until 6:30 p.m. She had in tow, however, the lumber-laden American schooner *Flora* as a prize.[3]

The following morning the prize was sent to Tangier Island, where her cargo would be put to good use in the construction of barracks for the latest Negro recruits and in the fortification works newly dubbed Fort Albion. Aboard the admiral's flagship the mood bordered on the expectant. Action seemed to be in the wind, although no one knew just where or when. Eight runaway slaves were brought aboard, having made their way out to the big warship with some difficulty. They undoubtedly brought with them the usual intelligence concerning American cattle and livestock locations on the mainland, information the British would characteristically put to excellent use. Aboard *Albion,* despite the expectant mood of an impending foray ashore, it was still business as usual. Day-to-day shipboard life went on as always: holystoning the decks, preparing the daily mess, and witnessing disciplinary actions. At noon the Articles of War were read, and one Thomas Harrison, seaman, was punished with twenty-six lashes for disobedience and neglect of duty.[4]

Finally, at 1:00 p.m. on July 4, the anchor was raised and the warship proceeded farther up the bay, finally coming to pause two miles offshore of St. Jerome's Creek. In the evening two armed barges, the ship's launch and gig, were sent ashore to obtain fresh livestock, undoubtedly basing their information of its location on the intelligence recently provided by the runaway slaves. The American families in St. Mary's County had borne much of the brunt of British depredations since the beginning of the enemy's occupation of the Chesapeake, and this evening was to be no exception. The raiders landed their vessels on the bay side of the county and took off sheep and cattle from a number of farms, including those belonging to the Widow Locker, Jenifer Taylor, and John Walsh. The barges returned to their mother ship about nine o'clock with the plunder in hand. Cockburn, however, had long before issued standing orders that all items confiscated, unless outright opposition was encountered, were to be paid for in full. Nearly six hours later the raiding party grudgingly returned to the shore under a white flag. The widow was roused and paid for all her cattle, sheep, and geese, the last article at fifty cents a head. Taylor was then visited and paid off, but "John Walsh," it was later noted, "not being present received no pay." Having already been looted once, Walsh was perhaps understandably unwilling to be present on the enemy's second visit. Nevertheless, the British foragers were skillful at their trade and had managed to secure six large bullocks, a number of sheep, and a quantity of geese for *Albion*'s larders.[5]

With stocks thus temporarily replenished, the flagship and her tender again weighed anchor and began working up the bay against variable winds toward the Patuxent. At noon on July 6 they finally dropped anchor in the river, joining Nourse's blockading squadron.[6]

About the same time Cockburn's foragers were setting out in their boats to raid the Southern Maryland countryside, a very dignified party of gentlemen was sitting down to a sumptuous dinner at McKeowan's Hotel on Pennsylvania Avenue in Washington, not far from the president's house, to celebrate the anniversary of American Independence "in style and spirit worthy of the occasion." The function was presided over by James H. Blake, mayor of the City of Washington, and assisted by Andrew Way and Colonel William Brent. The dignitaries and governmental officialdom were there in full regalia and included such notables as the attorney general, numerous members of Congress, various cabinet heads, the minister of France, and sundry "Strangers of Distinction." After the dessert had been served, the Declaration of Independence was read aloud by General John Mason. The reading was followed by a patriotic poem. Then, accompanied by patriotic strains delivered by the Marine Band of Music, sixteen toasts were raised. The eleventh toast was to the U.S. Navy, "whose thunder has awakened the Leviathan of the Ocean from a century's dream of invincibility."[7]

. . .

On the Patuxent the arrival of Leviathan in the form of HBMS *Albion* did not go unnoticed. Major John H. Briscoe of the St. Mary's County Militia, while stationed near the mouth of the river, had observed the approach of the great man-of-war and her tender and immediately headed off toward Nottingham with the news, arriving there on the evening of July 7. Now, besides the several warships on the river, the enemy reportedly had five schooners, "two of which are the same as heretofore, and three others (smaller) on which they have placed two cannon each." Briscoe also reported the enemy to be very busy "in working upon their launches & barges to fit guns & etc. from which he infers they mean an attack either on the flotilla, or elsewhere."[8]

Had he known, Barney might have taken some consolation in that the enemy had, for a change, been receiving some incorrect intelligence that may have accounted for the massing of forces. A British officer, it was later reported, had come ashore and claimed that it was known for a fact that the American flotilla was laid up, and that the commodore had departed for Baltimore to fit out the squadron lying there. Furthermore, the officer said, men were to be dispatched from Washington to man the commodore's vessels, and artillery was being sent down to be placed on a point of land where the two flotillas, the Baltimore fleet and the Patuxent fleet, were to convene and act in concert against the British. What the enemy had undoubtedly picked up was a muddled sequence of events concerning Rutter's departure to take command of the Baltimore flotilla. Nevertheless, the fact that the enemy knew even that much, had Barney been aware, would have been irritating to the old seadog.[9]

Upon the arrival of *Albion* on the Patuxent, the British proceeded to occupy themselves with taking on and distributing supplies as necessary from one ship to another. On July 7, taking advantage of the flotilla's neutered situation, Captain Brown was ordered to proceed with *Loire* and *St. Lawrence* on a cruise of the upper reaches of the Chesapeake to annoy the infant steamboat operations between Baltimore and Elkton by the steamer *Chesapeake*. Cockburn, who had no intention of staying long, was obviously confident that *Severn* and *Narcissus* would be sufficient to repel any attack or breakout attempt the Americans might make. It is also possible that he may have had some misgivings about Brown's capabilities should such an event occur—especially after the debacle at St. Leonard's Creek—and thus ordered him off on safer errands. If this was the case, however, he kept it to himself.[10]

In the meantime, Cockburn took the first opportunity he could to resupply his ship with water. A party of marines was thus landed soon after the departure of *Loire* and *St. Lawrence* "to reconnoitre and see if water could be procurred [*sic*]." On July 8 an early morning foray, consisting of *Albion's* marines and a hundred able seamen, was dispatched to scour the countryside. The raiders proceeded directly toward the St. Mary's County side of the river. And, as usual, the expedition was conducted without major opposition and only minor nuisance fire from the locals.[11]

The presence of government troops on one's property had long since become a distinct liability in Southern Maryland in view of the British policy of destroying any place foolish enough to offer quarter or aid to such forces. Father Francis X. Neale of the venerable old Catholic church at St. Inigoes, the oldest continuously operating Jesuit mission in English-speaking America, informed the superior at Georgetown College, Father Giovanni Grassi, in a letter dated July 8, of the problems this entailed. It had only recently been proposed by the local county militia commander, Lieutenant Colonel Athanasius Fenwick of the 12th Maryland Regiment, that the Jesuits' farm be employed as a stand for his troops. The priest had flatly opposed the notion. "I am informed," he had written, "that the English did express themselves to this purpose, that as they have never been fired on from this farm, and they understand it belongs to the Church, they will never molest anything on it." If Fenwick's militiamen were permitted to be stationed there, however, it was clear to Father Neale that he would be flirting with destruction.[12]

Cockburn's response to any such actions inimical to his men was indeed predictable. "The other day," he later wrote, regarding the most recent foray into St. Mary's, "two heroes on horseback fired at one of my Lieuts. when on shore and then rode off as hard as they could—I ascertained who they were & where they lived, & that night I sent to their house . . . destroyed every thing belonging to it and brought them & their horses on board." Father Neale's account of Cockburn's watering-cum-reconnaissance expedition and retaliation varied little from the admiral's. "On this day," he recorded, "at a very early hour of the morning, the English visited Mrs. Holton, took her two sons out of bed prisoners of war, kept them standing with no other dress than their linen, while they destroyed everything in the house excepting one looking glass which was begged of them by the youngest child of the family. Mrs. Holton was informed by the commanding officer that those two sons of hers were the cause of all this destruction for firing on the British the evening before. The house was saved from fire by the humble entreaties of Mrs. Holton; her two sons were taken on board by the English." The two brothers were eventually sent down to *Dragon* in Lynnhaven Bay for transshipment as prisoners of war to Halifax.[13]

In the meantime, the search for fresh water had continued. Finally, after locating a promising spot under Drum Point where water might be procured, working parties were sent ashore to dig wells. Numerous parties were thereafter dispatched every day for the next week to continue the work. More than ninety-nine tons of water, "as plentiful & better than at Tangier," was thus secured for the casks of *Albion,* enough for four to six weeks' consumption.[14]

. . .

Barney remained anchored upriver at Nottingham carefully studying his situation and the seemingly nonsensical motions of the American army and the local militia. Colonel Wadsworth and his regulars, he was informed, were now apparently lying in the rear of Benedict, "some say to cover the property of Clemm[ent] Dorsey during his harvest." Likewise, he was told that a body of Calvert County Militia under Colonel Taney, then at Nottingham, had been ordered out and told to proceed to St. Leonard's Creek, of all places. The commodore, never an admirer of the militia, thought even less of Colonel Taney, who he believed "has never done anything, nor do I believe, would, if in his power."[15]

Barney feared, perhaps with some justification, that should Taney's force cross over the Patuxent River, it might not be able to re-cross to defend the now all-important western shore route to the capital. Should the enemy come up and land on the Nottingham side, there would be no land forces to repel them nearer than Benedict to the south, a full day's march. Wadsworth, down at Benedict, would thus be flanked, and the road to Washington would be wide open. It was therefore the commodore's intention, should such an emergency arise, to meet the enemy with his entire force a mile south of the town's ferry landing, where the shores of the river were widest and commanded the narrowest part of the approach. This would permit a massive concentration of fire against a confined portal through which the enemy would be obliged to string out his vessels single-file to pass.[16]

There was, unfortunately, one hitch in the commodore's strategy. There were cliffs on the eastern side of the river, which he knew had to be occupied by troops and artillery. If the enemy managed to obtain possession of these heights with his marines, the flotilla's position at the mouth of the narrows would become untenable. "I do not fear them without troops," Barney contemplated, "but as they seem seriously employed at preparation, I think it very probable that they expect to have some. The troops under Col. Wadsworth can be of no real service at Benedict, or lower down, & even at Lower Marlborough as everything is destroyed below this place & perhaps higher up must be the object."[17]

Barney was soon to have the dubious benefit of a visit from Brigadier General William Henry Winder, the recently appointed commander of the new Tenth Military District, created by order of the War Department in July. Winder had been captured the previous year on the Canadian front and held until early 1814 as a prisoner of war at Quebec. Upon his negotiated release he had returned home to Washington to assume command of the newly created military district, to which President James Madison had appointed him. The district was comprised of the District of Columbia, Maryland, and the Virginia region between the Potomac and Rappahannock rivers. Though he was a native Marylander and an active officer, his appointment was in large measure due to a familial relationship with Levin Winder, the Federalist governor of Maryland, who had been a vigorous opponent to the war. The appointment of William Henry to the command of the upper Tidewater was, in fact, little more than a blatant attempt by the Madison administration, eternally in search of friends, to secure them wherever possible, and in the most propitious manner necessary. The attempt to curry favor with the uncooperative governor had thus resulted in the appointment of his nephew to a command of few regular troops, most of which were shut up in forts, and a mélange of poorly equipped, ill-trained militia, but of considerable strategic and political importance. Quality of leadership had not been a serious consideration, and though the general had achieved some notoriety serving on the Canadian front and was tireless, conscientious, and even zealous, he was at best a mediocre officer. The military district over which he was to exert authority, which had endured enormous devastation from the depredations of the enemy since February 1813, would ultimately suffer the consequences.[18]

With fewer than 500 regulars available in the Tenth Military District, on July 4 the government moved to call up 93,500 militia. However, Winder had been hamstrung from the onset by Secretary of War Armstrong, who prohibited the fielding of any militiamen unless there was imminent danger. And even when peril was clearly illustrated and forces were called for, the turnout was pitifully inadequate. On one occasion, when Governor Winder was requested to field 6,000 Marylanders, fewer than 250 would be in the field under General Winder's control 6 weeks later. Moreover, the general had no authority over any unit until it was formally organized, outfitted, armed, and released to him by the War Department.[19]

Winder held a brief consultation with Barney, during which several relatively unimportant points were discussed. The general, unfortunately, failed to provide the commodore with any insight into his own plans. Nor, apparently, did he seek to examine the commodore's. Despite the new reorganization, it soon became apparent to the commodore that little was likely to change and the flotillamen would have to continue to fend for themselves.[20]

. . .

Sunday, July 10, brought with it an urgent express from Annapolis to the regulars stationed near Benedict. The army, already leisurely moving upriver, was ordered to march immediately to the state capital. The call was in response to enemy warships that had come up from the Patuxent via the bay, namely *Loire* and *St. Lawrence*, and were believed to be menacing the capital of Maryland. Five hundred men were soon on their way, but they had not proceeded more than ten miles before receiving word that a large British force had reportedly visited the shores of Benedict once again. It was said that the enemy were landing no fewer than eight hundred soldiers from a frigate, two small schooners, and six barges. It was also reported that the enemy had ascended as far as the mouth of Hunting Creek. It mattered little to the local citizenry of the upper Patuxent that there were not eight hundred marines or soldiers aboard all of the ships in Cockburn's squadron combined, or that the landing was little more than a myth created in the panic-stricken minds of the few remaining townsfolk in Benedict stemming from the abandonment of their village by the regulars. Nevertheless, being well aware that there was a warehouse at the head of Hunting Creek that could be a likely target, Barney responded with alacrity. Thus, in the early morning darkness, the entire flotilla upped anchor and at 2:00 a.m. began moving south to surprise the enemy. At break of day, three and a half hours later, the fleet reached the creek only to find an empty stretch of river. Barney pressed on for Benedict.

While en route, a gun aboard one of the flotilla vessels, loaded and ready for combat, accidentally discharged. The sound reverberated down the Patuxent Valley and was heard in the town. Upon his arrival at the little river port soon afterward, the commodore learned to his dismay that the enemy had indeed landed the day before with not eight hundred but a hundred men, burned eight hogsheads of tobacco, and carried off several more in a scow brought along for the purpose. They had, in fact, intended on raiding Hunting Creek but had been unable to get up with the schooners, probably because of adverse winds and tide. Unfortunately, they too had heard the report of the accidental gun firing, and within ten minutes the invaders' vessels were under way downriver. The mysteriously large British invasion force was, it seemed, anything but large, but not entirely imaginary![21]

...

On July 14 *Loire* and *St. Lawrence* returned triumphant to the Patuxent from a successful cruise on the upper Chesapeake, in the course of which an even dozen American vessels had been taken as prizes. That same evening Cockburn was notified that several unidentified sails were observed standing up the bay. The following morning he was delighted to note the arrival of the major reinforcement he had been waiting for, 5 warships and 2 transports armed *en flute*, carrying a total of 186 guns and having on board a battalion of 350 marines and a full company of Royal Marine Artillery. The warships proved to be *Asia*, 74, *Regulus*, 44, and *Brune*, 38, accompanied by the long-awaited bomb ship *Aetna*, 8, and sloop-of-war *Manly*, 12. The two warships employed as transports were *Melpomene*, 38, and gun-brig *Thistle*, 12. Though still not adequately equipped to attack and take a major port or city, Cockburn now had both land and sea forces quite sufficient to intensify the level of incursions to something more than mere forays for food, water, and occasional plunder. And his contemplated expeditions would certainly be anything but imaginary. En route up the Chesapeake, in fact, the new arrivals had even got into the full swing of things by landing at Smith Point and burning the lighthouse there and several nearby buildings.[22]

Among other things, the reinforcement brought with it a set of long queries from Admiral Cochrane, the new commander-in-chief of the American Station, who fished for advice on where a major, perhaps decisive, attack might successfully be carried out on the American coast. Many considerations, some mere flights of fancy such as kidnapping the political leaders of the Madison administration, and others of considerably greater merit, had been laid out in detail, aired, and just as abruptly folded up and tucked away. He had yet to learn of the home government's wishes as to target selection or number of troops he would be allocated, but assumed the latter would be substantial. Nevertheless, he informed Cockburn that a strong invasion force would soon be available and wished to know where it might best be employed.

Poring over his maps at Bermuda, Cochrane had vacillated for weeks over what should be the primary target of the invasion force, perhaps as strong as twenty thousand men, be it Philadelphia, Baltimore, Richmond, or Washington. In mid-July he had even toyed with the idea of seizing Block Island in Long Island Sound, landing on Long Island, bombarding Brooklyn, and then capturing New York. Then it was Boston, New York, Philadelphia, and even New Orleans. He mulled over potential landing sites, ranging from New Castle and Chester on the Delaware to the Head of Elk, Baltimore, and Annapolis on the Chesapeake. "If troops arrive soon," he wrote on July 14, "and the point of attack is directed towards Baltimore, I have every prospect of success and Washington will be equally accessible." Yet, he still seemed unable to focus on a single course of action, and began to mention Norfolk and Portsmouth in Virginia, Charleston, South Carolina, and Savannah, Georgia, as other potential first-strike targets. Yet, whatever the British did, it was bound to be with a vengeance. On July 17 Cochrane received a message from Sir George Prevost, in Canada, informing him of American atrocities on the Canadian front, and in particular of the total destruction of the port of Dover. Retaliation was in order, and the admiral issued orders the following day to his captains "to destroy and lay waste such towns and districts upon the coast as you may find assailable." Then, on July 23, he declared that until October all efforts should focus only upon the northern states because of the illness that prevailed in the Chesapeake during the late summer. The following day, immediately after the arrival of Admiral Pulteney Malcolm's fleet and reinforcements from Europe, Portsmouth, New Hampshire, from which the army could be sent to fight its way overland to join General Prevost in Canada, was determined to be his most tempting target of interest—although Rhode Island offered an interesting alternative!²³

Cockburn countered with a confidence nurtured by his own experiences and those of his command in the Tidewater, and provided a specific target and point of invasion and a solid plan. The whole countryside about the Chesapeake, he informed Cochrane, with the exception of a few strong points such as Norfolk, was in a perfectly defenseless state. American morale was almost nonexistent, trade had been brought to a halt, the American treasury was empty, and "in short it is quite impossible for any country to be in a more unfit state for war than this is now." In a top-secret communication dispatched to Bermuda aboard *St. Lawrence* on July 17 he stated: "I feel no hesitation in stating to you that I consider the town of Benedict in the Patuxent, to offer us advantages for this purpose beyond any other spot within the United States . . . Within forty-eight hours after the arrival in the Patuxent of such a force as you expect, the City of Washington might be possessed without difficulty or opposition of any kind."²⁴

Cockburn cited many reasons to justify his selection of invasion sites: the facility and speed such an operation offered; the éclat of seizing the American center of government; the difficulty inherent in any assault attempt against Annapolis or Baltimore, yet the ease with which either might be taken from the main if the capital were secured. "If Washington (as I strongly recommend) be deemed worthy of our first efforts, although our main force should be landed in the Patuxent, yet a tolerably good diversion should at the time be sent up the Potomac with bomb ships & etc. which will tend to distract and divide the enemy, annoy Fort Washington, if it does not reduce it, and will most probably offer other advantages."²⁵

The Patuxent, the admiral pointed out, had finally been sounded as far as Benedict and roughly mapped, and an American pilot secured. With the relatively substantial naval forces at hand already, however, it might be foolhardy for him to remain in that river for long. There was always the danger that the Americans might gauge the true intentions of the British and respond accordingly. Thus, he proposed to proceed to the Potomac with the bulk of his squadron, primarily to allay American suspicions and draw attention to that waterway as the obvious main avenue for invasion. A visit to that river might also serve a useful purpose. Additional soundings could be taken, more data gathered, and a feel for the country entertained in the event that a diversion along this route should become a reality. As the black slave population inclined to join the British was more numerous along the Potomac than anywhere else in the upper Tidewater, the discord such a diversion might sow among the Americans was considerable. Yet, Cockburn's plan, in the final analysis, would never be more than that unless it had the blessings of the commander-in-chief. Convinced that his superior would be of the same mind, he fully intended on paving the way and proceeded to develop a broad format of destruction to mask his true strategy. As for the propriety of using the backdoor to the American capital, the Patuxent River, as the main invasion route, flotilla or no flotilla, Cockburn was smugly certain. It was, he later disclosed to Captain Barrie, "quite ridiculous the perfect dominion we have from the entrance of this river to Benedict—Mr. Maddison [*sic*] must certainly be either in confident expectation of immediate peace, or preparing to abdicate his chair."[26]

...

After Captain Skene of *Asia* was ordered down to Lynnhaven Bay, Virginia, to relieve *Dragon,* on blockade duty at the mouth of the Chesapeake, and *St. Lawrence* was hustled off to Bermuda with the critical proposal and other dispatches for Cochrane, Cockburn turned his full attention to implementing the first stage of his scheme.[27] The foray into the Potomac would, of course, embarrass and, perhaps, even terrify the Madison administration. It would certainly do much to further alienate the local Southern Maryland population from the government in Washington. And it would, of course, also greatly enrich the admiral's own coffers with prize money from captured tobacco and shipping. He even considered getting in a few licks against the obstreperous Virginians while he was at it.

To mask his intentions, Cockburn divided his fleet into two squadrons, one commanded by Captain Nourse, in *Severn,* and the other by himself, in *Albion.* The admiral's squadron would head for the Potomac. Nourse would be left in the Patuxent to maintain the blockade and carry on depredations as usual. To keep the Americans off balance, he was ordered to proceed immediately up the river with *Brune, Aetna, Manly,* and *Severn* "for the purpose of endeavouring to surprise & get possession of a store called Wilkinson's Store above Benedict where articles of considerable value are supposed to be deposited." He was then to bring off all stores possible, destroy the remainder, and cause "the enemy any other arrogance" that he might find practicable. After completion of the raid, he was to return to his anchorage under Drum Point and dispatch *Aetna* to the admiral with a full account of the expedition.

The remaining ships under his command were to stay under Drum Point and maintain a strict blockade "to prevent the possibility of the escape of [the] flotilla now shut up in the river."[28]

Cockburn's last order to Nourse was perhaps the most interesting. "You are to encourage," he directed, "by all possible means the emigration of negroes from the United States and you are to send all coloured emigrants you procure from the shore either to me or to Tangier Island. You are likewise to procure as many people as possible likely to prove useful as guards during our future operations on land in this part of the United States & are at liberty to promise them (if found competent) a regular stipend of 10s/ per day whilst employed in our service."[29]

Both Cochrane and Cockburn were cognizant of the importance of slave labor to the economic stability of Maryland and Virginia, as they were of the willingness of the slaves to fight when given the opportunity. One of Cockburn's officers, casually noting that many blacks frequently took advantage of British raiding forays to escape with their entire families, proclaimed their motivations to be quite clear. "Some of their first exclamations," he pointed out, "were 'me free man, me got cut massa's throat, give me musket,' which many of them did not know how to use when they had it." In order that they be given a chance to learn their use, however, the British, eternally short of manpower, had proceeded to induct and train as many blacks for military duty as possible. Most received their training at Tangier Island. Those found competent were inducted into the new Colonial Corps, the black marine unit that, though small, had been employed with considerable effect since spring.[30]

Some British officers were outraged at the very hypocrisy of the American concept of freedom, which flagrantly ignored the institution of slavery, although these same officers failed to note similar inequities in their own colonial system that girdled the entire earth. "Republicans," wrote one ardent critic, "are certainly the most cruel masters, and the greatest tyrants in the world toward their fellow man. They are urged by the most selfish motives to reduce every one to a level with, or even below themselves, and to grind and degrade those under them to the lowest stage of human wretchedness. But American liberty consists in oppressing the blacks beyond what other nations do, enacting laws to prevent their receiving instruction, and working them worse than a donkey—'But you call this a free country—when I can't shoot my nigger when I like, eh?'"[31]

Both Cochrane's and Cockburn's motives, however, lay not in the pros and cons governing the philosophy of the institution of slavery, but in the simple military expediency of manpower requirements. Simply put, with their army tied up in the war against Napoleon in Europe, the British lacked a sufficient land force suitable to conduct serious operations ashore in America. They could dominate the seas, but without land forces they could only hope to intimidate the Americans.

Cochrane was eager to employ blacks in any way feasible. As late as July 1 he had written Cockburn informing him that the main reasons for conducting forays ashore should be to support the escape of black slaves seeking British protection. "Let the landings you may make," he advised him, "be more for the protection of the desertion of the black population than with a view to any other advantage, the force you have is too small to accomplish an object of magnitude—the great point to be attained is the cordial support of the black population. With them properly armed & backed with 20,000 British troops, Mr. Madison will be hurled from his throne." Properly armed and trained, he even envisioned a Black Legion of Horse that could prove a strong asset to His Majesty's efforts against America. "The blacks are all good horsemen," he assured Cockburn, "and thousands will join upon their masters horses," and would require only to be clothed and accoutered, under good officers "to bring them into a little regularity." The fact that Cockburn lacked proper uniforms, accoutrements, or horses, seems not to have entered the equation.[32]

Unfortunately for the British, most of the slaves who escaped to the security of the Royal Navy were not found suitable for induction into the Colonial Corps and proved a considerable burden on the limited resources then available to Cockburn. They had to be fed, clothed, and housed, and there seemed to be three blacks unsuitable for military duty for every one inducted into service. Ultimately, the bulk of the freed slaves, between 1,500 and 2,000, would be shipped off to Halifax, Nova Scotia, where they suffered inordinate privations and death in the unfriendly climate, or to Trinidad, off the South American coast, where they would be given land in what would one day be called "company towns." Yet, the service of those who enlisted in the six companies of His Majesty's Colonial Corps of Marines would indeed prove an invaluable asset to British efforts in the Chesapeake Theater for the duration of the war.[33]

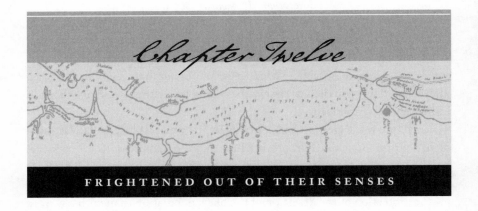

Chapter Twelve

FRIGHTENED OUT OF THEIR SENSES

The Patuxent arm of Cockburn's twin expeditions was soon under way. Nourse quickly had his squadron in motion upriver. There were to be depredations as usual, but not dangerous enough to alarm Washington. The first thrust was to be against the old county seat of Calvert County, the ancient town of Calverton, once known as Battle Town, which lay on the flat north shore floodplain abreast of the entrance to Battle Creek. The town was the first colonial urban settlement and the earliest civil center to be established on the Patuxent, dating from about 1669. Though now little more than a few random buildings, perhaps a storehouse or two, and some simple dwellings, the site was nevertheless considered important enough for Nourse to expend time and energy in destroying it. Interestingly, no effort whatsoever was taken to burn or plunder the great estate of Colonel Taney on the nearby slope that overlooked the town. After the usual arson, the British continued their advance up the river to Sheridan's Point, and the following day to Gods Grace Point, burning and plundering all the way. On the evening of Sunday, July 17, Nourse led three hundred men ashore at Gods Grace and proceeded on a forced march of seven miles with the intention of burning the tobacco warehouse at Huntingtown, at the head of Hunting Creek. The town was taken completely by surprise. The British promptly and efficiently commenced setting afire the warehouse and, lacking adequate water carriage to haul it off, the 130 hogsheads of tobacco within. The flames, unfortunately, spread from the warehouse to the houses of the town. Unrestrained by the hand of man, the blaze raced out of control, and within a short time the village was entirely consumed. The invaders returned by the same road whence they had come that evening. At Gods Grace they demanded twenty hogsheads of tobacco belonging to a Mr. Billingsley, a tenant farmer on the estate of the late George Mackall, and then proceeded to destroy much of the Gods Grace plantation itself. After leaving three hogsheads to an overseer or tenant of one Doctor Bell, they re-embarked aboard their boats with thirteen hogsheads of tobacco as their reward.[1]

...

The 36th and 38th Infantry Regiments, after the Second Battle of St. Leonard's Creek, had leisurely moved upriver, abandoning their positions near that waterway to cross over and take up another adjacent to the nearly deserted village of Benedict on the opposite side of the river. By Friday, July 8, they were at the Tanyard, near Nottingham, ostensibly, it is presumed, to protect Barney's flank and the road to Washington. Soon afterward they had received orders to march to the South River on Chesapeake Bay, below Annapolis. The Severn–South River region had only recently been threatened by *Loire* and *St. Lawrence*, a move by the British that nurtured a pet theory of General Winder's that the Maryland state capital was to be next on Cockburn's menu. The general was now in personal command of the two regiments, and, concerned for the safety of Annapolis, he ordered his men to march to its defense. On the evening of July 8 the general lodged in Upper Marlboro, and the following morning rode on ahead of his troops to the plantation of a certain Mrs. Berry at the head of South River. It was his intention to fix upon a spot at which a campsite might be established. On his return to Upper Marlboro, he received an urgent express informing him of the enemy's reinforcement on the Patuxent and Nourse's subsequent advance up the river. The artillery, which had just come up from Nottingham, was ordered back. The general and his aide set off immediately for the endangered town.[2]

Winder lingered about Nottingham for nearly a week, undoubtedly attempting to monitor Nourse's motions. At noon on July 15, dispatches reached Upper Marlboro from Winder calling upon General Stephen West of the Prince George's County Militia to assemble his entire brigade and march the whole force down to Nottingham. Another express reached the capital the same evening informing the War Department of the situation. Hot on the heels of Winder's orders to General West, another dispatch from Colonel Taney in Calvert County arrived in Upper Marlboro. Taney requested any and all aid West could afford to oppose the landing of a large force of horse and light artillery at Point Patience.[3]

West ignored Taney's plea, which was of questionable veracity since the enemy possessed no cavalry, but ordered his men to Nottingham. His brigade was composed of all of the Prince George's County Militia, a battalion of

the Montgomery County Militia, and Captain John C. Herbert's Bladensburg Troop of Horse. The District Volunteers, again called up by the War
Department, were slower to respond on this occasion than they had been
during earlier emergencies, and it was not until noon on Tuesday, July 19,
that they had formed to march. This time the District dispatched Davidson's
Light Infantry, Burch's Artillery, which were without swords as sidearms,
and Doughty's Rifles, which were armed with defective rifles, to join Winder
at Nottingham.[4]

As General West mustered his troops, Upper Marlboro throbbed with an
excitement heavily laced with pungent rumors. Occasionally, threads of fact
could be discerned amidst all the talk, but it took a bit of doing. Enemy barges, it was noted in one unverified report, had again reached as high as Lower
Marlboro, but Barney remained undisturbed in repose barely two miles above,
at White's Landing. The enemy, another report stated, had landed in Calvert
County with 1,500 men, put Huntingtown warehouse to the torch, and was
on the march toward Nottingham. Still other rumors had it that the Calvert
County Court House at Prince Frederick had been captured and burned by
only fifteen men. The enemy had then been allowed to return to their vessels
entirely without molestation by the local militia.[5]

Whatever the truth was, and the last report was quite prescient, the British
in the Patuxent were again causing considerable embarrassment to Washington and the State of Maryland. Jonathan, it seemed, was indeed still quite
befuddled.

. . .

If Colonel Taney wasn't exactly certain about just what the enemy was up
to, or what exactly to do about it, he certainly wasn't shy in continuing to request that reinforcements be sent to prevent the unforeseen from happening.
If General Winder wouldn't help, perhaps Governor Winder, the general's
uncle, would! Taney pleaded that more militia were needed. Within a short
time, Captain John Hall's troop of horse and Captain Jacob Franklin's militia
unit from Anne Arundel County had been called up and ordered to attach
themselves to the colonel's forces in Calvert County. These ill-trained and un-
ready citizen-soldiers were instructed to march from the outskirts of Annapolis to Sheridan's Point, where they would take up post on the plantation of one
Dr. John Gray, who had abandoned his home at the first sight of the British
squadron passing up toward Gods Grace. That Sheridan's Point should be
occupied made some military sense. In describing the area, William Wood,

a neighbor of Doctor Gray's, pointed out: "There is a very high eminence on this farm, (perhaps more so than any on the Patuxent river), which afforded a full view of the movements of the enemy, and from which our army kept a look-out, and could observe the British spying on our men." Moreover, the river channel passed within only a "few steps of the shore," making the spot a strategic choke point on the waterway. Upon their arrival, the Anne Arundel officers were ordered by the colonel to occupy the recently vacated Gray home for accommodations (without the doctor's permission), while their men were to find shelter in the kitchen (a separate outbuilding), and the four slave quarters, overseer's house, and barns on the farm.[6]

At first the quartermaster for Hall's men, Richard B. Watts, was able to provide ample rations of fresh food, salted pork, and beef for the troops, and grain, hay, and fodder for the horses. "Our meat," recalled Rezin Hammond, one of the Anne Arundel cavalrymen, "was cooked in doctor Gray's kitchen. We had free access to the buildings for our accommodation, and out-houses for our horses. We occupied them day and night."[7]

Taney made no effort to conceal his presence at Sheridan's Point, passing and repassing with his officers on horseback through the fields of the farm, and daily parading his troopers and those from Anne Arundel on the grounds at and near the house, sometimes in full view of the passing enemy shipping. Captain John G. Mackall's troop of Calvert County cavalry and other units of the county militia soon joined the growing force bivouacked on the rambling plantation estate.[8]

Captain Mackall was no stranger to the Gray plantation. His brother James G. Mackall lived on a farm adjoining the good doctor's property and had somehow managed to extract a promise, presumably in exchange for provisions or livestock when Nourse had landed earlier upriver, to protect his own estate. Ironically, the captain's own home at Hallowing Point had already succumbed to the enemy's fire and sword for even temporarily housing soldiers, and he was undoubtedly aware of the danger to the Gray holdings should the enemy decide to set another example. He may have been somewhat concerned, upon his arrival at the point, when he found that, unlike the Anne Arundel men, no rations for his troopers had been provided. He may have been further disturbed to discover another detachment already engaged, as per Taney's direct orders, in scavenging provisions for the regiment from the doctor's farm, and food for their horses from his stables and yard, as there was "no other place being near where we could get supplied." It began to appear to some that the Calvert County Militia and its colonel, who some believed was trading with the enemy to protect his own estate, were now little better than the marauding British![9]

...

On Sunday morning, July 17, Barney received word of the British movement up the river and immediately dropped the flotilla down to a convenient place below Nottingham to meet an expected attack. Throughout the day, he later informed Jones, "I received fifty different accounts of the movements of the enemy but none agreeing." With an unfavorable flood tide running and a wind blowing hard from the south, against which it was impossible to row or sail, it was perhaps fortunate the enemy had not chosen to assail the flotilla. Unable to take offensive measures, which would have been suicide in any event, the commodore could do little more than fume. No news was to be relied upon. Owing to the panic in the countryside, he had been unable to procure a single horse to go downriver to investigate. Moreover, he complained, "I cannot trust one of my officers for he would be betrayed by our internal foes." And without a small, fast gig or whaleboat to send down river for covert reconnaissance he was without eyes.[10]

...

July 18 was too rainy for Nourse to undertake operations but the steady drizzle failed to dampen the spirits of his men. On the following evening they were still eager for action and the captain decided on another landing. After a forced march of nine miles they reached the town of Prince Frederick, county seat of Calvert County. Upon arriving at their destination, they encountered a strong force of local militia that, true to form, provided little opposition. Nourse proceeded on with his business of destruction, and later reported of the raid: "I landed and marched nine miles to a place called the Court House in the County of Calvert denominated by the Americans a town and where the assizes are held—burnt the Court House and jail releasing one black man confined for endeavouring to escape to us—returned by the same road and re-embarked every one by four o'clock the same evening."[11] A tobacco warehouse, and the home belonging to Barney's purser, John Stuart Skinner, known as The Reserve, were also put to the torch. With the destruction of the court-house (which had been employed to house some military sick and wounded, and as a naval storehouse), unfortunately, many of the county records, some dating back to the earliest colonial times, were consumed. The countryside was driven into a panic-stricken frenzy. Rumors and alarms abounded. "The people," Barney noted, "are all frightened out of their senses running about the country like so many mad people."[12]

It has been stated by some historians that the British were driven from Prince Frederick and, realizing that they could expect little success in further forays, retreated posthaste down the Patuxent to Point Patience to await reinforcements. Such statements are grossly incorrect. In fact, Captain Nourse expanded upon the leeway in his orders to cause the Americans as much "arrogance" as possible. On the day following the attack on Prince Frederick he landed his forces two miles below Benedict, on the St. Mary's shore, probably in the vicinity of Trent Hall, and destroyed warehouses some four miles inland containing twenty-nine hogsheads of tobacco, and then carried off ten more found hidden in the woods. The raid was later reported in full in the Baltimore *Federal Republican:*

> The sailors were armed with boarding pikes and cutlasses (for the cavalry). They ascended into the country in quest of a quantity of tobacco, and other property belonging to Mr. W. Kilgour, which he had removed about three miles to a Mr. Alvey's, as a place of safety. The property was in a barn and covered with Alvey's wheat, this they deliberately removed for some time; they at length became tired and rolled out four hogsheads of tobacco, which they gave Alvey as an equivalent for the remaining wheat and a saddle they took from him—the barn was then burnt with all the tobacco. They then under the direction of a negro of Mr. Kilgour's, who had gone to them, patiently selected the bacon and other things . . . They found eight hogsheads of tobacco concealed in the woods near the water, which they carried off with a great deal of stock. Mr. Kilgour's loss is ruinous. As soon as General [Philip] Stuart received intelligence that the enemy were landing, he moved with his whole force in pursuit of them. He arrived at High Hill where he saw the enemy's barges prepared to cover the retreat of the men over the plain, and a frigate with her broadside ready for the same object. He could not receive any intelligence of the course they had taken till it was disclosed by the smoke ascending from Alvey's barn. To get between them and their shipping must necessarily have exposed his force to a galling fire from their shipping, and give their infantry the advantage of a high commanding situation; to get in their front, as to annoy them in their retreat, he must have taken a circuitous route of seven miles. Independent of all this, his force was much inferior to that of theirs; he therefore returned to his encampment; he has ordered out all of his brigade.[13]

As if the descent on Calvert and Charles had not been enough, a day or two later, a British deserter from *Severn* managed to come ashore in St. Mary's and brought the commodore even more disturbing information. The enemy's objectives, he said, were simply to plunder the shores of as much tobacco and slaves as possible, which was bad enough. But the most distressing news was that when they marched on Calvert County Courthouse, Nourse had been provided with horses for himself and his officers by none other than Michael Taney, the commander of the Calvert County Militia, by whom "they were well received and treated." In return, Taney was given "a written protection" that assured the survival of his plantation, less than a mile above Battle Creek and the smoldering ashes of old Calverton. The protection, however, had apparently not ensured that his slaves would remain, for every Negro on the estate had voluntarily run off to join the British.[14]

Nourse and Company had apparently moved down just ahead of the commodore. One of the probable reasons Barney had not responded to the enemy incursions before this time was that he had been seriously ill from constant exposure for three or four days with "hardly enough strength to keep up." It is possible he had contracted the flu or measles, both of which were reportedly passing among the citizenry of Nottingham. And it is also a possibility that he had simply dismissed the notice of Nourse's approach as another rumor, or even a fabrication of some Federalist designed to send him off on another pointless expedition downriver. "There are so many individuals that make it their business to give false and alarming news," he complained, "that we cannot believe any thing we hear."[15]

On the same day that Barney had moved down from Nottingham, Captain Nourse intended on dropping even farther down the Patuxent, but, finding the winds adverse, landed his marines instead, this time on both sides of the river, to conduct their usual business. The following morning, Friday, the squadron came to off Sandy Point and dropped anchor. Here in the vicinity, they had learned, were a number of undisturbed warehouses. The marines were again landed, marched five miles inland, and destroyed one warehouse containing twelve hogsheads of tobacco. For want of a conveyance, they were able to bring off only five.[16]

In the course of their pillaging expeditions, the British had managed to obliterate all evidence of a number of sizeable plantations and private estates situated along the banks of the river. Among these, of course, had been the estate of the late George Mackall at Gods Grace, which had been employed by Colonel Taney as a headquarters for militia units stationed in the Hunting Creek area.[17] Nor had the estate of Dr. John Gray at Sheridan's Point escaped their less than temperate attentions.

...

On his return downriver, Nourse paid one final visit to the shores of Calvert County. Observing the Gray plantation and its surrounding environs on the point clearly occupied by an apparently sizeable body of American light infantry and cavalry posted there, he ordered his ships to anchor opposite the farm. Within minutes *Severn*'s guns had opened fire and landing parties were sent toward the shore. Gray's overseer, William G. Jones, who had remained on the farm during Taney's occupation, later reported that the British "seemed to be much enraged, and commenced a heavy fire from the fleet at our light horse, who retreated from behind a hill."[18]

Captain Franklin immediately gave the order for his troop of horse to retire and to offer no resistance, "as the British showed signs of landing, and our force being incompetent to defend themselves." As the British barges shoved off with three or four hundred men, a virtual firestorm of between five and six hundred shots from the shipping drove the Americans helter-skelter from the plantation houses and surrounding terrain and into the countryside without receiving a single shot in response (see note 18: 5, 14, 20).

Immediately upon landing, the British made Overseer Jones a prisoner. After roughing him up a bit, they demanded information. Were there troops, they asked, behind the hills and hiding in wait in the pines? Jones replied in the negative, which failed to satisfy his inquisitors. The ships' fire was then redirected toward the hill, even as orders were circulated among the troops still landing to scour the pines (5, 10).

Disappointed that the Americans had again run off instead of offering a fight, the invaders began searching the houses for physical proof of military occupation. As the pillaging of the estate began, a military canteen was found. A gleeful soldier promptly placed it on his bayonet, raised it in the air, and shouted triumphantly to one of the officers: "We have found them out; their militia has been stationed here." If further justification for burning the estate was called for, it was provided soon afterward by a slave named Bill who had escaped from his masters. Erroneously believing that the farm belonged to Captain James Gray, he informed the British that it was indeed the property of an American military officer. At this, the British "appeared much exasperated, and gave orders to their men to fire the buildings." Overseer Jones was given one hour to remove his belongings, after which his own dwelling would be destroyed (10, 11, 14).

As one body of invaders saw to the destruction of the plantation—a dwelling, two tobacco houses, four slave quarters, the overseer's house, a corn house, and several outhouses, including the kitchen—another commenced methodically looting everything of use or interest. A supply of cedar timber was removed from one of the barns, 600 bushels of oats, 1,300 bushels of wheat, all of the vegetable stores, 26 cattle, 50 sheep, 40 hogs, and most of the household furniture was carried down to the waterside for transport to the ships. The corn crop, some of which had just been harvested, was taken off while the remainder in the fields was set alight. In all, over $5,000 in property was destroyed or pillaged within but a few hours (5, 10, 12, 14).

...

On July 23, finally glutted with the successes of their incendiarism and having sounded out the river as far as possible, Nourse and company finally dropped down to Drum Point. The captain had been unable to secure positive information regarding Barney, and that which he had obtained was questionable. He believed the flotilla was ensconced as high up the river as possible, and was supported ashore by as many as three thousand troops, which of course was far from the truth. Nevertheless, the product of his recent raids along the Patuxent Valley had been absolutely devastating to the Americans. He reported to Cockburn that "the people on either side of the Patuxent are in the greatest alarm and consternation many are moving entirely away from both Calvert & St. Mary's, and I think in a short time they will be nearly deserted." Those few inhabitants that remained on their farms and plantations had been almost entirely deserted by their slaves, most of whom had come over to the British. From the Plater plantation alone, on the St. Mary's shore opposite the mouth of St. Leonard's Creek, no less than thirty-nine black men, women, and children had come out to Nourse's squadron on the night of July 22 seeking freedom or to take up arms against their former masters. Unfortunately for the recruiters attempting to enlarge the ranks of the black Colonial Corps, out of the many Negro refugees being taken under the British wing, the greatest proportion were still women and children. It was a certainty, however, that "there would be no getting the men without receiving them." As for the American militia, it seemed that their main objective was to keep a respectable distance from the invaders.[19]

The captain was generous in his praise of the officers in his command. He could afford to be, since little opposition had been raised against any of his landings. "In all these operations," he reported with magnanimity, "I have been attended by Captain Kenah and Badcock and my first Lieutenant Mr. Gammon and received every assistance from their zeal and activity. I also find

Captain Cole commanding the detachment of marines a most zealous good officer."

Elated with the damage inflicted on the Americans, Cockburn later bragged about the ease with which such operations had been carried out but complained of an almost embarrassment of riches and lack of means to carry it off. "We go on here very prosperous by and pleasantly. We only want vessels to put our captured goods in for want of which much of the value is destroyed."[20]

. . .

Two days after returning to Drum Point, Nourse's squadron experienced one of the most frightening episodes of the campaign, not at the hands of the American flotilla, but at those of Mother Nature. As was common during the Tidewater summers, July 24 and the morning of July 25 had been extraordinarily close and sultry, indeed even stultifying. About midday on the latter, the sky rapidly filled with enormous black cumulus clouds blown in from the northwest. The storm that followed struck with incredible violence, with vivid flashes of lightning and loud claps of thunder punctuating its intensity. Its force was such that one of the frigates heeled over so far that her main gun deck nearly touched the water. A seventy-ton schooner, tender to *Severn*, with a long 18-pounder on board and at full anchor near the frigate, without topmasts, her sails furled and gaffs on deck, was suddenly capsized and turned bottom upwards. One man was drowned. Clinging to their seemingly puny craft, the British sailors watched in awe as immense trees along the nearby shoreline were torn up by their roots and barns collapsed without warning. In the water all that stood in the path of the suddenly voracious current was swept away or consumed.[21]

Amazingly, the fury of the blow was spent in less than ten minutes. "Trees and other things continued to be swept by us for some time," recalled one naval officer years later, "and when the tornado was over, we observed, at a turn of the river, so much large timber, lumber, and other articles floating down with the tide, that my gallant senior officer Capt. N[ourse] thought at first it was the American flotilla coming to attack us, and he was just on the point of returning to his ship to prepare for a fight, he having come on board to dine with me, when I discovered by means of a spy glass, the approaching flotilla was perfectly harmless."[22]

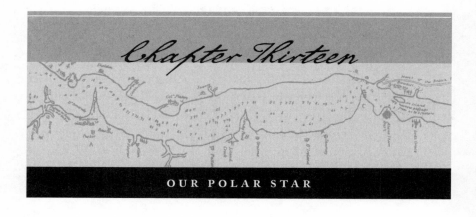

Admiral Cockburn prepared his diversionary incursions against the towns and plantations along the lower Potomac River with measured vigor. "I am myself with the rest of the force going into the Potowmac & after making a flourish or two there, sacking Leonards Town &c," he informed Captain Barrie, "I shall again move elsewhere, so as to distract Jonathan, do him all the mischief I can and yet not allow him to suspect that a serious and permanent landing is intended any where." He began by issuing fresh provisions and livestock to the various vessels of his squadron. The livestock, primarily cattle, had been captured during raids in and about the Maryland countryside, though *Albion*'s log attested to the fact that much of it had been "purchased by Mr. Williamson the Purser upon order of Rear Admiral Cockburn." The admiral's own flagship was now well supplied with sixty-three tons of fresh water and an extra complement of Royal Marines.[1]

Cockburn's squadron raised anchor in the Patuxent at 4:50 p.m. on July 16. Although *St. Lawrence* was obliged to sail for Bermuda the next day with the top-secret dispatches for Cochrane, and a tender called *Resolution* was ordered down to Tangier Island to deposit a large party of runaway slaves recently transferred from *Severn*, the admiral still had a formidable force on hand. And with Barney blockaded in the upper Patuxent by Nourse, the admiral would enjoy free rein on the Potomac. His force now consisted of *Albion, Loire, Regulus, Melpomene,* and *Thistle,* and a flotilla of tenders and barges, as well as the battalion of marines and marine artillery recently arrived and under the command of one Major George Lewis.[2]

. . .

The British departure from the Patuxent was closely watched; but as always, rumor reached the surrounding countryside well before the fact. The citizens of St. Mary's County were well aware that the enemy was preparing to move, not only on the Patuxent but possibly also to the Potomac as well. On Sunday, July 17, at the Jesuit Mission on St. Inigoes Creek, a diminutive but delightful little tributary of the St. Mary's River, Father Neale noted with justifiable apprehension the arrival of the enemy reinforcement on the Patuxent the preceding Thursday. It was obvious that British intentions were less than amicable, and despite the invader's assurances church property would not be harmed, the priest was deeply concerned. "I have made up my mind," he at last informed Father Grassi in Georgetown, "to move our stock, I mean our sheep and cattle, as they are a temptation if they remain here." Many in the hitherto untouched sectors of the county were soon following the priest's example, and with good reason.[3]

Sometime between nine and ten o'clock in the morning, Father Neale was in the midst of a church service when he received word that the enemy had just landed at the mouth of the Patuxent on the St. Mary's shore and was marching down in the direction of Point Lookout. "I was informed of the report," he noted, "while hearing confessions. I said Mass and gave them a few words of counsel to return home and keep their families quietly together; that if the enemy should pass, to behave with civility and keep to their houses. After sometime I found the report to be false." Yet, a visceral fear had already begun to grip the towns, hamlets, and farms all along the Potomac shores of the county. The enemy was on the move yet again.[4]

. . .

At Point Lookout Thomas Swann watched from his post on the isolated, mosquito-ridden tongue of sand projecting into the conflux of bay and river, meticulously recording and reporting to the War Department every arrival and departure of enemy shipping on the central Chesapeake. Day in and day out the astute coast watcher remained, usually with little to convey to Washington. July 18 was to be different. "This morning," he wrote hurriedly, "at 8 a.m. the fleet made sail with two 74s, one of which is the *Albion*, Admiral Cockburn, two frigates, one brig, a large topsail schooner, and seven smaller vessels, [and] shaped their course for the Potomac; the remainder of the fleet proceeded down the Bay."[5]

Cockburn's arrival on the Patuxent had stirred up considerable unrest in Washington, as had every operation the British undertook on that river, and numerous "erroneous and exaggerated reports had been circulated" as a result.[6] Now, with his sudden and unexpected movement to the Potomac, a fresh round of speculation was entertained, including some that Washington itself was again being threatened.

Attempting to downplay the danger, one armchair strategist at the *Daily National Intelligencer* in the capital wrote:

> The British squadron recently in the bay, availing itself of its wings, moves about from point to point, from river to river, and by this frequent motion induces a belief that there is more than one such squadron in the Bay. The enemy has probably now entered the Potomac for the purpose of watering only, as he has very few small vessels with him, and cannot ascend the river higher than Laidler's ferry even in the smallest of his vessels. The force now in the Potomac is evidently the same whose appearance (on Saturday and Sunday) in such force in the mouth of the Patuxent, caused the late requisition from the District, and the call for the militia of Prince George's and Charles counties. The force of the enemy and of its means of offense being now better understood, we hope to hear that our troops are speedily recalled to their families, whose apprehensions have been, as we think, rather unnecessarily excited on the present occasion.[7]

By 1:00 p.m. on July 18, Cockburn's squadron had already entered the Potomac and by evening had come to anchor southeast of the entrance to Breton Bay. Preparations for an attack on Leonardtown, county seat of St. Mary's County, were immediately undertaken. The admiral, it would soon become apparent, was after more than just fresh water, as he had been informed that the town "has many valuable stores deposited in it and principally belongs to people of the democratic faction."[8]

The admiral had certain intelligence that besides the sizeable supply of stores, an American regiment, believed to be the 36th Infantry, was stationed in the town. The squadron was therefore anchored as near as possible to the mouth of the little bay to minimize the distance the small craft would be obliged to travel. At 8:30 p.m. all of the armed boats, with the marines and marine artillery, were sent to assemble on *Loire*. A little over three hours later, having reconnoitered the waterway, Cockburn and his men shoved off for Breton Bay, fully prepared for action.[9]

At 2:00 a.m. on Tuesday, July 19, the "Battalion of marines, boats and tenders and the admiral proceeded up Leonards Creek [Breton Bay]." The sloop-of-war *Thistle* followed to provide whatever heavy gun support might be needed and to secure the retreat. At first light the troops landed near Newtown, a modest hamlet not far from the county seat, formed, and commenced their march.[10] That evening Cockburn reported in full to Admiral Cochrane the proceedings of the expedition:

At dawn of day the marines were put on shore at some distance from the town, and I directed Major Lewis to march round and attack it from the land side whilst the boats pulled up to it from the front. The enemy however, on discovering us, withdrew whatever armed force he had in the place and permitted us to take quiet possession of it. I found here a quantity of stores belonging to the 36th Regiment and a number of arms of different descriptions all of which were destroyed; a quantity of tobacco, flour, provisions and other articles likewise found in the town I caused to be shipped and brought away in the boats and schooner which we took laying off it. This occupied us the most of the day during the whole of which not a musket was fired at us nor indeed a single armed American discovered, in consequence of which conduct on the part of the enemy I deemed it prudent to spare the town, which we quitted in the evening and returned to the squadron without having sustained accident of any kind.[11]

In fact, several casualties were sustained. Three marines, all under the direction of Major Lewis, had been seriously injured during a boating accident on the return trip to the fleet. But the booty brought off more than made up for such incidents. Two small schooners, seventy hogsheads of tobacco, twenty barrels of flour, and forty stand of arms "which the enemy left behind they flying into the woods" were carried off to the waiting fleet. The brief stay of the invaders had not, in fact, been garnished with the usual incendiarism owing to the pacific reception they encountered. Indeed, it was later reported they behaved with the greatest politeness to the ladies and, by some accounts, respected private property where the proprietors had remained at home. Not everyone's property, public or private, however, was left untouched. A hundred barrels of supplies for Carberry's regiment, and the furniture, clothing, and bedding of Captains James Forrest, of the local cavalry, and Enoch J. Millard, of the county militia, were robbed. A stand of state-owned muskets, "only fit to stick frogs with," were discovered and broken to pieces. The town store, belonging to one Roger B. Haislip, was sacked of goods valued at $1,200 to $1,500. The county courthouse, however, had only been saved from being set alight by the intervention of two ladies, a Mrs. Thompson, and Miss Eliza Key, who persuaded the admiral that the building was also used as a place of divine worship.[12]

A visitor to the town the following day reported of the raid that

every housekeeper was plundered except one—to the Court House they did great injury; not a sash of glass but what they destroyed; much of the inside work cut to pieces, all the tobacco, about 70 hhds. carried off, and property belonging to individuals and the United States, to the amount of 4,000 dollars. Although [Rear]

Admiral [George] Cockburn gave to some of the inhabitants a guard, yet his men plundered almost within reach of the guard's muskets. The admiral and his officers, I hear, conducted themselves politely to a Mr. Key and his daughter, and to most of the inhabitants; in this way they were honorably remunerated for the loss and destruction to their property—no houses were burnt.[13]

Cockburn was, of course, full of praise for the conduct of his men. "I feel myself under much obligation for the zeal manifested on this occasion, and the assistance afforded me by Captain Brown of the *Loire,* who had the general superintendence of the naval operations, and by Captains Ramsay of the *Regulus,* and Rowley of the *Melpomene,* and Lieutenant Urmston 1st. [lieutenant] of this ship (acting as captain of her) who each commanded a division of the boats, and the several officers and men employed under them behaved to my entire satisfaction."[14]

...

The British campaign of depredation against Southern Maryland and American fear, inability, or reluctance to counter it was having a telling effect. Many of the citizens of the region were growing increasingly exasperated, blaming the president himself "for leaving them to their exposed situation." One letter from Leonardtown, extremely critical of the U.S. government, later reprinted in *The Times* of London, noted that the consternation and suffering of the people "are only exceeded by the high stock of irritable sensibility discovered by all classes of citizens, of whatever party, with scarcely an exception, whenever Madison or Barney's name is mentioned. The dethroned tyrant [Napoleon] is scarcely more excepted by the people of Paris, Lyon, or Bordeaux, then our President is by the good people of Calvert, Charles, and St. Mary's. Curses are poured upon him daily by thousands of mouths, for bringing the enemy upon them without affording protection."[15]

...

General Winder was unable to make up his mind just what to do about the dual incursions against Southern Maryland. Characteristically, he decided to do nothing. By the 21st of July the District Volunteers were encamped near the Woodyard, fourteen or fifteen miles from Washington, "in a position from which they can, at two hours notice, reach the banks of the Patuxent and Potomac, as either may be menaced." The grounds upon which the camp was situated were described as delightful, and it was generally expected that the volunteers would remain there unless the enemy directly threatened the capital or Annapolis. Yet no one seemed to know where Winder was from one moment to the next; nor was anyone sure where either the 36th or the 38th Regiments, continually moving about, were to be stationed. It was rumored in some circles that the general's headquarters were to be established on the east bank of the Patuxent, and that a reinforcement of 2,000 volunteers from Baltimore was expected to be acting in concert with him. But nothing was certain. In truth, the general had finally been authorized by the War Department on July 17 to call up 5,000 Pennsylvanians, 2,000 Virginians, and 2,000 District of Columbia militiamen. He had also requested, possibly at Barney's suggestion on July 8, that the secretary of the navy direct three of the navy's finest officers, Captains John Rodgers, Oliver H. Perry, and David Porter to come to Washington to assist in the capital's defense if needed. Unfortunately, fewer than several hundred men appeared and no state came close to making its quota.[16]

It had become all too clear that assistance from the regular army or the District of Columbia Militia would be limited in Southern Maryland, and that unless the capital itself was imperiled, neither force would again be moving about much at all. The flotilla seemed to be the only viable force capable of providing any organized opposition, and the strain was beginning to tell on Barney. On July 24 one of his officers reported that the commodore had been seriously ill, and was, in fact, still convalescing from the constant exposure and hard duty. The hostile attitude of the Southern Marylanders only added to his problems. The officer noted that his commander's illness was caused, in no small part, by the "anxiety founded on the knowledge that we should receive no information or assistance from the people [among] whom we are unfortunately placed; their inclination to deceive us is so great, that we are constantly kept in a state of alarm by their rumors."[17]

Fortunately, the commodore's health was improving, much to the relief of his men. "If anything had happened to him," the officer related, "we should have been lost indeed, although we have some excellent officers; he is in fact our Polar Star, every one looks to him as the leader in every enterprise, and the director of all our exertions that are to be crowned with success."[18]

Ironically, many in Washington were perplexed at the attitudes of those most exposed to enemy attack in Southern Maryland. Few observed that government had generally failed to provide any substantial support for the countryside against even the most minor incursions until it was too late or unless Washington itself was thought to be threatened. Yet, they were amazed that the foe could operate with such ease in hostile territory, and suffer so few losses. Almost no one faulted the militia system itself, but instead blamed the rural farmers for failing to mount their own defense. One Washingtonian observed:

> The villainous system of private depredation and predatory warfare carried on by the enemy in the neighboring water will reflect eternal disgrace on his naval character. Nothing escapes him of private property, from the tobacco-house to the hen roost. The most surprising circumstance attending his incursions on the shores of the Maryland rivers, is, the little resistance he has met with, and the impunity with which he has so far been permitted to invade the soil, in a country peopled by perhaps from 20 to 50 souls to the square mile. The population of any two or three plantations, if armed and faced to the enemy, might in many cases have repelled marauding parties which have ravaged a whole neighborhood.[19]

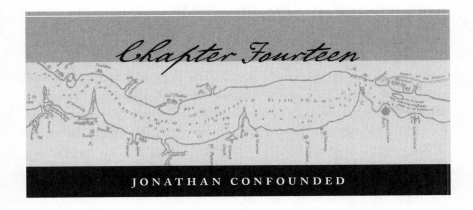

Chapter Fourteen

JONATHAN CONFOUNDED

By Saturday, July 23, the emergency caused by Nourse's raids on the Patuxent was determined to be at an end, the enemy, it was obliquely noted in Washington, thinking it "proper to decline advancing." General Winder promptly reviewed his troops at the Woodyard and discharged the entire body, publicly acknowledging their alacrity and patriotic zeal in turning out.[1]

The truth was anything but soothing to those living in Southern Maryland. Though Nourse had retired, Cockburn was far from finished with his work. In fact, the operation against Leonardtown was considered merely a warm-up for what was yet to come in a campaign intentionally designed to sow further confusion, fear, and panic in and about the entire region.

. . .

At 4:00 a.m. on July 20, even as Captain Nourse was returning from his last raid on the Patuxent, Cockburn was dispatching a boat party to sound out the Potomac between his fleet anchorage, a quarter-mile off Blackistone (modern St. Clement's) Island, and the Virginia shores of the Potomac. The Virginians had been monitoring Cockburn's motions on the river with both diligence and trepidation since the evening of July 18, when the first of his squadron appeared off the island. Having observed at least four large warships, a sloop of war, "and a great number of tenders and barges" coming to anchor under the island, the 25th Virginia Regiment, composed of militiamen from King George County under Colonel Richard E. Parker, began to assemble from dispersed positions along the river from Ragged Point and King Copsico, upstream to Haywood, Mattox Creek, and Chotank Neck to meet the expected attack. Anticipating a landing at any time, but poorly prepared to meet it, Parker dispatched an urgent request for immediate assistance and ammunition to Governor James Barbour. The enemy, he reported, was coming ashore and this time his destination was feared to be the Westmoreland County Court House.[2]

The subsequent engagement that took place in Nomini Creek must have proved quite tantalizing to those who had remained aboard the flagship, as only the slightest intimations of battle could be discerned. Cockburn's target was again a military one. Having learned that a body of Virginia militia, including an artillery unit, had been collecting at a ferry landing, some distance up the creek, he had decided to disperse them at the first opportunity. There was also reportedly a substantial assemblage of stores and several vessels there to sweeten the pot.[3]

As usual, Cockburn had arrayed his forces meticulously. First, the ships were moved as close as possible to the entrance of the creek. Then, at noon, three divisions of boats laden with marines under Captain Robyns, and a unit of marine artillery under Captain Harrison in tenders specially outfitted for the service, set out into the waterway, followed again by *Thistle*. Owing to the intricacy of the channel, however, only the boats could pass through to assail the American strongpoint at the ferry landing. The American position was a commanding one, on an eminence that projected well into the water, with a road leading from the landing up one side to the summit. The other side was a steep, heavily wooded slope the Virginians believed would not, or could not, be scaled.[4]

A party of marines was thus landed on the peninsula's wooded side and immediately began scaling its purportedly unclimbable clayey side to threaten the Virginians' flank. The main force, under the command of Captain Robyns, made directly for the ferry landing to attack up the main road. From *Albion* all that could be seen was the firing of *Thistle*'s guns and a random scatter of cannon fire upon the Virginians from several tenders.[5]

Upon discovering themselves being outflanked, the Virginians fell back as the British on the road aggressively pushed ahead, gained the summit, and formed ranks again. Within minutes the retreat became a rout, and the chase that ensued, which proceeded four or five miles into the countryside, was halted only by the onset of darkness and the British lack of intelligence regarding the lay of the land. The Virginia militia's field artillery, which might have been a factor in the defense, had been withdrawn early in the contest and hidden in the forest for fear that if left on the field it might fall into the hands of the invaders.[6]

The British now commenced the all-too-familiar routine of looting the surrounding region, and rounding up a few prisoners from the recent rout.

As usual, all of the available tobacco was loaded aboard their boats, and a quantity of cattle and other spoils of war were also taken off. Next came the plunder and destruction of the warehouses and private homes. The invaders labored throughout the night, stripping the area bare. Not until mid-morning of the following day were they able to exercise their considerable skills as master arsonists. By late morning the fires were visible all the way across the Potomac.[7]

Cockburn, however, had not finished with Nomini. After re-embarking aboard his boats, he and his men dropped down to another point in the creek where additional American movements had been observed. Once again a landing was made. A heavy volley greeted the assault, after which opposition again evaporated before the gleaming bayonets of charging Royal Marines. Following standard procedure, the admiral ordered everything in the neighborhood destroyed or brought off. Units were then sent in several directions into the surrounding countryside to assist in the escape of a considerable body of refugee slaves.[8]

Satiated with the destruction of all of human construction or produce that lay about Nomini Creek, the admiral finally decided to withdraw. About sunrise, two tenders carrying 135 black men, women, and children came alongside *Albion* to transfer their human cargoes. The admiral continued mopping-up operations in the creek until evening. At 7:40 p.m. he and his men returned to the squadron, having captured a heavily laden schooner, a large ferryboat schooner, fifty hogsheads of tobacco, some dry goods, and four American prisoners. The cost of the expedition had been one killed and three wounded in *Thistle*'s boats and a sergeant of marines attached to *Albion* seriously injured.[9]

By the time the first word of the raid reached Virginia's governor, James Barbour, the inflated number of invaders who had come to within a half mile of Westmoreland Court House, while sending the Virginia militia into full and ignominious retreat, was given as between 1,000 and 1,200 troopers. By the time the news had reached Falmouth, Virginia, the numbers of the enemy had grown to 1,500 and the entire region was in complete panic and disarray. The admiral's intended goal of generating fear and confusion was working far better than even he could have hoped.[10]

On July 22 the refugees freed at Nomini were transferred to *Thistle* for transport to Tangier Island, although two out of three were deemed to be of the wrong sex and age to be of any use by the British. Nevertheless, the pickings in both refugee slaves and prize goods had been so rich that Cockburn sent orders for Captain Watts at Tangier Island to convert several of the barracks and other buildings into storehouses until transports arrived from Bermuda "to take away our riches." Also to be sent to the island was an artillery detachment and forty of the Colonial Marines for use in operations on the Eastern Shore.[11]

Cockburn was pleased with the foray on Nomini Creek, although one incident during the operation caused him some upset. While his men were ashore, he charged, the Virginians had stooped quite below the normal bounds of civilized warfare in something of a repeat of the Benedict arsenic incident. It seemed that a bottle of poisoned whiskey had been enticingly exposed on the front porch of a Mrs. Thompson's house on the recently captured hill. Though an officer had accidentally broken the bottle, and absolute proof of its contents was not to be had, a formal complaint respecting the matter was sent to Brigadier General Hungerford of the Virginia State Militia. The general later ordered a court of inquiry, for which action he was severely criticized. It simply wasn't patriotic to bow to the wishes of an enemy the likes of Cockburn. Notwithstanding Hungerford's civility in the matter, the court ruled that the alleged bottle of poisoned whiskey never existed, and that the charge was "utterly without foundation." False or not, His Majesty's Royal Marines were sternly warned not to accept such entertainments again. It had, in fact, after the incident at Benedict, become an unwritten rule among the landing parties that "if we wished to eat or drink anything that was found in their houses placed out ready for us upon their tables, we used to force the natives to eat a part first, that in the event of its being poisoned, they might die with the Britishers."[12]

...

At 4:00 a.m. on July 23 Captain James K. White, Captain Ross's replacement as commander of Cockburn's flagship, took charge of yet another incursion. This time the invaders would put ashore on the Maryland side, in St. Clement's Creek. Again the marines, armed boats, and artillery formed, and within an hour and a half had landed with little opposition. Cockburn joined the expedition at 8:00 a.m., ostensibly to examine the surrounding countryside, but also to view the progress his boats were making in sounding out the creek. "The militia shewed themselves occasionally," he later noted, "but always retreated when pursued." Four schooners were captured, and another, which had sought refuge in the upper reaches of the creek, was destroyed. The local inhabitants remained docile, and as a reward Cockburn refused to permit harm to befall any of them—with a single exception. At one farm two musket shots were directed at the admiral's gig, whereupon he angrily ordered his forces ashore to destroy the entire plantation from whence the fire had come. Then, perhaps to tweak the War Department's nervousness, the admiral consoled one suffering individual, who had recently been stripped of his property, by informing him that he would not be visited again "as the reinforcement so long expected" had arrived, and the British would soon be proceeding on to Washington.[13] The blatant effort to plant disinformation, suggesting the Potomac would be the invasion route, quickly made its way to the capital city.

While the admiral cavorted on the shore, soundings were continually being made in the river by *Loire*'s boats, using a chain line of buoys to assist in charting the shoally natural obstructions in the river. Navigational buoys were laid to mark the channels whenever the opportunity presented itself. With the British continually taking soundings, the Americans were growing justifiably disturbed. On July 23, when *Loire* actually passed over the notorious Kettle Bottom Shoals, the deadliest hazard to navigation on the entire Potomac, taking soundings all the way, to discover a passage through for large ships, one American general quickly notified Washington. The Kettle Bottoms were indeed a most extensive, intricate, shifting complex of shallows and oyster bars, about a third of the way up the river. They were of various dimensions, some no longer than a small boat, and others acres in extent, running all the way from Nomini Cliffs on the Virginia side to Lower Cedar Point on the Maryland shore, and of major strategic importance to the security of both Washington and the ports of Alexandria and Georgetown. The few charts to be had of the river were sorely lacking in definition of the twisting channel near the Virginia shore, and knowledgeable pilots were out of the question. Even American frigates never tried the route without first taking off their guns, and even then passage to the mouth of the river could take up to a week or more.[14] The shoal, remarked General Stuart on learning of the British sounding effort, "is the only obstruction in the navigation of the river, which could create any serious delay to the enemy's shipping." And now that the enemy had found a way through, Secretary Jones half expected that he would press on at least as far as Maryland Point well above the shoals, if not farther, in his mapping operations.[15]

That the British were sounding the way, despite repeated groundings, was bad news indeed for Washington.

By this time the countryside was terrified, especially along the shores of St. Mary's and lower Charles counties. Rumors spread throughout the region that the enemy was on the march with 1,500 men. The venerable riverport of Port Tobacco was abandoned within hours, and the local militia was usually among the first of those fleeing the countryside. The War Department was in a dither as the enemy seemed to be ascending both the Potomac and Patuxent. Not everyone was convinced the capital might be their target. Secretary of War Armstrong was informed by the new commander of the military district, Brigadier General Winder, "that he expected him [the enemy] up the bay; and should not be surprised to find Annapolis his object; which he feared would fall, before five hundred men." Although there were several forts and earthen works, Horn, Madison, Nonsense, and Severn, defending the Severn River and the city, Secretary Jones was among those now in a high state of anxiety. Having more concern for the potential threat on the Potomac than that posed on the bay, he fell back upon the only man he could rely upon. On July 26 he asked Barney to consider if he could place the flotilla under one of his lieutenants and then with two hundred of his men proceed to the Washington Navy Yard to take command of three new barges and the new schooner *Lynx* "and such other forces as we have" and proceed down the Potomac to Maryland Point to keep an eye on the enemy and to erect a 6- or 8-gun battery and hot-shot furnace on the point. Soon afterward, the commodore received a countermanding order and instructions to continue with his present command. Barney's response to the understandably nervous secretary's letter can only be imagined.[16]

The following day, another enemy landing was launched from two schooners and eight barges against Lower Cedar Point with the objective of raiding and destroying the local warehouse. This time the raiders were met with resistance offered by Brigadier General Philip Stuart, commander of the 5th Brigade, Maryland Militia, with a small body of militiamen and two light 6-pounder field pieces. With the warehouse situated on a narrow peninsula surrounded by water, the defensive posture of the Marylanders was extremely poor. "I could not attack them with my infantry," wrote Stuart after the affair, "as it would expose them to the rake of the enemy's vessels and not assure to us the capture of the enemy." He thus employed his riflemen and artillery, and actually succeeded in driving the raiders back to their boats. There was no dealing with the big guns of the Royal Navy, though, especially on a peninsula surrounded by water. The British responded with a heavy barrage from the schooners and barges, including fire from their 32-pounders and rockets. For an hour the mêlée continued unabated. Soon the warehouse was afire, presumably set ablaze by a rocket, before the British hauled off, "not a little damaged" but far from discouraged.[17]

Cockburn launched yet another strike against the Virginia shore at 2:00 p.m. on July 26. Machodoc Creek was now to become the focal point of the untender attentions of the Royal Navy. The marines, brought in aboard twenty-two barges and three tenders, were landed without incident at a spot called The Narrows, between the mouths of Lower Machodoc and Nomini creeks, and proceeded to march overland toward the head of the Lower Machodoc while armed boats and tenders proceeded toward the same destination by water. Brigadier General John P. Hungerford, Virginia's pugnacious senior militia commander in the area, dispatched 250 men from his base, four miles from Yeocomico Church, where his forces had been mustering. The units' commander, however, believing the invaders numbered as many as 1,200 men, declined to engage "as the enemy was so great that would have been sheer madness to have met them." Thus, no opposition was encountered, and six American schooners were burned at the headwaters of the creek. The invaders returned to their squadron at 8:00 p.m., again unscathed.[18]

Cockburn had now "visited" every place in Maryland and Virginia within reach of his main anchorage off Blackistone, having "brought from these places everything worth bringing from there, about a hundred Hds [hogsheads] of tobacco, a small quantity of flour & other goods, some vessels and quantities of live stock," and a large number of black refugees.[19]

By evening, General Hungerford had arrived in person at Yeocomico Church, three or four miles from the port of Kinsale, to personally take command of the situation. He found the militia that had begun to muster there still too few in numbers to meet the enemy head on. These consisted of two companies of infantry from Westmoreland County, three from Caroline, three from Richmond, two from Essex, a company of horse from King George, another from Richmond County, as well as a company of riflemen and another of artillery from the same place. In all, only 650 officers and men had assembled, although more were expected at any time. Yet, even this small force lacked equipage of every kind, including medicine, camp kettles, axes, forage bags, canteens, and jugs. There were barely fifty tents to be had for the whole army. "Our force," wrote the general, "I consider as entirely inadequate at present to make any effectual defence against the enemy." No fewer than three thousand more men, in addition to those already assembled, he informed Governor Barbour, would be necessary to engage the enemy with any prospect for success.[20]

As the Virginians mustered and Hungerford attempted to predict the invader's next move, Cockburn decided to play cat and mouse and remove the fleet to another site farther upriver, just above Blackistone Island and near the mouth of the Wicomico River in Maryland. Just before departure, however, *Aetna* joined the squadron, in the midst of a violent thunderstorm, bringing the latest word from Nourse regarding the Patuxent expedition and Barney's flotilla.[21]

The admiral must have read Nourse's report of July 23 with considerable interest and a great deal of satisfaction. His raiding on the Patuxent, the river's abandonment by the inhabitants, and the ongoing rush of the Southern Maryland slave population to the British banner had been everything the admiral had wanted. There was, for once, a dearth of accurate intelligence available concerning the disposition of the American flotilla itself. Had there been, he might have expressed a note of sympathy for his opposite on the Patuxent, not for his military predicament, but for the indecisive leaders he was obliged to serve under. And for that indecision, Cockburn's plan was in large measure responsible. The admiral certainly would have taken some pleasure had he known that Secretary Jones was showing signs of major anxiety, in part inaugurated by the little raiding parties just downriver from the capital of the United States. He would also have taken great satisfaction had he known that Secretary Jones, again vacillating from one minute to the next regarding the latest crisis at hand, had dispatched orders—before abruptly rescinding them—for Barney to immediately abandon command of the flotilla and come to Washington with a force of two hundred to man barges and schooners in case of British attack.[22]

Cockburn was, fortunately, unaware of the goings-on in Washington. All he knew was what Nourse had informed him of. Yet all of the captain's officers agreed on one point—that Barney was "as high up the river as he can get and that he had made himself as strong as he can." A few nebulous reports that had leaked downriver suggested that there were as many as three thousand troops with the flotilla, though Nourse personally doubted such a figure. From his own experience it was clear that there were never more than a few cowardly militiamen or a band of regulars ever encountered on any forays, and he had raided quite close to the flotilla's main base at Nottingham.[23]

There was some irony in that much of the intelligence Nourse was securing was little more than the same rumors Washington was also hearing. On July 20, when the last landing at Benedict was made, he reported having heard that Cockburn had descended on the town of St. Mary's, Maryland's first capital, which was anything but true. As a consequence, the militiamen on the St. Mary's County side of the Patuxent, who had been lying in the woods opposite Drum Point, had timidly preferred to follow the movements of Nourse's small squadron rather than pursue the greater danger offered by Cockburn's main force. General Philip Stuart's main force was said to be ensconced for the moment at a place called Cool Springs, near Charlotte Hall, approximately seven miles from Benedict, and its only real objective, Nourse scoffed, was "to keep at a respectable distance."[24]

Though accurate intelligence was quite difficult to come by, there *were* some reliable sources available. Nourse had been quite fortunate in securing the services of an American traitor, one Mr. Hopewell of Drum Point, who regularly provided him with estimates of American troop strength, the latest news from Washington, and even current copies of the *Daily National Intelligencer.* Hopewell, it seems, was not alone in his activities. American turncoats were literally everywhere. On July 23 the *Intelligencer,* finally adopting a policy of silence concerning the publication of military data, published a suggestion that General Winder keep a vigilant lookout for enemy spies and American traitors. "We have little doubt that spies daily pass in and out of this city, and through the country. No man ought to be permitted to pass, and it is in these times the duty of good citizens as well as soldiers, to let no man pass within fifty miles in a direction to or from the enemy, who is not known, unless he can satisfactorily explain his character and business. It is no less their duty to apprehend all who are suspect, on good grounds, of affording information to the enemy."[25]

As meritorious as this suggestion was, given the bitter political dissension of the very region that surrounded the capital, it was totally impractical. Nourse, and indeed the entire British command, would rarely suffer from a total lack of information regarding their American opponents.

Nourse was impressed by the complete lack of support for the American war effort in Southern Maryland. "In one of our expeditions," he noted with relish, "an American told us he guessed we were the advanced guard of a considerable force intended to land at Benedict and march to Washington—I wish with all my heart this force was arrived for Jonathan I believe is so confounded that he does not know when or where to look for us and I do so believe that he is at this moment so undecided and unprepared that it would require but little force to burn Washington, and I hope soon to put the first torch to it myself."[26]

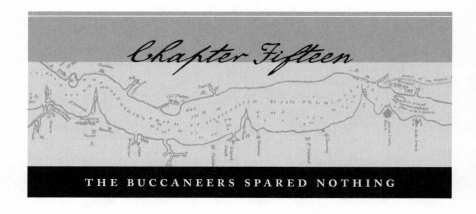

Chapter Fifteen

THE BUCCANEERS SPARED NOTHING

At 2:00 p.m. on July 28 Cockburn moved into the mouth of the Wicomico River, a major tributary of the Potomac, and promptly prepared for another raid.

> I proceeded with the marines under Major Lewis and the boats under the captains of the squadron (the whole of them invariably volunteer to accompany and assist me on every occasion) to reconnoitre this extensive inlet and its adjacent shores, on some part of which General Stuart was said to be stationed with twelve hundred men to oppose me. I landed at Hamburg and examined in the course of the evening the whole of the upper part of the river, and passing the night in the boats I landed at daylight [Saturday, July 30] with the marines about three miles below Chaptico, which place we marched to and took quiet possession of without opposition. I remained all day quietly in Chaptico whilst the boats shipped off the tobacco which was found there in considerable quantity, and at night I re-embarked without molestation. I visited many houses in different parts of the country we passed through, the owners of which were living quietly with their families and seeming to consider themselves and the whole neighborhood as being entirely at my disposal. I caused no further inconvenience to [them], than obliging them to furnish supplies of cattle and stock for the use of the forces under my orders.

Cockburn's raiders returned to the fleet at 2:40 a.m. on July 31, bringing along with them seventy hogsheads of tobacco as booty.[1]

American reports of the occupation of Chaptico differed radically from those of the admiral. American reports stated the British had been able to remove only thirty hogsheads of tobacco and no other plunder, "the inhabitants having removed all the property out of their grasp." On August 4, soon afterward, the *Intelligencer* published an account detailing the British desecration of Christ Church, an Episcopal house of worship, in which it was reported that the enemy had ruined the building's tile floors with their horses, destroyed the pipes of the church organ, employed the communion table as a dinner table and then smashed it, opened and robbed burial vaults, and even used sunken graves in the cemetery as barbecue pits. They plucked the feathers from stolen geese in the church. In one instance they broke into a vault in which lay the recently interred body of the wife of Judge Key, "a lady of the first respectability." They then proceeded to tear off the deceased's winding sheet and shred it to pieces, completely exposing the corpse, after which they looted the tomb. Several British officers, preferring the living over the dead, had a number of young women stripped stark naked and obliged them to stand before them for an hour and a half. Destruction of community property was not ignored as they smashed down doors and every window in the village. The town wells were filled in, and private homes torn to pieces. As one astonished visitor arriving on the scene after Cockburn's departure noted, "their conduct would have disgraced cannibals."[2]

Whether or not reports of such activities were founded in fact or were merely the creation of some active propagandist's mind is open to conjecture. Cockburn had few, if any, horses with his force, and the utility of employing gravesites as barbecue pits for the troops and robbing burial vaults seems a bit too time consuming and ghoulish even for the British. The public outrage was almost tactile. "During all this havoc," it was noted in Baltimore's *Niles' Weekly Register* on August 14, 1814, "not a man was in arms within fifteen miles of them, and they worked until ten o'clock at night, before they got the tobacco on board their vessels owing to the shallowness of the creek that leads up to Chaptico warehouse, they rolled more than half the tobacco one mile. General Stuart was encamped with the militia near sixteen miles from these free-booters; I presume he is waiting for a regular field action with the British. He has no confidence in our trees and bushes, as militia had in the revolutionary war." Such words of indignation, the facts of which were later confirmed by Stuart himself, were thought to be the stuff to stir up patriotic, anti-British sentiments in Southern Maryland. Unfortunately, all it succeeded in doing was further terrorizing an already paralyzed population and engendering citizen outrage over the failure of the American government to protect the region.[3]

...

Cockburn was now at a crossroads in decision-making. To proceed farther up the Potomac, conducting forays against the villages and plantations along the way, would undoubtedly prove both fruitful for the British and even more alarming for Washington. The capital would, of course, grow ever more frantic, and a great deal of energy would undoubtedly be expended to counter the advance. That would be counterproductive to the admiral's overall objective of diverting attention from the Patuxent. Indeed, he informed one of his captains, it must now be his intention to "steer downriver as the whole country is now alarmed, and they are I dare say beginning to feel uneasy at Washington which for the present I would rather avoid occasioning."[4]

Moreover, though he was not worried about the military opposition to such an ascent, he realized that his force was far too small to actually jeopardize the capital, and there were considerable obstacles to overcome in any further advance, the major ones being placed there by nature rather than by man. Cockburn had, of course, with the able assistance of Captain Brown of *Loire,* taking the soundings and charting the route, succeeded in discovering a hazardous passage through the Kettle Bottoms. Yet, negotiating a further advance with the forces in hand, though doable, would prove too time consuming and dangerous for the benefits to be had. Admiral Cochrane was tentatively expected with a convoy of transports at any time, and it was incumbent upon his second to be at the mouth of the Potomac to greet him. Thus, after another brief reconnaissance was made into the Wicomico, the British upped anchor and returned downriver, to play about Breton Bay and then some more about the Virginia shore.[5]

On August 2 a party of marines was landed two miles south of Breton Bay to investigate another large storehouse reported to be in the vicinity. The expedition returned at 5:00 p.m., and "there being no further object to induce me to remain longer in the higher part of this river," the admiral ordered the fleet to again weigh anchor and make sail for the mouth of the Yeocomico River, one of the many Virginia tributaries feeding the Potomac.[6]

. . .

Cockburn's next target was to be the town of Kinsale, near the head of a branch of the Yeocomico. At 2:00 a.m. on August 3, the admiral and his usual band of marauders, five hundred strong, proceeded up the little river directly against American positions established on the shore. At 5:15 a.m. it was observed from onboard *Albion* that a heavy musket and artillery fire had commenced against the approaching boat parties. "At 6," noted *Albion*'s log, "the marines landed. At 8 . . . observed several houses on fire."[7]

The attack on the Yeocomico had indeed met with substantially greater opposition than had been expected. General Hungerford had successfully rallied his militia units after the engagement at Nomini Creek and proceeded to track the enemy's motions up and down the Potomac with considerable diligence. On August 2 William Henderson, captain of a 2-gun artillery unit attached to Major Pemberton Claughton's battalion of the Northumberland County Militia regiment, was warned by Major John Tayloe Lomax that the enemy was at hand. Henderson's property, including dwellings, at Monday's Point on the Yeocomico, was considered situated as "the best in the upper part of the county for the annoyance of an invading force." The buildings on the site had already served for more than a year as militia barracks and mess and were strategically ensconced on the point. Now Henderson had been "advised" by his superiors to erect a breastwork for his defense in the event the enemy came ashore. Another militia unit under Major Henry Blackwell had already taken up a position on Oyster Shell Point, a mile and a half west of the artillery battery. Henderson immediately had his men throw up a substantial defense work for his two guns. The fortification consisted of a breastwork, "composed in front of large logs, covered very thickly with earth and sods, and a ditch in the rear."[8]

When Cockburn decided to put into the river, a warm reception awaited him—unlike those usually provided by the Marylanders across the river. Yet the results were ultimately the same. Offering a more determined resistance than usual, Henderson and his unit had stoutly met the invaders head on with their two guns until all their ammunition, with but two rounds of grape left each gun, was expended. As soon as the enemy stepped ashore, however, the militia around them gave way and retired, with Henderson being the last to leave. A short distance on, the captain rallied his men, but only for a few moments were they able to stand against the invaders. Then five hundred British marines followed them in hot pursuit "at almost a run" on the road to Richmond County Courthouse, for nearly six miles into the country, burning every house along the way (claimed by the British to also be military depots for militia use and ordnance stores). Henderson retired with his force intact, skirmishing with the enemy the whole way until the dogged pursuit was given up. Two of Henderson's men were wounded, and a 6-pounder field piece was captured. The fortification on Monday's Point was totally destroyed. The captain's principal dwelling in Richmond County, six or seven miles from the scene of action, including his kitchen, smokehouse, two storehouses, stable, stacks of wheat and hay, many bushels of oats, and another dwelling nearby, in which he had substantial furniture, valued at $6,045, was also burned to the ground in the process.[9]

At Kinsale, Hungerford rallied his available forces in hand, now reduced to approximately 570 or 580 men, even as Cockburn's tenders pressed into the shoally West Yeocomico River, firing at houses along the shoreline all the way. The admiral had already learned that the Virginians were regrouping in the town and determined to trounce them once again. "From the exposure on the bank to their cannon," reported Hungerford, "I knew nothing could be done for the relief of the place." After a single ineffectual volley, the Virginians again retired, and the British rushed the heights upon which the town was situated. Resistance again crumbled.[10]

The British capture and sack of Kinsale was brutal. As one express from the town reported,

> The buccaneers spared nothing but the hovel of a poor old negro woman. The houses (about 20 or 30) were burnt—every article was taken of which they could carry, the rest destroyed—all the tobacco, which they found in the ware-house was shipped, except about 20 H'hds, which they burnt, as night-fall prevented their carrying it on board. The unfortunate soldier, of Capt. Pitts' Company from Essex, who was killed by a grapeshot, was taken from the ground, where he fell, to within 10 steps of the spot where they dined—his pockets turned inside out and rifled—The enemy landed in Kinsale in 27 barges, which were supposed to contain near 1000 men. Admiral Cockburn is said to have been on shore, mounted on a grey horse—sanctioning by his presence as well as by his orders, all the atrocities which were perpetrated by his hand.[11]

When the storehouses had been put to the torch, the conflagration of the town had indeed become general. Two schooners and two artillery batteries had also been destroyed, after which the admiral had seen fit to retire to the fleet about ten o'clock at night. It had been a fair-sized haul—five schooners taken prize, sixty-eight hogsheads of tobacco, sundry quantities of flour, a field piece, five prisoners, and horses belonging to a senior American officer and his son. The losses had been trifling: two black Colonial Marines had been killed, along with a seaman belonging to *Loire*. Captain Lewis of the Royal Marines had been slightly injured, and two more marines and a seaman had been severely wounded. American losses were put at eight killed and five taken prisoner. Colonel Richard E. Parker, of the Virginia Militia, apparently serving as a brevet general, was ambushed, wounded, and unhorsed while retreating, and escaped only because of his proximity to and thickness of the nearby forest. Cockburn again commended his officers and men in the official report to Admiral Cochrane.[12]

The Virginians could only lament their vulnerability. "The situation of this part of the country is deplorable," wrote Hungerford to Governor Barbour, "and unless more vigorous efforts are made for its defense, it must become desperate." The slaves were flocking to the enemy from all quarters. "They leave us as spies . . . and they return upon as guides and soldiers and incendiaries," the general reported bitterly. Owing to their intimate knowledge of the landscape, they were capable of providing the foe with the details of every byway in the region, which could be put to troublesome use by the enemy, by preparing ambushes in the forests for American patrols. It was, in fact, in just such a manner that Parker and several of his men had been ambushed and nearly killed while being pursued by British marines during the retreat.[13]

On the evening of August 6 the fleet moved to yet another new anchorage, this time in the entrance of Coan River, the only major Virginia inlet on the south side of the lower Potomac yet to be visited, and prepared for another foray. Cockburn ordered *Loire, Aetna,* and *Thistle* to press in as far as their draft would admit, effectively sealing off the waterway. At midnight the artillerymen began embarking in tenders, and four hours later the expedition was under way. By 6:15 a.m. the boats, with both Cockburn and Captain Brown of *Loire* onboard, had begun working their way up the Coan. Again a staccato of fire from prepared breastworks and a cannonade from a single battery greeted them. A seaman from *Loire* was hit and severely wounded, collapsing in a bloody heap to the bottom of his boat. Another was wounded soon afterward. Undeterred, the British plodded on, landing directly in the face of the defenders' fire. As usual, the Americans were quickly driven from their posts and into the nearby woods, where soon "there was neither gun nor man to be seen." The battery was promptly destroyed, although the retreating defenders had carried off the artillery. Three boatloads of Royal Marines continued on along the right bank to the head of the Coan, where three schooners were discovered and quickly captured within two miles of the Northumberland County Courthouse. Before they could seize their prizes however, a company of Lancaster County militiamen arrived on the scene, driving the invaders from the schooners and cutting down their colors. The arrival of ten more boatloads of Royal Marine reinforcements almost immediately reversed the situation and the Virginians were once more driven from the field. As soon as the schooners were taken, the invaders landed on both sides of the river and burned every house within sight, including the property of Northumberland County Postmaster James Smith. At 1:00 a.m. Cockburn returned to the fleet with the prizes and twenty-one hogsheads of tobacco in hand.[14]

The raids along Virginia's Potomac shores had accomplished everything

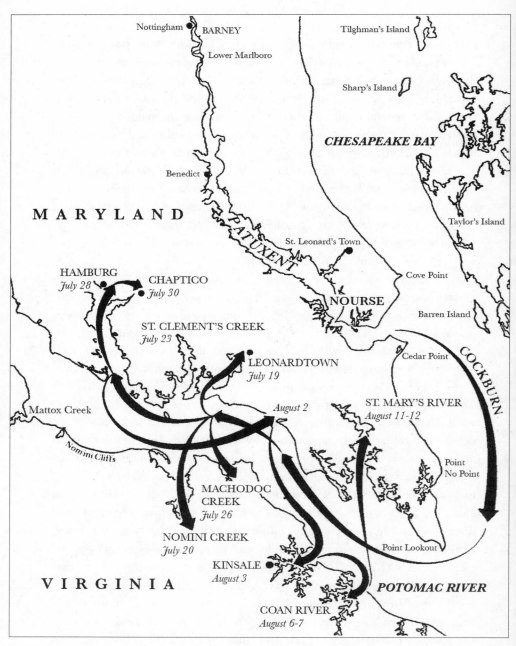

Nottingham • BARNEY

Tilghman's Island

Lower Marlboro

Sharp's Island

CHESAPEAKE BAY

Benedict •

MARYLAND

PATUXENT

Taylor's Island

St. Leonard's Town •

Cove Point

NOURSE

Barren Island

HAMBURG
July 28

CHAPTICO
• *July 30*

Cedar Point

COCKBURN

ST. CLEMENT'S CREEK
July 23

LEONARDTOWN
July 19

ST. MARY'S RIVER
August 11-12

Mattox Creek

August 2

Point
No Point

Nomini Cliffs

MACHODOC
CREEK
July 26

NOMINI CREEK
July 20

KINSALE
August 3

Point Lookout

POTOMAC RIVER

VIRGINIA

COAN RIVER
August 6-7

Rear Admiral George Cockburn's raid on the Potomac River, July–August 1814. *Map by Donald G. Shomette.*

the admiral had hoped for. By now more than 1,000 militiamen had mustered at Northumberland County Courthouse and 150 more at nearby Wicomico Church. The enemy fleet and its prizes anchored in the mouth of the Coan, it was being reported, numbered upwards of 30 vessels, and fear was universal. William Lambert, a Navy Department informant who had kept both the U.S. government and Virginia's Governor Barbour apprised of British movements on the Northern Neck, was less than optimistic about the situation. "The people of this part of Lancaster are in daily expectation of invasion, and it is their opinion that the war will be carried on against them with inveterate malignity." Yet, it was for Virginians not only the fear of invasion, but the enemy's insulting arrogance that was so offensive. "It is said that the language of these marauding Britons to persons who are or have been in their power, accords with their actions; and that among other terms of scurrilous indignity, the opprobrious, insulting epithet of 'rebels' has been applied to several native citizens of this state by some of the humane, well-bred disciples of Admiral Cockburn."[15]

And it wasn't going to improve.

. . .

Upon his return to the fleet, Cockburn was pleased to learn of the arrival of two more warships from Europe, *Menelaus*, 36, Captain Sir Peter Parker commanding, and *Hebrus*, 36, Captain Edmund Palmer commanding, and the heavily laden transport *Tucker*. He must have been even more elated over the news they brought with them. The war between Great Britain and France was definitely at an end. Napoleon had been thoroughly defeated, and a strong fleet of British warships and a respectable army of regulars were on the way.[16]

For the next several days Cockburn's fleet lay off Coan River taking on provisions from *Tucker* while the admiral refined his scheme for the invasion of America, a plan he would soon have the opportunity to personally press upon Cochrane. By August 10 loading had been completed. All told, the following quantity of provisions, a gauge of fleet consumption and requirements, had been loaded aboard *Albion*: 32,256 pounds of bread, 2,544 pounds of beef, 2,544 pounds of pork, 11,172 pounds of flour, 55 bushels of peas, 4,300 pounds of raisins, 3,255 gallons of rum, 8,009 pounds of sugar, 27 cases of lemon juice (an anti-scorbutic), and 350 gallons of vinegar.[17]

Reprovisioning having been completed, the admiral turned his attention briefly to the black refugees taken aboard the squadron. Orders were issued to Captain Urmston of the transport *Thistle* to proceed with the Negroes to

Tangier Island in company with the now empty *Tucker*. Captain Watts of *Jaseur*, temporarily stationed off the island, was directed to transfer the refugees to his vessel and proceed directly to Halifax, where they were to be disembarked.[18]

After attending to these transactions, Cockburn once more brought the squadron to the Maryland side of the Potomac. At 8:00 a.m. on August 11 the fleet came to anchor off the southeast point of St. George's Island, in the entrance to the St. Mary's River. Drinking water was again becoming of some concern, and with the impending arrival of a major fleet from Europe, the admiral wished to be ready to move at a moment's notice. Once again, parties were landed to dig wells and resupply the squadron with fresh water.[19]

Never one to let an opportunity pass, the admiral launched yet another landing on the mainland late that same evening. It seems likely that the expedition was intended to initiate the new arrivals into the arcane science of Tidewater raiding as much as to further throttle the Americans. The artillery and marines embarked, as usual, in the tenders, and by 2:00 a.m. on Friday, August 12, another foray was under way. The expeditionaries, divided into two divisions commanded by the newcomers, Captains Parker and Palmer, and followed by the admiral in *Albion*, landed at several locations on the shores of the St. Mary's River. Two hours later *Aetna* sailed up the beautiful little waterway. Units of the Maryland Militia were reportedly forming at a cotton manufactory in the vicinity, but the local inhabitants, considering it wiser to belie their opposition, submitted to the invaders without incident. The factory was taken without a shot being fired. The British "quietly marched through St. Inigoes Neck in small parties, collecting the stock, but paying for whatever they carried off (though some Americans had the boldness to complain of not having received the full value)." The usual depredations having been made, sans arson, they returned to their ships about midnight, August 12, leaving only *Aetna* in the creek to facilitate shipment of prize goods looted from the countryside. The admiral took particular delight now in boasting that "the inhabitants of this state appearing to have learnt that it is wiser for them to submit entirely to our mercy than to attempt to oppose us in arms."[20] Though few of those engaged realized it, the admiral's visit to the St. Mary's was not just a training exercise, but a dry run in preparation for a more important appointment soon to follow.

On August 14 the squadron lay at single anchor in the Potomac. The weather was fair, and the marines and seamen lounged about as best they could within the tight confines allowed them, enjoying a well-earned rest. After all, they had laid waste to about as much of the Southern Maryland shoreline as could reasonably be expected of such a small force, fought several spirited skirmishes in Virginia, and confounded Jonathan so badly he knew not what next to expect. The squadron had encountered little serious opposition, and there was certainly little reason to anticipate any surprises in the near future. Barney was locked in the upper Patuxent, and there appeared to be no one capable of deterring His Majesty's forces from taking whatever wealth or property from the Tidewater they desired.

The afternoon was hot; the shimmering waters of the Potomac on days such as this often produced mirages. At 2:00 p.m., however, it was no mirage the lookouts spotted, but several sails standing up the bay. Four hours later Vice Admiral Sir Alexander F. I. Cochrane, Knight of the Bath and commander-in-chief of the American Station, aboard his magnificent flagship HBMS *Tonnant*, 80, came to single anchor in the Potomac River. The vanguard of a vast armada of warships, the largest ever to be visited upon the waters of the upper Chesapeake, and an army of the world's finest troops, Wellington's Invincibles, were beginning to arrive.[21]

For the Americans, the war was about to take a distinct turn for the worse—if that was at all possible.

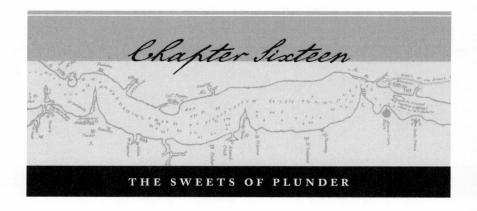

Chapter Sixteen

THE SWEETS OF PLUNDER

"I have considered the situation of the flotilla," Joshua Barney wrote on August 1 while aboard his flagship, "and passed in view the conduct of the enemy since I came into this river, and if I am to judge from what has passed, I am led to believe we have little to apprehend at present; it would appear that they have not a considerable force, and I do think the force now here, has been drawn from Bermuda for the express purpose of capturing the flotilla in St. Leonard's Creek, for from the first attack on the 8th June they declared they must have land or marine troops in order to take us where we were."[1]

From his narrow vantage point on the upper Patuxent, the commodore neither knew of, nor even suspected, the presence of the great forces that were at that very moment moving across the broad Atlantic to converge against him. Cockburn and Company were down on the Potomac sounding out the Kettle Bottom Shoals and wrecking havoc along the shores of Maryland and Virginia, and Nourse lay, for the moment at least, quietly off Drum Point contemplating what mischief he might next cause. Yet Barney realized that with the forces then at the enemy's disposal, there could not be any serious enterprise undertaken against any of the major towns and cities of the Tidewater. Unfortunately, he lamented, "they had tasted the sweets of plunder of tobacco & negroes," and were fully determined to continue the rapacious species of terror they had been so effectively carrying out. The commodore flattered himself that Cockburn did not wish to risk another attack on the flotilla for fear of impugning his reputation with another defeat. He even implied that the admiral had sought to excuse his own plundering ways by blaming the Madison administration for failing to end the war and the flotilla for failing to come to the defense of the Patuxent Valley as it supposedly should have.[2]

"The question now," Barney wrote, "is what is the best to be done with this part of the flotilla, should an occasion present for us to get out?" For the time being, escape to and then up the Potomac to Washington was entirely out of the question, and no guarantee of safety short of Baltimore would permit flight up the bay. But then there was the distinct probability that the blockade might be continued indefinitely, at least until winter, prohibiting movement altogether. At that very moment, in fact, *Severn, Brune,* a gun brig, and three schooners lay across the river at Drum Point with apparently no intention of moving. "This position," noted the commodore rather sarcastically, "would infer a settled blockade."[3]

Other options, however, were open.

On July 27 Secretary Jones, who believed that the British campaign of plundering had been nearly exhausted on the Patuxent, revisited his former pet concept for saving the flotilla. He queried Barney on the feasibility of bringing the squadron upriver to Queen Anne's Town, the old headwater terminus of Patuxent commercial navigation. From there the fleet could be carted overland to the South River by wagons, where it could be refloated, probably at the old port of London Town. Even if all of the warcraft could not be transported overland, he felt that Queen Anne's would be the safest refuge for them. From there, if need be, the flotillamen themselves could be readily moved to Baltimore, Annapolis, or Washington as the occasion required. To facilitate a sounding of the river between Nottingham and the venerable but silted-in upriver port, he sent a fast, light gig by wagon for Barney's use.[4] Not overly fond of the obvious resurrection of the plan introduced to him while on St. Leonard's Creek, the commodore nevertheless dutifully dispatched his son William to sound out the passage and examine the overland route that would have to be taken. The major returned from his reconnaissance mission on the evening of July 31 and immediately reported to his father. His report was succinct and to the point.[5]

> The depth of the water from this place (Nottingham) to Pig-point being already well known, I did not sound it. From Pig Point to Scotchmans hole about 4 miles higher up, is a sufficiency of water for the *Scorpion*, above that place she could not be carried without lightening, and then only about one mile—from this upwards there is not more than 4¼ to five feet at most—the river varies in width—above Pig Point and to within one mile of Queen Ann's it is narrow, not exceeding in some places 80 to 100 yards, its channel frequently crossing from side to side. For the last mile it is quite narrow and very winding but no where wider than to

admit more than one barge to row up at a time, as far as the bridge at the town. The road from Queen Ann's across to South River is generally good, the distance rather less than eight miles. There are 6 or 8 hills of gradual ascent to rise & as many to descend, all of which require more or less, and some of them considerable repairs: twelve or fifteen gates also intervene having large gate posts. There are two or three elbows in the road to obviate which several trees would have to be cut down; there are only two marshy places, and then very small; the shores at Queen Ann and South River are firm and rise gradually; the road in places and for short distances, passes between two banks which may require a little cutting away on each side.[6]

The commodore promptly prepared a full report, replete with computations on the weight of the flotilla, right down to the guns, tackle, and rigging. The entire squadron, replete with guns, shot, masts, rigging, yards, anchors, cables, water casks, small arms, and so forth, weighed 155 tons—perhaps a quarter of the weight of a good-sized man-of-war. Three horses per ton, he estimated, would be required to move the entire flotilla, not to mention 64 wagons and 56 pair of dray wheels. The whole operation, if properly managed and blessed with a little luck, might be completed in a single day and would require 465 horses.[7]

Then came his rebuttal to the secretary's scheme.

"Such a thing can be done," he informed Jones, "but can it be done with safety, & if done will we be better off in South River than in the Patuxent?" The commodore reminded the secretary of the enemies within, the spies and traitors who kept a constant watch on him, all of whom were quite willing to inform the British of every move the flotilla made. It was his own opinion that by the time his barges had reached the South River, the enemy would already have learned of the move and would be there to welcome him with their big guns. Nevertheless, should the secretary determine that such a plan should be followed, the commodore wrote, "I will cheerfully and expeditiously carry your orders into execution."

Barney's final consideration about what should be done was, given the information at hand, perhaps the most judicious of all. And that was simply to stay right where he was. He vigorously disagreed with Secretary Jones's view that the Patuxent Valley had nothing left for the British to plunder. His reasoning was quite logical and directly contradicted the secretary's own view that the wealth of the river valley had been exhausted by the raids of the enemy. Until now, the apparent British objective had been only to carry off as much booty as they could; and where else did such a "harvest" of material goods still present itself in such an unparalleled abundance in the Tidewater but at the still untouched headwaters of the Patuxent? He estimated that nearly six thousand hogsheads of tobacco worth more than $300,000 were still lying in warehouses at Nottingham, Pig Point, Upper Marlboro, and Queen Anne's, and in several private warehouses elsewhere on the river. And then there were at least a thousand or more slaves at and near those same places ready to go off with the invaders at the first opportunity. "This is a great temptation, more than can be presented to them throughout the U.S.; and I am well convinced had not the flotilla got out of St. Leonard's the sweep would have been made before this day." But worse, if the enemy received a sufficient reinforcement, it was likely they would have another go at it. Thus, it was imperative the flotilla remain where it was to stop or blunt such a threat.

The commodore was certain that his force was the only thing standing in the enemy's way between the upper Patuxent and total ruination of the region. Embittered by Federalist sentiments that had hitherto stymied defense efforts, he deftly pointed to recent events to buttress his conviction. "Sir, they [the British] never have, and I believe never will be resisted by the inhabitants near this river. The militia officers being mostly in their interest, encourage the enemy and discourage such as are disposed to aid [us] by exaggerated accounts of the enemy forces &c. If you had seen the panic that appears to strike all classes at hearing of the enemy, you would quickly agree with me in saying that when they see them (if they could be prevailed upon to stay & see them) they would make no defence whatever, for should 100 men land twenty miles below this, the number would increase (by report) to 1,000 before they reach here, and when the 100 did arrive, they would be looked upon as the advanced guard of 2,000 more; no resistance would be made for fear of the arrival of the supposed main army which was following. Thus sir, before the real number could be known the mischief would be done; I see it daily."

Several recent incidents fully illustrated Barney's statement. On one occasion the commodore had dispatched an officer and ten men downriver to bring up a pair of yawls belonging to the destroyed gunboats in St. Leonard's Creek. On their way back, "the militia which had not been stationed on the river, gave way in every direction at the appearance of these two boats," believing them to be the enemy. On another occasion a small schooner, which had also managed to escape the blockade of St. Leonard's Creek, had made its way up to Lower Marlboro. Upon the schooner's approach, the inhabitants ran out of the town, called upon the local militia officer in charge of the district, a certain William Contee, and reported that the enemy had arrived in the schooner with five hundred men.

Destitute of support on either shore, Barney had given up all thoughts of defending a position near the narrows. He now resolved that should the enemy make a landward thrust against Nottingham he would retire farther up until adequate support might be provided for his flanks. The town, of course, with well over a thousand hogsheads of tobacco, would have to be given up, and one suspects that Barney may have been of the opinion it would serve the citizens right for their apathy. The locals had already demonstrated their unwillingness to defend the place and had made their dislike for the commodore and his men quite clear. Yet, he noted, "the moment I leave Nottingham the inhabitants leave it also. They have no confidence in any other defense for the place."

There seemed to be an entire lack of willingness to submit to the disciplined requirements of war. The militia—those that turned out—only sluggishly accepted the directions of the government, and the citizenry, with some justification thanks to the usual indifference of the local militia, seemed to be suffering from extreme paranoia. The maintenance of order in the fleet amidst such chaos was for Barney becoming something of a problem in itself.

Some of the problems were with a handful of sailing masters whose performance was less than conspicuous. Lieutenant Rutter had requested that Sailing Master James Wright be discharged for intoxication and misconduct, which Barney complied with, even though he was short of officers. He had already been obliged to suspend another sailing master, Claude Beese, whose barge had been sunk under him in the battle on June 10, after which he had become so deranged that he had to be relieved of command. "My situation is almost that of a tyrant as I am obliged to punish from my own authority," he informed the navy secretary, "not having it my power to hold court martial for want of a sufficient number of commission[ed] officers, from which circumstance many escape from punishment, whilst I am obliged in other instances to be severe . . . We must begin at the head: for when petty officers & men see that, superiors are punished, we shall have but little trouble . . . thank God I have been able thus far to get forward with a few examples."[8]

The commodore was absolutely certain that the next major British offensive of any consequence would be in his quarter—first for the richness of the plunder, and second because, "if successful, they can march to the Capitol with as much ease and in as short a distance as from any other place." Should the flotilla receive adequate land support, however, he felt confident that a decisive effort might be made to "put an end to the war in this quarter, by completely beating them." His optimism on this last point seemed more a form of etiquette in reporting to his superior than of substance, for in light of recent events and the forces building against him, the commodore's observations on possible victory now possessed something of a hollow ring.[9]

Despite the almost sole island of sanity and security provided by the flotilla at Nottingham, the surrounding countryside was in total disarray. The slave population along the Patuxent now appeared to be literally flocking to the enemy from all quarters. "I have advised a number of persons in Calvert to get their negroes off," Barney reported, "and promised them to move down with the flotilla in order to cover and protect them when doing of it, and to be a check upon the black gentry—Altho Calvert deserves nothing from us, yet I conceive it a duty we owe our country."[10]

...

While Joshua Barney penned the pros and cons of the finer points of strategy for the edification of the secretary of the navy, and Cockburn ravaged the towns and plantations along the Potomac shores, Captain Nourse decided to initiate yet another raid of his own. He had ascertained from information provided by informants and spies that Barney, though constantly moving about on the upper Patuxent, rarely, if ever now, ventured below Benedict. It was even reported that he had again received orders to lay up his boats, but that the command had been countermanded. Coinciding with this news was information that a large body of militia was again moving about on the Calvert County side of the river, descending the Calvert peninsula as far south as the burnt-out county courthouse. A detachment of three hundred men, it was also reported, had been sent to guard a tobacco store on the bay side of the county, near the cliffs opposite the headwaters of St. Leonard's Creek.[11] It was also quite obvious that the Americans were not operating under any form of unified command, and that disorder, or at least some confusion over military priorities, reigned in the American camp. Indeed, the only organized opposition at all seemed to be the Chesapeake Flotilla.

If there was a seeming dearth of order on the American side, there was, perhaps, an overabundance of success in some areas on the British side. "The black refugees increase so fast," Nourse complained, "that I begin to be somewhat puz[z]led about them." On August 4 he had loaded as many as possible on a gunboat being sent with dispatches to the admiral, but had few available vessels to transport the bulk of them to Tangier. Yet it would be dealt with.[12]

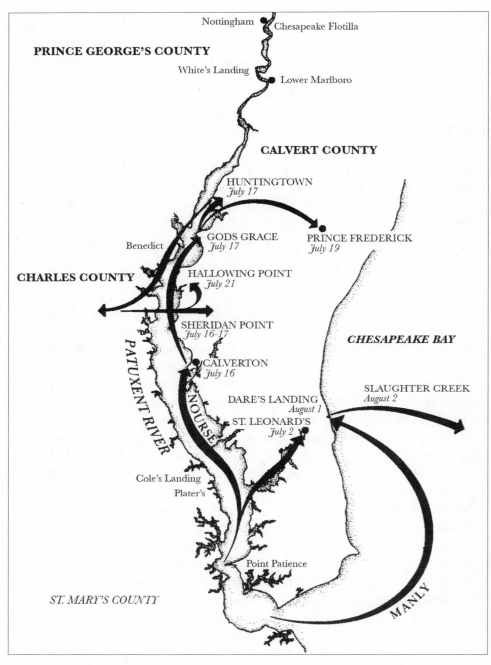

Captain Joseph Nourse's raids on the Patuxent River, July–August 1814. *Map by Donald G. Shomette.*

With Barney locked in upriver, Nourse felt quite secure in dispatching a detachment of warships from his squadron to counter any militia move, and to gather up more booty. Thus, on August 1, Captain Hugh Pearson, commander of HBM Brig *Manly*, with two gunboats belonging to *Severn* and as many marines as could safely be spared, was sent "to capture and drive away the militia and bring off the tobacco" on the bay side of the county.[13]

Pearson set off on his mission the same morning. By 2:00 p.m. he had landed his troops twenty miles above Drum Point, on the Chesapeake shoreline at or near Dares Landing, and promptly located the tobacco warehouse within a mile of the beach. The seamen and marines adeptly set about rolling the stocks down to the edge of the bay, where the plunder was taken aboard small boats and carried to the vessels in deeper water. Suddenly, a withering fire of musketry commenced from the nearby woods and an adjacent, hitherto-deserted house. A party of marine skirmishers commanded by a certain Captain Tunis was sent to drive the attackers from the building. The task was performed with alacrity, and the structure was immediately put to the torch. Within five minutes, "there was not one of them [Americans] to be seen."[14]

The business of looting was resumed, although the militiamen hidden in the woods soon afterward launched another pitifully brief attack. This assault was dispensed with celerity in the same manner as the previous one. Although never more than a dozen Americans were to be seen in the vicinity at one time, Pearson learned from several local blacks that more than 140 militiamen and several cavalrymen were skulking about the forest. The landing party nevertheless managed to successfully carry off twenty hogsheads of tobacco and burn that which they were unable to remove, all without suffering a single casualty.[15]

The following morning at daybreak, Pearson observed a strange sail, later identified as a schooner, standing up the Chesapeake. A gunboat was immediately dispatched under the command of a Lieutenant Griffin to investigate. The lieutenant pursued the vessel across the bay and into Hudson River, on the Eastern Shore, and then proceeded several miles up Slaughter Creek, where he discovered and burned five schooners. He later reported that there were many more American vessels in the Choptank River as well.[16]

Manly returned triumphant to Drum Point and to an undoubtedly pleased Captain Nourse.

. . .

Barney was hungry for reliable intelligence. The only source that he could count upon, however, was that which he himself provided. About the beginning of August he dispatched the six-oared gig recently sent from Washington to go down the Patuxent and spy on the British at Drum Point. On the morning of August 4 the recon party returned safely and with valuable information concerning the strength and motions of Nourse's squadron. The British were being kept in almost continual motion with their small schooners and barges, but seldom poked about north of Point Patience, and then only for a few hours at a time. The officer in charge had taken up an observation post the previous day on the St. Mary's County shore, on a hill behind James Hopewell's farm, near Town Creek, but had been obliged to retire when the enemy made a landing at the Carroll farm a short distance to the south. The enemy had come ashore from three schooners and eight barges with the supposed intent of destroying Clifton Factory, a cloth-manufacturing operation recently acquired by one Peter Gough, about four miles away. "The militia," Barney noted with no little sarcasm, "according to custom appeared after all was over." The data was promptly forwarded to Secretary Jones along with a sketch of the area. Convinced that the enemy was now about as weak as he was ever likely to be, Barney prepared to bring the flotilla down as far as Benedict for a visit. Below that point he would be in danger of exposing the squadron on open waters where the enemy frigates could operate with greater freedom.[17]

Enemy intelligence learned of the flotilla's motions, and on August 10 Nourse dispatched a small reconnaissance force of five boats upriver a distance of twenty miles or so to investigate. As the small force rowed upstream, a canoe was sighted pulling from St. Leonard's Creek for the opposite shore. The single occupant, a white man, on seeing the British approaching, desperately attempted to reach land, but stood little chance of success. Cut off from escape, he jumped overboard and drowned. "We had every reason to believe," noted the commander of the recon party, "he was one of our deserters." The remainder of the passage was without incident. On landing at Benedict, the party discovered, undoubtedly from informants in the town, that they had missed the commodore by two days.[18]

Myriad reports concerning Barney's activities were relayed to the British. One said that the commodore had been ordered not to leave the Patuxent. From a resident at Sandy Point, it was learned that the commodore had talked of bringing some guns onto the point, but the proprietor of the land, one Groom, had objected. Another report said that he had tried to discover where

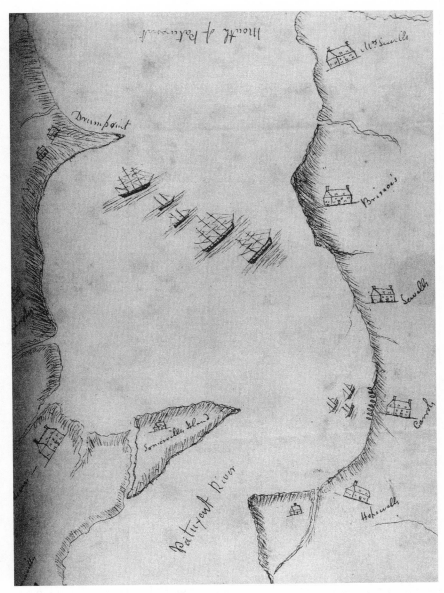

A sketch by Commodore Joshua Barney of the disposition of British naval forces blockading the mouth of the Patuxent River on August 2, 1814. Note the numerous plantations bordering the waterway. *National Archives and Records Administration, Washington, D.C.*

the British guard boats in the vicinity operated so that he might surprise them. Nourse also had been informed of his "meaning to get some people with black faces & hands to impersonate negroes begging to be taken off and to surprise our boat coming to fetch them" in the vicinity of Gods Grace. Another had it that Madison had ordered all of the militia to Washington but they had refused to go. And still another said that it was Barney's intention to regain his old anchorage in St. Leonard's Creek. None of the reports, however, were given much credence. Indeed, the captain seemed surprised that Barney had not considered something bolder, such as fitting out some small vessels as fire ships, which might throw some confusion into the British squadron. He was entirely unaware that the commodore had no suitable vessels available for such use. Nevertheless, the mere possibility caused the captain to move to a new anchorage on the south side of the Point Patience sandspit, which would stymie any such effort from upriver.[19]

On August 15 another reconnaissance was sent up to again try to ascertain Barney's movements, but learned little more than that he was at Nottingham with the flotilla.[20] The following day the British received intelligence that a body of American militiamen had slipped up behind the squadron's main watering site with the intention of ambushing an unwary landing party. Nourse responded in the most appropriate manner he knew. A force of three or four hundred marines and seamen was landed before daylight. The landing party was to be personally commanded by Nourse and accompanied by Captain William S. Badcock of the navy and Captain Nathaniel Coles of the marines, and separated into four units. The British hoped to be able to quietly encircle the Americans and cut them off, "but from the thickness of the woods and their knowledge of the country" the quarry was able to elude the trap.[21]

Despite the ambush attempt, Nourse of necessity was required to make frequent foraging excursions into the country for provisions and often led the landings himself. Occasionally, such raids provided the British with rare bits of humor. On one such expedition they were beset by a man described as a "Methodist Parson" who "put on his canonicals and began to whine and cant, and wished to preach a sermon on peace." Nourse, who was present on the occasion, very politely told the preacher to be off and "that we must attend to our 'calling' as well as he to 'his'—that Jim Madison had 'called us' and therefore we must perform our duty."[22]

The landing expeditions were sometimes the platforms upon which feats of gallantry or bravado were displayed. After the war, one of Nourse's officers related one such account concerning an Irish marine by the name of

Pat Gallaher or Gahagan who single-handedly "surrounded" three American dragoons and took both them and their horses prisoners.[23]

> He effected this extraordinary feat in the following manner: Whenever boats were sent for water, a sergeant's party of marines accompanied them, it being necessary to post videttes to watch for the approach of an enemy. The casks in the launch had been filled, and all the party except this man, who was placed near a stack of hay, had withdrawn. While the picket, who had to descend a cliff towards their boats were out of sight, Pat observed five dragoons ride down to the corner of a wood, near a gate. Keeping his eye on the party, he concealed himself behind the hay-rick; two of the men remained inside the gate, a long musket shot off, whilst the others, after ascertaining, as they thought, that no Britishers were near, came galloping up to see the boats go off, and without observing the sentry in his hiding place, halted. The marine very bravely putting his musket to his shoulder, called out, "you three d . . . d rascals, if you do not immediately jump off your horses and deliver yourselves up prisoners, I'll shoot the whole of you at once, for I have you all in a line." Off they got, and the sergeant at that moment shewing his head above the cliff to recall the vidette, they were very quietly taken to the beach, and themselves and horses brought safe on board.[24]

...

While the British continued their depredations, counting the hours until an army would arrive from Europe to totally chastise Jonathan, it seemed that no one in the American government could decide whether there was even a need to make provision for the defense of the capital of the United States. Some, of course, such as Barney and Jones expected an attack against both the flotilla and the capital. After all, if Washington was captured, government would be disrupted, the Madison administration humiliated, and the Navy Yard destroyed along with two major iron works. The peace negotiations, already in progress, would be directly influenced in favor of Great Britain. To counter such a strike, the Americans would have to quickly assume an advanced defensive posture. If the Chesapeake and its myriad tributaries were one of the major assets assisting the enemy in their depredations, they were also a potential danger. The weakness of the British fleet was that it could be blocked in if it passed too far up the winding, shallow waterways that laced the Tidewater. As Barney had so avidly stated, fire rafts, amphibious infantry, and aggressive cavalry to operate in concert with the naval forces ought to be assertively employed, and a telegraphic signaling system for communication should be adopted at once. Unfortunately, in stunning contrast to this point of view, Secretary of War John Armstrong vociferously argued that there were simply no grounds on which the enemy would find it worthwhile to assail the capital, which was barely over a decade old and could hardly be called a major city. He had repeatedly soothed the president's concerns by assuring him that he would take whatever action was deemed necessary to defend the place, and just as often turned a blind eye to the mounting tide of havoc. His faith in defense rested in militia and his interests were focused primarily upon the Canadian frontier. In fact, he kept his attention turned so consistently elsewhere that it was difficult to provide even for such irregular troops as did turn out in the vicinity.[25]

Chapter Seventeen

GATHERED LIKE A SNOW-BALL

"Now that the tyrant Bonaparte has been consigned to infamy," declared the *Times* of London in the glorious spring of 1814, "there is no public feeling in this country stronger than that of indignation against the Americans."[1] The British, it seemed, were now prepared to employ a major segment of their national military might, hitherto tied up in mortal combat with the French, to chastise the irksome Yankees. Rumors had already begun to circulate throughout the military establishment that between 13,000 and 20,000 soldiers would be sent to America.[2] Yet strategy was sketchy, and few considered the conservative nature of those responsible for administering finances necessary to carry on such a contest, especially after the years of costly and exhausting struggle against Napoleon. Manpower and money were, in fact, quite limited, necessitating restricted objectives in lieu of grand schemes and grandiose risk-taking by a war-weary nation. Now there seemed to be no one in authority ready to say attack this or that place, or indeed capable of making such a decision, primarily because no one could say for certain what military conditions would be necessary to force the Americans to sue for peace. Talks, of course, had been sputtering off and on, but nothing seemed definite about the chances for a favorable end to the war.

Vice Admiral Sir Alexander Cochrane, the new commander in charge of the American theater, for one, vacillated from one scheme to another almost as regularly as the ebb and flow of the tide as he waited impatiently at Bermuda for the arrival of what was expected to be a vast army of the Duke of Wellington's veterans. When he was finally issued orders, they proved conspicuously open-ended, so that, should a major defeat be incurred upon British arms, the field commanders would have no one to blame but themselves. His main mission on the coast of the United States was to principally serve as a diversion to take the stress off British forces defending Upper and Lower

Canada. Sir Alexander was ordered to simply employ the troops sent to him in "such operations as may be found best calculated for the advantage of H.M. service, and the annoyance of the enemy."[3]

About May 20 Major General Robert Ross, a popular forty-seven-year-old veteran of the Peninsular Campaign in Spain and reputedly one of Wellington's more reliable officers (there were many to choose from), had been selected to command the land forces being sent to Cochrane to club the Americans into submission. Perhaps not the most innovative or strategy-oriented of commanders, and a major general for barely a year, he was nevertheless as fine a choice as could have been made given the traditional political infighting that always accompanied such major military appointments. As a field officer, he had gained great respect from his men despite a reputation as a disciplinarian. During the long retreat to Coruña in the Peninsular Campaign, his 20th Foot, as a direct result of his severe drilling, reportedly suffered fewer losses than any other units involved. And, unlike other officers, he was not given to directing from the rear but shared the hardships and dangers of war along with his men. He was the complete professional line officer. In fact, at least two horses had been shot from under him, and he had been wounded twice in combat.[4]

Ross's orders, drawn up by Earl Bathurst, meticulously pointed out the general's relationship to Cochrane. The commander-in-chief would select the targets, but Ross was to freely provide his own opinions from a military point of view. He was to be given unilateral veto power over the deployment of his troops, and when they were finally ashore he was to be in total command of their operations. The specific objectives of his descent upon the coast were maddeningly imprecise. He was essentially instructed "to take possession of any naval or military stores," which were to be destroyed if not immediately removable, and take off or destroy "magazines belonging to the government, or their harbours, or their shipping," but no specific target or port was included in the orders. The only proviso was that he was "not to engage in any extended operations at a distance from the coast." In effect, the general was to be tied to the seaboard and obliged to attack only targets at or below the fall line.[5]

Bathurst's directions in this last arena of concern were directly linked to the sound advice offered up by no less a military personage than the Duke of Wellington. Riding the crest of immense popularity for his victorious Peninsular Campaign, Wellington possessed perhaps one of the few level heads in all of England concerning the direction the American war should take. Unlike the wildly ecstatic public, or the government-at-large, heady with victory, Wellington was wary of the prospects for successfully carrying out operations against the United States on its own territory. It was his solitary view that large-scale military operations in America would, at best, be severely retarded by the problems imposed by the primitive nature and vastness of the country, not the least of which were the lack of roads and the undeveloped state of the great hinterland itself. "You may go to a certain extent, as far as a navigable river or your means of transport will enable you to subsist, provided your force is sufficiently large compared with [those] which the enemy will oppose you," he warned Bathurst. "But I do not know where you could carry on such an operation which would be [so] injurious to the Americans as to force them to sue for peace, which is what one would wish to see. The prospect in regard to America is not consoling."[6] The wisdom of Wellington's warning was not lost on Bathurst, who quite correctly distilled the words and with some modifications installed them in Ross's final instructions.

Despite the rumors of an army of perhaps 13,000 to 20,000 men being assigned to the expeditionary force, the general would ultimately have to settle for barely 3,000. These would be drawn from the forces on the Continent and scattered about the Mediterranean, and though small in number were considered by the administration sufficient to drub the Americans into submission. Whatever feelings Ross may have had concerning the diminished number of troops he was being given, he did not object loudly. After all, men were also needed to defend the Canadian frontier against American invasion, and his operations, wherever they might be, were to be specifically designed to relieve some of the pressure in that theater.

Running counter to Cockburn's program of encouraging slaves to take up arms against their white overlords (an agenda heartily endorsed by Cochrane), Bathurst ordered Ross to "not encourage any disposition which may be manifested by the negroes to rise upon their masters," but authorized him to take off only those who assisted or joined his forces and who might be punished if left behind.[7] The order had not been lightly inserted in the packet of instructions communicated to the general, especially as it ran counter to the policy of the commander-in-chief. The question of slavery had, of course, reached considerable heights in England, culminating in Parliament's abolition of the trade altogether in 1807. The institution of universal abolition, however, had not yet been fully accepted, although it was on the books and was being bandied about in ever-widening circles. The fringes of the empire still relied heavily on the inhumane practice, and many members of the

British aristocracy outright feared the serious implications of the utilization of blacks against whites, and in particular the example such an undertaking would set. Slave uprisings and their unhappy consequences in the West Indies, as exemplified by the rebellion against the French in Santo Domingo, were still quite fresh in the memories of too many Englishmen to be ignored. The prosecution of the war in America would, Bathurst felt, proceed just as well without encouraging the employment of armed blacks under the British flag, with the notable exception of those already engaged in the newly formed black Colonial Corps of Marines.

...

On the morning of June 2, a British squadron commanded by Rear Admiral Pulteney Malcolm from aboard his flagship, HBMS *Royal Oak,* 74, upped anchor in Verdon Roads, at the mouth of the Gironde Estuary, west of Bordeaux, France. Included in this force were 3 frigates, 3 sloops-of-war, 2 bomb-ships, 5 vessels armed *en flute,* and 3 transports. Packed tightly aboard the transports and armed ships were the very best units of 3 regiments of the British army, Wellington's Invincibles, the 4th, 44th, and 85th Foot, totaling 2,814 men.[8]

"The military annals of England furnish no parallel of such a force as was there assembled," one veteran among them wrote, "a force composed of the *elite* of the finest army in the world—veterans of a hundred battles, and with whom 'to fight' and 'to conquer' were synonymous terms." Having helped dispose of the Bonapartist threat after years of bloody war, they were bound for Bermuda and then to America, where they would quickly bring the Americans to heel and perhaps return home in time for Christmas.[9]

At Bermuda, Vice Admiral Cochrane awaited the arrival of Malcolm's squadron with growing impatience. The new commander-in-chief harbored a strong personal distaste for anything American, having lost his brother during the Siege of Yorktown in 1781, and had spent the better part of his time continuing to concoct and then dispose of plans to mercilessly crush the foe. "They are a whining, canting race," he once said, "much like the spaniel and require the same treatment—[they] must be drubbed into good manners." Though flawed by a disturbing tendency toward indecision, his leadership during the war against France, proven during his blockade of the Spanish outports, and heroism in personally commanding a daring fireboat assault on the French fleet in Aix Roads, had stood him in high public and official esteem in England. His abundance of friends in high places, through whose influence he owed much of his command, had not hurt his career. Yet, he was a seasoned veteran and an able, aggressive, and highly organized officer. If anyone could bring the Americans to heel, reasoned the British government, it would probably be him—if he could only pick a target!

Whatever Cochrane did, however, it was bound to be with a vengeance, for on July 17, the same day *St. Lawrence* sailed from the Chesapeake with Cockburn's proposal, he received a message from Sir George Prevost, in Canada, informing him of American atrocities on the Canadian front, and in particular of the ruthless and total destruction of the port of Dover. Prevost had urged him to "deter the enemy from a repetition of such outrages." It mattered little that British forces on the Chesapeake had been ravaging crop and croft of the defenseless civilian population since their arrival in February 1813. Retaliation, total war without restraint, was in order. Thus, the admiral issued orders to his commanders on the North American Station the following day "to destroy and lay waste such towns and districts upon the coast as you may find assailable."[10]

Vice Admiral Sir Alexander F. I. Cochrane. *Oil painting by Sir William Beechey. National Maritime Museum, London, England.*

On July 21 HBMS *Pactolus* arrived at St. George's, Bermuda, several days in advance of Malcolm's main squadron, bringing word of the fleet's imminent approach and of the size of the expeditionary force. Cochrane, who maintained that an absolute minimum of five thousand men would be required to subdue America, was bitterly disappointed to learn of the reduced forces to be placed under his authority. Nevertheless, two days later Admiral Malcolm, in *Royal Oak,* with a great squadron of men-of-war leading the main convoy into the harbor, passed Cochrane's flagship, HBMS *Tonnant* (captured from the French by Lord Nelson at the Battle of the Nile), and was cordially greeted with a 15-gun salute, by a commander-in-chief still uncertain as to how he was going to use them.[11]

On July 26, three days after Malcolm's convoy had arrived at Bermuda, *St. Lawrence* came in with the secret dispatches from Cockburn on the Chesapeake that would remove the question of targets. In his communiqué, Cockburn had persuasively urged Cochrane to concentrate his entire attention on the Tidewater, and in particular on the Patuxent and Potomac, and with an abundance of solid reasons to reinforce his argument for doing so. His rationale was, of course, quite strong. The commander-in-chief surveyed the proposal and vacillated just once more. The Chesapeake it would be.[12]

Before further preparations could be undertaken, another reinforcement arrived. On the 29th a squadron of six frigates and several transports came in from the Mediterranean with three regiments of fusiliers aboard, the 21st, 29th, and 62nd, the latter two earmarked for Canada. The 21st Regiment, however, "a fine battalion, mustering nine hundred bayonets," was assigned to Ross, bringing his force up to well over 3,700 strong.[13]

Cochrane was anxious to be under way and ordered last-minute preparations to be undertaken immediately for the ten-day voyage to the Chesapeake. Stores of provisions, fresh water, ammunition, clothing, and an abundance of other necessaries were attended to in relatively short order. Shortages cropped up here and there—no medicine, no entrenching tools, and no maps—but, remarkably, everything somehow seemed to fall into place.[14]

On the morning of August 1 General Ross and his party joined the commander-in-chief aboard his enormous flagship, and before noon they had weighed anchor and were under way. Escorted by two frigates and a few tenders, and flying the red flag of a vice admiral, *Tonnant* cautiously edged her way past the treacherous island reefs, slipped into the open Atlantic, and pressed westward under full sail. Two days later, Malcolm's main troop convoy, twenty-four vessels strong, also weighed and stood out to sea.[15]

The navigation of any vessel past the teeth of the Bermuda reefs was a definite hazard; for an entire fleet, it was an accomplishment deserving of congratulations. "During the whole of this day," Lieutenant George Robert Gleig recorded aboard the transport *Golden Fleece,* "the wind was light and unsteady, consequently little progress was made, nor did the white rocks of Bermuda disappear till darkness concealed them; but toward morning a fresher and more favourable breeze sprung up, and the rest of the voyage was performed in reasonable time, and without the occurrence of any incident worthy of notice." As the fleet pressed on a northwesterly course, the heat became daily more oppressive, and the strict confinement aboard ship grew increasingly unpleasant, especially for most of the soldiers who hadn't touched solid ground for weeks. Only fishing, gambling, and an occasional "celebration" broke the tedium.[16]

Well ahead of the main convoy, Cochrane and his vanguard reached the low, sandy spears of the Virginia Capes on August 11. To the average Englishman entering the capes for the first time, they were both imposing and boring. "The coast of America, at least in this quarter," one officer wrote, "is universally low and uninteresting; insomuch that for sometime before the land itself can be discerned, forests of pines appear to rise, as it were out of the water. It is also dangerous, from the numerous shoals and sand-banks which run out, in many places, to a considerable extent into the sea; and which are so formidable, that no master of a vessel, unless he chance to be particularly well acquainted with navigation, will venture to approach after dark."[17]

En route to the Chesapeake, Cochrane had much time to reconsider Cockburn's scheme, the same plan that he had so readily adopted as militarily expedient in but a matter of hours after weeks of continued vacillation on his own. Now he was again no longer sure that the Tidewater befitted his attentions, but decided to delay making a final determination until after being briefed on the latest intelligence by Cockburn himself.

August 12 was extraordinarily hot, even for the Chesapeake region, and on the quarterdeck of *Tonnant* the record temperature reached well over 130 degrees. Nevertheless, the vanguard swept up the bay unhindered by the shimmering heat. On past the James and York rivers, past the Piankatank and Rappahannock it sailed unopposed, as if in command of the whole world. Finally, the mouth of the Potomac was in view. At 4:00 p.m. on August 14 the lookout sighted several large vessels at anchor in the river, one of which flew the ensign of a rear admiral. Simultaneously, the lookout aboard the anchored flagship in the river observed Cochrane's approach.[18]

It was not until dusk that Thomas Swann, the U.S. War Department's forward observer on the Potomac, was able to catch a glimpse of the enemy reinforcement from his low vantage point on the beach at Point Lookout. Unlike those aboard the two merging fleets, his was not a moment of celebration, but one of urgent duty. Hastily, he scribbled out a report of the new arrivals as they came up, informing Washington that Cockburn was to "be reinforced in a few hours by nine sail from below, which are now approaching the mouth of Potomac, viz. one seventy-four, two frigates (each mounting forty-six guns), two transports (a brig and a ship), one eighteen-gun brig, and three schooners."[19] More, he feared, would be coming in soon.

At 8:30 p.m. HBMS *Tonnant* dropped anchor in the Potomac River. Her visit to the shores of the Chesapeake Bay would be brief but most certainly unwelcome by her American hosts.[20]

. . .

Shortly after *Tonnant*'s arrival, Admiral Cockburn set off to pay his respects to the commander-in-chief and General Ross, and to place before them in person his own plans for a serious strike against Washington. He had, of course, already seen for himself, on numerous occasions, just how incapable the Americans, with the exception of Barney, were of defending themselves, and had frequently communicated his feelings along this line to Cochrane in several previous communiqués. "This country is in general in a horrible state," he had written in June. "It only requires a little firm and steady conduct to have it completely at our mercy." In July he had reiterated this opinion that "it is quite impossible for any country to be in a more unfit state of war than this is now." And now he would have the opportunity to express that point in person. His task would require every ounce of persuasion he could muster.[21]

Both Cochrane and Ross, whose mutual tendency toward vacillation had fed upon itself during nearly two uneventful weeks at sea, had drifted into the opinion that a strike against Washington was now neither safe nor feasible with the limited manpower available. Better, thought Cochrane, returning to one of his earlier stratagems, to make a combined effort with all of their forces against some other place such as Rhode Island. Yet, Cockburn's arguments and imposing persona were persuasive. He and his captains, he reminded his superior, had been aggressively attacking anywhere and everywhere at their own discretion, and with but a single battalion of marines. Numbers, he pointed out, meant little. General Ross, whose force had been cut back to less than a fifth of its expected manpower, remained doubtful but seemed willing to play it safe and go along with Cochrane's wishes. The commander-in-chief, however, remained undecided.

Undeterred, Cockburn proceeded to further elaborate on the plan he had sent to Cochrane on July 17, which suggested that a major landing be made on the Patuxent at Benedict, and a diversionary feint be sent up the Potomac; both of these undertakings would have Washington as their objective. The Patuxent had been charted as far as Benedict, above which it was unlikely that big warships could go, and Cockburn himself had sounded the Potomac in many places. Sir Alexander and the general were teased. Now Cockburn added a suggestion to further incite their interest. What if a landing was made at Benedict, as already proposed, but instead of marching directly for the capital, they headed up the Patuxent with Barney's flotilla as the apparent objective? The army could proceed by land, once Benedict had been adequately secured, and Cockburn with his marines and seamen would advance in small boats and barges by water. If the Americans believed the British target was the flotilla, they might be more concerned with the diversion on the Potomac than with Ross's main force and permit themselves to be caught off guard. At the very least, the Americans would again be confused, and a sudden thrust westward from the Patuxent might just succeed in surprising Washington from the rear. If nothing else, Barney's flotilla, hitherto the focal point of British naval concern, could finally be dispensed with and a considerable thorn in the Royal Navy's side removed once and for all. After all, hadn't Ross's instructions from Lord Bathurst been to capture or destroy the enemy naval stores and the shipping itself if possible?

Cochrane was swayed by Cockburn's case, but Ross, who would have to manage the land movement and would suffer the most direct consequences should the admiral's plan backfire, was still dubious. Obliged to relieve the general of his doubt, Cockburn offered to personally escort him on a typical outing deep into enemy territory with nothing more than his usual contingent of marines and sailors, that he might judge the level of American timidity for himself. If Royal Navy tars could do it, Wellington's battle-hardened veterans of countless engagements most certainly could too! Ross agreed to the trial run, and on the evening of August 14 Cochrane approved of the expedition.

At 5:00 a.m. the next morning Ross, Cockburn, Sir Peter Parker, Captains Palmer, Ramsay, and Rowley and others set off for St. Mary's with two divisions of scarlet-coated marines, seamen, and boats, followed by the bomb-ship *Aetna* and several tenders. The admiral's now quite intimate knowledge of the country, as well as a plan adopted to prevent surprise, enabled the two officers

to land at several points on the river and penetrate inland farther than prudence would have normally permitted, but in the usual manner honed from
months of experience. In his frequent forays into the countryside, the admiral
had invariably moved forward between two parties of marines, occupying in
open order the woods and thickets by a roadside. Each marine carried a bugle
to be used as a signal in case of casual separation or on the appearance of the
enemy. The rest of the force would then close ranks and deploy to confront
the threat at hand. And as he had expected, everything ran like clockwork.
The marines moved several miles inland from the St. Mary's River, destroyed
a factory in their own inimitable way, and returned to the fleet by 11:00 p.m.
without having met a single armed person or having fired a shot. Ross was
convinced and finally gave his blessing to Cockburn's scheme to capture and
destroy the infant capital of the United States of America.[22]

. . .

On the evening of August 15, even as Cockburn's expeditionaries were returning to their ships, Admiral Malcolm's convoy reached the Virginia Capes,
but owing to the dangerous Middle Ground Shoals was unwilling to hazard
entry after dark. "The fleet was accordingly anchored within a few miles of the
shore," recorded Lieutenant Gleig, "but no sooner had the day began to break,
than the sails were again hoisted; and the ships steering under the influence of
a leading wind, between the Capes Charles and Henry, stood in gallant style
up the Chesapeake."[23]

At 8:30 a.m. Sailing Master Joseph Middleton, a U.S. Navy lookout stationed at the Pleasure House, a popular inn near Cape Henry, spotted the
fleet. Middleton was able, with the aid of a spyglass, to pick out a rear admiral's blue flag flying from the mast of the leading ship, Malcolm's *Royal Oak*.
Through the bright glare of morning, he was able to count at least twenty-two
vessels in the armada: three ships-of-the-line, several frigates, a brig, a topsail
schooner, and nine transports. It was immediately feared that their objective
was to be Norfolk, and an express rider was dispatched to warn the local military establishment of the enemy's approach. Unexpectedly, the fleet turned
northward, and Norfolk's citizenry breathed a sigh of relief.[24]

Onboard the squadron few considered the trauma their appearance had
induced ashore; they contented themselves with scanning the generally low,
featureless countryside about the bay or in simply contemplating the martial
grandeur of a massive British armada under full sail. "This noble bay," wrote

Lieutenant Gleig, "is far too wide, and the land on each side, too flat to permit any but an indistinct glimpse of the shore, from the deck of a vessel which keeps towards the middle. We could distinguish nothing, therefore, on either hand, except the tops of trees, with, occasionally, a windmill, or a lighthouse; but the view of our own fleet was, in truth, so magnificent, as to prevent any murmuring on that account." Most aboard believed their first attack would be against Norfolk, but after communications from Cockburn, learned the upper bay was to be their destination.[25]

At 7:00 p.m. on August 16 American observers at Smith Point sighted Malcolm's convoy as it approached the mouth of the Potomac. Within a short time, the Chesapeake Bay reverberated with the great booming of saluting cannons as Cochrane's and Malcolm's squadrons greeted each other.[26] Only four times before had such massive concentrations of British warships threatened the Tidewater as they did now: once at the beginning of the Revolution when the Earl Lord Dunmore, the last colonial governor of Virginia, led a rag-tag armada in search of a stronghold from which to war against the rebels. In 1777 a British invasion force sailed to the head of the bay to land an army at the Head of Elk. A third fleet appeared in 1780 to ravage the lower bay and seized Hampton Roads. In October 1781 a fourth fleet had been rebuffed by a French squadron under Admiral Comte de Grasse off the Virginia Capes, permitting the incredible Franco-American victory at Yorktown that assured American independence.

Neither Cochrane nor Cockburn was about to permit a similar ending to their own grand campaign. Indeed, nothing seemed capable of standing in their way—nothing at all.

. . .

At dawn on August 17, Thomas Swann gazed in astonishment from his lookout post on Point Lookout at the enormous forest of masts and sails blanketing the Chesapeake. The combined British fleet was spread over a full two miles and consisted of every conceivable type and size of warship of the day: ships-of-the-line, frigates, bomb-ships, brigs, schooners, sloops-of-war, dispatch boats, transports, tenders, and, although the observer could not know it, even a ship fitted out specifically to fire barrages of rockets. The spectacle offered up as Cockburn's and Cochrane's combined squadrons joined Malcolm's main convoy force three miles off the point was indeed awesome to behold. After estimating the total number of enemy vessels at no less than forty-six sail, Swann dashed off a letter to Secretary of War John Armstrong and dispatched a trusted courier by the name of Carmichael to Washington with the frightening intelligence.[27]

Those who formed a part of it viewed with considerable delight the impressive gathering of a significant slice of the military might of the British Empire in one place at one time. "The sight," recalled Lieutenant Gleig years later, "was altogether as grand and imposing as any I ever beheld; because one could not help remembering that this powerful fleet was sailing in the enemy's bay, and was filled with troops for the invasion of the enemy's country. Thus, like a snow-ball, we had gathered as we went on, and from having set out a mere handful of soldiers, were now become an army formidable from its numbers as well as discipline."[28]

At 8:00 a.m. Admiral Cockburn and the captains of the battle fleet—"the squadron could now muster above twenty vessels entitled to display the pendant"—boarded Cochrane's flagship for a briefing and to receive their orders. Sir Alexander had by now fully warmed to Cockburn's strategy of employing the Patuxent as the main avenue of invasion, but couldn't prevent himself from tinkering with additional schemes for diversionary movements. A small squadron would, as Cockburn suggested, be sent up the Potomac led by Captain James Alexander Gordon in the frigate *Seahorse*, 38, to destroy American strong points along the river, draw off and confuse American forces, and provide an alternative escape route for Ross's army if necessary. Cochrane embellished the feint, however, by adding a second movement. The frigate *Menelaus*, 36, commanded by Sir Peter Parker, would be dispatched with several armed schooners to the headwaters of the Chesapeake, above Baltimore, to menace the Yankee lines of communication with Philadelphia and New York, and throw further panic into the already disorganized foe. Cockburn and Ross would lead the main thrust up the Patuxent.[29]

Cockburn reiterated for the assembled captains the reasons why the seemingly remote Patuxent River, which most had never heard of, had been selected as the main avenue for the invasion of America instead of the mighty Potomac. The most direct nautical route to Washington from Point Lookout was, of course, the Potomac River. If the principal invasion force were to be sent along this passage, a landing could indeed be made in safety at Port Tobacco, approximately fifty miles up, from which a "direct and good road" led to Washington. From there a march of thirty-two miles overland via the village of Piscataway would bring the invaders to a bridge over the Eastern Branch leading to the city. There were serious problems with this approach, however, not encountered with the Patuxent route. The first problem was the direct river passage to Port Tobacco, which was obstructed by the dangerous Kettle Bottom Shoals. The water route to the capital beyond Port Tobacco, though possible, would have to hazard the guns of Fort Washington, a dozen miles below the city. Moreover, the land route via Piscataway would bring the army to another major choke point, a bridge over the Potomac believed to be well defended by a strong body of troops, a heavy sloop-of-war, and an armed schooner, which might inflict higher than acceptable casualties.

A main thrust up the Patuxent, as Cockburn had proposed all along, and a march on Washington via the side door of Bladensburg, where the Eastern Branch of the Potomac could easily be forded if necessary, seemed to Cochrane the most appropriate alternative to his other schemes and offered the best chance of success. Barney's flotilla provided the perfect pretext for ascending the river in the first place, and by the time the actual objectives of the invasion had been discovered, it would be too late for the defenders. A perfect plan after all![30]

The fleet intended for the Patuxent was divided into three divisions, commanded by Captains John Wainwright of *Tonnant,* Joseph Nourse of *Severn,* and Andrew King of *Iphigenia,* from which fifty-four barges, launches, pinnaces, cutters, yawls, flats, and scows would be employed to ferry the troops, marines, sailors, and artillery from the transports and ships of war upriver to the designated landing site at the port of Benedict. The briefing was concluded about nine o'clock in the morning, and within half an hour the fleet was upping anchor, putting on all possible sail, and each element proceeding toward its particular objective, though not without witnessing an unsettling omen. "It was singular enough, that the ships had scarcely began to lift their anchors," recalled one officer, "when the sky, which had hitherto been calm and serene, became suddenly darkened, and overcast with heavy clouds; and the water, which before had been as smooth and bright as a mirror, began to rise in black waves tipped with foam, though there was not a breath of air to fill the sails." Yet no sooner had the fleet battened down than the expected hurricane dissipated into meandering squalls.[31]

An order was raised onboard *Tonnant* to begin preparing three days' provisions for the troops' landing. By early afternoon, signals were continuously being raised aboard the flagship of the Patuxent expedition. One signal was directed to the attention of the landing parties. "Make it known that enemy left poisoned spirits in house—great caution requisite." At 4:30 p.m., with the entrance to the Patuxent finally in sight, the fleet, clawing against adverse

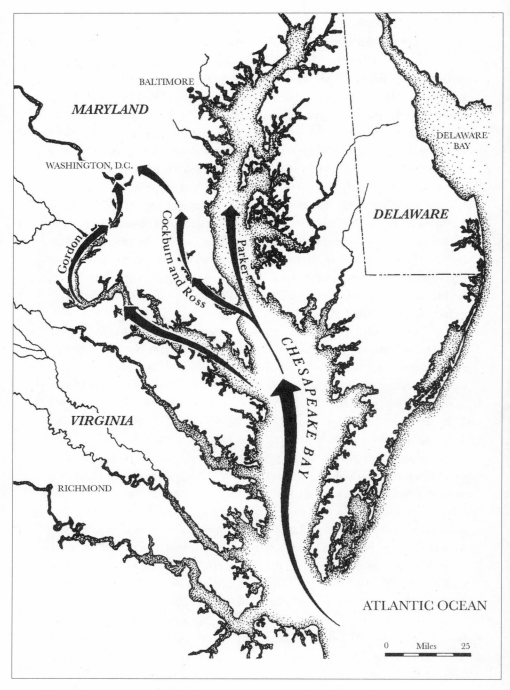

The British invasion of Maryland, August 1814. *Map by Donald G. Shomette.*

winds, was advised: "Troops will land tomorrow morning." A little over two hours later, the Royal Navy came to full anchor off the mouth of the river. The morning landing, it seemed, was likely to be later than anticipated.[32]

At 5:00 a.m. the following day, August 18, Cockburn's swollen squadron began to weigh anchor and stand into the Patuxent under the guidance of *Severn.* Captain Nourse, who had taken great pains to systematically sound the waters and a safe passage to Benedict over the past weeks, possessed the only accurate chart of the channel, not to mention intimate firsthand knowledge of the river itself. Nevertheless, the squadron encountered immediate difficulties despite his expert piloting. The morning breeze (when it saw fit to blow) was continually shifting, causing great distress in maneuvering the lumbering ships. From east, to variable, to calm, to southerly, and back to easterly the light winds blew. There was no end to navigational problems, especially at and below Point Patience, where the depth of water was 130 feet or more, with the point itself thrust like a knife directly across the river to within 200 yards of the opposite shore.[33]

· · ·

Aboard *Tonnant,* Admiral Cochrane sat in his cabin composing a letter to the American Secretary of State James Monroe. It was something of a preemptive justification of the havoc that the admiral hoped to soon invoke upon the United States.

> Having been called upon by the governor general of the Canadas to aid him in carrying into effect measures of retaliation against the inhabitants of the United States, for the wanton destruction committed by their army in Upper Canada, it has become imperiously my duty, conformably with the nature of the governor general's application, to issue to the naval force under my command, an order to destroy and lay waste such towns and districts upon the coast, as may be found assailable. I had hoped that this contest would have terminated, without my being obliged to the usage of civilized warfare, and as it has been with extreme reluctance and concern that I have found myself compelled to adopt this system of devastation, I shall be equally gratified if the conduct of the executive of the United States will authorize my staying such proceedings, by making reparation to the suffering inhabitants of Upper Canada; thereby manifesting that if the destructive measures pursued by their army were never sanctioned, they will no longer be permitted by the government.[34]

The ultimatum was clear, as was the admiral's intention. Washington was to be destroyed. Unfortunately, whether by design or not, Cochrane's letter

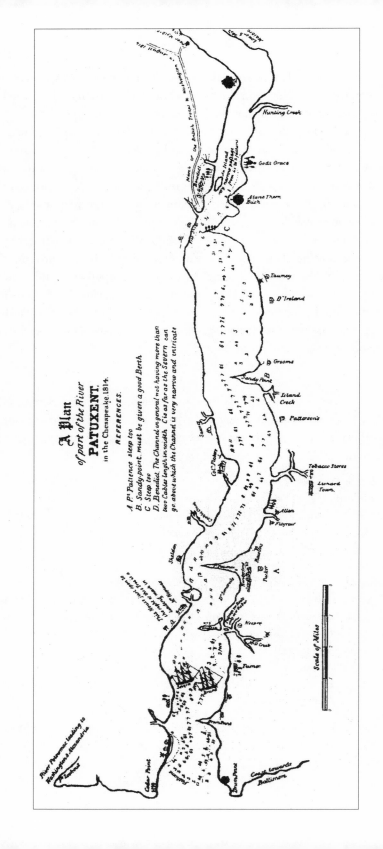

would not be delivered to the American secretary of state until August 31, by which time one of the most dramatic events of the war had already been carried out.[35]

...

As the bulk of the grand invasion armada came up off Somervell's Island, just below Point Patience, a calm brought all progress forward to a temporary halt to await a favorable breeze. Some aboard the fleet were amazed that the Americans had not mounted a half dozen heavy guns on the long spit of sand ahead of them, covered by riflemen in the woods, to put a check to the advance.[36] Cochrane took the opportunity offered by the lull to transfer the troops to lighter-draft vessels. Three companies of the 44th Regiment were shifted from HBMS *Dictator,* which dared proceed no farther than Point Patience, having lost an anchor in the deep waters there, to the frigate *Hebrus.* Several companies of troops aboard the transport *Diadem* were also transferred to frigates. Other units soon followed suit, and by 11:30 a.m. the troop transfers had been completed. Then the commander-in-chief moved his flag from *Tonnant* to the lighter-draft frigate *Iphigenia.* At noon, *Melpomene,* which had several American cavalrymen aboard as prisoners, was instructed to have them interrogated. Twenty minutes later, *Brune* was directed to send her principal prisoners aboard *Albion* and *Tonnant* for questioning. Cockburn was even at this late date attempting to glean whatever last-minute scraps of intelligence he could before the final commitment to a landing was made. It was obvious, however, that unless the wind picked up soon, a landing at Benedict within the next twenty-four hours was questionable and the element of surprise would most likely be lost. By 3:50 p.m. a light breeze finally began to whisper out of the south, and the squadron was soon under way again, tacking back and forth into the teeth of a stiff river current.[37]

Although of considerable draft, *Royal Oak* was among the lead vessels. As the fleet struggled up the waterway, a signal from Cochrane ordered the troops to be held in readiness to land at a moment's notice. Everything was therefore put in a state of forwardness. Provisions for three days had been

Facing page

Detail copy of a nautical chart of the Patuxent River from Drum Point to Benedict, August 1814, quite probably assembled from data gathered by Captain Joseph Nourse during his forays up the river. *Photocopy, Library of Congress, Washington, D.C.*

cooked and were now distributed to the troops—three pounds of pork and two and a half pounds of biscuits per man, or approximately eleven tons of food for the entire army to travel on. Cartouch boxes were supplied with fresh ammunition, and arms and accoutrements were handed out.[38]

"The fleet, however, continued to move on," noted Lieutenant Gleig, "without showing any inclination to bring up; till at length . . . the ships of the line began to take the ground; and in a little while after, even the frigates could proceed no farther. But, by this time, the sun had set, and darkness coming on; consequently, there was no possibility, for that day, of getting the troops on shore without much confusion, if not danger."[39]

The early morning hours of the 19th were rife with activity aboard the squadron, and the opportunity for sleep was minimal. At 2:00 a.m. boats were sent to begin disembarking the troops from the vessels lower down on the river that had been unable to pass the shallows. These smaller craft were run as high as prudence would permit under convoy of the gun-brigs and sloops-of-war. A lone gun-brig called *Anaconda* was sent up in advance of the main squadron to secure an anchorage less than 150 yards off Benedict, where the main landing was to be made, to provide covering fire if necessary. At 4:00 a.m. Admiral Cockburn debarked from *Albion,* which lay at anchor with the main fleet twelve miles below the town, and proceeded upriver in a small boat "to give the general every personal proof of his desire to assist him." In truth, the admiral did not wish to see Ross stricken with a case of cold feet this early in the game, and fully intended on "encouraging" him as often as possible.[40]

The first stages of debarkation had been carried out with efficiency and dispatch. Even the Light Division of Royal Artillery, with its two bulky field pieces, was taken off *Royal Oak* without incident. And everyone wondered just when Jonathan would make his appearance.[41]

...

Secretary Jones undoubtedly grew nervous when he opened an urgent dispatch from Captain Charles Gordon, dated the morning of August 16, for it presented to him for the first time an alarming description of a mighty invasion force coming in from the sea and pressing up the Chesapeake. At first count there were twenty-two sail in all: two 74-gun ships, one 64, a razee, seven frigates, seven transports, and two or three gun-brigs or schooners.[42] Upon receipt of the bad news, Jones fired off an express to Commodore Barney. "Appearances," he wrote, "indicate a design on this place, but it may be a feint, to mask a real design on Baltimore." If the enemy had arrived with a substantial land force, Washington would be their most likely target, and the secretary believed that it was probable they "would not waste much time with the flotilla." Thus, he ordered Barney to impede and retard the enemy's movements if possible to buy time to muster defense forces ashore. The commodore was further instructed to keep the secretary informed of his movements in order that an artillery unit and a detachment of U.S. Marines could be sent to reinforce him. In the event that it was possible to run the fleet safely up to Queen Anne's, as had been earlier considered, he would be permitted to do so, but was sternly warned: "you will run no hazard of capture." He was instructed without equivocation that, should the enemy "advance upon you, with an overwhelming force, you will effectually destroy the flotilla by fire, and with your small arms, retire as he advances, towards this place, opposing by all the means in your power, his progress." It was an order that would no doubt rankle the fire-eating commodore, whose only wish was to engage the oncoming enemy, but one that the secretary knew would be followed to the letter. At 2:00 p.m. an express rider was sent off with the orders and arrived at Nottingham seven hours later.[43]

The secretary's intelligence and directives came as no surprise to Joshua Barney, who had been the very first to learn of the main British presence on the Patuxent itself from two officers he had stationed at the river's mouth. That the enemy was coming up was, he believed, a good probability, and his ascent would be keenly monitored. On the morning of Friday, August 19, the commodore was able to fire off confirmed information of the enemy's numbers. They had arrived on the Patuxent with—at last count—an 80- or 90-gun ship, 2 74s, 6 frigates, 10 ships of at least 32 guns each, 4 small ships, one large 16-gun schooner, 2 barges, 13 large bay schooners, and a large flotilla of small craft. Soon afterward, he learned that at least 14 vessels had arrived at Benedict that same noon and within a few hours had begun disembarking troops. The enemy, it appeared, was finally committing himself to a massive invasion, for better or for worse, and information gathered by trusted forward observers verified the commodore's suspicions concerning their destination. Cockburn, it was reported, personally vowed to first annihilate the American flotilla, and then to "dine in Washington on Sunday."[44]

. . .

General Winder seemed in somewhat of a quandary as to what measures should be taken, as no one was certain what the intentions of the enemy might be. Even as Barney was sending off the latest news from the Patuxent, the general was flooding Secretary of War Armstrong with myriad scenarios and speculations. Would it be expedient, under the direction of the Navy Department, to have vessels ready to be sunk in the Potomac, at Fort Washington, or other points, at a moment's warning, to obstruct the navigation? Would it not be proper to put all the boats that could be propelled by oars at the City of Washington under the control of the navy at Fort Washington, to transport troops as events may require? Would it not be convenient to put the U.S. Marine Corps into service or at least be placed in readiness to reinforce Fort Washington at a moment's notice, or to be applied, as events require, to any point of defense? Should not the force under Commodore Barney be directed to cooperate with the commanding general, in case of the abandonment of the flotilla?[45]

...

The wooded shores and cliffs along the Patuxent drainage seemed to one British officer a throwback to primeval times, and the Royal Navy a predator stalking its prey through it. The stream was running strong, and many of the seamen were obliged to row fourteen or fifteen miles this way and that to combat the current before approaching their destination. Off Benedict the gun-brig *Anaconda* had moored fore and aft with spring cables and "was altogether as manageable as if she had been under sail." Her broadside was turned toward the shore, and her guns, loaded with grape and round shot, pointed directly at the beach and village beyond to cover the impending landing.[46]

A defense, although considered unlikely, was a possibility. "Had a few pieces of artillery," observed Gleig, "been mounted, indeed upon the high ground, afterwards taken possession of by us, some execution might have been done upon the boats, as they drew towards the beach; but even that would have been trifling, because, unless they had had leisure to heat their shot, no artillery in the open country could long stand before the fire of even a gun-brig, armed as this was, for the occasion, with long thirty-two pounders." The lieutenant had little positive to say about the town itself. It was, indeed, but "a small straggling place; the houses of which stand far apart from each other, and are surrounded by neat gardens, and apparently productive orchards. When we landed it was totally deserted by its inhabitants. The furniture however had not been removed, at least not wholly, from any of the houses, and not a few of the dairies were garnished with dishes of exquisite milk and delicate new cheese."[47]

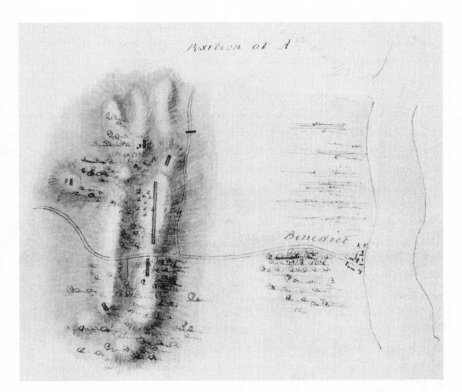

British engineer's map showing the town of Benedict and the disposition of General Robert Ross's army on the night of August 19, 1814. *Detail from a pen-and-ink "Sketch of the March of the British Army under M. Genl Ross from the 19th to the 29th Augt 1814," Beinecke Rare Book and Manuscript Library, Yale University Library, New Haven, Connecticut.*

The fleet was still, for the most part, strung out for a distance of ten or twelve miles below Benedict, but was crawling up slowly. With several frigates finally coming up, the advanced shore parties formed at 3:00 p.m. and prepared to land, still wondering all the while when the Americans would choose to make a stand.[48]

It would not be at Benedict. The initial landing was unopposed as the long anticipated invasion of America finally got under way. "Each boat load of soldiers," Gleig recalled, "likewise, drew up the moment they stepped on shore, forming line without any regard to companies or battalions." Reconnaissance parties were dispatched immediately to investigate the buildings in the town, while others established a temporary line behind a fronting of hedges near the shore. Regimental areas were soon sorted out on the beachhead, and the hospital and commissary stores were brought onto the beach, even as the main force of soldiers and marines was coming up in the frigates and transports.[49]

Aboard *Royal Oak,* which had finally ascended about as far up the Patuxent as possible for a ship of her size, the anchor was finally ordered dropped just northwest of Sandy Point. Not surprisingly, given the tricky navigational environment, the big warship had suffered a minor collision with a transport in coming up and had lost her flying jib. Carpenters were set to work immediately to make a new boom, even as the business of securing the nearby landing site went on without letup. Captain Edward Dix, commander of the ship, took the opportunity to attend to projects long delayed at sea. Armorers were set to work at the ship's forge, and sailmakers prepared a main deck awning and bags for the use of the artillery. Late in the evening, the remainder of the troops aboard and two howitzers per launch were sent ashore. Other vessels up and down the river were similarly employed throughout the night and well into the next morning.[50]

For many of the troops under General Ross's command, the landing provided them with the first feel of hard earth beneath their feet in more than eighty days. To put one's feet on solid land was for some, glorious indeed. Some were soon "lying at full length upon the grass, basking in the beams of a sultry sun, and apparently made happy by the very feeling of the green sod under them. Others were running and leaping about, giving exercise to the limbs which had so long been cramped and confined onboard ship." Yet discipline never flagged. The evening was taken up in establishing a defensive perimeter about the outskirts of the town and in distributing the expeditionary forces in proper order. The army moved up to an encampment site west of the town and overlooking the river. "In front was a valley," recorded one officer, "cultivated for some way and intersected with orchards; at the farther extremity of which the advanced picquets took their ground; pushing forward a chain of sentinels to the very skirts of the forest."[51]

Ross's right was anchored at a farmhouse, with its maze of enclosures and outbuildings, and his left upon the edge of a small hill. On the brow of the hill, and at the center of his line, loaded cannon were placed with lighted fuses beside them. The infantry bivouacked on the slope of the highland overlooking the town, and immediately under the ridge so that American observers could not discern their disposition and numbers. To ensure against surprise attack and any possibility of being cut off from the fleet, pickets were established at intervals circumventing the entire British line and running around both flanks.[52]

Ross paid meticulous attention to the details of organization as well as security. On the afternoon of the 19th, almost as soon as the initial beachhead had been established, he began to make a proper distribution of his army by dividing it into 3 brigades. The First, or Light Brigade, consisted of 1,100 men made up of the entire 85th Regiment, the light infantry companies of the 4th, 21st, and 44th Regiments, the black Colonial Corps of Marines, and a company of Royal Marines, all under the command of Colonel William Thornton, the brave and often impetuous commander of the 85th. The Second Brigade was composed of 1,460 men under the command of Colonel Arthur Brooke of the 44th, and made up of the main units of the 4th and 44th Regiments. The Third Brigade consisted of the 21st Regiment and a battalion of Royal Marines, totaling 1,460 men and commanded by Lieutenant Colonel William Paterson of the 21st. There was an abundance of miscellaneous personnel: 100 artillerymen, an equal number of teamsters, and a 100-man contingent of sailors from *Tonnant*, under the command of Lieutenant Lock, assigned to the army to haul artillery, stores, ammunition, and other necessaries. There was even a unit of 50 sappers and miners should fortification construction or destruction be necessary. A paucity of horses, it seemed, negated the use of a large train of artillery, and only two small 3-pounders and a single 6-pounder were brought ashore specifically for the march. Without horses to haul them, however, the remainder of the guns would be left to hold the beachhead.[53]

Now that the beachhead had been secured, General Ross permitted himself a good night's rest, even as the stream of troops continued flowing ashore unabated. Even as the eyes of the American secretary of state watched from the nearby hills.

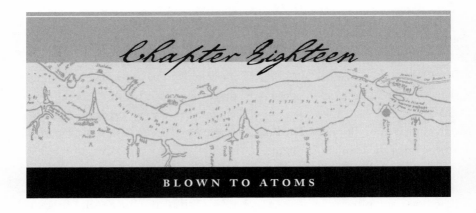

Chapter Eighteen

BLOWN TO ATOMS

Thomas Swann's express from Point Lookout had reached the U.S. secretary of the navy on the morning of August 18.[1] An enormous naval force was at hand at the mouth of the Potomac. If the size of the armada was commensurate with the number of land troops aboard, the entire Tidewater was indeed threatened. The horrific moment everyone had chosen to ignore, the enemy's designation of the Chesapeake as a major theater of land operations, at the very doorstep of the national government, had become a reality.

President Madison was immediately informed of the news, as were Secretary of War Armstrong, Secretary of State Monroe, and General Winder. Immediate action of some sort was imperative. Thus, orders went out to General John P. Van Ness to mobilize the District Militia; to General Samuel Smith, forty miles away in Baltimore, to federalize his Third Division and prepare to march at a moment's notice; and to General John Hungerford, 120 miles away in Virginia, to prepare to march with his two thousand militiamen.[2]

Intelligence began to flow in with ominous news, generally from points on the bay. British warships seemed to be everywhere. One frigate was even spotted off Annapolis, and enemy boat parties were believed to be laying out buoys and taking soundings, undoubtedly for charting purposes, in the nearby South River. Secretary of State James Monroe was among the first to learn of and respond to the threat. Calling on the president soon after the news had arrived at his office, the secretary was informed that the British had entered the Patuxent and were even then landing at Benedict. "I remarked," Monroe reported later, "that this city is their object. He concurred in the opinion." Characteristically, the secretary immediately volunteered to conduct a definitely un-statesmanlike function by leading a reconnaissance party to the bay shore for a firsthand look. Though far out of line from his normal cabinet function, Monroe yearned for action. Having served as a cavalry officer during the Revolution, and fought at the Battle of Trenton among others, he was certainly not unsuitable in a military sense for the task, and in the excitement of the emergency, Madison approved of the mission. A detachment of twenty-five or thirty of Colonel Thornton's Alexandria dragoons, commanded by a Captain Trist, was pressed into service and Monroe prepared to depart for Annapolis on what was to prove perhaps the most unusual mission ever conducted by a secretary of state.[3]

Despite the flurry of activity, no one in the American high command had the slightest indication of where the main British thrust would come from until Joshua Barney's express rider arrived. At 9:00 a.m. on August 19 the commodore had dispatched the report to Secretary Jones informing him of the enemy's movement into the Patuxent. Within five hours of his placing pen to paper, the capital knew. But it was still anyone's guess where the first blow would fall. General Winder contended that the enemy would strike against Annapolis; Secretary Armstrong, seeing no strategic advantage for the British to attack Washington, was certain it would be against Baltimore; Secretary Jones suspected the American flotilla at Nottingham was the main objective, but hadn't ruled out a feint designed to mask an attack on Baltimore. General Van Ness predicted a blow against Washington but was overruled by Armstrong. The president sided with Van Ness but for the moment refrained from strong comment. The only sure thing was that wherever the enemy attacked, at least one major arm, indeed probably his main thrust, would certainly originate from the Patuxent.[4]

If Winder wasn't panic-stricken, he had every right to be, for with Wellington's hard-bitten veterans about to march lord-knew-where, cruel reality was sweeping the capital. Pulling all of the numbers together, Winder discovered he had little more than a mélange of militiamen and regulars at his immediate disposal. General Hungerford was simply too far away and his forces too spread out to be of immediate service. There were only 330 men belonging to the 36th Regiment available at Piscataway on the Potomac, 140 cavalry at Georgetown, 240 Maryland militiamen at Bladensburg in nearby Maryland, and 1,400 assorted militiamen at Baltimore. Winder had a total available force, not including inactive militia, of barely 2,100 mostly part-time soldiers, the majority of which were poorly armed and ill-trained, to meet perhaps 4,000 to 6,000 veterans of the Napoleonic Wars![5]

Nevertheless, immediate mobilization of these standing forces and the summons to muster all inactive militia units were necessary. Orders were dispatched to Major General Samuel Smith in Baltimore to send down two regiments of county militia under General Tobias Stansbury; the 5th Regiment of Baltimore City Volunteers, a rifle battalion, and two companies of artillery under Brigadier General John Striker were also called up. The District of Columbia Militia, summoned on the 18th, was directed to report on the evening of the 19th for inspection. Many appeared without shoes, and others without weapons. One rag-tag company of riflemen, under the command of Captain John J. Stull, formed without so much as a single rifle in the entire unit. Disgusted by the showing, Winder had little alternative but to dismiss the men and order them to reassemble the next morning equipped and prepared to march. Without the means to provide for them himself, he desperately hoped they would somehow be ready. But that might only be possible with divine assistance.[6]

Secretary Jones also attempted to help fill in the manpower gap by dispatching an urgent express to Commodore John Rodgers in Philadelphia ordering him to come to Washington with three hundred seamen. Another order went out to Commodore David Porter in New York to gather what forces he could and come immediately to the capital. The Washington Navy Yard was stripped of all of the marines that could be spared, primarily Sam Miller's men, to join Commodore Barney on the Patuxent.[7]

James Monroe prepared to depart for Annapolis, but upon learning of the enemy force on the Patuxent, now altered his own plans. He would ride down to the river to watch for the enemy and then swing down to the Potomac to see what was going on there. At 1:00 p.m. he departed the capital and throughout the coming crisis would be addressed not as Mr. Secretary but as Colonel Monroe, a new role that he thoroughly relished.[8]

...

By the early morning hours of August 20 Joshua Barney had become woefully aware of the successful British landing operations even at that moment still under way at Benedict, and at 7:00 a.m. dispatched another urgent report to Secretary Jones. The enemy, it appeared, was indeed committing himself and had been coming ashore in a more or less steady stream since noon of the previous day. There did not, however, appear to be any sign of movement. "No doubt their object is Washington, and perhaps the flotilla."[9]

...

James Monroe, accompanied by Thornton's dragoons, arrived at 8:00 a.m. on August 20 at Aquasco, also known as Butler's Mill, four miles northwest of

Benedict, where it was rumored about the countryside that the British had marched. Finding the information to be without foundation, the secretary of state-turned-scout decided to probe even closer to the Patuxent. While at Aquasco, he learned that enemy pickets had taken station within a mile and a half's distance. To facilitate communications and expedite the carrying of information to the capital, he ordered several dragoons to be placed at a distance of ten or twelve miles apart from Aquasco all the way back to Washington. By 10:00 a.m., managing to avoid enemy pickets, he had closed in on Benedict enough to at least see the enemy shipping. His first express, which reached the president that same evening, was brief: "From a height between the mill and the river, I had a view of their ships," he reported, "but being at a distance of three miles, and having no glass, we could not count them . . . they are still debarking their troops, of the number of which I have not obtained any satisfactory information of. The general idea also is, that Washington is their objective, but of this I can form no opinion at this time."[10]

. . .

Colonel William Brent's 2nd Regiment of the District Militia began to assemble at around nine o'clock in the morning on the Capitol grounds. Three hours later, Colonel George Magruder's 1st Regiment arrived, but without its commander. Despite the proceedings of the evening before, disorder was minimal and, for a change, confined only to the high command. While Generals Winder and Van Ness reviewed the troops, a dispute arose between them over rank. The latter, a major general in the militia, was of the opinion that he outranked the former, a brigadier in the regulars. The bickering grew heated and was only resolved when Secretary Armstrong and then the president himself intervened. Van Ness was overruled. Piqued, the militia commander resigned in a fit of rage, and his command was turned over to Brigadier General Walter Smith.[11]

. . .

In his Navy Department office, Secretary Jones read Barney's dispatch, written early that morning, with alarm. It was now 11:30 a.m., and the courier had made excellent time from Nottingham—less than four and a half hours. Jones's first reaction to the commodore's intelligence was to find out exactly how far Benedict was from Washington and what type of road, if any, there was between the capital and the town, which is surprising given the constant action on the river in recent weeks. He learned, unhappily, that there was indeed a poor road, but quite direct, of some thirty-five miles in length. It could be covered in a day or two by foot soldiers under a heavy forced march.[12] The distance from Benedict to Nottingham had been computed by Barney at twenty miles with fine road, and from there another twenty-five to the capital. The commodore was of the opinion that the enemy would follow the latter. Yet from the head of navigation on the Patuxent, near Upper Marlboro, there were also good roads to both Washington and Annapolis and even Baltimore. It was still, unfortunately, unclear just what the British were up to.

The secretary considered the narrow alternatives available to Barney's flotilla, all of which depended on how the enemy committed his forces. He then composed a new set of orders for the commodore. "Should the enemy dash for this place," he wrote, "he will probably take this road [from Benedict], unless he should follow the bank of the river to Nottingham with his advance guard to drive back your flotilla and bring up his main body by water. This will have been discovered before you receive this, and you will immediately send the flotilla up to Queen Ann's Town with as few men as possible and a trusty officer to remain there and in the event of the enemy advancing upon the flotilla in force to destroy the whole effectually and proceed with his men to this place. Having given these directions you will retire before the enemy toward this place opposing his progress as well by your arms, as by falling trees across the road, removing bridges, and presenting every other possible obstacle to his march."[13]

The secretary informed Barney that at least a little help was on the way. The detachment of 110 marines from the Navy Yard, under Captain Sam Miller's command, with three 12-pounders and two long, light 18-pounders, would be ready to leave the capital on the morning of the 21st, and, on joining the flotilla force, was to be placed under the direct command of the commodore.[14]

Jones was obviously pessimistic about the chances of the flotilla's survival, but Barney's experienced, battle-hardened veterans were of considerably greater importance now than was the fleet itself. The commodore was thus instructed to employ the flotillamen as artillerists and Miller's marines as infantry. Since Miller had been placed under Barney's direct command, it was imperative that there be no disputes over the commodore's authority. Thus, the secretary enclosed a copy of established procedures entitled "Regulations of the War Department for the Government of Their Respective Commanders When Acting in Concert." There would be no repeat of the Winder–Van Ness tiff in his department if it could be helped. If the commodore had any further questions on the subject he was directed to "communicate freely" with General Winder on the matter.[15]

Almost as an afterthought, Jones queried Barney on his armaments. Did he have enough muskets and pikes? Would he require an additional supply of the former after manning his cannons? Should he need provisions, he was told he should draw directly from the Navy Department in Washington; Commodore Thomas Tingey, commandant of the Washington Navy Yard, would comply with his requisitions immediately. The secretary would also dispatch two men from the Navy Yard to ride express "in quick succession" during the crisis.[16]

Jones was well aware of Barney's unpleasant opinion of and working relationship with the U.S. Army and local militia forces. But it was imperative that he acquire just that capacity—and fast. Winder's requirements would soon dictate to what use the flotillamen could best be put, and Jones did not wish to interfere. Thus, he informed Barney that any modification of his orders "that yourself and General Winder shall agree upon" would be acceptable and automatically authorized by him.[17] Although he need not have said it, for Barney was undoubtedly aware of the fact already, the secretary added: "Your force on this occasion is of immense importance and is relied upon with the utmost confidence." They were, in fact, as events would prove, the only force that could be relied upon.[18]

...

At Benedict the last of Ross's troops were landed in the early morning hours of the 20th.[19] Those already ashore had been under arms at least an hour before daylight, and remained in that situation until well after the sun had risen. No one except the high command appeared to know just where the army was bound, but rumors floated about the camp "that a flotilla of gun-boats upon the Patuxent, commanded by the American commodore Barney, was the point of attack; and that while the land force advance up the river to prevent their retreat, armed boats from the fleet were to engage them in front." Everyone suspected that the army would be immediately put in motion, but those expecting to advance were quietly disappointed. The men were returned to their campsite of the night before to await orders. It was a classic case of "hurry up and wait" common to armies everywhere in the world—including the American army gathering in Washington.[20]

...

General Winder was relieved of at least one decision among the many being pressed upon him. With the receipt of the most recent intelligence concerning the landing at Benedict, he at least knew in which direction to march his troops, some of which had been standing about awaiting orders for nearly five hours. Even without precise information regarding the enemy's intentions, Winder proposed to march to the Woodyard, twelve miles east of the capital, where his force would be in a position to respond rapidly to any moves the invaders might make. Militia units coming in from the north and west were to rally at the port of Bladensburg, on the Northeast Branch of the Potomac. Unfortunately, the army with which this response was to be carried out was pitifully destitute of numerical strength as well as spiritual resolve.

Stirring words of encouragement, however, were not lacking, and appeared even in the general orders. "The enemy threaten the capital of your country, and are now pressing toward it with a force which will require every man to do his duty, without regard to sacrifice and privations. The zeal and promptitude evinced by those now in the field with the reinforcements which are rapidly pressing to your aid, afford the fairest promise that the enemy will receive the just chastisement of his temerity."[21]

Every man who could carry a gun, even those not legally required to turn out (the elderly, the young, and the infirm), was beseeched to muster to the defense of his capital and country. Cowardice would not be tolerated. "Let no man allow his private opinions, his prejudices or caprices in favor of this or that particular arm or weapon or annoyance be a pretended excuse for deserting his post, but seizing on those which can be furnished him, or he can command himself, resolutely encounter the enemy."[22]

In a move to preserve order in the army's rear and to prohibit the consequence of possible panic, Mayor Blake requested all persons exempted from militia duty to immediately enroll in civilian companies to patrol the city. All citizens were asked to be vigilant and report or "take up all suspected persons." A curfew of 10:00 p.m. was imposed, after which time any unauthorized persons found on the streets would be arrested.[23]

As Winder's men awaited their marching orders, the *Intelligencer* typesetters were blocking in a stunning story of American valor and triumph in Canada, and word of a Yankee military victory there quickly reached the forces mustered on the Capitol grounds. The British, it seemed, had been defeated in a bloody attack on Fort Erie, from which they had been repulsed with the loss of over six hundred in dead, wounded, and captured. Winder's troops roared their approval with a salute from Major Peter's artillery and a *feu de joi* from the infantry. The general completed the impromptu celebration by issuing a proclamation filled with heady words and noble assurances that thousands of reinforcements were on the way to Washington to help expel "the insolent foot of the invader." Three rousing cheers went up in response to his message.[24]

At 2:00 p.m. the American ranks, consisting of Brigadier General Walter Smith's 1st Columbian Brigade, barely 1,070 men strong, commenced the march to the Woodyard to take the offensive and meet the foe. The brigade included the 1st and 2nd Regiments under Colonels George Magruder, brother to the clerk of the U.S. House of Representatives, and William Brent; two companies of artillery, consisting of 210 men and a dozen 6-pounders; 2 companies of riflemen, totaling 170 men but armed with antiquated muskets, "the Secretary of war having declined or refused to furnish rifles"; a company of 40 grenadiers; 5 companies of light infantry, 250 men, in all 670 volunteers; and approximately 400 "residue," being defined as "common militia." Many were still without rifles or muskets, and others were still clad in their civilian clothes. Their now soaring spirits, however, temporarily made up for the material trappings of an army that sorely lacked every military accoutrement. Winder had already sent out an advance unit of Lieutenant Colonel Frisby Tilghman' dragoons belonging to the 1st Maryland Cavalry from Hagerstown, Washington County, under Major Otho Williams, toward the Woodyard "to fall upon the enemy, to annoy, harass, and impede their march, by every means possible, to remove or destroy forage and provisions from before the enemy, and gain intelligence." Captain Elias B. Caldwell, with his Washington Light Horse, was dispatched with the same view toward Benedict, by way of Piscataway, as it was uncertain which route the enemy might take if Washington was his intention.[25]

...

At the very moment that the American army was setting out from Washington, Admiral George Cockburn began moving up the Patuxent River with his flotilla of armed boats and tenders, barges, cutters, gigs, and miscellaneous vessels drafted from the ships of the fleet, laden with both black and white marines. His mission was designed specifically "to keep up with the right flank of the army, for the double purpose of supplying it with provisions, and, if necessary, to pass it over to the left bank of the river, into Calvert county, which secured a safe retreat to the ships, should it be judged necessary." Oxen had been slaughtered and fresh provisions for the troops had been transferred to two of the tenders ascending the river with the flotilla. Unlike his opponents, there were no irregularities in the accoutrements of his marines, although a few creases may have appeared in their heavy coats and trousers as they sat stiffly erect in the stifling midday heat.[26]

The marines had been placed under the overall command of Captain Robyns, and the marine artillery under that of Captain Harrison, aboard their respective tenders. The frigates *Severn* and *Hebrus* and sloop-of-war *Manly* were to follow close behind, as far upriver as possible. As far as most of the rank-and-file knew, their main objective was simply to destroy the American flotilla and to offer support and/or protection to General Ross's command. Like the soldiers ashore, few realized that Washington was the main target. Cockburn's meticulous arrangement of his mini-armada reinforced this belief. The boats and tenders were divided into three divisions. The first division was placed under the command of Captain Thomas Ball Sullivan, senior commander employed on the occasion, and William Stanhope Badcock. The second division fell under the direction of Captains James Somerville and Rowland Mony. The third division was placed under the command of Captain Robert Ramsay. Superintendence and immediate management of the whole operation was given to Captain John Wainwright, skipper of *Tonnant*. Cockburn embarked aboard the tender *Resolution*, and was personally attended to by First Lieutenant James Scott of *Albion*, who served as his aide-de-camp.[27]

Ashore, the British army remained poised to march, but it was not until 4:00 p.m. that General Ross suddenly appeared in the camp. Cheers resounded amidst the ranks as he rode through. Bugles were sounded, and within minutes the regiments had formed in marching trim. Soon afterward orders were dispensed and the army started out on the sandy road to Nottingham, an estimated twenty miles distant.[28]

There had been fewer horses at Benedict than had been anticipated, and only the general officers and their staffs rode. Thus, lacking cavalry, the eyes of an army on the march, Ross was obliged to proceed with caution—the same caution that marked his careful selection of an encampment site in the heart of enemy territory. His officer in charge of gathering intelligence in the region, Captain Harry Smith, fortunately, had managed to secure the services of two American renegades, a leper named Calder, "a shrewd, intelligent fellow," and another collaborator named Brown. With these two men willing to serve as guides and scouts, the advance guard consisted of twenty men marching a hundred yards ahead. But even this unit was preceded by two files sent forward to prevent surprise and to warn of the approach of hostile forces.

Flank patrols of fifty to sixty men each marched parallel with the head of the three companies, extending perpendicular from each side of the column and sweeping the forests and fields for nearly half a mile. At an interval of 100 to 150 yards behind the advanced guard came the Light Brigade, which also sent flankers to prevent ambush. Next came the Second Brigade, then the three artillery pieces drawn by the seamen. Last came the Third Brigade with a detachment at the same distance from the rear of the column as the advance guard was from the front.[29]

The march was not an easy one for men who had been cooped up aboard ships for the better part of three months, trekking through a hostile countryside quite suitable for ambush and "annoyance" from the enemy. They had grown unused to the burdens of heavy arms and backpacks, and soon began to chafe under their loads. Each soldier carried, besides his weapons and sixty rounds of ball cartridges, a knapsack containing shirts, shoes, stockings, a blanket, a haversack with provisions for three days, and a canteen or wooden keg filled with water. As the afternoon wore on and the temperatures hovered at a sultry level, the water in the canteens disappeared, and the miles seemed to grow longer with every step. More than a third of the army fell out of position, and stragglers were everywhere. Many broke into houses along the way and consumed any liquids available. No one paid attention to the warnings of potentially poisoned beverages. More troops dropped from the ranks on the march beneath the Tidewater sun, one veteran officer of the 85th noted, than had ever fallen out in any march three times the length and difficulty undertaken during the entire Peninsular Campaign. Ross soon realized he had little alternative but to bring the column to rest—barely six miles from its starting point at Benedict.[30]

The gentle eminence selected for the bivouac area was fronted by an open, pleasingly cultivated countryside, and was crowned by several houses with barns and walled gardens attached to them. "Neither flank," recalled Gleig of their position, "could be said to rest upon any point peculiarly well defended, but they were not exposed; because, by extending or condensing the line, almost any one of these houses might be converted into a protecting redoubt. The outposts . . . extended completely round the encampment, enclosing the entire army within a connected chain of sentinels; and precluding the possibility of even a single individual making his way within the line." Fires were lit, and the bone-weary troops at last settled down to rest. The night, however, would prove far from comfortable.[31]

At 7:00 p.m. a violent Tidewater thunderstorm rolled in from the southeast

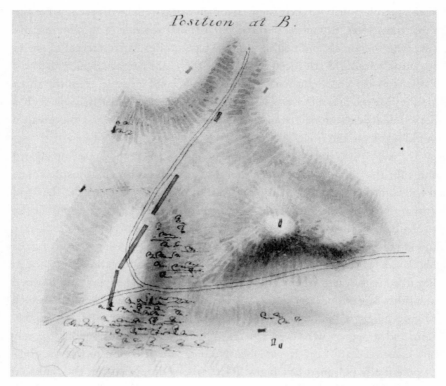

The disposition of the British army on the night of August 20, 1814, on the road to Nottingham. *Detail from "Sketch of the March of the British Army under M. Genl Ross from the 19th to the 29th Augt 1814," Beinecke Rare Book and Manuscript Library, Yale University Library, New Haven, Connecticut.*

as Lieutenant Gleig and his comrades watched in wonderment. "The effect of the lightning, as it glanced for a moment upon the bivouac, and displayed the firelocks piled in regular order, and the men stretched out like so many corpses beside them, was extremely fine." The downpour, which immediately followed, was something else. The soldiers, devoid of shelter, were soon drenched to the skin and spent the remainder of the night in utter misery.[32]

. . .

The British were not alone in their discomfort. Winder's army had also found the going somewhat unpleasant during the heat of the day. They had marched off in the afternoon full of zeal from the Capitol grounds down Pennsylvania

Avenue to the Eastern Branch of the Potomac. Crossing the lower of two bridges over this waterway, they proceeded in the direction of the Woodyard, but managed to cover only four sweat-soaked miles before calling a halt for the day. It was then that they learned that no one seemed to know where the tents or camp equipment were, or if they had even been requisitioned. This army, too, was obliged to spend the night in restless, near drowned repose.[33]

Perhaps the only person on either side able to pass the evening in comfort was James Monroe. Having quickly tired of waiting for the enemy to move from Benedict, the secretary of state had galloped out of Aquasco Mills south to Charlotte Hall, headquarters for the St. Mary's County Militia, to spend the evening in moderate comfort. His intention was to proceed the next day, perhaps as far as the Potomac, to view the situation in that region. On the morning of the 21st, before departing, he had finally been able to secure a view of the entire British fleet near Benedict, and downriver to a distance of eight or ten miles. Though he counted at least twenty-three square-rigged vessels, few others were to be seen and very few barges. With the enemy taking up its march soon after his departure the day before, Monroe had missed gathering extremely important intelligence and had also unwittingly permitted Ross to come between himself and the capital. He immediately inferred, however, that the enemy was moving upriver, "either against Commodore Barney's flotilla at Nottingham, confining their views to that object, or taking that in their way, and aiming at the city, in combination with the force on the Potomac."[34]

Abandoning his original plan to next spy out the enemy strength on the Potomac, Monroe determined to follow his movements on the Patuxent, which he believed "might be more important for the government to be made acquainted with." Instantly, he and Thornton's dragoons wheeled about and headed north to intercept, or at the very least shadow, the invaders on the road to the capital. They found nothing there also, and decided to next try Nottingham, where they might at least find Barney's flotilla, which the secretary now believed was the primary target. The tiny force spurred their sweating horses and galloped off toward the town.[35]

. . .

Commodore Barney had kept a close watch on the enemy, to determine which road they intended on taking. The direct route to Washington meant they hoped to fall upon the capital before resistance could be mounted. The better road to Nottingham, however, meant that they intended on keeping the Americans in the dark about their destination until the last possible moment,

James Monroe. *Oil painting by John Vanderlyn, 1816. Photocopy, Library of Congress, Washington, D.C.*

be it Washington, Annapolis, or even Baltimore. But one thing was certain: his fleet was in the way. At 11:00 a.m. on August 20 he received intelligence that the enemy was finally on the march to Nottingham and would probably reach the town by evening.[36]

When Joshua Barney was given an order, he generally carried it out with exemplary promptness, although he must have cringed at the thought of his flotilla possibly going up in flames without even offering combat. Yet Secretary Jones's command to retire to Queen Anne's Town and destroy the squadron should the enemy approach it was to be no exception. His orders were clear. It was time to move out. Within hours after receiving the secretary's instructions and the latest intelligence from below, the commodore's gallant little fleet had upped anchor and abandoned Nottingham to its own devices.[37]

The town, since 1810 an official Maryland Port of Entry, was at that time one of the more notable, thriving villages on the upper Patuxent. It consisted of four short streets, two running parallel with the river and two others crossing at right angles. "The houses," one British chronicler noted, "are not such as indicate the wealth or grandeur of the owners, being in general built of wood, and little superior to cottages; but it is surrounded by others of a much better description, which convey the idea of good substantial farmhouses, a species of mansion very common in the United States." Lieutenant Gleig estimated that the town contained between 1,000 and 1,500 inhabitants, and approved of its position, perched as it was amidst fields covered by an "abundant and luxuriant" crop of tobacco. Many barns filled with proof of the season's fine harvest dotted the landscape about the town. Yet with Barney's flotilla abandoning the site, the few citizens who had endured earlier enemy incursions into the region now commenced a general exodus, many departing in such haste as to leave all their earthly belongings behind.[38]

. . .

The British army resumed its march early on the 21st. Within a short time, the land seemed to alter in character as the open, cultivated fields gave way to thick stands of forests. The rural aspects of the countryside, the random farmhouses and fields of corn on both sides of the road, gradually disappeared and were replaced by wilderness savannahs. From some of the country folk encountered along the way, the British learned that numerous parties of American riflemen lay ahead, lurking in the brush and thickets, preparing to ambush the invaders at the slightest opportunity. This intelligence had an electrifying effect in the soldiery, "and the very expectation of something to do, created on the troopers a degree of excitement which, till now, we had not experienced." As a consequence of the danger, Ross strengthened his flank patrols and extended their reach outward from the central column to command even more of the field. The advance guard marched at a greater distance from the lead column, and the entire army assumed an even more cautious demeanor than before.[39]

Whenever intelligence came in regarding the possible presence of American patrols in the immediate vicinity, flying squads of troopers were sent out to investigate. On one occasion, information came in that a company of riflemen had passed the night in a particular section of the nearby forest, and Lieutenant Gleig was dispatched with a party of soldiers to surprise them. Gleig later recalled,

> On reaching the place, I found they had retired, but I thought I could perceive something like the glitter of arms a little farther towards the middle of the wood. Sending several files of soldiers in different directions, I contrived to surround the spot, and then moving forward, I beheld two men dressed in black coats, and

armed with bright firelocks, and bayonets, sitting under a tree; as soon as they observed me, they started up and took to their heels, but being hemmed in on all sides, they quickly perceived that to escape was impossible, and accordingly stood still. I hastened towards them, and having got within a few paces of where they stood, I heard the one say to the other, with a look of the most perfect simplicity, "Stop, John, till the gentlemen pass." There was something so ludicrous in this speech, and in the cast of countenance which accompanied it, that I could not help laughing aloud; nor was my mirth diminished by their attempts to persuade me that they were quiet country people, come out for no other purpose than to shoot squirrels. When I desired to know whether they carried bayonets to charge the squirrels, as well as musquets to shoot them, they were rather at loss to a reply; but they grumbled exceedingly when they found themselves prisoners, and conducted as such to the column.[40]

On the Patuxent, Admiral Cockburn did his best to advance in tandem with the troops ashore. "I endeavoured," he reported, "to keep the boats and tenders as nearly as possible abreast of the army of General Ross that I might communicate with him as occasion offered." Accordingly, near midday, the admiral anchored at the ferry house at White's Landing, opposite Lower Marlboro, and met with the general, in keeping with earlier plans. Here the army halted for several hours while the two commanders conferred, Cockburn no doubt taking the opportunity to once more bolster Ross's somewhat flagging enthusiasm for the entire operation. Afterward, they again set out upon their separate ways toward Nottingham.[41]

By late afternoon Ross's column had advanced to within a few miles of the town, and the troops were again looking forward to a halt. To many, it seemed that the extreme measures taken to prevent surprise attack were unnecessary in light of the relative safety in which they had traveled thus far. Yet, the intelligence provided by the locals was beginning to take on the appearance of fool's news perpetrated by ignorant country bumpkins. Forays to flush out hidden ambushers had turned up a few simple militiamen, but that was all. It hardly seemed worth the effort. Again the ranks began to distend, and an orderly line of march was becoming difficult to maintain. Suddenly, as the column neared the outskirts of the town, shots were heard somewhere ahead and to the right.[42]

...

James Monroe had galloped into Nottingham at about five o'clock in the afternoon, having circumvented the entire British line of march without realizing it. Unhappily, he discovered that the flotilla, which he had undoubtedly hoped to find there, had already retired upriver. The place was entirely deserted with but a "scattering militia" about and only two muskets to be found in town. An exodus of some size had apparently been carried out in great haste, for in several houses bread was later found still baking in the ovens. It was unclear to the secretary of state whether or not he was behind or in front of the enemy army. Within a few minutes, however, he would find out.

Shortly before 5:30 p.m. three of Cockburn's barges were spotted rounding the bend in the river below town. Excitedly, Monroe dashed off a message to General Winder suggesting that he immediately dispatch five hundred or six hundred men to the town. Although they might not be able to save the little community, it was just possible that they might cut off the enemy's retreat or sever his rear. Before the ink on the communiqué was dry, the number of barges had increased to ten or twelve, then thirty or forty more hove in sight, and the Alexandria dragoons opened a desultory fire, which was immediately returned from the barges.[43]

As Cockburn's flotilla closed on the town, the right flank of Ross's column also came up. The firing had given the soldiers in the column new life. Everyone was expecting—indeed, eager for—a meeting with Jonathan, and it was supposed that the anxiously awaited American stand would be made at Nottingham. Recklessly, General Ross led three or four of his mounted officers in a charge. Then, as the sun was setting, Monroe and his dragoons wisely wheeled about and galloped off in the direction of the Woodyard.[44]

The British were discouraged at not finding Barney at Nottingham. General Ross, in particular, was not a little disturbed that the American naval force, lurking somewhere ahead on his right flank, had yet to be encountered much less destroyed. Cockburn did his best to persuade the general that the flotilla was as good as captured or burned. Ross had nothing to fear from that point. Captains Nourse and Palmer, of the *Severn* and *Hebrus* frigates, without a doubt helped the admiral convince the general of the security of the army's flank. Both captains had just joined the barge force after finding the passage above deep-water navigation north of Benedict impossible for their ships.[45]

That night the British remained at Nottingham, with Cockburn's tenders, boats, and barges anchored comfortably in the river off the town or rowing guard. Ross's troops lay with their right on the river and their left extending a considerable distance in a half circle beyond the town, secured from surprise by a connected chain of outposts extending a full three miles beyond the encampment.

. . .

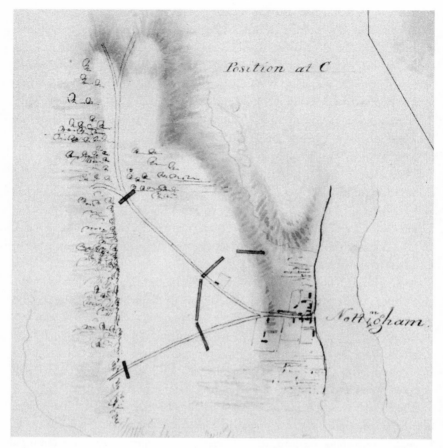

The disposition of the British army at Nottingham on the nights of August 21 and
27, 1814. Note the forward position of pickets. *Detail from "Sketch of the March of the British
Army under M. Genl Ross from the 19th to the 29th Augt 1814," Beinecke Rare Book and Manuscript
Library, Yale University Library, New Haven, Connecticut.*

The American flotilla, having retreated about as far up the Patuxent as possible, was intentionally grounded in the shallows a little above the bend of
Pig Point. It was absolutely impossible for *Scorpion* to proceed higher than
Scotchman's Hole, and the order to take the squadron, with the exception of
a few of the small barges, up as far as Queen Anne's was out of the question.
It was apparent now that the little force, which had so valiantly withstood
the might of the Royal Navy practically alone for nearly three months, was
doomed. And the commodore who had guided it through its inception, birth,

and growth, and courageously fought it against a far superior enemy through-out its short life, would not be permitted to see it die as he had vowed. It was Barney's sad duty to leave the business to the flotilla's junior commander, Lieutenant Solomon Frazier. The lieutenant's orders were simple: proceed with 120 flotillamen, including the sick and wounded, with the fleet to Queen Anne's. Should the enemy appear in force, as he most assuredly would, the lieutenant and a small party of men were to set fire to every boat and see them in full conflagration before escaping ashore and joining the commodore.[46]

After attending to a few final details, Barney put ashore with nearly 400 of his men, leaving behind not 120 but 103 sailors and the entire collection of personal belongings, most of the baggage, and all of the bedding of the flo-tillamen. Within minutes, carrying only three days' worth of provisions, he was on the march to Upper Marlboro, through a heavy forest and dense cedar thickets, where his men would spend the night. From the town he would pro-ceed by the Woodyard Road to link up with Miller's marines, and hopefully the U.S. Army.[47]

...

General Walter Smith's 1st Columbian Brigade, the largest component of General Winder's army, albeit without the commander-in-chief in company, had finally reached the vicinity of the Woodyard at dusk, after a most debili-tating and exhaustingly hot march, and set up camp. At the Woodyard Smith discovered 350 men belonging to Colonel William Scott's 36th Infantry and Tilghman's cavalry already encamped.[48]

About midnight Winder arrived in camp, followed soon afterward by Monroe with news of the enemy's arrival at Nottingham by land and water "with considerable force." Shortly after the secretary of state rode in, Colonel William D. Beall, a fifty-nine-year-old Revolutionary War veteran, militia officer, former commander of the 5th U.S. Infantry, and now commander of the 17th Maryland Militia, came in after having been sent out earlier to watch the enemy's motions. The British were at Nottingham. At least that much was agreed on—but that was about all. The secretary of state-turned-colonel es-timated Ross's force at six thousand. Beall thought it was closer to four thou-sand. Winder still wondered what the enemy's main objective would be, and vacillated from moment to moment, guessing at first one place and then an-other. At first he thought it would be Baltimore, but then considered an attack on Fort Washington from the rear a distinct probability, which was fright-ening since the fort was deemed "in several respects to be incomplete." And then came Washington itself.[49] Smith was ordered to be prepared to march immediately and to inform Scott that he was also to awaken and muster his men. Two hours later the drums beat reveille and the weary American army to parade. It was now Winder's intention to confront the enemy rather than to await his approach, whatever his destination might be. Quickly tents were struck, baggage wagons reloaded, and the troops mustered to arms. Then, 1,800 men stood at the ready, not knowing what to expect, until sunup.[50]

James Monroe went to bed. Colonel Beall rode off to Annapolis to fetch more troops. And General William Henry Winder spent the next few hours writing out orders and mulling over just what in heaven's name was to be done next.[51]

...

The American commander at the Woodyard was not the only general facing a moment of indecision. On the morning of August 22 General Ross again failed to set his army in motion at the crack of dawn as was his usual practice. Perhaps, as Lieutenant Gleig recorded, there "seemed indeed to be something like hesitation as to the course to be pursued, whether to follow the gunboats, or to return to the shipping." Ross was going through yet another crisis of resolve, for his forces were now a considerable distance from the sea and the sanctuary offered by the Royal Navy. They would soon be obliged to turn westward and out of sight and support of Cockburn's barge squadron. Whatever the cause for the delay, however, a final resolution was made to continue, and the army was set in motion at about eight o'clock in the morning in the direction of Upper Marlboro.[52]

The road was a good one, generally hard but often dusty. In some places isolated exposures of sandy soil were encountered; but always the marchers were surrounded by thick forests that sheltered them from the melting heat of the sun, "a circumstance which, in a climate like this, is of no slight importance." Throughout the march Ross insisted that the same precautions hitherto employed to prevent surprise be continued. Gradually the line angled away from the river and contact with the barge force was lost. Though Cockburn was personally accompanying him to spur him on, Ross was in command of a small army now devoid of all support. He was entirely on his own in a foreign land of which he knew little, marching across enemy terrain, to destroy the new capital of an infant nation his own country had spawned.[53]

...

At sunrise, the American column at the Woodyard, having sluggishly formed and then been obliged to wait for several hours for some unidentified bureaucratic reason, finally marched off toward Nottingham. Three hundred of Major George Peter's District Militia with twelve 6-pounders, which included two companies of riflemen and infantry under Captains Stull and Davidson, marched in the vanguard, with orders "to reconnoitre and hold the enemy in check." They were followed by elements of the 36th Infantry under Colonel Scott. Colonel Tilghman's cavalry had already been ordered to proceed on to the Marlboro-Nottingham road, and to rendezvous with Winder at a Catholic chapel near Upper Marlboro, most likely St. Thomas Church, later in the morning. The general himself, and James Monroe, accompanied by Dr. Hanson Catlett, an army surgeon with the 1st Regiment, sagaciously galloped off ahead of Peter's vanguard to examine the lay of the land.[54]

After riding five miles the three "scouts" came to a halt just before reaching a strategic juncture on the Woodyard Road. Here they came upon a tobacco plantation called Bellefields situated within a short distance from a most important junction. The plantation belonged to one Colonel Benjamin Oden, a staunch supporter of the war effort. As owner of 125 slaves, he had much to lose if the British came his way and absconded with his labor force as they had done to so many other planters. Beyond Oden's farm, approximately a quarter of a mile to the west, the road forked north and south. The north branch led to Upper Marlboro; the other led south to Nottingham from whence the enemy was approaching. It was an important junction to monitor, and a better one to command. "The country here," Dr. Catlett later remarked, "from the heights and fields, was admirably calculated to afford observations of the enemy." Should the British have the flotilla as their primary objective, they would have to take the branch to Upper Marlboro; should they have the Woodyard, Fort Washington, or even the capital in their sights, Ross would likely swing left onto the very route over which Winder had just ridden. If the British took this route, a collision with the American army was inevitable. At Oden's Winder took a brief respite to draft orders for another unit of U.S. cavalry that had arrived at the Woodyard during the evening from Carlisle, Pennsylvania, commanded by one Lieutenant Colonel Jacint Lavall. The colonel was to take the Marlboro road, post himself at the chapel near town, and send out patrols on all roads leading to Nottingham.[55]

In less than half an hour, the horsemen came thundering back with a report that the enemy was approaching the junction. At the same time, the advance brigade of the American forces, consisting of Peter's artillery, Davidson's infantry, and Stull's riflemen (armed with muskets rather than rifles), came up behind Oden's. In the meantime, the bulk of the army had continued along behind Peter until within an estimated two miles of the advanced guard. General Smith ordered them to take up defensive positions on high ground. Here they unexpectedly encountered Captain Miller and his marines, who had come in from Washington and had "judiciously posted" their own five guns. Smith, however, deemed the marine position unsuitable for his infantry, and rode briskly ahead to discover a better one, albeit without any luck. He thus determined to throw a portion of his light infantry into the woods and leave the remainder who were directed "to act according to circumstance."[56]

At that moment, from the south, Ross's vanguard suddenly appeared marching directly toward an apparent collision with the American van. "After taking such positions as would afford the best view of the enemy," Peter's command, forward of the main army, "partially formed in order of battle," and prepared to meet the oncoming enemy.[57]

At 8:30 a.m. the British advance reached the forks. To the left was the American camp at the Woodyard, and to the right was the way to Upper Marlboro. Winder fully expected the enemy to take the route toward the Woodyard and Washington. Instantly the British spotted a party of cavalry skulking about in the road ahead and to the left. The Americans were at first thought to be the rear guard of a column of infantry evacuating Upper Marlboro. Ross immediately wheeled his column onto the Woodyard Road to counter the threat. Perhaps a quarter of a mile east of Oden's farm, Winder's advance units, who were now barely three or four hundred yards ahead of the oncoming van, "in a most prompt and animated manner" steeled themselves behind forest cover to meet the enemy.[58]

. . .

On the Patuxent, Cockburn's flotilla moved with greased precision, albeit slowed by winds blowing directly down the narrow Patuxent Valley. With the advance of his tenders all but stymied, the admiral pressed on in his small craft. On approaching Pig Point, where it was reported that the American squadron had been drawn up, Captain Robyns's marines were landed with orders to march around and attack the village from the east. The ancient little river port, more a hamlet now than a proper town, was situated just below a point of land jutting into the Patuxent, and Robyns's marines would, he hoped, draw the attention of whatever troops might be stationed there away from his main barge force.[59]

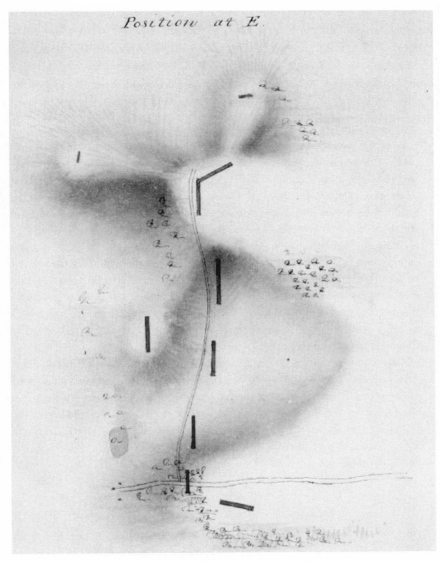

The temporary position of the British army as it turned up the road to the Woodyard and Washington, narrowly missing an engagement with Brigadier General William Henry Winder's advance units of the U.S. Army. The road to Upper Marlboro is at lower right. *Detail from "Sketch of the March of the British Army under M. Genl Ross from the 19th to the 29th Augt 1814," Beinecke Rare Book and Manuscript Library, Yale University Library, New Haven, Connecticut.*

Shortly before eleven o'clock in the morning the admiral began to focus his attention on the capture of Barney's flotilla itself, situated about three miles above Pig Point. Proceeding forward with his barge flotilla, he rounded the reach above the town, where he "plainly discovered Commodore Barney's broad pendant in the headmost vessel (a large sloop) and the remainder of the flotilla extending in a long line astern of her." With at least forty barges, all firing cannons and rockets, he advanced on the Americans

as rapidly as possible but on nearing them we observed the sloop bearing the broad pendant to be on fire, and she very soon afterwards blew up. I now saw clearly that they were all abandoned and on fire with trains to their magaz[ines], and out of the seventeen vessels which composed this formidable and so much vaunted flotilla sixteen were in quick succession blown to atoms, and the seventeenth (in which the fire had not taken) we captured, the commodore's sloop was a large armed vessel, the others were gun boats all having a long gun in the bow and a carronade in the stern, but the calibre of the guns and the number of the crew of each differed in proportion to the size of the boat, varying from 32 prs. and 60 men, to 18 prs. and 40 men—I found here laying above the flotilla under its protection thirteen merchant schooners, some of which not being worth bringing away I caused to be burnt, such as were in good condition, I directed to be moved to Pig Point—Whilst employed taking these vessels a few shots were fired at us by some of the men of the flotilla from the bushes on the shore near us, but Lieut. Scott whom I had landed for that purpose, soon got hold of them and made them prisoners—Some horsemen likewise shewed themselves on the neighbouring heights, but a rocket or two dispersed them, and Captain Robyns who had got possession of Pig Point without resistance now spreading his men through the country the enemy retreated to a distance and left us in quiet possession of the town, the neighbourhood, and our prizes.[60]

. . .

General Ross, lacking a cavalry screen, was entirely unaware of the American units ahead as he approached the critical crossroads near the Oden farm and viewed the appearance of American dragoon in the same light as the other minor encounters with the few minutemen along the way. Ahead, Winder and Monroe observed the enemy and soon saw a part of his column turn onto the Woodyard Road "and penetrate a skirt of wood, which hid the junction of the Marlborough and Woodyard road from view, and then halt within a quarter of a mile of Oden's house." He had already posted Scott's and Peter's units in the most favorable position to hopefully check the enemy's advance with as little risk as possible. For an hour or so the enemy column hesitated, seemingly uncertain as to its intended route. As the moments ticked by, the late morning hush was suddenly ripped asunder by the sound of tremendous explosions echoing down the Patuxent Valley.

Perhaps it was the demoralizing effect of hearing the demolition of the entire American fleet, which was believed by some to have been the enemy's first objective, or perhaps it was the very real possibility that the numerically superior invaders would turn up the Woodyard road at any minute. Whatever the motivation may have been, General William Henry Winder immediately ordered the van and then his entire army to retreat. Leaving behind his assistant adjutant for the Tenth Military District, Major Robert Hite, to actually determine which road the enemy would take, the general and the army's vanguard expeditiously began to retrace its steps toward camp. Several hundred yards away, satisfied that its right flank was no longer threatened by the flotilla, and that the American horsemen ahead posed not the slightest menace, the British army wheeled about, retraced its own steps, and took the fork leading to Upper Marlboro. In his report of the maneuvers, Winder later reported simply that the enemy "declined the combat." [61]

Yet, even the American retreat, without having fired a single shot, was rife with confusion. As they hurried back toward the camp, Peter's men suddenly collided with Lavall's cavalry, followed by Tilghman's unit, and then the 36th Regiment, in all about four or five hundred men coming down the road toward the forks as the forward element of the main force.[62] Not long afterward, Major Hite, who actually observed the British retrace their steps to take the Marlboro road, reported on the enemy's motions as well as his greatest weakness. The invaders, he informed his superior, had indeed peeled off onto the road to Upper Marlboro but what he had seen as they did so was of significant importance. "Their entire want of cavalry was observable, from their being none with their advance, to which we were so near." Nor, it was later determined, was any substantial artillery to be seen. The enemy, it appeared, was devoid of its eyes or major firepower, giving the Americans, who possessed both cavalry and artillery, a distinct tactical advantage.

Though the apparent lack of cavalry in the enemy formation might have seemed like something Winder could have taken advantage of, in truth most of his mounted force was untested, and in Lavall's case poorly trained. Lavall's men had been riding recently purchased and untrained horses all the way from Pennsylvania. The majority of the infantry had been up most of the night on standby after a forced march and were weary and footsore; his

"The Taking of the City of Washington . . . by the British Forces Under Major Genl. Ross on Augt. 24, 1814," a British montage depicting the Washington campaign. At *bottom* Admiral Cockburn's barge squadron bombards an already burning Chesapeake Flotilla. At *top right* the British army descends on Washington, D.C. The president's house burns (*center top*), while the Eastern Branch bridge is destroyed. The city of Washington, the U.S. Capitol, and the city ropewalk (*top left*) also are afire, while incendiaries set the Washington Navy Yard afire along with a vessel on the stocks (*center left*). *Library of Congress, Washington, D.C.*

riflemen were armed with antiquated and defective muskets; and his militia was untried in battle and were now facing (if Monroe was correct) as many as six thousand of the finest troops in the world. It was, perhaps given the stark realities of the moment, why Winder had given the order for his whole force to fall back.[63]

As far as the general was concerned, the British had at that moment committed themselves even though they were headed for Upper Marlboro. He was now certain that Washington was to be the enemy's ultimate target, and he hastily ordered all of his troops to retire toward the capital. In but an instant William Henry Winder had completely abandoned his offensive before it had even begun, and resolved to assume a defensive posture. Perhaps it was the appalling successive explosions emitting from Barney's flotilla from which "it was . . . inferred, that the enemy had ascended the Patuxent in force, that a column of troops had co-operated, by taking the road in that direction, which was soon afterwards confirmed." From the valley of the Patuxent the

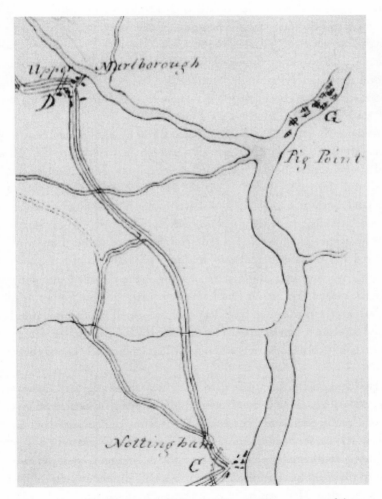

Detail from a British engineer's drawing showing the position of the Chesapeake Flotilla wrecks above Pig Point on August 22, 1814. *"Sketch of the March of the British Army under M. Genl Ross from the 19th to the 29th Augt 1814," Beinecke Rare Book and Manuscript Library, Yale University Library, New Haven, Connecticut.*

black smoke from the burning, sinking fleet, which could be seen rising above the tree line, only accentuated the general's opinion.[64]

The decision by William Henry Winder to retire from the Woodyard proved a pivotal moment that would become one of the most contentiously debated issues of the whole campaign. The general himself was certain of Ross's destination—at least for the moment. "A doubt, at that time," he later testified, "was not entertained by any body of the intentions of the enemy to proceed direct to Washington." Scott and Peter were ordered to occupy "the first eligible position" between the forks and the road the army was taking. Orders were also sent to Smith to have all baggage left in the camp removed west on the road to Washington and for the troops to retire slowly along the same road "to take post at the points where the roads from Washington city and the Woodyard, to Marlborough, unite."[65]

At about this time Commodore Barney and his flotillamen arrived from Upper Marlboro and joined the army. Among the first troops they encountered after entering the American lines were Captain Miller and his marines. The commodore was pleased that it was Miller's unit being placed under his command, but was astonished to discover that a general retreat had just been ordered. His disgust at such a move was not recorded, but his puzzlement over the retreat, which he considered injudicious at best, was. Finally, Winder appeared and Barney queried him, undoubtedly rather brusquely, about why the army was retiring. The general, having just confirmed that the enemy had backtracked and was at that moment heading toward Upper Marlboro, from which the flotillamen had just come, informed the commodore that he wished to place his troops between the British and the capital. Disgruntled but obedient to orders, Barney and his flotillamen dutifully joined the retiring force.[66]

Elsewhere on the field, James Monroe was apparently still unaware that the enemy had backtracked to Upper Marlboro when he dashed off an urgent dispatch to the president. "The enemy," he wrote, "are advanced six miles on the road to the Woodyard, and our troops retiring. Our troops were on the march to meet them, but in too small a body to engage. General Winder proposes to retire till he can collect them in a body. The enemy are in full march for Washington. Have the materials prepared to destroy the bridges."[67]

Almost as an afterthought, the secretary of state suggested: "you had better remove the records."[68]

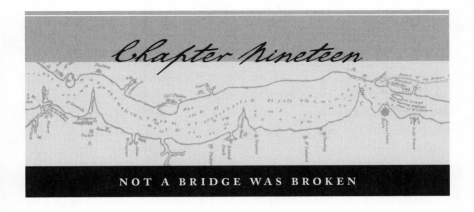

Chapter Nineteen

NOT A BRIDGE WAS BROKEN

Major General Robert Ross could not have picked a more pleasant site along the entire Patuxent River to bivouac his army. His men had hitherto encountered terrain that was relatively flat and boring, but upon approaching the vicinity of the village of Upper Marlboro they found the ground broken into graceful swells and rolling hills, generally stripped of timber to within a short distance of their summits. Yet the crests of these gentle terrestrial ridges were crowned with ancient and venerable forests. The village itself lay in a slight valley cradled by two such hills nearly two miles apart and surrounded by fields of corn, hay, and the all-important tobacco. The slopes were sprinkled with grazing sheep that accentuated the pastoral atmosphere of the setting.[1]

Upper Marlboro, county seat of Prince George's County, could only loosely be called a town, although it had been in existence as such for well over a century, indeed since 1695, when Scottish Presbyterians first settled there. Though it had originally been laid out in a formal grid pattern, its houses lay scattered about a wide area, on the plain, and even about the slopes of the hills. Orchards and gardens, abounding in peaches and other delightful fruits, hugged many of the buildings closely. Enhancing this charming setting was a small rivulet, the Western Branch, navigable in colonial times but at this point too silted up to permit any but the most rudimentary water carriage. The little creek trickled through the bottomlands of the village, wound its way around the foot of one of the hills, and ultimately melded with the mother Patuxent at Mount Calvert.[2]

The British, absolutely fatigued from their long, hot slog, were instantly taken with the town as they marched in, around two o'clock in the afternoon on August 22, and but an hour or two after the destruction of Barney's flotilla. A few junior officers and their men foraged about a number of deserted homes, finding bread, flour, chickens, and whiskey, which was passed about among them beneath the shade of a copse of trees. General Ross quickly selected as his temporary headquarters the home of Dr. William Beanes, a prominent medical practitioner and one of the few individuals in the place who had not fled in mortal fear before the British invaders. The good doctor was one of Upper Marlboro's leading citizens, a landholder of note, proprietor of a large gristmill, and owner of one of the better houses in the town. The general's host, who presented himself as an ex-patriot Scotsman of twenty years or so, at sixty-five, seemed amicable enough. He had "retained his native dialect in all its doric richness," appeared to be a perfect gentleman, and possessed certain Federalist sympathies—or so it seemed—which, together with his ingratiating charm, secured the commander's full trust. Beanes declared he was prepared to give his uninvited guests anything they wanted; he was nevertheless paid in full for the horses and provisions. "There was nothing," Gleig later noted, "about his house or farm to which he made us not heartily welcome; and the wily emigrant was no loser by his civility." On the assumption that to pay for the milk, tea, and sugar that was laid before him as a guest would be insulting, Gleig paid him nothing.[3]

For the first time in several days, General Ross had the opportunity for a moment of genuine respite and time to reflect on his situation. His right flank had been secured by the destruction of Barney's flotilla, but when the American naval force went up in smoke, so did his purported reason for being so far away from the main Royal Navy anchorage. He had already ascended some thirty miles up from the main fleet at Benedict, and though Washington lay only sixteen miles to the west, the Americans seemed to slip away from him at every step. Unfortunately, there was now, of all times, a decided lack of reliable intelligence. Nothing whatsoever seemed certain as to what lay between Upper Marlboro and the District of Columbia. Once again, Ross's resolve began to melt away with the heat of the day.[4]

The general had served for years in the British army with great loyalty and considerable efficiency. He had distinguished himself in all ranks as an officer, gaining enormous experience in Egypt, Italy, Portugal, France, and now America. Yet he had always served under a superior director, the last of which had been the great Wellington himself, whose troops he now commanded. As a general of a brigade, he had learned the art of war from the finest tutor in the world; but now he had to depend upon his own judgment. Obedience had been easy. Decision-making was something else. Upon his actions now depended the fate of a campaign, perhaps the entire course of the war. As one

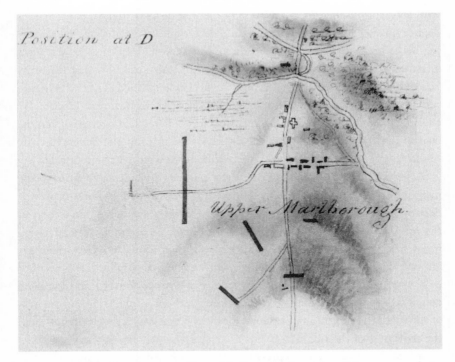

Disposition of the British army at Upper Marlboro on the nights of August 22 and 26, 1814. *Detail from "Sketch of the March of the British Army under M. Genl Ross from the 19th to the 29th Augt 1814," Beinecke Rare Book and Manuscript Library, Yale University Library, New Haven, Connecticut.*

of his junior officers sadly noted, "the great error of General Ross appears to have been a sufficient confidence in himself."[5]

Ross was at a crossroads. From Upper Marlboro he could either march west against the capital of the United States of America or retire to the fleet, the supposed objective of his endeavor, destruction of the Chesapeake Flotilla, having been successfully achieved. No one would question his decision should he choose to retire, for he was already near the end of the allotted tether permitted him by Earl Bathurst. Many of his staff, painfully aware of his crisis of resolve, were of the opinion that a move against Washington would decide the issue in His Majesty's favor, but Ross was not convinced. The general's hesitation at both Nottingham and Upper Marlboro was sensed throughout the ranks "and produced a delay which might have been attended with serious consequences." Lieutenant George de Lacy Evans, the general's deputy quarter master general and aide de camp, was vociferous in expressing his opinion that the capital be taken. Jonathan had yet to show any signs of strong resistance, and it was simply absurd to turn tail now that the army was so close to the Americans' center of government. Several of the general's staff in favor of a move west quietly decided to enlist Admiral Cockburn's considerable influence in the matter. Since the scheme had been his from the beginning, the very least he could do would be to prod the general a little further along. Perhaps another sixteen miles or so would do quite nicely.[6]

After all, thus far, as one critic of the campaign would later write of the insignificant American defense, "not a bridge was broken—not a causeway destroyed—not an inundation attempted—not a tree fallen—not a rood of the road obstructed, nor a gun fired at the enemy, in a march of nearly forty miles from Benedict to Upper Marlborough, by a route on which there are ten or a dozen difficult defiles, which, with a few hours' labour, six pieces of light artillery, 300 infantry, 200 riflemen, and 60 dragoons, could have been defended against any force that could approach them—such is the narrowness of the road, the profundity of the ravines, the steepness of the acclivities, and the sharpness of the ridges."[7]

If Cockburn was eager to press the general onward, his own superior, Admiral Cochrane, who was waiting at Benedict, was anything but, and already anxious to end the invasion. Cochrane was nervous. Rear Admiral Edward Codrington, who was with the commander-in-chief, was of a like mind, and believed an advance on Washington would be imprudent. The army lacked both cavalry and the horses to haul artillery, and Cockburn had already accomplished far more than his country could have expected of him or the army he was cajoling along. To risk it in an attack on the enemy capital might jeopardize future plans, such as an attack on New Orleans, the capture of which would give Great Britain control of the Mississippi and the American West. After some consultation between them, they decided that the attack should be aborted. Cockburn must return to Benedict.[8] Upon receiving word that the flotilla had been destroyed, the commander-in-chief sent a cordially curt note congratulating both Cockburn and Ross, ending with the thought that "as this matter is ended, the sooner the army get[s] back the better; I will not longer detain the boat that she may save tide up." Though not a direct order, the meaning was clear.[9]

Cockburn ignored the note, as it was not a direct order, and proceeded to secure Pig Point, placing the village in the hands of Captain Robyns and the

Royal Marines and Captain Nourse with two divisions of boats. Of course, the "large quantity of Tobacco" found in the town could not be ignored, and within a short time was being transferred from the village to several light schooners that had not gone down with the flotilla, along with the one captured American barge, "which is a good vessel for these waters." The third division of boats was moved up to an anchorage off Mount Calvert, at the truly majestic confluence of the Western Branch and Patuxent.[10]

On the following morning, August 23, Cockburn debarked from aboard the tender *Resolution* at Mount Calvert and rode horseback into Upper Marlboro, four miles away, with his aide Lieutenant James Scott and the two self-appointed emissaries from Ross's staff. Whatever was said between the two commanders at their meeting soon afterward, the admiral was apparently at his persuasive best. Ross emerged convinced that a move on Washington could be made with a reasonably good chance of success. The admiral couched to his superior the proceedings of the conference in terms that seemed to suggest the initiative had been Ross's all along. "I came here this morning to consult with him," he informed Cochrane, "& learn his future plans, & I find he is determined (in consequence of the information he has received & what he has observed of the enemy), to push on towards Washington, which I have confident hopes he will give account of." They were, he later reported, "not long in agreeing on the propriety of making an immediate attempt on the City of Washington." The admiral minimized his own role, that of mother hen herding her chicks along, by adding, almost as an afterthought, "I shall accompany him and of course afford him every assistance in my power."[11]

Offering every assistance to the army meant moving the third division of Cockburn's flotilla from Mount Calvert up the Western Branch to Upper Marlboro to maintain a communication between the army and the fleet, while the rest of the barges were to remain at Pig Point. Orders were dispatched to the marine artillery under Captain James H. Harrison, stationed at Pig Point, to cross the river to Mount Calvert and join the army. Captain Wainwright was directed to bring over the seamen from the British flotilla, and Captains Nourse and Palmer were sent to join the army with their men. When Ross finally moved out, Captain Robyns and his unit of marines would hold Upper Marlboro. The remainder of the Royal Marines and marine artillerymen would accompany the army to whatever ground it would occupy on the route.[12]

. . .

Though General William Henry Winder's army was retiring in orderly albeit hasty fashion, it was not destined to go where he wanted. The position he had ordered it to take, he later reported, was either "incorrectly delivered, or misunderstood." As it turned out, however, and by his own admission, the new location proved far superior to the one he had originally intended. Indeed, the "only position where the troops could be tolerably accommodated, or posted to advantage," he later stated, "was at Dunlap's, or, as it is generally called, the long, or Battalion Old Fields," midway on the sixteen mile road between Washington and Upper Marlboro. The cavalry under Tilghman and Herbert, who had come in with his Bladensburg Troop of Horse, was charged with hovering about the enemy on all roads leading from Bladensburg, from the north, and from Annapolis to Upper Marlboro. Lavall was advanced "to the nearest and most convenient positions between the Woodyard and Marlborough," and one or two prisoners "who had straggled beyond the enemy's pickets" confirmed that Ross had quietly halted at the latter and had no intention of leaving that day. There was little consolation, however, in that the enemy picket line would soon extend a full five miles beyond the town, and barely three miles from Battalion Old Fields itself.[13]

When the army arrived at its destination near the close of August 22, General Winder was still in the vicinity of Upper Marlboro, personally monitoring the motions of the enemy. Finally, as late afternoon was upon him, he determined that the invaders would likely remain in and about town, at least for the night. The disposition of the British was both disturbing and heartening. The general again revised his opinion regarding the enemy's intentions and now believed Ross might be waiting to link up with Gordon's squadron, which was at that moment slowly ascending the Potomac, perhaps at Piscataway. But there were potential possibilities for initiating an American offensive if the enemy remained in the town for a day or two more by launching an assault on them from the neighboring hills. The notion, however, was quickly dispelled in the late afternoon heat and dust of his ride to rejoin the army at Battalion Old Fields.[14] Upon his arrival late in the day Winder took a mental muster of the troops under his command, which had finally reached Battalion Old Fields about four o'clock in the afternoon, and immediately established camp. They now numbered, including the approximately 620 sailors and marines belonging to Barney and Miller, a little over 2,400 men.[15]

As if the enemy was not headache enough, upon his arrival at Battalion Old Fields, Winder also learned that the president and members of his cabinet had arrived at a house a mile in the rear of the camp. He dutifully dispatched a captain's guard to provide for their security, but there was little time at the moment for him to personally meet with the commander-in-chief of the United States. Instead, he dispatched Lavall's cavalry to monitor the roads from Marlboro with orders to patrol "as close upon the enemy as possible during the course of the night." He then set himself to wading through "the infinite applications, consultations, and calls, necessarily arising from a body of two thousand five hundred men, not three days from their homes, without organization, or any practical knowledge of service on the part of their officers, and being obliged to listen to the officious but well intended information and advice of the crowd, who, at such a time, would be full of both."[16]

In his own tent a mile in the rear of the army, Commodore Joshua Barney met with Secretary of the Navy Jones and invited him to spend the night, with both old seafarers recounting their own versions of the events of the recent days and the dangers ahead. One gets the feeling that they spent the evening not as master and subordinate, but as friends. The night was not destined to be passed in repose, however, as sometime between two o'clock and three o'clock in the morning, an alarm gun was sounded, and the troops were roused and formed. The alarm proved false, although the state of alert was maintained until sunrise, and few in the American army, standing at arms, got much sleep.[17]

. . .

The morning of August 23 dawned with all the promise of another exceedingly sticky hot and sultry day. Shortly after sunup, Winder ordered the tents struck, baggage wagons loaded, and the troops made ready to march in an hour. He then rode over to the quarters of the president to brief him, Secretary of War Armstrong, and Secretary of the Navy Jones upon the situation and to arrange for a review of the troops. The general was again uncertain as to whether Washington or even Annapolis was to be the enemy's main objective, for from their position at Upper Marlboro good roads led to both. He now tended, having changed his mind yet again in the last twenty-four hours, to believe Annapolis was the enemy target, "a fine port, where his ships could lie in safety; it afforded abundant and comfortable quarters for his men; magazines and store for all his stores and munitions of every description; was capable, with very little labor, of being rendered impregnable by land, and he commanded the water." From there both Washington and Baltimore were within striking range. As for the enemy fleet ascending the Potomac, he now assumed the move to be a feint, to mask Ross's intended attack on Annapolis.

But then again, he waxed lyrically, it might be possible Gordon intended "to unite with the land force, and co-operate in a joint attack on Washington," after first taking Fort Washington in the rear "where it is wholly defence-less." It was anyone's guess! The president, succumbing to the latest theory emanating from the general's ever-vacillating thoughts, was apparently reassured that the immediate object of enemy intentions was probably Annapolis. Moreover, he had been convinced by the general that the enemy, having been many weeks at sea and lacking any appreciable cavalry and artillery, and after hard marching in the heat and dust, were certainly in no condition to assail the capital.[18] Commodore Barney, who knew better, said nothing.

Upon Winder's return to camp about eight o'clock in the morning, accompanied by the president and his entourage, he was informed of rumors that the enemy had taken the road from Upper Marlboro to Queen Anne's Town, from which another road led directly to South River and Annapolis. Believing that Tilghman and Herbert's cavalry, which had been posted to cover the roads in that area, could not have missed such a move, he quickly discredited the story. Nevertheless, he dispatched a party of fifteen or twenty mounted volunteers, who had just come in from Washington, to investigate. About noon they confirmed that the enemy was definitely not marching on the Annapolis road. In the meantime 150 Prince George's County militiamen under Major Samuel Maynard of the 22nd Regiment arrived, the first of a number of reinforcements heading toward the field.[19]

After the troops at Battalion Old Fields had finally been readied, they formed up to be formally reviewed by the president. Winder was able to again take stock of the forces that had assembled or were coming in to join the now nearly 3,000 men of the growing army, including Barney's flotillamen and Miller's marines. He took heart in also knowing that there were reportedly 1,350 troops from Baltimore that had just arrived at Bladensburg under the command of Brigadier General Tobias E. Stansbury and were preparing defenses atop Lowndes Hill, overlooking the town. An additional 800 Baltimoreans in Lieutenant Colonel Joseph Sterret's 5th Regiment were expected at any time.[20] Colonel William D. Beall would be coming in with another 800 from Annapolis. In all, the American army forming at Bladensburg and Battalion Old Fields to meet the enemy would, if all went well, amount to nearly 6,000 men.[21]

The review of the troops at Battalion Old Fields was brief but impressive. Afterward the president scribbled a short letter to his wife Dolley noting that the troops were "in high spirits & [made] a good appearance." Secretary

Jones was also impressed with Barney's sailors and Miller's marines, the only truly combat-tested men on the field, "whose appearance and preparations for battle promised all that could be expected from cool intrepidity, and a high state of discipline."[22]

With the formalities concluded, Winder returned to the business of the day and ordered an advanced corps, composed of the same units that had been employed the previous day under Peter, Davidson, and Stull, to be sent forward to further monitor the British. He then dispatched orders to Stansbury, who had arrived at 5:00 p.m. the previous evening at Bladensburg, to advance toward Upper Marlboro and take a position at the junction where the Battalion Old Fields–Queen Anne's road crossed the Bladensburg–Upper Marlboro pike, about four miles from Battalion Old Fields itself and six miles from the enemy. He then informed the president that he was going to meet Stansbury at the appointed junction "to be situated in a position where he might more

James Madison. *Oil painting by Gilbert Stuart, 1804. Photocopy, Library of Congress, Washington, D.C.*

conveniently communicate with the troops from Baltimore." General Smith would be left with directions where he might find the commander at the crossroads. Before departing, however, Winder left orders for Smith to have Peter's advance unit reconnoiter the enemy, and "approach him as near as possible without running too much risk, and to annoy him, either in his position or in his movements, by all the means in his power." Smith and the army were to remain for the time being at Battalion Old Fields "and act according to the intelligence [he] should receive of the movements of the enemy." If they moved upon Bladensburg, however, he was to approach them by the intersecting road from Battalion Old Fields and attack their left flank. If they approached from the Upper Marlboro–Old Fields road, he was, as conditions warranted, to either receive them or retire to Bladensburg or Washington.[23]

At 11:00 a.m. Major Peter's battalion was joined by Captain Caldwell's light cavalry unit, which had just come in, and together, numbering approximately two hundred men, set out about noon on one of the two roads leading to Upper Marlboro, one being a stage road of eight miles and the other a "not so good road" of six miles but more direct. The major was ordered to send back reports every hour.[24]

Not long after his departure, several British deserters and prisoners were brought into camp and cross examined by General Smith, but apparently proved of little value. Then, the sound of gunfire was heard from the direction of Upper Marlboro. The president and his party headed for Washington. General Smith began to prepare for action.[25]

...

Major Peter's advanced unit had taken position on a hilltop not far from the enemy lines. They had received a tip from a nearby resident that British officers had stopped by a bit earlier in the day and mentioned that Ross would be getting under way with his army about midday—and their destination was Washington. The major thus established his 6-gun battery on the road over which the invaders would be marching, flanked on both sides by riflemen armed only with muskets, and prepared to stall the enemy as best he could. Then, at the same moment he was alerted by Caldwell's dragoons that the enemy was approaching, an order from General Winder arrived instructing everyone to pull back.[26]

The British army, with elements of the Royal Navy, Royal Marines, and black Colonial Corps of Marines in company, had already moved out of Upper Marlboro by 2:00 p.m. on the final leg of their march on Washington.[27]

As Ross approached the hill upon which the Americans had only moments before been ensconced, and were even then in the process of descending, Major Peter shouted out for his men to shoot. A brief but ill-directed fire from antiquated muskets sent balls whistling in every direction but where the enemy was coming from. In a flash, a mounted British officer charged, hurtled a fence, and pressed on as the scurrying defenders dropped their weapons and ran for the brush. Somehow, Peter managed to extract his men at the cost of only one man wounded, but for years afterward believed that if his men had been armed with rifles, the outcome might have been different.[28]

The Americans retired toward Battalion Old Fields, even as the British juggernaut, believing Peter's force numbered at least 1,200 Americans, began to outflank the position the major had just held. As he managed his retreat, Peter dashed off an express informing Smith of the British advance from Upper Marlboro with a force that he estimated to be 6,000 strong. The message arrived at Smith's camp between four and five o'clock in the afternoon. The general immediately dispatched Lavall's cavalry to cover the major's retreat, and ordered the entire army under arms and the baggage train sent off to cross the Eastern Branch.[29]

A nervous General Smith quickly conferred with Commodore Barney, the most battle-tested officer in camp, and resolved to make a stand at Battalion Old Fields, a decision "with which, with his [Barney's] characteristic gallantry, he promptly acquiesced, professing his willingness to co-operate in any measures that might be deemed advisable." The troops were immediately formed in order of battle, which extended nearly a quarter of a mile on either side of the road. Commodore Barney, with the heavy artillery and Miller's marines, was posted on the right, flanked by the 36th and 38th Regiments (the same units that had abandoned the battlefield at St. Leonard's Creek). The District troops and "residue" militia were stationed on the left. As the advanced troops returned, they too took their station in the line. The artillery, which it was now ascertained, was superior to any the British had, was posted on the grounds best suited to it. Still nervous about making such decisions in Winder's absence, Smith dispatched his aide, Major Thomas L. McKenney, to find the commander.[30]

Undoubtedly buoyed by the core strength provided by the presence of Barney and his men, Smith was optimistic despite his trepidations. The American position, combined with an overwhelming superiority of artillery and cavalry, gave his forces, though inferior in numbers, a great advantage over the enemy. Indeed, "so strong did we deem our position in front, that we were apprehensive that the enemy, upon viewing us, would forebear to assail us by day-light, or that, availing of his numbers, he would endeavor to outflank us." Light troops and cavalry were immediately dispatched to cover both flanks.[31]

...

Four or five miles from Bladensburg, Major McKenney overtook General Winder, then en route to meet with Stansbury, and informed him of the situation, and that the enemy had marched to within three miles of the American line. The two officers instantly wheeled their horses around and returned to camp about five o'clock in the afternoon, as the hot August sun began to lower in the west. Winder immediately reviewed and approved of Smith's disposition of the troops. The enemy, however, had stopped only a few miles from Battalion Old Fields, which led him to a single conclusion. As Winder rode along the line, he remarked: "It is well arranged, but the manifest object of the enemy is to attack us in the night. We have not the material for a night fight." He gave as his reasoning that in a night attack, American superiority in artillery would be of little value. Moreover, the inexperience of the troops would "subject them to certain infallible, and irremediable disorder, and probable destruction, and thereby occasion the loss of a full half of the force which I could hope to oppose, under more favorable circumstances, to the enemy." He may also have been fearful of such a contest, illuminated in the dark only by the flash of gunfire, possibly recalling how he had been captured during a night action at Stoney Creek on the Canadian front on June 6, 1813. It was a situation he was not eager to revisit. The line of battle was maintained for only a short time after Peter's men returned and briefly took their position in it. Then, about sunset, after a short meeting with Barney, orders were issued and passed down the line to begin an immediate retreat, "as it was said the enemy was too strong for us."[32]

Winder was a whirlwind of activity as he organized the withdrawal. Captain Benjamin Burch's Washington Artillery, among the most recent arrivals on the scene, was ordered to remain in position as a rear guard until the rest of the troops had marched, and then, every fifteen minutes, send off two of his pieces with the appropriate number of men, until all six guns had been dispatched. If the enemy appeared he was to open upon them until he could no longer in safety do so, and then join the main body.[33] The commander-in-chief had already dispatched orders to Stansbury to reverse course, fall back, and "take the best position in advance of Bladensburg." There he was to link up with Lieutenant Colonel Joseph Sterett's eight hundred riflemen and artillerymen who were at that moment believed to be racing down from Elkridge, near Baltimore, and whose arrival was expected in the evening. Should the enemy come Stansbury's way to attack him, he was ordered to resist as long as possible. If obliged to retire, he was to fall back toward Washington. Winder now recommended to Barney that the heavy artillery also be withdrawn, with the exception of a single 12-pounder, to help Burch protect the eight-mile retreat toward the strategic long bridge over the Eastern Branch at Washington.[34]

Quickly the army began to move out, until finally, all were en route west. After sending off only his second set of guns, even Burch was ordered to quit the scene immediately. The only remnant left to indicate that an army, now swollen to nearly three thousand men, had mustered at Battalion Old Fields were several casks of flour and whiskey lying around that had to be destroyed in haste and left behind. The rush toward the Eastern Branch soon became more than a dash—it was a race that left all engaged absolutely out of breath and exhausted.[35]

At 7:00 p.m., even as Winder's army was racing toward Washington, General Stansbury arrived at Bladensburg, eight miles west of Battalion Old Fields, with his "fatigued, undisciplined, and inexperienced troops" which, one colleague blatantly admitted, should never be placed in the front lines. Stansbury fixed his encampment on Lowndes Hill, by the side of the road from Upper Marlboro and between it and the Eastern Branch. The position was a moderately defensible one, thanks to the efforts of many Washington and Bladensburg volunteers who, exempted from military service owing to age or infirmities, had hastily organized to dig earthworks. Winder had even provided a trained engineer to oversee their efforts. Even five hundred free people of color had been urged to answer the call and pitched in with unvarnished zeal. The smell of freshly turned earth was still in the air when about sunset, almost as soon as Stansbury had set up camp, Colonel Sterett's 5th Regiment, 3rd Maryland Brigade, marched into the town about eleven o'clock at night and encamped a short distance away. With many of their number being from the finest families in Baltimore, they were, perhaps, among the most colorful troops in the army, dressed as they were in blue jackets faced with crimson, white pantaloons, black gaiters, white cross-belts, and heavy leather helmets topped with two black and red sweeping plumes. Although 800 men had been expected, this weary force was somewhat undermanned. It consisted of 2 companies of artillery with 6 6-pounders, commanded by Captains Myers and Magruder, amounting to 150 men, and 3 companies belonging to

Major William Pinkney's battalion, commanded by Captains Dyer, Aisquith, and Baden, amounting to 180 rank-and-file.[36]

...

Although the enemy was approaching from the east, Winder still fretted over which road the enemy would take toward Washington. He also knew that they would have to cross at one of three bridges over the Eastern Branch to reach the city. The first crossing, known as the lower bridge, or Eastern Branch bridge (at the convergence of modern Pennsylvania and Kentucky avenues), was about a mile northeast of the Washington Navy Yard. The upper crossing, also known as Stoddert's Bridge, was on the southwest side of Bladensburg, at the convergence of a road to Baltimore and another from Upper Marlboro via Battalion Old Fields, and at the head of navigation on the Eastern Branch where the river was only forty yards wide and in some places only three feet deep. A third overpass was farther upstream of the town. If the enemy came by way of Battalion Old Fields, he would have to take one of the first two crossings. Winder now toyed with the idea of posting a guard on the lower bridge and destroying it. That in itself, however, might not deny the enemy a way across. Several miles upstream at Bladensburg was Stoddert's Bridge, and a shallow ford near the fork made by the Northeast and Northwest branches of the Eastern Branch. The ford could be "reached from Bladensburg, by first crossing the northeast branch in the present Baltimore road, and then running to the left."[37]

Upon arriving on the Eastern Branch about eight o'clock at night, Winder ordered his column to halt on high ground and began to position Smith's troops in the most advantageous situation he could. After four days of marching two and fro, Smith's men were exhausted, having drawn but two days' rations the whole time, because the army's wagons had been impressed into service by government agents to remove federal records from the capital.[38] One group was dispatched to burn the Eastern Branch bridge. An infantry company was sent out a half mile beyond to provide early warning of the enemy's approach. He also began to establish his main defensive position on the Washington side of the bridge. Having left no one behind to ghost the British approach, however, he had absolutely no idea of where they were—or if they were even on the march!

...

Almost as soon as they had arrived at Bladensburg, Joseph Sterett and William Pinkney were summoned to General Stansbury's tent, where his principal officers were assembled for a council of war. The militia commander informed them that he had just been told that Winder was retiring to Washington across the Eastern Branch via the lower bridge. He then asked their advice as to what course his own army might take, and if the officers thought Winder expected him to fight where he was if the enemy came through Bladensburg. Sterett reported that his own troops were exhausted from both the heat and their forced march from Baltimore. Stansbury's citizen-soldiers were not much better, according to Pinkney, and consisted "altogether of militia unused to service, amounting to little more than two thousand men, and deprived of all prospect of support from any quarter, was in no condition to withstand nearly thrice its number of regular troops, in a position which presented no peculiar facilities for defence," especially since Winder's own force, which was now substantially larger than his own and included regulars with heavy artillery, had been compelled to place itself behind the Eastern Branch. It was an opinion in which Stansbury himself totally concurred. For this reason, the council of war agreed that the entire army at Bladensburg should withdraw across Stoddert's Bridge, closer to the capital, and put itself "in a situation with that of General Winder, and to receive and execute the orders of that general, whatever they might be, for the protection of the capital." It was also agreed that the campsite, which had been established only a few hours earlier, be immediately broken up and the entire army marched across the bridge. It was nothing less than disobedience of a direct order. And it made absolute sense.[39]

. . .

Burch's Washington Artillerymen were so fatigued from their trek from Battalion Old Fields, almost at a run, as if the devil himself was on their tail, that "they could scarcely stand by their guns." They were the last of Winder's force to reach Washington. Burch later wrote: "After we had crossed the bridge into the city, and pitched our tents, between twelve and one o'clock at night, General Winder came to my tent and called me out: he observed, that he knew my men were worn down with fatigue and from loss of rest; but that in all probability, one of the last good acts which it might be in my power to do for my country, would be that night."[40]

Winder ordered the captain to take thirty men, with three guns, and defend the lower Eastern Branch bridge "as he had reason to believe that the enemy would attempt the passage of it that night." The general also told him he had already visited the Navy Yard and left directions that "a boat be sent to the bridge, with combustibles to blow it up, in case it became necessary."[41]

Winder was now entirely unaware of the enemy's whereabouts, or that the enemy advance from Upper Marlboro had been minimal. The British army had indeed moved out of that town on the morning of August 23, but had only progressed a mere five miles closer to their destination before making camp in the vicinity of a plantation called Melwood, belonging to Thomas Sim Lee and his wife Mary Carroll Digges. There, it had again rested as General Ross resumed pondering whether or not to proceed. Admiral Cockburn had been joined there by Captains Palmer of *Hebrus,* Mony of *Trave,* and Wainwright of *Tonnant,* the admiral's aide, Lieutenant James Scott (now acting First Lieutenant of *Albion*), along with the seamen, and marine artillery under Captain Harrison. Cockburn would now need all of his persuasive powers to keep Ross moving ahead.[42]

. . .

As the night slowly passed, the 5th Maryland, undoubtedly cursing their officers for marching them so soon after they had come to rest from their last amble, tromped across the bridge to a position about a mile and a half from Bladensburg and on a high ground on the main road to Washington. From here the enemy's approach could easily be seen if he should advance from the direction anticipated.[43]

About six miles to the southwest, the march of men that evening across the Eastern Branch bridge had also been notable. Although not the last to cross, Joshua Barney, Sam Miller, and their little legion of weary sailors and marines, having left everything but the clothes on their backs behind in the flotilla, and many of them without shoes, had trudged across the bridge dragging their five great artillery pieces, and marched to the Washington Navy Yard. At the marine barracks they took up quarters for the night to sleep for the first time in many weeks in actual beds. Barney, however, perhaps hoping

Facing page

The British line of march from Benedict to Washington and back, August 19–28, 1814. *Detail from "Sketch of the March of the British Army under M. Genl Ross from the 19th to the 29th Augt 1814," Beinecke Rare Book and Manuscript Library, Yale University Library, New Haven, Connecticut.*

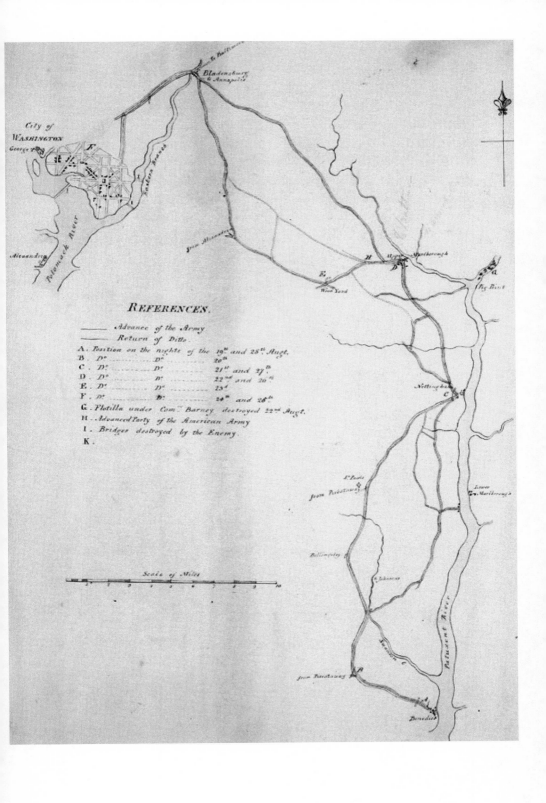

City of
WASHINGTON
George T.

Alexandria

Potomack River

Bladensburg
to Annapolis

Eastern Branch

from Alexandria

H   Upper Marlborough
E   D
Wood Yard   Pig Point   G

Nottingham   C

St Pauls
from Piscataway

Lower
Marlborough

Bellingsley   Patuxent River

J. Johnsons

from Piscataway   B

A
Benedict

REFERENCES.

———— Advance of the Army
———— Return of Ditto.

A. Position on the nights of the 19ᵗʰ and 28ᵗʰ Augᵗ.
B. Dᵒ .... Dᵒ 20ᵗʰ
C. Dᵒ .... Dᵒ .... 21ˢᵗ and 27ᵗʰ
D. Dᵒ .... Dᵒ .... 22ⁿᵈ and 26ᵗʰ
E. Dᵒ .... Dᵒ 23ᵈ
F. Dᵒ .... Dᵒ .... 24ᵗʰ and 25ᵗʰ
G. Flotilla under Comʳ Barney destroyed 22ⁿᵈ Augᵗ.
H. Advanced Party of the American Army
I. Bridges destroyed by the Enemy.
K.

Scale of Miles

for a full night's rest before the inevitable battle, slept fitfully at the residence of the yard's commandant, Captain Thomas Tingey.[44]

For General William Henry Winder, sleep proved an inconvenient luxury that he could not indulge as he rode off to find the president of the United States and then pay a visit to Tingey at the Navy Yard to prepare, if necessary, for the yard's destruction. For Commodore Joshua Barney, who was awakened at 2:00 a.m. by the hyperactive general who came to personally search for combustibles with which to destroy the bridge, it was the eve of the last great fight of his life. It was also to become one of both his and his young country's darkest hours ever.[45]

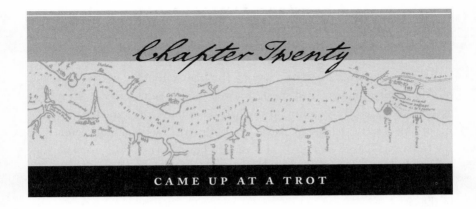

Chapter Twenty

CAME UP AT A TROT

Dr. Hanson Catlett was unquestionably *the last* in the American army to leave the vicinity of Battalion Old Fields. Unlike the troops that had rushed toward Washington at a trot, he had calmly camped in the open only a mile from the army's former campsite. Quite early on the morning of the 24th he had dispatched a man to see if the British were yet on the march. The man returned soon after and informed him the enemy was not yet advancing, after which the doctor rode toward Washington. As he had pressed toward the lower bridge, he could see in the distance the 822-foot-long span afire. The blaze was apparently not enough to consume it, for upon his arrival, about eight o'clock in the morning, he was able to cross and witnessed preparations being made to blow it up. Indeed, a boat loaded with eight barrels of gunpowder had already been placed beneath the span earlier in the morning and more vessels packed with explosives were coming up. Colonel Decius Wadsworth had already ordered that firewood be hauled up to burn the bridge in its entirety if necessary, and within a short time troops were tearing up fences and pulling down the tollhouse and a small nearby shed for additional wood.[1] On the Washington side of the river the good doctor discovered everything in motion, troops marching to and fro, orders shouted, horses and wagons on the move. There was also no lack of confusion.

Catlett proceeded on to the capital, where he found disorder and bewilderment running amok. Rumors abounded, and no intelligence seemed reliable. One report stated the enemy was only two and a half miles away, and that his objective was the lower bridge crossing. Exaggerated estimates of as many as nine thousand enemy troops were bandied about, although British prisoners could identify only four regiments, headed by a single general and seconded by a colonel acting as a brigadier. "I examined several [prisoners] myself, with all the address I could," the doctor later reported, "and would certainly have risked my life upon their almost entire want of artillery and their want of cavalry."[2]

There was no lack of discord among the high command either. Secretary of War Armstrong, who had strongly advocated the superiority of the militia system over a costly standing army, had discounted the capital as being a major objective of the enemy. Now, when cornered by the ailing secretary of the treasury, George Campbell, and asked if he approved of the troop deployments, Armstrong adeptly dodged the question. Winder, the secretary of war retorted, was in command and he presumed that he had a plan for the defense of the city.[3]

A mile and a half to the rear of Stoddert's Bridge General Stansbury was already placing his men on the top of the hill above Tuncliffe's Bridge, which crossed a small creek and ravine, when, at 9:00 a.m. Major Woodyear returned with new orders from Winder. Stansbury was to retrace his steps toward the crossing and "contest the enemy at the bridge." The commander-in-chief would rejoin him later. Like it or not, both Stansbury's and Sterett's raw Maryland militiamen would be at the front, the forward line that was to face the finest troopers the British Empire could field if they should come by way of Bladensburg. Despite their apprehensions, between 10:00 and 11:00 a.m., the tired Baltimore militiamen soon moved back to Stoddert's Bridge and halted at an apple orchard on the left of the road to Washington and not far from the crossing. Some of the hungry troops, who had not eaten in a day, broke ranks and rushed into the orchard to feast on the hanging fruit.[4]

Stansbury, having taken stock of his new position, was well aware that there were two ways to cross from Bladensburg, one route being by the bridge and the second being across the shallow ford, somewhat above the crossing. The position he had taken commanded both the passage across the bridge and the shallow ford. He immediately ordered forty horsemen, presumably Lavall's men, to take axes and "cut away this bridge before the near approach of the enemy." He later reported: "It is certain the enemy could have forded the stream above, but I considered it would, in some degree, impede their progress, and give our artillery and riflemen more time and opportunity to act with effect against them." For whatever reasons, unfortunately, even though he saw the men milling about with their axes, the order was never executed. The failure to do so would prove costly, if not pivotal to the outcome of the approaching battle.[5]

In the meantime, Colonel Wadsworth had set to work preparing an earthwork, "a small breastwork of dirt" for the Baltimore artillery of Captains Myers and Magruder, fifty yards in front of the 5th Regiment under Colonel Sterett. The battery itself was situated between four and five hundred yards from the bridge. Though the work was deemed quite suitable for heavy cannon, it would soon become evident it was not for the lighter guns of the Baltimore artillery. The parapets were simply too lofty for their 6-pounders. With time being short, the men desperately used sticks to dig embrasures so the guns could be aimed at the bridge.[6] Major William Pinkney, in charge of the rifle companies, whose own 1st Rifle Battalion numbered about 150 men, well knew there was no time to reduce the parapets and thus set his men to masking the works with bushwood. Their own position would be to the right of the battery, "behind a fence, and among the bushes, upon the slope of the bank which terminates the field, and also beyond the slope, as near to the bridge and ford as was practicable." Pinkney himself, along with his adjutant and sergeant major, would take station some yards in the rear and on the top of the bank where they could get an uninterrupted view of the advancing enemy.[7]

Colonel Sterett, unable to locate Winder to receive his orders, had soon encountered Monroe, who placed him on the left and in line with Stansbury's brigade. That Monroe was not happy that such raw militia were being placed in the front line may be gauged when he mentioned to Sterett as the first line was forming: "Although you see that I am active, you will please to bear in mind that this is not my plan."[8]

Two companies of Stansbury's brigade acting as riflemen, although armed with muskets, were posted near a barn, behind the battery, near to and beyond a path that flanked it called Mill Road, to watch that road and the upper ford, and to march to the aid of or supply other detachments as needed.[9]

As Pinkney's men worked furiously preparing the battery and Sterett's troopers moved into their assigned positions, a cloud of dust, stirred by marching men, was seen approaching from Bladensburg along the Annapolis Road. The alarm was raised and Pinkney's men readied themselves to engage the invaders head on. The approaching troops, however, proved to be a regiment of Maryland militia under Lieutenant Colonel Beall, who had just hobbled in after a long and fatiguing sixteen-mile forced march from Annapolis. Upon his arrival, Beall was met by one of Winder's aides and informed that his position was to be on Veitch's Hill, on the far right in the last line of defense.[10]

Finally, Winder himself appeared on the field and again tinkered with the positions, ordering Pinkney to shift a portion of his riflemen to the left of his battery. The major promptly detached a company of sharpshooters under Captain Asquith from behind the fence line, but retained two companies in their former station, and replaced Asquith's unit with another under Captain Doughty.[11]

...

No one could fault William Henry Winder for want of zeal. He had been up the better part of the night, scurrying hither and yon. About midnight or one o'clock in the morning he had roused Commodore Tingey from his bed to address the matter of burning of the lower bridge and an hour later had done the same with Commodore Barney, while in search of combustible to conduct the job. The general had also found time to confer with Secretary of War Armstrong, who seemed entirely noncommittal in his views and support. Then he had learned "with considerable mortification" of Stansbury's abandonment of Bladensburg, but in ordering him back had merely told him to "post himself to the best advantage," which the Marylander decided was to be found on the west side of the river instead of on the outskirts of the town itself. Nevertheless, Winder had also taken great pains to send out cavalry units to monitor all of the roads leading to Washington, Bladensburg, and Fort Washington to prevent any untoward surprises by the enemy. He had also attempted to address errant commanders such as the egregiously unavailable Colonel Carberry, who had seemingly just disappeared from the scene altogether, much as he had managed to do with regularity on the Patuxent. Then, about three or four o'clock in the morning, while making his way back to the Navy Yard, he was thrown from his horse into a ditch and injured his right arm and ankle. Nevertheless, though exhausted and limping badly, he managed to reach camp afoot and prepare for the defense and demolition of the lower bridge.[12]

By early morning Winder had sent a message to the president requesting a conference at the Washington Navy Yard. He also dispatched a note to Joshua Barney directing him to move his men and artillery to take command of the defense of the lower bridge, where Burch's and Peter's units were already posted. Wasting no time, the commodore hastened with a party of flotillamen to position one of his guns in the most advantageous position possible to protect the crossing, even though the bridge was by then burning, and barges and scows, laden with gunpowder were being readied to blow up at a moment's notice and had been lodged beneath it. Miller's marines and the rest of the flotillamen men were left behind at the barracks.

Upon the commodore's arrival at the Eastern Branch bridge, the artillery units already there were relieved and ordered to Bladensburg. Burch was instructed to leave one gun and fifteen men at the bridge, and another two on the main road, and report with the remaining three to General Winder. The two guns left on the main road were borrowed by Wadsworth and soon after placed on the Washington Road to the rear of a forward battery site to be occupied by Baltimore artillery. Secretary Jones, en route to the meeting with the president, found the commodore busily planting his battery on a hill near the head of the bridge and preparing the first line of defense should the enemy march that way.[13]

. . .

At 9:00 a.m. the meeting with the president and his cabinet was convened at the quarters of Dr. Andrew Hunter at the Navy Yard. In attendance were the president, the attorney general, the secretary of the navy, the secretary of the treasury, General Winder, and several other military officers. Monroe was with Smith or at Bladensburg. Secretary of War Armstrong was nowhere to be seen. The proceedings were conducted in a charged atmosphere. It had been less than twenty-four hours earlier that the president had been convinced by Winder that Washington would not be the enemy's target. By now the general had morphed into the opinion that the invaders would first strike at Fort Washington and then, only after the fort was taken, against the capital itself. Then a messenger arrived with a dispatch for Winder "considered by him decisive." The enemy had been observed by one of Lavall's pickets turning off onto the road to Bladensburg.[14] At that moment Armstrong finally appeared and smugly opined that even if the British marched on the capital, without the ability to conduct a siege or hold the terrain, it would be nothing more than "a mere Cossack hurrah," a short sortie followed by a brisk retreat to their ships. Why not entice the enemy into the very environs of the U.S. Capitol, and ambush him with artillery, five thousand infantry, and several hundred cavalry? In any event, he mused, the defense of Washington was still Winder's problem, not his.[15]

At that, about ten o'clock in the morning, the meeting broke up and the president and several members of his entourage headed for Bladensburg, and Winder again began to scurry about organizing the defense. He quickly sent orders to General Smith, who was camped some distance from the lower bridge, to detach one piece of artillery and an infantry company to the bridge itself and to march with his troops and the 36th Infantry and other regular and militia units in support of Stansbury, whom he believed was probably still at Bladensburg. He then rode off for a firsthand look.[16]

As President Madison, Secretary Jones, and other members of the president's party passed by the lower bridge while en route to the probable scene of action at Bladensburg, they almost immediately encountered Commodore Barney, whose guns had just been placed. Displeased with his position well to the rear of the coming fight, to guard a half-burned bridge that could be blown up in an instant if necessary by half a dozen men as well as by five hundred, the commodore pointed out the obvious. The lower crossing could be easily defended by a handful of men, while he and his flotillamen, the most experienced fighters in the region, might be better employed on the field of action. The president readily concurred and directed the commodore to draw off his guns and proceed toward Bladensburg. Barney quickly arranged with Tingey for some of his men to take over at the bridge. Master Commandant John Orde Creighton was thus placed in charge of a sergeant's guard of marines with orders to blow up the bridge if the enemy appeared, and then to help destroy the Navy Yard if necessary.[17]

Barney instantly dispatched an officer back to the Marine Barracks to hurry on his men, all of whom soon "came up in a trot." The six- or seven-mile march was undoubtedly a bit unpleasant for the men. "The day was hot," Barney later wrote, "and my men very much crippled from the severe marches we had experienced the days before; many of them being without shoes; which I had replaced that morning." While en route to the scene of action, the commodore, who was in advance of his men by some distance, was informed that the enemy was within a mile of the town. The flotillamen hastened the pace, manually dragging their five guns behind, with Barney pressing on ahead to select the best position to place his battery on a high ground, beside Smith's brigade and commanding Tuncliffe's Bridge.[18]

. . .

The field upon which the coming battle would be fought heavily favored the Americans. Though there were fordable places from Bladensburg above Stoddert's Bridge, the post road from the town to Washington was eminently defensible. The eastern extremity along the riverbank was low, marshy ground, which gently sloped up for several hundreds of yards to the west. Approximately seventy to eighty yards west of the bridge, Washington Road was intersected at a near forty-five-degree angle by a road from Georgetown, northwest of Washington, but also within the District of Columbia. Within the V formed by the two roads, and adjacent to it, the apple orchard and several farm buildings were the only sheltered areas governing an otherwise open expanse of cultivated fields. Nearly a mile farther west of the intersection, Tuncliffe's Bridge traversed a small creek and ravine. From here the road to the capital took a slightly southerly approach toward the city as it progressed to a defensible ridge, approximately a third of a mile farther west and running on a north-south axis. Here and there the ridge was segmented by gullies that drained into the ravine below.[19]

It was not until 11:00 a.m. that General Smith received the orders from Winder to march his troops to take up a position opposite Bladensburg in support of General Stansbury. Smith's troops were put into motion immediately. After marching from their encampment, with "Colonel" Monroe in company, they had found Stansbury posted about noon on the west side of the river, with his right flank on the main Bladensburg-Washington road, about five to six hundred yards from the bridge, with his line extending in a northwesterly direction and his left near a small creek. "An extensive apple orchard was in his front, and one hundred to two hundred yards in advance, a work thrown up, commanding the bridge, occupied by a corps of artillery, with five or six pieces, and appeared to be supported by some rifle and light companies. In his rear, on the right, was a thick undergrowth of wood, and directly behind that a deep hollow or ravine, open or cleared, of about sixty yards width, which the main road crosses. The ravine terminates on the left in a bold declivity, about two hundred yards from the road; the rest of the ground in his rear was open, unbroken, and gradually ascending fields."[20]

Smith positioned his own force as carefully but as quickly as possible. One hundred and fifty yards to the rear of Stansbury's right, Lieutenant Colonel Scott's 36th U.S. Infantry and part of the 38th was posted in an open field on the left of the road, with his right on it and commanding the road's descent into the ravine, with the rest of his line commanding the ascent from the ravine.[21]

About a hundred yards to the rear of Scott's position, Colonel Richard B. Magruder's American Artillery Company was stationed with part of the 1st Regiment of the 1st D.C. Brigade, commanded by Colonel George Magruder. The artillery unit's right rested on the road, with its left advanced somewhat obliquely to the road and situated so as to cover and support the 36th Regiment.[22]

At the same time, Major Peter with his six 6-pounders, Captain Davidson's light infantry, and Captain Stull's riflemen took possession of the declivity terminating in the ravine. From their position they commanded not only the ravine and the road crossing it, but the ground over which Stansbury's front line—if forced—might have to retire over. As the approach was over broken ground, however, another position suitable for artillery was soon found. Because Peter's new artillery position would be firing principally through the field occupied by Scott's infantry it was decided by Smith that one or the other would have to be moved. Thus the 36th was drawn back a hundred yards, losing some advantage of elevated ground and leaving the road. The position of George Magruder's 1st Regiment was thus also somewhat altered and it fell back the same distance and nearly in line with the 36th.[23] Lieutenant Colonel Kramer with his battalion of Maryland draft militia was posted in the woods on the right of the road and commanding the ravine, which continued in that direction.[24]

Among the troops that had arrived on the field in the night were Lavall's light dragoons, which had been reduced to about 125 men owing to sickness and other wounds, although reports circulated that he had as many as 500 men. A number of his horses were unable to proceed much farther, having come all the way from Carlisle, Pennsylvania, in quick time, to the Navy Yard, then to the Battalion Old Fields, and then back to Washington, which had been reached at 11:00 p.m. the previous evening. Both men and horses were famished with hunger and "harassed with fatigue" when they reached the city. Not until the next morning were the troopers able to assuage their hungry steeds with the purchase of a stack of hay. Then, while the men "were in the act of fetching the hay on their heads," a trumpet sounded and they were ordered to mount up immediately and ride to Bladensburg, as the arrival of the enemy was at hand. When Lavall's dragoons reached the town they had been unable to find Winder and were without orders until Secretary Monroe appeared. At that moment the cavalry commander and his men, who had never been to Bladensburg, were watering their horses by the Eastern Branch. Lavall informed the secretary of state that he was totally unacquainted with the place. Monroe immediately pointed out a position to take on the far left of the American line. Moments later, General Stansbury rode by and approved of the position, on his own left, assigned him by Monroe.[25]

Lavall was not the only officer looking for Winder. Captain Burch, who had just arrived on the field with only half of his guns, had also set out to locate the commander-in-chief to receive his orders. He had proceeded to within a short distance of Bladensburg, but discovered the general was nowhere to be found. He later reported, "I rode up and down the whole line in search of him, and when I returned, I found that my guns had been moved off to the left; I followed on and overtook them just as they were formed in battery, near the extreme left of the line." The captain soon discovered that while he was off searching for the general, the British were observed entering the outskirts of Bladensburg as "the arms of a large body of them were seen glittering in the sun, about a mile from the town." John Law, a sergeant in Burch's unit, at that moment had spotted Winder and marched a detachment over to him and asked where the artillery should be posted. The general, mistakenly addressing the sergeant as captain, directed him to place it on the far left of Stansbury's Baltimore militia. Almost as if he were already resigned to defeat, he then pointed toward the pike leading from Digge's Mill northwest into the countryside and added: "When you retreat, you must retreat by the Georgetown Road." Soon afterward, Burch arrived just as the battery was being formed, dismounted, took command of his guns, and then encountered the general and asked for directions. Pointing toward Bladensburg, where the enemy was coming into plain view, the general replied: "Captain, there is the enemy . . . take charge of your pieces."[26]

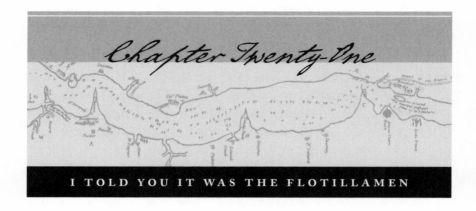

Chapter Twenty-One

I TOLD YOU IT WAS THE FLOTILLAMEN

The volunteer from Georgetown, an ex-government accountant named William Simmons, would probably not have been considered scout material given his background and certainly not one likely to save the president of the United States from possible capture. Having been a federal employee in the War Department for nearly two decades, he had only recently been fired by the president for alleged hostility toward the government and his superiors. His case, however, had caused something of a ruckus when he charged that his boss, Secretary Armstrong himself, had orchestrated his cashiering after quarreling with him over "accounting procedures."[1]

Regardless of whatever feelings he may have harbored for the president or Armstrong, Simmons was nevertheless anxious for action, and had ridden to Washington to offer his services. When he arrived at the lower bridge he found only a few sailors and a piece or two of artillery waiting to destroy the crossing if necessary. The battlefront, he soon learned, was to be at Bladensburg. Galloping off toward the town, he soon encountered Colonel Monroe near Stoddert's Bridge, just in the rear of the front line. No one, including Monroe, seemed certain about the actual whereabouts of the British or when they were likely to appear; Simmons quickly volunteered to cross the bridge as a scout, and let him know when they were coming.[2]

Within minutes the accountant-turned-scout had ridden into Bladensburg as far as Ross's Tavern, not far from the bridge, where he halted to talk with a few militiamen standing about. He learned little more from them than the enemy was coming down the river road. Mounting up again, he pressed on to a heights called Lowndes Hill, "which had a commanding prospect of the river road for a considerable distance, and which was almost fronting the hill." From this vantage point, he could see the river and the road upon which the British would be marching for several miles. He did not have long to wait.

306

Soon he saw at a great distance "a great cloud of dust rise to a great degree." The enemy was approaching.

Soon, a few horsemen, clad only in civilian clothes, undoubtedly riding horses confiscated from farms and plantations along the line of march, were observed reconnoitering ahead of the column. The army itself, Simmons later reported,

> appeared to march very slow, and in close order, not less than twenty-four or thirty abreast in front, and the horsemen . . . sometimes in front, and at other times a little to the right of front; which position they marched in until they nearly approached the foot of the hill, and not more than a gunshot from me, where I was sitting on my horse, and the road in full sight for near a mile, and that filled with British troops, and still approaching. At this time there was not a person in sight of me, other than the enemy, except one dragoon, who appeared to have been posted there a little to my left, upon the same hill, where I left him, and have since understood he was taken by the advance party of the enemy.

Expecting at any moment to have his retreat cut off, Simmons descended the hill in front of the Christopher Lowndes house. As he crossed the bridge, he looked back and saw the advance party of enemy horsemen peel off onto the Annapolis Road, to the east of the house, and another two dozen of them head up the road to Baltimore. Six or eight were left at the entrance to the latter. The town was now effectively sealed off from escape by anyone therein except across the bridge.

Although the veracity of events that next transpired, based upon Simmons's own subsequent written testimony to a congressional court of inquiry, was rejected by some and attributed to his possible upset with the government for terminating his career, they clearly echoed the confusion that was prevalent in the American high command.

Several months afterward, on November 28, 1814, Simmons reported to Congress on his scouting expedition. On his return across Stoddert's Bridge, he claimed, he encountered President Madison, Attorney General Rush, Secretary of War Armstrong, and Secretary of State Monroe, all on horseback, "considerably in advance of all our troops, going immediately into Bladensburg."

As they stopped for a moment in passing, he addressed the president: "Mr. Madison, the enemy are in Bladensburg!"

"The enemy in Bladensburg!" replied the chief executive in utter amazement.

Without a further word, the president's party all turned their horses and galloped "with considerable speed" toward the Washington side of the river.

Simmons called out as they raced off: "Mr. Madison, if you stop I will show them to you; they are now in sight."

The leadership of the United States of America scampered on. Then, reining in his horse, Attorney General Rush suddenly halted and declared, almost incredulously, that the horsemen in town couldn't be the enemy for they were not in uniform. Simmons reiterated that they were the advance guard and the regulars were behind them. At that moment the British army appeared in two sections, some in the rear and others in front of the Lowndes House and forming on the Annapolis Road.

The attorney general of the United States sped off, his hat falling off as he went. "I am satisfied," he shouted as he rode away.

Simmons yelled, "Mr. Rush, come back and take up your hat," which he did, and then pursued his company with all haste.

. . .

At the first sight of British troops in Bladensburg, Stansbury's men opened a nervous and sporadic fire with artillery, albeit from too far away and too early to be of any effect, and then musketry. As the last American to leave Bladensburg galloped across the narrow 120-foot-long bridge, Simmons immediately rode up the hill behind the lines in hopes of rejoining the president or some of the cabinet "to endeavor to get them to stop the firing, till it could be more effectual." Finally, he found General Winder, informed him he had just come in from Bladensburg, "and that there was but a very small party of the enemy in the town; that they [Stansbury's line] had commenced firing too early; and that, if they would reserve their fire for a few minutes, the British troops were then coming down the hill, and were about to form on the Annapolis road, when they would be able to do some execution." Winder paid the volunteer little heed.

Whether the Americans were ready or not, the Battle of Bladensburg had already begun and, as they were all painfully aware, the fate of the still infant capital of the United States of America hung in the balance.

If the numerically superior American army was hamstrung by confusion, indecision, and ineptitude, the British were in many ways equally disadvantaged, albeit in different ways. They had broken camp near Melwood at dawn, with the 85th Light Infantry being the first to get underway, and had been marching for nearly seven hours. Dr. Catlett even recognized that they had reached the opposite side of Bladensburg only "by a necessarily extraordinary effort, for men immediately from ship board."[3] They had pressed on, marching four abreast, first on an open road and through cleared fields in the early morning, and then through woods, thickets, and brush, where they were for a while at least sheltered from the sun's exhausting rays. Finally, upon leaving the wooded part of the countryside, they entered a landscape normally more hospitable and welcoming, one of farms and fields bearing the fruits of an abundant summer. Now with the soldiers openly exposed to the sapping heat of the sun, the pace of the march, albeit but two miles an hour, began to take its toll. A few men began to fall by the wayside, hoping to catch up as soon as they could. Ross's aide, Captain Thomas Fell, was among them, as he collapsed from his horse, a victim of sunstroke. Soon "they were dropping off in considerable numbers." After marching nine miles, an hour and a half rest at 10:00 a.m. beside a stream helped recoup the strength and spirits of many. Yet, it was discipline and duty, forged in the cauldron of the Napoleonic Wars in Europe, that kept most going.[4]

Now, as the British army marched along the river road, a small detachment of artillery drivers, commanded by Captain William Lempriere of the Royal Artillery, acting as cavalry on a range of captured horses, were the first to enter the outskirts of Bladensburg ahead of the main column. As they viewed the American forces still assembling on the opposite side, they could also readily see the killing grounds they would soon have to traverse. Their entire army, no more than 4,500 strong, including 150 sailors (armed only with cutlasses) and Royal Marines, one 6-pounder howitzer, and a pair of 3-pounder field pieces, had its day's work laid out for it. It would first have to be funneled across a narrow bridge where the Americans would likely concentrate their muskets and superior artillery fire, cut through a first line of defense, charge up hills against secondary and tertiary positions flanked by cavalry and again against superior artillery, and then drive on to Washington, where God only knew what lay awaiting them. Though Ross estimated the Americans to number between 8,000 and 9,000 men, with 300 to 400 cavalry, Winder later reported that he was enabled, "by the most active and harassing movements of the troops, to interpose before the enemy at Bladensburg about five thousand men, including three hundred and fifty regulars and Commodore Barney's command." Another estimate provided by Captain John Law of the Washington Artillery stated the American defense force consisted of 3,160 men who had come in from Battalion Old Fields, 2,000 men from Baltimore, 500 militiamen under Colonel Beall, 18 6-pounders under Majors Peter and Burch, and Captain Magruder, and 2 18-pounders and 3 12-pounders under Commodore Barney, in all 5,660 men and 23 guns.[5]

For approximately twenty minutes the forward-most British column halted to await the rear to come up, as the two armies were "pretty much in view of each other," separated by only perhaps three-quarters of a mile and the river.[6] The British had little time to take note of the little gem of a town they were occupying, which had been founded in 1742 as a Maryland port of entry and was now a thriving village of perhaps 1,500 inhabitants situated on the main north-south post road. Though the river had silted in early on, denying the town its direct seafaring trade, a nearby shipyard founded by the Lowndes family, as well as a hearty profit in the Potomac fisheries, tobacco warehousing, and a gunpowder factory, had helped sustain it. It had gained some notoriety in 1784, when Peter Carnes released the first unmanned hot-air balloon in American history near the town. An ill-famed dueling ground nearby, where half a hundred bloody "affairs of honor" were held, had also earned it a bit darker niche in local history.

Upon his entry in the town, General Ross and several of his officers quickly located a two-story house called Parthenon Manor on Lowndes Hill, belonging to Reverend John Bowie, from which they could clearly view the American positions on the other side of the bridge. From his perch, he later reported, "the enemy was discovered strongly posted on a very commanding heights formed in two lines his advance occupying a fortified house which with artillery covered the bridge over the Eastern Branch across which the British troops had to pass. A broad and streight [sic] road leading from the bridge to Washington ran through the enemy's position which was carefully defended by artillery and riflemen."[7] It was readily discerned that the bridge across the river had for some inconceivable reason not been destroyed, which the Americans had every opportunity to do, but it was barely wide enough for three men abreast to pass.

For once in the campaign, Ross was neither hesitant nor indecisive. Though his troops were exhausted with fatigue from the long march, and only a portion of the army, primarily Colonel Thornton's light brigade, had come up, the general was inclined to seize the initiative. The Americans, it appeared, were still marching about in a hurried attempt to establish their positions. Moreover, Thornton made it known that he was eager to begin a direct assault across the bridge immediately.

Other experienced officers, such as Captain Harry Smith, objected strenuously, saying that it would be foolhardy to attack right away. None of the other brigades had yet come up or would be in a position to support the operation and Thornton would certainly be repulsed. It would be necessary for the light division to first probe the enemy for weak points. Perhaps, it was suggested, if the colonel insisted on marching ahead, a feint could be made against the American left, by crossing the ford north of the bridge![8]

Ross, with Thornton aggressively pressing for a direct frontal attack, was unyielding and determined to move without delay. The colonel's light brigade, the 85th Regiment, distinctly identifiable by the dark green plume on their shakos, with a few light companies of the 4th, 21st, and 44th, would lead the assault; they would be followed by the remainder of 4th and 44th led by Brooke. The 4th regiment would form a line after crossing the bridge to the left to attack the American right, including the gun battery. The 44th would form a line to the right to attack the American left along the Georgetown Road. The 3rd brigade, the 21st Regiment, which was still straggling into Bladensburg, would be held in reserve.[9]

Precisely when the attack began in earnest varies with the source. Major William Pinkney, a former U.S. minister to the Court of St. James and one-time U.S. attorney general, stated that the enemy descended down Lowndes Hill about noon "in a very fine style, and showed his intention to force his way by the bridge." Dr. Catlett states the British had not even reached the town until 1:00 p.m.[10] Yet now, as they had done so many times before in another war far away, at the sounds of drums beating and bugles sounding, Thornton's men formed in two columns and then began moving down the hill at a trot and then onto the road leading to the 120-foot-long bridge. A young midshipman from HBM brig *Espoir* was awestruck by the conspicuous bravery of his fellow countrymen as they formed to storm through the narrow defile under what would prove to be a dreadful fire from American artillery and musketry. As the British soldiers now reached the foot of the hill, the Americans on the other side of the bridge suddenly "gave three cheers, and fired a tremendous volley, appearing, as if it was an expiring effort."[11]

As Thornton's men charged, they did so without their normal covering fire of sharpshooters. The three pieces of British artillery were just being un-limbered near the old George Washington House on the Baltimore road. However, the British army's Rocket Brigade and a unit of the Royal Marine Rocket Corps, under the overall command of a Captain Deacons, had already taken up a position and set up their launchers behind a warehouse close to the water, and began firing their unnerving but inaccurate projectiles at the American line and the president and his entourage, who were clustered together behind to observe the engagement. "It was suggested to them [Madison and his cabinet], I think by General Winder," Dr. Catlett later recalled, "to take a more responsible distance." The president's response was succinct. "Let us go," he said, "and leave it to the commanding general." For most of the Americans, the display of rocketry was merely watched in awe, but a few panicked.[12]

The British columns now pushed ahead at double quick time toward the head of the bridge. "While we were moving along the street," Gleig recalled, "a continued fire was kept up with some execution, from those guns which stood to the left of the road; but it was not till the bridge was covered by our people that the 2-gun battery upon the road itself began to play. Then, indeed, it also opened, and with tremendous effect; for at the first discharge almost an entire company was swept down." Confusion among the British ranks on and about the bridge was considerable, so much so "that their officers could now be seen actively engaged [in] preventing their retreating, and pushing them on to the bridge," but to no effect.[13]

Burch's Washington battery, concentrating its fire upon the road and bridge, had devastated the column, forcing the attackers to seek shelter in a number of houses nearby. Although after only fifteen rounds had been fired one of the guns was masked by the slight advance of the 5th Regiment of Baltimore and had to be discontinued, the bombardment with shot and grape "proved to be very galling to the enemy." Several British officers and a number of men lay dead on the road and bridge, and others, still living but mutilated and dying, sat or lay nearby. The Americans were exhilarated at having stopped the first attempt by the invaders dead in its tracks. The artillery continued to fire, now focusing upon the warehouse and the enemy's rocketry, which was interrupted, albeit only temporarily. Lieutenant Gleig, who had retreated to the cover of the houses and the warehouse, endured the bombardment stoically, even when the occasional cannonball snuffed out a life or severed a limb of a comrade nearby.[14]

If the first assault had been blunted, British spirit was not. Lieutenant James Scott would later recall that a wounded Scotsman, his bloody arm dangling, shouted across the river defiantly: "Dinna halloo, my fine lads. You're no' yet oot of the wood. Wait a wee bit, wait a wee, wie your skirling."[15]

. . .

As the battle was beginning and rockets "announced the arrival of the enemy," Barney's and Miller's men were just arriving on the field; they were instructed by General Winder to join the rearmost position as a supportive artillery unit, half a mile from the river on a slight hill overlooking the shallow valley, Tuncliffe's Bridge, and the creek running beneath it. On the other side of the valley, toward the river and on another but lower elevation, the commodore could plainly see the forward line of defense composed of elements of Stansbury's 11th Maryland Militia Brigade. And beyond that was the other half of the forward defense, closest to Bladensburg and the bridge, also made up of his brigade. Although not entirely pleased with his own position so far from the scene of action, Barney nevertheless immediately placed his five guns in a battery in the middle of the Washington road and quickly deployed the marines and flotillamen. Miller's men were stationed on the commodore's right, and a hundred yards in front of the battery. Near them were the flotillamen not engaged in manning the battery who, under Sailing Master John Webster, one of the commodore's best officers, were also to act as infantry and provide flank support for the artillerymen working their pieces. To the far right of the marines and flotillamen Colonel William D. Beall's 17th Maryland Militia Regiment and the attached 32nd Battalion of Anne Arundel County Militia under Lieutenant Colonel Thomas Hood had just taken up position. On the commodore's left was Colonel George Magruder's 1st Regiment of the D.C. Militia. As everyone hastily readied for combat in the rearmost tier of defense, all could plainly see the surge of the engagement below assuming a new level of intensity.[16]

. . .

Colonel Thornton, described by some as an impetuous officer, was not lacking in courage. Mounted upon his gray horse, with sword drawn, he almost single-handedly rallied his men for another charge. "Now my lads, forward," he shouted above the sound of musketry, rifle, and cannon fire. "You see the enemy. You know how to serve them." Then, above the din of battle, bugles sounded the charge even as Thornton raced across the bridge, sagaciously hurtling his horse over the bodies of his fallen and wounded comrades, followed close behind by the men of the 85th. Miraculously, though bullets, grape, and round shot whizzed by, the colonel reached the other side of the bridge without a scratch, though more than a half dozen men fell behind him. Ross immediately ordered Captain Smith to hurry up the 4th and 44th, and then also boldly galloped into the fray, heedless of his own safety, shouting, "Come on, my boys."[17]

The choke point against which all of the forward American fire had concentrated had been breeched, even as Gleig and others now began to effectively snipe at the American riflemen across the river from windows in houses by the bank. Now men began to also press across the creek itself, "which was every where fordable, and in most places lined with bushes or trees, which were sufficient . . . to conceal the movements of light troops," who acted singly or in small units. Soon, they had secured the shelter of the far side of the apple orchard, from which they began sniping at the troops on Stansbury's left.[18] Once across the main bridge, clusters of men now automatically began to form in line, but not without paying a price. Captain John Knox, among those who successfully crossed intact, had serious misgivings about his own chances after passing the bloodied bodies of three officers and eight or nine troopers of the 85th Regiment lying dead or wounded on the ground. "Before

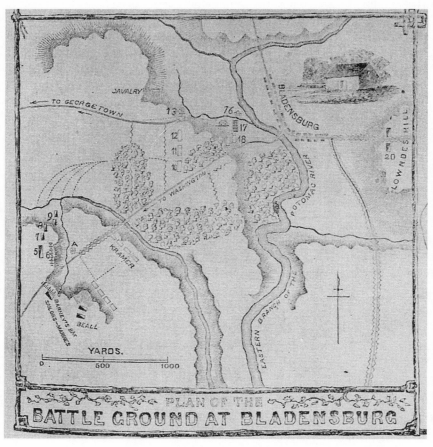

Plan of the Battle of Bladensburg, August 24, 1814, by Benson J. Lossing, *The Pictorial Field Book of the War of 1812* (New York: Harper & Bros., 1869).

we had been a quarter of an hour under fire, thinks I to myself," he recalled incredulously, "thinks I, by the time the action is over the devil is in it if I am not either a walking major or a dead captain." It was, indeed, the worst fire he had experienced in his career.[19]

"This, too," Pinkney reported of the second attack, "was encountered by the artillery in the battery, but not with its former success, although it was served with great spirit, and commanded by officers of acknowledged skill and courage." As a consequence, a large column of the enemy was soon formed on the Washington side to menace the American battery and the inadequate force that defended it.[20]

As the clusters of British soldiers began to form in regular formation and more men began crossing the bridge amidst raking fire from the 5th Regiment batteries of Magruder and Myers, some of the defenders were astonished at how the attackers seemed to take no notice of it. Private Henry Fulford, a militiaman from Baltimore, wrote after the battle, "their men moved like clock-work; the instant a part of a platoon was cut down it was filled up by the men in the rear without the least noise and confusion whatever, so as to present always a solid column to the mouths of our cannon."[21]

The relentless onslaught of the British was more than the American riflemen in the line could take, and they quickly broke band and ran. Doughty's company of seventy-one D.C. volunteers, just arriving on Pinkney's right, were just in time to fire six to eight shots before the enemy was within range, and then fled despite efforts of the captain and Pinkney to stop them. As they ran, Doughty later stated, one of Winder's aides appeared and ordered them to fall back to the heights beyond Georgetown.[22]

Now the entire focus of the enemy attack came to bear on Pinkney's two companies, both of which had followed the example set by Doughty's men by firing too early without pausing to aim. The effect produced only a momentary hesitation in the ranks of the attackers. Again, the British light infantry pressed forward and was close at hand when the artillery ceased fire, as it could do no more now. Pinkney's right was threatened, as the enemy had almost reached it. Unfortunately, the attackers were very nearly "out of the line of fire which the half formed embrasures of the battery would admit; and I should presume that it would have been difficult, if not impracticable, to depress the guns in those embrasures (the ground of the battery being considerably elevated) so as to touch the enemy after his near approach." Believing that they were all there was to stop the oncoming wall of bayonets, unaware of the lines that had been set up behind them, and being flanked on the right with Asquith's unit too weak to hold the left, Pinkney's own small force of about a hundred men now stood little chance of stopping the enemy, even if he attacked on the front. They, too, did not await orders to retreat.[23]

Only one of Pinkney's companies had bayonets, and, "under these circumstances of urgent peril, both the companies began at the same instant to move towards the artillery, now in the act of limbering its guns." He later reported "the retreat of my men and the artillery appeared to be simultaneous. The whole fell back upon the regiment." They halted upon reaching the bushes to Sterett's left, where they were re-formed by Captain Dyer, the adjutant and sergeant major. Pinkney himself was barely able to escape, having been seriously wounded by a ball that had struck his right arm, slightly above the elbow, and splintered the bone as it coursed through. On foot he managed to bring up the rear and was nearly captured. As he loped toward the nearest rally point, the 5th Regiment, he was certain that had his men remained at their post longer they would have been slaughtered or taken prisoner.[24]

It was now Sterett's turn to bear the brunt of the enemy assault. Only moments before, in the brief visit of hubris after the first attack on the bridge had been repelled, Winder ordered the 5th Regiment from their initial position on the left of Stansbury's line to advance and "sustain the artillery." For a short time, the American fire had been overwhelming and the regiment "kept its ground with exemplary steadiness, and maintained a regular and spirited fire." But now, with the right and center crumbling, the situation had changed dramatically.[25]

Though the enemy had also advanced to the cover of the forward edge of the orchard, Winder still hoped to be able to prevent their further progress with the forces at hand. The return fire by British marksmen concealed behind trees, however, began to take effect. In an effort to draw the enemy from the orchard and beyond the shelter of their covering rocket fire, Winder ordered a retreat up the hill toward a wood on the left and a little to the rear. However, thinking better of the command and fearing that his raw troops might be more inclined to run from the field altogether in utter confusion than conduct an orderly retirement to a new position, he immediately countermanded the order and directed that return fire be aimed at a barn on the left of the orchard, behind which the enemy were believed to be sheltered.[26] The confusion caused by the two back-to-back orders to the ill-trained citizen-soldiers was nearly universal.

Burch's Washington Artillery, all three 6-pounders, began firing at the barn, perhaps 350 yards or so ahead, and on the other side of the Georgetown road. After getting off a few rounds per gun, however, Winder personally appeared and, worried that the unit might be enveloped as the right wing collapsed, ordered Captain Burch to limber his guns and to also retire. "I did not do so immediately," the captain later testified, "but fired two or three rounds, when the General repeated his order in a peremptory manner. We retreated a few yards, when he observed to me that he thought I might venture to unlimber one of my pieces and give them another fire. I was in the act of doing so, but as the enemy advanced so rapidly, he countermanded it, and again ordered me on."[27]

Some in the Washington Artillery were astonished at the order to retreat as the British began advancing from the barn. Captain John Law was among them. "Not a man of our company had been touched by the fire of the enemy, and I thought that the battle was only then seriously commencing." His own piece would never again see action, nor would any order be given as to where the battalion was to rally.

Burch would see no more of General Winder that day. Like many on both sides, suffering from lack of sleep and the unforgiving sun, the fatigued captain was unable to keep up with his guns and fainted in the sweltering heat by the side of a fence, unobserved by the retreating artillerymen of his battalion. When he awoke, he was ill with a burning fever, but nevertheless found a horse and made his way to Washington to rejoin his men. Many of them were not there, for, on the road they had taken from the battlefield, they had eventually come to a three-way intersection, with spurs leading to the capital, to Georgetown, and another via Rock Creek Church to Tenleytown and Montgomery Court House, in Maryland. Each man had gone the route of his choosing. Eventually, Burch rejoined most of his unit many miles away at Montgomery Court House.[28]

· · ·

Colonel Jacint Lavall and his little squadron of the 1st U.S. Dragoons, "all green recruits, and upon raw horses" (purchased only two days before leaving Carlisle and unused to the sounds of gunfire), had patiently awaited orders in the shallow ravine 1,500 feet west of the barn. When the colonel peered over the edge of the ravine to observe the progress of the fight, he was stunned as he watched the enemy "advancing rapidly under a shower of fire, besides a column of about seven or eight hundred which had gained considerably on our right." When later criticized for failure to assail the enemy's right flank, and "cut to pieces four or five thousand of the British troops with fifty-five men . . . the consequences are so obvious, that I did not think myself justified to make so certain, so inevitable a sacrifice, without a hope of doing any good; there is a distinction between madness and bravery."[29]

Lavall waited impatiently for orders until it was clear that a retreat had either been ordered elsewhere on the field or had been forced by the enemy. "All of a sudden our army seemed routed; a confused retreat appeared to be about in every corner of the battle ground, and the place we were occupying seemed to have been the one by which it was to be effected. They poured in torrents by us; my right wing being outside the ravine, covered, unfortunately, a gate which it appeared was much wanted. An artillery company drove through before we could clear it; several of my men were crushed down, horses and all, and myself narrowly escaped having my thigh broken by one of the wheels which nearly took off my horse. All this created much confusion in the right wing of the squadron; they, however, soon got in order, and the stream of the running phalanx considerably abated." By then all Lavall had standing with him were fifty-five cavalrymen.[30]

"We then, and only then . . . marched off between the flanking column and our disordered army." They continued west, "walking our horses as slow as horses can walk," when they encountered Monroe unhurriedly making his way back to the capital and leading his own horse on foot. The president and the remainder of his entourage were not far off on the same road.[31]

. . .

As the front was in the process of caving in, General Stansbury did his best to keep his infantry from wavering. "I rode along the line," said the general after the battle, "and gave orders to the officers to cut down those who attempted to fly, and suffer no man to leave our lines." Yet, there was no counter to the fear now imposed by the enemy's rocketry, the seemingly unstoppable line of approaching bayonets, and light infantry fire from the orchard. At the right and center he found Lieutenant Colonel Jonathan Schutz's men giving way, despite all efforts of Schutz and several of his other officers to rally them. Lieutenant Colonel John Ragan's regiment from western Maryland was also succumbing to panic, despite that officer's gallant efforts to stem the tide.[32] Winder also did his desperate best to halt the flight and rode swiftly across the field "towards those who had shamefully fled, and exerted my voice to the utmost to arrest them." For a moment they halted, began to reform, and returned to their positions. Satisfied that their officers would take over the rally, the general turned his attention to the 5th Maryland, whose rapidly failing position was critical and from which point he could better view the battlefield.[33]

Then, to his "astonishment and mortification," both regiments he had just turned back were seen flying from the field "in the utmost precipitation and disorder." Only two companies of the 1,300 men in the two regiments, barely eighty men, had been successfully reformed and returned to the fight, but the remainder were racing from the field in utter terror, their flight here and there only briefly interrupted by a fence or some other obstacle. Ragan himself was thrown from his dying horse and injured, rendering him unable to further rally his men.[34]

Sterett's 5th was by now also collapsing, being driven from the field well before encountering British bayonets. Private John Pendleton Kennedy recalled only that "we made a fine scamper of it." His own company of sixty-six men suffered at least eight wounded and all were retreating. While carrying from the field Corporal James W. McCulloch, a wounded comrade who had his leg broken by an enemy bullet, he had given his own musket to a friend to carry during the melee. Soon afterward, the friend was also wounded and the weapon lost, but Kennedy merely chalked it and the battle up in later years as the adventure of youth.[35]

Another soldier in the 5th Regiment, Henry Fulford, was confident that had they stayed ten minutes longer, all would have been killed or captured. His flight was perhaps typical of the panic that had swept the American line. "When the retreat was ordered, I shaped my course for a wood in the rear, where I intended to lay down and rest, being almost fatigued to death, but the bullets and grape shot flew like hailstones about me and I was compelled to make headway for a swamp where I remained until I had strength sufficient to get to a little farm house where I was hospitably received and got refreshed."[36]

With the front lines fleeing in disarray on the roads to Washington and Georgetown, many without having been given a rallying point, the panic soon spread to the second line of defense, Colonel William Scott's 36th Regiment and Colonel William Brent's 2nd Regiment of D.C. militiamen. As the mass of men from the forward lines swarmed like ants toward them, the second line was swept by panic and joined in the rout. Only a few moments earlier, Scott had repositioned his troops a bit farther from Barney's left to counter an enemy thrust against the extreme left of the American line, which might have been particularly effective had the collapse of the front line, especially on its right, not thwarted the defenders' resolve. Brent's militiamen, positioned in a gully and wooded area a few hundred yards behind Scott, were swept along in the exodus, having never fired a shot. To the left, Stansbury's whole command was soon in flight on the Georgetown road. Utterly frustrated by the militia, Winder now ordered a general retreat.[37] Unfortunately, he was obliged to dispatch a messenger to General Smith, rather than deliver the order in person as his horse was exhausted from galloping all morning about the field. The consequences were, nevertheless, to produce additional confusion.

Winder immediately dispatched a messenger to President Madison to inform him that the army was falling back but that he hoped to make another stand between his present position and the capital. And still the enemy came on, up the Washington road. The 4th Regiment soon gained the road crossing the ravine and relentlessly drove ahead, now pressing back Lieutenant Colonel Kramer's command, which had been posted on the right of the road to Washington in a facing wood and in advance of Barney's position. Having maintained his position despite the retirement to his left and front, Kramer, too, was forced to withdraw, but unlike others, continued firing as he retreated, causing much hurt to his attackers but failing to even slow their inexorable advance. Now the enemy became exposed to the oblique fire from Major Peter's battery, which had been situated on the left, "which was kept up with great animation," until it too was swept up in the general retreat.[38]

No one bothered to inform Barney of Winder's orders, although it was quite obvious to him that the entire front was dissolving before his eyes, even as he steeled himself for combat against now hopeless odds.

...

As the British 85th Light Infantry advanced, inspired by Colonel Thornton's heroic charge across the bridge, they had been joined soon after by Colonel Arthur Brooke's 2nd Brigade, composed of the 4th Regiment under Major Alured D. Faunce and the 44th Regiment under Major Thomas Mullins. Major Mullins's men had moved to the right of the bridge, where it had turned the American flank in that quarter, and Faunce had advanced on the left. With studied discipline, each soldier marched in a line ten paces from the man on his left and right, bayonet forward, making the least possible target for grape shot or grouped American musket fire. Ahead, clusters of defenders provided ready targets for the attackers, even as artillery fire continued to crater the fields all about the attackers. Here and there men were felled not only by shot and ball, but by the punishing heat, which killed no fewer than eighteen men on the march and in the assault, at least three of which belonged to the 4th Regiment who died while climbing the hill, another nine from the 21st, and six more from the 85th.[39]

Despite the merciless heat, the offensive continued unabated. At a fence line dividing a grove from a cultivated field, the line of advance was halted only momentarily. A young junior officer ahead of Lieutenant Gleig taunted him: "Who will be the first in the enemy's line!" Stay with your men, Gleig warned his comrade, and do not get ahead of the line. Before the words were out of his mouth, a musket ball smashed into the junior officer's neck, killing him in an instant. Another musket shot struck Gleig's sword scabbard, breaking it, and a third caused a slight flesh wound on his arm. Yet, the line did not waver and, rallied by the lieutenant and others, the infantry pressed onward past the fence and up the hill.[40]

If the Americans could find little to rally around, the British had no want of brave leaders to spur them on. By now General Ross himself had come up leading the 4th Regiment to lend further support for the assault. As balls tore through his clothing, though not touching his flesh, he continued to cry out, "Charge! Charge!"[41] Nor was Admiral Cockburn to be left in the rear. Elegantly dressed in his Royal Navy uniform, gold laced hat, and admiral's epaulettes, and mounted upon a beautiful white horse, he was perhaps one of the most conspicuous senior officers—and targets—on the field, riding to and fro less than 140 yards from the second American line of defense. When his aide pleaded with him to seek shelter behind a small quarry to his right, he scoffed, "Nonsense!" He watched in delight as his marine artillery, now moved forward from their previous position, began to launch rockets at the American lines almost horizontally, which seemed to distill even more panic amidst their wavering ranks. "Capital! Excellent!" Then, when a ball sliced his stirrup, having passed between the saddle flap and his leg, he quickly dismounted. As a marine and an aide began lacing the strap together, another shot killed the marine.[42]

· · ·

As the British pushed along the main road in force, now driving the Americans before them like hares pursued by foxes, they soon came within view of Barney's battery in the direct center of the road to Washington. For a brief moment they arrested their advance before what had only minutes before been the center of the rearmost American line. It was now all that stood between them and the capture of the capital of the United States of America.

The commodore, who had faced down seemingly unbeatable odds many times in his life, was not the least bit intimidated by the enemy rockets and bayonets or influenced by the panic that had gripped the forward lines, still to be seen fleeing into the countryside. As he sat astride his horse to conduct the last fight of his life against his most enduring adversary, he may have considered the irony in that it was to be on dry land and not from the deck of a ship.

For a few pregnant moments, the two sides continued to stand facing each other. And then the fight began its bloodiest and final phase. "I reserved our fire," the commodore later reported. "In a few minutes the enemy again advanced, when I ordered an 18 lb. to be fired." The grapeshot ripped through the ranks of the oncoming British and completely cleared the road.[43]

Stunned for a moment, the enemy recoiled, regained his composure, reorganized, and bravely charged once more into the maw of certain death, and again was felled in considerable numbers by another wall of grape. Again the attackers charged, this time led by Colonel Thornton himself, mounted on horseback, leading the 85th. This charge too was cruelly crushed as the enemy sprinted across the creek and for the first time appeared to threaten Barney's right flank. For a full half hour, the repeated assaults had been repelled, and for a moment the invader's offensive was stopped in its tracks.[44] To the British, as it had been throughout the campaign on the Patuxent, it was now clear that direct frontal assault against the flotillamen and their battery was sheer suicide.[45]

The defenders held firm, but their assailants were no less resolute: they had not been dubbed Wellington's Invincibles for nothing. If they could not overcome Barney's position, they would attempt to lay into his immediate right flank. To do so, Thornton would have to cross an open field and then deal with both the battery of three 12-pounders and the flotillamen acting as infantry, as well as the commodore's big 18-pounders which had been turned obliquely in that direction.[46]

It was here that the most ferocious fighting of the entire battle was to be engaged with both shot and cold steel. Rallied by their impetuously brave Colonel Thornton with sword in hand, the 85ths once again formed and charged across the open field. Again they were met by a cascade of fire, but pushed on to within fifty yards of Miller's line of marines. Being a mounted officer at the head of the charge, Thornton and his steed proved ample targets for American marksmen. Suddenly, a shot smashed into the horse, felling him in an instant. Undismayed, the colonel rebounded to his feet and, with sword waving, continued to lead the charge afoot. As he was almost upon the

American line, grape shot shredded his coat and a bullet tore into his thigh, felling him in mid-stride, severely wounded, but not dead.[47]

With their leader down, the British advance momentarily wavered. Seeing his opportunity, Barney ordered Miller to countercharge and engage the enemy head on. Though his ranks of just 114 men had already been thinned by enemy fire, the captain and seventy-eight U.S. Marines, with their cutlasses waving madly over their heads, at once swarmed from their defensive nest like angry wasps, screaming, "Board 'em! Board 'em!" The stunned invaders, taken completely by surprise, were soon hotly pursued and ran for cover, but there was none to be found.[48]

Farther and farther back down the road and across the open field they were driven at breakneck speed. Most leaped over a stone wall topped by a wooden fence and into a ravine nearly two hundred yards in their rear. Here they found cover and time to catch their breath in the scalding midday heat. Many among their number, both rank-and-file alike, had suffered from musket, cutlass, and bayonet wounds. Many more of their officers and comrades lay on the field behind them, including Thornton, his second and third ranking officers, Lieutenant Colonel William Wood, and Major George Brown. Some were luckier than others. Thornton later told Barney that "his men had passed very near him in their advance, and that he expected every instant to be discovered as he lay prostrate, and made prisoner; but they missed him; and on their return from the charge, they took another route, leaving him some distance to their right."[49]

Miller's rush, with too few men to maintain momentum, proved but a forlorn hope, for at that moment Ross himself rode up mounted on a beautiful Arabian horse and personally took command of Thornton's brigade and began to regain the ground. As he rallied his soldiers, his appearance was indeed imposing. One of Barney's own black flotillamen, Charles Ball, who was helping to man one of the cannon on the commodore's immediate left, later recalled that the general was "one of the finest looking men that I ever saw on horseback." At that moment Barney's guns again opened, sending grapeshot once more toward the advancing British. Ross's steed, a veteran of the Peninsular Campaign, crumpled beneath him, mortally wounded, throwing the general to the ground. Yet the American counterattack was blunted and the U.S. Marines became stalled and then forced back by the exacting fire from enemy marksmen. Captains Miller and Sevier were both seriously wounded. Miller had been felled by a bullet in his arm and Sevier by a wound in the neck, though both temporarily escaped capture. Before all was said and done, the marines would count eleven dead and sixteen wounded among them, having suffered a nearly 25 percent casualty rate. Captain Miller himself would be hospitalized for nearly a year and partially handicapped for the rest of his life.[50]

Having been rebounded by Barney, then Miller, General Ross turned his full attention to the unseasoned militiamen under Beall and Hood, on the commodore's extreme right, still winded and exhausted from their sixteen-mile forced march from Annapolis in the morning. Because of the commanding elevation they were ensconced upon, Barney expected more from these units than he perhaps should have. Not surprisingly, as the 85th charged, Beall's and Hood's militiamen, somewhere between five and six hundred strong, fired once or twice without much effect. As the oncoming British regulars, perhaps half the number of Marylanders in front of them, pressed up the hill with bayonets poised at the front, the American right quickly faltered. The colonel tried without success to rally his troops even as "they ran like sheep chased by dogs" before British steel. In an instant, Barney's right flank simply evaporated.[51]

The commodore's left flank, composed of the 1st Regiment of the D.C. Militia, under Colonel George Magruder, became the next objective of British attack, this time by fresh troops of the 4th and 44th Regiments under Lieutenant Colonel Brooke. At first the attack was met by substantial fire and with some success. To one of the American regimental commanders, taking heart from the flotilla artillerists on their right who were firing without letup, there seemed no reason to retire. General Winder, however, thought better of it and, upon observing the fresh attack on the left, issued orders to fall back. The 1st Columbians pulled back, initially about eighty paces. Then the order for a further withdrawal was issued. As the militiamen attempted to regroup and fall back again, the whole left flank began to cave in before the British onslaught. As they retired another six hundred paces, a third order came in for a full retreat to the heights of Washington itself. Like Beall's men, the D.C. Militia, too, virtually dissolved.[52]

Now, flanked on both their left and right, the flotillamen and U.S. Marines, who had single-handedly and repeatedly turned back every massive assault launched against them, became the subject of the undivided attention of the enemy. The fire from the entire British army was now leveled against them, with devastating consequences. From the heights to the right, only minutes earlier occupied by Beall and Hood, sharpshooters rained a killing fire upon the Americans. Standing between his two big 18-pounders, Barney's horse was pierced by two balls and fell dead. The situation was becoming worse by the second. "Our ammunition was expended," Barney later informed Jones, "and unfortunately the drivers of my ammunition wagons had gone off in the general panic." Then, while he stood near one of his guns, a bullet smashed into the commodore's thigh, leaving him unable to walk and bleeding badly.[53]

In the chaos of combat, Barney was momentarily able to keep his wound a secret to prevent his own men from panicking, but could take no steps to staunch the flow of blood. As he looked about him, he readily determined the situation was desperate. Sailing Master Warner had been killed while standing at his side manning one of the guns. Sailing Master James H. Martin had also fallen severely wounded as had Sailing Master William Martin, who also commanded one of the guns. Yet, "as fast as their companions & mess mates fell at the guns they were instantly replaced from the infantry."[54]

Now finding the enemy working around to his rear, leaving his position defenseless, without ammunition, and faced with overwhelming odds against him, the bleeding commodore ordered the guns spiked and his men to retire. Three officers, Surgeon Thomas Hamilton, Sailing Master Jesse Huffington, and Midshipman Thomas Dukehart, attempted to assist him off the field, but the profuse loss of blood, he later recorded, "occasioned such a weakness that I was compelled to lie down." Calmly but forcefully he directed the officers to escape while they still could, but they declined until he issued a direct command. Knowing he faced certain capture, imprisonment, and an uncertain future, Huffington nevertheless again refused and faithfully remained by his commander. At that moment, and before Hamilton and Dukehart had gone, Barney's temporary aide de camp, a steward named George I. Wilson, galloped by on horseback, and Huffington beseeched him to assist in removing the commodore from the battlefield. The steward galloped on, shouting back that he too was wounded, then disappeared to the west. Barney was enraged at the "wretch" and remained convinced that if he had reined in his horse, all would have escaped capture.[55]

Though Barney had ordered retreat, some in the battery refused to quit and continued to fight on, even as sweating troopers of the 85th swarmed across the guns, shooting or bayoneting anyone who stood in their way, including some of the flotillamen with lit fuses in their hands. Here and there steel engaged steel as cutlasses crossed and guts were spilled onto the ground.[56]

Within minutes, as the field was no longer contested, the carnage subsided, even as the last Americans retired in "double quick time" from the battery.

Sailing Master John Webster was one of the last to leave. Bullets whizzed by him, one passing through his hat and another shooting his horse out from under him. His final view of the battery as he pressed ahead on foot was of his beloved commander being supported by a British officer.[57]

...

Still lying in the battery in a pool of his own spreading blood, Joshua Barney had spotted a British regular and had him summoned. The soldier was asked to seek an officer and within a few minutes Lieutenant James Scott, Cockburn's aide de camp, appeared, followed by Captain John Wainwright, both of who were among the few Royal Navy officers on the battlefield. The commodore was at first a little surprised at meeting Wainwright, as he "was a very young looking man, and being dressed in a short, round jacket," was at first mistaken for a midshipman. The two captains, however, "were soon mutually announced to each other, and the moment Captain W. learned the name of his prisoner . . . went in search of the Admiral, who soon afterwards made his appearance, accompanied by the general, Ross." Now, for the one and only time in their lives, the two adversaries met face to face, Barney and Cockburn, who had fought for three months in a battle of will, skill, and enterprise. Given the savagery of the encounter all had participated in only a few minutes earlier, Barney's captors were as attentive, respectful, and polite as if they had just met in a coffee house. An army surgeon was immediately summoned to attend to the commodore's wounds as the three enemies exchanged pleasantries.[58]

"Well, admiral, you have got hold of me at last," said the commodore.

"Do not let us speak on that subject, commodore," Cockburn replied. "I regret to see you in this state. I hope you are not seriously hurt."

"Quite enough to prevent my giving you any trouble for some time," said Barney.[59]

Then the general spoke.

"I am really very glad to see you, Commodore."

"I am sorry I cannot return you the compliment, General," replied Barney, obviously in great pain.

A wide grin may have passed across the general's face as he turned to Cockburn. "I told you it was the flotillamen!"

"Yes! You were right, though I could not believe you. They have given us the only fighting we have had."

The two officers spoke quietly between themselves for a few moments and then, abruptly turning to face Barney, Ross spoke in a commanding tone: "Commodore Barney, you are paroled. Where do you wish to be conveyed?"[60]

Both the commodore and Huffington were given liberty to proceed to either Washington or Bladensburg. The sailing master, who had faithfully remained by his commander, ordered a litter on which to carry him to Bladensburg. At Cockburn's command Captain Wainwright was delegated to accompany the litter. The captain remained with the commodore throughout the day "and behaved to me," Barney recalled, "as if I was a brother."[61]

As the litter moved along, the intense pain from the only major wound he had ever received in his many battles showed on Barney's face. Wainwright ordered the soldiers to put the litter down, saying "they did know how to handle a man," and then directed a naval officer to "bring a gang of sailors" to convey him. And as the captain predicted they "handled him like a child."[62]

As the commodore was carried along, an American prisoner, whose arm was hanging at his side connected only by a small piece of skin, passed the litter, knelt by the side of his commander, seized one of his hands and kissed it repeatedly with apparent affection, and then burst into tears. "The effect of this action upon the British sailors was electric—they began to wipe their eyes, and blow their noses, in concert, and one of them at length broke out— with, 'Well d—n my eyes! If he wasn't a kind commander, that chap wouldn't ha done *that!*'"[63]

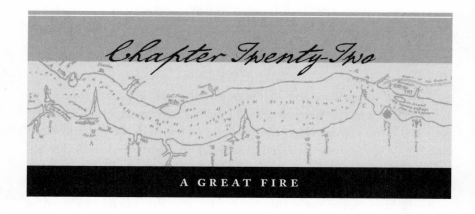

Chapter Twenty-Two

A GREAT FIRE

The British occupation of Benedict, while the war was becoming very warm elsewhere, was for the most part uneventful. Aboard *Royal Oak,* sailmakers were busily employed in making a new foresail and deck awning for the schooner *Anna Maria,* one of the many fleet tenders at anchor nearby. Elsewhere, the ship's company was ashore gathering water and wood, and carpenters were busily employed in fitting a new foretopmast stay.[1] On *Albion,* the traditional problems incurred by hard discipline, hard duty, and, occasionally, hard liquor, were dealt with in the traditional way. On August 21, even as Ross's army was marching northward to its rendezvous with destiny, the usual solutions to such problems were meted out with the customary severity of the Royal Navy and dutifully recorded in the ship's log. "Read the Articles of War," wrote the log-keeper, "and punished Henry Farley (S) with 40 and Peter Anderson (M) with 14 lashes for drunkeness, Michl Sullivan (S) with 18 lashes for neglect of duty, Wm Smith (M) with 48 lashes for drunkeness and sleeping on his post, Jno. Sheridan (Arts) with 48 lashes and Henry Halls (M) with 36 lashes for drunkeness and violence." The following day, more of the same was offered up. Aboard *Hebrus,* carpenters were put to work making coffins.[2] And so it went as everyone waited for news from the front.

At 1:00 p.m. on August 25 the fleet at Benedict was subjected to the thrashing of another violent storm. The sky was aglow with jagged blades of lightning and the winds funneled down the Patuxent Valley with hurricane force. *Albion* was driven from her single anchor a full cable's length to the east, and many vessels were nearly upended. By 8:00 p.m., however, the worst was over as the storm marched grudgingly westward, leaving behind a moody, cloud-covered sky. An hour later a significant entry was scribbled into *Albion*'s logbook, almost as if the event recorded had been heralded by the gale: "Observed a great fire in the direction of Washington."[3]

General Ross had been successful. The capital city of the United States of America was in flames.

...

By the late afternoon of August 27, the British army had returned to its former campsite at Upper Marlboro, weary and footsore from a forced march beneath the searing Tidewater sun. The troopers were as pleased with a solid victory gained over the Americans opposite the little town on the Eastern Branch called Bladensburg as they were with the capture and sack of Washington. Though losses at Bladensburg had been high, 64 dead and 185 wounded against 71 American losses (most of whom had been Barney's flotillamen and U.S. Marines), it had been a victory to crow about. It had been for Jonathan the final link in a chain of disasters that had started when the British entered the Chesapeake what seemed an eternity before. The news, of course, spread quickly about the fleet. At the Battle of Bladensburg, Ross and Cockburn utterly humiliated the American forces with one glaring exception. A stout resistance, which had held off the entire British army before succumbing to overwhelming numbers, had been made by the gallant Barney and his small band of flotillamen and marines. Even Barney's mortal enemy acknowledged the heroism of his redoubtable sailors and marines. But it had not been enough.

Soon after Washington had been captured, Captain Gordon had managed to ascend the Potomac, pass the obstacles proffered by the Kettle Bottoms, force the destruction of Fort Washington, and then accept the surrender of the City of Alexandria, Virginia, just opposite the American's national capital. President Madison was said to yet be in the countryside in hiding, and the smashed and thoroughly demoralized American army no longer worried anyone but General Ross. The general insisted, after his sack of the capital had been completed, on a forced march back to the Patuxent in case Jonathan was organizing a pursuit. Indeed, upon his hasty departure, he had been obliged to leave behind upwards of eighty wounded officers and men at Bladensburg.[4]

...

Commodore Joshua Barney suffered greatly from the bullet in his thigh while ensconced at Ross's Tavern in Bladensburg, to which he had been taken at his own request. Soon after his arrival, Captain Miller had joined him in his room. The captain, during his gallant charge, had also been severely wounded and was eventually taken prisoner. Though surrounded by his fellow comrades who mourned their defeat, the paroled commodore continued to attend, unofficially, to his duty and his men. On the day Ross had entered Washington, he had sent Barney a list of officers, "for his ratification," whom he had agreed to parole. Soon afterward, the guard stationed at his door disappeared, an action that he surmised to mean the enemy was already moving out. On the morning of August 26, he received a message from the secretary to the British Commissary of Prisoners that Ross was retiring to Upper Marlboro "and to request that he would send for some of his own men, for the purpose of keeping order in the town and preventing mischief from stragglers and deserters." A guard, provided to attend to the British wounded who had been left behind, would be surrendered, but the officers were to be paroled. The general also informed him "that a party of his men should be sent out to pick up stragglers, and a few posted in the village to preserve order."[5]

With these duties addressed, Joshua Barney, attended by the flotilla surgeon, Dr. Hamilton, with his wife and son William, was conveyed upon a bed to his farm at Elkridge, where many failed attempts would be made to extract the ball that had lodged behind the head of his femur.[6] His battle-weary flotillamen, however, had already marched off to the defense of Baltimore, which many believed would be the enemy's next target.

. . .

During the British army's trek back to Upper Marlboro, many slaves had pleaded with the troopers to take them along and had joined the long column, "offering to serve either as soldiers or sailors, if we would give them their liberty." The Crown's new policy regarding the utilization of slaves had, of course, been well outlined by Lord Bathurst during the drafting of instructions for the campaign. General Ross, who personally considered the slaves to be the private property of his foe, "persisted in protecting private property of every description" and thus permitted only a few to accompany the army.[7]

After a good night's rest at Upper Marlboro, the army rose early the next morning and took up the march to Nottingham, where they arrived several hours later. Here Ross permitted his men to rest and recuperate for the remainder of the day. A gun-brig and a number of ships, launches, and longboats had already made their way up against the stream and come to anchor opposite the town to await them. Many of the troopers wounded during the engagement at Bladensburg had been left behind on the fields of Maryland, but the walking casualties had remained with the main army and were now carried aboard the brig. Large quantities of flour and tobacco, the only substantial spoils of war brought away, were transferred to the smaller vessels and shipped downstream.[8]

At daylight on August 29, the wounded, the artillery, and the plunder having already been sent downriver by boat, the army broke camp and commenced the tedious march to Benedict. Cockburn's marines had it much easier traveling by water and several elements of the vanguard of this force reached the fleet anchorage as early as 10:00 a.m. At 6:00 p.m. a signal was raised aboard HBMS *Surprize* to send all boats, large and small, to commence bringing aboard the troops, primarily the marine artillery, which by then was coming down in advance of the army. Two hours later Admiral Cockburn with his mini-armada arrived with the main body of marines. Ross's foot-weary troopers were, at about this time, observed marching down the sandy road to the town, and soon afterward began occupying the grounds beneath the ridge upon which they had first encamped on August 19. A number of officers, Lieutenant Gleig among them, were only too ready to relax in the first serviceable home available. "The luxury I enjoyed," the lieutenant confided to his diary, "in turning into clean sheets is beyond description."[9]

...

The departure of the British army from Upper Marlboro had been greeted by the local citizens with a general sigh of relief. The town and its inhabitants had been spared the unfortunate fate of many others on the Patuxent. Not the least of those who breathed a bit easier was Dr. William Beanes, who promptly arranged a small dinner party at his home on Academy Hill. Among those invited were former Governor of Maryland Robert Bowie, Dr. William Hill, Philip Weems, his own brother, Dr. Bradley Beanes, and William Lansdale of nearby Queen Anne's Town. Their celebration was to be short lived.[10]

The British withdrawal through the Maryland countryside had left behind more than wounded soldiers in its wake. Deserters and stragglers abounded. At least III men had unaccountably vanished. Many had taken the opportunity to escape from the harsh military life offered in His Majesty's service, while others thought only of raiding, plundering, and pillaging in the civil vacuum created by a retiring victorious army. Most of the looting was carried out against the pitifully poor dirt farmers who could offer little resistance. The holdings of many wealthy plantation owners, it was widely rumored, were occasionally protected by troops of the British army or were spared such attacks.[11]

Robert Bowie, who owned property in Nottingham, was not about to stand for such "barbaric" activity. As a former military man, he refused to accept the departure of the invaders from the neighborhood as evidence of the return to complete normalcy. Indeed, while the enemy was still on the march from Washington to Upper Marlboro, he had dispatched his son, Robert W. Bowie, and Benjamin Oden off to reconnoiter their march. On the 27th he set out to pay a visit to Dr. William Beanes. When he arrived at the good doctor's farm in the company of William Lansdale soon after the enemy's departure from Upper Marlboro, he encountered a British soldier named Tom Holden in the doctor's garden attempting "to steal the refreshments." The thief was quickly "compelled to surrender." The soldier readily admitted to being a deserter and was taken to the doctor's house.[12]

To Beanes, Ross's erstwhile host, British gentlemen such as the general were one thing, but scavengers and deserters were something else. Beanes and Bowie readily determined to take action to maintain order, with the good doctor, perhaps, attempting to save face for his earlier friendly reception of the enemy. Within a short time, several local volunteers were recruited to gather up as many British stragglers and deserters as possible. Within a short time three more enemy soldiers were promptly captured and sent into the town by Oden, Bowie's son, and others. Unfortunately, several more escaped toward Nottingham to tell the tale. Holden and the other three new captives were soon assembled at Upper Marlboro, where their very presence soon caused great alarm among the citizens, who feared certain retaliation by the enemy.[13] After all, the British had destroyed whole towns elsewhere in the Tidewater with far less justification!

Concerned that the locals would release the prisoners, Bowie called upon two trustworthy brothers, John and Robert Hodges, to remove them to a more secure place. With the assistance of Oden, Bowie himself took charge of the fourth prisoner, the deserter Holden. Three of the captives were marched upriver to Queen Anne's Town, where they were placed under the guard of one John Randall and safely incarcerated. Holden, the fourth prisoner, was conveyed on horseback by William Lansdale and reached the town about midnight. Upon the captives' arrival, at Bowie's request, a guard of young men, including John Randall, Solomon and Thomas Sparrow, and a man named Wells, was mounted to keep watch over them. In a letter informing Governor Winder of the captures, Bowie was generous in his praise of the Hodges, stating that "if it had not been for their promptness and patriotism, he could not have got the prisoners out of Marlborough."[14]

In the meantime, while at Nottingham General Ross took the opportunity offered by the army's temporary halt to dispatch Lieutenant George de Lacy Evans with a body of horsemen, on captured horses, back as far as Upper Marlboro to discover whether or not the American army had regrouped and taken up pursuit, unlikely as that prospect may have been. Simultaneously, one of the stragglers who had escaped capture managed to run directly into the arms of the mounted scouts just as they were preparing to return to Nottingham from the outskirts of Upper Marlboro. The penalty for desertion was death. Thus, perhaps to save his own skin, the deserter informed his comrades that the inhabitants of the town, led by none other than their former host Dr. Beanes, had risen in arms upon the army's departure and, "falling upon such individuals as strayed from the column, put some of them to death, and made others prisoners," only half of which was true.[15]

Enraged by the deserter's tale despite the questionable veracity of the source, fifty or sixty British horsemen wheeled about and galloped into the village in the middle of the night, directly up to the home of William Beanes' brother, Dr. Bradley Beanes. After searching the house for men and arms and finding nothing, they departed and proceeded to William's home, burst in, and yanked the elderly physician from his bed, as well as two houseguests, Hill and Weems, who had decided to stay the night. Yet it was William Beanes, a citizen "universally esteemed and respected—in whose situation every one would feel an interest," who had become the focal point of the enemy's wrath. The doctor and his guests were ordered to dress with such speed he failed to locate his eyeglasses. His captors then "compelled him, by threat of instant death, to liberate his prisoners; and mounting him before one of the party, brought him in triumph to the camp" at Nottingham, where he was placed in solitary confinement. Other townsmen were also rounded up, including the wives and children of the Hodges brothers, and temporarily taken as hostages as well.[16]

Within a short time a local militia captain named Brooke, "very much agitated," visited Bradley Beanes and informed him that the British had carried off his brother and others and told him of the threats. He then implored the doctor to go with him to the residence of John and Robert Hodges to "persuade them to go to Queen Anne and bring back some of the prisoners, and to Robert Bowie, who had another." The two brothers agreed to set off immediately.[17]

The British soldiers, who were now perhaps more feared than Satan himself, had made their demands quite clear. If the captives were not returned before noon the next day, Evans had declared, he would leave Upper Marlboro in ashes. The shock effect was instantaneous. "Never was people so universally alarmed on God's earth as the people of Upper Marlborough," Bowie later testified. "Death and destruction were threatening them every moment if they refused to deliver up these men" (see note 17: 10, 12, 13).

The Hodges, at Captain Brooke's urging, fearing the possible loss of their families, friends, homes, and the town itself, took it upon themselves to comply with the enemy demands. Riding at full gallop to Queen Anne's, they arrived early Sunday morning and demanded the prisoners, including Holden, be turned over to them. The deserter appealed to Bowie, begging that his name not be given up to the British, knowing full well the fate that awaited him should he be sent back, and pleaded "that *he* must not be delivered up; his blood would be at their door" (12, 14). Taking considerable pity on him, Bowie "strenuously contended that they [the Hodges] had no right to demand his prisoner, as he [Bowie] did not live in the town, and acted independently of the town." If his prisoner was returned "it would be murder: he actually shed tears in speaking of the fate of the man." He had already discussed the issue with Bradley Beanes, who suggested that he should not worry about the deserter as "that thing could be managed—by which he thought Mr. Bowie might understand that an opportunity would be given to the deserters to make their escape" (17–18). A resident of Queen Anne's named William Caton also went to the deserter's defense, telling Hodges that "if he [John Hodges] surrendered the deserter he was no American—he would stain his hands with human blood" (10).

At first, Randall, in whose care the prisoners had been placed, refused to release them until the two Hodges reiterated to him in no uncertain terms of what would happen to Upper Marlboro and their families if the prisoners were not turned over to the enemy. "Every American must do his duty," implored John Hodges, "without regard to danger or inconvenience." A heated debate between Bowie and Lansdale quickly erupted, and was only silenced when the ex-governor refused to continue, stating, "they had enough to do to fight the enemy." When Thomas Sparrow, who had been guarding the prisoners, queried Bowie on what should be done, the ex-governor said, "it was very hard—that the capture was legal, but he supposed they must submit." Now, with the ex-governor himself having second thoughts, Randall released the captives to Lansdale and the Hodges, albeit not without some negotiation and a compromise regarding Holden. It was soon agreed that the deserter would be removed only as far as Hall's Mill, about a mile from Upper Marlboro. Bowie and Brooke would enter the enemy lines to determine precisely what their demands were. Gustavus Hay, a volunteer, was recruited to help the Hodges in returning the remaining prisoners to the British, following behind Bowie at a distance (11–13, 15, 16).

After proceeding about eight miles, the party approached the British lines. Bowie and Lansdale proceeded ahead to negotiate the surrender of the captives. After leaving Holden and another prisoner in the custody of Benjamin Oden in a stone house at Oden's farm, Bellfields, and not far from Bowie's own mill, they and two of the prisoners still in their own custody were met by Evans at a bend in the road. The British officer minced no words. He demanded that all the prisoners be given up immediately or Upper Marlboro would "be utterly destroyed." When asked who gave these orders, the officer responded sharply, "the general." The two Americans then expressed their desire to speak to Ross in person and were conducted to him. Seeing only two prisoners when he had been told by Bowie for some unexplained reason that there were six, Evans exclaimed: "By ——, gentleman, you'll all be ruined; you are keeping them prisoners yet. Where are the other two? . . . You wanted to sneak off with two, did you?" "No, we don't," said one of the two Americans, "they are up at that house," pointing to Oden's farm, where Holden and another prisoner had been kept. The general then ordered Lansdale to go back for them. Soon afterward, Evans and a troop of horse rode off toward the house to make sure they were turned over (13–14).

As the British approached the house, both Holden and his comrade, who had also just confessed to being a deserter, bolted. In a heartbeat, Evans had entered the building, knocked Oden to the ground, and demanded to know where the deserters had gone. Oden proclaimed ignorance, whereupon the officer threatened to set the house afire. A panicked woman, presumably the mistress of the estate, pointed out the direction the two men had taken, and the invaders departed. A few minutes later, John Hodges and several others appeared and, with a full British detachment now in sight and coming up, suggested they had all better clear out (12, 14, 16).

Within a short time, both deserters had been taken. Tom Holden, fortunately for him, would escape a second time and would never be heard from again. Robert Bowie, Dr. Hill, and Philip Weems were held by the British until the following day and then released. Dr. William Beanes (possibly because Holden remained at large) was taken to Benedict, where he was confined aboard HBMS *Tonnant* on August 29.[18]

Upper Marlboro was spared. Some time afterward, John Hodges was tried for treason in U.S. Circuit Court by Judge Gabriel Duvall of Prince George's

County for aiding and abetting the enemy by returning the prisoners without government authority. He was ably defended by none other than William Pinkney and was found innocent of all charges. The last major event of the Patuxent Campaign had seemingly come to a close.

...

Early on the morning of August 30 *Albion* and the other ships anchored off the little port of Benedict dispatched all their boats ashore to re-embark the troops. The beach was soon covered with sailors who welcomed the victorious warriors with loud and lusty cheers. Within a few hours the entire British army was removed from the town without incident or accident. At 6:00 a.m. the next morning, the Royal Navy weighed anchor and began to wend its way down the Patuxent.[19]

At 11:00 p.m. the fleet was becalmed, and Cockburn took the opportunity to have the squadron's surgeons examine "all people on expedition and give medicine in turn." Prize lists were prepared, and appropriate reports of the recent excursion to Washington were to be filed.[20]

On September 2 the fleet came safely to anchor under Drum Point and immediately began preparations for another expedition. Some said it would be against Baltimore, and others said Annapolis. Even the high command hadn't made up its own mind yet. Nevertheless, the squadron required tidying up. Orders were raised throughout the day: "Send refugees not engaged on board . . . repairs to *Madagascar* immediately . . . how many casks of tobacco on board . . . what number of spare muskets on board . . . all prize tobacco [and] prisoners to be sent to *Albion* . . . send all copper sheets & nails you can spare to *Ramilles*." All the last-minute preparations and housekeeping necessary before another thrust could be made anywhere was being carried out with typical Royal Navy efficiency. The Marine Artillery and the black Colonial Corps were transferred from *Albion*, scheduled to depart soon, to *Ramilles*; *Melpomene* was supplied with cases of lemon juice (considered an anti-scorbutic) and raisins; *Regulus* was provided with bales of marine clothing and flannel waistcoats; *Albion* received flour, rice, and rum from *Iphigenia*, *Benson*, and *Diadem*. Carpenters aboard *Royal Oak* were put to work cutting timber to build additional flatboats. Some forty boxes of money, each containing $5,000, were transferred to Admiral Malcolm's flagship. And so, on and on it went.[21]

At 5:30 p.m. on September 4 a major portion of the fleet weighed anchor and departed the Patuxent, although Malcolm's troop convoy lingered until the 6th.[22] Rumors were rampant as to their next destination. Baltimore was still on everyone's tongue, but by now both Ross and Cochrane had discussed other possibilities: Rhode Island, a supposedly easier and surer prize, still beckoned. Cochrane still feared the unhealthy climate of the Tidewater, now upon them; and Ross worried that its debilitating effects might substantially reduce his army's numbers through sickness.

The fleet headed southward, lingered about Tangier Island a bit, menaced the Potomac until Captain Gordon's squadron came down, and on September 9 was spotted off the mouth of the Patuxent once again. Where it was bound seemed anyone's guess. The following morning, the still-massive armada was observed heading up the bay under a full press of sail. Cockburn, it appeared, was again about to have his way, for he had successfully pushed upon Ross and Cochrane a plan for a devastating strike against the Port of Baltimore. Such a strike, he felt, if successful, could end once and for all the war in the Tidewater, if not in America.

. . .

When the British departed the Patuxent, they left behind them what seemed a ruined land. The few houses and farms that remained along the river's banks lay untended and deserted. Fields of unharvested corn still abounded, often around the burnt-out shells of once-pleasant dwellings and modest farms. Many of the major plantations had been completely destroyed while others had been mysteriously spared. Here and there flocks of sheep could still be found grazing, tended by a slave or two who had refused to run off to face a somewhat uncertain future in Canada or the West Indies.[23]

Yet the scene of total ruination and destruction extended, for the most part, barely two miles inland from the river. The scar upon the hearts and minds of the people, however, extended much deeper. The march on Washington had produced traumatic repercussions amidst the natives of the Maryland countryside. Cottages throughout the region were now largely depopulated of young men—or so it appeared to Lieutenant Gleig, who seized an opportunity to make a final visit to the Patuxent shores. They were, he believed, all gone off to take up arms against the British army.[24] Though the campaign on the Patuxent was at an end, perhaps the spirit of American resistance, so lacking hitherto on the river, with the exception of the flotillamen and marines, had somehow been galvanized into solid defiance by the burning of Washington. Perhaps the capture and destruction of Baltimore, as many suspected to be in the offing, would not be the simple matter Admiral Cockburn had supposed it to be. What if Wellington's Invincibles were not invincible after all?

. . .

The British offensive against Baltimore will long be remembered for father-ing one of the truly memorable moments in American military history: the noble defense of Fort McHenry and the gallant resistance by the citizens of Maryland and the soldiers of the nation at the Battle of North Point. Upon the invaders, whose soldiery had beaten the might of a Napoleon, a blow was inflicted from which there could be little recourse except an ignominious re-treat to the sanctuary of the wooden walls of the British Royal Navy.

Among those Americans present to participate in the conflict on the Pa-tapsco were many whose fortunes had been inextricably linked to the cam-paign on the Patuxent. Among them were the battle-tested Chesapeake flo-tillamen whose service would prove pivotal to the defense of Fort McHenry and the City of Baltimore by denying the enemy armada direct access to the city harbor. It was the flotillamen who capably manned the big guns of Fort McHenry's Water Battery on Whetstone Point, the mosquito fleet of remain-ing flotilla barges lined across the entrance to the harbor behind a barricade of sunken ships, and the guns of the Lazaretto that effectively kept the Royal Navy from closing with the fort. And it was the flotillamen who defended the right flank of Fort McHenry from envelopment by enemy landing par-ties at Fort Babcock. Ironically, though many would be ascribed the deserved honors and fame for the gallant resistance offered those fateful two days, Ar-mistead, Smith, Striker, Rodgers, and others, little would be attributed to the flotillamen.

With Barney recuperating at Elkridge, Lieutenant Rutter had been placed under the command of Commodore John Rodgers of the U.S. Navy on Sep-tember 3 and was to take charge of the Lazaretto, a gun battery, and 11 barges armed with long 8- and 12-pounders and 18-pounder gunnades.[25] A 3-gun battery near the Lazaretto was to be managed by Lieutenant Frazier and 45 flotillamen. Sailing Master Solomon Rodman and 60 flotillamen would man the main Water Battery at Fort McHenry. A 6-gun battery at Fort Babcock, on the Ferry Branch of the Patapsco to the southwest of Fort McHenry, was to be placed under a 50-man detachment of flotillamen commanded by the redoubtable Sailing Master John A. Webster.[26]

The attack on Fort McHenry that ensued on September 13–14, 1814, has, of course, become one of the seminal moments of American history. Lieuten-ant Colonel George Armistead's resolute endurance of the twenty-five-hour bombardment by the mighty British fleet would serve to partially erase the sordid scars of almost perpetual defeat that had beleaguered America's trial by arms. His triumph was in large measure owing to the undaunted courage and tenacity of the men of the U.S. Chesapeake Flotilla. As Joshua Barney's niece, Mary Barney, would later write, "the greater part of the credit, in fact, which was so lavishly bestowed upon the commander and officers of Fort McHenry—whose merit consisted in not abandoning the fort—was due to the officers of the flotilla, whose batteries executed the only damage which the enemy received in their attempt to land above the fort."[27]

When the initial bombardment had begun on Tuesday morning, September 13, from a range of two miles, it had been the flotillamen's guns, in the fort, the Lazaretto, and on the barge line in the Patapsco, that answered in angry response. "We opened our batteries and kept up a brisk fire from our guns and mortars," Armistead later reported, "but unfortunately our shot and shells all fell considerably short of him." Yet not a man shrunk from his duty as massive enemy bombs burst with impunity upon the defenses. When the enemy brought three bomb-ships within striking distance, they were driven off with alacrity. Then the long-range shelling of the fort continued with little intermission.[28]

At 1:00 a.m. on September 14, hoping to cause a diversion to favor Ross's motions ashore, Admiral Cochrane sought "to avail himself of the darkness of night" and dispatched a force of twenty barges with several hundred men—later inflated by the Americans to 1,250 picked men—into the Ferry Branch, to the right of Fort McHenry. (The troops were also reported by the American press to be carrying scaling ladders, to reconnoiter the shore, cause a diversion, and, if possible, storm the fort.) The attack was, in fact, far less grandiose, albeit equally perilous, and was to be led by Captain Charles Napier, commander of HBMS *Euraylus,* 38. Cochrane's orders to Napier were succinct. He wrote,

> You are to proceed with the boats placed under your command and execute the following services. The boats to proceed up the Patapsco (to be supplied with an additional quantity of blank cartridges) to fire for the intention of drawing the notice of the enemy. When the boats leave this ship their oars must be muffled. They will in the first place proceed direct for the shore abreast *Meteor* bomb [ship] then tow up close to the shore until they round the point of the Patapsco, and proceed up that river about one or one and a half miles. Then let them drop their grapnels and remain perfectly quiet until one o'clock, at which hour the bombs will open upon the fort and star rockets will be thrown up when you will begin a regular fire directed upon the opposite side of the river occasionally using blank cartridges only.[29]

The night was thick and hazy, with occasional showers. A rocket signaled the diversionary movement into the Ferry Branch to commence. The nighttime maneuver against the defenses on the flank of Fort McHenry was later reported in the pages of *Niles' Weekly Register.*

> At this time, aided by the darkness of the night and screened by a flame they had kindled, one or two rocket or bomb vessels, and many barges, manned with 1200 chosen men, *passed fort McHenry and proceeded up the Patapsco* to assail the town and fort in the rear, and, perhaps, effect a landing. The weak sighted mortals now thought the great deed was done—they gave three cheers, and began to throw their missive weapons. But alas! Their cheering was quickly turned to groaning, and the cries and screams of their wounded and drowning people soon reached the shore; for forts McHenry and Covington [and Babcock], with the City Battery and the Lazaretto and barges [of the flotilla] vomited an *iron flame* upon them, and a storm of heavy bullets flew upon them from the great semicircle of large guns and gallant hearts. The houses of the city were shaken to their foundations; for never perhaps, from the time of the invention of the cannon to the present day, were the same number of pieces fired with so rapid succession. Barney's flotilla men, at the City Battery, maintained the high reputation they had before earned.[30]

Armistead attributed the enemy's repulse directly to the "animated" and destructive fire from the naval detachment at Fort Covington, under Lieutenant Henry S. Newcomb, and Sailing Master John Webster's 6-gun battery at Fort Babcock. "The only means we had of directing our guns," Armistead later reported, "was by the blaze of their rockets and the flashes of their guns." The loss suffered by the enemy was uncertain, although one of their partially sunken seventy-five-foot barges was found with two dead men in it, and other bodies were observed the next morning floating in the river. "Had they ventured to the same situation in the day time," the colonel noted, "not a man would have escaped."[31]

Nevertheless, the horrendous bombardment of Fort McHenry continued without letup until 7:00 a.m. Armistead estimated that between 1,500 and 1,800 shells had been thrown by the enemy over a twenty-five-hour period, many bursting directly over the fort. Incredibly, only four men had been killed and twenty-four more wounded. By 9:00 a.m. the enemy, having been defeated at North Point and rebuffed at Fort McHenry, had had enough. The Battle of Baltimore was over. And the American flag continued to fly over Fort McHenry.[32]

In his report to Secretary Jones, Commodore John Rodgers was lavish in his praise of the men under his command, in particular the flotillamen, whose

Pencil sketch of the bombardment of Fort McHenry, September 13–14, 1814. At *lower
left* is the Lazaretto. Eight Chesapeake Flotilla barges, their flags flying at the mastheads, lie behind a line of sunken ships protecting Baltimore Harbor. Fort McHenry
is at *right,* sustaining a bombardment by the British fleet (*top*). Note the leeboards
on the barges and individual barge numbers on pennants beneath the national flags.
Photocopy courtesy of Scott S. Sheads.

management of the big guns that had turned back the British naval attack and
then repulsed the attempted landing on the Ferry Branch had perhaps saved
the fort.

The enemy's repulsion from the Ferry Branch on the night of the 13th: inst after
he had passed Fort McHenry with his barges and some light vessels was owing to
the warm reception he met with from Forts Covington and Babcock commanded
by Lt. Newcomb and S. Master Webster, whom with all under their command
performed the duty assigned to them, to admiration.

To Lt. Frazier commanding the three gun battery at the Lazaretto, great praise
is due for the constant and animated fire with which he at times assailed the en-

emy during the whole bombardment, altho' placed in a very exposed situation to rockets and shells.

Great praise is justly due to Lt. Rutter for his prompt execution of my orders, as well as the zeal and coolness with which he performed all the duties of his station, altho' continually exposed for near 24 hours to the enemy's rockets and shells.

Similar praise is due to the officers and men in the several barges of the flotilla which were immediately under his command, who without regard to the enemy's rockets and shells maintained their position with firmness in the passage between Fort McHenry and the Lazaretto.

Sailing Master Rodmond [*sic*] stationed in the Water Battery of Fort McHenry with 60 seamen of the flotilla, did his duty in a manner worthy of the service to which he belongs.[33]

...

Aboard the British fleet, as Admiral Cochrane and Cockburn agonized over their failure and prepared to put the best face on things in their reports to the home government, Dr. Beanes remained locked up in the forecastle of a warship. The Upper Marlboro physician's situation had not gone unnoticed by his fellow Americans, and efforts had been launched immediately after his capture to arrange for a prisoner exchange for his release. One of the two agents who had diligently attempted to free the old Marylander was Barney's own purser and U.S. agent for prisoner exchange, John S. Skinner. The other was a young lawyer by the name of Francis Scott Key, who had come to plea for the doctor's release. During the abortive attack on Fort McHenry, Key had watched from aboard the flag-of-truce sloop *President* as the giant American flag continued to wave above the embattled fortress. Deeply moved, he had written a memorable poem commemorating the stirring patriotism the scene evinced in his breast. The stanzas of this poem were later to become a popular song entitled "The Star Spangled Banner," and ultimately the American National Anthem.

Of course, practically the entire British army and Royal Navy forces employed in the Patuxent Campaign also suffered through the Baltimore offensive. The blood of many soldiers, sailors, and marines was spilled during the Battle of North Point, including that of General Robert Ross. The brave but sometimes hesitant general had been mortally wounded by a sniper's bullet while in advance of his army, riding in company with Admiral Cockburn, not long after boasting that he would dine in Baltimore that evening or in hell. The army had suffered badly, and the navy, after testing the strength of Fort McHenry with seemingly endless hours of artillery and rocket fire, finally sailed away on September 17, bloodied and in humiliation, albeit quite intact.

Once more, the fleet stood toward the Patuxent. Late in the afternoon of the 18th the squadron was again off the cliffs of Calvert County and approaching the mouth of the river. At 3:45 p.m. *Albion,* leading the van, came to full anchor between Cove and Cedar points, directly in the middle of the river's entrance.[34]

Parties were sent ashore to dig for fresh water and to obtain livestock. Captured flour stocks were baked into biscuits, and every indication seemed to point to a long voyage in the making. Here the fleet was to be divided, with Admiral Malcolm's squadron heading for the Potomac and Admiral Cochrane's force, including *Tonnant* and several frigates and gun-brigs, making sail for Halifax. British morale was incredibly low aboard Cockburn's squadron, which remained for a while in the Patuxent. No one talked of future enterprises, and many were dispirited over the loss of General Ross and the army's humiliating abandonment of the field of battle. To make matters worse, dysentery now riddled both the army and the navy. The unhealthy season, as both Cochrane and Ross had called it, was indeed upon them.[35]

Cockburn must have viewed the beautiful little river with mixed feelings. The waterway, which had added considerably to his own personal wealth through plunder, save for the gallant defense offered by Barney and his flotillamen, had succumbed perhaps a little too easily. Perhaps he had been misled, even beguiled, by the diminutive waterway. Even though he had personally never led a single foray against its shores until the march against Washington, it had somehow permeated, perhaps fatally, the very fiber of his planning for the course of the war in the Chesapeake Tidewater. Not to worry though. The Royal Navy would at least have the opportunity of visiting upon it one last salute.

At 6:20 p.m., before departing for Canada, *Tonnant* raised a signal ordering the entire fleet to anchor under Drum Point. Aboard the flagship, two seamen, James Crosby of *Tonnant* and Michael Welch of *Weser,* lay in chains. Both men had been found guilty of desertion only the day before and were sentenced to death for their crimes. At 5:00 a.m. the following morning, each vessel in the fleet dispatched boats to the flagship to attend the hanging. Almost a planned format was offered up to the representatives of His Britannic

344 FLOTILLA

Majesty's Royal Navy. The Articles of War were read, and several seamen, "for seditious & mutinous expressions," and for drunkenness, were flogged. The main event, the executions, followed on schedule.[36]

At 5:30 p.m. the British fleet weighed anchor and set sail, departing the Patuxent River forever.[37]

Chapter Twenty-Three

THE OUNCE OF BRITISH INFLUENCE

In the history of the United States of America, our nation has suffered from three heinous attacks on its soil by powerful enemies intent on bringing us down. Every American student knows that December 7, 1941, was the day of the infamous Japanese attack on Pearl Harbor, a Day of Infamy as President Franklin Delano Roosevelt called it, which heralded our country's entry into the bloody cauldron of World War II. And what American cannot but mourn the events of September 11, 2001, when a new form of threat was hurled upon us, altering forever our way of life and perhaps the very future of humankind itself? Unfortunately, few remember August 19, 1814, when our young nation suffered from the first event of the terrible trilogy, the British invasion of American soil and the soon-after destruction of our infant national capital. Today, the scars of December 7 and 9/11 are deeply etched into the very being of our social fabric, but the wounds of the first attack upon the United States of America, in those trying and distant days of the summer of 1814, are more subtly concealed, discretely hidden by time and tide, beneath our soils and waters, and barely recalled.

Though profound and numerous, the footprints of the War of 1812 on the Chesapeake Tidewater are seldom discernible, save for the inspiring tale of Francis Scott Key and the Star-Spangled Banner, preserved today in our National Anthem and the imposing defense works of Fort McHenry, one of America's greatest national monuments and shrines. They are the grist meat for every American child's elementary school education. Yet, few today have ever heard of the indefatigable Commodore Barney, who had tested his mettle and that of his brave fellow officers and men on the muddy waters of the Patuxent River to prevail against an unbeatable foe, or of the tiny squadron with which they dared the impossible. Oddly enough, the long-forgotten tale of the flotillamen and their diminutive squadron after its loss are almost as tortured as the short life of the U.S. Flotilla Service itself had been.

Joshua Barney convalesced at his farm at Elkridge for several weeks until he was able to return to service. On October 5, 1814, though still seriously incapacitated by the ball in his hip and unable to walk, he departed the Washington Navy Yard to negotiate with Rear Admiral Malcolm, whose fleet still lay in the Piankatank River, Virginia, a prisoner exchange of all men captured by both sides at Bladensburg. Two days later the transfer was completed and Barney, now officially released from his parole, returned to Baltimore on October 10 to resume his command only to discover the flotilla in total disorder. Though the Baltimore squadron was increasing in size, with several new barges in operation and even a steam frigate on the stocks and nearly ready to launch, without the commodore the fleet had been hemorrhaging seamen, who were again being lured from service by privateering syndicates. Owing to the bankrupt state of the federal government, none of the flotillamen had been paid. Moreover, Congress had outright refused to compensate them for clothing and other private effects lost during the late campaign. During debate on Capitol Hill over the requested indemnity, "there seemed to be a willful disposition to misunderstand, or to misrepresent, the merits of the question, on the part of many of the members; by whom it was averred, either from inexcusable ignorance or some still worse motive, that the enemy were not within a day's march of the flotilla, when it was blown up—thus intimating that the destruction had been a wanton act of mischief or cowardice, for which it would be just to leave the sufferers without relief." On October 20 the House of Representatives, already in search of a scapegoat for the humiliation at Bladensburg and the burning of Washington, vigorously debated on the indemnity and then laid it on the table.[1]

The commodore was infuriated and addressed a public letter to the *Daily National Intelligencer* meticulously and effectively repudiating every charge against both him and the flotilla. Another letter was addressed to Congressman Pleasants of Virginia, chairman of the indemnity subcommittee, reminding him that "when *orders* were given to *blow up* the flotilla, that the enemy were firing upon them from 40 barges with cannon and rockets, and had landed a body of marines at Pig Point, within a mile of the flotilla." The fleet went down with "most of the baggage and all of the bedding of the men."[2] On November 2 the House passed the bill by a narrow margin, fifty-three to forty-seven, but with the proviso that officers were not to be indemnified on the grounds that "it would set a bad precedent for remuneration of officers in other cases where they should lose baggage, which frequently occurred."[3]

Weeks passed and $4,000 was allowed to pay off flotillamen whose time had expired, but nothing more. As fall turned to winter, many men, whose families were "in the greatest distress" and who were themselves still without clothing or pay, refused to remain in service. Desertion was rampant. Yet, somehow, Barney kept most of his men together, conducting salvage work on the sunken fleet, assisting the Baltimore Committee of Vigilance in further securing the harbor by placing obstructions in the channels, transporting timber to Fort McHenry, loading vessels and wagons with guns for the defense of New York, and rigging and outfitting the USS *Ontario*.[4]

By December the situation of the flotillamen had not improved. Unpaid and still lacking winter clothing they were now ordered by the new Acting Secretary of the Navy Benjamin Homans, the Navy Department's chief clerk who had temporarily replaced Jones after his resignation on November 30, to recover the numerous merchantmen scuttled in the Patapsco as obstructions.[5]

The demands upon Barney and his men seemed now too much to endure. He determined to resign his commission, but was counseled to hold off by his friend and former Secretary of the Navy William Jones. Finally, on January 3, he submitted his resignation. "The flotilla service in the spring, will be no object, but few men will serve in it," he warned, "if they can get other employment; the conduct of Congress to those under my command has been infamous, and I see no honour and (certainly no profit) to be gained by commanding a few boats badly mann'd; much will [be] expected from us, and we must disappoint public expectation to our discredit—which is a situation I would not wish to be in. Congress I fear will do nothing good for the Navy or themselves, all seem to be going the wrong way."[6]

On December 24, 1814, British and American negotiators finally brought the war to an official close with the signing of the Treaty of Ghent. Yet, it would be weeks before the news arrived on the American side of the Atlantic. For all intents and purposes, in the United States the war was still on and business as usual had to be attended. Fortunately, the flotilla would never again have to be tested in combat.

When a new secretary of the navy, Benjamin Crowninshield, a Massachusetts sea captain, merchant, and politician, was appointed to permanently replace William Jones, one of his first efforts was to bring a still irate Barney back into the fold despite the obstacles. On February 14, 1815, Barney was again offered a commission as captain in the Flotilla Service of the United States: the document was personally conveyed to him by the hand of his trusty lieutenant Solomon Rutter. With talks of a treaty agreement growing ever stronger, four days later the old commodore agreed to accept. "I do most solemnly pledge myself not to quit the service, or lay down my sword, until death, or a peace such as our country ought to obtain; external enemies and internal traitors, notwithstanding."[7] Then, only three days later, on February 17, 1815, upon ratifications of the treaty being exchanged by both nations, President James Madison declared the war was officially over.

On February 27, 1815, less than two weeks after Barney had resumed command, Congress passed legislation formally disestablishing the U.S. Flotilla Service as an agency of the government.[8] On March 9, Secretary Crowninshield ordered the commodore to dismantle and cover the barges in the fleet. He was to deliver all armaments and stores to Navy Agent James Beatty and provide a list of all vessels under his command.[9] By April 15 all but a handful of officers and men had been discharged from service. Finally, on May 2 Commodore Joshua Barney, who had superintended the creation, fielding, fighting, and finally the dissolution of the U.S. Chesapeake Flotilla, one of the most unique experiments in American riverine naval warfare, was issued his discharge by Secretary Crowninshield:

> In the discharge of your duty as an officer commanding the U.S. Flotilla on the Chesapeake, and waters adjacent, I recognize with pleasure the character you had previously sustained, as a vigilant, active and brave commander to whom your country, and your government, have unequivocally bestowed the meed of praise, and the well earned tribute of thanks; to these I cordially add my testimony and approbation . . . In compliance with the Act before mentioned [of February 27, 1815], the term of your services has expired, and having honorably discharged your duty, settled up your accounts and given evidence of your integrity, and fidelity in your prompt compliance with the law; and orders of this department, you will receive the pay and emoluments of a Commander of the Flotilla, to the 30th. of April past."[10]

On December 1, 1818, Commodore Joshua Barney, the Maryland naval hero who had fought more sea and land engagements in behalf of his country than any other American, died during a visit to Pittsburg, Pennsylvania, while still convalescing from the "ounce of British influence" he had labored under, ever since the Battle of Bladensburg.[11]

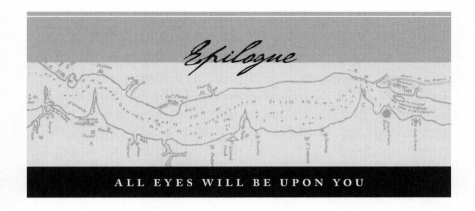

Epilogue

ALL EYES WILL BE UPON YOU

Even before the final destruction of the majority of Commodore Joshua Barney's Chesapeake Flotilla in the Patuxent River, some of the vessels of the fleet, sunk in St. Leonard's Creek, had already become the subject of indiscriminate plundering by local inhabitants. Sailing Master Geoghegan had quickly put a stop to the looting on the creek. But not long after the British departure from Washington, looters had also descended upon the wrecks of the main flotilla squadron and, presumably, the merchantmen sunk with it near Upper Marlboro. The navy was quickly contacted by a local resident named John Weems, of Richards, Maryland, who had notified the government of the looting and had taken matters into his own hands. He was soon contracted to raise the main fleet and salvage the government effects upon it. Establishing a base of operations on the river at Mount Pleasant Landing, near a creek called Ferry Branch, Weems salvaged twenty-two of thirty-two cannons, along with quantities of munitions, anchors, and other items, all of which were sent to Baltimore and stored until an officer of the Flotilla Service could evaluate them. The salvage mission proved far more difficult and costly for the salvor than had been anticipated, however, and increased logistical support, which Weems alone could not provide, was necessary. He therefore requested the assistance of two navy vessels to raise Barney's flagship *Scorpion* so that he might burn her down to extract metal fittings. Naval assistance was not forthcoming, and although the salvor was able to recover two vessels, he found the flagship, though still very valuable, impossible to raise. When payment for his work was not forthcoming from the now totally bankrupt government, the salvor reluctantly abandoned the project. The Flotilla Service then attempted to pick up where Weems had left off.[1]

In November 1814 two of Barney's midshipmen and twenty to twenty-five flotillamen "went with pleasure to the Patuxent . . . and there saved from the bottom of the river all the guns, gun carriages, cambooses, anchors, cables, shot, &c. belonging to their late flotilla which had been destroyed." This salvage work, however, was apparently initially conducted at Queen Anne's Town, where the sailors managed to drag one of two barges found there onto the shoreline. They were dismayed to find it stove in owing to an explosion in the second barge, which lay nearby. Neither of the second-class vessels, the only ones to make it up to the town, could be salvaged. That they also conducted some salvage on other vessels of the fleet is likely, for on November 17 Barney informed Secretary Jones that his men had already been at work on the river for several weeks and had been very successful "in getting up the guns of the late flotilla, with a very considerable quantity of other articles." Those goods that were recovered from them were carried downriver by a contractor named Christopher Lambert to the schooner *Asp*, anchored off Mount Calvert, for transport to Baltimore.[2]

Salvage sputtered along through the first week of April, while Barney, though still in very ill health, occupied himself with paying off his petty officers and men and settling disputes among his senior officers over retaining their warrants and four months' "gratification" offered them for their service. At the beginning of the month he had dispatched *Asp*, the lookout boat, and a gunboat back to the Patuxent to bring off whatever materials remained there that had been recovered from the fleet. On April 4 the lookout boat returned with iron ballast and was ordered back to bring up a second load. The following day, *Asp* and the gunboat returned "having brought every thing except the guns & a few shot."[3]

On April 27, 1815, Secretary Crowninshield ordered the salvaged goods that had been recovered near Queen Anne's Town sold at auction in Baltimore. One of the barges that had been saved by Weems and remained in the Patuxent was given by the salvor, who had not been paid for his services, to a Dr. James Tongue.[4]

. . .

With the war officially over, as after all such conflicts, its detritus soon began to provide legal headaches for the U.S. government. That which was related to the Patuxent Campaign would prove to be especially troublesome for decades.

Although two major efforts to salvage the fleet were undertaken, by Weems and the Flotilla Service, and most of the guns and munitions belonging to Barney's vessels were recovered, the wreck of the hired schooner *Islet* and her military cargo, which may have included items removed from *Nos. 137* and *138* prior to or following the retreat from St. Leonard's Creek, remained untouched, presumably because the vessel was not government owned.

Congress, however, was unprepared to address the barrage of claims from hundreds, if not thousands, of citizens who had suffered damages or financial losses as a result of war-related activities of the American military. Lacking an adequate mechanism to address the many war claims and petitions for compensation that began to bombard Congress, the government passed legislation authorizing the payment for private property lost, captured, or destroyed by the enemy while such properties were employed in or by the military services of the United States.

On December 16, the new secretary of the navy, Benjamin W. Crowninshield, provided to Bartlett Yancey, chairman of the Committee of Claims, copies of letters relating to a petition from O'Neale and Taylor for restitution of losses, with the notation that when Barney ordered Frazier to burn the flotilla, "no allusion was made to the schooner *Islet,* that vessel being from the beginning at the sole and exclusive risk of the owner; and the certificate obtained from Lieutenant Frazier [submitted with the letters] forms the only pretense for O'Neale and Taylor's claim." The secretary noted that the vessel's actual service time of forty-six days, which technically had not begun until the fleet was at Nottingham, had already been fully paid for and submitted as proof the owners' receipt for a warrant on the U.S. Treasury for receipt of payment on September 26, 1814, for the amount of $460.

"The vessel," declared Crowinshield, "cannot be fairly considered as discharged from the service previously to being sunk, as there were then, and are now, some ordnance, shot, &c. on board," even though the whole time of the vessel's service had already been compensated for.

As early as October 2, 1814, Richard Bland Lee of the Office of Claims wrote to Crowninshield: "Having adjudged to Messrs. William O'Neale and Robert Taylor, the owners of the schooner *Islet,* sunk in the Patuxent, by orders of Commodore Barney, during the late war, while in the service of the United States, the value of the said vessel, I consider it my duty to apprize you of the circumstance, as from this date the said vessel in her present condition must be regarded as the property of the nation . . . It will rest with you to decide whether any attempt should be made to save the vessel and the articles in her hold."

In 1815 the schooner's owners filed a petition with the U.S. House of Representatives Committee of Claims seeking full compensation equal to the value of the vessel "and such further relief as may be just." On January 5, 1816, the petition was presented to the full House with the opinion of the committee that the petitioners, "having undertaken in their contract to be at all risks of the vessel," and the vessel having been sunk by her commander, were not entitled to relief. The committee recommended that the petitioners not be granted compensation.

The Committee of Claims, which had already become masterful in bureaucratic delaying tactics, soon reported that after examining all the available evidence and reviewing the claims, as well as the extended construction which had been given to the existing law, and the erroneous decisions made under it, the committee was of the opinion that the act should be amended so as to repeal a part of its provisions and transfer the settlement of claims under it to the War Department. The committee was induced to recommend this course, they said, because the cases provided for would there be determined, according to uniform principles observed in the settlement of claims under the control and responsibility of the head of that department, and would pass through several offices in the usual way of transacting business, and subject to the usual checks known to be so salutary in the settlement of accounts. In later years, the action would have been termed "passing the buck."

On December 17 the committee reported to the full House a bill to that effect, and the act was amended. The owners of *Islet* were awarded $4,000, the valuation according to affidavits filed with the Commissioners of Claims. No evidence was ever located to suggest that salvage efforts to retrieve the ship or the ordnance aboard were ever undertaken thereafter.[5]

The mode of adjudicating claims proved awkward and difficult at best. Thus, on April 9, 1816, the legislation, entitled "Act Authorizing Payment for Property Destroyed by the Enemy During the War with Great Britain," was modified again but was still far from perfect. In December 1816, under continuing pressure from numerous complainants, the 14th Congress of the United States considered additional modifications. Three specific cases were examined by the Committee of Claims and were employed as primary examples for the need to revise the Act. These three cases included: a petition by Daniel Carroll of Dudington, for the loss of property in Washington that had been occupied by American troops and destroyed by the British thereafter; a petition by Tench Ringgold, W. and C. Smith, and Philip Key, for the loss of a ropewalk employed by the navy and destroyed by the enemy as a consequence of its military use; and the petition of O'Neale and Taylor, for compensation for the loss of *Islet*.

Despite fine-tuning the machinery for just compensation, salvage issues and legal claims against the government for damages incurred during the fighting on the Patuxent continued to proliferate. Among them were claims from property owners at St. Leonard's Town, such as John Ireland and Mary Frazier, who had lost much if not all during the British raid of July 2, 1814, and along the shores of the Patuxent itself. Unfortunately, some cases, such as those pressed by Dr. Gray and his descendants for the loss of property at Sheridan's Point and by Benjamin Mackall and his heirs for the loss of the family estate at Hallowing Point on June 15, 1814, would go on for decades. The longest such legal claims effort, the Mackall case, would not be resolved until March 8, 1860, and would be ruled against the claimants.[6]

. . .

By 1878, sixty-four years after the abandonment of Barney's barges, some of the hulks were still visible in the shallow river shoals and occasionally a source of curiosity to those who ventured onto the waters, especially fishermen and hunters. During the spring of 1892 members of a local hunt club avidly collected artifacts from the main barge fleet. On June 4 of that year, a local newspaper reported: "The Patuxent Gun and Rod Club at Hill's Landing have had the Patuxent River dredged a little north of the [Hills] bridge, in search of Commodore Barney's flotilla, which was sunk during the War of 1812. Two pieces, well preserved, have been secured and they will be placed among the curiosities of the club house. The nails, which are hand-made, are in an excellent state of preservation, considering the many years that they have lain in the water and mud. At a very low tide several pieces of this old fleet can be seen."[7]

In 1907, ninety-three years after their loss, Spencer Cosby, of the Baltimore District U.S. Army Corps of Engineers, after surveying the river for a proposed dredging project, reported: "A short distance above Hills landing [modern Green Run Landing] there are visible at extreme low tide the hulks of some old vessels reported to have been sunk by the British during their attack upon Washington in the War of 1812." The dredging project was never carried out.[8]

As the river rapidly began to silt up, owing to poor farming practices (and later on urban development), the wrecks of the Chesapeake Flotilla, both on St. Leonard's Creek and near Upper Marlboro, continued to be visited from time to time by fishermen and hunters who neither knew nor cared what they were. When the occasional cannonball was found on the muddy shore or an ancient anchor was fished from the waters tangled in a hapless waterman's net, they were viewed as curiosities and then forgotten. For construction man Arthur Cox, who spent his weekends fishing in the lovely isolation above old Hills Bridge, one of the old hulks had proved an excellent mooring for his boat. For Harry Brooke Watkins, a young African American boy living in Hardesty (old Queen Anne's Town), two old wrecks once witnesses to history itself, now lying half submerged in the river nearby, had been little more than perches from which he and his friends could dive and frolic in the chilly waters on a hot summer's day. To the farm boys living on the banks of St. Leonard's, the old wrecks at the head of the creek were just as inviting.[9]

In August 1932 Norris and Winifred Harris of Baltimore, with the assistance of C. W. Mitchell, Hendrick George Mitchell III, Milton T. Mitchell, and Lee Suit of Prince George's County, recovered seven timbers from what was believed to be remains of the Chesapeake Flotilla found less than two miles above Hills Bridge in Prince George's. The timbers, Mrs. Harris reported, had been exposed by "an extremely low tide, due to the wind being down the river, at which time they were approximately six feet below the surface of the water." Four years later, three of the timbers were presented as a gift to Fort McHenry National Park through the National Society, United States Daughters of 1812, in Maryland.[10]

As the upper Patuxent reaches began to fill in and the channel itself migrated, by as much as a half mile, the wrecks slowly disappeared until only one or two remained visible. By 1938, when the U.S. Department of Agriculture conducted the first comprehensive aerial photographic survey mapping of the United States, one vessel remained still exposed. By 1951, the wreck's location could only be identified by the roiling of the river waters as they passed over the obstruction that lay just beneath them.

In 1958 a party of wreck divers, including Carl DiJulio, Joseph E. Besche, Joseph Hollar, Charles Mills, Jr., and John Remington, arrived on the Patuxent to revisit the site located during the Harris investigation, as well as others on the river. Near Nottingham they encountered a wooden wreck and, mistakenly believing it to be one of Barney's vessels, tied a line from it to a vehicle on the shore and dragged several large frames from its hull onto the narrow beach, where they were reportedly left to rot. At the Harris site another wreck was located and also ravaged for artifacts.[11]

. . .

In 1977 planning for the first systematic archaeological effort to locate and examine the remains of the Chesapeake Flotilla was begun and launched the following year by Nautical Archaeological Associates, Inc., of Upper Marlboro, Maryland, under the direction of the author, and the Calvert Marine Museum, of Solomons, Maryland, under Dr. Ralph E. Eshelman. In St. Leonard's Creek, investigation of potential War of 1812 wrecks was undertaken with questionable results. In June 1979 a limited magnetometer survey of the upper river between Mill Creek, two thousand feet south of Hills Landing, and the south end of Spyglass Island, formerly known as Tincan or Snake Island, was carried out in what was believed to be the main fleet resting area, not far from Upper Marlboro. A total of seven significant targets were registered, although numerous minor targets were also acquired. One target, dubbed the "Turtle Shell Wreck" after the first item found on it (a turtle shell sans its original occupant), was ground-truthed and in 1980 archaeologically tested. The site proved to be the nearly intact remains of a naval vessel belonging to the Chesapeake Flotilla, possibly even Barney's own flagship *Scorpion*. Test excavation and mapping of a component of the warship was undertaken in June the same year, during which time limited sampling of only 151 artifacts was carried out (owing to limited conservation facilities and funding). After the month-long investigation was terminated, the wreck itself was reburied beneath more than five feet of sediment to ensure its continued preservation. The artifacts, which included military, medical, nautical, and shipboard domestic items as well as architectural features of the ship itself, were conserved at Solomons, Maryland, and entered into the collections of the Calvert Marine Museum, where they were put on display the following year in a major exhibition entitled "War on the Patuxent: 1814."[12]

On April 21, 1996, a second, more comprehensive remote sensing survey of the upper Patuxent, between Bristol Landing and Mount Pleasant Ferry Landing, was carried out during Phase I of a new investigative program dubbed the Chesapeake Flotilla Project, under the direction of the author and with the assistance of the University of Baltimore, the Maryland Historical Trust, and the Applied Sonics Corporation.[13]

The following year, with the support of myriad organizations and individuals, including the University of Baltimore, the Trust, the U.S. Navy, the U.S. Department of Agriculture, the Calvert County Soil Conservation District Office, and graduate students in marine archaeology from East Carolina University, further intensive remote sensing of the upper reaches of the river

Artifacts recovered during the author's 1980 archaeological excavation of the "Turtle Shell Wreck," a nearly intact vessel belonging to the Chesapeake Flotilla sunk near Upper Marlboro on August 22, 1814. From *top left (clockwise)* is a gray-and-blue stoneware inkwell, a dinner plate, a large Liberty Head penny, a Revere lantern, a grog ration cup with the initials "CW" scratched in its surface (believed to belong to cook Caesar Wentworth), a pair of padlocks for prisoners, and, *center,* a metal button. *Photographs by Donald G. Shomette.*

and St. Leonard's Creek was carried out under the author's direction. The technologies employed, including aerial infrared photography, side-reading sonar, magnetometry, and sub-sediment radar, resulted in the comprehensive examination of over eleven miles of waterway. A campaign of hands-on survey of discrete targets by divers and hydro-probing in the sediment-filled waters wherein Barney's "much vaunted flotilla" was documented as going down, was conducted to a sub-sediment depth of twenty-five feet in the upper waterway. The meticulous, labor-intensive hydro-probing investigation covered more than half a million square feet of lateral sub-surface area of the river, albeit with depressingly negative results. On St. Leonard's Creek, however, the remains of gunboats *Nos. 137* and *138* were finally discovered by the author not far from the foot of old St. Leonard's Town itself, along with possible fragments of one or more of the merchant vessels destroyed alongside of them.[14] In 1998 and 1999 graduate students from East Carolina University under the direction of marine archaeologist Dr. Lawrence E. Babits expertly excavated both gunboats.

But where was the main fleet, and why hadn't it been found by the most intensive, state-of-the-art archaeological assault ever launched on the Chesapeake? The historic record was, after all, quite clear as to where it went down.

Subsequent research into the geological and cartographic record by the author and colleague William Clark, head of the Calvert Soil Conservation Office, revealed just why the main fleet had not been discovered. During several episodic periods in the late nineteenth and early twentieth centuries, the river had dramatically changed course, turning the once main channel in which the fleet had gone down into a secondary channel, and then slowly filling it in with sediment. As the same volume of water continued to flow, a new channel evolved, in the process cutting across old tributaries that once flowed directly into the ancient river course. Much to our surprise, we discovered that the Turtle Shell Wreck, the nearly intact vessel archaeologically tested in 1980, lay smack in the middle of the intersection of one of these tributaries and the modern channel.

Had the only vessel of the main fleet wreck area discovered to date (which the archaeological evidence suggested may have been used as a hospital ship during her last days) been seeking refuge up one of these minor backwaters? Had she been hoping to evade capture until the last minute? Or had she been towed up during salvage operations later on, only to be abandoned? Was it, indeed, Barney's own flagship *Scorpion*, as the archaeological evidence also suggested?

Although many such questions abounded, the answer to the big one had been discovered. The venerable bones of the U.S. Chesapeake Flotilla no longer lay beneath the waters of the river upon which it had waged its gallant fight nearly two centuries before in defense of the American homeland. It now lay beneath the newly created shoreline banks and wetlands of the Patuxent, beneath the very soil of the nation it had fought so hard to defend.

Postscript

On December 11, 2006, the U.S. Chesapeake Flotilla Memorial Committee was formed to establish a permanent monument to honor the memory and service of the officers and men of the Chesapeake Flotilla who served and died for their country during the War of 1812. "Your force is our principal shield," said Secretary of the Navy William Jones to the commodore and his brave flotillamen as they prepared to sail against overwhelming odds, "and all eyes will be upon you."

And one day they will be again.

Muster of the U.S. Chesapeake Flotilla from Its Inception
to Its Dissolution

Source: RG 4S, Naval Records, Collector of the Office of Naval Records and Library, Muster Book U.S. Flotilla, National Archives and Record Service, Washington, D.C., recorded 3 March 1815.

No.	Entry Year	Month	Day	Appear on board	From where	Name	Station	Discharged, dead, or run away	When Month	Day	Year	Whither or for what reason / pay due
1	1813	Sept.	23			Joshua Barney	CO					
2	1813	Sept.	20			Solomon Rutter	LT	Discharged	Apr.	1	1815	349.38
3	1813	Sept.	6			James Nicholson	SM	Discharged	Apr.	1	1815	555.35
4	1813	Sept.	21			Jesse Huffington	SM					
5	1813	Sept.	18			Henry Worthington	SM	Discharged	Apr.	15	1815	481.30
6	1813	Sept.	22			John Warner	SM	Died	Aug.	24	1814	112. Killed at Bladensburg
7	1813	Oct.	12			John M. Breese	SM	Discharged	Apr.	15	1815	454.98
8	1813	Oct.	16			John Kiddall	SM					
9	1813	Sept.	10			Claudius Besse	SM	Discharged	Apr.	15	1815	692.37
10	1813	Sept.	11			Andrew Dorgan	SM					
11	1813					Robert Ormsby	P	Discharged	Apr.	6	1815	
12	1813	Sept.	1			Lewis Barney	CL	Discharged	Dec.	15	1813	
13	1813	Dec.	16			James C. Armstrong	CL	Discharged	Apr.	1	1815	181.27
14	1813	Dec.	22			Thomas Hamilton	SU	Discharged	Apr.	1	1815	1135.60
15	1813	Sept.	25	Apr. 7		Girard Gorsuch	MM	Discharged	Mar.	9	1814	
16	1813	Sept.	25	Apr. 7		Moses Middleton	MM	Discharged	Apr.	1	1815	137.7
17	1813	Sept.	27	Apr. 7		Mathias Isley	MM	Discharged	Jan.	7	1814	
18	1813	Sept.	28	Apr. 7		Lewis Beaudsin	MM	Discharged	Mar.	15	1814	
19	1813	Sept.	28	Apr. 7		James Elliott	MM	Discharged	Mar.	26	1814	
20	1813	Sept.	28	Apr. 7		William B. Benson	MM	Discharged				53.0 or 2
21	1813	Sept.	28	Apr. 7		John Besse	MM	Discharged	Dec.	15	1814	

No.	Enlisted				Name	Rank	Discharged/Died				Remarks
22	1813	Sept.	28	Apr. 7	James Hall	MM	Discharged	Dec.	16	1814	
23	1813	Sept.	19	Apr. 7	John Bassin	MM	Discharged	Dec.	16	1814	
24	1813	Oct.	20	Apr. 7	H. W. Bassett	MS	Discharged	Mar.	2	1814	
25	1813	Sept.	28	Apr. 7	Simmon Besse	MS	Discharged	Dec.	16	1814	
26	1813	Sept.	28		Solomon Rutter	MS	Discharged	Mar.	5	1814	48.7
27	1813	Oct.	27	Apr. 7	Benjamin F. Fearson	MS	Discharged	Nov.	5	1814	
28	1813	Nov.	9	Apr. 7	William Street	MS	Discharged	Apr.	1	1815	97.94
29	1813	Sept.	29		Valentine Rutter	MM	Discharged	Feb.	9	1814	
30	1813	Nov.	1	Apr. 7	Thomas Dukehart	MM	Discharged	Dec.	11	1814	
31	1813	Sept.	18	Apr. 7	James Jones	BT	Discharged	Sept.	26	1814	
32	1813	Sept.	27	Apr. 7	Nathan Foster	BT	Discharged	Oct.	28	1814	
33	1813	Sept.	30	Apr. 7	William Redding	BT	Discharged	Sept.	30	1814	
34	1813	Sept.	30	Apr. 7	Elie Dill	BT	Discharged	Jan.	5	1815	
35	1813	Oct.	6	Apr. 7	Joseph Crooker	BT	Discharged	Oct.	13	1814	
36	1813	Sept.	24	Apr. 7	Edward Burrows	BT	Discharged	Oct.	10	1814	ES
37	1813	Oct.	12	Apr. 7	John Howard	BT	Discharged	Oct.	12	1814	
38	1813	Oct.	16	Apr. 7	Peter Roderick	BT	Discharged	Oct.	16	1814	ES
39	1813	Oct.	16	Apr. 7	Henry Howard	BT					
40	1813	Sept.	28	Apr. 7	Benjamin Gordon	BT	Discharged	Oct.	12	1814	
41	1813	Sept.	16	Apr. 7	Jacob S. Bundy	G	Discharged	Sept.		1814	
42	1813	Sept.	28	Apr. 7	David Chambers	G	Discharged	May	11	1814	
43	1813	Sept.	28	Apr. 7	Isaac Van Blake	G	Died	Aug.	24	1814	Killed at Bladensburg
44	1813	Sept.	28	Apr. 7	William Barling	G	Discharged	Sept.	28	1814	

Abbreviations: AG, Assistant Gunner; AR, Armourer; BT, Boatswain; BY, Boy; CA, Carpenter; CK, Cook; CL, Clerk; CO, Commandant; GB, Gunner's Boy; G, Gunner; GM, Gunner's Mate; LA, Landsman; LT, Lieutenant; MM, Master's Mate; MS, Midshipman; OS, Ordinary Seaman; P, Purser; PL, Pilot; QM, Quartermaster; S, Seaman; SM, Sailing Master; ST, Steward; SU, Surgeon.

No.	Entry Year	Entry Month	Entry Day	Appear on board	From where	Name	Station	Discharged, dead, or run away	When Month	When Day	When Year	Whither or for what reason / pay due
45	1813	Oct.	12	Apr. 7		William Gutrige	G	Discharged	Oct.	12	1814	
46	1813	Oct.	16	Apr. 7		Norris Luke	G	Discharged	Oct.	16	1814	
47	1813	Oct.	30	Apr. 7		Joseph Stewart	G	Discharged	Oct.	30	1814	
48	1813	Nov.	12	Apr. 7		Thomas Moohol	G	Discharged	Nov.	14	1814	84.91
49	1813	Sept.	14	Apr. 7		Thomas Barker	S	Discharged	Oct.	6	1814	131.49. Sick
50	1813	Sept.	14	Apr. 7		George Lucas	S	Discharged	Sept.	14	1814	
51	1813	Sept.	14	Apr. 7		Alexander Weir	S	Discharged	Sept.	14	1814	
52	1813	Sept.	18	Apr. 7		Robert Green	S	Died	Aug.	16	1814	105.79. Baltimore of disease
53	1813	Sept.	27	Apr. 7		Michael Pluck	S	Discharged	Sept.	27	1814	
54	1813	Sept.	27	Apr. 7		David Dick	S	Discharged	Sept.	27	1814	15.62
55	1813	Sept.	30	Apr. 7		James Scarlett	S	Discharged	Sept.	30	1814	ES
56	1813	Sept.	30	Apr. 7		John Everett	S	Discharged	Sept.	30	1814	ES
57	1813	Sept.	30	Apr. 7		George Williams	S	Discharged	Oct.	5	1814	ES
58	1813	Sept.	30			James Dickenson	S	Discharged	Feb.	20	1814	
59	1813	Sept.	30			John V. Phelan	S	Discharged	Dec.	30	1813	
60	1813	Sept.	30			William Smith	S	Run away	Jan.	29	1814	
61	1813	Oct.	12	Apr. 7		John Bates	S	Discharged	Oct.	13	1814	
62	1813	Oct.	12	Apr. 7		Joseph Morris	S	Discharged	Oct.	12	1814	
63	1813	Oct.	15	Apr. 7		Francis Mitchell	S	Discharged	Oct.	15	1814	
64	1813	Oct.	16	Apr. 7		Robert Harrington	S	Discharged	Oct.	16	1814	
65	1813	Oct.	18	Apr. 7		Isaac Dicks	S	Discharged	Oct.	18	1814	

No.	Year	Month	Day	Re-enlisted	Name	Rating	Status	Month	Day	Year	Remarks
66	1813	Oct.	18	Apr. 7	Charles Siffit	S	Discharged	Oct.	18	1814	ES
67	1813	Oct.	23		James Johnson	S	Died	Dec.	5	1813	
68	1813	Nov.	4	Apr. 7	Thomas P. Gilbert	S	Died	June	10	1814	Killed at St. Leonard
69	1813	Nov.	9	Apr. 7	Nicholas Fleming	S	Discharged	Nov.	9	1814	
70	1813	Nov.	11		Edward Oliver	S	Discharged	Dec.	7	1813	In jail
71	1813	Nov.	14		Peter C. Betworth	S	Run away	Mar.	19	1814	
72	1813	Oct.	5	Apr. 7	Emanuel Santo	S	Discharged	Nov.	14	1814	97.87
73	1813	Oct.	13	Apr. 7	John Teshy	S	Discharged	Oct.	13	1814	
74	1813	Oct.	14	Apr. 7	John Vinn	S	Discharged	Nov.	14	1814	
75	1813	Oct.	18		John Hall	S	Discharged	Jan.	16	1814	
76	1813	Oct.	20		Joseph Tabinis	S	Run away	Nov.	6	1813	
77	1813	Nov.	1	Apr. 7	William Bowmaker	S	Discharged	Nov.	1	1814	
78	1813	Nov.	3	Apr. 7	Michael Miller	S	Discharged	Nov.	3	1814	
79	1813	Nov.	4		Lawrence Lezar	S	Discharged	Dec.	10	1813	
80	1813	Nov.	10	Apr. 7	Joseph Miller	S	Discharged	Oct.	10	1814	
81	1813	Nov.	16	Apr. 7	William Smith	S					Transferred to GB
82	1813	Oct.	6	Apr. 7	James Harvey	S	Discharged	Oct.	7	1814	
83	1813	Oct.	21	Apr. 7	John Christy	S	Discharged	May	1	1814	For Geo. Wood enlisted
84	1813	Oct.	27	Apr. 7	John Gordon	S	Discharged	Oct.	27	1814	
85	1813	Oct.	27	Apr. 7	James Correw	S	Discharged	Oct.	27	1814	
86	1813	Oct.	29	Apr. 7	Matthew Cobbits	S	Discharged	Oct.	29	1814	
87	1813	Oct.	30	Apr. 7	John Ignacious	S	Discharged	Oct.	30	1814	

Abbreviations: AG, Assistant Gunner; AR, Armourer; BT, Boatswain; BY, Boy; CA, Carpenter; CK, Cook; CL, Clerk; CO, Commandant; GB, Gunner's Boy; G, Gunner; GM, Gunner's Mate; LA, Landsman; LT, Lieutenant; MM, Master's Mate; MS, Midshipman; OS, Ordinary Seaman; P, Purser; PL, Pilot; QM, Quartermaster; S, Seaman; SM, Sailing Master; ST, Steward; SU, Surgeon.

No.	Entry Year	Month	Day	Appear on board	From where	Name	Station	Discharged, dead, or run away	When Month	Day	Year	Whither or for what reason / pay due
88	1813	Nov.	1	Apr. 7		Charles David	S	Discharged	Nov.	1	1814	
89	1813	Sept.	14	Apr. 7		Matthew Taylor	ST	Discharged	May	21	1814	
90	1813	Oct.	12	Apr. 7		Anthony Potale	ST	Discharged	Oct.	12	1814	88.66
91	1813	Oct.	5	Apr. 7		John Frew	ST	Discharged	Oct.	5	1814	
92	1813	Sept.	15	Apr. 7		John Tobin	ST	Discharged	May	24	1814	
93	1813	Oct.	9			Robert Shortiles	ST	Discharged	Jan.	27	1814	
94	1813	Oct.	7			John Harris	ST	Run away	Feb.	9	1814	
95	1813	Sept.	15	Apr. 7		Matthias Butler	CK	Discharged	Sept.	21	1814	Capt. Wound.
96	1813	Sept.	16	Apr. 7		Daniel Cassidy	CK	Discharged	Sept.	21	1814	
97	1813	Sept.	20	Apr. 7		John Amos	CK	Discharged	Sept.	27	1814	
98	1813	Sept.	25	Apr. 7		John Walker	CK	Discharged	Sept.	26	1814	
99	1813	Sept.	28	Apr. 7		Henry Bartley	CK	Discharged	Sept.	28	1814	
100	1813	Sept.	15	Apr. 7		Elisha Braden	CK	Discharged	Sept.	23	1814	
101	1813	Oct.	20	Apr. 7		Cato Pattison	CK	Discharged	Oct.	10	1814	
102	1813	Oct.	16	Apr. 7		Daniel Fuller	OS	Discharged	Sept.	16	1814	
103	1813	Oct.	18	Apr. 7		Joseph Hardy	OS	Discharged	Sept.	28	1814	
104	1813	Oct.	25	Apr. 7		John Piles	OS	Discharged	Sept.	26	1814	
105	1813	Oct.	25	Apr. 7		Thomas Deile	OS	Discharged	Oct.	7	1814	
106	1813	Oct.	12	Apr. 7		John Boyd	OS	Discharged	Oct.	12	1814	
107	1813	Oct.	16	Apr. 7		Robert Sawyer	OS					
108	1813	Oct.	30	Apr. 7		William O. Vickers	OS	Discharged	Nov.	11	1814	

#	Year	Month	Day	Date	Name	Rank	Status	Month	Day	Year	Notes
109	1813	Nov.	11	Apr. 7	William Blackburn	OS	Discharged	Nov.	12	1814	51.3
110	1813	Nov.	19	Apr. 7	Richard Merchant	OS	Discharged	Nov.	19	1814	
111	1813	Oct.	10	Apr. 7	Charles Massington	OS	Died	Sept.	13	1814	Killed at Ft. McHenry
112	1813	Oct.	13	Apr. 7	George Miller	OS	Discharged	Oct.	13	1814	
113	1813	Nov.	2	Apr. 7	John Lowry	OS	Discharged	Nov.	2	1814	
114	1813	Nov.	12	Apr. 7	Henry Argan	OS	Discharged	Nov.	12	1814	
115	1813	Oct.	2	Apr. 7	John Jenkins	OS	Discharged	Oct.	2	1813	
116	1813	Oct.	17	Apr. 7	James Rowlins	OS	Discharged	Oct.	17	1814	
117	1813	Oct.	25	Apr. 7	John Crow	OS	Discharged	Oct.	25	1814	
118	1813	Oct.	27	Apr. 7	Thomas Gordon	OS	Discharged	Oct.	27	1814	
119	1813	Sept.	25	Apr. 7	Buril Artias	LA	Discharged	Oct.	7	1814	
120	1813	Sept.	29	Apr. 7	Abraham Dogwood	LA					
121	1813	Sept.	29	Apr. 7	Ezekial McClemmy	LA					
122	1813	Sept.	29	Apr. 7	John Crawford	LA					
123	1813	Sept.	30	Apr. 7	Samuel Hawkins	LA	Discharged	Sept.	30	1814	23.12
124	1813	Sept.	30	Apr. 7	John Emolds	LA	Discharged	Oct.	18	1814	40.13
125	1813	Nov.	20	Apr. 7	Caleb Martin	LA	Discharged	Nov.	20	1814	
126	1813	Oct.	6	Apr. 7	Benson L. McCormick	LA	Discharged	Oct.	7	1814	
127	1813	Oct.	8	Apr. 7	William Young	LA	Discharged	Oct.	7	1814	
128	1813	Nov.	2	Apr. 7	William Lowry	LA	Discharged	Nov.	2	1814	
129	1813	Oct.	1	Apr. 7	Isaac Martin	LA	Discharged	June	24	1814	See entry 999
130	1813	Sept.	20	Apr. 7	Jacob Wilson	BY	In jail	Oct.	30	1813	

Abbreviations: AG, Assistant Gunner; AR, Armourer; BT, Boatswain; BY, Boy; CA, Carpenter; CK, Cook; CL, Clerk; CO, Commandant; GB, Gunner's Boy; G, Gunner; GM, Gunner's Mate; LA, Landsman; LT, Lieutenant; MM, Master's Mate; MS, Midshipman; OS, Ordinary Seaman; P, Purser; PL, Pilot; QM, Quartermaster; S, Seaman; SM, Sailing Master; ST, Steward; SU, Surgeon.

No.	Entry Year	Entry Month	Entry Day	Appear on board	From where	Name	Station	Discharged, dead, or run away	When Month	When Day	When Year	Whither or for what reason / pay due
131	1813	Sept.	20			John Fee	BY	Run away	Feb.	25	1814	
132	1813	Sept.	20	Apr. 7		George Gallagher	BY	Discharged	Mar.	24	1815	17.62. Lost in action
133	1813	Sept.	25			Samuel T. Hardy	BY	Discharged	Dec.	4	1813	
134	1813	Sept.	29	Apr. 7		Henry Jones	BY	Discharged	Nov.	2	1814	
135	1813	Sept.	15			Francis T. Tobin	BY	Discharged	Nov.	15	1813	
136	1813	Oct.	13			William J. Bruff	BY	Discharged	Nov.	15	1813	
137	1813	Oct.	27	Apr. 7		James Gordon	BY	Discharged	Oct.	27	1814	
138	1813	Nov.	16	Apr. 7		William Sturges	S	Discharged	Nov.	19	1814	Promoted? See entry 854
139	1813	Sept.	28	Apr. 7		Isaac Nicholson	CK	Discharged	Sept.	28	1814	
140	1813	Oct.	29	Apr. 7		John H. Hindman	S	Discharged	Nov.	29	1814	
141	1813	Oct.	12			William Barnard	S	Died	Dec.	19	1813	
142	1813	Oct.	16			George McKiff	S	Discharged	Oct.	28	1813	
143	1813	Oct.	30	Apr. 7		William Gore	LA	Discharged	Oct.	6	1814	
144	1813	Oct.	11			John McCarty	OS	Run away	Oct.	20	1813	
145	1813	Oct.	19	Apr. 7		Hendric Hrulle	S	Discharged	Oct.	30	1814	
146	1813	Nov.	10			Matthias Billowry	CK	Run away	Nov.	28	1813	
147	1813	Nov.	13	Apr. 7		John Caldwell	AR	Discharged	Nov.	17	1814	
148	1813	Nov.	2	Apr. 7		Thomas Lashford	OS	Discharged	Nov.	22	1814	
149	1813	Nov.	12	Apr. 7		Daniel Patterson	OS	Discharged	Nov.	22	1814	74.93
150	1813	Nov.	2	Apr. 7		Stephen Blaston	S	Discharged	Nov.	22	1814	

No.	Year	Month	Day		Name	Rank	Status	Month	Day	Year	Remarks
151	1813	Nov.	17		John Stokes	S	Run away	Dec.	27	1813	
152	1813	Nov.	17		John Hartman	S	Run away	Dec.	11	1813	
153	1813	Nov.	27		David Ellison	S	Run away	Mar.	12	1814	
154	1813	Nov.	17		Thomas Dunningham	S	Run away	Mar.	12	1814	
155	1813	Nov.	27	Apr. 7	Dorsey Robinson	OS	Died	Oct.	2	1814	90.28
156	1813	Dec.	1	Apr. 7	James Spencer	S	Discharged	Dec.	1	1814	92.58
157	1813	Sept.	27		John C. Ausward	S	Run away	Dec.	24	1813	
158	1813	Dec.	6	Apr. 7	John Miller	S	Died	Sept.	3	1814	67–69. Shot & killed by ensign
159	1813	Dec.	10	Apr. 7	William Cobb	LA	Discharged	Dec.	11	1814	To Flotilla
160	1813	Dec.	16	Apr. 7	John Garrish	S	Died	Oct.	13	1814	
161	1813	Nov.	19	Apr. 7	Henry Fox	OS	Discharged	Nov.	19	1814	17.82
162	1813	Nov.	19	Apr. 7	William Wilson	OS	Discharged	Nov.	19	1814	40.0
163	1813	Nov.	19	Apr. 7	Fisher Morris	LA	Discharged	Nov.	26	1814	(Illegible)
164	1813	Nov.	19	Apr. 7	Thomas Pierce	OS	Discharged	Nov.	19	1814	31.20½
165	1813	Nov.	19	Apr. 7	Robert Williams	OS	Discharged				
166	1813	Dec.	7	Apr. 7	Henry Johnson	OS	Discharged	Dec.	7	1814	
167	1813	Dec.	7	Apr. 7	Elisha Jackson	S					
168	1813	Dec.	7	Apr. 7	William Hendric	S	Discharged	Dec.	7	1814	55.30½
169	1813	Dec.	7	Apr. 7	Thomas Murphy	OS					
170	1813	Dec.	7	Apr. 7	George Howland	OS	Discharged	Dec.	7	1814	29.61
171	1813	Dec.	7	Apr. 7	John Eaton	OS	Discharged	Dec.	7	1814	(Illegible)
172	1813	Dec.	7	Apr. 7	William Miller	OS					
173	1813	Dec.	8	Apr. 7	William Foster	OS	Discharged	Dec.	10	1814	6.55

Abbreviations: AG, Assistant Gunner; AR, Armourer; BT, Boatswain; BY, Boy; CA, Carpenter; CK, Cook; CL, Clerk; CO, Commandant; GB, Gunner's Boy; G, Gunner; GM, Gunner's Mate; LA, Landsman; LT, Lieutenant; MM, Master's Mate; MS, Midshipman; OS, Ordinary Seaman; P, Purser; PL, Pilot; QM, Quartermaster; S, Seaman; SM, Sailing Master; ST, Steward; SU, Surgeon.

No.	Entry Year	Entry Month	Entry Day	Appear on board	From where	Name	Station	Discharged, dead, or run away	When Month	When Day	When Year	Whither or for what reason / pay due
174	1813	Dec.	9	Apr. 7		Bennett McClean	S	Discharged	Dec.	9	1814	
175	1813	Dec.	9	Apr. 7		John Burnes	S	Discharged	Dec.	9	1814	
176	1813	Dec.	9	Apr. 7		Wesley Stone	OS	Run away	May	22	1814	
177	1813	Dec.	9	Apr. 7		William Watson	S	Discharged	Dec.	9	1814	
178	1813	Dec.	9			William Stritch	OS	Discharged	Jan.	27	1814	
179	1813	Dec.	9	Apr. 7		Joseph Ward	OS	Discharged	Dec.	9	1815	
180	1813	Dec.	10	Apr. 7		George Morrison	OS	Discharged	Dec.	10	1814	
181	1813	Dec.	18			Jacob Bowen	LA	Discharged	Feb.	28	1814	
182	1813	Dec.	16			Isaac Webster	LA	Discharged	Jan.	29	1814	
183	1813	Dec.	8	Apr. 7		William Bermina (?)	S	Discharged	Dec.	8	1814	
184	1813	Dec.	20			John Collins	LA	Run away	Dec.	10	1813	
185	1813	Dec.	30			Peter Inez	OS	Run away	Feb.	27	1814	
186	1814	Jan.	3			Asia Allen	S	Run away	Jan.	24	1814	
187	1814	Jan.	3			Henry Huge	OS	Discharged	Feb.	2	1814	
188	1814	Jan.	3			John Armstrong	OS	Discharged	Jan.	20	1814	
189	1814	Jan.	3	Apr. 7		John Stafford	S	Discharged	Jan.	3	1815	
190	1814	Jan.	3	Apr. 7		Joshua Rook	S	Discharged	Jan.	3	1815	32.40½
191	1814	Jan.	3	Apr. 7		John T. Cochrane	MM	Discharged	Jan.	3	1815	45.0
192	1814	Jan.	3	Apr. 7		Samuel Inez	OS	Discharged	Jan.	3	1815	
193	1814	Jan.	3	Apr. 7		Richard Gibbs	S	Discharged	Jan.	3	1815	
194	1814	Jan.	3			Edward Quinn	S	Discharged	Feb.	16	1814	
195	1814	Jan.	3			Richard Ratcliff	OS	Run away	Feb.	27	1814	

No.					Name		Status				
196	1814	Jan.	5	Apr. 7	John Nicholes	S	Discharged	Jan.	5	1815	66.20
197	1814	Jan.	5	Apr. 7	John P. Evans	S	Discharged	Jan.	5	1815	
198	1814	Jan.	5	Apr. 7	Samuel Dunlap	ST	Discharged	Dec.	10	1814	111.73½. Ship 58 by Articles
199	1814	Jan.	6	Apr. 7	John Isley	OS	Discharged	Feb.	20	1814	
200	1814	Jan.	8	Apr. 7	William Hook	G	Discharged	Jan.	28	1815	
201	1814	Jan.	8	Apr. 7	Launcelot Davidson	S	Discharged	Feb.	5	1815	129.64
202	1814	Jan.	9	Apr. 7	Jacob Turner	S	Discharged	Jan.	9	1815	
203	1814	Jan.	11		John Sanford	S	Run away	Jan.	22	1814	
204	1814	Jan.	12	Apr. 7	Hollingsworth Rook	S	Run away				
205	1814	Jan.	12		William Martin	SM					
206	1814	Jan.	13	Apr. 7	Tristram S. Palmer	OS	Discharged	Jan.	13	1815	
207	1814	Jan.	13	Apr. 7	William Milfield	S	Discharged	Apr.	1	1815	124.98
208	1814	Jan.	17	Apr. 7	John Haywood	OS	Discharged	Feb.	5	1815	79.43½
209	1814	Jan.	17	Apr. 7	Andrew Anderson	S	Discharged	Jan.	17	1815	102.26
210	1814	Jan.	21	Apr. 7	Levi Stallings	OS	Discharged	Jan.	24	1815	
211	1814	Jan.	22	Apr. 7	James Caldwell	OS	Discharged	Jan.	28	1815	
212	1814	Jan.	22	Apr. 7	Richard Hill	S	Discharged	Jan.	30	1815	
213	1814	Jan.	22	Apr. 7	William Beach	S	Discharged	Jan.	24	1815	
214	1814	Jan.	22	Apr. 7	Thomas Cochran	MM	Discharged	Jan.	22	1815	12.0
215	1814	Jan.	25	Apr. 7	William McClanahan	LA	Discharged	Jan.	25	1815	
216	1814	Jan.	26	Apr. 7	Samuel Bobbit	S	Discharged	Jan.	26	1815	76.47
217	1814	Jan.	26	Apr. 7	George Smith	BY	Discharged	Jan.	26	1815	2 dollars (illegible)

Abbreviations: AG, Assistant Gunner; AR, Armourer; BT, Boatswain; BY, Boy; CA, Carpenter; CK, Cook; CL, Clerk; CO, Commandant; GB, Gunner's Boy; G, Gunner; GM, Gunner's Mate; LA, Landsman; LT, Lieutenant; MM, Master's Mate; MS, Midshipman; OS, Ordinary Seaman; P, Purser; PL, Pilot; QM, Quartermaster; S, Seaman; SM, Sailing Master; ST, Steward; SU, Surgeon.

No.	Entry Year	Entry Month	Entry Day	Appear on board	From where	Name	Station	Discharged, dead, or run away	When Month	When Day	When Year	Whither or for what reason / pay due
218	1814	Jan.	26	Apr. 7		Charles Jones	S (OS)	Discharged	Jan.	26	1815	63.86
219	1814	Jan.	26	Apr. 7		George Willet	S	Discharged	Jan.	30	1815	
220	1814	Jan.	27	Apr. 7		Christian Strummel	LA	Discharged	Jan.	28	1815	
221	1814	Jan.	27	Apr. 7		James Sellers	SM	Discharged	Dec.	14	1814	377.70 (illegible)
222	1814	Jan.	29	Apr. 7		William Warren	OS	Discharged	Jan.	30	1815	
223	1814	Feb.	1	Apr. 7		Henry Jones 2d	OS	Discharged	Feb.	1	1815	
224	1814	Feb.	1	Apr. 7		Robert Pindergast	OS	Died	Sept.	3	1814	
225	1814	Feb.	1	Apr. 7		Daniel Croacher	S	Discharged	Feb.	1	1815	100.78
226	1814	Feb.	2	Apr. 7		Richard Pritchard	S	Discharged	May	7	1814	Promoted BT Mate 98.0
227	1814	Feb.	3	Apr. 7		Moses Adams	OS					
228	1814	Feb.	8	Apr. 7		John Whitemore	S	Discharged	Feb.	12	1815	25.72
229	1814	Feb.	9	Apr. 7		James Murry	S	Discharged	Feb.	9	1815	100.75
230	1814	Feb.	10	Apr. 7		Daniel Cloud	LA	Discharged	Feb.	10	1815	
231	1814	Feb.	12	Apr. 7		Stephen B. Onion	MM	Discharged	May	21	1814	
232	1814	Feb.	15	Apr. 7		Robert Cashaden	MM	Discharged	Aug.	10	1814	
233	1814	Feb.	15	Apr. 7		George Lowder	S					
234	1814	Feb.	17	Apr. 7		Samuel Peaters	OS	Discharged	Feb.	7	1815	
235	1814	Feb.	17	Apr. 7		Frederick Linderman	S					
236	1814	Feb.	19	Apr. 7		William Conner	S	Discharged	Feb.	19	1815	5.76
237	1814	Feb.	26	Apr. 7		Benjamin Atwell	OS	Discharged	Feb.	26	1815	
238	1814	Feb.	26	Apr. 7		Edward Pulley	OS	Discharged	Feb.	26	1815	

No.	Yr.	Mo.	Day	Date	Name	Rating	Disposition	Mo.	Day	Yr.	Remarks
239	1814	Feb.	25	Apr. 7	Elisha Thompson	OS	Discharged	Feb.	26	1815	56.64
240	1814	Feb.	26	Apr. 7	James Elliston	OS	Discharged	Apr.	1	1815	48.65
241	1814	Mar.	2	Apr. 7	Francis Clark	OS	Discharged	Feb.	25	1815	62.17
242	1814	Feb.	24	Apr. 7	John Smith 1st	S	Discharged	Feb.	22	1815	
243	1814	Feb.	22	Apr. 7	James Lorand	S	Discharged	Feb.	25	1815	29.92
244	1814	Feb.	25	Apr. 7	Andrew Lundgram	S	Died	Apr.	26	1814	
245	1814	Feb.	24	Apr. 7	John Waddell	S	Discharged	July	4	1814	See entry 988
246	1814	Mar.	1	Apr. 7	James H. Martin	MM	Discharged	Jan.	5	1815	30.22
247	1814	Feb.	25	Apr. 7	George W. Duvall	MM	Discharged	May	23	1814	
248	1814	Mar.	2	Apr. 7	James D. Taylor	MM	Discharged	Dec.	15	1814	89.26. His request
249	1814	Feb.	28	Apr. 7	Joseph Jenny	MS	Discharged	Feb.	17	1815	100.21½
250	1814	Feb.	17	Apr. 7	Thomas King	S	Discharged	Feb.		1815	
251	1814	Feb.	22	Apr. 7	Henry Harper	S	Died	Nov.	12	1815	Sick
252	1814	Feb.	23	Apr. 7	Robert Huza	S	Discharged	Feb.	23	1815	
253	1814	Feb.	25	Apr. 7	Samuel Adams	S	Discharged	Feb.	25	1815	
254	1814	Mar.	6	Apr. 7	Samuel Vinton	S	Died	Jan.	4	1815	20.70½. See entry 464
255	1814	Mar.	6	Apr. 7	Charles Neale	S	Discharged	Jan.	7	1815	63.41½
256	1814	Mar.	2	Apr. 7	Lambert Abbit	S	Discharged	Apr.	1	1815	72.98½
257	1814	Feb.	12	Apr. 7	Robert Elliott	LA	Discharged	Apr.	1	1815	99.27. Prisoner
258	1814	Feb.	19	Apr. 7	Nicholas Dawson	S	Discharged	Feb.	19	1815	
259	1814	Mar.	2	Apr. 7	James Wilson	LA	Discharged	Mar.	2	1815	49.72½
260	1814	Feb.	19	Apr. 7	Ralph Gustiff	OS	Discharged	Feb.	19	1815	

Abbreviations: AG, Assistant Gunner; AR, Armourer; BT, Boatswain; BY, Boy; CA, Carpenter; CK, Cook; CL, Clerk; CO, Commandant; GB, Gunner's Boy; G, Gunner; GM, Gunner's Mate; LA, Landsman; LT, Lieutenant; MM, Master's Mate; MS, Midshipman; OS, Ordinary Seaman; P, Purser; PL, Pilot; QM, Quartermaster; S, Seaman; SM, Sailing Master; ST, Steward; SU, Surgeon.

No.	Entry Year	Entry Month	Entry Day	Appear on board	From where	Name	Station	Discharged, dead, or run away	When Month	When Day	When Year	Whither or for what reason / pay due
261	1814	Feb.	19	Apr. 7		John Vickers	OS	Discharged	Feb.	20	1815	
262	1814	Feb.	19	Apr. 7		Ennolds Nalum	OS	Discharged	Feb.	19	1815	
263	1814	Feb.	25	Apr. 7		Jacob Cuff	OS					
264	1814	Feb.	19	Apr. 7		Benjamin Brooks	OS	Died	June	26	1814	Killed at St. Leonard
265	1814	Feb.	14	Apr. 7		William Flemming	BY	Discharged	Apr.	1	1815	58.28½
266	1814	Mar.	1	Apr. 7		Robert L. Porter	ST	Discharged	Jan.	2	1815	
267	1814	Jan.	2	Apr. 7		John Green	S	Discharged	Jan.	28	1815	36.07
268	1814	Mar.	9	Apr. 7		John Scott	S	Discharged	Mar.	7	1815	
269	1814	Mar.	10	Apr. 7		William Sutton	S	Run away	Mar.	21	1814	
270	1814	Feb.	7	Apr. 7		John Small	OS	Discharged	Apr.	1	1815	90.50
271	1814	Mar.	12	Apr. 7		Robert Adams	S	Discharged	Apr.	1	1815	95.96
272	1814	Mar.	12	Apr. 7		George Caso	S					
273	1814	Mar.	11	Apr. 7		David Birch	S					Prisoner
274	1814	Mar.	14	Apr. 7		Lorne Maryjohn	S	Discharged	Apr.	1	1815	113.98
275	1814	Mar.	8	Apr. 7		Thomas Duck	OS	Discharged	Mar.	8	1815	40.56
276	1814	Mar.	7	Apr. 7		Levin Smith	OS	Discharged	Mar.	7	1815	66.69
277	1814	Mar.	7	Apr. 7		Joseph Watts	OS	Discharged	Mar.	9	1815	
278	1814	Mar.	10	Apr. 7		William Taylor	OS					
279	1814	Mar.	11	Apr. 7		Francis Hall	OS	Discharged	Mar.	12	1815	2.50
280	1814	Mar.	9	Apr. 7		Henry Webb	OS	Discharged	June	5	1814	For Geo. Fields as substitute
281	1814	Mar.	8	Apr. 7		James Pints	OS	Discharged	Mar.	8	1815	

No.	Enlisted				Name	Rating	Status	Discharged			Notes
282	1814	Mar.	15	Apr. 7	Ezekiel Stokes	S	Discharged	Mar.	15	1815	
283	1814	Mar.	9	Apr. 7	Thomas Harris	S					Prisoner
284	1814	Mar.	9	Apr. 7	Gabriel Venams	BY	Discharged	Mar.	9	1815	13.28½
285	1814	Mar.	15	Apr. 7	Joshua Chillcut	OS	Discharged	Apr.	1	1815	81.80½
286	1814	Mar.	1	Apr. 7	Edmund F. Duvall	MS	Discharged	Apr.	1	1815	91.99
287	1814	Mar.	10	Apr. 7	Solomon Rodman	MM	Discharged	June	21	1814	SM. See entry 991
288	1814	Mar.	1		William Peterkin	MM	Discharged	July	6	1814	
289	1814	Mar.	1		Josiah Rutter	SM	Discharged	Apr.	1	1815	431.75
290	1814	Mar.	1		John Davis	SM	Discharged	Feb.	1		
291	1814	Mar.	1		Beverly Diggs	SM	Discharged	Feb.	1		
292	1814	Mar.	3	Apr. 7	Daniel Gallatin	MM	Discharged	Mar.	6	1815	110.76
293	1814	Mar.	10	Apr. 7	William Achison	MM	Discharged	July	7	1814	SM. 90.00
294	1814	Mar.	10	Apr. 7	James Taylor Jr.	MM	Discharged	Aug.	10	1814	
295	1814	Mar.	10	Apr. 7	Thomas Foster	MM	Discharged	Dec.	26	1814	
296	1814	Mar.	10	Apr. 7	John Bowen	MM	Discharged	Apr.	1	1815	195.16
297	1814	Mar.	11	Apr. 7	William Abraham	MM	Discharged	Apr.	1	1815	108.85
298	1814	Mar.	12	Apr. 7	William Hill	MM					
299	1814	Mar.	1		John A. Webster	SM	Discharged	Apr.	1	1815	303.73
300	1814	Mar.	15	Apr. 7	James Thompson	MM	Discharged	July	2	1814	31.28
301	1814	Mar.	7	Apr. 7	Joseph L. Barry	MS	Discharged	Apr.	1	1815	78.90
302	1814	Mar.	11	Apr. 7	Charles A. Hardisty	MS	Discharged	Apr.	1	1815	65.33½
303	1814	Mar.	16	Apr. 7	John Oram	MS	Discharged	June	5	1814	See entry 994
304	1814	Mar.	22	Apr. 7	Benjamin Perkins	MS	Discharged	Mar.	22	1815	

Abbreviations: AG, Assistant Gunner; AR, Armourer; BT, Boatswain; BY, Boy; CA, Carpenter; CK, Cook; CL, Clerk; CO, Commandant; GB, Gunner's Boy; G, Gunner; GM, Gunner's Mate; LA, Landsman; LT, Lieutenant; MM, Master's Mate; MS, Midshipman; OS, Ordinary Seaman; P, Purser; PL, Pilot; QM, Quartermaster; S, Seaman; SM, Sailing Master; ST, Steward; SU, Surgeon.

No.	Entry Year	Month	Day	Appear on board	From where	Name	Station	Discharged, dead, or run away	When Month	Day	Year	Whither or for what reason / pay due
305	1814	Mar.	23	Apr. 7		Aymond Dunan	MS	Discharged	Aug.	24	1814	
306	1814	Mar.	4	Apr. 7		James Gannon	S	Discharged	Apr.	1	1815	82.75
307	1814	Mar.	5	Apr. 7		William Waddell	BY	Discharged	Apr.	1	1815	8.14
308	1814	Mar.	10	Apr. 7		John Anderson	S	Discharged	Apr.	1	1815	104.65
309	1814	Mar.	15	Apr. 7		Jeremiah Grandison	OS	Discharged	Sept.	13	1814	
310	1814	Mar.	17	Apr. 7		James Hooker	ST	Discharged	May	20	1814	
311	1814	Mar.	17	Apr. 7		John O. Conway	S	Run away	Mar.	10(?)	1814(?)	
312	1814	Mar.	19	Apr. 7		William Davidson	LA	Run away	Feb.	1	1814	
313	1814	Mar.	18	Apr. 7		George Webber	S	Discharged	Apr.	1	1815	
314	1814	Mar.	19	Apr. 7		Hicks Rooks	BY	Discharged	Apr.	1	1815	106.17
315	1814	Mar.	20	Apr. 7		Thomas Gilham	OS	Discharged	Apr	1	1815	7.38
316	1814	Mar.	21	Apr. 7		John McCallister	LA	Run away	Feb.	28	1815	
317	1814	Mar.	21	Apr. 7		Charles McCallister	BY	Run away	Feb.	28	1815	
318	1814	Mar.	22	Apr. 7		John Risk	OS					
319	1814	Mar.	22	Apr. 7		William Nabbs	LA	Died	June	26	1814	Killed at St. Leonard
320	1814	Mar.	23	Apr. 7		James Hunt	LA	Discharged	Apr.	1	1815	35.3
321	1814	Mar.	23	Apr. 7		Joshua Gale	S	Discharged	Apr.	1	1815	32.12
322	1814	Mar.	23	Apr. 7		Levin Carmichael	S	Discharged	Apr.	1	1815	113.15
323	1814	Mar.	23	Apr. 7		Benjamin L. Conway	S	Discharged	Apr.	1	1815	59.25
324	1814	Mar.	24	Apr. 7		Hugh Montgomery	BY	Discharged	Apr.	1	1815	35.27
325	1814	Mar.	24	Apr. 7		Peter Owens	S					
326	1814	Mar.	24	Apr. 7		George Briscoe	OS	Discharged	Apr.	1	1815	87.92
327	1814	Mar.	24	Apr. 7		John Conway	OS	Discharged	Mar.	24	1815	21.95

#	Year	Mo.	Day	Date	Name	Rate	Status	Mo.	Day	Year	Amount/Notes
328	1814	Mar.	25	Apr. 7	Thomas Graham	OS	Discharged	Apr.	1	1815	93.73
329	1814	Mar.	26	Apr. 7	William Brown	S	Discharged	June	7	1814	Promoted to Gunner
330	1814	Mar.	26	Apr. 7	John Gibbons	S	Died	Jan.	7	1815	
331	1814	Mar.	2	Apr. 7	William Thompson	OS	Discharged	Apr.	1	1815	64.56
332	1814	Mar.	28	Apr. 7	Isaac Garraway	OS	Discharged	Apr.	1	1815	97.41
333	1814	Apr.	8	Apr. 7	John Fowler	OS	Run away				
334	1814	Mar.	17	Apr. 7	John McClellan	ST	Died	July	28	1814	25.18
335	1814	Mar.	28	Apr. 7	John Pasco	S	Discharged	Apr.	1	1815	127.1
336	1814	Mar.	29	Apr. 7	Noah Phillips	OS					
337	1814	Mar.	29	Apr. 7	Henry M. Horn	S	Discharged	July	9	1814	See entry 1000
338	1814	Mar.	28	Apr. 7	Isaac Shillingsburg	S	Discharged	Apr.	1	1815	93.82
339	1814	Mar.	29	Apr. 7	John Carter	S					
340	1814	Mar.	31	Apr. 7	John Goodman	LA	Discharged	Apr.	1	1815	45.89
341	1814	Apr.	4	Apr. 7	John Neptner	OS	Discharged	Apr.	1	1815	111.69½
342	1814	Apr.	4	Apr. 7	Joseph Founder	OS					
343	1814	Apr.	5	Apr. 7	Nathaniel Card	S	Discharged	Apr.	1	1815	115.1
344	1814	Apr.	5	Apr. 7	William McKay	S	Discharged	Apr.	1	1815	69.87
345	1814	Apr.	1	Apr. 7	C. Davis	MM					
346	1814	Apr.	1	Apr. 7	Henry Taylor	BT	Discharged	Apr.	1	1815	206.28
347	1814	Apr.	1	Apr. 7	Peter Buddy	ST	Discharged	Dec.	24	1814	34.49
348	1814	Apr.	2	Apr. 7	James Smith	S	Discharged	Apr.	1	1815	118.93
349	1814	Apr.	2	Apr. 7	Naem Patterson	S	Discharged	Apr.	1	1815	101.63
350	1814	Apr.	2	Apr. 7	Frederic Coy	S	Discharged	Apr.	1	1815	133.47

Abbreviations: AG, Assistant Gunner; AR, Armourer; BT, Boatswain; BY, Boy; CA, Carpenter; CK, Cook; CL, Clerk; CO, Commandant; GB, Gunner's Boy; G, Gunner; GM, Gunner's Mate; LA, Landsman; LT, Lieutenant; MM, Master's Mate; MS, Midshipman; OS, Ordinary Seaman; P, Purser; PL, Pilot; QM, Quartermaster; S, Seaman; SM, Sailing Master; ST, Steward; SU, Surgeon.

No.	Entry Year	Month	Day	Appear on board	From where	Name	Station	Discharged, dead, or run away	When Month	Day	Year	Whither or for what reason / pay due
351	1814	Apr.	2	Apr. 7		Thomas Buckley	MS					
352	1814	Apr.	2	Apr. 7		Charles Green	S	Discharged	Apr.	1	1815	139.43. Wounded in service
353	1814	Apr.	5	Apr. 7		John Bates 2nd	S	Discharged	Apr.	1	1815	140.61
354	1814	Apr.	5	Apr. 7		John Marie	S	Discharged	Apr.	1	1815	128.93
355	1814	Apr.	5	Apr. 7		George Medcalf	S	Discharged	Apr.	1	1815	59.44
356	1814	Apr.	6	Apr. 7		John Cook	BY					
357	1813	Nov.	15	Apr. 7		Joseph Thomas	LA					
358	1813	Dec.	2	Apr. 7		Lloyd Jones	OS	Comn. servant	Apr.	1	1815	308.54
359	1814	Jan.	3	Apr. 7		Matthias Benno	S					
360	1814	Apr.	2			Jonathan Plummer	OS	Discharged	Apr.	1	1815	60.89
361	1814	Apr.	3			James Plummer	OS	Discharged	Apr.	1	1815	57.18
362	1814	Apr.	23			Philamen Porter	S	Discharged	Apr.	1	1815	93.47
363	1814	Apr.	11			Alen Larimore	S	Discharged	Apr.	1	1815	91.8½
364	1814	Feb.	5			Nathan Townsend	MM	Discharged	May	25	1814	See entry 939
365	1814	Mar.	31			Woolman Dawson	S	Discharged	Apr.	1	1815	91.46
366	1814	Apr.	11			Benjamin Lowry	S	Discharged	Apr.	1	1815	104.46
367	1814	Mar.	3			Richard Kinnemont	S					See entry 380
368	1814	Mar.	16			James Harrison	S	Discharged	Apr.	1	1815	100.64
369	1814	Jan.	21			Stephen W. Pindel	MM	Discharged	Apr.	1	1815	232.79
370	1814	Feb.	22			John H. Smoot	MM	Discharged	Apr.	1	1815	103.19½
371	1814	Mar.	28			John Wheeler	MM	Discharged	Apr.	1	1815	144.2½

#	Name	Rating	Enl. Month	Enl. Day	Enl. Year	Status	Disch. Month	Disch. Day	Disch. Year	Amount / Notes
372	Henry Jenkins	MS			1814					
373	John Jefferson	OS	Mar.	19	1814	Discharged	Apr.	1	1815	92.14
374	Thomas Larimore	S	Mar.	31	1814	Died	May	13	1814	
375	James Bowden	OS	Mar.	31	1814	Discharged	Apr.	1	1815	57.94
376	Thomas Auld	LA	Apr.	7	1814	Discharged	Apr.	1	1815	76.62
377	Thomas Roberts	S	Apr.	10	1814	Discharged	Apr.	1	1815	58.6
378	Thomas Cockey	BT	Apr.	3	1814	Discharged	Apr.	1	1815	154.16
379	Purnel Taylor	CK	Mar.	27	1814	Discharged	Apr.	14	1815	157.56
380	Richard Kinnemont	S	Apr.	3	1814	Discharged	Apr.	1	1815	116.68. See entry 367
381	William Ross	OS	Mar.	16	1814					
382	John Carr		Mar.	25	1814					See entry 403
383	Joseph Hardesty		Mar.		1814					
384	Hadaway Sinclair	S	Mar.	29	1814	Discharged	Apr.	1	1815	96.8
385	Asa Hambleton	OS	Apr.	7	1814	Discharged	Mar.	5	1815	26.5
386	John Boy	BY	Apr.	13	1814					
387	James Kirby 1st	S	Mar.	26	1814	Discharged	Apr.	1	1815	131.87
388	Benjamin Cooper	S	Apr.	3	1814	Discharged	Apr.	1	1815	76.90
389	Jeremiah Phillips	LA	Apr.	14	1814	Discharged	Apr.	1	1815	29.39
390	John Bisbee (Ontario)	AR	Mar.	17	1814	Died	Aug.	28	1814	
391	Archibald Eideston	LA	Jan.	1	1814	Discharged	Jan.	1	1815	6.15
392	Ross Frazier	MM	Feb.	12	1813	Discharged	Dec.	16	1814	
393	James Frazier	MS	Mar.	1	1813	Discharged	Dec.	16	1814	
394	John Williams 1st	LA	Mar.	28	1814	Discharged	Apr.	1	1815	57.11

Abbreviations: AG, Assistant Gunner; AR, Armourer; BT, Boatswain; BY, Boy; CA, Carpenter; CK, Cook; CL, Clerk; CO, Commandant; GB, Gunner's Boy; G, Gunner; GM, Gunner's Mate; LA, Landsman; LT, Lieutenant; MM, Master's Mate; MS, Midshipman; OS, Ordinary Seaman; P, Purser; PL, Pilot; QM, Quartermaster; S, Seaman; SM, Sailing Master; ST, Steward; SU, Surgeon.

No.	Entry Year	Entry Month	Entry Day	Appear on board	From where	Name	Station	Discharged, dead, or run away	When Month	When Day	When Year	Whither or for what reason / pay due
395	1814	Mar.	28			Samuel Southerton	LA	Discharged	Apr.	1	1815	48.73
396	1814	Mar.	28			Thomas Hubbard	LA	Died	June	26	1814	Killed at St. Leonards
397	1814	Mar.	28			Richard Thomas	LA	Discharged	Apr.	1	1815	47.51½
398	1814	Apr.	1			Henry Jenkins	MS	Discharged	Apr.	1	1815	121.69
399	1814	Apr.	30			John Steiger	LA	Discharged	Apr.	1	1814	60.87
400	1814	Apr.	1			Solomon Jackson	LA	Discharged	Apr.	1	1815	56.27
401	1814	Mar.	21			Richard Griffin	CK	Discharged	Apr.	1	1815	155.42
402	1814					Pernnel Jenkins						
403	1814	Mar.	24		Baltimore	John Carr	LA	Discharged	Apr.	1	1815	48.65
404	1812	Aug.	26	Apr. 7	Scorpion	John Peck	MM	Discharged	Sept.	9	1814	Exp. service
405	1814	Apr.	28			Andrew McDonough	S	Discharged	Apr.	1	1815	70.72
406	1814	Mar.	6			Wlilliam C. Blades	S	Discharged	Apr.	1	1815	30.79
407	1814	Apr.	2			Greenbury Foster	LA	Discharged	Mar.	6	1815	82.39
408	1814	Apr.	6			Nicholas Parish	OS					Same as entry 450
409	1814	Mar	26			James Jenkins	LA					Same as entry 451
410	1813	Nov.	1			John Wilson	S					
411	1814	Feb.	10			Daniel Cloud	LA					Same as entry 230. Right marine
412	1813	Nov.	16	Apr. 14		John Harker	BY					Josh Barney
413	1814	Mar.	15		Ontario	Frederich Soderstach	OS	Discharged	Dec.	6	1814	For Ontario

#	Year	Month		Day	Ship	Name	Rate	Status	Month	Day	Year	Amount
414	1814	Mar.		15	Ontario	John Thompson	OS	Discharged	Dec.	6	1814	For Ontario
415	1813	Nov.	Apr. 14	15		John McCormick	OS	Discharged	Dec.	6	1814	For Ontario
416	1813	Nov.	Apr. 14	16		Alexander Thompson	S	Discharged	Dec.	6	1814	For Ontario
417	1814	Mar.		10		Robert F. Martin	MM	Discharged	Apr.	1	1815	58.65
418	1814	Apr.		28		Jacob Walters	S					
419	1814	Apr.		28		James Lloyd	S	Discharged	Apr.	1	1815	101.6½
420	1814	May		2		John Tonlson	S	Discharged	Jan.	29	1815	84.84
421	1813	Jan.		22	Scorpion	John Burgess	OS	Discharged	Jan.	29	1815	10.78½
422	1814	Apr.		4		James W. Clife	ST	Discharged	Apr.	1	1815	174.28
423	1814	Mar.		30		William Dean	ST	Discharged	Dec.	31	1814	
424	1814	Mar.		30		Melville Dean	ST	Run away	Apr.	1	1815	190.38
425	1813	Feb.		10	Scorpion	Daniel Brown	S	Discharged	Jan.	15	1815	
426	1813	Jan.		25	Scorpion	Nathaniel Read	OS	Discharged	Jan.	28	1815	
427	1814	Apr.		23		James Brown	OS					
428	1812	Dec.		7	Scorpion	Thomas Pritchard	OS	Discharged	Dec.	7	1814	7.25½
429	1813	Feb.		1	Scorpion	Noah Dearing	OS	Discharged	Feb.	1	1815	36.48
430	1813	Jan.		12	Scorpion	Joseph Chase	OS	Discharged	Feb.	16	1815	44.99
431	1814	Mar.		26		James Joshua	LA					
432	1814	Apr.		6		William Assrayders ?	OS	Discharged	Apr.	1	1815	68.54
433	1814	Mar.		12		George Kinsey	S	Discharged	Mar.	9	1815	49.63
434	1814	Mar.		8		Charles G. Cockle	LA	Discharged	Mar.	8	1815	
435	1814	Mar.		11		Francis Hall	OS					See entry 279
436	1814	Apr.		16		Nathaniel Chapman	LA	Discharged	July	5	1814	

Abbreviations: AG, Assistant Gunner; AR, Armourer; BT, Boatswain; BY, Boy; CA, Carpenter; CK, Cook; CL, Clerk; CO, Commandant; GB, Gunner's Boy; G, Gunner; GM, Gunner's Mate; LA, Landsman; LT, Lieutenant; MM, Master's Mate; MS, Midshipman; OS, Ordinary Seaman; P, Purser; PL, Pilot; QM, Quartermaster; S, Seaman; SM, Sailing Master; ST, Steward; SU, Surgeon.

No.	Entry Year	Entry Month	Entry Day	Appear on board	From where	Name	Station	Discharged, dead, or run away	When Month	When Day	When Year	Whither or for what reason / pay due
437	1814	Mar.	18			Benjamin G. Brown	S	Died	June	26	1814	Killed at St. Leonards
438	1814	Apr.	4			Henry Gadd	OS	Discharged	Apr.	1	1815	72.75
439	1814	Apr.	4			William Bartheson	S	Discharged	Apr.	1	1815	119.81
440	1812	July	28		No. 137	George Nesbit	S	Discharged	Aug.	17	1814	
441	1813	Feb.	12		Shark	James Vermilion	OS	Discharged	Feb.	13	1815	12.39
442	1813	Jan.	19		No. 137	Urban Rice	OS	Discharged	Mar.	27	1814	Made ST. See entry 985
443	1813	Jan.	14		No. 137	Charles Gowen	OS	Discharged	Jan.	18	1815	
444	1813	Jan.	21		No. 137	Daniel Seward	OS	Discharged	Jan.	6	1815	
445	1814	Mar.	14			John W. Cooper	S	Discharged	Mar.	16	1815	
446	1814	Jan.	27			Christian Strummel	LA	Discharged	Jan.	28	1815	Same as entry 220
447	1813	Feb.	5		Shark	Haven Lanbon	S	Discharged	Feb.	5	1815	
448	1814	Feb.	1			William Byus	SM	Discharged	Apr.	1	1815	636.38
449	1814	Mar.	26			Thomas Cary	S	Discharged	Apr.	1	1815	103.53
450	1814	Apr.	6			Nicholas Parish	OS	Discharged	Apr.	1	1815	50.33
451	1813	Nov.	25		Ontario	Henry Gray	S					
452	1814	Apr.	18			Isaac Gardiner	OS	Discharged	Apr.	1	1815	62.93
453						Thomas Nashville						
454	1814	Mar.	18			George Webber	S					Same as entry 313
455	1814	Mar.	18		?	John Wilson 1st	LA	Discharged				40.10

No.	Enl. Year	Enl. Month	Enl. Day	Vessel	Date	Name	Rating	Status	Disch. Month	Disch. Day	Disch. Year	Notes
456	1814	Mar.	15	Ontario		Armon Miller	LA	Discharged	Dec.	6	1814	For Ontario
457				P. Flotilla		Benjamin Hodges						E. Services
458	1813	Nov.	11		Mar. 30	John Francis	BY	Discharged	Feb.	1	1815	
459	1812	Sept.	22	Shark	Apr. 7	Thomas Foreman	OS	Discharged	Sept.	26	1814	
460	1813	Feb.	23	137		William Averill	S	Discharged	Feb.	23	1815	
461	1812	Sept.	17	137		William Harrison	G	Discharged	Sept.	28	1814	
462	1813	Jan.	26	137		John Underwood	OS	Discharged	Jan.	24	1815	
463	1814	Jan.	1	Shark		Francis Russell	OS	Run away	Apr.	1	1815	84.94
464	1814	Mar.	6			Samuel Vinton	S	Died	Jan.	4	1815	
465	1814	Dec.	5	Ontario		Richard Richmond	S	Discharged	Dec.	6	1814	Ontario
466	1813	Feb.	3	137		Joseph Littlefield	S	Discharged	Feb.	3	1815	37.98
467	1813	Mar.	8	137		Samuel Davis	OS					
468	1813	Feb.	15	137		Benjamin Goodridge	OS	Discharged	Feb.	15	1815	
469	1813	Jan.	21	137		David Williams	OS	Discharged	Jan.	21	1815	
470	1812	May	21			William Melville	OS					
471	1814	Jan.	18			Ira Amsden	OS	Discharged	Apr.	1	1815	52.24
472	1814	Feb.	12			John Hubbard	S	Discharged	Feb.	12	1815	83.49
473	1814	Apr.	1			John Jacobs 1st	S					
474	1814	Feb.	6	Shark		Joshua Lambert	S	Discharged	Oct.	18	1814	Sick
475	1813	Nov.	27		Apr. 18	William Stanton	S	Discharged	Dec.	6	1813	83.49
476	1813	Jan.	26	137		Joseph Simpson	S	Discharged	Jan.	30	1815	78.76
477	1814	May	5			Kelly Johnson	S					
478	1814	Apr.	6			John Turner	S					
479	1814	Mar.	25			Patrick Dominic	ST	Discharged	Mar.	24	1814	37.48

Abbreviations: AG, Assistant Gunner; AR, Armourer; BT, Boatswain; BY, Boy; CA, Carpenter; CK, Cook; CL, Clerk; CO, Commandant; GB, Gunner's Boy; G, Gunner; GM, Gunner's Mate; LA, Landsman; LT, Lieutenant; MM, Master's Mate; MS, Midshipman; OS, Ordinary Seaman; P, Purser; PL, Pilot; QM, Quartermaster; S, Seaman; SM, Sailing Master; ST, Steward; SU, Surgeon.

No.	Entry Year	Entry Month	Entry Day	Appear on board	From where	Name	Station	Discharged, dead, or run away	When Month	When Day	When Year	Whither or for what reason / pay due
480	1813	Dec.	27		Ontario	George Viahara	OS					For Ontario
481	1813	Nov.	15	Apr. 14		Thomas Brown 1st	S	Discharged	Dec.	6	1814	Ontario
482	1814	Mar.	15		Ontario	Elijah Loring	QM	Discharged	Dec.	6	1814	
483	1812	May	21		Shark	Thomas Dixon	OS	Discharged	May	21	1814	
484	1812	Sept.	28		Scorpion	George Bamberger	BY	Discharged	Oct.	1	1814	
485						John Murry						
486	1814	Jan.	22		Ontario	Joseph Breese	S	Discharged	Dec.	6	1814	Ontario
487	1814	Mar.	15		Ontario	John Orr	OS	Discharged	Dec.	6	1814	Ontario
488	1814	Apr.	19			William Porter	S	Discharged	Apr.	1	1815	114.58½
489	1814	Mar.	15		Ontario	Hiram Dandsey	OS	Died	Aug.	24	1814	Killed at Bladensburg
490	1814	Mar.	9			William Jones	BY	Discharged	Apr.	1	1815	32.39
491	1814	Apr.	3			Richard Kinny	ST	Discharged	Apr.	1	1815	196.0
492	1813	Aug.	20		Scorpion	Richard Dunn	OS					
493	1813	Dec.	22	Apr. 7		Charles Smith	S					
494	1814	Apr.	3			Elihu Ellis	OS	Discharged	Apr.	1	1815	69.14
495	1812	Jan.	18		Scorpion	Thomas Hill	S					Transferred Dec. 14
496	1814	Nov.	23	Apr. 14	Ontario	Robert Stephenson	OS	Discharged	Dec.	6	1814	For Ontario
497	1813	Sept.	10	Apr. 7	138	George Wright	BY					
498	1814	Jan.	22		Ontario	Michael White	S	Discharged	Dec.	6	1814	Ontario
499	1813	June	9		Scorpion	Simon Garden	OS	Discharged	Jan.	9	1815	
500	1812	Sept.	17	Apr. 7		Richard Jenkins	CK	Discharged	Sept.	26	1814	

No.	Year	Mo.	Day		Vessel	Name	Rating	Status	Mo.	Day	Year	Remarks
501	1813	Sept.	10	Apr. 7	138	Henry Ennis	BY	Discharged	Mar.	2	1815	Ontario
502	1814	Mar.	28	Apr. 7	138	William Monday	S	Discharged	Oct.	11	1814	
503	1813	Oct.	11	Apr. 7	137	Thomas Valiant	OS	Discharged	Feb.	17	1815	6.82
504	1812	Dec.	26		Shark	James Daniels	BY	Discharged	Jan.	21	1815	
505	1812	Jan.	21		Shark	Samuel Ireson	S	Discharged	Jan.	6	1815	
506	1814	Mar.	6			Samuel Neale	S	Discharged	Mar.	3	1815	18.97
507	1812	Feb.	3		Shark	Robert Page	OS	Discharged	Feb.	2	1815	
508	1813	Jan.	26		Shark	George Dennett	OS	Discharged	Jan.	23	1815	
509	1812	Nov.	23		Scorpion	James Bryson	S	Discharged	Nov.	12	1814	34.86
510	1813	Jan.	22		Scorpion	Andrew Matthews	OS	Discharged				
511	1814	Mar.	2			John H. Lovedy	ST	Discharged	Nov.	6	1814	
512	1814	Jan.	28		Ontario	Peter Johnson	S	Discharged	Dec.	29	1814	Ontario
513	1812	Dec.	21		Ontario	William Peach	OS	Died	Sept.	6	1814	
514	1814	Feb.	4		Ontario	Cornelius Boyce	S	Discharged	Dec.	1	1814	Ontario
515	1814	May	2			Samuel Shammeau	S	Discharged	Apr.	22	1815	105.17
516	1813	Jan.	31		Scorpion	Joseph Averill	S	Discharged				
517	1812	Sept.	18		Scorpion	Frederick Earnest Airnes	S	Discharged				Same as 814
518	1814	Apr.	11			John Frazier	S	Discharged	Dec.	11	1814	Promoted BT. See entry 649
519	1813	Feb.	5		Shark	James Williams	S	Discharged				26.97
520	1813	Jan.	25		Shark	Benjamin Doliner	OS	Discharged	Jan.	24	1815	30.85
521	1813	Feb.	6		Shark	Joseph Haley	OS	Discharged	Feb.	6	1815	54.80
522	1813	Feb.	19		Shark	William Carnes		Discharged	Feb.	19	1815	560

Abbreviations: AG, Assistant Gunner; AR, Armourer; BT, Boatswain; BY, Boy; CA, Carpenter; CK, Cook; CL, Clerk; CO, Commandant; GB, Gunner's Boy; G, Gunner; GM, Gunner's Mate; LA, Landsman; LT, Lieutenant; MM, Master's Mate; MS, Midshipman; OS, Ordinary Seaman; P, Purser; PL, Pilot; QM, Quartermaster; S, Seaman; SM, Sailing Master; ST, Steward; SU, Surgeon.

No.	Entry Year	Entry Month	Entry Day	Appear on board	From where	Name	Station	Discharged, dead, or run away	When Month	When Day	When Year	Whither or for what reason / pay due
523	1813	Jan.	19		137	Lemuel Holbrook	OS	Discharged	Jan.	19	1815	
524	1813	Jan.	21		Shark	Ebenezer Harris	OS	Discharged	Nov.	13	1814	
525	1814	Mar.	5		Ontario	George Carrie	OS	Discharged	Dec.	6	1814	Ontario
526	1814	Mar.	31			William Vaughn	MM	Discharged	Feb.	4	1815	30.59
527	1814	Mar.	26			Henry Bullen	ST					
528	1814	Feb.	19		Ontario	Ebenezer Evans	BY	Discharged	Mar.	1	1815	Lost sight 26 June St. Leonard
529	1814	Apr.	6			Joseph I. Wilson	ST					
530	1814	May	10			John Donaldson	BY	Discharged	Apr.	1	1815	20.82
531	1814	May	9			Henry Bevans	OS					
532	1814	May	9			Martin Pradier	S		.			
533	1814	Apr.	15			Samuel Wingate	ST	Discharged	Dec.	28	1814	Captured
534	1814	Apr.	23			Washington Lee	ST	Died	Nov.	9	1814	Sick
535	1814	Jan.	7		Ontario	John Peters 1st	QM	Discharged	Dec.	6	1814	Ontario
536	1813	Feb.	2		Scorpion	John De Groot	S	Discharged				
537	1814	Jan.	7		Ontario	Peter Dutell	OS	Discharged	Dec.	6	1814	Ontario
538	1813	Dec.	29		Ontario	Joseph Baily	AG	Discharged	Dec.	6	1814	Ontario
539	1814	Jan.	5		Ontario	John Martin	S					
540	1814	Apr.	25			George Wilson	S					
541	1814	Mar.	10			Josiah Lockerman	MS	Discharged	Apr.	1	1815	98.63½
542	1814	Mar.	20			Edward Dawson	ST	Discharged	Mar.	28	1814	
543	1812	Dec.	31		Scorpion	Francis Lemouse	S	Discharged	Dec.	31	1814	

No.						Name						
544	1813	Mar.	1		Scorpion	Jotham Gilpatrick	S	Discharged	Mar.	1	1815	53.78
545	1814	May	11			Daniel Sanders	LA	Discharged	Apr.	1	1815	59.92
546	1813	Mar.	2		Shark	Jonathan Davis	OS	Run away				Onboard Ontario
547	1814	Mar.	4	Apr. 7		Andrew Mason	S	Run away				(or missing)
548	1813	Sept.	10		138	William Woodward	OS	Discharged	Jan.	20	1815	107.48
549	1812	Jan.	20	Apr. 15	Scorpion	John Smith 2nd	S	Discharged	Dec.	6	1814	Ontario
550	1813	Mar.	23			John Lord	QM	Discharged	Apr.	1	1815	87.12
551	1814	Mar.	26		Shark	James Jenkins	OS	Discharged	Nov.	13	1814	Same as entry 524
552	1813	Jan.	21		Shark	Ebenezer Harris	OS	Run away				
553	1813	Feb.	4		Shark	William Grant	S	Discharged	Feb.	4	1815	101.93
554	1812	Nov.	17		Ontario	Benjamin Hodges	BY					
555	1814	Mar.	15		Ontario	James Foster	AG					
556	1814	Mar.	15		Shark	James Shefton	S	Discharged	Apr.	1	1815	225.83½
557	1813	Mar.	3			Daniel Emmory	S	Discharged	Mar.	3	1815	154.46
558					Shark	George Coke						Same as entry 624
559	1812	Sept.	17		Shark	James Tucker	S					
560	1813	Feb.	19		Shark	William Couran	BY	Discharged	Feb.	9	1815	
561	1813	Feb.	3		Shark	Theodore Hutchings	OS	Discharged	Feb.	3	1815	16.63½
562	1813	Feb.	3		137	Edward Moor (Moon?)	S					Prisoner
563	1813	Mar.	15		Ontario	William Norman	S	Discharged	Dec.	6	1814	Ontario
564	1814	Dec.	18		Shark	James Glenn	S	Discharged	Dec.	18	1814	
565	1812	July	18		Shark	James Roach	S	Discharged	Aug.	17	1814	57.26

Abbreviations: AG, Assistant Gunner; AR, Armourer; BT, Boatswain; BY, Boy; CA, Carpenter; CK, Cook; CL, Clerk; CO, Commandant; GB, Gunner's Boy; G, Gunner; GM, Gunner's Mate; LA, Landsman; LT, Lieutenant; MM, Master's Mate; MS, Midshipman; OS, Ordinary Seaman; P, Purser; PL, Pilot; QM, Quartermaster; S, Seaman; SM, Sailing Master; ST, Steward; SU, Surgeon.

No.	Entry Year	Entry Month	Entry Day	Appear on board	From where	Name	Station	Discharged, dead, or run away	When Month	When Day	When Year	Whither or for what reason / pay due
566	1812	Dec.	22		Scorpion	John Simpson	OS	Discharged	Dec.	22	1814	
567	1813	Jan.	13		Shark	Ichabod Shaw	CK	Discharged	Jan.	30	1815	
568	1814	May	9			Allen Steward	S	Run away	Sept.	30	1814	
569	1813	Jan.	9		Scorpion	Lewis R. Criff	AG					
570	1813	Jan.	1		Shark	William Ratcliff	BY	Died	Nov.	12	1814	Sick
571	1813	Jan.	2		Scorpion	John B. Carr	BY	Discharged	Jan.	2	1815	
572	1814	Feb.	3	Apr. 7		Samuel Holland	OS	Discharged	Dec.	6	1814	Ontario
573	1814	Mar.	25		ES	Tristan Stoker	OS	Discharged	Apr.	1	1815	71.55
574	1813	Apr.	28	Apr. 7	Ontario	Richard Montgomery	MM	Discharged	June	6	1814	(Illegible)
575	1812	Dec.	26		Scorpion	Thomas Baste	BY	Discharged	Oct.	26	1814	32.11
576	1814	May	5			Lloyd Wright	LA					Discharged 1 Apr. 1815
577	1814	May	4			Charles Smith 2nd	LA	Run away	June	28	1814	Tkn 3 Dec. 1814
578	1814	May	4			Thomas Bell	LA					
579	1814	May	4			Joseph Edwards	LA	Run away	Aug.	(24)	1814	From Bladensburg
580	1814	Apr.	25			John Wightman	MM	Discharged	Jan.	13	1815	
581	1814	Apr.	6			Thomas N. Harvey	S	Discharged	May	14	1814	G. See entry 973
582	1814	Feb.	2		Ontario	Michael Nigler	S	Discharged	Dec.	6	1814	Ontario
583	1814	Apr.	23			George W. Ash	LA	Discharged	Dec.	29	1814	Ontario
584	1814	Feb.	5		Ontario	John Smith 3rd	S					
585	1813	Dec.	23		Ontario	Peter Gordon	QM	Run away				

No.	Year	Month	Day	Note	Amt.	Ship	Name	Rate	Disposition	Month	Day	Year	Remarks
586	1814	May	7	Apr. 7			Thomas Dorman	MS	Discharged	Apr.	1	1815	57.77
587	1813	Jan.	4				John Peters 2	S	Discharged	Sept.	19	1814	Asp. seaman
588	1813	Sept.	10	Apr. 7	138		George Schwickardt	ST	Died	Apr.	23	1814	57.94. Sick
589	1814	Sept.	7	Apr. 7	138		Casar Wentworth	CK	Discharged	Feb.	23	1815	161.25
590	1814	May	7				Charles Butler	S					
591	1814	Apr.	25				Andrew Uhl	S	Run away	or in jail			
592	1814	Mar.	14				James Sollers	S	Run away				23 (Died?)
593	1814	May	23				John Cooper	OS	Discharged	Apr.	1	1815	53.11
594	1814	Apr.	9				Nathan Hunt	OS	Run away				
595	1813	Dec.	9			Ontario	William Levering	OS	Discharged	Dec.	6	1814	Ontario
596	1814	May	9				Peter G. Holden	S	Run away	Sept.	30	1814	
597	1813	Feb.	24			Scorpion	Asa Roberts	S	Discharged	Feb.	24	1815	
598	1812	Apr.	5	Apr. 7			Charles Fleming	CA	Discharged	Sept.	9	1814	Asp. seaman
599	1814	Feb.	3				William Young 2nd	S	Discharged	Dec.	6	1814	Ontario
600	1813	Sept.	10				William Carter	MM	Discharged	Nov.	11	1814	Same as entry 852
601	1812	Dec.	19			Scorpion	James Minzies	BT	Discharged	Dec.	21	1814	His request
602							Solomon Frazier	LT					
603							William Dotson	SM	Discharged	Apr.	1	1815	351.35
604	1814	May	17				John Hambleton	LA					
605	1814	Apr.	16				Rowland Kimbol	S	Run away	Jan.	23	1815	
606	1814	Apr.	23				Stacy Hay	LA	Run away	Oct.		1814	
607	1814	Jan.	31			Ontario	Thomas Jones	OS	Discharged	Dec.	6	1814	Ontario
608	1814	Mar.	15			Ontario	Nathan Glen	OS	Discharged	Dec.	6	1814	Ontario

Abbreviations: AG, Assistant Gunner; AR, Armourer; BT, Boatswain; BY, Boy; CA, Carpenter; CK, Cook; CL, Clerk; CO, Commandant; GB, Gunner's Boy; G, Gunner; GM, Gunner's Mate; LA, Landsman; LT, Lieutenant; MM, Master's Mate; MS, Midshipman; OS, Ordinary Seaman; P, Purser; PL, Pilot; QM, Quartermaster; S, Seaman; SM, Sailing Master; ST, Steward; SU, Surgeon.

No.	Entry Year	Month	Day	Appear on board	From where	Name	Station	Discharged, dead, or run away	When Month	Day	Year	Whither or for what reason / pay due
609	1814	Mar.	10			John I. Steward	ST	Discharged	Dec.	28	1814	
610	1814	May	12			Gabriel Harman	OS	Discharged	Apr.	1	1815	76.89
611	1814	May	16			Constant Labec	S	Died	Aug.	24	1814	Killed at Bladensburg
612	1814	May	16			John Peters 2nd	BY	Discharged	Apr.	1	1815	47.48
613	1814	Apr.	14			Thomas J. Smith	LA	Discharged	Apr.	1	1815	73.56
614	1814	Apr.	23			William Smith 3rd	LA	Discharged	Apr.	1	1815	73.50
615	1814	Apr.	14			Charles McMahon	OS	Discharged	Apr.	1	1815	100.21
616	1814	Mar.	10			John Thompson 3rd	MM	Discharged	Apr.	1	1815	234.86
617	1814	Mar.	4			Philip Marshall	ST	Discharged	Mar.	10	1815	122.63
618	1814	Mar.	25			Larkins Kelly	G	Discharged	Apr.	1	1815	212.35
619	1814	Mar.	30			Thomas Jenkins	ST	Discharged	Dec.	29	1814	
620	1814	Mar.	10			James Wheeler	MS					
621	1814	Apr.	14			Robert Ray	ST	Discharged	Apr.	1	1815	112.26
622	1812	June	10	Apr. 7	Scorpion	Timothy Stevens	S	Discharged	July	21	1814	
623	1813	Nov.	16	Apr. 7	Ontario	John Tucker	S	Discharged	Dec.	6	1814	Ontario
624	1813	Feb.	3		P. Flotilla	George Coke	S	Discharged	Feb.	3	1815	55.32
625	1814	Mar.	16			Joseph Devetrie (?)	S	Discharged	Apr.	1	1815	79.24
626	1814	Mar.	1			Alexander Beard	SM	Discharged	Apr.	1	1815	507.80
627	1814	Nov.	10			James Hubbard	MM	Discharged	Apr.	1	1815	197.57
628	1814	Feb.	19		Ontario	James Ward	OS					
629	1813	Dec.	30		Ontario	David Wilson	BY	Discharged	Dec.	6	1814	Ontario

No.	Year	Mo.	Day		Ship	Rating	Name	Status	Mo.	Day	Year	Amount/Notes
630	1814	May	19			OS	John Paine					
631	1814	Mar.	6			S	Andrew Stocker	Discharged	Mar.	6	1815	51.18
632	1813	Nov.	12	Apr. 7	Ontario	S	Andrew Baxter	Discharged	Dec.	6	1814	Ontario
633	1814	May	19			MS	Francis C. Andrew					
634	1814	Feb.	12		Ontario	OS	Joseph Peterson	Discharged	Dec.	12	1814	Ontario
635	1814	Feb.	19		Ontario	OS	Stephen Elderkin	Discharged	Jan.	3	1815	
636	1814	Apr.	17			SM	William B. Barney		Aug.	14	1814	
637	1814					SM	Henry Thomas	Discharged	July	1	1815	327.85
638	1814	Jan.	16			S	Edmund Blades	Discharged	Apr.	1	1815	112.40
639	1814	Apr.	15		Ontario	OS	Joseph Francino	Discharged	Dec.	6	1814	Ontario
640	1813	Dec.	7		Ontario	QG	Thomas Burke	Discharged	Dec.	6	1814	Ontario
641	1814	Apr.	14			OS	Thomas Lewis	Discharged	Apr.	1	1815	33.38
642	1814	May	14			S	John Roach		May	14	1814	
643	1812	Dec.	10		Ontario	BY	Matthew Strickers	Discharged	Dec.	6	1814	Ontario
644	1814	Mar.	26			S	Francis Gossage	Discharged	Mar.	21	1815	95.33
645	1814	Apr.	10			OS	William Martin	Discharged	Apr.	1	1815	86.6
646	1812	May	15				William Harrington		May	15	1812	
647	1814	Mar.	8			SM	Thomas Moore	(Illegible)	Aug.	27	1814	
648	1814	May	24			LA	John Peck	Discharged	Apr.	1	1815	33.26
649	1814	Apr.	12			BT	John Frazier	Discharged	Jan.	11	1815	Substitute for Wm Hook
650	1814	May	12			S	John Taylor	Discharged	Apr.	1	1815	97.29. Punishment
651	1814	May	3			S	Forbes Hague					

Abbreviations: AG, Assistant Gunner; AR, Armourer; BT, Boatswain; BY, Boy; CA, Carpenter; CK, Cook; CL, Clerk; CO, Commandant; GB, Gunner's Boy; G, Gunner; GM, Gunner's Mate; LA, Landsman; LT, Lieutenant; MM, Master's Mate; MS, Midshipman; OS, Ordinary Seaman; P, Purser; PL, Pilot; QM, Quartermaster; S, Seaman; SM, Sailing Master; ST, Steward; SU, Surgeon.

No.	Entry Year	Month	Day	Appear on board	From where	Name	Station	Discharged, dead, or run away	When Month	Day	Year	Whither or for what reason / pay due
652	1814	May	21			Robert Lousine	OS					
653	1814	Apr.	20			Stephen Winingdon	G	Discharged	Dec.	26		49.22
654	1814	Mar.	15		Ontario	Asa Elwell	OS	Discharged	Dec.	6		Ontario
655	1814	Feb.	10		Ontario	John Brown	OS	Run away	Aug.	24		From Bladensburg
656	1813	Feb.	9		137	James Webber	OS	Discharged	Feb.	17		32.70
657	1814	Apr.	14			Emanuel Roulson	S	Discharged	Apr.	1		127.97
658	1814	Mar.	14			Garison James	S	Discharged	Apr.	1		107.80
659	1813	Dec.	1		Ontario	John Graves	OS	Discharged	Dec.	6		Ontario
660	1813	Nov.	24	Apr. 15	Ontario	Gabriel Roulson	S	Run away				
661	1814	Mar.	15		Ontario	John Mortimer	S	Discharged	Dec.	6		Ontario
662						Ross (?) Steward						
663	1813	Dec.	28		Ontario	David Kay	OS					
664	1814	Apr.	23			Frederick Williamson	OS					
665	1812	May	18		137	Edward Sealy	OS					
666	1813	Dec.	28		Ontario	Thomas Strong	BY	Discharged	Dec.	6	1814	Ontario
667	1814	Apr.	16			John Way	MM					
668	1814	May	26			James R. Simmons	MS	Discharged	Nov.	24	1814	
669	1814	Mar.	6			David Townsend	S	Died	July	11	1814	Sick
670	1814	May	27			James Dugan	MM	Discharged	Nov.	3	1814	6.62. Requested
671	1814	May	28			Samuel L. Isetts	MS	Discharged	Jan.	13	1815	40.42
672	1814	May	14			Samuel Wall	BT					

Entry	Name	Rating	Enlisted	Note	Status	Disch. Month/Day	Disch. Year	Remarks
673	Ruben Mitchell	G	Apr. 5, 1814		Discharged	Apr. 1	1815	85.43
674	Cawsford Cleat	S	May 6, 1814		Died		1815	
675	Henry Young	OS	May 27, 1814		Run away		1814	
676	John Rusk	OS	May 24, 1814		Discharged	Apr. 1	1815	22.64
677	Daniel McBain	OS	May 23, 1814		Run away	Aug. 31	1814	
678	David Coulson	OS	May 27, 1814		Discharged	Apr. 1	1815	45.5
679	Timothy Conner	OS			Run away	May	1814	
679*	Samuel Moore	OS	Apr. 28, 1814		Discharged	Sept. 16	1814	
680	John Stevens	CK	Mar. 16, 1814		Discharged	Apr. 1	1815	214.49
681	Richard Dixon	S	Jan. 24, 1814		Run away	July 4	1814	
682	George Wood	S	May 22, 1814		Discharged	Oct. 21	1814	Subt. John Christian
683	Stephen Sparrow	OS	Mar. 3, 1813	Asp	Discharged	Mar. 3	1815	
684	Philip Collins	OS	May 31, 1814					
685	Sylvester Brown	G	Apr. 20, 1814		Discharged	Apr. 1	1815	211.15
686	James Pembroke	CK	May 23, 1814		Died	May 29	1814	Sick
687	John Ascom	S	May 7, 1814	May 8	Died	Oct. 7	1814	Sick
688	William Laurence	S	May 7, 1814		Discharged	Apr. 1	1815	121.13
689	Benjamin M. Carr	S	May 7, 1814					
690	John Baggate	S	May 4, 1814					See entry 948
691	Thomas C. Elliston	S	May 7, 1814		Run away	Aug. 31	1814	
692	Samuel Roads	S	May 17, 1814	May 20				See entry 761
693	John Franciscus	S	May 19, 1814		Discharged	Apr. 1	1815	121.1

Abbreviations: AG, Assistant Gunner; AR, Armourer; BT, Boatswain; BY, Boy; CA, Carpenter; CK, Cook; CL, Clerk; CO, Commandant; GB, Gunner's Boy; G, Gunner; GM, Gunner's Mate; LA, Landsman; LT, Lieutenant; MM, Master's Mate; MS, Midshipman; OS, Ordinary Seaman; P, Purser; PL, Pilot; QM, Quartermaster; S, Seaman; SM, Sailing Master; ST, Steward; SU, Surgeon.

*Same number repeated on original muster document for both Conner and Moore.

No.	Entry Year	Entry Month	Entry Day	Appear on board	From where	Name	Station	Discharged, dead, or run away	When Month	When Day	When Year	Whither or for what reason / pay due
694	1814	May	19			Archibald Cade	S	Discharged	Apr.	1	1815	122.16
695	1814	May	25			Osburn Garend	S	Discharged	Apr.	1	1815	76.47
696	1814?	Aug	26			George Ervin	S	Run away	July	9	1814	
697	1814	May	27			Thomas Barrett	S	Discharged	Apr.	1	1815	99.49
698	1814	May	31			Lester Mortimer	S	Discharged	Apr.	1	1815	78.62
699	1814	May	31			Frederich Frieze	S	Run away	July	9	1814	
700	1814	May	31			Thomas Tate	S	Discharged	Apr.	1	1815	86.69
701	1814	Mar.	31			William Bennett	OS	Discharged	Apr.	1	1815	74.54
702	1814	May	31			Barnett Thompson	S					
703	1814	Feb.	16			James Wright	SM	Discharged	Feb.	1	1815	78.0
704	1814	June	2			John Powers	S					
705	1814	June	2			John Kennedy	LA	Run away	June	18	1814	
706	1814	June	1			John Noble	BY					
707	1814	June	5			Ferdinand Boyer	LA					
708	1813	Feb.	12	Apr. 7	Asp	Joseph N. Dommit	S	Discharged	Feb.	12	1815	
709	1813	Feb.	2		Asp	Ruben Hammond	S					
710	1813	Jan.	13	Apr. 7	Asp	John McDonough	S	Discharged	May	17	1814	G. See entry 984
711	1813	Jan.	26		Asp	John Gray	OS	Discharged	Jan.	28	1815	
712	1812	Dec.	21	Apr. 7	Asp	Thomas Woodford	S	Discharged	May	16	1814	Gunner
713	1813	Feb.	3		Asp	Enoch Drew	OS	Discharged	Feb.	3	1815	14.87
714	1814	Jan.	8			William Brown	G					191.34. See entry 329
715	1814	June	6			Daniel Daily	S	Discharged	Apr.	1	1815	126.89

No.	Year	Month	Day		Name	Rating	Status	Month	Day	Year	Remarks
716	1814	June	6		Samuel Peterson	S	Discharged	Apr.	1	1815	62.94
717	1814	June	4		Joseph Wilson 2nd	S	Discharged	Apr.	1	1815	61.4
718	1814	June	6		George Fields	OS	Discharged	May	9	1815	4.71 Sub. for Benjamin Wilson
719	1814	June	10		Edward Cooper	OS	Discharged	Apr.	1	1815	65.63½
720	1814	June	4		William Farr	OS					
721	1812	July	4	Asp	Thomas Oldham	S	Discharged	(July)	(1)	1814	E. Served
722	1814	Apr.	5		Adam Teabolt	S	Discharged	Apr.	1	1815	113.36
723	1814	Apr.	7		Peter Griffin	OS					
724	1814	Apr.	8		Paul Edwards	G					
725	1814	Apr.	13		Peter Chrisall	OS	Run away	Apr.	17	1814	
726	1814	Apr.	14		James Ellis	OS					
727	1814	Apr.	14		John Heinzman	OS	Discharged	Apr.	1	1815	79.41
728	1814	Apr.	14		Richard F. Peabeck	OS	Discharged	Apr.	1	1815	79.3
729	1812	Dec.	23	Asp	John William 2nd	OS					
730	1814	Apr.	15		Thomas Glenn	G	Discharged	Apr.	1	1815	221.27
731	1814	June	8		James Doniven	OS	Run away	July	10	1814	
732	1814	May	24		William I. Young	MM	Discharged	Dec.	31	1814	His request
733	1814	June	10		William Craig	OS					
734	1814	Apr.	22		William Woolford	S	Discharged	Apr.	1	1815	90.44
735	1814	Apr.	23		Robert Bromwell	OS	Discharged	Apr.	1	1815	
736	1814	Apr.	26		Thomas Harris	OS	Discharged	Apr.	1	1815	95.80
737	1814	Apr.	27		Nathaniel Harvey	S	Discharged	Mar.	8	1815	
738	1814	Apr.	28		George Christie	MM	Discharged	Aug.	14	1814	

Abbreviations: AG, Assistant Gunner; AR, Armourer; BT, Boatswain; BY, Boy; CA, Carpenter; CK, Cook; CL, Clerk; CO, Commandant; GB, Gunner's Boy; G, Gunner; GM, Gunner's Mate; LA, Landsman; LT, Lieutenant; MM, Master's Mate; MS, Midshipman; OS, Ordinary Seaman; P, Purser; PL, Pilot; QM, Quartermaster; S, Seaman; SM, Sailing Master; ST, Steward; SU, Surgeon.

No.	Entry Year	Entry Month	Entry Day	Appear on board	From where	Name	Station	Discharged, dead, or run away	When Month	When Day	When Year	Whither or for what reason / pay due
739	1814	May	4			Samuel Haynie	MM					Same as 911
740	1814	May	17			Timothy Conner	OS	Run away	May		1814	
741	1814	May	19			Hugh Sherwood	MM	Discharged	Apr.	1	1815	133.21
742	1814	May	19			Davis Robinson	LA	Discharged	Apr.	1	1815	125.38
743	1814	Dec.	17			John Frazier	MM	Died	July	17	1814	99.26. Sick
744	1813	Mar.	24			Thomas Linthicum	MM					
745	1814	Apr.	7			Thomas Kelly	ST					
746	1814	Apr.	13			John Thomas	G					
747	1814	Apr.	8			Joshua Beaty	S	Discharged	May	18	1814	S. See entry 977
748	1814	Apr.	22			Sylvester A. Lost	S	Discharged	Apr.	1	1815	120.31
749	1814	Apr.	22			Joseph Pinto	S					
750	1814	Apr.	18			Samuel Overholtz	OS	Discharged	Apr.	1	1815	61.98
751	1814	June	11			Levin Wingate	BT					See entry 805
752	1814	June	6			William Brown	S					
753	1814	June	8			William Aimes	OS	Discharged	Apr.	1	1815	47.20
754	1814	June	9			Zachariah Sterling	OS	Discharged	Apr.	1	1815	69.57
755	1814	June	14			Nathaniel Johnson	OS	Discharged	Apr.	1	1815	25.22
756	1814	June	14			Patrick Doyle	OS	Died	Oct.	28	1814	
757	1814	Apr.	15			Charles Harrison	OS	Run away	July	2	1814	Sloop War, LB
758	1814	Apr.	16			Peter Koon	S	Discharged	Apr.	1	1815	79.99
759	1814	Apr.	18			George Bing	S					
760	1814	Apr.	23			John Wilson	OS					

No.	Year	Month	Day	Name	Rating	Status	Month	Day	Year	Amount
761	1814	May	17	Samuel Roads	S					Seaman 692
762	1814	Mar.	26	Thomas Kerry	S					Seaman 449
763	1814	Apr.	3	Perry Jones	BY	Discharged	Apr.	1	1815	122.7
764	1814	Apr.	15	Edward Bowman	S	Discharged	Apr.	1	1815	101.40
765	1814	Apr.	15	William Samson	S	Run away	Jan.	18	1815	
766	1814	Apr.	16	Nathaniel Kennard	S	Run away	Apr.	22	1814	
767	1814	May	3	William Weightman	OS					
768	1814	May	5	William R. Jones	OS	Discharged	Apr.	1	1815	218.5
769	1814	May	17	William Grant 2nd	S	Run away	Aug.	5	1814	
770	1814	June	7	George Halsey	OS	Discharged	Apr.	1	1815	53.11
771	1814	June	26	James Daily	LA	Discharged	Apr.	1	1815	39.9
772	1814	July	9	William Harris	LA	Run away	Sept.		1814	
773	1814	July	22	John Fearson	MS	Discharged	Jan.	2	1815	
774	1814	June	15	Peter Nouvell	S	Discharged	Apr.	1	1815	59.18 Prisoner
775	1814	July	11	Henry Palmer	LA	Run away	Nov.	11	1814	32.57
776	1814	July	15	James Truet	LA	Discharged	Apr.	1	1815	
777	1814	July	12	Benjamin Taylor	OS	Run away	Dec.	26	1814	44.26
778	1814	July	28	Daniel Wellslager	LA	Discharged	Apr.	1	1815	103.39
779	1814	Apr.	2	John Montell	S	Discharged	Apr.	1	1815	32.15
780	1814	July	15	William Fleming		Discharged	Apr.	1	1815	90.91
781	1814	July	12	John Billings	S	Discharged	Apr.	1	1815	56.48
782	1814	July	19	James Connan	S	Discharged	Apr.	1	1815	14.92
783	1814	July	11	John Marshall	MM	Discharged	Dec.	16	1814	
784	1814	July	20	Thomas Andrews	MS					

Abbreviations: AG, Assistant Gunner; AR, Armourer; BT, Boatswain; BY, Boy; CA, Carpenter; CK, Cook; CL, Clerk; CO, Commandant; GB, Gunner's Boy; G, Gunner; GM, Gunner's Mate; LA, Landsman; LT, Lieutenant; MM, Master's Mate; MS, Midshipman; OS, Ordinary Seaman; P, Purser; PL, Pilot; QM, Quartermaster; S, Seaman; SM, Sailing Master; ST, Steward; SU, Surgeon.

No.	Entry Year	Entry Month	Entry Day	Appear on board	From where	Name	Station	Discharged, dead, or run away	When Month	When Day	When Year	Whither or for what reason / pay due
785	1814	July	29			John Reynolds	OS					
786	1814	July	21			Timothy Lynch	S					
787	1814	July	30			Kenneth Tracy	S	Discharged	Mar.	16	1815	
788	1814	June	8			William Cox	OS					
789	1814	July	15			Robert Walker	MM					
790	1814	July	23			Jacob Krebs	OS	Run away				LB
791	1814	July	11			Benjamin Main	OS					
792	1814	May	24			John Hand	MM	Run away	Dec.	23	1814	
793	1814			See 755		Edward Johnson						
794	1814	July	10			Benjamin Jones	S	Discharged	Apr.	1	1815	57.82 68.32
795	1814	July	28			Jacob Hymer	LA	Discharged	Apr.	1	1815	34.33
796	1814	June	16			Daniel Wallender	S	Discharged	Apr.	1	1815	51.93
797	1814	Aug.	1			John Nicholas	S					
798	1814	Apr.	29			Thomas Gibbons	LA	Discharged	July	26	1814	Transfer
799	1814	July	25			Jasper Laderrman	OS	Run away	Jan.	25	1815	
800	1814	July	27			George Houlton	S					
801	1814	July	25			Henry Davidson	LA	Run away	Jan.	19	1815	
802	1814	July	11			William Barron	LA	Discharged	Apr.	1	1815	31.17
803	1814	July	15			William Baird	LA	Discharged	Apr.	1	1815	35.37
804	1814	Mar.	15		Ontario	James Benjamin	OS	Discharged	Oct.	6	1814	
805	1814	June	8			Levin Wingate	BT	Discharged	Dec.	26	1814	J. Stines subs. for 978

No.	Year	Month	Day	Name	Ship	Rating	Status	Month	Day	Year	Notes
806	1814	June	14	Benjamin Dungan		OS	Discharged	Apr.	1	1815	56.72
807	1814	June	16	George Asquith		MS	Died	June	26	1814	Killed at St. Leonards
808	1814	July	9	Stephen White		MM	Discharged	Apr.	1	1815	119.74
809	1814	July	9	John Barry		MM	Discharged	Jan.	26	1815	LB
810	1814	July	11	Joseph Wilkinson		OS	Discharged	Apr.	1	1815	64.57
811	1814	July	11	Anthony Trenton		S	Discharged	Apr.	1	1815	61.28
812	1813	Feb.	22	William Clifford	Asp	S					
813	1813	Jan.	11	John Maria	Scorpion	OS	Died	Aug.	24	1814	Killed at Bladensburg
814	1812	Sept.	18	Frederick Earnest Airns	Scorpion	S					187.20½ same as 517
815	1814	July	16	James Wilson 2nd		MM	Discharged	Nov.	17	1814	
816	1814	Aug.	2	William Penn		S					
817	1814	July	17	Sutton Boice		LA	Discharged	Apr.	1	1815	49.58
818	1814	July	17	William Flannel		OS					
819	1814	July	21	Robert Baker		OS	Run away	Nov.	21	1814	
820	1814	July	21	Christopher Shillingsburg		OS	Discharged	Apr.	1	1815	37.71
821	1814	July	25	David English		S	Discharged	Apr.	1	1815	78.36
822	1814	July	27	Henry Fisher		S	Discharged	Apr.	1	1815	62.4
823	1814	July	28	James Winters		S	Discharged	Apr.	1	1815	90.38
824	1814	July	29	Thomas Oldham		S					
825	1814	July	14	Peter Martin		G	Discharged	July	16	1814	Made G. See entry 964
826	1814	July	14	Samuel Taylor		LA	Discharged	Apr.	1	1815	53.2

Abbreviations: AG, Assistant Gunner; AR, Armourer; BT, Boatswain; BY, Boy; CA, Carpenter; CK, Cook; CL, Clerk; CO, Commandant; GB, Gunner's Boy; G, Gunner; GM, Gunner's Mate; LA, Landsman; LT, Lieutenant; MM, Master's Mate; MS, Midshipman; OS, Ordinary Seaman; P, Purser; PL, Pilot; QM, Quartermaster; S, Seaman; SM, Sailing Master; ST, Steward; SU, Surgeon.

No.	Entry Year	Entry Month	Entry Day	Appear on board	From where	Name	Station	Discharged, dead, or run away	When Month	When Day	When Year	Whither or for what reason / pay due
827	1814	July	30			Joseph Jarboe	S	Discharged	Aug.	5	1814	Promoted MM. See entry 972
828	1814					No. omitted in original book						
829	1814	July	30			John Foble	LA					
830	1814	Aug.	8			William Lawson	S	Discharged	Apr.	1	1815	78.88
831	1814	Aug.	10			George Paulding	OS	Run away	Oct.	2	1814	
832	1814	Aug.	7			John Giddleman	OS	Discharged	Apr.	1	1815	59.67
833	1814	Aug.	8			Charles Pasture	OS	Run away				LB
834	1814	Aug.	9			Peter Parker	S					
835	1814	Aug.	11			James Mitchell	OS					
836	1814	Aug.	12			Henry Fletcher	S					
837	1814	Aug.	6			Seabert Sollers	OS	Run away	Nov.	13	1814	
838	1814	Aug.	3			William Somerfield	OS	Discharged	Apr.	1	1815	55.12
839	1814	Aug.	8			Walter Dunn	OS	Discharged	Apr.	1	1815	73.97
840	1814	Aug.	3			Philip Cloues	OS					
841	1814	July	13			Charles Fullerton	G	Discharged	Apr.	1	1815	
842	1814	Aug.	3			John Mars	OS					
843	1814	Aug.	2			James Slater	OS					
844	1814	Aug.	4			William Martin 3rd	S	Discharged	Aug.	20	1814	BT. See entry 931
845	1814	Aug.	3			Benjamin Lucas	S	Same as 859				
846	1814	Aug.	6			Alexander Deshield	G	Discharged	Apr.	1	1815	152.6
847	1814	Aug.	8			William Anderson	LA	Discharged	Apr.	1	1815	44.56

No.	Year	Month	Day	Ref	Name	Rating	Status	Month	Day	Year	Remarks
848	1814	Aug.	5		Joseph White	OS	Died	May	12	1814	
849	1814	July	26		John Townsley	S	Discharged	Nov.	14	1814	
850	1813	Sept.	5	Apr. 7	John Geoghegan	SM	Discharged	Sept.	27	1814	
851	1813	Sept.	10	Apr. 7 / 138	George Moony	MM	Discharged	Sept.	26	1814	Drowned in submarine boat
852	1813	Sept.	10	Apr. 7 / 138	William Carter	MM	Discharged	Sept.	7	1814	Same as 600
853	1813	Sept.	10	138	Ebenestus Weed	S	Discharged	Sept.	7	1814	150,000
854	1814	Mar.	20	July 19 / 138	William Sturges	G	Discharged	Sept.	24	1814	See entry 138
855	1814	July	17		Anthony Thompson	SM	Discharged	Sept.	7	1814	As requested
856	1814	Aug.	16		Robert Rattles	OS					
857	1813	Jan.	26	137	John Launey	OS					
858	1814	Aug.	15		Abraham Detter	LA					
859	1814	Aug.	14		Benjamin Lucas	S					Same as 845
860	1814	Aug.	13		William Williams	S					
861	1814	Aug.	11		Greenbury Leverton	OS	Discharged	Apr.	1	1815	65.72
862	1814	Aug.	11		Thomas Abbot	OS					
863	1814	Aug.	15		Thomas M. Nichols	OS	Discharged	Apr.	1	1815	66.64
864	1814	Aug.	15		John Jory	OS	Run away				
865	1813	Sept.	10	Apr. 7 / 138	John Batis 3rd	BY					
866	1814	Mar.	18	Apr. 7 / 138	Ownes Diddolph	G	Discharged	Apr.	1	1815	142.7
867	1814	Aug.	19	Aug. 21	Hans Walker	OS	Discharged	Apr.	1	1815	57.84
868	1814	Aug.	16	Aug. 22	Jonathan Kelly	OS	Discharged	Apr.	1	1815	64.00
869	1814	Aug.	18	Aug. 22	Robert Halfpenny	OS	Run away				LB
870	1814	Aug.	19	Aug. 21	Conyman Gardiner	LA	Discharged	Apr.	1	1815	42.68
871	1814	Aug.	14	Aug. 22	John Weeks	LA	Discharged	Apr.	1	1815	56.0

Abbreviations: AG, Assistant Gunner; AR, Armourer; BT, Boatswain; BY, Boy; CA, Carpenter; CK, Cook; CL, Clerk; CO, Commandant; GB, Gunner's Boy; G, Gunner; GM, Gunner's Mate; LA, Landsman; LT, Lieutenant; MM, Master's Mate; MS, Midshipman; OS, Ordinary Seaman; P, Purser; PL, Pilot; QM, Quartermaster; S, Seaman; SM, Sailing Master; ST, Steward; SU, Surgeon.

No.	Entry Year	Entry Month	Entry Day	Appear on board	From where	Name	Station	Discharged, dead, or run away	When Month	When Day	When Year	Whither or for what reason / pay due
872	1814	Aug.	17	Aug. 20		Jonas Jones	S	Discharged	Mar.	5	1815	6.85
873	1814	Aug.	16	Aug. 22		William Stines	S	Discharged	Apr.	1	1815	64.10
874	1814	Aug.	19	Aug. 22		Peter Martin	S	Same as 964				
875	1814	Aug.	19	Aug. 22		Peter Butler	S					
876	1813	Oct.	28	Apr. 13		Robert Harper	GM	Discharged	Apr.	23	1814	
877	1813	Nov.	13	Apr. 13		Asakel Roberts	BY					
878	1813	Nov.	16	Apr. 14		Ceazar Farmer	S	Discharged	Dec.	6	1814	For Ontario
879	1813	Nov.	23	Apr. 13		Hugh Dougherty	S	Discharged	Dec.	6	1814	Ontario
880	1813	Nov.	27	Apr. 17		George Richardson	S	Discharged	Dec.	6	1814	Ontario
881	1814	July	26		Patuxent	John Neal	OS					
882	1814	Jan.	25			John H. Buckley	S					
883	1814	Aug.	25			James Much	S	Discharged	Apr.	1	1815	58.25
884	1814	Aug.	1			Peter Lucas	OS					
885	1814	Mar.	15	Apr. 7	Ontario	Dennis McAllen	S	Died	Oct.	11	1814	
886	1814	Aug.	26			Joseph Belt	OS	Discharged	Apr.	1	1815	51.35
887	1814	June	14	June 14		John Woods Jr.	MM	Discharged	Aug.	10	1814	
888	1814	June	27	Apr. 7	Ontario	James Cook	S	Discharged	Dec.	6	1814	Ontario
889	1814	July	18			Thompson Moon	MS					Ontario
890	1814	June	6		Ontario	Joseph Henry	OS	Discharged	Dec.	6	1814	Ontario
891	1814	July	31		Patuxent	John H. Carrol	MS	Discharged	Mar.	1	1815	67.84
892	1814	Mar.	15		Ontario	Jacob Philips	OS					
893	1814	May	20	May 20		James W. Peace	SM	Discharged	Apr.	1	1815	

No.	Year	Month	Day		Vessel	Name	Rank	Disposition	Month	Day	Year	Remarks
894	1814	July	26		Patuxent	Dennard James	OS	Discharged	Apr.	1	1815	53.86
895	1814	Mar.	5			John Morris						
896	1814	July	18			John B. Burnham	G	Discharged	Apr.	1	1815	79.68
897	1814	Jan.	1	Apr. 7	Ontario	John Abbott	S	Run away				
898	1814	Jan.	22	Apr. 7		Thomas Brown 2nd on Ont	S	Died	Sept.	29	1814	37.43 76.58½ Files for him Captured
899	1814					Samuel (alias Henry) Parker*	S	Discharged	Dec.	6	1814	Ontario
900	1814	Jan.	1		Ontario	David Auterbridge	S	Discharged	Dec.	6	1814	Ontario
901	1814	Aug.	1			William Gannon	LA					
902	1814					Richard Ricaud	SM					
903	1814	Jan.	27		Ontario	Thomas Tooley	S	Discharged	Dec.	6	1814	Ontario
904	1814	Apr.	14			Emanuel Holmes	S	Run away	Dec.	2	1814	Ontario
905	1814	Jan.	31		Ontario	James Brown 2nd	OS	Discharged	Dec.	6	1814	Ontario
906	1813	Dec.	23		Ontario	Philip Holiday	BY	Discharged	Dec.	6	1814	Ontario
907	1814	Mar.	15		Ontario	Michael Mathis	S	Discharged	Feb.	28	1815	Ontario
908	1813	Feb.	10			James Brown 3rd	S	Discharged	Feb.	18	1815	73.52½
909	1814	Feb.	2		Ontario	Edward Brown	S	Discharged	Dec.	6	1814	Ontario
910	1814	Aug.	25			Peter Blakeman	S					
911	1814	May	4			Samuel Haynie	MM	Run away	Jan.	13	1815	
912	1814	May	3			Robert M. Hambleton	SM	Discharged	Nov.	15	1814	
913	1814	July	12			Thomas Cooper	MM					
914	1814	Jan.	24	Apr. 7	Ontario	John Paulson	S					

Abbreviations: AG, Assistant Gunner; AR, Armourer; BT, Boatswain; BY, Boy; CA, Carpenter; CK, Cook; CL, Clerk; CO, Commandant; GB, Gunner's Boy; G, Gunner; GM, Gunner's Mate; LA, Landsman; LT, Lieutenant; MM, Master's Mate; MS, Midshipman; OS, Ordinary Seaman; P, Purser; PL, Pilot; QM, Quartermaster; S, Seaman; SM, Sailing Master; ST, Steward; SU, Surgeon.
*Run from Ontario & taken in Patuxent by flotilla marines.

No.	Entry Year	Entry Month	Entry Day	Appear on board	From where	Name	Station	Discharged, dead, or run away	When Month	When Day	When Year	Whither or for what reason / pay due
915	1814	Mar.	12	Apr. 7		Henry Amby	CK	Discharged	Apr.	1	1815	258.72
916	1814	June	7		Ontario	Jesse Nicholson	S	Discharged	Dec.	6	1814	Ontario
917	1814	Sept.	15			Sam. A. Whittington	SM	Discharged	Dec.	25	1814	His request
918	1814	Feb.	12		Ontario	Joab Daniels	OS					
919	1813	Feb.	6		137	John Jacobs 2nd	S	Discharged	Feb.	6	1815	115.80
920	1814	Mar.	22			James Kirby 2nd	OS	Discharged	Apr.	1	1815	69.56
921	1814	Aug.	15			George Abbot	OS	Discharged	Apr.	1	1815	50.56
922					Fort	James Bowie						
923	1813	Dec.	22			John Denny	S	Discharged	Dec.	6	1814	Ontario
924	1814	Jan.	24			Emanuel Huff (Kuff)	S	Run away	Aug.	26	1814	Bladenbg tkn later Flotilla marines
925	1814	Apr.	1			James Ellis	OS	Discharged	Apr.	1	1815	75.2
926						Richard Johnson						
927	1814	Jan.	24		Ontario	John (Illegible)	S	Died	Aug.	24	1814	Killed at Bladensburg
928	1814	Jan.	6		Ontario	William Denight	BY	Discharged	Dec.	6	1814	For Ontario
929						Richard Suitor	MS	Run away				
930	1814	Feb.	10		Ontario	James Hooper	S	Died	Sept.	1	1815	From wound at Bladensburg
931	1814	Aug.	21			William Martin	BT	Discharged	Apr.	1	1815	121.79. See entry 844
932	1814	Feb.	4		Ontario	Timothy Denight	S	Run away	Apr.	17	1814	
933					Ontario	Thomas Butcher		Run away	Apr.	17	1814	976

No.	Year	Month	Day	Name	Vessel	Rank	Status	Month	Day	Year	Notes
934	1814	Jan.	22	John Brant	Ontario	S	Run away	Aug.	25	1814	Bladensburg
935	1814	Jan.	24	James Harvey	Ontario	S	Run away	Apr.	21	1814	
936	1814	Feb.	5	Thomas Lang	Ontario	GM					
937	1814	Mar.	15	William Brown	Ontario	S					
938	1814	Mar.	15	George Miller	Ontario	MM/SM					
939	1814	Feb.	5	Nathan Townsend		S	Discharged	Apr.	1	1815	148.7½
940	1814	Mar.	13	Thomas Hill	Ontario	OS					
941	1814	Feb.	23	George Cain	Ontario	S					
942	1814	Jan.	1	Thomas Davis	Ontario	S		Aug.	8	1814	Per standing command at sea
943	1813	Jan.	20	Asa Holbrook	Shark	OS					
944	1814	July	2	Daniel Quigins		MM	Discharged	Apr.	1	1814	
945	1814	July	3	Samueal Peale		MM	Discharged	Dec.	23	1814	
946	1813	Dec.	23	John Nichols 2nd	Ontario	OS	Discharged	Dec.	6	1814	Ontario
947				John T. Winder							
948				John Baggate							
949	1813	Nov.	29	John Shephard	Ontario	OS					
950	1814	Jan.	3	William Moor	Ontario	OS					
951	1813	Dec.	31	Zachariah Fuller	Ontario	S	Died	May	22	1814	
952	1814	Dec.	5	James Mullinex	Ontario	OS	Discharged	Dec.	6	1814	Ontario
953	1814	Jan.	22	John Davison	Ontario	S	Run away				
954	1814	Jan.	28	John Baxter	Ontario	S					
955	1814	Feb.	7	Joseph Godfrey	Ontario	S					

Abbreviations: AG, Assistant Gunner; AR, Armourer; BT, Boatswain; BY, Boy; CA, Carpenter; CK, Cook; CL, Clerk; CO, Commandant; GB, Gunner's Boy; G, Gunner; GM, Gunner's Mate; LA, Landsman; LT, Lieutenant; MM, Master's Mate; MS, Midshipman; OS, Ordinary Seaman; P, Purser; PL, Pilot; QM, Quartermaster; S, Seaman; SM, Sailing Master; ST, Steward; SU, Surgeon.

No.	Entry Year	Month	Day	Appear on board	From where	Name	Station	Discharged, dead, or run away	When Month	Day	Year	Whither or for what reason / pay due
956	1814	Feb.	17		Ontario	Pursel Newbold	OS					Prisoner
957	1814	Feb.	17		Ontario	Adam Bastian	OS					Prisoner
958	1814	Aug.	20			Robert Taylor alias Tyler	S	Discharged	Apr.	1	1815	76.51
959	1814	Aug.	25			(Negro) David Bell	OS	Discharged	Apr.	1	1815	44.29
960	1814	Aug.	25			Joseph Peck	OS	Discharged	Apr.	1	1815	46.0
961	1814	Aug.	25			John Sauer	OS	Discharged	Apr.	1	1815	43.74
962	1814	Oct.	29	See 533		Samuel Wingate	CA	Discharged	Apr.	1	1815	66.83
963	1814	Apr.	29			Frank B. Fedrolph	S	Discharged	Apr.	1	1815	92.39
964	1814	Aug.	19			Peter Martin	S	Discharged	Apr.	1	1815	63.60
965	1814	Aug.	3			John Murr	OS	Discharged	Apr.	1	1815	73.29
966	1814	July	9			John Edmonds (?)	S	Discharged	Apr.	1	1815	43.9
967	1814	Feb.	1			Hugh Perry	LA/BY	Discharged	Apr.	1	1815	141.66
968	1814	Nov.	21			Daniel H. Stover	MS	Discharged	Apr.	1	1815	55.44
969	1814	Nov.	21			George Hyatt	MS	Discharged	Apr.	1	1815	68.6
970	1814	July	24	Sept. 11		William W. Polk	SM	Discharged	Dec.	2	1814	From the Station
971	1814	Apr.	2			Joseph Wiseman	MS	Discharged	Apr.	1	1815	42.0
972	1814	Aug.	6			Joseph Jarboe	MM	Discharged	Dec.	16	1814	See entry 827
973	1814	May	5			Thomas N. Harvey	G	Discharged	Jan.	11	1815	85.69. See entry 581
974	1814	May	19			Thomas Woodford	G	Discharged	Dec.	21	1814	
975	1814	Sept.	8			Stephen Guilford (Fullford)	OS	Discharged	Apr.	1	1815	118.0

No.	Month	Year	Age	Vessel/Prior	Name	Rating	Disposition	Month	Day	Year	Remarks
976	Apr.	1814	15		Thomas Butcher	OS	Run away				See entry 933
977	May	1814	17		Joshua Beaty	ST	Discharged	Jan.	8	1815	See entry 747
978	Dec.	1814	27	Ontario	John Stines	BT	Discharged	Apr.	1	1815	104.50 sub. for Levin Wingate
979	Jan.	1815	9		John Rutter	MS	Discharged	Apr.	1	1815	54.6
980	Jan.	1815	9		Edward Rutter	MM	Discharged	Apr.	1	1815	50.63
981	Dec.	1814	12		Joseph M. Byrus	MM	Discharged	Apr.	1	1815	87.34
982	Jan.	1815	12		William Hook	BT	Discharged	Apr.	1	1815	114.26 Sub./John Frazier 649
983	Jan.	1815	23		Thomas Cochran	MM	Discharged	Apr.	1	1815	108.20 Sub./ Thomas Cooper See entry for 913
984	May	1814	18		John McDonough	BT	Discharged	Jan.	24	1815	See entry 442
985	Mar.	1814	28		Urban Rice	ST	Discharged	Feb.	15	1815	Stolen prsoner (?)
986	May	1814	28		John Pritchard	BT	Discharged	Feb.	2	1814/5	
987	July	1814	8	See 293	William Achison	SM	Discharged	Apr.	1	1815	476.43
988	July	1814	5		James H. Martin	SM	Discharged	Apr.	1	1815	486.41
989	Apr.	1814	16		James Dixon	ST	Discharged	Apr.	1	1815	
990	Apr.	1814	16		John S. Skinner	P					
991	June	1814	22		Solomon Rodman	SM	Discharged	Apr.	1	1815	426.6½
992	Sept.	1814	13		Jeremiah Grandison	CK	Discharged	Mar.	15	1815	44.32
993	Jan.	1815	18		Jacob Turner	G	Discharged	Apr.	1	1815	133.46
994	June	1814	6	See 303	John Oram	MM	Discharged	Apr.	1	1815	221.88
995	July	1814	6	See 436	Nathan Chapman	CK	Discharged	Apr.	1	1815	157.51

Abbreviations: AG, Assistant Gunner; AR, Armourer; BT, Boatswain; BY, Boy; CA, Carpenter; CK, Cook; CL, Clerk; CO, Commandant; GB, Gunner's Boy; G, Gunner; GM, Gunner's Mate; LA, Landsman; LT, Lieutenant; MM, Master's Mate; MS, Midshipman; OS, Ordinary Seaman; P, Purser; PL, Pilot; QM, Quartermaster; S, Seaman; SM, Sailing Master; ST, Steward; SU, Surgeon.

| No. | Entry | | | From where | Appear on board | Name | Station | Discharged, dead, or run away | When | | | Whither or for what reason / pay due |
	Year	Month	Day						Month	Day	Year	
996	1814	May	20		See 735	Robert Bromwell	BT	Discharged	Apr.	1	1815	211.80
997	1815	Mar.	9		See 737	Daniel Crocker	S	Discharged	Apr.	1	1815	57.83
998	1814	Dec.	27		See 653	Thomas Mahool	G	Discharged	Apr.	1	1815	143.26
999	1814	June	25		See 129	Isaac Martin	CK	Discharged	Oct.	1	1814	56.17
1000	1814	July	10		See 337	Henry M. Horn	ST/PL	Discharged	Apr.	1	1815	170.60

Abbreviations: AG, Assistant Gunner; AR, Armourer; BT, Boatswain; BY, Boy; CA, Carpenter; CK, Cook; CL, Clerk; CO, Commandant; GB, Gunner's Boy; G, Gunner; GM, Gunner's Mate; LA, Landsman; LT, Lieutenant; MM, Master's Mate; MS, Midshipman; OS, Ordinary Seaman; P, Purser; PL, Pilot; QM, Quartermaster; S, Seaman; SM, Sailing Master; ST, Steward; SU, Surgeon.

Cost and Type of Materials and Workmanship for Building and
Equipping the Row Galley *Black Snake*

In 1813 Secretary of the Navy William Jones directed that the U.S. Navy galley *Black Snake*, built at the Washington Navy Yard, be employed as the model for all barges to be built for the Chesapeake Flotilla. It is probable that the galley's content and equipment also served as a model for the standard barge outfit. The listing below is extrapolated from the inventory and costs record incurred in building and fielding *Black Snake*.

Article 1: Materials & workmanship, in the hulls, masts, spars, sweeps, with small boats & oars, &c

2952 feet 1½ pine planks @ 4½ cents	$ 132.84	
375 feet 3 white oak planks @ 9 cents	33.75	
765 feet 3 white oak planks @ 10½ cents	80.32½	
327 feet 4 white oak planks @ 12 cents	39.24	
105 feet 6 white oak planks @ 18 cents	18.90	
525 feet 1 white oak plank @ 3 cents	15.75	
30 white oak knees 180 inches @ 30 cents	54.00	
17 white oak knees 158 inches @ 45 cents	71.0	445.90½
222 lbs. oakum @ 6 cents	13.32	
1 ⅔ barrel naval stores @ $3.60	6.00	19.32
1 main mast	4.00	
making main mast 37 feet long 10 inches diameter 370 @ 3 cents	11.10	
1 foremast	3.80	
making foremast 35 feet long 9½ inches diameter 332½ @ 3 cents	9.97½	
1 main and 1 fore yard, cost and making	15.24	
3 booms with oak jaws	9.30	
1 main topmast	2.31	
1 fore topmast	1.92	
1 main topsail yard	1.53	
1 fore topsail yard	1.33	
2 manacles	1.68	
25 white oak horn cleats @ 15 cents	3.45	
24 white oak stop cleats @ 5 cents	1.20	
44 sweeps 1947 feet pine, reduced measure @ 3 cents	58.41	
370 feet white pine, for store rooms &c @ 3 cents	11.25	

Article 1: Materials for Hull & workmanship—continued

350 feet cedar – rood of awning @ 3½ cents	12.25	
20 ash stantions – to room of awning @ 50 cents	10.00	158.74½
Canvas covering to awning and curtains 4 bolts Russia ducks @ $30	120.00	
Making up canvas covering to awning @ $4.00	16.00	
4 lbs. twine @ 80 cents	3.20	139.20
1 pump 5 feet @ 50 cents	2.50	
2 sets of boxes for pump	2.75	
1 pump brake	.75	6.00
Amount carried over $		769.17
Ironwork: Bolts, rings, spikes, nails &c &c.	254.97	
Eye and ring bolts	11.14	
Rudder braces and gudgeons	8.46	
Yoke tiller with brass sheaves 72 lbs @ 20 cents	14.40	
Thole pins for sweeps, 44 @ 50 cents	22.00	
Hinges, screws bolts &c. for store rooms	3.40	314.37
Paints &c: 5 kegs white lead @ $6.50	32.50	
4 lbs. lamp black @ 12½ cents	.50	
50 lbs. Spanish whiting @ 3½ cents	1.75	
5 lbs. literage @ 25 cents	1.25	
10 lbs. Spanish brown @ 6 cents	.60	
15 gallons linseed oil @ 60 cents	15.00	
4 gallons spirits turpentine @ 60 cents	2.40	54.00
Workmanship, viz.		
Carpenters & boat builders wages	913.74	
Caulker & laborers wages	114.14	
Joiners work	65.00	
Mast makers, making 44 sweeps @ $1.00	44.00	
Painters 20 days work … Various	23.70	1,160.58
		2298.12

Article 2 – Sails, rigging anchor & c.

Main & fore sails 6 bolts American duck @ $22.50	135.00	
Main and fore topsail 2½ Ravens duck @ $16.00	40.00	
Bolt rope lbs. @ 20 cents	9.20	
Twine 8½ lbs. @ 80 cents	6.80	
Welded thimbles 12 @ 6 cents	.72	
Making & fitting sails with 8½ bolts canvas @ $4.00	34.00	225.72
Rigging masthead pendants & tackles 107¼ (lbs. ?)		
Tyes, hallyards, sheets &c. 200 (ft. ?)		
Rudder & tiller ropes & stoppers 12		
Lanyards &c for sweeps 37¾/357¼ @ 17 cents	60.73	

Article 2: Rigging &c—continued

Pendant hallyards, white line 6 @ 62½ cents	3.75	
Half tanned leather, fitting rigging &c	7.92	
Old canvas 20 yards fitting rigging @ 20 cents	4.00	
1 cable 90 fathoms 3½ inch 202¾ lb.		
1 cable 82 fathoms 5 inch 415¼ inch 618 lb @ 17 cents	105.06	
1 anchor with iron stock 238 lb		
1 anchor with iron stock 128 lb – 366 lbs @ 15 cents	54.90	

Amount carried over	$	236.36	769.17

12 single 8 inch blocks bushed @ 70 cents	$	8.40	
16 single 6 inch blocks bushed @ 50 cents		8.00	
8 single 5 inch blocks bushed @ 25 cents		2.00	
10 hooks and thimbles 27 lbs. @ 20 cents		5.40	
29 open and welded thimbles @ 6 cents		1.74	
Caps, travellers, yard straps, &c. 111 lbs. @ 14 cents		13.87½	
Sheaves, sheaving & coppering lower & topmasts		6.00	
Sheave and sheaving davit for the anchors		1.00	287.77½

	$508.49½

Article 3: Armaments & gunners stores, viz.

1 long cannon, 18 pounder	230.00
1 sliding carriage for 18 pounder complete with bed & quoin	100.00
2 breechings, 9 fathoms 7 inch 95 lb.	
2 tackle falls & strapping, 18 fathoms 3 inch 37 lb.	
2 tackle falls & strapping 11 fathoms 2½ inch 13 = 145 lb 2.17	24.65
4 double 10 inch bushed blocks @ $1.94	7.76
4 single 10 inch bushed blocks @ 97 cents	3.88
2 large hooks and thimbles for breechings 31 lb. @ 16 cents	4.96
8 hooks and thinbles for tackles 28 lb. @ 16 cents	4.48
1 cannon lock, fitted	14.50
1 rammer and sponge	2.50
1 worm and ladle	2.75
3 gunners handspikes iron shod @ $1.50	4.50
1 mallet and spike	1.20
1 pouch barrel copper hooped & leathered	3.75
1 leather cartrdige passing box	2.50
200 quill tubes filled @ 2.80	5.60
1 powder horn, copper mounted	1.25
2 priming wires @ 12½ cents	.25
1 boring bitt	.25
1 training bar to carriage 10½ lb @ 16 cents	1.68
80 round shot, 18 pound @ 65 cents	52.00
30 stand grape, 18 pound 540 lbs. @ 8 cents	43.20
10 cannister, 18 pound 180 lbs. @ 10 cents	18.00
80 flannel cartrdiges, 18 pound, filled @ $3.96¼	317.00

Article 3: Armament &c—continued

20 lbs match rope @ 67 cents	13.40	
100 wads @ 5 cents	5.00	
2 tube boxes and belts @ $1.00	2.00	
Amount carried over	$ 867.06	
2 Match tubes @ $1.25	2.50	
2 lbs. putty	.16	
1 apron and cap for lock 24 lbs lead @ 18 cents	4.32	
1 tompion	.10	
1 carronade 32 pounder	160.00	
1 sliding carriage for 32 pounder complete	100.00	
1 carronade lock fitted	14.00	
1 elevating screw and brass cap	12.00	
4 tackles 22 fathoms 2½ inch rope 26 lbs @ 17 cents	4.42	
2 breechings 6 fathoms 7 inch rope 63 lbs @ 17 cents	10.71	
4 double 7 inch blocks bushed @ $1.10	4.40	
4 single 7 inch blocks bushed @ 55 cents	2.20	
10 hooks and thimbles 46 lbs. @ 16 cents	7.36	
1 worm and ladle for 32 pounder	3.00	
1 rammer and sponge for 32 pounder	2.50	
1 training bar 10 lbs @ 16 cents	1.60	
1 mallet and spike	1.20	
1 pouch barrel, copper hooped and leathered	3.50	
1 leather cartridge passing box	2.50	
1 powder horn, copper mounted	1.25	
1 priming wire and boring bitt	.37½	
1 carronade apron & 35 lbs lead @ 18 cents	4.30	
1 tompion for 32 pounder	.12½	
80 round shot for 32 pounder 2560 lbs @3-6/10 cents	92.16	
10 stand grape for 32 pounder 320 lbs @ 8 cents	25.60	
30 cannister for 32 pounder 960 lbs @ 10 cents	96.00	
100 wads for 32 pounder @ 8 cents	8.00	
80 flannel cartridges fitted @ $1.73¼	138.60	
2 match staffs @ 25 cents	.50	
3 powder chests lined with flannel	31.80	
copper hasps & staples for 3 powder chests	1.80	1604.04

Article 4: Small arms, armourers stores, &c.

36 muskets, bayonets & cartridge boxes with belts @ $12.00	432.00	
1800 musket balls cartridges filled @ $1.20	70.20	
150 flints	1.80	
30 boarding pikes @ $1.00	30.00	
40 cutlasses @ $2.00	80.00	
11 pair handcuffs @ $1.25	13.75	
Amount carried over	$ 627.75	

Article 4: Small arms, armourers stores, &c—continued

11 pair leg shackles and bolts	$ 16.50	
1 screw driver	.20	
3 smith's files	.75	
1 stone jug & 1 quart sweet oil	1.75	646.95

Article 5: Masters stores

1 wood compass	3.50	
1 American ensign 10 feet by 6	11.00	
1 American pendant 15 feet	1.50	
1 spyglass	10.00	
2 half hour glasses, solid joint @ $2.50	4.20	
1 hand trumpet	1.50	
1 horn lantern	3.00	
1 hand lead 5 lbs. @ 15 cents	.75	
1 hand lead line 6 lbs. @ 62½ cents	3.75	
1 grapling & chain 41 lbs @ 20 cents	8.20	
8 50 gallon casks @$4.50	36.00	
8 15 gallon breakers @ $2.00	16.00	
1 log reel	.75	
6 sail needles @ 3 cents	.18	
1 topping (?) needle	.04	
1 palm iron	.26	100.63

Article 6: Boatswains stores

1 Quisil (?) 2½ inch rope 150 lbs @ 17 cents	25.50	
4 boat hooks & staffs @ $1.25	5.00	
1 marline spike	1.00	
2 hickory brooms @ 12½ cents	.25	
4 scrubbing brushes @ 62¼ cents	2.50	34.25

Article 7: Carpenters stores

1 tool chest	3.00	
1 logger head 9 lbs @ 16 cents	1.44	
1 broad axe	3.00	
2 cold chisels @ 25 cents	.50	
1 claw hammer	.75	
2 nail gimblets @ 10 cents	.20	
2 lb. wrought nails @ 16 cents	.32	
100 pump tacks @ 60 cents	.06	9.27

Article 8: Cooks stores, &c

1 coffee pot	$ .75	
1 hatchet	.62½	
2 iron pots	1.80	
1 pair flesh forks and ladle	1.25	
1 frying pan	1.60	
1 grid box	1.87½	

1 tinder box, steel flints	.50	
1 tin funnel	.25	
1 tin lanthern	.75	
1 set tin measurers, quart, pint, ½ pint, ¼ pint	1.86	
1 set scales and weights	7.50	
1 iron fire lamp 36 lbs @ 20 cents	7.20	
1 iron ash pan 30 lbs @ 20 cents	6.00	
1 hand pump	3.00	
2 harness tubes @ $3.00	6.00	40.96

Contingencies

Scraping the hull, decks, &c.	10.00	
Masting, rigging, fitting rigging & bending sails	31.25	
Mounting the guns & lading all materials onboard	16.20	57.45

Recapitulation

Article 1. Hull and workmanship	$	2,298.12
Article 2. Sails, rigging, &c.		508.49½
Article 3. Armament &c.		1604.04
Article 4. Small arms & armourer stores		646.95
Article 5. Masters department stores		100.63
Article 6. Boatswains stores		34.25
Article 7. Carpenters stores		9.27
Article 8. Cooking utensils &c.		40.96
Contingencies		57.45
		$5,300.16½

Source: Thomas Tingey to Secretary of the Navy, 20 October 1813 (Cost of Outfit of Row Galley Black Snake), Letters Received by the Secretary of the Navy from Captains, 1805–1831, M 125, R 32, Vol. 32, National Archives.

Fleet Maneuver Exercises for the U.S. Chesapeake Flotilla

Commodore Barney prepared a small handwritten notebook illustrating the formations and manner in which the flotilla was to be managed as a fleet. The notebook's remains, just four pages of an estimated eight, were found lodged within the pages of the U.S. Flotilla Muster Book in the National Archives. The commodore's original text described at least nineteen maneuvers for the flotilla, seven of which (nos. 13 to 19) are extant in the notebook. These are accompanied by four diagrams. The diagrams show nine vessels, which are divided into three divisions. No. 13 describes and illustrates line forward motion of the line under close hauled sails. No. 14 describes the order of front, or forward motion, with wind aft. No. 15 describes the order of the chase. No. 16 describes the order of retreat. Nos. 17, 18, and 19, all text (not pictured), address sailing in line forward, following the wake of the preceding vessel, the normal placement of each division, and sailing in two columns. The illustrations here are courtesy of the National Archives and Records Administration, Washington, D.C.

Order of front, supposing the wind aft, or any cause that may be signaled, conserving the line of front

N[ote]. by this signal, the Vessels manoeuvre to place in a line aloof the wind, in order of N[o]s, but if the comm[ander] adds signal 17 to place the 2d division on the left, then the Vessels will place themselves with the N[o]s reversed, N[o]9 will take the place of N[o]1 on the right, and N[o]1 will take the extremity of the left line & so on according to N[o]. Then they will steer the course ordered —

15 Order of Chase, formed by two lines of close hawl, the form.n in the Center, the course wind aft. or large

16. Order of Retreat. formed by the two lines of close hawl the form.n to windward in the Center, the course, wind aft or large

African Americans from the Patuxent Valley Enlisted in the Royal Colonial Marine Corps

Name	Date	Owner	Location
1st Company			
Buey [Bucy, Bury, Bowie], James	June 12, 1814	Plater, John R.	St. Mary's County, St. Leonards Creek
Clarke, Randle	July 21, 1814	Unknown	Patuxent River
Cole, Job	June 5, 1814	Thompson, Peter W.	St. Mary's County, Patuxent River
Coventry [Covington], Alexander (Sandy)	August 1, 1814	Rawlings, Susan	Calvert County, Patuxent River
Cully [Cowley], Benjamin	July 17, 1814	Unknown	Calvert County, Patuxent River
Handy, William – **Sergeant**	July 27, 1814	Hopewell, James	St. Mary's County, Patuxent River
Jackson, Philip	July 18, 1814	Carroll, John Charles	Prince George's County, Upper Marlboro
Spawley, John	July 19, 1814	Unknown	Calvert County, Patuxent River
Wood, George [Joshua]	August 4, 1814	Unknown	Patuxent River
Wood, Joseph	June 12, 1814	Plater, John R.	St. Mary's County, Patuxent River
2nd Company			
Dawson, Woolsey [Holsey, Holdsworth]	July 16, 1814	Broome, Mary Ann	Patuxent River
Gant, Richard	June 19, 1814	Gant, Thomas C.	Calvert County
Gray, Benjamin*	July 13, 1814	Unknown	Patuxent River
Groves [Grose], Henry, 2nd	July 17, 1814	Unknown	Patuxent River
Mason, Ben	July 12, 1814	Brook, John J.	Calvert County, Patuxent River
Pam [Pain], Dymond	July 17, 1814	Parran, Jane	Calvert County, Patuxent River
Sewell, Peter	July 13, 1814	Somerville, W. & W.C.	Calvert County, Patuxent River

Name	Date	Owner	Location
Smith, Nat	July 14, 1814	Somerville, W. & W.C.	Calvert County, Patuxent River
Somwell [Somerville?], Francis	June 6, 1814	Somerville, W. & W.C.	Calvert County, Patuxent River
Speaks, Joseph	July 17, 1814	Billingsby, Thomas	Calvert County, Patuxent River
3rd Company			
Dukes, Sorney [Sorrow, Alexander]	September 4, 1814	Cox, Sarah	Calvert County
Gaines, Edward	July 21, 1814	Unknown	Patuxent River
Grace, Moses	July 18, 1814	Bond, James T.	Calvert County, Patuxent River
Handy, James	July 27, 1814	Unknown	Patuxent River
Jones, Prince	July 18, 1814	Williams, Benjamin	Calvert County, Patuxent River
Meynard, Daniel	July 18, 1814	Wilkinson, George	Calvert County, Patuxent River
Parker, Daniel	July 31, 1814	Unknown	Patuxent River
Sewell, John	July 13, 1814	Somerville, W. & W.C.	Calvert County, Patuxent River
Skinner, Guy**	July 17, 1814	Parrann [Parran?], Jane	Calvert County, Patuxent River
4th Company			
Brookes, John, 1st	August 2, 1814	Dawkins, William C.	Calvert County, St. Leonard's Creek
Butler, Barsle – **Sergeant**	July 13, 1814	Somerville, W. & W.C.	Calvert County, Patuxent River
Hoy, Sanuek	August 2, 1814	Dawkins, William C.	Calvert County, St. Leonard's Creek
Limbo, David	August 7, 1814	Unknown	Patuxent River
Patterson, William	August 2, 1814	Bourne, James E.	Calvert County, Patuxent River
Smith, Esau [Jesse]	August 8, 1814	Unknown	Patuxent River
5th Company			
Wiggin, Bessick – **Sergeant**	June 6, 1814	Ball, Thomas	Northumberland, Va., Patuxent River
6th Company			
Hall, John	August 30, 1814	Unknown	Patuxent River
Family Members Bought Off			
Boom, Robert***	July 12, 1814	Brook, John J.	Calvert County
Handy, Dolly	August 13, 1814	Gray, John M.	Calvert County
Handy, Sophy	August 13, 1814	Gray, John M.	Calvert County
Ransom, Hannah	September 1, 1814	Towny, Miles	Calvert County

Name	Date	Owner	Location
Sewll, Bill - Child	July 12, 1814	Somerville, W. & W.C.	Calvert County
Sewell, Clarissa - Child	July 12, 1814	Somerville, W. & W.C.	Calvert County
Sewell, Fanny - Child	July 12, 1814	Somerville, W. & W.C.	Calvert County
Sewell, Rachel - Child	July 12, 1814	Somerville, W. & W.C.	Calvert County
Turner, Ben - Child	July 18, 1814	Turner, Samuel	Calvert County

Source: John McNish Weiss, *The Merikens: Free Black American Settlers in Trinidad, 1815–1816* (London: McNish & Weiss, 2002).
*Moved to 4th Company.
**Freeman.
***With Ben Mason of 2nd Company.

Abbreviations

ASPMA	*American State Papers: Military Affairs*
ASPNA	*American State Papers: Naval Affairs*
Cockburn Papers	Admiral Sir George Cockburn Papers
CVSP	*Calendar of Virginia State Papers*
LC	Library of Congress, Washington, D.C.
MHS	Maryland Historical Society, Baltimore, Md.
NARA	National Archives and Record Service, Washington, D.C.
NW	*The Naval War of 1812: A Documentary History*
SNCL	Secretary of the Navy Confidential Letters Sent
SNLC	Secretary of the Navy Letters to Congress
SNLO	Secretary of the Navy Letters to Officers
SNCLR	Letters Received by the Secretary of the Navy: Captains' Letters
SNMLR	Letters Received by the Secretary of the Navy: Miscellaneous Letters

Chapter 1

Depredations of the Usual Character

1. William M. Marine, *The British Invasion of Maryland 1812–1815* (1913; rpt., Hatboro, Pa.: Tradition Press, 1965), 21.

2. G[ilbert] Auchinleck, *A History of the War Between Great Britain and the United States of America During the Years 1812, 1813 & 1814* (1855; rpt., Toronto, London, and Redwood City, Calif.: Arms and Armor Press and Pendragon House, 1972), 26.

3. Ibid., 37.

4. *Federal Republican*, June 20, 1812.

5. *Federal Gazette*, June 24, 1812; Marine, *The British Invasion*, 1–10.

6. Auchinleck, *A History of the War*, 43.

7. The number of enemy vessels captured by American privateers during the course of the war varies with the authorities cited. *Niles' Weekly Register* estimated the whole number of prizes taken at 2,500, of which 720 were recaptured, but was able to admit of a satisfactory accounting of only 1,634. Coggeshall, whose historic accuracy has occasionally been found wanting, places the number at somewhat in excess of 2,000. By an estimate of the merchants, manufacturers, and shipowners of the Port of Glasgow, at a meeting held on December 7, 1814, somewhat before the close of the war, it was stated that 800 vessels

had been taken. Emmons, who attempted to meticulously itemize the captures of every known American privateer that held a commission, along with their engagements, recaptures, and so on, has most often been the source cited in histories of the war. However, Cranwell and Crane, who more accurately documented 126 private-armed vessels operating out of Baltimore during the war, noted that only 53 were commissioned privateers, and accounted for more than 500 prizes. *Niles' Weekly Register*, 7:190; George Coggeshall, *History of American Privateers* (New York: privately printed, 1856); Marine, *The British Invasion*, 15; George F. Emmons, *The Navy of the United States from the Commencement, 1775 to 1853* (Washington, D.C.: Gideon and Co., 1853), 170–210.

8. Mary Barney, ed., *A Biographical Memoir of the Late Commodore Joshua Barney: From Autobiographical Notes and Journals in Possession of His Family, and Other Authentic Sources* (Boston: Gray and Bowen, 1832), 252; Fred W. Hopkins Jr., *Tom Boyle, Master Privateer* (Cambridge, Md.: Tidewater Publishers, 1976), 13–55.

9. Marine, *The British Invasion*, 16.

10. *Daily National Intelligencer,* March 11, 1813.

11. "Declaration of His Majesty's Government," January 9, 1813, *Naval Chronicle* (London), 1749–1818, 29:141–49; *Buffalo Gazette*, in Earnest A. Cruickshank, *Documentary History of the Campaigns upon the Niagara Frontier in 1813 and 1814,* 9 vols. (Welland, Ont.: Lundy's Lane Historical Society, n.d.), 5:122; Glenn Tucker, *Poltroons and Patriots: A Popular Account of the War of 1812* (Indianapolis: Bobbs-Merrill Co., 1954), 287.

12. Lords Commissioners of the Admiralty to Admiral Sir John B. Warren, December 26, 1812, *NW,* 1:633–34.

13. Auchinleck, *A History of the War,* 43–44; Marine, *The British Invasion,* 21.

14. Marine, *The British Invasion,* 16.

15. Spencer A. Tucker, ed., *Naval Warfare: An International Encyclopedia,* 3 vols. (Santa Barbara, Calif.: ABC-Clio, 2002), 1:232; Walter Lord, *The Dawn's Early Light* (New York: W. W. Norton & Co., Inc., 1972), 50–51. That Cockburn was not averse to severe punishment, which was frequently meted out for even the slightest infractions of conduct, is exemplified by the punishment of an ordinary seaman belonging to HBMS *Narcissus* ordered by court martial on February 17, 1813. The seaman was to receive two hundred lashes with a cat of nine tails on the bare back. After receiving forty-eight lashes alongside *Narcissus,* the prisoner was "then to be towed by the boats ordered to attend" to receive in succession aboard six other ships of the fleet between twenty-four and twenty seven lashes on each. The punishment could be stopped by *Narcissus*'s surgeon only if the "prisoner cannot bear more with safety." Rear Admiral George Cockburn, General Memo, February 17, 1813, Cockburn Papers, vol. 43, LC.

16. Marine, *The British Invasion,* 22, 27.

17. Ibid., 28, 29.

18. Ibid., 32; Auchinleck, *A History of the War,* 264–72.

19. Marine, *The British Invasion,* 52.

20. Henry, Earl Bathurst to Colonel Sir Thomas Sidney Beckwith, March 20, 1813, *NW,* 2:325.

21. Auchinleck, *A History of the War,* 273–78.

22. James Jarboe Papers, MHS.

23. Ibid.; Arthur Hecht, "The Post Office Department in St. Mary's County in the War of 1812," *Maryland Historical Magazine* 52, no. 2 (June 1957): 146.

24. G. N. Causins and James Forrest to Major James Thomas, April 9, 1813, Gift Collection, Box G 176/260, Hall of Records, Annapolis, Md.

25. Edwin W. Beitzell, *The Jesuit Missions of St. Mary's County, Maryland* (1960; rpt., Abell, Md.: privately printed, 1976), 158.

26. Ibid.

27. Ibid., 158–59.

28. Hecht, "The Post Office Department," 146.

29. Edwin W. Beitzell, "A Short History of St. Clements Island," *Chronicles of St. Mary's* 6, no. 11 (November 1958): 246; Regina Combs Hammett, *History of St. Mary's County, Maryland* (Ridge, Md.: privately printed, 1977), 95; Admiral Sir John B. Warren to First Secretary of the Admiralty John W. Crocker, July 29, 1813, *NW*, 2:369.

30. Marine, *The British Invasion*, 53; *Niles' Weekly Register* 4, no. 22 (July 31, 1813), and 4, no. 23 (August 7, 1813).

31. *Niles' Weekly Register* 4, no. 22 (July 31, 1813), and 4, no. 23 (August 7, 1813).

32. *Daily National Intelligencer*, September 25, 1813.

33. Ibid.

34. "Cockburn Memo," June 1, 1813, Cockburn Papers, vol. 24, LC; Captain John R. Lumley to Rear Admiral George Cockburn, June 12, 1813, Cockburn Papers, vol. 38, LC; Commander Frederick Hickey to Rear Admiral George Cockburn, June 15, 1813, Cockburn Papers, vol. 38, LC.

35. Beitzell, *Jesuits*, 160.

36. "A Personal Narrative of Events by Sea and Land, from the Year 1800 to 1815 Concluding with a Narrative of Some of the Principal Events in the Chesapeake and South Carolina, in 1814 and 1815," *Chronicles of St. Mary's* 8, no. 1 (January 1960): 9; Lord, *The Dawn's Early Light*, 27.

37. "Personal Narrative," 9.

38. Marine, *The British Invasion*, 53.

39. Ibid., 2, 3, 197.

40. Ibid., 196.

41. Ibid., 3, 197.

42. Hecht, "The Post Office Department," 143.

43. Hammett, *History of St. Mary's County*, 96.

44. Marine, *The British Invasion*, 53, 54.

45. Ibid., 54–56; Captain Robert Barrie to Mrs. George Clayton, September 4, 1813, *NW*, 2:385.

46. Marine, *The British Invasion*, 57; Lieutenant George Pedlar to Captain Robert Barrie, November 5, 1813, *NW*, 2:395; Captain Robert Barrie to Admiral Sir John B. Warren, November 14, 1813, *NW*, 2:395.

47. Beitzell, *Jesuits*, 160–61.

48. Vice Admiral Sir John B. Warren to Sir George Prevost, September 21, 1813, C680/97, Public Archives of Canada, Ottawa; Vice Admiral Sir John B. Warren to Robert S. Dundas, 2d Viscount Melville, August 24, 1813, Warren Papers, National Maritime

Museum, Greenwich, England; Alfred T. Mahan, *Sea Power in Its Relation to the War of 1812*, 2 vols. (Boston: Little, Brown & Co., 1919), 2:21; Henry Adams, *The War of 1812*, ed. H. A. DeWeerd (Harrisburg, Pa.: Infantry Journal Press, 1944), 129.

49. Marine, *The British Invasion*, 54–56; Barrie to Warren, November 14, 1813, *NW,* 2:395–96.

Chapter 2
No Other Mode of Defense

1. For the early life and naval career of Joshua Barney, see Mary Barney, ed., *A Biographical Memoir of the Late Commodore Joshua Barney: From Autobiographical Notes and Journals in Possession of His Family, and Other Authentic Sources* (Boston: Gray and Bowen, 1832); Hulbert Footner, *Sailor of Fortune: The Life and Adventures of Commodore Barney, U.S.N.* (New York: Harper & Brothers, 1940); and Louis Arthur Norton, *Joshua Barney: Hero of the Revolution and 1812* (Annapolis, Md.: Naval Institute Press, 2000).

2. Mary Barney, *A Biographical Memoir,* 250.

3. Ibid., 250–51.

4. Ibid., 252–53; Log of the *Rossie,* U.S. Naval Academy Library, Annapolis, Md. The *Rossie* log has been published in full in *NW,* 1:248–60. A very abbreviated and much quoted form of the log appears in J. Thomas Scharf, *The Chronicles of Baltimore: Being a Complete History of "Baltimore Town" and Baltimore City from the Earliest Time to the Present Time* (Baltimore: Turnbull Brothers, 1874), 358–59.

5. Mary Barney, *A Biographical Memoir,* 252; Footner, *Sailor of Fortune,* 257.

6. Gilbert Byron, *The War of 1812 on the Chesapeake Bay* (Baltimore, Md.: Maryland Historical Society, 1964), 64; *Daily National Intelligencer,* May 25, 1813; Scott S. Sheads, *The Rockets' Red Glare: The Maritime Defense of Baltimore in 1814* (Centreville, Md.: Tidewater Publishers, 1986), 12, 15–16, 20–21.

7. Gilbert Byron, *The War of 1812 on the Chesapeake Bay* (Baltimore, Md.: Maryland Historical Society, 1964), 64; *Daily National Intelligencer,* May 25, 1813; Scott S. Sheads, *The Rockets' Red Glare: The Maritime Defense of Baltimore in 1814* (Centreville, Md.: Tidewater Publishers, 1986), 15–16, 20–21.

8. *Daily National Intelligencer,* June 5, 1813.

9. Ibid.

10. Ibid.

11. Ibid.; Joshua Barney, "Defence of the Chesapeake Bay," July 4, 1814, James Madison Papers, ser. 1, vol. 52, no. 73, LC.

12. Secretary of the Navy William Jones to President James Madison, June 6, 1813, James Madison Papers, ser. I, vol. 52, no. 50, LC.

13. Ibid.

14. Secretary of the Navy William Jones to Senator Samuel Smith, June 17, 1813, RG 45, SNLC, vol. 2, 177–78, NARA. The balance of the citations in this section are from this source.

15. Barney, "Defence of the Chesapeake Bay." In his lifetime, Barney would be credited with fighting at least twenty-six engagements, far more than John Paul Jones, who was

later adopted as the Father of the U.S. Navy. The balance of the citations in this section are from this source.

16. U.S. Statutes at Large, 3:3.

17. Secretary of the Navy William Jones to Joshua Barney, August 20, 1813, RG 45, SNLO 1813, vol. 11, 56–58 (M 149, R 11), NARA.

18. Ibid.

19. Ibid.

20. Ibid.

21. Mary Barney, *A Biographical Memoir,* 253.

Chapter 3
A Commander of Capacity and Influence

1. Secretary of the Navy William Jones to Joshua Barney, August 20, 1813, RG 45, SNLO 1813, vol. 11, 56–58 (M 149, R 11), NARA.

2. Ibid.

3. Secretary of the Navy William Jones to Acting Master Commandant Joshua Barney, August 27, 1813, RG 45, SNLO, vol. 11, 62–64 (M 149, R 11), NARA. The design plan of the new barges had been produced by Naval Constructor James Doughty, probably in his office at the Washington Navy Yard. Howard Chapelle, in his classic *History of the American Sailing Navy,* states that the vessels were double-enders, somewhat like large whaleboats, armed with either a single gun or with one long gun aft and a carronade forward. The barges were sometimes rigged for sailing with one or two lateen sails, but the smaller were often fitted for rowing only. The first design was for a 50-foot barge, made in June 1813, and building, according to Chapelle, began on the plan in July and August. The new design called for boats 50 feet long, 12-foot molded beam, and 3½-foot total depth. In September Doughty made another design, this time for a barge 75 feet over all, 15-foot beam, and 4-foot depth in hold. The boats built from it were usually rigged with one or 2 lateen sails. These barges were intended for Lakes Champlain and Ontario, the Chesapeake, and rivers, and were not in any way seagoing coastal defense gunboats. The American barges were, in fact, the counterparts of the large launches carried by some British blockading ships for boat attacks and raids inshore. Chapelle's description, at least regarding the sails and rigging of the barges, may be somewhat in error. According to bills later paid to contractors engaged in building barges for the flotilla, both on the Eastern Shore and at Baltimore, some of the vessels would appear to have been square rigged. The 75-foot craft carried 32-foot tall masts 8 inches in diameter, topmasts 17 feet tall and 4½ inches in diameter, a main yard 20 feet in length by 5½ inches in diameter, and a topsail yard 10 feet in length and 4½ inches in diameter. A typical second-class barge carried a single 24-foot tall mast 7½ inches in diameter, a topmast 11 feet tall and 3¾ inches in diameter, a main yard 32 feet in length by 3¾ inches in diameter, and a topsail yard 15 feet in length and 2¾ inches in diameter. Secretary Jones later reported that at least several of the first class vessels employed 2 lugsails and carried 40 oars. A lugsail is a quadrilateral sail with the forward end shorter than the aft edge, with the yard set obliquely to the mast. The lateen

sail, which Chapelle states the barges were usually outfitted with, were long triangular sails attached by their foremost edges to long yards that were hoisted at an angle to the masts. A similar sail with the extreme foremost corner cut off to make it quadrilateral was also occasionally referred to as a lateen sail, wherein the confusion may lie. James Beatty's Accounts in the Fourth Auditor of the U.S., May 15, 1814. Bills paid to Joseph Kemp and Perry Spence.

Reference is made in at least one communication between Secretary Jones and Commodore Barney that the vessels might be outfitted with leeboards. A single pencil drawing, included in this book's illustrations, showing eight barges lined up behind sunken vessels between Fort McHenry and the Lazaretto during the September 1814 British attack on the fort suggest that the barges were indeed fitted with leeboards on both sides of the craft. The vessels are also fitted with awnings to shelter the crews from the weather.

4. Jones to Barney, August 20, 1813.

5. Mary Barney, *A Biographical Memoir,* 254; Hulbert Footner, *Sailor of Fortune: The Life and Adventures of Commodore Barney, U.S.N.* (New York: Harper & Brothers, 1940), 263; Louis Arthur Norton, *Joshua Barney: Hero of the Revolution and 1812* (Annapolis, Md.: Naval Institute Press, 2000), 170–71.

6. *Boston Gazette,* September 11, 1813; Mary Barney, *A Biographical Memoir,* 254–55.

7. Acting Master Commandant Joshua Barney to Secretary of the Navy William Jones, August 31, 1813, RG45, SNMLR, 1813, vol. 5, no. 154 (M 124, R 57), and vol. 6, no. 3½ (M 124, R 58), NARA.

8. Ibid.

9. Defense of Baltimore Papers, MS 2304, R 2, MHS, Baltimore, Md.; Howard I. Chapelle, *The History of The American Sailing Navy: The Ships and Their Development* (New York: W. W. Norton and Co., Inc., 1949), 246. The row galley *Vigilant* first appears in the historic record in the muster of naval vessels fielded by the City of Baltimore for its own defense during the spring of 1813. Following the series of devastating raids by British naval forces in the upper Chesapeake, and with but a single U.S. Navy gunboat available to defend the Patapsco against the enemy, the city had moved quickly to field its own naval force. A flotilla of six armed barges and the recently acquired *Vigilant* were soon afloat in the Patapsco River. The galley, and presumably the remainder of the flotilla, appears to have made its entrance upon the scene about mid-April as evidenced by city payment records and later efforts by the city to secure federal reimbursements for expenses incurred while it was in municipal service. It is possible that *Vigilant* was originally built as a large schooner-rigged revenue cutter in 1811 by Benjamin Marble at Newport, Rhode Island, and subsequently cut down for service as a row galley for the city's defense in 1813 and prior to its acquisition for Barney's flotilla. This city force was attached to the Sea Fencibles, then under the overall command of Captain M. Simmones Bunbury, based at the Lazaretto, on the north shore of the Patapsco opposite Fort McHenry. Captain James Chaytor was to serve as commodore of the fleet, and Captain John Kiddell (Keddell) would serve as the first commander of *Vigilant,* although he would later be replaced by Captain John Rutter. Abraham Boyche would serve as the galley gunner, and Richard Berry as boatswain. The Sea Fencibles, who boarded *Vigilant* to serve as marines about July 1813, were paid $15 a month, while the galley's crewmen were to receive $16 a month.

There remains some confusion as to whether the barges Barney first examined were those of the Baltimore flotilla or the U.S. vessels. Document no. 39, 20th Congress, 1st Session, House of Representatives; Treasury Department, *Report of the Secretary of the Treasury on the Memorial of the Mayor and City of Baltimore, for Pay and Allowance for Money Advanced and Supplies Furnished During the Late War January 2, 1828. Referred to the Committee of Claims* (Washington: Printed by Gales & Seaton, 1828), 12–17.

10. Footner, *Sailor of Fortune*, 263–64; Naval History Division, *Dictionary of American Naval Fighting Ships*, 8 vols. (Washington, D.C.: Navy Department, 1959), 1:68.

11. Secretary of the Navy William Jones to Acting Master Commandant Joshua Barney, September 2, 1813, RG 45, SNLO, 1813, vol. 11, 72–74 (M 149, R 11), NARA. By March 1814, with recruitment lagging, it was advertised that seamen would be advanced four months' wages upon enlisting. *Baltimore Commercial & Daily Advertiser*, March 16, 1814.

12. Acting Master Commandant Joshua Barney to Secretary of the Navy William Jones, March 1, 1814, RG 45, SNMLR, 1814, vol. 2, no. 57 (M 124, R 61), in *NW*, 3:36; Flotilla Muster, NARA. Huffington had served as first mate, and Gorsuch as second mate aboard the Baltimore 6-gun privateer *Lottery*, which had been captured in Lynnhaven Bay after a fight with HBMS *Belvidera* in February 1813. *American Watchman & Delaware Republican*, February 27, 1813.

13. Footner, *Sailor of Fortune*, 263; *ASPNA*, 1:305–6.

14. Footner, *Sailor of Fortune*, 263; *ASPNA*, 1:305–6; *Report of the Secretary of the Treasury on the Memorial of the Mayor and City Council of Baltimore*, 12; Footner, *Sailor of Fortune*, 263–64.

15. See Spencer C. Tucker, *The Jeffersonian Gunboat Navy* (Columbia: University of South Carolina Press, 1993), 36–64; George F. Emmons, *The Navy of the United States from the Commencement, 1775 to 1853* (Washington, D.C.: Gideon and Co., 1853), 22; and Chapelle, *History of the American Sailing Navy*, 276, for descriptions of gunboat series armaments and barge outfits. The carronade was a British invention, first produced by the Carron Foundry from which its name was derived. This particularly destructive species of artillery was short and stubby in appearance, rapidly loaded, and capable of being fired quickly, while throwing twice the weight in shot (up to a 68-pound ball) that could be fired by the standard long gun of the day. It was also quite accurate at close range after its designers had reduced its windage to overcome the disadvantages of a very short gun. Its range, however, was quite limited, though the weapon became an American and British favorite in close combat. It was affectionately termed "the smasher" by the English and "the devil gun" by the French. See Chapelle, *History of the American Sailing Navy*, 33; A. B. C. Whipple, *Fighting Sail* (Alexandria, Va.: Time-Life Books Inc., 1978), 60; and Spencer C. Tucker, *Arming the Fleet: U.S. Navy Ordnance in the Muzzle-Loading Era* (Annapolis, Md.: Naval Institute Press, 1989), 120–30, for further descriptions and accounts of carronades.

16. Thomas Kemp Papers, Wades Point Farm, McDaniel, Md.; James Beatty's Accounts in the Fourth Auditor of the U.S., May 15, 1814, NARA.

17. Secretary of the Navy William Jones to Acting Master Commandant Joshua Barney, September 15, 1813, RG 45, SNLO, 1813, vol. 11 (M 149, R 11), NARA.

18. Chapelle, *History of the American Sailing Navy*, 27.

19. Secretary of the Navy William Jones to Master Commandant Daniel T. Patterson, October 18, 1813, RG 45, SNLO, 1813, vol. 11, 122–24 (M 149, R 11), NARA; Secretary of the Navy William Jones to Master Commandant Thomas Macdonough, December 7, 1813, RG 45, SNLO, 1813, vol. 11, 163 (M 149, R 11), NARA; Secretary of the Navy William Jones to Acting Master Commandant Joshua Barney, September 2, 1813, RG 45, SNLO, 1813, vol. 11, 72–74 (M 149, R 11), NARA.

Barney's selection of Spencer is not surprising in that Perry Spencer, probably together with his brother Richard, had built the famed U.S. Navy schooner *Enterprize* in 1799, and produced a number of privateer schooners such as *Valona, Manilus,* and *Hussar* for Baltimore interests during the War of 1812.

20. Chapelle, *History of the American Sailing Navy,* 222, 223, 225. Chapelle states that these vessels were 64 feet, 5 inches long on deck, 16 feet, 10 inches abeam, and 6 feet, 6 inches deep in the hold.

21. William Price to Secretary of the Navy, June 4, 1806, RG 45 SNMLR, 1806 (M 124, R10), NARA.

22. Secretary of the Navy William Jones to Master Commandant Arthur Sinclair, February 17, 1813, RG 45, SNLO, 1813, M 149, vol. 10 (M 149, R 10), NARA; Secretary of the Navy to Captain Charles Gordon, April 15, 1813, RG 45, SNLO, 1813, M 149, vol. 10 (M 149, R 10); Captain Charles Gordon to Secretary of the Navy William Jones, April, 18, 1813, RG 45, SNCLR, 1813, vol. 3, no. 58 (M 125, R 28), NARA; Captain Charles Gordon to Secretary of the Navy William Jones, April 27 1813, RG 45, SNCLR, 1813, vol. 3, no. 58 (M 125, R 28), NARA; Captain Charles Gordon to Secretary of the Navy William Jones, April 27 and, May 7 and 9, 1813, RG 45, SNCL, 1813, 23–24, 29, NARA; Captain Charles Gordon to Secretary of the Navy William Jones, June 21, 1813, RG 45, SNCLR, 1813, vol. 4, no. 98 (M 125, R 29), NARA. Soon after her arrival at Baltimore, having little admiration for the sluggish and poor sailing gunboats as warships, Barney had *No. 137*'s 24-pounders removed and the vessel converted to serve as a Chesapeake Flotilla storeship.

23. Chapelle, *History of the American Sailing Navy,* 226; Emmons, *The Navy of the United States,* 22–23; Captain James Barron to the Secretary of the Navy, May 8, June 3, October 4, December 7, 1806, and January 18, 1807, RG 45, SNCLR, 1807 (M 125, R 4, 5, 6, and 7), NARA; Secretary of the Navy William Jones to Joshua Barney, February 18, 1814, R G45, SNLO, Ships of War, 1813, vol. 11, 219–20 (M 149, R 11), NARA.

24. Mary Barney, *A Biographical Memoir,* 257; Sailing Master Commandant Joshua Barney to Secretary of the NavyWilliam Jones, March 1, 1814, RG 45, SNMLR, 1814, vol. 2, no. 57 (M 124, R 61); Captain Robert Barrie to Admiral Sir George Cockburn, June 1, 1814, Cockburn Papers, vol. 38, LC. When Barney selected *Scorpion* for his flagship, she was a vessel that had been gainfully employed in anything but static defense. By the time she was ready for fielding with the Chesapeake Flotilla, she was both speedy and apparently quite maneuverable. Barney described her as a cutter, but the British referred to her as only a large sloop. That the commodore had selected her for his flagship may also have been due to her record, having been tested in combat at the Battle of Craney Island, Virginia, in early 1813, and later briefly in an engagement on Yeocomico River, one of the many tributaries of the Potomac, where she had been forced to show the enemy her heels.

25. *NW,* 3: 37, note 1; Muster Book U.S. Flotilla, Naval Records, Collector of the Office

of Naval Records and Library, RG 45, NARA (hereafter Muster Book); Footner, *Sailor of Fortune*, 264.

26. Acting Master Commandant Joshua Barney to Secretary of the Navy William Jones, December 15, 1813, RG 45, SNMLR, 1813, vol. 7, no. 96 (M 124, R 59), NARA.

27. Secretary of the Navy William Jones to Acting Master Commandant Joshua Barney, December 17, 1813, RG 45, SNLO, 1813, vol. 11, 174–75 (M 149, R 11), NARA.

28. *American & Commercial Daily Advertiser* (Baltimore), December 25, 1813, March 25, and May 10, 1814.

29. The placement of free blacks with the flotilla, of which there were a substantial number in Baltimore, went with little notice as many such were employed in the maritime trades. The employment of slaves aboard vessels of the fleet, however, did not apparently meet with the approval of the senior commanders. Lieutenant Rutter ordered the removal of one such individual named Richard Owens, an ordinary seaman, because of his slave status. Other blacks such as Joseph Ball (who, being a runaway, enlisted under an alias), or probable blacks such as cooks Cato Patterson and Cesar Wentworth served throughout, fighting in all of the flotillamen's engagements from Cedar Point to Bladensburg and the Battle of Baltimore. Muster Book, NARA.

30. *ASPNA*, 1:307.

31. Footner, *Sailor of Fortune*, 264; *ASPNA*, 1:308; Secretary of the Navy William Jones to Acting Master Commandant Joshua Barney, April 14, 1814, RG 45, SNLO, 1814, vol. 11, 277 (M 149, R 11); Muster Book; Acting Master Commandant Joshua Barney to Secretary of the Navy William Jones, April 15, 1814, RG 45, SNMLR, 1814, vol. 3, no. 80 (M124, R62), NARA. The commissioned and warrant officers from *Ontario* were sent to Sacketts Harbor to flesh out the naval manpower needs on Lake Ontario. Captain Robert T. Spence, whose ill health would not allow him to go with his officers, was obliged to remain behind with but a petty officer and three or four men to take care of *Ontario*. Jones to Barney, April 14, 1814.

32. Footner, *Sailor of Fortune*, 264; *American & Commercial Daily Advertiser,* May 10, 1814; Acting Master Commandant Joshua Barney to Secretary of the Navy William Jones, March 1, 1814, RG 45, SNMLR, 1814, vol. 2, no. 57 (M 124, R 61), NARA; Acting Master Commandant Joshua Barney to Secretary of the Navy William Jones, March 17, 1814, RG 45, SNMLR, 1814, vol. 2, no. 112 (M 124, R 61), NARA.

33. Acting Master Commandant Joshua Barney to Secretary of the Navy William Jones, April 4, 1814, RG 45, SNMLR, 1814, vol. 3, no. 40 (M 124, R 62), NARA.

34. *ASPNA*, 1:305–6; *American & Commercial Daily Advertiser,* March 25, 1814; Acting Master Commandant Joshua Barney to Secretary of the Navy William Jones, March 25, 1814, RG 45, SNMLR, 1814, vol. 3, no. 12 (M 124, R 62), NARA; Muster Book, NARA; Barney to Jones, April 4, 1814; *NW,* 3:54, n4. A pilot-boat, presumably *Shark,* had been acquired for $500 and was intended to carry a single 24-pounder on pivot. Acting Master Commandant Joshua Barney to Secretary of the Navy William Jones, March 1, 1814, RG 45, SNMLR, 1814, vol. 2, no. 57 (M124, R61), NARA.

35. Secretary of the Navy William Jones to Acting Master Commandant Joshua Barney, February 18, 1814, RG 45, SNLO, 1814, vol. 11, 219–20 (M 149, R 11), NARA.

36. Footner, *Sailor of Fortune*, 264, 265.

Chapter 4
Miserable Tools

1. Acting Master Commandant Joshua Barney to Secretary of the Navy William Jones, April 12, 1814, RG 45, SNMLR, 1814, vol. 3, no. 66 (M 124, R 62), NARA; Hulbert Footner, *Sailor of Fortune: The Life and Adventures of Commodore Barney, U.S.N.* (New York: Harper & Brothers, 1940), 265; *American & Commercial Daily Advertiser,* April 12, 1814. Skinner was also the American agent for prisoner exchange at Annapolis. He would not be formally enrolled as purser for the flotilla until April 16 pending approval of Congress. Muster Book, NARA. Captain Allen's vessel is reported as both *Eliza* and *Eliza Ann,* and may have been owned by brothers John and James Allen, proprietors of a small shipping company at Fredericktown, on the Sassafras River. The Allen firm had been all but wiped out in May 1813 during the British attack and destruction of Fredericktown and Georgetown.

2. Barney to Jones, April 12, 1814.

3. *Daily National Intelligencer,* April 19, 1814.

4. Colonel Thomas M. Bayley to Governor James Barbour, April 14, 1814, *CVSP,* 11: 320.

5. Secretary of the Navy William Jones to Acting Master Commandant Joshua Barney, April 14, 1814, RG 45, SNLO, 1814, vol. 11, 277 (M 149, R 11), NARA.

6. Acting Master Commandant Joshua Barney to Secretary of the Navy William Jones, April 15, 1814, RG 45, SNMLR, 1814, vol. 3, no. 80 (M 124, R 62), NARA.

7. Ibid.; Acting Master Commandant Joshua Barney to Secretary of the Navy William Jones, April 18, 1814, RG 45, SNMLR, 1814, vol. 3, no. 91 (M 124, R 62), NARA.

8. Mary Barney, ed., *A Biographical Memoir of the Late Commodore Joshua Barney: From Autobiographical Notes and Journals in Possession of His Family, and Other Authentic Sources* (Boston: Gray and Bowen, 1832), 255; Barney to Jones, April 18, 1814; Acting Master Commandant Joshua Barney to Secretary of the Navy William Jones, April 22, 1814, RG 45, SNMLR, 1814, vol. 3, no. 101 (M 124, R 62), NARA.

9. Footner, *Sailor of Fortune,* 265; Barney to Jones, April 18, 1814. By May 11 Barney notes he had six hundred men in service. Acting Master Commandant Joshua Barney to Secretary of the Navy William Jones, May 11, 1814, RG 45, SNMLR, 1814, vol. 4, no. 25 (M 124, R 63), NARA.

10. *American & Commercial Daily Advertiser,* April 28, 1814.

11. *NW,* 3:57; Footner, *Sailor of Fortune,* 265.

12. *Daily National Intelligencer,* April 27 and May 2, 1814; John G. Joynes to Colonel Thomas M. Bayley, April 13, 1814, *CVSP,* 11:319.

13. Captain Joshua Barney to Secretary of the Navy William Jones, April 29, 1814, RG 45, SNMLR, 1814, vol. 3, no. 129 (M 124, R 62), NARA.

14. Ibid.; Captain Joshua Barney to Secretary of the Navy William Jones, May 1, 1814, RG 45, SNMLR, 1814, vol. 3, no. 138 (M 124, R 62), NARA.

15. Barney to Jones, May 1, 1814.

16. Captain George Edward Watts to Rear Admiral George Cockburn, May 2, 1814, Cockburn Papers, vol. 38, LC; Rear Admiral George Cockburn to Vice Admiral Sir Alexander F. I. Cochrane, May 9, 1814, Cockburn Papers, vol. 24, LC.

17. Barney to Jones, May 11, 1814.

18. Rear Admiral George Cockburn to Captain Robert Barrie, April 25, 1814, *NW*, 3:49; *American & Commercial Daily Advertiser,* June 9, 1814.

19. *American & Commercial Daily Advertiser,* June 9, 1814; Footner, *Sailor of Fortune,* 265–66.

20. *Daily National Intelligencer,* May 6, 1814; Barney to Jones, May 11, 1814; Regina Combs Hammett, *History of St. Mary's County, Maryland* (Ridge, Md.: privately published, 1977), 102. William C. Somerville was part owner with William Hebb and Peter Gough in the Clifton Factory cotton mill, weaving house, and tannery complex, St. Mary's County's only manufacturing industrial site at that time. The factory would later be destroyed during a British raid. Hammett, *History of St. Mary's County,* 162. Peckatone, also referred to as Picatone, was an early Georgian mansion and plantation site erected in 1750 by Gawen Corbin. It was named after a local Indian chief by Nicholas Jernew, the original patentee of the 900-acre tract in 1650, which was acquired by Henry Corbin in 1660. Walter Biscoe Norris Jr., ed., *Westmoreland County Virginia* (Montross, Va.: Westmoreland County Board of Supervisors, 1983), 308–9.

21. Barney to Jones, May 11, 1814.

22. Ibid.The increased elevation of the washboards was determined in 1980 from the author's archaeological survey of one of the wrecks of the flotilla found in the upper Patuxent. Donald G. Shomette and Ralph E. Eshelman, *The Patuxent River Submerged Cultural Resource Survey, From Drum Point to Queen Anne's Bridge, Maryland: Reconnaissance, Phase I, and Phase II* (Maryland Historical Trust Manuscript Series no. 13: April 1981), 422.

23. Barney to Jones, May 1 and 11, 1814.

24. Barney to Jones, May 11, 1814.

25. *Niles' Weekly Register,* November 5, 1814, 7:133.

26. *NW,* 2:356; 3:38; Vice Admiral Sir Alexander F. I. Cochrane to Rear Admiral George Cockburn, rApril 1, 1814, Cockburn Papers, vol. 38, LC.

27. H[ugh] Noel Williams, *The Life & Letters of Admiral Sir Charles Napier, K.C.B. (1786–1860)* (London: Hutchinson & Co., 1917), 41.

28. Vice Admiral Sir Alexander F. I. Cochrane to Governor-General Sir George Prevost, March 11, 1814, *NW,* 3:39–40; John McNish Weiss, *The Merikens: Free Black American Settlers in Trinidad 1815–16* (London: McNish & Weiss, 2002), 5, 7.

29. Vice Admiral Sir Alexander F. I. Cochrane to Rear Admiral George Cockburn, April 28, 1814, Cockburn Papers, vol. 38, LC; Alexander Cochrane, "A Proclamation," April 2, 1814, *NW,* 3:60.

30. Lieutenant Colonel Leaven Gayle to Rear Admiral George Cockburn, March 22, 1814, Cockburn Papers, vol. 38, LC; Rear Admiral George Cockburn to Lieutenant Colonel Leaven Gayle, March 24, 1814, Cockburn Papers, vol. 24, LC.

31. Rear Admiral George Cockburn to Vice Admiral Sir John Borlase Warren, April 13, 1814, Cockburn Papers, vol. 24, LC; Lieutenant Colonel Thomas M. Bayley to Governor James Barbour, June 11, 1814, *CVSP,* 11:341. Tradition claims that the 2nd Virginia Regiment took advantage of winds and tide to cut the vessel's anchor cables, allowing her to be driven ashore, and was the action that precipitated the British attack on Pungoteague. Personal communication, Ralph E. Eshelman, August 24, 2007. *Hiram* was documented as later taken by the local militia, and the wreck sold at auction.

32. Cockburn to Warren, April 13, 1814; Joynes to Bayley, April 13, 1814.

33. Cockburn to Warren, April 13, 1814; Joynes to Bayley, April 13, 1814; Cockburn to Cochrane, May 9, 1814.

34. Rear Admiral George Cockburn to Vice Admiral Sir Alexander F. I. Cochrane, April 13, 1814, *NW,* 3:46–49; Cockburn to Warren, April 13, 1814; Thomas M. Bayley to Governor James Barbour, [April 14, 1814], *CVSP,* 11:320–21.

35. David Hardgrave Statement, May 30, 1814, *CVSP,* 11:333; Lieutenant Colonel R. E. Parker to Governor James Barbour, June 11, 1814, *CVSP,* 11:338.

36. *American & Commercial Daily Advertiser,* June 9, 1814; Rear Admiral George Cockburn to Vice Admiral Sir John Borlase Warren, April 27, 1814, *NW,* 3:52.

37. Footner, *Sailor of Fortune,* 260.

Chapter 5
Sails and Oars

1. Captain Robert Barrie to Rear Admiral George Cockburn, June 1, 1814, Cockburn Papers, vol. 38, LC.

2. Rear Admiral George Cockburn to Captain Robert Barrie, May 30, 1814, Cockburn Papers, Container 10, vol. 25, LC.

3. Barrie to Cockburn, June 1, 1814.

4. Ibid.; *American & Commercial Daily Advertiser,* June 8, 1814.

5. Barrie to Cockburn, June 1, 1814; Captain Joshua Barney to Secretary of the Navy William Jones, June 3, 1814, RG 45, SNMLR, 1814, vol. 4, no. 86 (M 124, R 63), NARA.

6. Barrie to Cockburn, June 1, 1814. As the flotilla was divided into red, white, and blue divisions, the French flag reported by Barrie may simply have been the blue squadron pennant. It is also possible that Barney was flying the pennant of his former command in the French navy as an intended slight against his avowed enemy, the British.

7. Barrie to Cockburn, June 1, 1814; *American & Commercial Daily Advertiser,* June 8, 1814.

8. *American & Commercial Daily Advertiser,* June 8, 1814; Barney to Jones, June 3, 1814.

9. Barrie to Cockburn, June 1, 1814.

10. Barney to Jones, June 3, 1814; *American & Commercial Daily Advertiser,* June 8, 1814.

11. Ibid.

12. See Donald E. Graves, *Sir William Congreve and the Rocket's Red Glare* (Alexandria Bay, N.Y.: Museum Restoration Service, 1989); and Richard R. Hibbs, "Congreve War Rockets, 1800–1825," *U.S. Naval Institute Proceedings* 94 (March 1968): 80–88, for discussions on Congreve rockets and their applications in naval and land warfare.

13. Barrie to Cockburn, June 1, 1814; Rear Admiral George Cockburn to Captain Robert Barrie, June 3, 1814, *NW,* 3:83.

14. *American & Commercial Daily Advertiser,* June 8, 1814; Barney to Jones, June 3, 1814.

15. *American & Commercial Daily Advertiser,* June 8, 1814; Barrie to Cockburn, June 1, 1814.

16. *American & Commercial Daily Advertiser,* June 8, 1814; Barrie to Cockburn, June 1, 1814.

17. Barrie to Cockburn, June 1, 1814.

18. Barney to Jones, June 3, 1814; *Daily National Intelligencer,* June 7, 1814; *American &
Commercial Daily Advertiser,* June 8 and 9, 1814.

Chapter 6
Pen the Flotilla Within

1. Captain Joshua Barney to Secretary of the Navy William Jones, June 4, 1814, RG
45, SNMLR, 1814, vol. 4, no. 87 (M 12 R 63), NARA; *Daily National Intelligencer,* June 7,
1814.

2. Rear Admiral George Cockburn to Captain Robert Barrie, June 3, 1814, *NW,* 3:82;
Rear Admiral George Cockburn to Captain Alexander R. Kerr, June 3, 1814, Cockburn
Papers, vol. 24, LC. For the next few weeks Cockburn was left with but a single tender,
converted from a prize sloop, to keep open the line of communications with *Acasta* in
Hampton Roads. Rear Admiral George Cockburn to Vice Admiral Sir Alexander Co-
chrane, June 23, 1814, Cockburn Papers, vol. 24, LC.

3. Captain Robert Barrie to Rear Admiral George Cockburn, June 11, 1814, Cockburn
Papers, vol. 38, LC; "Log of H.M.S. *Loire,*" June 6, 1814, *Chronicles of St. Mary's* 8, no.
10 (October 1960); "Log of H.M.S. *Jaseur,*" June 6, 1814, *Chronicles of St. Mary's* 8, no. 12
(December 1960); "Log of H.M.S. *St. Lawrence,*" June 6, 1814, *Chronicles of St. Mary's* 11,
no. 12 (December 1963); "Log of H.M.S. *Dragon,*" June 6, 1814, *Chronicles of St. Mary's* 13,
no. 8 (August 1965); Cockburn to Barrie, June 3, 1814; Rear Admiral George Cockburn to
Captain George Edward Watts, June 3, 1814, Cockburn Papers, vol. 25, LC; Statement of
David Hargrave, April 18, 1814, *CVSP,* 11:333; Hulbert Footner, *Sailor of Fortune: The Life
and Adventures of Commodore Barney, U.S.N.* (New York: Harper & Brothers, 1940), 269.

4. "Log of H.M.S. *Loire,*" June 7 and 8, 1814; "Log of H.M.S. *Jaseur,*" June 7, 1814; "Log
of H.M.S. *St. Lawrence,*" June 7, 1814; "Log of H.M.S. *Dragon,*" June 7, 1814.

5. Commodore Joshua Barney to Secretary of the Navy William Jones, June 9, 1814,
RG 45, SNMLR, 1814, vol. 4, no. 105 (M 124, R 63), NARA; Barrie to Cockburn, June 11,
1814; Commodore Joshua Barney to Secretary of the Navy William Jones, June 16, 1814,
RG 45, SNMLR, 1814, vol. 4, no. 119 (M 124, R 63), NARA. In his report to Cockburn,
Barrie notes that he proceeded in pursuit of Barney on the morning of June 7, but the
logs of *Loire* and *Jaseur* note that the pursuit was made on the morning of June 8. "Log of
H.M.S. *Loire,*" June 6 and 8, 1814; "Log of H.M.S. *Jaseur,*" June 8, 1814; *American & Commercial Daily Advertiser,* June 9, 1814; Barrie to Cockburn, June 11, 1814.

6. Barrie to Cockburn, June 11, 1814; "Log of H.M.S. *Loire,*" June 6, 1814; "Log of
H.M.S. *St. Lawrence,*" June 8, 1814.

7. Barrie to Cockburn, June 11, 1814.

8. John Smith, *The Generall Historie of Virginia, New England, and the Summer Isles*
(London: Printed by I. D. and I. H. for Michael Sparkes, 1624); Charles Francis Stein, *A
History of Calvert County, Maryland* (Baltimore, Md.: published in cooperation with the
Calvert County Historical Society, 1960), 129–30.

9. Stein, *A History of Calvert County,* 77, 301; *Archives of Maryland* (Baltimore: Maryland Historical Society), 22:306–7.

10. *Archives of Maryland*, 26:636; 39:170; 21:21.

11. Footner indicates that Barney was two miles up the creek when the British arrived, but Barrie notes that he found the flotilla anchored nearly six miles from the entrance. The creek is slightly less than five miles in length from its head to the bar that slashes across its mouth. Barney would have undoubtedly found the defensive position two miles up, midway between modern Breedens Point and Johns Creek, indeed favorable. Here the channel depth shallows to eleven feet and would have prohibited penetration by Barrie's deeper-draft warships while permitting the flotilla close proximity to its only portal of escape. Footner, *Sailor of Fortune*, 269; Barrie to Cockburn, June 11, 1814; Barney to Jones, June 9, 1814.

12. Barney to Jones, June 9, 1814; *Daily National Intelligencer*, June 11, 1814. Although Mary Barney notes that the commodore made the red, white, and blue unit designations about June 26, it is probable that such undertakings would have been made well before the flotilla became locked in St. Leonard's Creek. Mary Barney, ed., *A Biographical Memoir of the Late Commodore Joshua Barney: From Autobiographical Notes and Journals in Possession of His Family, and Other Authentic Sources* (Boston: Gray and Bowen, 1832), 257, 259.

13. Footner, *Sailor of Fortune*, 269. William B. Barney also held a commission in the Baltimore City Militia, Fifth Regimental Cavalry District. *NW*, 3:102n2.

14. Barney to Jones, June 9, 1814; Mary Barney, *A Biographical Memoir*, 256.

15. Barney to Jones, June 9, 1814; Mary Barney, *A Biographical Memoir*, 256.

16. *American & Commercial Daily Advertiser*, June 13, 1814; Mary Barney, *A Biographical Memoir*, 257; Muster Book, NARA; Barney to Jones, June 9, 1814.

17. Mary Barney, *A Biographical Memoir*, 257–58.

18. Commodore Joshua Barney to Secretary of the Navy William Jones, June 20, 1814, RG 45, SNMLR, 1814, vol. 5, no. 4 (M 124, R 64), NARA.

19. Rear Admiral George Cockburn to Captain Alexander R. Kerr, June 13, 1814, Cockburn Papers, vol. 25. *St. Lawrence* struck ground at 8:00 a.m. and attempted to kedge herself off with her small anchor. By noon, however, she was still unable to free herself and had to be towed off by a small tender called *Eris*. At 2:00 p.m. she was finally refloated, and by 5:00 p.m. came to off the mouth of St. Leonard's Creek. "Log of H.M.S. *St. Lawrence*," June 8, 1814; "Log of H.M.S. *Loire*," June 8, 1814; Barrie to Cockburn, June 11, 1814.

20. Barrie to Cockburn, June 11, 1814.

21. "Log of H.M.S. *Loire*," June 8 and 9, 1814; "Log of H.M.S. *St. Lawrence*," June 8 and 9, 1814.

22. Barney to Jones, June 9, 1814. The purser, Robert Ormsby, previously sent to Baltimore, apparently had not sailed with the fleet.

23. "Log of H.M.S. *St. Lawrence*," June 9, 1814; "Log of H.M.S. *Loire*," June 9, 1814; Mary Barney, *A Biographical Memoir*, 256; Commodore Joshua Barney to Secretary of the Navy William Jones, June 11, 1814, *NW*, 3:88.

24. "Log of H.M.S. *Loire*," June 10, 1814.

25. *American & Commercial Daily Advertiser*, June 18, 1814; *Daily National Intelligencer*, June 27, 1814. The site of the battery, indicated on a diagram of the battle drawn by Barney after the engagement, was situated on one of the highest elevations on the creek. The remains of the emplacement lasted well into the final third of the twentieth century and

were adopted into the geographical nomenclature of the region under the name "Fort Hill." The works were bulldozed down in the 1970s to make way for a private home. A one-gun battery site on the opposite shore was archaeologically mapped and then partially bulldozed down in late 1980 to make way for a housing development. Details of Barney's positions and movements have been drawn from the comparison of his map data with modern geodetic charts and on-site investigations.

26. "Log of H.M.S. *Loire*," June 10, 1814.

27. Footner notes that the commodore removed his masts after the battle, but Barrie's report indicates that the vessels were entirely invisible when protected by the southern lip of the mouth of St. Leonard's. The vessels had apparently been built in such a way that the masts could be easily and quickly unstepped in just such a situation. Footner, *Sailor of Fortune*, 271; Barrie to Cockburn, June 11, 1814.

28. Commodore Joshua Barney to Secretary of the Navy William Jones, June 20, 1814, RG 45, SNMLR, 1814, vol. 5, no. 4 (M 124, R 64), NARA; Mary Barney, *A Biographical Memoir*, 256.

29. Mary Barney's documentation of the American forces participating in the engagement of June 10 is not entirely acceptable. A count of vessels in the commodore's flotilla made only several days before indicate eighteen craft, yet in his memoirs only thirteen barges, *Scorpion*, and gunboats *Nos. 137* and *138* are accounted for. See Mary Barney, *A Biographical Memoir*, 256; and Barney to Jones, June 20, 1814.

30. Barney to Jones, June 11, 1814; Barrie to Cockburn, June 11, 1814. Barney estimated British manpower arrayed against him in the upper creek at 800, a number accepted by Mary Barney and Footner. By four British deserters who made their escape from their ship on June 14, a slightly modified estimate of between 600 and 700, including 200 marines, is given, together with a breakdown of men per vessel. The "1st and 2nd barges and pinnace and rocket boat, with their crews and 22 marines from admiral Cochrane's [*sic*] ship in the sound; all the boats with their crews and marines from the *Dragon;* all the boats from the *Loire* frigate, and all the crew that could be got together with the marines; all the boats and nearly all the crew, and the marines of the *Jaseur* brig—the boats of the *St. Lawrence* schr. Of 18 guns and their crews—The *St. Lawrence* herself towards the close of the action—a smaller gaff topsail sch. With a long 18, and full of men, and a craft which they had taken, full of men, with two 32 lb. carronades; 2 of the launches also had 18 lb. carronade; so that they might warrantably calculate upon." *American & Commercial Daily Advertiser*, June 17, 1814; Barney to Jones, June 20, 1814; Footner, *Sailor of Fortune*, 270; *Daily National Intelligencer*, June 21, 1814.

31. "Log of H.M.S. *Loire*," June 10, 1814; Barney to Jones, June 11, 1814; Commodore Joshua Barney to Secretary of the Navy William Jones, June 13, 1814, RG 45, SNMLR, 1814, vol. 4, no. 111 (M 124, R 63), NARA; Mary Barney, *A Biographical Memoir*, 256.

32. Barney to Jones, June 11, 1814; *Daily National Intelligencer*, June 13, 1814. Although Barrie's stated purpose was to draw Barney down to the range of his big guns at the mouth of the creek, he was apparently somewhat lax in communicating his intentions to his officers. The commander of *Jaseur* simply noted the flight of the British barges as a retreat, the "enemy being much too powerful." "Log of H.M.S. *Jaseur*," June 10, 1814; *American & Commercial Daily Advertiser*, June 17, 1814; Mary Barney, *A Biographical Memoir*, 256.

33. Barney to Jones, June 13, 1814; Commodore Joshua Barney to Secretary of the Navy William Jones, July 21, RG 45, SNMLR, 1814, vol. 5, no. 67 (M 124, R 64), NARA; Mary Barney, *A Biographical Memoir,* 256.

34. The sequence of events during the engagement varies with each British ship log. *St. Lawrence* was sent up to her station in the creek an hour before the British retreat occurred. *Loire* noted the sighting of the American flotilla from the mouth of the creek at 3:30 p.m. *Jaseur,* however, states that both she and *Loire* had already opened fire at 3:00 p.m., and that Barney commenced his withdrawal at 3:30 p.m., moments before the landing of the marines. *Dragon,* anchored off the mouth of the Patuxent, noted that the sounds of battle were heard at 4:00 p.m. The *St. Lawrence* log states that she had not even moved to her station in the creek until 5:00 p.m. and was run aground at 6:00 p.m. I have accepted the sequence of events as given by the *Loire* log as the most reasonable. "Log of H.M.S. *St. Lawrence*," June 10, 1814; "Log of H.M.S. *Jaseur*," June 10, 1814; "Log of H.M.S. *Loire*," June 10, 1814; "Log of H.M.S. *Dragon*," June 10, 1814.

35. "Log of H.M.S. *Loire*," June 10, 1814; Mary Barney, *A Biographical Memoir,* 256.

36. A. B. C. Whipple, *Fighting Sail* (Alexandria, Va.: Time-Life Books Inc., 1978), 35–43.

37. "Log of H.M.S. *Loire*," June 10, 1814; Mary Barney, *A Biographical Memoir,* 256; Barney to Jones, June 11, 1814; Barrie to Cockburn, June 11, 1814.

38. Commodore Joshua Barney to Secretary of the Navy William Jones, June 13, 1814; *American & Commercial Daily Advertiser,* June 17, 1814.

39. *American & Commercial Daily Advertiser,* June 17, 1814; "Log of H.M.S. *Loire*," June 10, 1814; Mary Barney, *A Biographical Memoir,* 256–57.

40. Barrie to Cockburn, June 11, 1814.

41. Barney to Jones, June 13, 1814; *American & Commercial Daily Advertiser,* June 17, 1814; "Log of H.M.S. *Loire*," June 10, 1814; Mary Barney, *A Biographical Memoir,* 256–57; Barrie to Cockburn, June 11, 1814; "Log of H.M.S. *Jaseur*," June 10, 1814.

42. "Log of H.M.S. *Loire*," June 10, 1814; Barrie to Cockburn, June 11, 1814; Barney to Jones, June 13, 1814.

43. *Jaseur* reported two killed and two wounded; *St. Lawrence* noted the loss of a single man, seaman John Dundas; and *Loire* recorded three men killed and five wounded in the ship's launches. Barrie later reported only three dead and two wounded. "Log of H.M.S. *Jaseur*," June 10, 1814; "Log of H.M.S. *St. Lawrence*," June 11, 1814; "Log of H.M.S. *Loire*," June 10, 1814; Barrie to Cockburn, June 11, 1814.

44. Commodore Joshua Barney to Secretary of the Navy William Jones, July 21, 1814, RG 45, SNMLR, 1814, vol. 5, no. 67 (M 124, R 64), NARA; Muster Book, NARA. Mary Barney notes that the barge was sunk but was afterward raised. Mary Barney, *A Biographical Memoir,* 257; *American & Commercial Daily Advertiser,* June 18, 1814.

45. Barney to Jones, June 13, 1814; Mary Barney, *A Biographical Memoir,* 258.

46. Captain Robert Barrie to Rear Admiral George Cockburn, June 19, 1814, Cockburn Papers, vol. 38, LC; Cockburn to Kerr, June 13, 1814.

Chapter 7
They Opened All the Feather Beds

1. [George Robert Gleig], *A Narrative of the Campaigns of the British Army, at Washington, Baltimore, and New Orleans, under the Generals Ross, Packenham, & Lambert, in the Years 1814 and 1815 With Some Account of the Countries Visited* (Philadelphia: M. Carey & Sons, 1821), 90–91.

2. Ibid., 90.

3. Ibid., 91.

4. "Log of H.M.S. *Jaseur*," June 11, 1814, *Chronicles of St. Mary's* 9, no. 1 (January 1961); "Log of H.M.S. *Loire*," June 11, 1814, *Chronicles of St. Mary's* 8, no. 10 (October 1960).

5. "Log of H.M.S. *Jaseur*," June 11, 1814; "Log of H.J.S. *Loire*," June 11, 1814.

6. "Log of H.M.S. *Loire*," June 11, 1814; *American & Commercial Daily Advertiser*, June 17, 1814. Barney later testified in writing that "Pattison would not suffer a man to go on his place for its defence, but declared he would shoot the first man that attempted to do so, rather trusting the enemy than the protection of the militia. This statement was made to me immediately after his declaration, and soon after his house was burnt, which could have been defended with ease, had not Mr. Pattison prevented it." Skinner's family estate, situated on Smith's Point, on the right bank of the Patuxent "at the north entrance of St. Leonard's Creek," also suffered the destruction of "every shingle on it." As Skinner was then also serving as the agent for flags of truce and prisoners of war, he had already established some congenial communication with the enemy who, as a consequence, soon afterward expressed much regret to him for the loss of his property. On July 13, 1814, Cockburn issued orders that no outbuildings or stock belonging to Skinner, and particularly his extremely valuable Merino sheep, be molested or destroyed. Such exception did not extend to many others, as the British had also conducted some kidnapping, making off with a planter named Jabo, or Jarbo, and his overseer while raiding elsewhere on the same day as the landing at St. Leonard's Creek. *Public Documents Printed by Order of the United States Senate During the First Session of the Twenty-Sixth Congress, Begun and Held At the City of Washington, December 2, 1839* (hereafter *Public Documents . . . Twenty-Sixty Congress*), 8 vols. (Washington: Printed by Blair and Rivers, 1840), 1st Session, Committee of Claims, Report, February 21, 1840, 5:2; *American Farmer*, June 16, 1837, no. 52, vol. 8, 414; *Daily National Intelligencer*, June 10, 1814.

7. U.S. Congress, Senate, 36th Congress, 1st Session, Rep. Com., no. 118, 2; Charles Francis Stein, *A History of Calvert County, Maryland* (Baltimore, Md.: published in co-operation with the Calvert County Historical Society, 1960), 292–93. Mackall had been commissioned on July 28, 1812, as a Maryland Militia officer in the 3rd Cavalry District, covering Calvert and Anne Arundel counties. William M. Marine, *The British Invasion of Maryland 1812–1815* (1913; rpt., Hatboro, Pa.: Tradition Press, 1965), 367.

8. U.S. Congress, Senate . . . no. 118, 2. Captain George McWilliams received his commission on October 31, 1812. Lieutenant William G. Neale, of Captain William T. Lee's Company, received his commission on May 23, 1812. Marine, *The British Invasion*, 355, 369.

9. U.S. Congress, Senate . . . no. 118, 3.

10. "Log of H.M.S. *Jaseur*," June 12, 1814, *Chronicles of St. Mary's* 8, no. 12 (December 1960).

11. Captain Robert Barrie to Rear Admiral George Cockburn, June 19, 1814, Cockburn Papers, vol. 38, LC; *Maryland Republican*, June 18, 1814; Stein, *A History of Calvert County*, 246.

12. *Daily National Intelligencer*, June 18, 1814.

13. Barrie to Cockburn, June 19, 1814. Plater's plantation, later known as Sotterly, would one day be designated a National Historic Register Site. The salvation of the plantation was related by Lieutenant, later Captain, James Scott, Cockburn's aide de camp. "Colonel [John Rousby] Plater . . . told the [Rear] Admiral [George Cockburn] that he had done his utmost to bring forward his regiment (militia) to beat him back, but that they had deserted him, and he surrendered himself a prisoner, feeling he was entirely at his mercy. This candour at once gained the favour and protection of Admiral Cockburn, and the most rigid orders were issued, and sentinels placed around, to secure the premises from molestation or injury. The gallant Colonel himself remained at perfect liberty . . . For his conduct, Colonel Plater was held up by democratic portion of the republican press as something akin to a traitor." Captain James Scott, *Recollections of a Naval Life*, 3 vols. (London: Bentley, 1834), 3:227.

14. Mary Barney, ed., *A Biographical Memoir of the Late Commodore Joshua Barney: From Autobiographical Notes and Journals in Possession of His Family, and Other Authentic Sources* (Boston: Gray and Bowen, 1832), 258.

15. "Log of H.M.S. *Loire*," June 13, 14, 15, 1814; "Log of H.M.S. *Jaseur*," June 13 and 14, 1814; "Log of H.M.S. *Jaseur*," June 15, 1814, *Chronicles of St. Mary's* 10, no. 2 (February 1962); Rear Admiral George Cockburn to Captain Robert Barrie, June 10, 1814, Cockburn Papers, vol. 25, LC.

16. *Daily National Intelligencer*, June 21, 1814.

17. Barrie to Cockburn, June 19, 1814.

18. Ibid.

19. Ibid.

20. U.S. Congress, Senate . . . no. 118, 3. In their policy of not attacking or burning any site that remained peaceful, the British justified their actions on the grounds that the house and environs had been used as a bivouac for American soldiers, from which one of their marines had been hit by American gunfire. The view that the house had been used as a barracks by the Americans was upheld by the U.S. Congress as late as 1860 during the long-delayed processing of claims for restitution that were unsuccessfully carried on against the government by Mackall's heirs. Some historians, such as Stein, have erroneously attributed the loss of Captain Mackall's estate at Hallowing Point to the Nourse raids later on, which is directly contradicted by eyewitnesses in later claims hearings held by the federal government. Ibid., 2–9; Stein, *A History of Calvert County*, 153.

21. Barrie to Cockburn, June 19, 1814. Barrie was apparently under the misconception that Upper Marlboro and Lower Marlboro, the latter being the town to which he referred simply as Marlborough, were one and the same, and consequently mistook the latter's proximity to Washington, D.C., for that of the former. His mistake, in which he believed

he was only eighteen miles from the American capital, is echoed in local histories of the region, which incorrectly claim that Upper Marlboro was sacked.

22. Stein, *A History of Calvert County,* 56.

23. Barrie to Cockburn, June 19, 1814; "Log of H.M.S. *Jaseur,"* June 16, 1814.

24. *American & Commercial Daily Advertiser,* June 20, 1814; Barrie to Cockburn, June 19, 1814; *Maryland Republican,* June 25, 1814.

25. Barrie to Cockburn, June 19, 1814; "Log of H.M.S. *Jaseur,"* June 17, 1814. The value of tobacco lost at Lower Marlboro is based on Barney's estimate of $50 per hogshead as of August 1, 1814. Commodore Joshua Barney to Secretary of the Navy William Jones, August 1, 1814, RG 45, SNMLR, 1814 (M 124, R 64), NARA. For a brief review of Captain David's service in the Maryland State Navy, see Donald G. Shomette, *Lost Towns of Tidewater Maryland* (Centreville, Md.: Tidewater Publishers, 2000), 120.

26. Barrie to Cockburn, June 19, 1814; *NW,* 3:127n2.

27. Barrie to Cockburn, June 19, 1814.

28. *American & Commercial Daily Advertiser,* June 20, 1814; Barrie to Cockburn, June 19, 1814; "Log of H.M.S. *Jaseur,"* June 17, 1814; *The Times* (of London), August 9, 1814. An unidentified merchant claimed that 1,100 hogsheads had been destroyed in Magruder's warehouse alone, although the British report attests to only 300. New York *Herald,* June 25, 1814.

29. New York *Herald,* June 25, 1814.

30. In late August 1814, at the time of the main British army approach on Upper Marlboro, James Goddard, a resident of the town and assistant collector in the Fifth District of Maryland, who maintained in his house "a number of papers belonging to the office of the collector," would also move important documents to Mount Lubentia. These documents, all relating to the revenue of the state, were normally kept "closely and secretly locked up in his desk." When the British arrived in the town, they destroyed Goddard's house and property "in consequence of his being a collector of revenue." He later filed a claim with the federal government for restitution, but on December 20, 1816, was denied relief. The author has examined fragments of several documents found stuffed in the ceiling, left behind, and later found during restoration of Mount Lubentia. *ASPMA,* Claims (Washington, D.C.: Printed by Gales and Seaton, 1834), 1:439.

31. Commodore Joshua Barney to Secretary of the Navy William Jones, June 20, 1814, RG 45, SNMLR, 1814, vol. 5, no. 4 (M 124, R 64), NARA.

32. "Log of H.M.S. *Loire,"* June 13, 1814; "Log of H.M.S. *Jaseur,"* June 13, 1814, *Chronicles of St. Mary's* 9, no. 1 (January 1961).

33. Barney to Jones, June 20, 1814.

34. Commodore Joshua Barney to Secretary of the Navy William Jones, June 16, 1814, RG 45, SNMLR, 1814, vol. 4, no. 119 (M 124, R 63), NARA.

35. Barney to Jones, June 20, 1814.

36. *ASPNA,* Claims, 1:552–55; James Beatty Expenses, Fourth Auditor Records, NARA. Buildings in the town, the few for which some record exists, were quite modest. Ireland's tobacco warehouse, the largest structure in the setting, was 48 feet long, 24 feet wide, and 12 feet high, with sheds on two sides and a shed at one end, and was valued at

$2,500. A nearby dwelling and store occupied by Hezekiah Coberth measured 14 feet long, 16 feet wide, and 10 feet high. A second nearby store joined to Coberth's establishment measured 18 feet long, 16 feet wide, and 10 feet high, with an 18-foot by 12-foot shed, and was worth $2,000. *Public Documents . . . Twenty-Sixth Congress,* 1st Session, Committee of Claims, Report, February 21, 1840.

37. *Public Documents . . . Twenty-Sixth Congress,* 1st Session, Committee of Claims, Report, February 21, 1840.

38. Ibid.

39. Secretary of the Navy William Jones to Commodore Joshua Barney, June 6, 1814, RG 45, SNLO, 1814, vol. 11, 333 (M 149, R11), NARA.

40. Ibid., 334.

41. *ASPNA,* Claims, 1:454, 486–87, 488.

42. Commodore Joshua Barney to Secretary of the Navy William Jones, June 13, 1814, RG 45, SNMLR, 1814, vol. 4, no. 111 (M 124, R 63), NARA; Barney to Jones, June 16; Mary Barney, *A Biographical Memoir,* 258, 262.

43. Barney to Jones, June 16, 1814; Hulbert Footner, *Sailor of Fortune: The Life and Adventures of Commodore Barney, U.S.N.* (New York: Harper & Brothers, 1940), 273.

44. Commodore Joshua Barney to Secretary of the Navy William Jones, June 18, 1814, RG 45, SNMLR, 1814, vol. 5, no. 1 (M 124, R 64), NARA.

45. Colonel Henry Carberry to Commodore Joshua Barney, June 16, 1814, RG 45, SNMLR, 1814, vol. 4, bound with no. 125 (M 124, R 63), NARA; Barney to Jones, June 20, 1814. See correspondence regarding the inter-service dispute in RG 45, SNMLR, 1814, vol. 4, nos. 119, 120, 125, 126 (M 124, R 63), and vol. 5, nos. 1 and 2 (M 124, R 64), NARA.

46. Secretary of the Navy William Jones to Commodore Joshua Barney, June 14, 1814, RG 45, SNCL, 1814, 152, NARA; Barney to Jones, June 16, 1814.

47. Barney to Jones, June 18, 1814; Footner, *Sailor of Fortune,* 273.

48. *The Times* (of London), August 9, 1814.

49. Barney to Jones, June 13, 1814; *American & Commercial Daily Advertiser,* June 17, 1814.

50. Barney to Jones, June 13, 1814; Jones to Barney, June 14, 1814; Barney to Jones, June 16, 1814.

51. Commodore Joshua Barney to Secretary of the Navy William Jones, June 21, 1814, RG 45, SNMLR, 1814, vol. 5, no. 5 (M 124, R 64), NARA.

52. "Log of H.M.S. *Loire,*" June 18, 1814.

53. The British landed at Benedict at 3:00 p.m. on June 16 and took possession without opposition. The party of marines from *Jaseur,* who had seized the town, was left with a tender for support when Barrie's main force pushed on upriver to Lower Marlboro. "Log of H.M.S. *Jaseur,*" June 16, 1814, *Chronicles of St. Mary's* 10, no. 2 (February 1962).

54. *Daily National Intelligencer,* June 20, 1814. The balance of the citations from Dorsey's story in this and the following sections are from this source.

55. *American & Commercial Daily Advertiser,* June 27, 1814; Marine, *The British Invasion,* 270. One British officer noted in his memoirs of the caution that he and his men were obliged to exercise when dining in enemy territory as a result of the Benedict arsenic incident. "In consequence of what had taken place, if we wished to eat or drink anything that was found in their houses placed out ready for us upon their tables, we used to force

the natives to eat a part first, that, in the event of its being poisoned, they might die with the Britishers. "A Personal Narrative of Events by Sea and Land, from the Year 1800 to 1815 Concluding with a Narrative of Some of the Principal Events in the Chesapeake and South Carolina, in 1814 and 1815," *Chronicles of St. Mary's* 8, no. 1 (January 1960): 8.

56. *Daily National Intelligencer,* June 20, 1814.

57. Ibid.

Chapter 8
By the Light of the Blaze

1. *ASPM,* 1:525; *Daily National Intelligencer,* June 20, 1814.

2. *ASPM,* 1:525, 527; *Daily National Intelligencer,* June 20, 1814.

3. Rear Admiral George Cockburn to Captain B. H. Ross, June 20, 1814, Cockburn Papers, vol. 24, LC; Rear Admiral George Cockburn to Vice Admiral Sir Alexander F. I. Cochrane, June 25, 1814, Cockburn Papers, vol. 25, LC; Lieutenant Colonel Thomas M. Bayly to Governor James Barbour, June 23, 1814, *CVSP,* 11:348.

4. Rear Admiral George Cockburn to Captain Robert Barrie, June 17, 1814, Cockburn Papers, vol. 24, LC.

5. Rear Admiral George Cockburn to Captain B. H. Ross, June 20, 1814, Cockburn papers, vol. 24, LC; Rear Admiral George Cockburn to Vice Admiral Sir Alexander F. I. Cochrane, June 25, 1814, Cockburn Papers, vol. 25, LC; Lieutenant Colonel Thomas M. Bayly to Governor James Barbour, June 23, 1814, *CVSP,* 11:348.

6. Rear Admiral George Cockburn to Captain Robert Barrie, June 17, 1814, Cockburn Papers, vol. 24, LC.

7. Lieutenant Colonel Thomas M. Bayly to Governor James Barbour, June 23, 1814, *CVSP,* 11:348.

8. Rear Admiral George Cockburn to Captain Sir Edward T. Trowbridge, June 19, 1814, Cockburn Papers, vol. 25, LC.

9. Cockburn to Cochrane, June 25, 1814.

10. Vice Admiral Sir Alexander F. I. Cochrane to Rear Admiral George Cockburn, May 26, 1814, *NW,* 3:67; Captain Robert Barrie to Rear Admiral George Cockburn, June 19, 1814, *NW,* 3:114; Cockburn to Cochrane, June 25, 1814; Rear Admiral George Cockburn to Captain George Edward Watts, July 9, 1814, Cockburn Papers, vol. 25, LC.

11. "Log of H.M.S. *Loire,*" June 20, 1814, *Chronicles of St. Mary's* 8, no. 10 (October 1960); Rear Admiral George Cockburn to Captain Sir Edward T. Troubridge, June 23, 1814, Cockburn Papers, vol. 38, LC.

12. "Log of H.M.S. *Loire,*" June 21, 1814; Captain Thomas Brown to Rear Admiral George Cockburn, June 23, 1814, Cockburn Papers, vol. 38, LC; "Log of H.M.S. *St. Lawrence,*" June 21, 1814, *Chronicles of St. Mary's* 13, no. 4 (April 1965).

13. Brown to Cockburn, June 23, 1814; "Log of H.M.S. *St. Lawrence,*" June 21, 1814.

14. *American & Commercial Daily Advertiser,* June 20 and 23, 1814; *The Times* (of London), August 9, 1814, reprinted from Washington, June 22, 1814.

15. Harrison was undoubtedly responding to the British probes sent into the vicinity of Hall's Creek, just below Nottingham. *American & Commercial Daily Advertiser,* June 20 and 23, 1814.

16. *Daily National Intelligencer,* June 18, 1814.

17. *Daily National Intelligencer,* June 24, 1814.

18. Ibid.

19. Ibid.; Brown to Cockburn, June 23, 1814; "Log of H.M.S. *St. Lawrence,*" June 21, 1814.

20. *Daily National Intelligencer,* June, 18, 1814; "Log of H.M.S. *Loire,*" June 22, 1814.

21. *Daily National Intelligencer,* June 18, 1814. Brown to Cockburn, June 23, 1814, says four field pieces were employed in the action.

22. *Daily National Intelligencer,* June 18, 1814. The British were accused by the Baltimore press of firing a number of copper balls (deemed capable of inducing blood poisoning when embedded in a victim) in the skirmish at Benedict, as "a number of Cartridges were found in Benedict containing these balls, which are now in the hands of proper authority." *American & Commercial Daily Advertiser,* June 27, 1814.

23. *Daily National Intelligencer,* June 18, 1814.

24. *Daily National Intelligencer,* June 24 and 27, 1814; "Log of H.M.S. *Loire,*" June 22 and 23, 1814; Brown to Cockburn, June 23, 1814; General Philip Stuart to Secretary of War John Armstrong, June 23, 1814, in *Official Letters of the Military and Naval Officers of the United States During the War with Great Britain in the Years 1812, 13, 14, & 15,* comp. and ed. John Brannan (Washington City: Way & Gideon, 1823), 342; *Federal Republican,* June 23, 1814. The British, acting under the mistaken assumption that Mahiou was still alive, dispatched a flag of truce to Colonel Plater's estate on June 23 in an effort to arrange for a prisoner exchange. They wished to trade a certain Mr. Reynolds, a citizen of Lower Marlborough kidnapped during their raid on that place, for the unfortunate marine sergeant.

25. *American & Commercial Daily Advertiser,* June 24, 1814.

26. *Daily National Intelligencer,* June 27, 1814.

27. *American & Commercial Daily Advertiser,* June 23, 1814.

28. Secretary of the Navy William Jones to Commodore Joshua Barney, June 10, 1814, RG 45, SNCL, 1814, 149–50.

29. Hulbert Footner, *Sailor of Fortune: The Life and Adventures of Commodore Barney, U.S.N.* (New York: Harper & Brothers, 1940), 272; Harrison Bird, *Navies in the Mountains* (New York: Oxford University Press, 1962), 186–95; Commodore Joshua Barney to Secretary of the Navy William Jones, June 14, 1814, RG 45, SNCL, 1814, 152–53, NARA.

30. *American & Commercial Daily Advertiser,* June 18, 1814; *Daily National Intelligencer,* June 27, 1814; Barney to Jones, June 13, 1814.

31. Commodore Joshua Barney to Secretary of the Navy William Jones, June 16, 1814, RG 45, SNMLR, 1814, vol. 4, no. 119 (M 124, R 63), NARA.

32. Ibid.; Commodore Joshua Barney to Secretary of the Navy William Jones, June 20, 1814, RG45, SNMLR, 1814, vol. 5, no. 4 (M 124, R 64), NARA.

33. Secretary of the Navy William Jones to Commodore Joshua Barney, June 18, 1814, RG 45, SNCL, 1814, 154–55, NARA.

34. Barney to Jones, June 20, 1814.

35. Secretary of the Navy William Jones to Commodore Joshua Barney, June 20, 1814, RG 45, SNCL, 1814, 155–58, NARA.

36. Commodore Joshua Barney to Secretary of the Navy William Jones, June 21, 1814, RG 45, SNMLR, 1814, vol. 5, no. 5 (M 124, R 64), NARA.

37. Ibid.

38. Commodore Joshua Barney to Secretary of the Navy William Jones, June 22, 1814, RG 45, SNMLR, 1814, vol. 5, no. 6 (M 124, R 64), NARA.

39. Jones to Barney, June 21, 1814.

40. Ibid.

41. Barney to Jones, June 22, 1814.

42. Commodore Joshua Barney to Louis Barney, June 22, 1814, Dreer Collection, Pennsylvania Historical Society, Philadelphia, Pa.

Chapter 9
An Act of Madness

1. Secretary of the Navy William Jones to Captain Joshua Barney, June 10, 1814, RG 45, SNCL, 1814, 150, NARA.

2. Captain Thomas Brown to Rear Admiral George Cockburn, June 23, 1814, Cockburn Papers, vol. 38, LC.

3. *Daily National Intelligencer,* June 22 and July 7, 1814.

4. Captain Joshua Barney to Secretary of the Navy William Jones, June 20, 1814, RG 45, SNMLR, 1814, vol. 5, no. 4 (M 124, R 64), NARA.

5. Ibid., with enclosure.

6. "Log of HMS *Loire,*" June, 20, 1814, *Chronicles of St. Mary's* 8, no. 10 (October 1960); Brown to Cockburn, June 23, 1814; "Log of HMS *St. Lawrence,*" June 22, 1814, *Chronicles of St. Mary's* 11, no. 12 (December 1963).

7. Brown to Cockburn, June 23, 1814.

8. Ibid.

9. *Daily National Intelligencer,* June 22, 1814.

10. *American & Commercial Daily Advertiser,* June 27, 1814.

11. Mary Barney, ed., *A Biographical Memoir of the Late Commodore Joshua Barney: From Autobiographical Notes and Journals in Possession of His Family, and Other Authentic Sources* (Boston: Gray and Bowen, 1832), 259.

12. Ibid.; *Daily National Intelligencer,* July 9, 1814.

13. *Daily National Intelligencer,* July 7, 1814; Mary Barney, *A Biographical Memoir,* 259; Captain Joshua Barney to Louis Barney, June 27, 1814, U.S. *NW,* 3:123, 125. Captain Barney's letter to his brother was published in part in the *American & Commercial Daily Advertiser* on June 29, 1814.

14. Mary Barney, *A Biographical Memoir,* 259.

15. Sailing Master John Geoghegan to Captain Joshua Barney, Official Report of the Transactions at the Battery on the 25th & 26th June 1814, RG45, SNMLR, vol. 5, no. 54, enclosure (M 124, R 64), with Captain Joshua Barney to Secretary of the Navy William Jones, July 14, 1814 (hereafter Official Report).

16. A similar version of Wadsworth's comments to Geoghegan was related by Lieuten-

ant Carter to T. P. Andrews: "At last the Colonel informed Capt. Gohagen [*sic*], that he might, as he was to fight it, choose the position of the fort himself." *Daily National Intelligencer*, July 9, 1814; Mary Barney, *A Biographical Memoir*, 261.

17. Official Report; *Daily National Intelligencer*, July 9, 1814.

18. Official Report.

19. *Daily National Intelligencer*, June 29, 1814; Colonel Decius Wadsworth to Secretary of War John Armstrong, June 26, 1814, in *Official Letters of the Military and Naval Officers of the United States During the War with Great Britain in the Years 1812, 13, 14, & 15*, comp. and ed. John Brannan (Washington City: Way & Gideon, 1823), 345.

20. Official Report; Wadsworth to Armstrong, June 26, 1814, 345.

21. *Daily National Intelligencer*, July 7 and 9, 1814; *American & Commercial Daily Advertiser*, June 23, 1814; Wadsworth to Armstrong, June 26, 1814, 345.

22. *Daily National Advertiser*, July 7 and 9, 1814.

23. *Daily National Advertiser*, June 29, 1814; Wadsworth to Armstrong, June 26, 1814, 344.

24. *Daily National Advertiser*, June 29, 1814; Wadsworth to Armstrong, June 26, 1814, 344.

25. *Daily National Advertiser*, July 9, 1814; Wadsworth to Armstrong, June 26, 1814, 344.

26. Official Report.

27. *Daily National Intelligencer*, June 28 and July 7, 1814; "Log of HMS *Loire*," June 26, 1814; Captain Joshua Barney to Secretary of the Navy William Jones, June 26, 1814, 10 a.m., RG45, SNMLR, 1814, vol. 5, no. 12 (M 124, R 64), NARA; Joshua Barney to Louis Barney, June 27, 1814; Official Report; Captain Thomas Brown to Rear Admiral George Cockburn, June 27, 1814, *NW*, 3:127.

28. Mary Barney, *A Biographical Memoir*, 261.

29. *Daily National Intelligencer*, July 7 and 9, 1814; Mary Barney, *A Biographical Memoir*, 261; Wadsworth to Armstrong, June 26, 1814, 345.

30. Brown to Cockburn, June 27; Wadsworth to Armstrong, June 26, 1814, 345; *Daily National Intelligencer*, July 2 and 7, 1814.

31. *Daily National Intelligencer*, July 2, 7, and 9, 1814; Joshua Barney to Louis Barney, June 27, 1814; Mary Barney, *A Biographical Memoir*, 259; Brown to Cockburn, June 27, 1814.

32. It was noted in a letter to the *Intelligencer* that "from the narrowness of the water only the large barges of our flotilla could engage the enemy." *Daily National Intelligencer*, June 28 and July 9, 1814; Mary Barney, *A Biographical Memoir*, 259–60.

33. *Daily National Intelligencer*, June 28 and July 2, 1814.

34. Ibid, June 29 and July 7 and 9, 1814; Wadsworth to Armstrong, June 16, 1814, 344; Official Report.

35. *Daily National Intelligencer*, July 7, 1814; Official Report.

36. *Daily National Intelligencer*, June 29 and July 7, 1814; Official Report; Muster Book, NARA; Wadsworth to Armstrong, June 16, 1814, 344.

37. *Daily National Intelligencer*, July 2 and 7, 1814; Official Report.

38. *Daily National Intelligencer*, July 7, 1814.

39. *Daily National Intelligencer,* July 7 and 9, 1814.

40. *Daily National Intelligencer,* June 29, 1814.

41. Ibid.; Official Report.

42. *Daily National Intelligencer,* June 29, 1814; Official Report.

43. Barney to Jones, June 26, 1814, 10:00 a.m.; Barney to Louis Barney, June 27, 1814; Mary Barney, *A Biographical Memoir,* 260; *Daily National Intelligencer,* June 28, 1814; *American & Commercial Daily Advertiser,* June 29, 1814.

44. Mary Barney, *A Biographical Memoir,* 260.

45. *Daily National Intelligencer,* July 9, 1814.

46. Ibid.

47. Ibid.

48. Ibid.

49. Captain Thomas Brown to Rear Admiral George Cockburn, June 29, 1814, Cockburn Papers, vol. 38, LC.

50. "Log of HMS *Loire,*" June 26, 1814; Barney to Jones, June 26, 1814, 10:00 a.m. Barney reports the enemy was warping around Point Patience at 10:00 a.m., indicating they were heading to the southern side.

51. Brown to Cockburn, June 29, 1814.

52. "Log of HMS *Loire,*" June 26, 1814; *American & Commercial Daily Advertiser,* June 27, 1814. The Somervells, who had already lost at least one slave to the British on June 6, would also lose at least four children and a male adult slave on July 12 and 13, 1814. One of the adults, Barsle Butler, would enlist in the Royal Colonial Marine Corps and serve as a sergeant of Company B. John McNish Weiss, *The Merikens: Free Black American Settlers in Trinidad 1815–16* (London: McNish & Weiss, 2002), *passim.*

53. Brown to Cockburn, June 27, 1814.

54. Barney to Jones, June 26, 1814, 10:00 a.m.; Barney to Louis Barney, June 27, 1814.

Chapter 10
Old Barney in Hell

1. *Daily National Intelligencer,* June 29, 1814.

2. Ibid.

3. Ibid.

4. Mary Barney, ed., *A Biographical Memoir of the Late Commodore Joshua Barney: From Autobiographical Notes and Journals in Possession of His Family, and Other Authentic Sources* (Boston: Gray and Bowen, 1832), 261.

5. An extraordinary controversy raged soon after the battle. The uncalled-for retreat of the infantry, Barney's belated arrival on the scene of combat, the independent motions of Captain Miller's unit, and the apparent breakdown in the chain of command became sources of conflict in the press and in the military. Captain Miller faced a Court of Inquiry for his movements, but emerged fully exonerated. Keyser, defending his movement in joining the flight from the field, blamed Wadsworth and the cloudy chain of command. Carberry simply made himself unavailable for public discussion, and Barney refused to comment, preferring to let the victory he had achieved speak for him. The split between

the army and the navy was never so wide as after the Second Battle of St. Leonard's Creek. There was even disagreement over whether or not the hot shot fired from the Wadsworth Battery had set the enemy vessels afire. Sailing Master John Geoghegan to Commodore Joshua Barney, Official Report of the Transactions at the Battery on the 25th & 26th June 1814, enclosure with Commodore Joshua Barney to Secretary of the Navy William Jones, July 14, 1814, RG 45, SNMLR, 1814, vol. 5, no. 54, (M 124, R 64), NARA; *Daily National Intelligencer*, June 28 and 29, and July 2, 7, 9, and 14, 1814; *American & Commercial Daily Advertiser*, June 28 and 29, 1814; Mary Barney, *A Biographical Memoir*, 258–60; "Log of H.M.S. *Loire*," June 25, 1814, *Chronicles of St. Mary's* 8, no. 10 (October 1960).

6. *Daily National Intelligencer*, June 29, 1814; Colonel Decius Wadsworth to Secretary of War John Armstrong, June 26, 1814, in *Official Letters of the Military and Naval Officers of the United States During the War with Great Britain in the Years 1812, 13, 14, & 15*, comp. and ed. John Brannan (Washington City: Way & Gideon, 1823), 342.

7. Captain Joshua Barney to Louis Barney, June 27, 1814, *NW*, 3:123, 125; Mary Barney, *A Biographical Memoir*, 262.

8. Colonel Decius Wadsworth to Secretary of the Navy William Jones, July 7, 1814, RG 45, SNMLR, 1814, vol. 5, no. 38 (M 124, R 64), NARA; Secretary of the Navy William Jones to Captain Joshua Barney, July 12, 1814, RG 45, SNLO, 1814, vol. 11, 372 (M 149, R 11), NARA; Samuel Miller Court of Inquiry, July 26–August 15, 1814, Records of General Courts-Martial and Courts of Inquiry of the Navy Department, RG 125, vol. 5, no. 169 (M 273, R 7), NARA; Captain Joshua Barney to Secretary of the Navy William Jones, July 13, 1814, RG 45, SNMLR, 1814, vol. 5, no. 53 (M 124, R 64).

9. *Daily National Intelligencer*, July 2 and 7, 1814.

10. *Daily National Intelligencer*, July 7, 1814; Official Report. Thomas Carberry would one day become mayor of the City of Washington.

11. *Daily National Intelligencer*, July 2, 7, and 9, 1814.

12. Official Report; Captain Joshua Barney to Secretary of the Navy William Jones, June 27, 1814, RG 45, SNMLR, 1814, vol. 5, no. 15 (M 124, R 64), NARA.

13. Acting Lieutenant Solomon Rutter to Captain Joshua Barney, July 3, 1814, RG 45, SNMLR, 1814, vol. 5, no. 31a (M124, R64), NARA, enclosure with Barney to Jones July 4, 1814, RG 45, RG 45, SNMLR, 1814, vol. 5, no. 31, NARA, in which Barney reports he is soon going to move the flotilla up to Nottingham.

14. Official Report; Rutter to Barney, July 3, 1814.

15. Ibid.

16. "Log of H.M.S. *Loire*," June 27 and July 1, 1814; "Log of H.M.S. *St. Lawrence*," June 30 and July 1, 1814, *Chronicles of St. Mary's* 13, no. 4 (April 1965); *Niles' Weekly Register* 7, no. 160 (October 6, 1814): 50.

17. Captain Joseph Nourse to Rear Admiral George Cockburn, July 4, 1814, Cockburn Papers, vol. 38, LC.

18. "Log of H.M.S. *Loire*," July 1, 1814; "Log of H.M.S. *St. Lawrence*," July 1, 1814.

19. "Log of H.M.S. *Loire*," July 2, 1814; "Log of H.M.S. *St. Lawrence*," July 2, 1814; Nourse to Cockburn, July 4, 1814. Rutter reported there were eleven barges and a schooner in the British force. Rutter to Barney, July 3, 1814.

20. Rutter to Barney, July 3, 1814.

21. Ibid.

22. Nourse to Cockburn, July 4, 1814; Captain Joshua Barney to Secretary of the Navy William Jones, July 8, 1814, RG 45, SNMLR, 1814, vol. 5, no. 43 (M 124, R 64), NARA; Rutter to Barney, July 3, 1814; "Log of H.M.S. *St. Lawrence*," July 2, 1814; Rear Admiral George Cockburn to Captain Robert Barrie, July 11, 1814, *NW*, 3:151.

23. Rutter to Barney, July 3, 1814.

24. Barney to Jones, July 8, 1814.

25. Thomas Tingey to Captain Joshua Barney, July 29, 1814, Barney Papers, Dreer Collection, Historical Society of Pennsylvania, Philadelphia, Pa.; Receipt from Buller Cocke, June 28, 1814, Barney Papers.

26. Secretary of the Navy William Jones to Captain Joshua Barney, June 28, 1814, RG 45, SNCL, 160, NARA; *Daily National Intelligencer*, July 2, 1814. Mary Barney states that the commodore received on Friday, July 1, Secretary Jones's letter requesting his presence in Washington. However, the *Intelligencer* of Saturday, July 2, notes that Barney had already arrived in the city on Thursday evening, June 30. Mary Barney, *A Biographical Memoir*, 262; *Daily National Intelligencer*, July 2, 1814.

27. Mary Barney, *A Biographical Memoir*, 262.

28. Ibid.; *Daily National Intelligencer*, July 2, 1814.

29. Clement Hollyday to Urban Hollyday, July 12, 1814, LC.

30. Thomas B. King to Benjamin King, July 14, 1814, Transcript, King Family Files/ War of 1812, Calvert County Historical Society, Prince Frederick, Md.

Chapter 11
Leviathan Awakened

1. "Log of H.M.S. *Albion*," July 2, 1814, Cockburn Papers, LC.

2. Rear Admiral George Cockburn to Vice Admiral Sir Alexander F. I. Cochrane, June 25, 1814, Cockburn Papers, vol. 25, LC; Rear Admiral George Cockburn to Captain George Edward Watts, July 9, 1814, Cockburn Papers, vol. 25, LC.

3. "Log of H.M.S. *Albion*," July 3, 1814, Cockburn Papers, LC.

4. Ibid., July 4, 1814.

5. Ibid., July 4 and 5; Edwin W. Beitzell, *The Jesuit Missions of St. Mary's County, Maryland* (Abell, Md.: privately published, 1976), 161.

6. "Log of H.M.S. *Albion*," July 5, 1814, Cockburn Papers, LC.

7. *Daily National Intelligencer*, July 6, 1814.

8. Commodore Joshua Barney to Secretary of the Navy William Jones, July 8, 1814, RG 45, SNMLR, 1814, vol. 5, no. 43 (M 124, R 64), NARA.

9. Ibid.

10. "Log of H.M.S. *Albion*," July 7, 1814, Cockburn Papers, LC; Rear Admiral George Cockburn to Captain Thomas Brown, July 7, 1814, Cockburn Papers, vol. 44, LC; Rear Admiral George Cockburn to Captain Robert Barrie, July 11, 1814, *NW*, 3:151.

11. "Log of H.M.S. *Albion*," July 7 and 8, 1814, Cockburn Papers, LC.

12. Father Francis X. Neale, SJ, to Father John Grassi, SJ, July 8, 1814, in *Woodstock Letters* (Baltimore: privately printed by the Society of Jesuits), 32:8.

13. Cockburn to Barrie, July 11, 1814.

14. "Log of H.M.S. *Albion*," July 8–15, 1814, Cockburn Papers, LC; Cockburn to Watts, July 9, 1814.

15. Barney to Jones, July 8, 1814.

16. Ibid.

17. Ibid.

18. *ASPM,* 1:524; William M. Marine, *The British Invasion of Maryland 1812–1815* (1913; rpt., Hatboro, Pa.: Tradition Press, 1965), 70; Walter Lord, *The Dawn's Early Light* (New York: W. W. Norton & Co., Inc., 1972), 23.

19. *ASPMA,* 1:524–99, "Recapitulation," in *Niles' Weekly Register,* December 17, 1814, 7:249–50.

20. Mary Barney, ed., *A Biographical Memoir of the Late Commodore Joshua Barney: From Autobiographical Notes and Journals in Possession of His Family, and Other Authentic Sources* (Boston: Gray and Bowen, 1832), 262.

21. "Log of H.M.S. *Loire*," July 14, 1814, *Chronicles of St. Mary's* 8, no. 12 (December 1960); "Log of H.M.S. *St. Lawrence*," July 14, 1814, *Chronicles of St. Mary's* 13, no. 4 (April 1965); Commodore Joshua Barney to Secretary of the Navy William Jones, July 13, 1814, RG 45, SNMLR, 1814, vol. 5, no. 53 (M 124, R 64), NARA.

22. "Log of H.M.S. *Albion*," July 14, 1814; "Log of H.M.S. *Loire*," July 15, 1814, *Chronicles of St. Mary's* 8, no. 12 (December 1960); "Log of H.M.S. *St. Lawrence*," July 15, 1814; *Daily National Intelligencer,* July 16, 1814.

23. Vice Admiral Alexander F. I. Cochrane to Rear Admiral George Cockburn, July 1, 1814, Cockburn Papers, vol. 38, LC; Vice Admiral Alexander F.I. Cochrane to Rear Admiral George Cockburn, July 14, 1814, *NW,* 3:131–32; Vice Admiral Alexander F. I. Cochrane to Rear Admiral George Cockburn, July 17, 1814, *NW,* 3:133; Vice Admiral Alexander F. I. Cochrane to Rear Admiral George Cockburn, July 23, 1814, *NW,* 3:135.

24. Rear Admiral George Cockburn to Vice Admiral Sir Alexander Cochrane, July 17, 1814, *NW,* 3:136. Rear Admiral George Cockburn to Vice Admiral Sir Alexander Cochrane, Secret Copy, July 17, 1814, Cockburn Papers, vol. 24, LC.

25. Cockburn to Cochrane, Secret Copy, July 17, 1814.

26. Rear Admiral George Cockburn to Captain Robert Barrie, July 16, 1814, *NW,* 3:153.

27. "Log of H.M.S. *Albion*," July 15, 1814, Cockburn papers, LC.

28. Rear Admiral George Cockburn to Captain Joseph Nourse, July 15, 1814, Cockburn Papers, vol. 44, LC.

29. Ibid.

30. "A Personal Narrative of Events by Sea and Land, from the Year 1800 to 1815," *Chronicles of St. Mary's* 8, no. 1 (January 1960): 3.

31. Ibid.

32. Cochrane to Cockburn, July 1, 1814; Cochrane to Cockburn, July 14, 1814.

33. "A Personal Narrative," 3.

Chapter 12
Frightened Out of Their Senses

1. Captain Joseph Nourse to Rear Admiral George Cockburn, July 23, 1814, Cockburn Papers, vol. 38, LC; Rear Admiral George Cockburn to Captain George Edward Watts, July 17, 1814, Cockburn Papers, vol. 25, LC; Charles Francis Stein, *A History of Calvert County, Maryland* (Baltimore, Md.: published in cooperation with the Calvert County Historical Society, 1960), 153; Baltimore *Federal Republican,* July 27, 1814; *Niles's Weekly Register* 7, no. 161 (October 6, 1814): 50.

2. *Daily National Intelligencer,* July 15 and 22, 1814.

3. *Daily National Intelligencer,* July 22, 1814.

4. *Daily National Intelligencer,* July 19 and 22, 1814; Correspondence of the Secretary of War and General William Henry Winder, *ASPMA,* 1:525.

5. *Daily National Intelligencer,* July 22, 1814.

6. U.S. Congress, 29th Congress, Rep. no. 131, 1st Session, Ho. of Reps., 5, 14, 15, 16.

7. Ibid., 16, 20.

8. Ibid., 5, 12, 13.

9. Ibid., 5, 12.

10. Captain Joshua Barney to Secretary of the Navy William Jones, July 21, 1814, RG 45, SNMLR, 1814, vol. 5, no. 67 (M 124, R 64), NARA. It is presumed the lookout boat, a large pilot boat schooner, would have proved to be unsuitable for reconnaissance on the river in that she would have been too easily spotted, and perhaps unfit for operation in the narrow confines of the waterway.

11. Nourse to Cockburn, July 23, 1814; Stein, *A History of Calvert County,* 153.

12. Barney to Jones, July 21, 1814.

13. Nourse to Cockburn, July 23, 1814; Stein, *A History of Calvert County,* 153; *Federal Republican,* July 27, 1814; *Niles' Weekly Register* 7, no. 161 (October 6, 1814): 50–51.

14. Commodore Joshua Barney to Secretary of the Navy William Jones, July 24, 1814, RG 45, SNMLR, 1814, vol. 5, no. 87 (M 124, R 64), NARA.

15. *Daily National Intelligencer,* July 29, 1814; Barney to Jones, July 24, 1814.

16. Nourse to Cockburn, July 23, 1814.

17. Stein, *A History Calvert County,* 153.

18. U.S. Congress, 29th Congress, 10, 14. Additional page numbers for this source in this section appear parenthetically.

19. Nourse to Cockburn, July 23, 1814.

20. Ibid.; Cockburn to Watts, July 17, 1814.

21. "A Personal Narrative of Events by Sea and Land, from the Year 1800 to 1815," *Chronicles of St. Mary's* 8, no. 1 (January 1960): 3, 4.

22. In the October 1963 issue of *Chronicles of St. Mary's,* the editors suggest that the storm that upended the unidentified British schooner occurred on August 25. Several facts indicate that this assumption is incorrect. There were indeed violent storms on both July 25 and August 25. However, the author of "Personal Narrative" states that the disaster occurred on July 25 about the time he was dining aboard his ship in the Patuxent with Captain Nourse. He noted that the floating debris cast into the river as a result of the

storm was initially mistaken to be the American flotilla. If the disaster had occurred on August 25, he could not have been dining with Nourse, who was on that date documented as being with Admiral Cockburn. Furthermore, the American flotilla had already been destroyed by August 22, a fact that was immediately communicated to the entire British fleet in the Patuxent, and which would have precluded the case of mistaken identity noted by the author of "Personal Narrative." The severity of the storm of July 25 was such as to drive *Severn* before it in the Patuxent, and was noted in both the logs of both *Severn* and *Albion*, then in the Potomac. No mention is made of the sinking of any vessel in the logs of any of the vessels in the Patuxent on August 25. See "Log of H.M.S. *Albion*," July 25 and August 25, 1814, Cockburn Papers, LC; "Log of H.M.S. *Severn*," August 25, 1814, *Chronicles of St. Mary's* 14, no. 8 (August 1966); "Log of H.M.S. *Hebrus*," August 25 and 26, 1814, *Chronicles of St. Mary's* 15, no. 10 (October 1967); "A Personal Narrative," 3, 4; Rear Admiral George Cockburn to Vice Admiral Sir Alexander F. I. Cochrane, August 22, 1814, Cockburn Papers, vol. 24, LC; and *Chronicles of St. Mary's* 11, no. 10 (October 1963): 78–79.

Chapter 13
Our Polar Star

1. Rear Admiral George Cockburn to Captain Robert Barrie, July 16, 1814, *NW*, 3:153.
2. Ibid.
3. "Log of H.M.S. *Albion*," July 16, 17, and 18, 1814, Cockburn Papers, LC.
4. Father Francis X. Neale, SJ, to Father John Grassi, SJ, July 17, 1814, in *Woodstock Letters* (Baltimore: privately printed by the Society of Jesuits), 32.
5. *ASPMA*, 1:527. The Swann data was published two days later in the *Daily National Intelligencer*, July 20, 1814.
6. *ASPMA*, 1:525; *Daily National Intelligencer*, July 20, 1814.
7. *Daily National Intelligencer*, July 20, 1814.
8. "Log of H.M.S. *Albion*," July 18, 1814, Cockburn Papers, LC; Rear Admiral George Cockburn to Vice Admiral Sir Alexander F. I. Cochrane, July 17, 1814, *NW*, 3:156; Rear Admiral George Cockburn to Vice Admiral Sir Alexander Cochrane, July 19, 1814, Cockburn Papers, vol. 24, LC. The motions of the British were keenly watched and reported upon from the Virginia shores of Westmoreland County by Lieutenant Colonel Richard E. Parker, of the Virginia State Militia, who noted that the fleet came to anchor a little below Blackistone Island about five o'clock in the afternoon. Lieutenant Colonel Richard E. Parker to Governor James Barbour, July 18, 1814, *CVSP*, 11:355.
9. "Log of H.M.S. *Albion*," July 18, 1814, Cockburn Papers, LC; Cockburn to Cochrane July 19, 1814.
10. "Log of H.M.S. *Albion*," July 19, 1814, Cockburn Papers, LC.
11. Cockburn to Cochrane, July 19, 1814.
12. "Log of H.M.S. *Albion*," July 19, 1814; *Niles' Weekly Register* 7, no. 161 (October 6, 1814); *Maryland Gazette and Political Intelligencer*, August 4, 1814.
13. *Niles' Weekly Register*, July 19, 1814.
14. Cockburn to Cochrane, July 19, 1814.
15. *The Times* (of London), September 6, 1814.
16. *Daily National Intelligencer*, July 21 and 23, 1814; Brigadier General William Henry

Winder to Secretary of War John Armstrong, July 20, July 23, and August 13, 1814, *ASP-MA*, 1:544, 539, 546.

17. *Daily National Intelligencer,* July 29, 1814.

18. Ibid.

19. *Daily National Intelligencer,* July 21, 1814.

Chapter 14

Jonathan Confounded

1. *Daily National Intelligencer,* July 28, 1814.

2. Lieutenant Colonel Richard E. Parker to Governor James Barbour, July 18, 1814, *CVSP,* 11:355; "Log of H.M.S. *Albion,*" July 20, 1814, Cockburn Papers, LC; Robert K. Krick, *9th Virginia Cavalry* (Lynchburg, Va.: H. E. Howard, Inc., 1982), extract reprinted in *Westmoreland County, Virginia 1653–1983,* ed. Walter Biscoe Norris Jr. (Montross, Va.: Westmoreland County Board of Supervisors, 1983), 357.

3. Rear Admiral George Cockburn to Vice Admiral Sir Alexander Cochrane, July 21, 1814, *NW,* 3:163, 165–66.

4. Ibid.

5. "Log of H.M.S. *Albion,*" July 20, 1814; Cockburn to Cochrane, July 21, 1814; *Chronicles of St. Mary's* 10, no. 7 (July 1960): 72.

6. Cockburn to Cochrane, July 21, 1814; *Chronicles of St. Mary's* 10, no. 7 (July 1960): 72.

7. Cockburn to Cochrane, July 21, 1814; "Log of H.M.S. *Albion,*" July 21, 1814, Cockburn Papers, LC. General Hungerford sent a letter to Cockburn on August 5, 1814, protesting the capture of six prisoners. Of these, Elisha Williams, 66, Luke Dameton, 53, and Thomas Beuehum, 45, he stated, were all above military age and not in service. Also taken were Christopher Dawson, John King, and Thomas Nutt. None of the men were taken under arms, and all had been forcibly carried off though "peaceably remaining in their homes," several of which were burned. Cockburn replied that he simply did not agree. Brigadier General John P. Hungerford to Rear Admiral George Cockburn, August 5, 1814, reprinted in *Niles' Weekly Register,* Supplement to Vol. VII, 155; Rear Admiral Cockburn to Brigadier General John P. Hungerford, August 11. 1814, reprinted in *Niles' Weekly Register,* Supplement to Vol. VII, 156.

8. "Log of H.M.S. *Albion,*" July 20 and 21, 1814; Cockburn to Cochrane, July 21, 1814.

9. Cockburn to Cochrane, July 21, 1814; "Log of H.M.S. *Albion,*" July 22 and August 11, 1814, Cockburn Papers, LC.

10. Lieutenant Colonel Austin Smith to Governor James Barbour, July 21, 1814, *CVSP,* 11:358; Lieutenant Colonel S. H. Peyton to Governor James Barbour, July 22, 1814, *CVSP,* 11:359.

11. Rear Admiral George Cockburn to Captain George Edward Watts, July 22, 1814, Cockburn Papers, vol. 25, LC.

12. "Log of H.M.S. *Albion,*" August 17, 1814, Cockburn Papers, LC; *Chronicles of St. Mary's* 10, no. 7 (July 1960): 74–75; "A Personal Narrative of Events by Sea and Land, from the Year 1800 to 1815," *Chronicles of St. Mary's* 8, no. 1 (January 1960): 3. Correspondence between Cockburn and the Virginians regarding the Nomini poison incident was

published, along with the investigation results, in *Niles's Weekly Register,* Supplement to Volume VII, 155–56.

13. "Log of H.M.S. *Albion*," July 23, 1814; Rear Admiral George Cockburn to Vice Admiral Sir Alexander F. I. Cochrane, July 24, 1814, *NW,* 3:166; Brigadier General Philip Stuart to Secretary of War Armstrong, July 24, 1814, *NW,* 3:167. The British expedition retired safely to the fleet at 9:00 p.m. without casualty or further incident.

14. Stuart to Armstrong, July 24, 1814; Rear Admiral George Cockburn to Vice Admiral Sir Alexander F. I. Cochrane, August 4, 1814, *NW,* 3:168–69; Secretary of the Navy William Jones to Commodore Joshua Barney, July 26, 1814, RG 45, SNCL, 1814, 172, NARA.

15. H[ugh] Noel Williams. *The Life & Letters of Admiral Sir Charles Napier, K.C.B. (1786–1860)* (London: Hutchinson & Co., 1917), 42.

16. Commodore Joshua Barney to Secretary of the Navy William Jones, July 24, 1814, RG 45, SNMLR, 1814, vol. 5, no. 87 (M 124, R 64), NARA; Secretary of the Navy William Jones to Commodore Joshua Barney, July 26, 1814, RG 45, SNCL, 1814, 172, NARA; Secretary of the Navy William Jones to Captain Joshua Barney, July 27, 1814, RG 45, SNCL, 1814, 173, NARA; *ASPMA,* 1:525.

17. Stuart to Armstrong, July 24, 1814. Stuart's overall force in the region was reported by General Winder to be eight hundred men, but they appear to have been dispersed at various points along the Potomac. *ASPMA,* 1:525.

18. "Log of H.M.S. *Albion,*" July 26, 1814, Cockburn Papers, LC; Rear Admiral George Cockburn to Vice Admiral Sir Alexander F. I. Cochrane, July 31, 1814, Cockburn Papers, vol. 24, LC; Brigadier General John P. Hungerford to Governor James Barbour, July 27, 1814, *CVSP,* 11:362–63.

19. "Log of H.M.S. *Albion,*" July 26, 1814; Cockburn to Cochrane, July 24, 1814.

20. Hungerford to Barbour, July 27, 1814.

21. "Log of H.M.S. *Albion,*" July 26, 1814.

22. Hulbert Footner, *Sailor of Fortune: The Life and Adventures of Commodore Barney, U.S.N.* (New York: Harper & Brothers, 1940), 277.

23. Captain Joseph Nourse to Rear Admiral George Cockburn, July 23, 1814, Cockburn Papers, vol. 24, LC.

24. Ibid.

25. *Daily National Intelligencer,* July 23, 1814.

26. Nourse to Cockburn, July 23, 1814.

Chapter 15
The Buccaneers Spared Nothing

1. Rear Admiral George Cockburn to Vice Admiral Sir Alexander F. I. Cochrane, July 31, 1814, Cockburn Papers, vol. 24, LC; "Log of H.M.S. *Albion*" July 31, 1814, Cockburn Papers, LC.

2. *Daily National Intelligencer,* August 4, 1814, also republished in *Niles' Weekly Register* 7, no. 7 (November 5, 1814): 136; *Chronicles of St. Mary's* 8, no. 9 (September 1960): 4, 5.

3. *Niles' Weekly Register* 7, no. 4 (October 6, 1814): 61.

4. Rear Admiral George Cockburn to Captain Alexander Skene, July 29, 1814, Cockburn Papers, vol. 25, LC.

5. Rear Admiral George Cockburn to Vice Admiral Sir Alexander F. I. Cochrane, August 4, 1814, *NW,* 3:168–69.

6. "Log of H.M.S. *Albion,*" August 2, 1814.

7. Ibid., August 3, 1814; Cockburn to Cochrane, August 4, 1814, Cockburn Papers, LC.

8. "Log of H.M.S. *Albion,*" August 4, 1814, Cockburn Papers, LC; Cockburn to Cochrane, August 4, 1814; *Chronicles of St. Mary's* 10, no. 7 (July 1960): 72; Walter Biscoe Norris Jr., ed., *Westmoreland County, Virginia* (Montross, Va.: Westmoreland County Board of Supervisors, 1983), 358; William Lambert to Secretary of the Navy William Jones, August 12, 1814, RG 45, SNMLR, 1814, vol. 6, no. 20 (M 124, R. 65), NARA; *ASPNA,* Claims (Washington: Printed by Gales and Seaton, 1834), 1:795–800.

9. Ibid; Cockburn to Cochrane, August 4, 1814; Brigadier General John P. Hungerford to the Adjutant General [Claiborne W. Gooch], August 5, 1814, *CVSP,* 11: 367–69. The British claimed they had pursued the artillerymen for ten miles. One of Henderson's men would later die of his wounds.

10. Ibid.

11. Norris, *Westmoreland County,* 359.

12. Cockburn to Cochrane, August 4, 1814.

13. Hungerford to the Adjutant General, August 5, 1814.

14. "Log of H.M.S. *Albion,*" August 7 and 8, 1814, Cockburn Papers, LC; Rear Admiral George Cockburn to Vice Admiral Sir Alexander F. I. Cochrane, August 8, 1814, Cockburn Papers, vol. 24, LC; Lambert to Jones, August 12, 1814; *Chronicles of St. Mary's* 10, no. 7 (July 1960), 73; William Lambert to Governor James Barbour, August 12, 1814, *CVSP,* 11: 371–72; Regina Combs Hammett, *History of St. Mary's County, Maryland* (Ridge, Md.: privately published, 1977), 98.

15. Lambert to Jones, August 12, 1814.

16. "Log of H.M.S. *Albion,*" August 8, 1814, Cockburn Papers, LC.

17. Ibid., August 8, 9, and 10, 1814.

18. Ibid., August 10 and 11, 1814.

19. Ibid., August 12, 1814.

20. Ibid., August 11, 1814; *Daily National Intelligencer,* August 17, 1814; Rear Admiral George Cockburn to Vice Admiral Sir Alexander F. I. Cochrane, August 13, 1814, *NW,* 3:172–73.

21. "Log of H.M.S. *Albion,*" August 14, 1814, Cockburn Papers, LC.

Chapter 16

The Sweets of Plunder

1. Captain Joshua Barney to Secretary of Secretary of the Navy William Jones, August 1, 1814, RG 45, SNMLR, 1814, vol. 5, no. 103 (M 124, R 64), NARA.

2. Ibid.

3. Ibid.

4. Secretary of the Navy William Jones to Captain Joshua Barney, July 27, 1814, RG 45, SNCL, 1814, 173, NARA.

5. Barney to Jones, August 1, 1814.

6. Report of W. B. Barney, enclosure, with Barney to Jones, August 1, 1814.

7. Barney to Jones, August 1, 1814. The balance of the citations from the report in this section are from this source.

8. Captain Joshua Barney to Secretary of Secretary of the Navy William Jones, August 4, 1814, RG 45, SNMLR, 1814, vol. 5, no. 111 (M 124, R 64), NARA.

9. Barney to Jones, August 1, 1814.

10. Barney to Jones, August 4, 1814.

11. Captain Joseph Nourse to Rear Admiral George Cockburn, August 4, 1814, Cockburn Papers, vol. 38, LC.

12. Ibid.

13. Ibid.

14. Commander Hugh Pearson to Captain Joseph Nourse, August 3, 1814, Cockburn Papers, vol. 38, LC.

15. Ibid.

16. Ibid.

17. Barney to Jones, August 4, 1814; Regina Combs Hammett, *History of St. Mary's County, Maryland* (Ridge, Md.: Privately published, 1977), 162.

18. "A Personal Narrative of Events by Sea and Land, from the Year 1800 to 1815 Concluding with a Narrative of Some of the Principal Events in the Chesapeake and South Carolina, in 1814 and 1815," *Chronicles of St. Mary's* 8, no. 1 (January 1960): 4.

19. Captain Joseph Nourse to Rear Admiral George Cockburn, August 12, 1814, Cockburn Papers, vol. 38, LC.

20. "A Personal Narrative," 4.

21. Ibid. The author of "Personal Narrative" was quite likely the officer in command of HBMS *Brune,* Captain William S. Lovell.

22. "A Personal Narrative," 4.

23. Ibid.

24. Ibid., 4, 5.

25. Thomas L. McKenney, *Memoirs, Official and Personal,* 2 vols. (New York: Paine and Burgess, 1846), 1:5.

Chapter 17
Gathered Like a Snow-ball

1. *The Times* (of London), April 15, 1814.

2. Walter Lord, *The Dawn's Early Light* (New York: W. W. Norton & Co., Inc., 1972), 36; Vice Admiral Alexander F. I. Cochrane to Rear Admiral George Cockburn, July 1, 1814, Cockburn Papers, vol. 38, LC.

3. First Secretary of the Admiralty John W. Crocker to Vice Admiral Sir Alexander Cochrane, March 30, 1814, *NW,* 3:72n2; First Secretary of the Admiralty John W. Crocker to Vice Admiral Sir Alexander Cochrane, April 4, 1814, *NW,* 3:70–71; Secretary of State

for War and the Colonies Earl Bathurst to Major General Edward Barnes, May 20, 1814, *NW*, 3:72; Lord, *The Dawn's Early Light*, 37.

4. Lord, *The Dawn's Early Light*, 37–38.

5. Bathurst to Barnes, May 20, 1814.

6. Lord, *The Dawn's Early Light*, 36.

7. Bathurst to Barnes, May 20, 1814.

8. William M. Marine, *The British Invasion of Maryland 1812–1815* (1913; rpt., Hatboro, Pa.: Tradition Press, 1965), 72; Lord, *The Dawn's Early Light*, 41.

9. "Recollections of the Expedition to the Chesapeake, and Against New Orleans, in the Years 1814–15 By An Old Sub," *United Service Journal* (April 1840), reprinted in *News and Notes from the Prince George's County Historical Society* 9, no. 9 (September 1981): 57.

10. Lord, *The Dawn's Early Light*, 44; Vice Admiral Alexander F. I. Cochrane to Commanding Officers of the North American Station, July 18, 1814, *NW*, 3:140–41.

11. Lord, *The Dawn's Early Light*, 44; Cochrane to Commanding Officers, July 18, 1814; Marine, *The British Invasion*, 72; Vice Admiral Alexander F. I. Cochrane to Secretary of the Admiralty John W. Crocker, August 11, 1814, *NW*, 3:190. The men-of-war included HBMS *Pomona, Menelaus, Despatch, Rover, Meteor, Devastation, Diadem, Dictator, Trave, Weser*, and *Thames*.

12. Lieutenant David Boyd, new commander of *St. Lawrence*, was ordered by Cockburn on July 17 to proceed to Bermuda with the critical dispatches that were to influence Cochrane's decision to descend on the Chesapeake. "Log of H.M.S. *Albion*," July 17, 1814, Cockburn Papers, LC; Rear Admiral George Cockburn to Vice Admiral Sir Alexander Cochrane, July 17, 1814, Cockburn Papers, vol. 24, LC; Rear Admiral George Cockburn to Vice Admiral Sir Alexander Cochrane, July 17, 1814, Cockburn Papers, vol. 24, LC; Lord, *The Dawn's Early Light*, 48.

13. [Gleig, George Robert], *A Narrative of the Campaigns of the British Army, At Washington, Baltimore, and New Orleans, under the Generals Ross, Packenham, & Lambert, in the years 1814 and 1815 With Some Account of the Countries Visited* (Philadelphia: M. Carey & Sons, 1821), 85–86; Vice Admiral Alexander F. I. Cochrane to Secretary of the Admiralty John W. Crocker, August 11, 1814.

14. [Gleig], *A Narrative*, 86; Lord, *The Dawn's Early Light*, 49.

15. [Gleig], *A Narrative*, 86; Cochrane to Crocker, August 11, 1814, *NW*, 3: 189–90.

16. [Gleig], *A Narrative*, 86–87.

17. Lord, *The Dawn's Early Light*, 50; [Gleig], *A Narrative*, 87.

18. Lord, *The Dawn's Early Light*, 50; "Log of H.M.S. *Albion*," August 14, 1814, Cockburn Papers, LC.

19. *Daily National Intelligencer*, August 17, 1814; *Maryland Republican*, August 20, 1814.

20. "Log of H.M.S. *Albion*," August 14, 1814.

21. Rear Admiral George Cockburn to G.P. Hurlburt, June 25, 1814, Cockburn Papers, vol. 15, LC; Rear Admiral George Cockburn to Vice Admiral Alexander F. I. Cochrane, June 25, Cockburn Papers, vol. 24, LC; Rear Admiral George Cockburn to Vice Admiral Sir Alexander Cochrane, July 17, 1814, Cockburn Papers, vol. 24, LC.

22. "Log of H.M.S. *Albion*," August 12, 1814, Cockburn Papers, LC; Rear Admiral George Cockburn to Vice Admiral Alexander F. I. Cochrane, August 13, 1814, Cockburn

Papers, vol. 24, LC; Rear Admiral George Cockburn to Vice Admiral Alexander F. I. Cochrane, August 15, 1814, Cockburn Papers, vol. 24, LC; Marine, *The British Invasion,* 72.

23. Gleig claims that the Virginia Capes were sighted on the evening of August 14. The log of HBMS *Royal Oak* notes the sighting on the evening of August 15. American sightings of the fleet were first made on the morning of August 16, placing Gleig off by a full day, a mistake that was often made when sailing across the Atlantic, when a day was either lost or gained in the crossing. [Gleig], *A Narrative,* 87; "Log of H.M.S. *Royal Oak,*" August 15, 1814, *Chronicles of St. Mary's* 15, no. 2 (February 1967); Sailing Master Joseph Middleton to Captain Charles Gordon, August 16, 1814, RG 45, SNMLR, 1814, vol. 6, no. 34 (M 124, R 65), NARA.

24. Middleton to Gordon, August 16, 1814. Word was relayed to Richmond as well, but not until August 16 was Governor Barbour himself informed. When General Porter of the U.S. Army requested the 8th Brigade, Virginia State Militia, called up, he was refused. Brigadier General M. Porter, USA, to Governor James Barbour, August 16, 1814, *CVSP,* 11:373.

25. [Gleig], *A Narrative,* 88; "Recollections . . . By An Old Sub," 57.

26. *Alexandria Gazette,* August 20, 1814; Lord, *The Dawn's Early Light,* 20.

27. Thomas Swann to Secretary of War John Armstrong, August 17, 1814, Letters Received by the Secretary of War, ser. S-191 (8) RG 45 (M 222, R 14), NARA.

28. [Gleig], *A Narrative,* 88.

29. Ibid.; "Log of H.M.S. *Albion,*" August 17, 1814, Cockburn Papers, LC; Marine, *The British Invasion,* 72–73.

30. Vice Admiral Alexander F. I. Cochrane to Lord Bathurst, September 27, 1814, reprinted in *Niles' Weekly Register,* Supplement to Volume VII, 141. In late July Port Tobacco was defended by 300 to 350 infantry and forty dragoons under the command of Captain William D. Beall. *ASPMA,* 1:525.

31. *NW,* 3:192–93; "Log of H.M.S. *Albion,*" August 17, 1814; [Gleig], *A Narrative,* 90; "Log of H.M.S. *Severn,*" August 17, 1814, *Chronicles of St. Mary's* 14, no. 6 (June 1966).

32. "Log of H.M.S. *Albion,*" August 17, 1814.

33. Ibid., August 18, 1814; "Log of H.M.S. *Royal Oak,*" August 18, 1814, *Chronicles of St. Mary's* 15, no. 2 (February 1967); "Log of H.M.S. *Hebrus,*" August 18, 1814, *Chronicles of St. Mary's* 15, no. 2 (February 1967); "Log of H.M.S. *Severn,*" August 18, 1814, *Chronicles of St. Mary's* 14, no. 8 (August 1966). Lord notes that Captain Nourse possessed the only map of the Patuxent, probably developed during his forays up the river. The author of "Personal Narrative" included a chart of the Patuxent that was undoubtedly a copy of Nourse's original chart, and which may be the first known navigational chart ever produced of the river and is undoubtedly derived from the same as in the Poultney Malcolm Collection in the William L. Clements Library at the University of Michigan, Ann Arbor. Lord, *The Dawn's Early Light,* 56; "A Personal Narrative of Events by Sea and Land, from the Year 1800 to 1815 Concluding with a Narrative of Some of the Principal Events in the Chesapeake and South Carolina, in 1814 and 1815," *Chronicles of St. Mary's* 8, no. 1 (January 1960): 4.

34. Sir Alexander F. I. Cochrane to Secretary of State James Monroe, August 18, 1814, reprinted in *Niles' Weekly Register,* September 24, 1814, 17.

35. Ibid., 18.

36. "Recollections . . . By An Old Sub," 58.

37. "Log of H.M.S. *Albion*," August 18, 1814, Cockburn Papers, LC; "Log of H.M.S. *Royal Oak*," August 18, 1814; "Log of H.M.S. *Hebrus*," August 18, 1814; "Log of H.M.S. *Severn*," August 18, 1814.

38. "Log of H.M.S. *Albion*," August 18, 1814; "Log of H.M.S. *Royal Oak*," August 18, 1814; [Gleig], *A Narrative*, 93.

39. [Gleig], *A Narrative*, 93.

40. "Log of H.M.S. *Albion*," August 19, 1814, Cockburn Papers, LC; [Gleig], *A Narrative*, 94; "Recollections . . . By An Old Sub," 57. *Anaconda*, formerly a New York privateer, had been captured as a prize by Cockburn on July 11, 1813, during a British raid on Ocracoke Inlet, North Carolina, and then taken into Royal Navy service.

41. "Log of H.M.S. *Royal Oak*," August 19, 1814, *Chronicles of St. Mary's* 15, no. 2 (February 1967)..

42. Captain Charles Gordon to Secretary of the Navy William Jones, August 16, 1814, RG 45, SNMLR, 1814, vol. 5, no. 105 (M 125, R 38), NARA; Report from the Navy Department, Including the Official Report of Commodore Barney, October 3, 1814 (hereafter Navy Department Report), *ASPMA*, 1:575.

43. Secretary of the Navy William Jones to Captain Joshua Barney, August 19, 1814, RG 45, SNCL, 1814, 181, NARA.

44. Commodore Joshua Barney to Secretary of the Navy William Jones, August 19, 1814, RG 45, SNMLR, 1814, vol. 6, no. 30 (M 124, R 65), NARA; Lord, *The Dawn's Early Light*, 59; Hulbert Footner, *Sailor of Fortune: The Life and Adventures of Commodore Barney, U.S.N.* (New York: Harper & Brothers, 1940), 278; Mary Barney, ed., *A Biographical Memoir of the Late Commodore Joshua Barney: From Autobiographical Notes and Journals in Possession of His Family, and Other Authentic Sources* (Boston: Gray and Bowen, 1832), 262.

45. Brigadier General William Henry Winder to Secretary of War John Armstrong, August 19, 1814, *ASPMA*, 1:547.

46. Lord, *The Dawn's Early Light*, 56; [Gleig], *A Narrative*, 94.

47. [Gleig], *A Narrative*, 95.

48. Ibid., 94.

49. Ibid., 95.

50. "Log of H.M.S. *Royal Oak*," August 18, 1814.

51. [Gleig], *A Narrative*, 97.

52. Ibid. By the time intelligence had reached Washington concerning the establishment of a British picket line about Benedict, it had grown in the telling to monumental proportions. It was said that the British had "infiladed" the entire peninsula "by establishing a line of pickets from Benedict to a point on the Potomac, at which lies another squadron of ships." *Daily National Intelligencer*, August 22, 1814.

53. There is some discrepancy concerning the number of guns carried ashore and later used by the army. Gleig notes that a single 6-pounder and two 3-pounders were all that were brought along and "all the other guns had to be left behind." The log of *Royal Oak* indicates that each boat and launch going ashore carried two howitzers per boat. Gleig states that the limitation on the amount of artillery permitted ashore was due to a lack of horses to drag them overland when the army marched. "Except those belonging to the general

and staff officers," he wrote, "there was not a single horse in the army. To have taken on shore a large park of artillery would have been, therefore, absolute." It is probable that the majority of guns taken ashore were employed for the defense of the beachhead. [Gleig], *A Narrative,* 96; "Log of H.M.S. *Tonnant,*" *Chronicles of St. Mary's* 14, no. 8 (August 1966); Lord, *The Dawn's Early Light,* 64–65.

Chapter 18
Blown to Atoms

1. Walter Lord, *The Dawn's Early Light* (New York: W. W. Norton and Co., Inc., 1972), 27–28.

2. Ibid., 29; *Daily National Intelligencer,* August 22, 1814.

3. Narrative of General Winder (hereafter Winder Narrative), September 26, 1814, *ASPMA,* 1:554; Letters of Colonel Monroe, then secretary of state, November 13, 1814, *ASPMA,* 1:536.

4. Secretary of the Navy William Jones to Commodore John Rodgers, August 19, 1814, *NW,* 3:199; Walter Lord, *The Dawn's Early Light* (New York: W. W. Norton & Co., Inc., 1972), 61. Annapolis was among the more poorly defended of the potential targets and most assessable of all. General William Henry Winder, in a letter dated July 16, 1814, to Secretary of War John Armstrong, had expressed his embarrassment in relation to the situation of Annapolis, and gave as his opinion that a large force and many additional works would be necessary to defend it against a serious attack by land and water. He noted its importance to the enemy, and the ease with which it might be maintained by them if taken, as they could easily command the waters surrounding the town, along with an entrenchment of seven or eight hundred yards, protected by batteries. One of the two major city defenses, Fort Madison, was exposed, and unhealthy in the months of August and September, and had been provided with two 50-pound columbiads, two 24-pounders, two 18-pounders, one 12-pounder, and one 4-pounder, which, if taken, might be turned with success against nearby Fort Severn. He suggested that these guns should be removed, and arrangements made to blow up the fort, but opined the importance of defending the town if the means could be obtained. Correspondence of the Secretary of War and General Winder, *ASPMA,* 1:525.

5. Winder's Narrative, September 26, 1814, *ASPMA,* 1:552; Lord; *The Dawn's Early Light,* 29.

6. Lord, *The Dawn's Early Light,* 60.

7. Secretary of the Navy William Jones to Commodore John Rodgers, August 19, 1814, *NW,* 3:199; Secretary of the Navy William Jones to Commodore David Porter, August 19, 1814, RG 45, SNLO, 1814, vol. 11, 140 (M 19, R 11), NARA.

8. Winder's Narrative, September 26, 1814, *ASPMA,* 1:554; Letters of Colonel Monroe, then secretary of state, November 13, 1814, *ASPMA,* 1:536.

9. Captain Joshua Barney to Secretary of the Navy William Jones, August 20, 1814, RG 45, SNMLR, 1814, vol. 6, no. 31 (M 124, R 65), NARA.

10. Copy of a letter from James Monroe to the president of the United States, August 20, 1814, *ASPMA,* 1:537, reprinted also in Stanislaus Murray Hamilton, ed., *The Writings of*

James Monroe, vol. 5 (New York: G. Putnam's Sons, 1901), 289; Letters of Colonel Monroe, November 13, 1814, *ASPMA,* 1:536; Winder's Narrative, September 26, 1814, *ASPMA,* 1:554. The dispatch quoted by Hamilton appeared in the local press sans author and may have been penned by someone other than Monroe. Monroe's official dispatch, from Horse Road, near Acquasco, and represented in *Writings,* contains much the same information.

11. General Van Ness's Statement, November 23, 1814, *ASPMA,* 1:581–82; Major General John P. Van Ness to Secretary of War John Armstrong, August 20, 1814, *ASPMA,* 1:583; Lord, *The Dawn's Early Light,* 61.

12. Secretary of the Navy William Jones to Captain Joshua Barney, August 20, 1814, Barney Papers, Dreer Collection, Historical Society of Pennsylvania, Pa.

13. Ibid.

14. Ibid.; Report from the Navy Department, Including the Official Report of Commodore Barney (hereafter Navy Department Report), October 3, 1814, *ASPMA,* 1:576.

15. Jones to Barney, August 20. Jones did not inform Winder that Barney was to operate under his command until after the order had been sent. He called upon the general on August 20 at his headquarters in the capital, at McKeown's Hotel on Pennsylvania Avenue, to inform him of the transfer and to also apprise him that he would also be turning over the mechanics at the Washington Navy Yard to serve as axmen to fell trees in the enemy's path, and to send the U.S. Marines to help defend Fort Washington if necessary. Navy Department Report, October 3, 1814, *ASPMA,* 1:576.

16. Jones to Barney, August 20, 1814.

17. Ibid.

18. Ibid.

19. "Log of H.M.S. *Royal Oak,*" August 20, 1814, *Chronicles of St. Mary's* 15, no. 2 (February 1967); "Log of H.M.S. *Albion,*" August 20, 1814, Cockburn Papers, LC.

20. [Gleig, George Robert], *A Narrative of the Campaigns of the British Army, at Washington, Baltimore, and New Orleans, under the Generals Ross, Packenham, & Lambert, in the Years 1814 and 1815 With Some Account of the Countries Visited* (Philadelphia: M. Carey & Sons, 1821), 99.

21. *Daily National Intelligencer,* August 22, 1814.

22. Ibid.

23. Ibid.

24. Ibid.; Lord, *The Dawn's Early Light,* 62.

25. Winder's Narrative, *ASPMA,* 1:554–55; General W[alter] Smith's Statement (hereafter Smith's Statement), October 6, 1814, *ASPMA,* 1:563; Lord, *The Dawn's Early Light,* 62.

26. Vice Admiral Sir Alexander F. I. Cochrane to Lord Bathurst [John Wilson Crocker], September 27, 1814, reprinted in *Niles' Weekly Register,* Supplement to Volume VII, 146.

27. Rear Admiral George Cockburn to Vice Admiral Sir Alexander F. I. Cochrane, August 22, 1814, Cockburn Papers, vol. 24, LC; [Gleig], *A Narrative,* 99.

28. [Gleig], *A Narrative,* 100.

29. Ibid., 100–101; Christopher T. George, *Terror on the Chesapeake: The War of 1812 on the Bay* (Shippensburg, Pa.: White Mane Books, 2000), 85.

30. [Gleig], *A Narrative,* 102–3.

31. Ibid., 103.

32. Ibid., 104; "Log of H.M.S. *Royal Oak*," August 20, 1814; "Log of H.M.S. *Albion*," August 20, 1814.

33. Lord, *The Dawn's Early Light*, 62.

34. James Monroe to the president of the United States, August 21, 1814, *ASPMA*, 1:537.

35. Ibid.

36. Captain Joshua Barney to Secretary of the Navy William Jones, August 21, 1814, RG 45, SNMLR, 1814, vol. 6, no. 36 (M 124, R 65), NARA.

37. Ibid.

38. [Gleig], *A Narrative*, 107.

39. Ibid., 104–5.

40. Ibid., 106–7.

41. Cockburn to Cochrane, August 22, 1814.

42. [Gleig], *A Narrative*, 107.

43. James Monroe to Brigadier General William Henry Winder, August 21, 1814, *ASPMA*, 1:537. Winder received Monroe's report shortly after crossing the Eastern Branch of the Potomac and undoubtedly hastened his pace. Winder's Narrative, *ASPMA*, 1:555. Lord has treated the rush by General Ross against Monroe and his dragoons as two separate incidents. A close reading of Gleig, however, suggests that Gleig's account and a foray against American units by Ross somewhat earlier were actually one and the same. [Gleig], *A Narrative*, 107; Lord, *The Dawn's Early Light*, 66–67.

44. *Severn, Hebrus,* and *Manly* were directed to follow Cockburn's barge force upriver "as far as might prove practicable." However, none of the vessels were able to move up higher than a mile or so above Benedict. Cockburn to Cochrane, August 22, 1814; "Log of H.M.S. *Severn*," August 23, 1894, *Chronicles of St. Mary's* 14, no. 8 (August 1966). Dr. Hanson Catlett states Monroe departed Nottingham about sunset which, on August 21, arrived about 7:56 p.m. If the British arrived at 5:00 p.m. as Madison reported, he would have waited in the vicinity for nearly three hours, which seems quite unlikely. Dr. Catlett's Statement, *ASPMA*, 1:584.

45. [Gleig], *A Narrative*, 109.

46. Barney to Jones, August 21, 1814. The size of the detachment of flotillamen left behind to destroy the American flotilla, and the actual number of vessels that were destroyed are questions of some interest. In a letter to the editors of the *Daily National Intelligencer*, republished in *Niles' Weekly Register*, Barney states that he detailed 103 men to destroy the flotilla, which he numbered at "14 open row boats (not gun boats) and one tender." On October 30, 1814, he wrote to U.S. Representative Pleasants of Virginia informing him that he left "only eight men in each barge to take care of them as the case might be, but by no means to let them fall into the hands of the enemy." In another letter to the *Intelligencer* republished in an undated supplement to *Niles' Weekly Register*, the commodore stated that he left 6 or 8 men in every barge. If 15 vessels, as his own count claims, was the correct number of boats left, a total of 120 men would have been left behind, according to his letter to Pleasants. By Admiral Cockburn's count, there were a total of 17 vessels belonging to the flotilla, 16 of which were blown up, and a 17th one captured. There were also 13 merchantmen above the flotilla, which Barney never mentions, 5 of which were captured and

the remainder burned by the British. Joshua Barney to Mr. Pleasants, October 30, 1814, in *Niles' Weekly Register,* November 5, 1814, reprinted in Mary Barney, ed., *A Biographical Memoir of the Late Commodore Joshua Barney: From Autobiographical Notes and Journals in Possession of His Family, and Other Authentic Sources* (Boston: Gray and Bowen, 1832), 321–23; "British Official Account Set Right," *Niles' Weekly Register,* Supplement to Volume VII, 159; Cockburn to Cochrane, August 22, 1814.

47. Barney to Jones, August 21, 1814; Barney to Pleasants, October 30, 1814; Charles Ball, *A Narrative of the Life and Adventures of Charles Ball* (Lewistown, Pa., 1836), 362; Lord, *The Dawn's Early Light,* 68. Some historians such as Whitehorne state that Barney retired from the fleet taking as much equipment and as many guns as possible. Norton, apparently confusing the armament brought to the Woodyard by Miller's marines, states that Barney and his men were exhausted when they reached Upper Marlboro, having just dragged two naval 18-pounders and three 12-pounders with them overland. This is definitely not the case, as the commodore himself states they carried but three days' provisions and nothing else. Many of his men were shoeless and carried only the clothes on their backs. His October 30, 1814, letter to Representative Pleasants states he arrived at the Woodyard "where I found the marine corps and five pieces of heavy artillery, which the secretary of the navy had the precaution to send forward from Washington and place under my command." Later salvage reports on the fleet indicate that all the cannon had gone down with the squadron, the majority of which were later recovered. Joseph A. Whitehorne, *The Battle of Baltimore 1814* (Baltimore: The Nautical & Aviation Publishing Company of America, 1997), 121; Louis Arthur Norton, *Joshua Barney: Hero of the Revolution and 1812* (Annapolis, Md.: Naval Institute Press, 2000), 179; Barney to Pleasants, October 30, 1814. See Epilogue for account of salvage efforts.

48. Smith's Statement, *ASPMA,* 1:563.

49. Ibid.; Catlett's Statement, *ASPMA,* 1:584; Winder's Narrative, *ASPMA,* 1:554–55; Navy Department Report, October 3, 1814, *ASPMA,* 1:576; Whitehorne, *The Battle of Baltimore,* 120.

50. Smith's Statement, *ASPMA,* 1:563.

51. Winder's Narrative, *ASPMA,* 1:554–55; Navy Department Report, October 3, 1814, *ASPMA,* 1:576; Lord, *The Dawn's Early Light,* 67–68. Jones reported on October 3 that Miller's force consisted of "a detachment of about one hundred and ten marines," not the 120 reported by Winder on September 26, who was at the Woodyard when they came in. I have accepted Winder's report as the most likely accurate of the two. Whitehorne, *The Battle of Baltimore,* 122, states that Miller's unit consisted of 103 marines, obviously confusing the marine count with Barney's account of the men left behind to destroy the flotilla. Norton, *Joshua Barney,* 179, states the marines, who arrived in company with Secretary Jones, numbered only seventy-eight, which is the number the unite had been reduced to at the Battle of Blandensburg.

52. [Gleig], *A Narrative,* 109.

53. Ibid.

54. Lord, *The Dawn's Early Light,* 70; Smith's Statement, *ASPMA,* 1:563; Winder's Narrative, 555; Captain Burch's Statement (hereafter Burch's Statement), October 12, 1814, *ASPMA,* 1:574.

55. Winder's Narrative, *ASPMA,* 1:555; Catlett's Statement, *ASPMA,* 1:584.

56. Smith's Statement, *ASPMA,* 1:563.

57. Burch's Statement, *ASPMA,* 1:574

58. [Gleig], 110; Winder's Narrative, *ASPMA,* 1:555; *Daily National Intelligencer,* August 23, 1814; Catlett's Statement, *ASPMA,* 1:584; Lord, *The Dawn's Early Light,* 71.

59. Cockburn to Cochrane, August 22, 1814.

60. Ibid.; Barney to Pleasants, October 30, 1814. Cochrane to Bathurst, September 27, 1814, states the position of the fleet as three miles above Pig Point. Lieutenant James Scott later reported a colorful account of the firing on Cockburn's gig, and his own foray ashore. Two of the captives were found to be British seamen who had deserted from the fleet. Captain James Scott, *Recollections of a Naval Life,* 3 vols. (London: Bentley, 1834), 3:378–79.

61. Winder's Narrative, *ASPMA,* 1:555.

62. Catlett's Statement, *ASPMA,* 1:584; Smith's Statement *ASPMA,* 1563; Lt. Colonel [Jacint] Lavall [Statement], *ASPMA,* 1:570.

63. Catlett's Statement, *ASPMA,* 1:584; Burch's Statement *ASPMA,* 1:574.

64. Smith's Statement, *ASPMA,* 1:563; Catlett's Statement, *ASPMA,* 1:584.

65. Smith's Statement, *ASPMA,* 1:563; Winder's Narrative, *ASPMA,* 1:555.

66. Mary Barney, *A Biographical Memoir,* 263–64.

67. James Monroe to the president of the United States, August 21, 1814, *ASPMA,* 1:436.

68. Ibid.

Chapter 19

Not a Bridge Was Broken

1. [Gleig, George Robert], *A Narrative of the Campaigns of the British Army, at Washington, Baltimore, and New Orleans, under the Generals Ross, Packenham, & Lambert, in the Years 1814 and 1815 With Some Account of the Countries Visited* (Philadelphia: M. Carey & Sons, 1821), 110.

2. Ibid.

3. Ibid., 45–46, 150; Irvin Molotsky, *The Flag, The Poet & The Song: The Story of the Star-Spangled Banner* (New York: Dutton, 2001), 71; Walter Lord, *The Dawn's Early Light* (New York: W. W. Norton & Co., Inc., 1972), 79.

4. [Gleig], *A Narrative,* 150; Molotsky, *The Flag, The Poet & The Song,* 71; Lord, *The Dawn's Early Light,* 79.

5. William M. Marine, *The British Invasion of Maryland 1812–1815* (1913; rpt., Hatboro, Pa.: Tradition Press, 1965), 159; [Gleig], *A Narrative,* 150.

6. Lord, *The Dawn's Early Light,* 80; [Gleig], *A Narrative,* 111.

7. [Gleig], *A Narrative,* 105.

8. Vice Admiral Sir Alexander F. I. Cochrane to Secretary of State for War and the Colonies Earl Bathurst, July 14, 1814, *NW,* 3:131.

9. Vice Admiral Sir Alexander F. I. Cochrane to Rear Admiral George Cockburn, August 22, 1814, *NW,* 3:197.

10. Rear Admiral George Cockburn to Vice Admiral Sir Alexander F. I. Cochrane, August 22, 1814, Cockburn Papers, vol. 24, LC.

11. Rear Admiral George Cockburn to Vice Admiral Sir Alexander F. I. Cochrane, August 23, 1814, Cockburn Papers, vol. 24, LC.

12. Cockburn to Cochrane, August 22, 1814,

13. Winder's Narrative, *ASPMA*, 1:555.

14. Ibid., 1:555, 556.

15. Smith's Statement, *ASPMA*, 1:563; Winder's Narrative, *ASPMA*, 1:555.

16. Assembled at Battalion Old Fields, according to General Smith, was 1,070 District volunteers and militia, 350 of Scott's 36th U.S. Infantry; 240 of Lieutenant Colonel Kramer's battalion of drafted militia; 150 of Major Henry Waring's battalion of Prince George's Militia; a total of about 1,800 men. Colonel Barney's 400 and Miller's 120 made the count 2,320. Assuming Barney's detachment left behind to destroy the fleet had also come in the total would be 2,423. Smith's Statement, *ASPMA*, 1:563.

17. Winder's Narrative, *ASPMA*, 1:555.

18. Navy Department Report, *ASPMA*, 3:576; Mary Barney, ed., *A Biographical Memoir of the Late Commodore Joshua Barney: From Autobiographical Notes and Journals in Possession of His Family, and Other Authentic Sources* (Boston: Gray and Bowen, 1832), 264; Winder's Narrative, *ASPMA*, 1:555; Smith's Statement, *ASPMA*, 1:563.

19. Winder's Narrative, *ASPMA*, 1:555.

20. Smith's Statement, *ASPMA*, 1:563; Winder's Narrative, *ASPMA*, 1:555. Stansbury's force then consisted of 550 men in Lieutenant Colonel John Ragan's 1st Regiment of riflemen, and 803 in Lieutenant Colonel Jonathan Shutz's 2nd Regiment. General Stansbury's Report, November 15, 1814 (hereafter Stansbury's Report), *ASPMA*, 1:560.

21. Colonel Beall had departed the Woodyard almost as soon as he arrived in order to proceed to Annapolis to take command of Prince George's County militiamen that had been earlier dispatched to that place to counter a perceived British threat.

22. Smith's Statement, *ASPMA*, 1:563; Winder's Narrative, *ASPMA*, 1:55, 556; President James Madison to Mrs. Madison, August 22, 1814, in *The Writings of James Madison*, ed. Galliard Hunt (New York: G. P. Putnam's Sons, 1908), 8:293–94.

23. Winder's Narrative, *ASPMA*, 1:555.

24. Madison to Mrs. Madison, August 22, 1814; Navy Department Report, *ASPMA*, 1:576; Mary Barney, *A Biographical Memoir*, 264.

25. Smith's Statement, *ASPMA*, 1:563–64; Winder's Narrative, *ASPMA*, 1:555–56. Smith (564) says Winder departed at noon, but later stated that Peter's unit left at 11:00 a.m., which would have meant that the order was relayed at or before that time, probably immediately after the parade inspection.

26. Smith's Statement, *ASPMA*, 1:564.

27. Ibid.

28. Anthony S. Pitch, *The Burning of Washington: The British Invasion of 1814* (Annapolis, Md.: Naval Institute Press, 1998), 57.

29. [Gleig], *A Narrative*, 111.

30. Winder's Narrative, *ASPMA*, 1:556; Pitch, *The Burning of Washington*, 57.

31. Smith's Statement, *ASPMA*, 1:564; Burch's Statement, *ASPMA*, 1:574; Major General Robert Ross to Secretary of State for War and the Colonies Earl Bathurst, August 30, 1814, *NW*, 3: 224; Winder's Narrative, *ASPMA*, 1:556.

32. Smith's Statement, *ASPMA*, 1:564; Captain Joshua Barney to Secretary of the Navy William Jones, August 29, 1814, RG 45, SNMLR, 1814, vol. 6, no. 57 (M 124, R 65), NARA; Winder's Narrative, *ASPMA*, 1:556; Navy Department Report, *ASPMA*, 1:576.

33. Burch's Statement, *ASPMA*, 1:574.

34. Winder's Narrative, *ASPMA*, 1:556; Smith's Statement, *ASPMA*, 1:564; Thomas L. McKenney, *Memoirs, Official and Personal*, 2 vols. (New York: Paine and Burgess, 1846), 1:45–46); Barney to Jones, August 29, 1814; Burch's Statement, *ASPMA*, 1:574; Smith's Statement, *ASPMA*, 1:564.

35. Burch's Statement, *ASPMA*, 1:574; Catlett's Statement, *ASPMA*, 1:584; Lieutenant Colonel Joseph Sterett's Statement, November 22, 1814 (hereafter Sterett's Statement), *ASPMA*, 1:568.

36. Major William Pinkney's Statement, November 16, 1814 (hereafter Pinkney's Statement), *ASPMA*, 1:571; *Daily National Intelligencer*, August 18 and 21, 1814.

37. Winder's Narrative, *ASPMA*, 1:556–57.

38. Ibid., 1:557; Smith's Statement, *ASPMA*, 1:564.

39. Pinkney's Statement, *ASPMA*, 1:572.

40. Burch's Statement, *ASPMA*, 1:574.

41. Ibid.

42. Cockburn to Cochrane, August 27, 1814, *NW*, 3:220–21.

43. Stansbury Report, *ASPMA*, 1:560, 561; Henry T. Tuckerman, *Life of John Pendleton Kennedy* (New York: 1871), excerpt reprinted in Marine, *The British Invasion*, 112.

44. Winder's Narrative *ASPMA*, 1:556; Barney to Jones, August 29, 1814.

45. Barney to Jones, August 29, 1814.

Chapter 20
Came Up at a Trot

1. Catlett's Statement, *ASPMA*, 1:584; Burch's Statement, *ASPMA*, 1:574; Anthony S. Pitch, *The Burning of Washington: The British Invasion of 1814* (Annapolis, Md.: Naval Institute Press, 1998), 64.

2. Catlett's Statement, *ASPMA*, 1:584.

3. Memorandum by James Madison, August 24, 1814, James Madison Papers, LC; Pitch, *The Burning of Washington*, 63. See George W. Campbell's Letter, December 7, 1814, *ASPMA*, 1:597–99, for the tiff between Armstrong and Campbell.

4. Stansbury's Report, *ASPMA*, 1:561; Pinkney's Statement, November 16, 1814, *ASPMA*, 1:572; J. Lavall to R. M. Johnson, and George Hoffman to John Hoffman, September 9, 1814, War of 1812 Collection, MHS. Catlett's Statement, *ASPMA*, 1:584, states Stansbury's move was made at 11:00 a.m.

5. Stansbury's Report, *ASPMA*, 1:562.

6. Ibid., 1:561; Pinkney's Statement, *ASPMA*, 1:572.

7. Stansbury Report, *ASPMA*, 1:560; Pinkney's Statement, *ASPMA*, 1:571–74.

8. Pinkney's Statement, *ASPMA*, 1:572; Lieutenant Colonel Joseph Sterett's Statement, November 22, 1814, *ASPMA*, 1:568.

9. Pinkney's Statement, *ASPMA*, 1:572.

10. Ibid.; Colonel William D. Beall's Statement, November 22, 1814, *ASPMA*, 1:571.

11. Pinkney's Statement, *ASPMA*, 1:572–73.

12. Winder's Narrative, *ASPMA*, 1:556–57; Captain Joshua Barney to Secretary of the Navy William Jones, August 29, 1814, RG 45, SNMLR, 1814, vol. 6, no. 57 (M 124, R 65), NARA.

13. Navy Department Report, *ASPMA*, 1:576; Winder's Narrative, *ASPMA*, 1:557, Barney to Jones August 27; James Madison, Memorandum, August 24, 1814; Burch's Statement, *ASPMA*, 1:574, noted he was relieved at 10:00 a.m. by Barney, which would have been off by an hour as Secretary Jones was at the meeting, which convened at 9:00 a.m. Jones did not leave the meeting until 10:00 a.m., and almost immediately encountered Barney already laying out his position. Law's Statement, *ASPMA*, 1:585, says that Burch's unit received the order to march at 11:00 a.m., which is a more likely time.

14. Law's Statement, *ASPMA*, 1:599; Navy Department Report, *ASPMA*, 1:576.

15. Pitch, *The Burning of Washington*, 65.

16. Navy Department Report, *ASPMA*, 1:576; Smith's Statement, *ASPMA*, 1:564.

17. Barney to Jones, August 27, 1814; Navy Department Report, *ASPMA*, 1:576; Secretary of the Navy Jones to Master Commandant John O. Creighton, August 24, 1814, *NW*, 3:206.

18. Barney to Jones, August 27, 1814; Navy Department Report, *ASPMA*, 1:576.

19. Joseph A. Whitehorne, *The Battle of Baltimore 1814* (Baltimore: The Nautical & Aviation Publishing Company of America, 1997), 129.

20. Smith's Statement, *ASPMA*, 1:564; Navy Department Report, *ASPMA*, 1:576.

21. Smith's Statement, *ASPMA*, 1:564.

22. Ibid.

23. Ibid.

24. Ibid.

25. J. Lavall to R. M. Johnson (undated), *ASPMA*, 1:570.

26. Burch's Statement, *ASPMA*, 1:574; Law's Statement, *ASPMA*, 1:585–86.

Chapter 21
I Told You It Was the Flotillamen

1. *Daily National Intelligencer*, July 7, 8, 14, and September 20, 1814; *Federal Republican*, July 8, 11, 18, 1814.

2. William Simmons Letter, November 28, 1814, *ASPMA*, 1:596. The cites that follow that deal with Simmons are from this source.

3. Catlett's Statement, *ASPMA*, 1:584.

4. [Gleig, George Robert], *A Narrative of the Campaigns of the British Army, at Washington, Baltimore, and New Orleans, under the Generals Ross, Packenham, & Lambert, in the Years 1814 and 1815 With Some Account of the Countries Visited* (Philadelphia: M. Carey & Sons, 1821), 118; Catlett's Statement, *ASPMA*, 1:585.

5. Major General Robert Ross to Secretary of State for War and the Colonies Earl Bathurst, August 30, 1814, *NW*, 3:224; Winder's Narrative, *ASPMA*, 1:543; Law's Statement, *ASPMA*, 1:586; Stansbury's Report, *ASPMA*, 1:561.

6. Catlett's Statement, *ASPMA,* 1:584.

7. Ross to Bathurst, August 30, 1814.

8. Rear Admiral George Cockburn to Vice Admiral Sir Alexander F. I. Cochrane, August 27, 1814, *NW,* 3:220; Ross to Bathurst, August 30, 1814, *NW,* 3: 223; Sir Harry Smith, *The Autobiography of Lt.-Gen. Sir Harry Smith* (London: Murray, 1903), 199.

9. Ross to Bathurst, August 30, 1814; William James, *A Full and Correct Account of the Military Occurrence of the Late War between Great Britain and the United States of America* (London: Black, Kingsbury, Parbury, & Allen, 1818), 2:496–97.

10. Pinkney's Statement, *ASPMA,* 1:573; Catlett's Statement, *ASPMA,* 1:584.

11. *Niles' Weekly Register,* Supplement to Volume VII, 150.

12. Catlett's Statement, *ASPMA,* 1:584; Walter Lord, *The Dawn's Early Light* (New York: W. W. Norton & Co., Inc., 1972), 25. Monroe stated that the president said they should retire to the rear, "leaving the military movement to military men." Monroe letter, November 13, 1814, *ASPMA,* 1:537; Catlett's Statement, *ASPMA,* 1:584; Ross to Bathurst, August 30, 1814, *NW,* 3: 225; Stansbury's Report, *ASPMA,* 1:562; [Gleig], *A Narrative,* 122.

13. [Gleig], *A Narrative,* 122–23; Stansbury's Report, *ASPMA,* 1:562.

14. Stansbury's Report, *ASPMA,* 1:562; Burch's Statement, *ASPMA,* 1:574; Pinkney's Statement, *ASPMA,* 1:573; [Gleig], *A Narrative,* 122–23.

15. Captain James Scott, *Recollections of a Naval Life,* 3 vols. (London: Bentley, 1834), 3:286.

16. Captain Joshua Barney to Secretary of the Navy William Jones, August 29, 1814, RG 45, SNMLR, 1814, vol. 6, no. 57 (M 124, R 65), NARA; Smith's Statement, *ASPMA,* 1:565; List of Marines at Bladensburg, and Samuel Miller to David Henshaw, December 24, 1843, (Samuel) Miller Papers, including List of Marines at Bladensburg, Personal Papers Collection, Marine Corps History and Museums Division, Washington, D.C.; Anthony S. Pitch, *The Burning of Washington: The British Invasion of 1814* (Annapolis, Md.: Naval Institute Press, 1998), 67.

17. General Ross and William Elliott to William Thornton, March 11, 1815, William Thornton Papers, LC; [Gleig], *A Narrative,* 71; "The Triumphant Mob . . . Victorious British Army," *Federal Republican,* September 2, 1814; Harry Smith, *The Autobiography of Lt.-Gen. Sir Harry Smith* (London: Murray, 1903), 199.

18. Pinckney's Statement, *ASPMA,* 1:571–72; Winder's Narrative, *ASPMA,* 1:558.

19. Captain John Knox to unidentified recipient, November 23, 1814, in [R. R. Gubbins], *The 85th King's Light Infantry,* ed. C. R. B. Barrett (London: Spottiswoode, 1913), 153.

20. Pinkney's Statement, *ASPMA,* 1:573.

21. Henry Fulford letter, August 26, 1814, reprinted in William M. Marine, *The British Invasion of Maryland 1812–1815* (1913; rpt., Hatboro, Pa.: Tradition Press, 1965), 114.

22. Pinckney's Statement, *ASPMA,* 1:573. Pinkney says they fired only once. Doughty corrected the account in a letter dated January 14, 1815, published in *Daily National Intelligencer,* February 2, 1815.

23. Pinckney's Statement, *ASPMA,* 1:573, 574.

24. Winder's Narrative, *ASPMA,* 1:558; Pinckney's Statement, *ASPMA,* 1:573.

25. Winder's Narrative, *ASPMA,* 1:558; Pinckney's Statement, *ASPMA,* 1:573; Stansbury's Report, *ASPMA,* 1:562.

26. Burch's Statement, *ASPMA,* 1:574.

27. Ibid.

28. Mr. John Law's Statement, November 10, 1814, *ASPMA,* 1:586.

29. Lavall's Statement, *ASPMA,* 1:569–70.

30. Ibid., 1:570.

31. Ibid., 1:571.

32. Stansbury's Report, *ASPMA,* 1:562.

33. Winder's Narrative, *ASPMA,* 1:558.

34. Ibid.; Stansbury's Report, *ASPMA,* 1562; Brigadier General William Henry Winder to Secretary of War John Armstrong, August 27, 1814, *ASPMA,* 1:548.

35. Kennedy, in William M. Marine, *The British Invasion of Maryland 1812–1815* (1913; rpt., Hatboro, Pa.: Tradition Press, 1965), 112–13.

36. Fulford letter, in Marine, *The British Invasion,* 114.

37. Winder's Narrative, *ASPMA,* 1:558.

38. Ibid.; Smith's Statement, *ASPMA,* 1:565.

39. Pitch, *The Burning of Washington,* 80–81.

40. [Gleig], *A Narrative,* 73.

41. Harry Smith, *Autobiography,* 199–200.

42. Scott, *Recollections,* 3:289.

43. Barney to Jones, August 29, 1814.

44. Ibid.

45. Ibid.

46. Ibid.

47. John Webster to Brantz Mayer, July 22, 1853, War of 1812 Collection, MHS; Scott, *Recollections,* 3:287; [Gleig], *A Narrative,* 75; [Robert J. Barrett], "Naval Recollections of the Late American War," *United Service Journal and Naval and Military Magazine,* Part 1 (April 1841): 459.

48. Captain Joshua Barney to *Daily National Intelligencer,* n.d., in Mary Barney, ed., *A Biographical Memoir of the Late Commodore Joshua Barney: From Autobiographical Notes and Journals in Possession of His Family, and Other Authentic Sources* (Boston: Gray and Bowen, 1832), Appendix, 321.

49. Pinckney's Statement, *ASPMA,* 1:571–74; Mary Barney, *A Biographical Memoir,* 265–66, 316; Lord, *The Dawn's Early Light,* 130.

50. Pinckney's Statement, *ASPMA,* 1:571–74; Mary Barney, *A Biographical Memoir,* 265–66, 316; Samuel Miller to David Henshaw, December 24, 1843; Charles Ball, *Slavery in the United States: A Narrative of the Life and Adventures of Charles Ball, a Black Man* (1836; rpt., Detroit, Mich.: Negro History Press, 1970), 362; "The Triumphant Mob . . . Victorious British Army," *Federal Republican,* September 2, 1814; Mary Barney, *A Biographical Memoir,* 266; *Niles' Weekly Register,* October 1, 1814, 41.

51. Barney to Jones, August 29, 1814; Winder's Narrative, *ASPMA,* 1:558; *Niles' Weekly Register,* December 17, 1814; Ball, *Slavery in the United States,* 362.

52. Barney to Jones, August 29, 1814; Pitch, *The Burning of Washington,* 82; Lieutenant Colonel J. Thompson to Brigadier General Walter Smith, October 5, 1814, Select Committee Papers and Reports (HRI 3A-D15-3), RG 233, NARA.

53. Barney to Jones, August 29, 1814; Mary Barney, *A Biographical Memoir,* 266; Webster to Mayer, July 22, 1853.

54. Mary Barney, *A Biographical Memoir,* 266. James H. Martin was later noted by Mary Barney as being a fine young man who was severely wounded. William Martin "was so good an officer that the loss of his services was deeply felt." Mary Barney, *A Biographical Memoir,* 266; Barney to Jones, August 27, 1814.

55. Mary Barney, *A Biographical Memoir,* 266, 267; Baltimore *Federal Gazette,* February 16 and 17, 1815; Hulbert Footner, *Sailor of Fortune: The Life and Adventures of Commodore Barney, U.S.N.* (New York: Harper & Brothers, 1940), 290; Pitch, *The Burning of Washington,* 83; Captain Joshua Barney to Secretary of the Navy William Jones, September 7, 1814, William Jones Correspondence, Uselma Clarke Smith Collection, Historical Society of Pennsylvania, Philadelphia, Pa.

56. [Gleig], *A Narrative,* 67; *Historical Record of the Fourth, or the King's Own, Regiment of Foot* (London: Longman, Orme, 1839), 119; Pitch, *The Burning of Washington,* 83–84.

57. Webster to Mayer, July 22, 1853.

58. Mary Barney, *A Biographical Memoir,* 267; Barney to Jones, August 29, 1814.

59. Scott, *Recollections,* 3:291.

60. Mary Barney, *A Biographical Memoir,* 267.

61. Barney to Jones, August 29, 1814, *ASPMA,* 1:580; Mary Barney, *A Biographical Memoir,* 267.

62. Mary Barney, *A Biographical Memoir,* 267–68.

63. Ibid., 268.

Chapter 22

A Great Fire

1. "Log of H.M.S. *Royal Oak,*" August 22, 1814, *Chronicles of St. Mary's* 15, no. 10 (October 1967).

2. "Log of H.M.S. *Albion,*" August 21 and 22, 1814, Cockburn Papers, LC; "Log of H.M.S. *Hebrus,*" August 25, 1814, *Chronicles of St. Mary's* 15, no. 10 (October 1967).

3. "Log of H.M.S. *Albion,*" August 25, 1814, Cockburn Papers, LC.

4. Mary Barney, ed., *A Biographical Memoir of the Late Commodore Joshua Barney: From Autobiographical Notes and Journals in Possession of His Family, and Other Authentic Sources* (Boston: Gray and Bowen, 1832), 268.

5. Ibid., 268–69.

6. Ibid., 268.

7. [Gleig, George Robert], *A Narrative of the Campaigns of the British Army, at Washington, Baltimore, and New Orleans, under the Generals Ross, Packenham, & Lambert, in the Years 1814 and 1815 With Some Account of the Countries Visited* (Philadelphia: M. Carey & Sons, 1821), 148.

8. Ibid.

9. Ibid., 149; "Log of H.M.S. *Albion,*" August 29, 1814, Cockburn Papers, LC; Walter Lord, *The Dawn's Early Light* (New York: W. W. Norton & Co., Inc., 1972), 187.

10. R. Lee Van Horn, *Out of the Past: Prince Georgeans and Their Land* (Riverdale, Md.: Prince George's County Historical Society, 1976), 262; *Report of the Trial of John Hodg-*

es, Esq. on a Charge of High Treason. Tried in the Circuit Court of the United States for the Maryland District, at the May Term, 1815 ([Baltimore, 1815]), Photocopy, Darnall's Chance Manuscript Collection, Upper Marlboro, Md. (hereafter *Hodges Trial*), 12.

11. Lord, *The Dawn's Early Light*, 185.

12. *Hodges Trial*, 11, 14, 16; Van Horn, *Out of the Past*, 262.

13. *Norfolk Herald*, September 6, 1814; Lord, *The Dawn's Early Light*, 186; *Hodges Trial*, 10–12, 16; Van Horn, *Out of the Past*, 262.

14. *Norfolk Herald*, September 6, 1814; Lord, *The Dawn's Early Light*, 186; *Hodges Trial*, 10–12, 14, 15, 16.

15. *Norfolk Herald*, September 6, 1814; Lord, *The Dawn's Early Light*, 186; [Gleig], *A Narrative*, 149; William M. Marine, *The British Invasion of Maryland 1812–1815* (1913; rpt., Hatboro, Pa.: Tradition Press, 1965), 183–84.

16. *Norfolk Herald*, September 6, 1814; Lord, *The Dawn's Early Light*, 186; [Gleig], *A Narrative*, 149; William M. Marine, *The British Invasion of Maryland 1812–1815* (1913; rpt., Hatboro, Pa.: Tradition Press, 1965), 183–84; *Hodges Trial*, 10–11, 16–17; Van Horne, *Out of the Past*, 263.

17. *Hodges Trial*, 17. Additional page numbers for this source in this section appear parenthetically.

18. Van Horn, *Out of the Past*, 263.

19. "Log of H.M.S. *Albion*," August 30, 1814, Cockburn Papers, LC; [Gleig], *A Narrative*, 150.

20. "Log of H.M.S. *Albion*," August 30, 1814.

21. Ibid., September 2, 3, and 4, 1814; "Log of H.M.S. *Royal Oak*," September 2 and 3, 1814, *Chronicles of St. Mary's*, 15, no. 2 (February 1967).

22. "Log of H.M.S. *Albion*," September 4, 1814, Cockburn Papers, LC; [Gleig], *A Narrative*, 167.

23. [Gleig], *A Narrative*, 164.

24. Ibid.

25. Lieutenant Solomon Rutter to Commodore John Rodgers, September 11, 1814, *NW*, 3:264; Secretary of the Navy William Jones to Lieutenant Solomon Frazier, September 3, 1814, RG 45, SNLO, 184, vol. 11, 411–12 (M 149, R 11), NARA.

26. Commodore John Rodgers to Major General Samuel Smith [September 11, 1814], *NW*, 3:264; Commodore John Rodgers to Secretary of the Navy William Jones, September 23, 1814, RG 45, SNCLR, 1814, vol. 6, no. 89 (M 125, R 39), NARA. After the war, John Adam Webster was awarded a gold-mounted sword by the State of Maryland, and another sword by the citizens of Baltimore. With money given to him for the loss of his horse, he purchased a set of silver. For full citations accompanying the awards, see *The Patriotic Marylander*, 1, no. 1 (December 1914): 38–39.

27. Mary Barney, *A Biographical Memoir*, 270–71.

28. Lieutenant Colonel George Armistead to Acting Secretary of War James Monroe, September 24, 1814, RG 107, Letters Received by the Secretary of War, Registered Series, A-68 (8) (M 221, R 59), NARA, reprinted in *NW*, 3:303.

29. Vice Admiral Sir Alexander F. I. Cochrane to Captain Charles Napier, September 13, 1814, *NW*, 3:278.

30. Mary Barney, *A Biographical Memoir*, 318.

31. Lieutenant Colonel George Armistead to Acting Secretary of War James Monroe, September 24, 1814.

32. Ibid.

33. Commodore John Rodgers to Secretary of the Navy William Jones, September 23, 1814, RG 45, SNCLR, 1814, vol. 6, no. 89 (M 125, R 39), NARA.

34. "Log of H.M.S. *Albion*," September 18, 1814, Cockburn Papers, LC.

35. [Gleig], *A Narrative*, 203.

36. "Log of H.M.S. *Albion*," September 19, 1814, Cockburn Papers, LC.

37. Ibid.

Chapter 23
The Ounce of British Influence

1. Mary Barney, ed., *A Biographical Memoir of the Late Commodore Joshua Barney: From Autobiographical Notes and Journals in Possession of His Family, and Other Authentic Sources* (Boston: Gray and Bowen, 1832), 271–73, 322.

2. Joshua Barney to Mr. Pleasants, October 30, 1814, reprinted in ibid., 322–33.

3. Ibid., 323.

4. Barney to Jones, November 17, 1814, RG 45, SNMLR, 1814, vol. 8, no. 1 (M 124, R 64), NARA.

5. Acting Secretary of the Navy Benjamin Homans to the Commanding Naval Officer Baltimore [Master Commandant Robert T. Spence], December 9, 1814, RG 45, SNLO, vol. 11, 475 (M 149, R 11), NARA; Acting Secretary of the Navy Benjamin Homans to Captain Joshua Barney, December 27, 1814, RG 45, SNLO, vol. 11, 493 (M 149, R 11), NARA.

6. Captain Joshua Barney to Acting Secretary of the Navy Benjamin Homans, January 3, 1815, RG 45, SNMLR, 1815, vol. 1, no. 7 (M 124, R 68), NARA.

7. Secretary of the Navy Benjamin W. Crowninsield to Captain Joshua Barney, February 14, 1815, RG 45, SNLO, vol. 12, 35 (M 149, R 12), NARA; Captain Joshua Barney to Secretary of the Navy Benjamin W. Crowninsield, February 18, 1815, RG 45, SNMLR, 1815, vol. 2, no. 72 (M 124, R 69), NARA.

8. *U.S. Statutes at Large*, 3:217–18.

9. Secretary of the Navy Benjamin W. Crowninsield to Captain Joshua Barney, March 9, 1815, RG 45, SNLO, vol. 12, 55 (M 149, R 12), NARA.

10. Secretary of the Navy Benjamin W. Crowninshield to Captain Joshua Barney, May 2, 1815, RG 45, SNLO, vol. 12, 116 (M 149, R 12), NARA.

11. Mary Barney, *A Biographical Memoir*, 294, 296.

Epilogue
All Eyes Will Be upon You

1. James Randall to Secretary of the Navy William Jones, March 21, 1815, RG 45, SNMLR, 1815 (M 124, R 41), NARA.

2. Captain Joshua Barney to Secretary of the Navy William Jones, November 17, 1814, RG 45, SNMLR, 1814, vol. 8, no. 1 (M 124, R 67), NARA.

3. Captain Joshua Barney to Secretary of the Navy Benjamin W. Crowninshield, April 17, 1814, RG 45, SNMLR, 1815, vol. 4, no. 43 (M 124, R 71), NARA.

4. Captain Joshua Barney to Secretary of the Navy William Jones, March 24 and April 17, 1815, RG 45 SNMLR, 1815, (M 124, R 70), NARA.

5. *ASPNA,* I, Claims (Washington: Printed by Gales and Seaton, 1834), 454, 486–87, 488.

6. Ibid., 552–55; *U.S. Congress, Senate, 36th Congress, 1st Session, Rep. Com., No. 118,* 1–9.

7. Dawson Lawrence, "Historical Sketch of Prince George County, Md.," in *Atlas of Fifteen Miles Around Washington Including the County of Prince George, Maryland* (Philadelphia: G. M. Hopkins, 1878), 8; Marlborough *Gazette,* June 4, 1892.

8. U.S. Congress, House, 60th Congress, 1st Session, Document no. 531, 2.

9. Arthur Cox, personal communication, Waysons Corner, Md., June 15, 1980; Harry Brooke Watkins interview, Hardesty, Md., March 21, 1998, audio tape, Fred Tutman Collection, Queen Anne's, Md.

10. Mrs. Norris Harris to George A. Palmer, Superintendent, Fort McHenry National Park, August 12, 1936, included in National Park Service Accession Receiving Report, Accession No. 14, Catalogue numbers 714–716, April 12, 1989, Fort McHenry Library, Fort McHenry National Monument and Historic Shrine, Baltimore, Md.

11. *Sunday Sun Magazine,* October 19, 1958, 19–22.

12. Donald G. Shomette and Fred W. Hopkins Jr., "The Search for the Chesapeake Flotilla," *The American Neptune* 43, no. 1 (January 1893): 5–19.

13. Donald G. Shomette, "The Chesapeake Flotilla Project: Remote Sensing. Phase I." Report prepared for the Maryland Historical Trust, May 1996.

14. Donald G. Shomette, "The Chesapeake Flotilla Project. Final Report, Phase I and Phase II Research: St. Leonard's Creek and Hills Bridge Transects, 1 January 1996 to 31 December 1997." Report prepared for the University of Baltimore, Baltimore, Md., and the Maryland Historical Trust, 1998.

Adams, Henry. *The War of 1812,* edited by H. A. DeWeerd. Harrisburg, Pa.: Infantry Journal Press, 1944.

Admiral George Cockburn Papers. Washington, D.C.: Manuscript Division, Library of Congress.

American & Commercial Daily Advertiser (Baltimore, Md.).

American Farmer (Baltimore, Md.).

American State Papers, Documents, Legislative and Executive, of the Congress of the United States. Washington, D.C. 38 vols. Washington, D.C.: Gales & Seaton, 1832–61.

American Watchman & Delaware Republican (Wilmington, Del.).

Anonymous. "A Personal Narrative of Events by Sea and Land, from the Year 1800 to 1815 Concluding with a Narrative of Some of the Principal Events in The Chesapeake and South Carolina, in 1814 and 1815." *Chronicles of St. Mary's* 8, no. 1 (January 1960).

Archives of Maryland. Vols. 21, 22, 26, and 39. Baltimore: Maryland Historical Society.

Auchinleck, G[ilbert]. *A History of the War Between Great Britain and the United States of America During the Year 1812, 1813 & 1814.* Toronto, London, and Redwood City, Calif.: Arms and Armor Press and Pendragon House, 1972.

Ball, Charles. *Slavery in the United States: A Narrative of the Life and Adventures of Charles Ball.* Lewistown, Pa., 1836.

Baltimore Commercial & Daily Advertiser (Baltimore, Md.)

Barney, Joshua. Defense of the Chesapeake. Washington, D.C.: Manuscript Division, Library of Congress.

Barney, Mary, ed. *A Biographical Memoir of the Late Commodore Joshua Barney: From Autobiographical Notes and Journals in Possession of His Family, and Other Authentic Sources.* Boston: Gray and Bowen, 1832.

Barney Papers. Dreer Collection, Pennsylvania Historical Society, Philadelphia, Pa.

[Barrett, Robert J.]. "Naval Recollections of the Late American War." *United Service Journal and Naval and Military Magazine,* Part 1 (April 1841).

Beitzell, Edwin Warfield. "A Short History of St. Clements Island." *Chronicles of St. Mary's* 6, no. 11 (November 1958).

———. *The Jesuit Missions of St. Mary's County, Maryland.* Abell, Md.: 1960; rpt. privately printed, 1976.

Bird, Harrison. *Navies in the Mountains.* New York: Oxford University Press, 1962.

Boston Gazette (Boston, Mass.).

Brannan, John, comp. and ed. *Official Letters of the Military and Naval Officers of the United States During the War with Great Britain in the Years 1812, 13, 14, & 15.* Washington City: Way & Gideon, 1823.

Byron, Gilbert. *The War of 1812 on the Chesapeake Bay.* Baltimore: Maryland Historical Society, 1964.

Calendar of Virginia State Papers. Ed. William P. Palmer. 11 vols. Richmond, 1873–93.

Causins, C. N., and James Forrest to Major James Thomas, April 9, 1813. Gift Collection, Box G 176/260. Annapolis: Maryland Hall of Records.

Chapelle, Howard I. *The History of The American Sailing Navy: The Ships and Their Development.* New York: W. W. Norton and Co., Inc., 1949.

Chronicles of St. Mary's 8, no. 9 (September 1960); 10, no. 7 (July 1976); 11, no. 3 (October 1963).

Coggeshall, George. *History of American Privateers.* New York: privately printed, 1856.

Cranwell, John Philips, and William Bowers Crane. *Men of Marque: A History of Private Armed Vessels out of Baltimore During the War of 1812.* New York: W. W. Norton & Co., Inc., 1940.

Cruickshank, Earnest A. *Documentary History of the Campaigns upon the Niagara Frontier in 1813 and 1814.* 9 vols. Welland, Ont.: Lundy's Lane Historical Society, n.d.

Daily National Intelligencer (Washington).

Defense of Baltimore Papers. Maryland Historical Society. Baltimore, Md.

Dictionary of American Naval Fighting Ships. 9 vols.. Washington, D.C.: Naval History Division, 1959–91.

Document no. 39, 20th Congress, 1st Session. House of Representatives. Treasury Department, *Report of the Secretary of the Treasury on the Memorial of the Mayor and City of Baltimore, for Pay and Allowance for Money Advanced and Supplies Furnished During the Late War January 2, 1828. Referred to the Committee of Claims.* Washington: Printed by Gales & Seaton, 1828.

Dudley, William S., and Michael J. Crawford, eds. *The Naval War of 1812: A Documentary History.* 3 vols. Washington, D.C.: Naval Historical Center, Department of the Navy, 1985–2002.

Emmons, George F. *The Navy of the United States from the Commencement, 1775 to 1853.* Washington, D.C.: Gideon and Co., 1853.

Federal Gazette (Baltimore, Md.).

Federal Republican (Baltimore, Md.).

Footner, Hulbert. *Sailor of Fortune: The Life and Adventures of Commodore Barney, U.S.N.* New York: Harper & Brothers, 1940.

George, Christopher T. *Terror on the Chesapeake: The War of 1812 on the Bay.* Shippensburg, Pa.: White Mane Books, 2000.

[Gleig, George Robert]. *A Narrative of the Campaigns of the British Army, at Washington, Baltimore, and New Orleans, under the Generals Ross, Packenham, & Lambert, in the Years 1814 and 1815 With Some Account of the Countries Visited.* Philadelphia: M. Carey & Sons, 1821.

Gift Collection, Box G 176/260, Hall of Records, Annapolis, Md.

Graves, Donald E. *Sir William Congreve and the Rocket's Red Glare.* Alexandria Bay, N.Y.: Museum Restoration Service, 1989.

[Gubbins, R. R.]. *The 85th King's Light Infantry,* edited by C. R. B. Barrett. London: Spottiswoode, 1913.

Hamilton, Stanislaus Murray, ed. *The Writings of James Monroe.* Vol. 5. New York: G. P. Putnam's Sons, 1901.

Hammett, Regina Combs. *History of St. Mary's County, Maryland.* Ridge, Md.: privately printed, 1977.

Hecht, Arthur. "The Post Office Department in St. Mary's County in the War of 1812." *Maryland Historical Magazine* 52, no. 2 (June 1957).

Herald (New York).

Hibbs, Richard R. "Congreve War Rockets, 1800–1825." *U.S. Naval Institute Proceedings* 94 (March 1968): 80–88.

Historical Record of the Fourth, or the King's Own, Regiment of Foot. London: Longman, Orme, 1839.

Hollyday, Clement, to Urban Hollyday, July 12, 1814. Washington, D.C.: Manuscript Division, Library of Congress.

Hopkins, Fred W., Jr. *Tom Boyle, Master Privateer.* Cambridge, Md.: Tidewater Publishers, 1976.

Hunt, Galliard, ed. *The Writings of James Madison.* Vol. 8. New York: G. P. Putnam's Sons, 1908.

James Beatty Expenses, Fourth Auditor Records, National Archives and Record Service, Washington, D.C.

James Jarboe Papers. Baltimore: Maryland Historical Society.

James Madison Papers. Manuscript Division, Library of Congress.

James, William. *A Full and Correct Account of the Military Occurrence of the Late War between Great Britain and the United States of America.* 2 vols. London: Black, Kingsbury, Parbury, & Allen, 1818.

King Family Files/War of 1812, Calvert County Historical Society, Prince Frederick, Md.

Lawrence, Dawson. "Historical Sketch of Prince George County, Md." In *Atlas of Fifteen Miles Around Washington Including the County of Prince George, Maryland.* Philadelphia: G. M. Hopkins, 1878.

Letters Received by the Secretary of War, 1814, RG 45, National Archives and Record Service, Washington, D.C.

"Log of H.M.S. *Dragon.*" *Chronicles of St. Mary's* 13, no. 8 (August 1965).

"Log of H.M.S. *Hebrus.*" *Chronicles of St. Mary's* 15, no. 10 (October 1967).

"Log of H.M.S. *Jaseur.*" *Chronicles of St. Mary's* 8, no. 12 (December 1960); 9, no. 1 (January 1961); 10, no. 2 (February 1962).

"Log of H.M.S. *Loire.*" *Chronicles of St. Mary's* 8, no. 10 (October 1960); 8, no. 12 (December 1960).

"Log of H.M.S. *Royal Oak.*" *Chronicles of St. Mary's* 15, no. 2 (February 1967).

"Log of H.M.S. *St. Lawrence.*" *Chronicles of St. Mary's* 11, no. 12 (December 1963); 13, no. 4 (April 1965).

"Log of H.M.S. *Severn.*" *Chronicles of St. Mary's* 14, no. 8 (August 1966).

"Log of H.M.S. *Tonnant.*" *Chronicles of St. Mary's* 14, no. 8 (August 1966).

Log of the *Rossie.* U.S. Naval Academy Library, Annapolis, Md.

Lord, Walter. *The Dawn's Early Light.* New York: W. W. Norton and Co., Inc., 1972.

Mahan, Alfred T. *Sea Power in Its Relation to the War of 1812.* 2 vols. Boston: Little, Brown & Co., 1919.

Marine, William M. *The British Invasion of Maryland 1812–1815.* 1913; rpt., Hatboro, Pa.: Tradition Press, 1965.

Maryland Gazette and Political Intelligencer (Annapolis).

Maryland Republican (Annapolis).

McKenney, Thomas L. *Memoirs, Official and Personal.* 2 vols. New York: Paine and Burgess, 1846.

Miller Papers. Personal Papers Collection, Marine Corps History and Museums Division, Washington, D.C.

Miscellaneous Letters of the Secretary of the Navy. Old Army and Navy Branch, National Archives, Washington, D.C.

Molotsky, Irvin. *The Flag, The Poet & The Song: The Story of the Star-Spangled Banner.* New York: Dutton, 2001.

Muster Book U.S. Flotilla, Naval Records, Collector of the Office of Naval Records and Library, RG 45, National Archives and Record Service, Washington, D.C.

Naval Chronicle (London, England).

Niles' Weekly Register (Baltimore, Md.).

Norfolk Herald (Norfolk, Va.).

Norris, Walter Biscoe, Jr., ed. *Westmoreland County, Virginia.* Montross, Va: Westmoreland County Board of Supervisors, 1983.

Norton, Louis Arthur. *Joshua Barney: Hero of the Revolution and 1812.* Annapolis, Md.: Naval Institute Press, 2000.

Pitch, Anthony S. *The Burning of Washington: The British Invasion of 1814.* Annapolis, Md.: Naval Institute Press, 1998.

Poultney Malcolm Collection. William L. Clements Library, University of Michigan, Ann Arbor, Mich.

Public Documents Printed by Order of the United States Senate During the First Session of the Twenty-Sixth Congress, Begun and Held At the City of Washington, December 2, 1839, 8 vols. Washington: Printed by Blair and Rivers, 1840.

"Recollections of the Expedition to the Chesapeake, and Against New Orleans, in the Years 1814–15 By An Old Sub." *United Service Journal* (April 1840), reprinted in *News and Notes from the Prince George's County Historical Society* 9, no. 9 (September 1981).

Records of General Courts-Martial and Courts of Inquiry of the Navy Department, RG 125, National Archives and Record Service, Washington, D.C.

Report of the Trial of John Hodges, Esq. on a Charge of High Treason. Tried in the Circuit Court of the United States for the Maryland District, at the May Term, 1815 ([Baltimore, 1815]), Photocopy, Darnall's Chance Manuscript Collection, Upper Marlboro, Md.

Rouse, Park, Jr. "Low Tide at Hampton Roads." *Naval Institute Proceedings* 95, no. 797 (July 1969).

Scharf, J. Thomas. *The Chronicles of Baltimore: Being a Complete History of "Baltimore Town" and Baltimore City from the Earliest Time to the Present Time.* Baltimore: Turnbull Brothers, 1874.

Scott, Captain James. *Recollections of a Naval Life.* 3 vols. London: Bentley, 1834.

Secretary of the Navy Letters, 1813, 1814, 1815, RG 45, National Archives and Record Service, Washington, D.C.

Select Committee Papers and Reports (HRI 3A-D15-3), RG 233, National Archives and Record Service, Washington, D.C.

Sheads, Scott S. *The Rockets' Red Glare: The Maritime Defense of Baltimore in 1814.* Centreville, Md.: Tidewater Publishers, 1986.

Shomette, Donald G. *Lost Towns of Tidewater Maryland.* Centreville, Md.: Tidewater Publishers, 2000.

———. "The Chesapeake Flotilla Project: Remote Sensing. Phase I." Report prepared for the Maryland Historical Trust, May 1996.

———. "The Chesapeake Flotilla Project. Final Report, Phase I and Phase II Research: St. Leonard's Creek and Hills Bridge Transects, 1 January 1996 to 31 December 1997." Report prepared for the University of Baltimore, Baltimore, Md., and the Maryland Historical Trust, 1998.

Shomette, Donald G., and Ralph E. Eshelman. *The Patuxent River Submerged Cultural Resource Survey, From Drum Point to Queen Anne's Bridge, Maryland: Reconnaissance, Phase I, and Phase II.* Maryland Historical Trust Manuscript Series Number 13: April 1981.

Shomette, Donald G., and Fred W. Hopkins, Jr. "The Search for the Chesapeake Flotilla." *The American Neptune* 43, no. 1 (January 1983): 5–19.

Smith, Sir Harry. *The Autobiography of Lt.-Gen. Sir Harry Smith.* London: Murray, 1903.

Smith, John. *The Generall Historie of Virginia, New England, and the Summer Isles.* London: Printed by I. D. and I. H. for Michael Sparkes, 1624.

Statutes at Large, The Public Statutes at Large of the United States of America, from the Organization of the Government in 1789, to March 3, 1845. 8 vols. Ed. Richard Peters. Boston: Little, Brown, 1846–67.

Stein, Charles Francis. *A History of Calvert County, Maryland.* Baltimore, Md.: published in cooperation with the Calvert County Historical Society, 1960.

Sunday Sun Magazine, October 19, 1958, 19–22.

The Patriotic Marylander 1, no. 1 (December 1914): 37–40.

The Times (London, England).

Thomas Kemp Papers. Wades Point Farm, McDaniel, Md.

Tilp, Frederick. *This Was Potomac River.* Alexandria, Va.: privately printed, 1978.

Tucker, Glenn. *Poltroons and Patriots: A Popular Account of the War of 1812.* Indianapolis: Bobbs-Merrill Co., 1954.

Tucker, Spencer C. *Arming the Fleet: U.S. Navy Ordnance in the Muzzle-Loading Era.* Annapolis, Md.: Naval Institute Press, 1989.

———. *The Jeffersonian Gunboat Navy.* Columbia: University of South Carolina Press, 1993.

Tucker, Spencer A., ed. *Naval Warfare: An International Encyclopedia.* 3 vols. Santa Barbara, Calif.: ABC-Clio, 2002.

U.S. Congress, 29th Congress, Rep. no. 131, 1st Session, Ho. of Reps.

U.S. Congress, Senate, 36th Congress, 1st Session, Rep. Com., no. 118.

U.S. Congress, House, 60th Congress, 1st Session, Document no. 531.

Van Horn, R. Lee. *Out of the Past: Prince Georgeans and Their Land.* Riverdale, Md.: Prince George's County Historical Society, 1976.

Warren Papers, National Maritime Museum, Greenwich, England.

Watkins, Harry Brooke, interview, Hardesty, Md., March 21, 1998, audio tape, Fred Tutman Collection, Queen Anne's, Md.

Weiss, John McNish. *The Merikens: Free Black American Settlers in Trinidad 1815–16.* London: McNish & Weiss, 2002.

Whipple, A. B. C. *Fighting Sail.* Alexandria, Va.: Time-Life Books Inc., 1978.

Whitehorne, Joseph A. *The Battle of Baltimore 1814.* Baltimore: The Nautical & Aviation Publishing Company of America, 1997.

William Jones Correspondence. Uselma Clarke Smith Collection, Historical Society of Pennsylvania, Philadelphia, Pa.

Williams, H[ugh] Noel. *The Life & Letters of Admiral Sir Charles Napier, K.C.B. (1786–1860).* London: Hutchinson & Co., 1917.

Woodstock Letters, vol. 32. Baltimore, Md.: privately printed by the Society of Jesuits.

Breton Bay, Md., 69, 192, 208
Brewhouse, 87
Briscoe, Maj. John H., 169
Bristol Landing, Md., 355
British Admiralty Office, 71
British Army, 2, 232, 260, 265, 275, 280, 288,
294, 308, 309, 311, 324, 329–31, 336, 337, 342;
First Brigade, 251, 261, 311, 323; Rocket
Brigade, 311; Second Brigade, 251, 261, 320;
Third Brigade, 251, 261, 311; 4th Regiment,
232, 251, 311, 313, 320, 321, 324; 20th Regi-
ment, 230; 21st Regiment, 234, 251, 256, 311,
321; 29th Regiment, 234; 44th Regiment,
232, 245, 251, 311, 313, 320, 324; 62nd Regi-
ment, 234; 85th Regiment, 232, 251, 261,
308, 311, 313, 314, 320–22, 324–25
Brooke, Lt. Col. Arthur, BA, 251, 311, 320,
313, 324
Brooke, Capt., 333, 334
Broome, Capt. John, VII, 105, 115
Broome's Island, Md., 105
Brown, Maj. George, BA, 323
Brown, Capt. Thomas, RN, 159, 170, 208,
211; and attack on St. Leonard's Town,
162; Cockburn praises, 194; downplays St.
Leonard's Creek defeat, 155, 156; and flo-
tilla's escape, 155; joins Barrie's squadron,
85; and Patuxent blockade, 125, 128, 139,
140, 141; at Second Battle of St. Leonard's
Creek, 147, 148, 149, 150
Bryantown, Md., 119
Bunbury, Capt. Matthew Simmones, 59
Burch, Capt. Benjamin, 291, 300, 304–5, 309,
317
Burdett, Capt. George, RN, 7
Butler's Mill, Md., 254. *See also* Aquasco, Md.
Byron, Capt. Richard, RN, 7

Caicard, [William Molleson]. *See* Carcaud,
William Molleson
Caldwell, Capt. Elias B., 124, 259, 288
Calvert County, Md., 17, 62, 103, 120, 164,
181, 259; Barney and, 165, 221; British at,
182, 343; Court House at, 161, 182, 184, 186;
defenseless status of, 18, 136; flotilla carried
across, 134; militia of, 16, 91, 104, 115, 171,

183, 186, 221; Nourse and, 180, 184, 187–88;
St. Leonard's Town's importance to, 88,
119; 31st Regiment, 91, 115
Calvert County Soil Conservation District
Office, 355, 357
Calvert Marine Museum, 355
Calverton, Md., 180, 186
Campbell, George, 298, 301
Canada, 2, 117, 176, 230, 337; American
campaign against, 6, 21, 71; American vic-
tory in, 258; British response to American
atrocities in, 175, 233, 243; British troops
sent to, 234; refugee slaves given land in,
72, 337; *Tonnant* sails for, 343
Canadian Chasseurs, 10
Cape Charles, Va., 238
Cape Henry, Va., 238
Cape May, N.J., 23
Capitol Hill, 346
Carberry, Col. Henry, USA, 129, 144,
193; Barney and, 115, 116; during Battle
of Bladensburg, 300; Keyser and, 146;
Leonardtown's defense and, 68; at Second
Battle of St. Leonard's Creek, 150, 159, 193;
at St. Leonard's Creek, 115, 140
Carberry, Capt. Thomas, USA, 144, 159, 160
Carcaud, William Molleson, 110
Carlisle, Pa., 271, 304, 317
Carnes, Peter, 310
Caroline County, Va., 203
Carroll, Daniel, of Dudington, 352
Carter, Capt. Thomas, RM, 98, 105, 111
Carter, Lt. William, USFS, 150, 154
Catlett, Dr. Hanson, 271, 297, 308, 311
Caton, William, 334
Cedar Point, Md., 79, 82–85, 343
Chaptico, Md., 206, 207
Charles County, Md., 16–17, 104, 107, 121, 159,
192, 194, 201
Charles County Militia, 107
Charleston, S.C., 175
Charlotte Hall, Md., 205, 263
Chesapeake Bay, 1, 9, 14, 16, 18, 49, 56, 60, 65,
67, 73, 76–78, 84, 125, 161, 167–68, 177, 181,
215, 223, 236, 329, 343, 345, 348; American
defense of, 8, 22, 27, 29, 33–38; Barney's